D0646623

# dreaming the future

# WORKS BY CLIFFORD A. PICKOVER

# dreaming the future

the fantastic story of prediction

# clifford a. pickover

**Prometheus Books**

59 John Glenn Drive
Amherst, New York 14228-2197

**HOUSTON PUBLIC LIBRARY**

R01211 00056

Cover art by Alex Grey, *Sacred Mirrors*.

Published 2001 by Prometheus Books

*Dreaming the Future: The Fantastic Story of Prediction.* Copyright © 2001 by Clifford A. Pickover. All rights reserved. No part of this publication may be reproduced, stored in a retrieval system, or transmitted in any form or by any means, digital, electronic, mechanical, photocopying, recording, or otherwise, or conveyed via the Internet or a Web site without prior written permission of the publisher, except in the case of brief quotations embodied in critical articles and reviews.

Inquiries should be addressed to
Prometheus Books
59 John Glenn Drive
Amherst, New York 14228–2197
VOICE: 716–691–0133, ext. 207
FAX: 716–564–2711
WWW.PROMETHEUSBOOKS.COM

05 04 03 02 01    5 4 3 2 1

Library of Congress Cataloging-in-Publication Data

Pickover, Clifford A.
    Dreaming the future : the fantastic story of prediction / Clifford A. Pickover.
        p. cm.
    Includes bibliographical references and index.
    ISBN 1–57392–895–X (alk. paper)
    1. Divination. 2. Fortune-telling. 3. Prophecies (Occultism). I. Title.

BF1750 .P53 2001
133.3—dc21                                                    00–051838

Printed in the United States of America on acid-free paper

This book is dedicated to the New York Yankees,
winners of the 2027 World Series.
This book is also dedicated to all
of my readers who can
divine the meaning of
ᛏᚾᛊᚾ ᚩᛗᚾᛏᚤᛊᛊᚢᚾ ᚩᚤᚾᚾᚨᚩᚤ

先見之明

Translation: *the wisdom of prediction*.
This familiar Chinese idiom is
pronounced "xian jian zhi ming."
The small square at the bottom
encloses the name of the calligra-
pher, Siu-Leung Lee.

We are in the position of a little child entering a huge library whose walls are covered to the ceiling with books in many different tongues. . . . The child does not understand the languages in which they are written. He notes a definite plan in the arrangement of books, a mysterious order which he does not comprehend, but only dimly suspects.

♌ Albert Einstein (20th Century)

A strange and wonderful instrument exists in the earth, but it is concealed from minds and souls. It is an instrument that has the power to change the atmosphere of the whole earth. . . . The sun of justice will rise from the horizon of the unseen realm. Soon will the present-day order be rolled up, and a new one spread out in its stead.

♍ Baha'u'llah (19th century)

He calmly rode on, leaving it to his horse's discretion to go which way it pleased, firmly believing that in this consisted the very essence of adventures.

♐ Miguel de Cervantes (17th Century)

# Contents

# Preface

*A cloud does not know why it moves in just such a direction and at such a speed. It feels an impulsion . . . this is the place to go now. But the sky knows the reasons and the patterns behind all clouds, and you will know, too, when you lift yourself high enough to see beyond horizons.*
> —Richard Bach, *Illusions*

*Though it is not widely accepted or even well known to the public, it is a fact that no occult, paranormal, psychic, or supernatural claim has ever been substantiated by proper testing.*
> —James Randi, *An Encyclopedia of Claims, Frauds, and Hoaxes of the Occult and Supernatural*

*We should all be concerned about the future because we will have to spend the rest of our lives there.*
> —Charles Kettering, *Seed for Thought*

## DREAMING WITH THE GODS

*If we wish to understand the nature of reality, we have an inner hidden advantage: we are ourselves little portions of the universe and so carry the answer within us.*
> —Jacques Boivin, *The Single Heart Field Theory*

If there were a way to predict the moment of your death, would you choose to know? If you are single, do you want to know whom you will

**11**

marry? Would you like to know the price of IBM stock next week? The practice of foretelling the future, or gaining secret knowledge, is called *divination*. Ancient and modern civilizations have explored divination using an incredible assortment of techniques—from dreams to drugs, from patterns in the stars to messages in the Magic 8-Ball®, a children's toy with admittedly limited fortune-telling potential.

Most of you have probably heard of the more popular divination methods that make use of astrology, tarot cards, or the ubiquitous Chinese fortune cookie. But many exotic methods have been used through history that seem truly fantastic or quirky. Consider, for example:

- *Kephalonomancy*, an ancient practice in which one burns a piece of carbon on the head of an ass while reciting the names of suspected criminals. (Ouch!)[1] If a crackling sound is heard when a person's name is mentioned, the poor schlub is guilty as charged.
- *Onychomancy*, divination by observing the sun's reflection in a person's fingernails.
- *Haruspicy*, a pre-Roman method of entrail reading, or more bluntly, divination by studying the shapes of animal guts. (If this turns your stomach, you don't even want to think about *anthropomancy*—divining by studying the organs of freshly sacrificed humans.)

In short, this book provides a sweeping reference of fortune-telling practices, ranging from tea-leaf readings (*tasseography*) to predictions based on the shapes of holes in Swiss cheese (*tiromancy*) to divining God's will by fire or flame (*pyromancy*). One thing is certain: humans have always wanted to know what the future holds. Because some cultures, even today, believe that the universe is controlled by higher beings or planetary influences, many divination systems rely on these spiritual beings and paranormal forces. The ancient Greeks saw dreams as visitations from gods and the souls of the dead. People who were skilled at reading dreams formed an integral part of the Greek world. Today, many divination methods have undergone a popular resurgence due to the New Age movement. The New Age sections of bookstores grow ever-larger, filled with books on topics ranging from rune stones to crystal reading.

Sometimes divination methods are meant to give the practitioner insight into solutions for problems instead of suggesting future events. The methods point out possible challenges, hidden dangers, and paths of opportunity. Many divination methods for predicting the future were not intended to take away people's freedom to alter their lives. Rather, the methods suggested future trends and allowed querents to creatively maneuver through the waters of their destiny. (A "querent" is a person performing a divination ritual in order to obtain answers to questions.)

Divination is everywhere these days. Right now as I write this book, there are more professional astrologers than astronomers. Let me give a few contemporary examples of divination. Indira Gandhi, prime minister of India from 1966 to 1977, used astrology to help her in scheduling and making decisions. Nancy Reagan, former First Lady to President Ronald Reagan, consulted an astrologer and used the advice to organize her husband's daily activites.[2] In the sixties and seventies, Ronald Reagan consulted regularly with astrologer Jeane Dixon during his visits to Washington. The meetings were held secretly in the Mayflower hotel and were carefully concealed so Democrats couldn't make fun of the then governor Reagan.[3]

At the time, White House Chief of Staff Donald Regan was depressed by the fact that "virtually every major move and decision the Reagans made during my time as White House Chief of Staff was cleared in advance with a woman in San Francisco who drew up horoscopes to make certain that the planets were in favorable alignment for the enterprise."[4] When George Bush raised a question about President Reagan's schedule, Donald Regan told him it was in the hands of an astrologer. Bush replied, "Good God, I had no idea."[5]

California Astrologer Joan Quigley said, "I was responsible for timing all press conferences, most speeches, the State of the Union addresses, and the takeoffs and landings of Air Force One."[6] She also alleges that she wielded considerable influence in the creation of major U.S. policy, including the handling of the Bitburg crisis,[7] the INF Treaty,[8] and President Reagan's historical shift from viewing Russia as the evil Empire to accepting Mikhail Gorbachev as a peace-seeking leader. She asserts that she picked the time for Reagan's presidential debates, briefing for various summits, and medical operations.[9]

Modern divinatory practices are certainly not restricted to the United States. The large Hong Kong Bank, designed by the Western Architect Sir Norman Foster, was built to conform to guidelines and provided by the tenets of feng-shui ("wind-water"), a form of Chinese geomancy that you will learn about later in this book.[10] Among other things, feng-shui and geomancy practitioners examine various aspects of the surrounding land to determine the most favorable locations of buildings. If a building is erected on a site that is not in harmony with the surrounding ch'i (or energy), the building inhabitants will presumably suffer.

Even serious business people today seem to be interested in various forms of divination, and divination is also flourishing on the Internet. For example, Paul O'Brien, founder of the multimedia company Visionary Networks and author of *Intuitive Decision-Making in an Age of Chaos,* uses ancient divination systems to make businesses more creative. In particular, he uses the *I Ching,* an ancient Chinese divination system, to stimulate intuition and suggest new business directions. Just to give you a flavor of some current thinking, consider how some wealthy people use the *I Ching.* Paul writes:

> We live and work in an age of uncertainty and chaos. Face it, good decision-making is more an art than a science. Having harnessed powerful computers—the ultimate models of left-brain processing—can we now humbly admit that our commitment to any given course of action is based largely on gut-feel? Can we find systematic ways to train or stimulate our intuitive function? Fortunately, a number of people—including prominent scientists and business leaders—have rediscovered ancient technologies for intuitive decision-making and creativity. One such is an ancient Chinese oracle known as the *I Ching.* [As just one example], consider multimillionaire Paul Wenner, founder of the health-food company Wholesome & Hearty, Inc., who used the *I Ching* in the form of a software program appropriately named Synchronicity to stimulate intuition and support critical decision-making. Wenner states that "the Synchronicity program played a major role in my company's success and growth." A surprising number of people use the *I Ching* oracle at home or work as a method of centering themselves when engaged in delicate negotiations—whether with a potential business partner or a teenage child. One customer of ours claims to have closed a three-million-dollar deal with Intel using an oracle program to reorient himself during the lengthy negotiations. Before every meeting, he would consult the oracle on his PC to stimulate his intuition.[11]

This history of divination deals with a timeless realm, a place of archetypes where diviners take on big issues—love, death, birth, the fate of nations, and our place in the universe.[12] The grandest prophets thought big—about the fate of our species, our entire planet, and our relationship with divine beings. Shakespeare wrote that we are the stuff that dreams are made of. This book is going to show you some of the most beautiful and most haunting of those dreams. Whether divination is more than a dream has yet to be seen.

## Ψ GODS, GUTS, GHOSTS

> *At all the moments of death, one lives over again his past life with a rapidity inconceivable to others. This remembered life must also have a last moment, and*

*this last moment its own last moment, and so on, and hence, dying is itself eternity, and hence, in accordance with the theory of limits, one may approach death but can never reach it.*

—Arthur Schnitzler, *Flight Into Darkness*

*There's a world behind the world we see that is the same world but more open, more transparent, without blocks. . . . To touch this world no matter how briefly is a help in life.*

—Gary Snyder, *The Practice of the Wild*

Imagine yourself transported back in time. It is Valentine's Day in nineteenth-century England. You stare at a field besides a barn and notice a girl dropping melted wax into a puddle of cold water, hoping to find true love. She looks intently at the still water. In her mind, the shapes of the cooled wax sometimes resemble letters of the alphabet. "It's Nicholas!" she screams, certain that the wax has formed the letter "N." She, along with many people of the time, believes that wax letters indicate the letters in the names of their future marriage partners. Is this divination? You bet. This is just one of the European methods popular in the past and still used in Central America.

The following Valentine's Day recipe was also quite popular in nineteenth-century England: "Let a single woman go out of her own door very early in the morning, and if the first person she meets be a woman, she will not be married that year: if she meet a man, she will be married within three months."[13]

As you can probably divine by this point, this book will allow you to travel through time and space, and you needn't be an expert in divination or any magical arts. To facilitate your journey, I include lots of "do-it-yourself" recipes so that you can get an intimate feel for the various methods. Beginners may use the recipes to explore a range of topics, from divination with spiders to crystal gazing. Chapter 4, "Science and the Will to Believe" describes some of my scientific, skeptical experiments in several areas related to divination.

Not all of my divination examples will be as tame as the girl dripping wax into puddles. Divination has had a wild, gory past in history and mythology. For example, in Homer's *The Odyssey*, Odysseus summons the shades of the dead by sacrificing animals. The animal's warm blood drains into a pit, and the hungry spirits eagerly come, seeping upward from the underworld. Odysseus holds them back with his sword until a particular spirit comes forward, laps up the congealing blood, and then prophesies events in the future. This scene combines the themes of fear, slaughter, death, the Underworld, and ghosts that are common to the history of divination.

The blood-licking ghosts remind me that many forms of divination have involved food. For instance, some recipes for divination on Halloween advise you to take a candle, stand next to a mirror in a dark room, and eat an apple while looking into the mirror.[14] The face of your lover, or a demon, will appear standing behind you. A variation of this approach suggests you can cut an apple into several equal parts and eat all but one piece, which you toss in the air. If you turn quickly, you will see your future mate.[15] (Gypsy girls and Celtic queens chose their consorts by tossing them an apple.) Couples who want information about their relationships were advised to place a pair of nuts in the fire. Unfortunately the advice on how to interpret them varies.[16] Some say if the nuts pop at the same time, the couple will marry. Others say this means they will grow apart. This is one feature of divination that can make implementations problematic. Not everyone agrees as to the best interpretation.

Enough talk about food. Ready to start? Prepare yourself for a strange journey as *Dreaming the Future* unlocks the doors of your imagination with thought-provoking mysteries, puzzles, and problems on topics ranging from the prophecies of Nostradamus, to reading the coils of sheep intestines, to hypnotic *future-life progression*—the opposite of the well-known *past-life regression* in which clients attempt to recall past lives. I have scoured the Earth for strange diviners and bizarre beliefs, and I give lists of some of the most wonderfully offbeat methods practiced by humans to predict their destiny.

Please note that his book is not a comprehensive survey of all divination methods and diviners, although I give concise definitions for a very large number of practices. In fact, I have focussed on just a few methods that personally fascinate me or that I might treat with a fresh perspective. Since the term "divination" can refer to finding secret knowledge, I sometimes describe practices that are not specifically aimed at the future; for example, as I already mentioned, the Chinese practice of feng-shui is used to divine suitable locations for buildings, graves, or other constructions, and not for divining the future.

As in all my previous books, I encourage you to pick and choose from the smorgasbord of topics. Many of the sections are brief and give you just a flavor of an application or method. Often, additional information can be found in the referenced publications. In some cases, my shorter descriptions reflect our current, limited knowledge of certain subjects. For example, we know a lot more about the history of tarot cards than the practice of tiromancy, rigorously defined as the art of prediction by interpreting the holes (or mold) in cheese—an art that is no longer practiced today but was popular in the Middle Ages.

Some information is repeated so that each chapter contains sufficient background information. The basic philosophy of this book is that creative thinking is learned by experimenting. By actually trying some of the divination methods, you will get a better feel for people's belief systems. You will better remember some of the ancient ways and concerns. Early humans developed divination methods to understand an incomprehensible world. The best place for us to begin our studies is by looking at some of the millennium-old methods. We may consider them merely entertaining artifacts, but the ancients regarded them as much, much more.

# Acknowledgments

*A rock pile ceases to be a rock pile the moment a single man contemplates it, bearing within him the image of a cathedral.*
— Antoine-Marie-Roger de Saint-Exupery, *Flight to Arras*

In exploring the history of divination, I would like to note and thank the "Ten Outstanding Skeptics of the Twentieth Century": James Randi, Martin Gardner, Carl Sagan, Paul Kurtz, Ray Hyman, Isaac Asimov, Philip J. Klass, Bertrand Russell, Harry Houdini, and Albert Einstein. These ten were chosen for the distinction in 1999 by the Fellows and Scientific Consultants of the Committee for the Scientific Investigation of Claims of the Paranormal (CSICOP).

One of my favorite, highly imaginative books on divination is Damon Wilson's *The Mammoth Book of Nostradamus and Other Prophets*. John Hogue's *The Millennium Book of Prophecy* is a great source for quotations of the great seers. Stephen Karcher's *The Illustrated Encyclopedia of Divination* and Eva Shaw's *Divining the Future* also contain a wealth of fascinating information. For a very insightful and scholarly treatise, see Michael Loewe's and Carmen Blacker's *Oracles and Divination*, and for a skeptical look, see two books by James Randi, *An Encyclopedia of Claims, Frauds, and Hoaxes of the Occult and Supernatural* and *The Mask of Nostradamus*.

The Magic 8-Ball® is a registered trademark of Tyco Toys®, Inc. The poems "Return of the Haruspex," "Plight of the Auspex," and "Augery" are by Keith Allen Daniels. See Daniels's book *Satan Is a Mathematician* published by Anamnesis Press for more poetry. I thank Ken Inoue for answering several questions relating to Japanese forms of divination.

I also thank David Zeitlyn for information on Mambila spider divination. David is a Senior Lecturer in Social Anthropology at the University of Kent in Canterbury, UK. The Chinese calligraphy after the dedication was contributed by Dr. Siu-Leung Lee (http://www.asiawind.com). Dr. Lee has been practicing the art of calligraphy for more than forty years, and his calligraphy is collected by people around the world. Capable of writing in many styles, Dr. Lee has created his own style evolving from those of the Han and Jin dynasties.

Numerous Web sites provided useful background material for this book, and these are credited in the Notes and Further Reading section. I owe a special debt of gratitude to Ellie Crystal, John Opsopaus, Kevin Knight and creators of the New Advent Web site, Steven Barrett, Robert Todd Carroll, William Cassidy, Waverly Fitzgerald, Fortune Cookie Ltd. (Europe's largest fortune cookie maker), Alan G. Hefner, Mell Paul, M. Turford, James Lett, Brendan McKay, David Rose, Mell Paul and M. Turford, Gavin Cloggie and Paragon Publishing Ltd., Kevin Bugeja, Doron Witztum, and David Zeitlyn for their imaginative, important, and stimulating Web sites. Additionally, *Encyclopedia Britannica Online*, www.eb.com, is always a source of valuable facts and ideas. Finally, and most importantly, I thank my editor at Prometheus Books, Linda Greenspan Regan, for her wonderful comments and suggestions.

The frontispiece artwork for chapter 3 is by Paul Hartal, Ph.D. for Clifford Pickover. The figure on the dedication page is often said to be a sixteenth-century German woodcut, although its origin is probably much more recent. The figure is from Stephen Karcher, *The Illustrated Encyclopedia of Divination* (New York: Barnes & Nobles Books, 1997), p. 117.

The cover artwork for this book is a detail of a much larger work titled "Sophia" (acrylic on canvas, 84 × 46 inches) by my favorite artist, Alex Grey. For more information on Grey, see his Web page http://www.alexgrey.com/ and his book Alex Grey, *Sacred Mirrors: The Visionary Art of Alex Grey* (Rochester, Vt.: Inner Traditions International, 1990). A complete "Sophia" can be found in Grey's book.

---

**Disclaimer:** Divination methods are presented for educational purposes only. The author and publisher are not responsible for rash acts committed by readers as a result of performing the divination rituals. Please exercise caution when handling spiders. Please do not perform entrail readings. Please do not kill goats or sheep. Be cautious, be kind, be intelligent, and you will prosper.

# Introduction

*As the island of knowledge grows, the surface that makes contact with mystery expands. When major theories are overturned, what we thought was certain knowledge gives way, and knowledge touches upon mystery differently. This newly uncovered mystery may be humbling and unsettling, but it is the cost of truth. Creative scientists, philosophers, and poets thrive at this shoreline.*
—W. Mark Richardson, "A Skeptic's Sense of Wonder," *Science*

## ⚘ HOW I BECAME INTERESTED IN DIVINATION

*I contend that we all suffer from prophet's block. Most of us have been pro-grammed to act like ostriches, to hide our heads from premonitions of change.*
—John Hogue, *The Millennium Book of Prophecy*

I first became fascinated by the notion of divination when reading Roger Zelazny's science-fiction novel *Creatures of Light and Darkness*. The book contains a hilarious (although gruesome) divination scene in which one seer is "reading" the entrails of a competing seer as he lies dying, and they're both arguing over the interpretation. They use *scrying*, a divination technique that uses some kind of physical object—like a crystal ball, flame, or reflecting pool—as a point of focus. In Zelazny's book, scryer Boltag has just called scryer Freydag a fraud and a "mighty misreader of innards":

> "Liar!" cries Freydag, scrambling to his side and seizing Boltag by the beard. "This ends thy infamous career!" and he slits the other's belly. Reaching in,

he draws forth a handful of entrails and spreads them upon the floor. Boltag cries, moans, lies still.[1]

A moment later Freydag begins to examine Boltag's entrails and divine the future. After Freydag makes a few pronouncements, it is the wounded Boltag who speaks:

> "Strangely, thou hast read that part all right. But thy failing vision was clouded by the bit of mesentery thou has erroneously mixed into things."
>
> "Silence!" cries Freydag. "I did not call thee in for a consultation!"
>
> "They are my innards! I will not have them misread by a poseur!"

Many questions flew around in my brain after reading *Creatures of Light and Darkness*. I knew that divination was not confined just to science-fiction stories. But I did not know that people around the world still practiced divination using numerous strange techniques. Why are we so interested in divination today? Why were our ancient cultures fascinated by divination? Can the wrinkles in a sheep liver really give accurate information about the future? To what degree did the ancients believe in these fantastic methods? What hardships would they suffer to see visions and hear voices from the other side? Clearly, the ancients suffered greatly for their practice. Sometimes they would go so far as to place herbal salves directly into their eyes. These concoctions, called collyria, often contained harmful or irritating substances. For example, the medieval manuscript *The Marvels of the World* gives the following recipe:

> If thou wilt see that other men cannot. Take the gall of a male Cat, and the fat of a Hen all white, and mix them together, and anoint thy eyes, and though shalt see it that others cannot see.[2]

Luckily for diviners, most divination methods are easier on the eyes than the ancient collyria. In fact, divination has become so popular that some methods have become part of curious parlor-room games. For example, probably many of you have heard of or used Ouija boards. I had one as a teenager, about the same time as I read Zelazny's book, and the board also stimulated my interest in divination.

The Ouija board, and its brother the planchehtte, are automatic writing devices. The planchette is a triangular plate mounted on little wheels. Several people place their fingertips on it and wait for messages to be written by a pencil that is attached to the device. The more complex Ouija board consists of a smooth board containing the words "yes" and "no," the alphabet, and numbers from 0 to 9. Users place their fingers on a small heart-shaped device attached to felt-tipped legs. In a few seconds, the device begins to wander around the board to spell messages and answer questions. Exactly how this mysterious movement occurs is discussed in the section on "ideomotor action" (unconscious muscle movement) in chapter 1. In the 1800s (and still today), some people thought that the messages emanated from spirits. Often the device spelled out embarrassing or obscene messages.

Did you know that there was a patent granted for the first modern Ouija board? Elijah J. Bond got the patent in 1891, and the game and board were produced the following year by William Fuld, who started to manufacture his "Oriole Talking Boards" at the Southern Novelty Company of Baltimore, later to be renamed the Baltimore Talking Board Company. One of William Fuld's first public relations tricks was to reinvent the history of the Ouija board. He claimed to have invented the board and that the name Ouija was a combination of the French and German words *oui* and *ja* for "yes." In actuality, the name probably derives from the legendary Moroccan city Oujda. In 1966, Parker Brothers bought the rights to the Ouija board and manufactured it in Salem, Massachusetts. Salem, of course, is where the infamous witchcraft trials took place in the late 1600s, but this may have had no relationship to why Salem was chosen. In its first full year of sale at Salem, the board outsold the famous Parker Brothers favorite, *Monopoly*. Over two million copies were shipped. The psychedelic sixties was the perfect decade to bring out such a cool device.

## ⅄ WHAT IS DIVINATION?

> *Time is a relationship that we have with the rest of the universe; or more accurately, we are one of the clocks, measuring one kind of time. Animals and aliens may measure it differently. We may even be able to change our way of marking time one day, and open up new realms of experience, in which a day today will be a million years.*
>
> —George Zebrowski, *OMNI*

The term *divination* means many different things to researchers, historians, and the general public. Academicians Michael Lowe and Carmen Blacker in their book *Oracles and Divination* define divination as the attempt to elicit from some higher power the answers to questions beyond the range of ordinary human understanding.[3] Similarly, divination is often an attempt to discern the will of the gods. Divination is also commonly understood as using supernatural means for foretelling future events or discovering hidden information. Through the centuries people have asked questions about the future, about mysterious past disasters, about secret things that could not be seen, about proper behavior, about other people, and about religious worship. People have used divination to arrange marriages, start journeys, choose treatments for the sick, settle legal disputes, and recover lost items.

Eva Shaw, author of *Divining the Future*, defines divination as the ability to forecast the future by *intuitive* means that are not necessarily unscientific.[4] For Shaw, interpreting omens is a form of divination. Often a diviner answers a person's question after observing manmade or natural objects. For example, in Bangladesh the diviner may use parrots that pick up grain scattered on handwritten messages. The diviner interprets the results for his clients. Evidence of ancient divination comes in many forms. For example, archeologists have found old divination manuals and clay models of livers used in entrail reading. Diviners have studied cracks on turtle shells in China, the movement of horses in Germany, the guts of sacrificed animals in Babylon, or the flight of birds in ancient Greece.

Practitioners of divination have often believed two things: (1) they can understand the divine will, and (2) gods send messages through various natural signs and extraordinary phenomena. In ancient Greece and Rome, diviners gave readings for the government. Here, the diviners did not restrict themselves to prognosticating on the future but also gave advice on whether a certain action was in accordance with the gods' wills.

Many of the divination methods in this book can be divided into *inductive* and *deductive* systems. The inductive methods require visions or trances in which the diviner receives information. This is sometimes called *mediumistic divination*. The deductive systems require the diviner to carefully study signs around him and analyze them according to a fixed set of rules and meanings.

The great Roman statesman and writer Marcus Tullius Cicero once wrote that there are two type of divination, one derived from "art" and the other from "nature." By "art," Cicero meant divination though human skill and training, such as would be required for tea-leaf, entrail reading, or astrology. By "nature" Cicero referred to dreams, visions, and other contact with the supernatural. As you will see later in this book, many diviners like John Dee and Nostradamus seemed to induce visions by gazing at reflective surfaces like waters and crystals.

One of my goals in this book is to show just how pervasive divination has been through the ages. Just as humans create gods and religions that rise and fall with time, humans also seem to be locked into cycles of divination. In Islam and Judaism, divination continues despite Old Testament prohibitions and the warnings of Mohammed.

Many people still seem to find divination a fascinating subject. It's of particular interest to social anthropologists, admirers of synchronicity (the theory that there is a mysterious connectedness of objects and events in space and time), and some psychologists who suggest that the divination apparatuses (for example, crystal balls, cracks in turtle shells, intestines, and tarot cards) focus the conscious mind so that subconscious insights bubble up like water from a fountain. In the Bible, Joseph was renowned for his ability to interpret the dreams of the pharaoh, and in many cultures dreaming is regarded as a divinatory state. Belief in the powers of divination was not restricted to the uneducated or foolish. Many of the great minds of the classical world believed in divination. Roman statesman Cicero, in his book *On Divination*, suggested that all the ancient famous philosophers—including Aristotle, Plato, and Socrates—believed in divination.

My favorite Icelandic saga is *Grettir's Saga* or *The Saga of Grettir the Strong*, written in the early fourteenth century by an unknown author. (You can find many versions on the World Wide Web should you wish to study it further.) Grettir is a complicated and stubborn protagonist who saves his people from the evil ghost of Glam the shepherd. One particular line in the story is relevant to divination. Here, Thorian the Wise has just guessed that Grettir is his son Bardi's new ally. Bardi replies, "*Spá er spaks geta.*"[5] Translators have rendered this phrase in many ways including: "The guess of the wise is truth," "Prophecy is the wise man's guess," or "The wise person's guess reveals hidden truths." In much of Icelandic literature, we find that people with special powers can know the future through divination. Sometimes when people ask me what divination is all about, I look them in the eye and say "*Spá er spaks geta.*" I pause and then give them my dissertation, which has now evolved into this book.

## ᚼ WHAT IS PROPHECY?

> *Tell us what the future holds, so we may know that you are gods. Do something, whether good or bad, so that we will be dismayed and filled with fear.*
> —Isaiah 41:23

Today we are used to thinking of fortune telling and divination as directed towards individuals and personal destiny. Astrology, tarot cards, and palmistry are well-known examples of this kind of tailored divination. *Prophecy* often refers to predictions applied to a larger group, such as a city, nation, or the planet.[6] In this general sense, examples of prophecy can include the general predictions of psychics, astrologers, and futurists, as well as the prophecies of Nostradamus and the biblical sages. A prophets differs from a magician and a seer in that the prophet is often concerned with more spiritual matters such as God's will, the spiritual health of a society, and warnings of disaster. The prophet's utterances tend to be more revolutionary and of general importance. Some of the most famous non-biblical prophets of natural upheaval are Nostradamus, Gordon Michael Scallion, Lori Toye, and Edgar Cayce. Nostradamus (1503–1566), predicted earthquakes and drought. Edgar Cayce (1877–1945), the sleeping prophet, foretold the coming of enormous earthquakes and said that New York, San Francisco, and Los Angeles would not exist after the year 2000. In the 1900s, Cayce, Scallion, and Toye have all drawn inspired maps of the earth after these natural disasters. Most of the maps show California and New York under water and the Great Lakes pouring into the central states. Perhaps because New York, Los Angeles, and Chicago are the three largest cities in America, the psychics' prediction of disasters in these regions gives the prophecies additional impact.

Sometimes the origins of prophecies found through archeological excavations are obscure and shrouded in mystery. As one modern example, consider the famous "Flowering Almond Tree" of Berlin. In the year 1944, Allied bombers destroyed Berlin. In the ruins of a church, they found a lead tube containing a document titled "The Flowering Almond Tree." The document seemed to be written by a nineteenth-century Benedictine monk. Upon the old parchment was a cryptic prediction for each year. No one knows who wrote the predictions and why they were stored in a lead tube.

≈   ≈   ≈

In this book, the line between closely related words like "diviner" and "prophet" grow thin, and sometimes I use them almost interchangeably. The term prophet comes from the Greek *prophetes*, meaning "forthteller." Although prophecy usually expresses the overall future for groups of people, prophecy also often implies speaking by divine inspiration. Some prophets believe they are gods' messengers, receiving his communications in visions or by divinatory practices. The term prophet also applies to someone like Nostradamus, the sixteenth-century physician and astrologer, and one of the best-known prophets of all time. He said he believed that his prophecies were the result of a form of divine or spiritual revelation, and his unorthodox views caused conflict with the church authorities.

Other differences exist between prophecy and divination. In this last section, we noted how divination often refers to the means and techniques for looking into the future. Prophets believe that they do not *choose* to receive revelations about the future and sometimes even resist the role.[7] Most prophets feel that they have been chosen to transmit their prophecies, whereas a person does divination by choice. Also, divination is often done to get an answer to a specific question, while prophecy usually happens spontaneously. Some prophets say they are unaware of their messages' importance.

By these definitions, Nostradmus was both a prophet and a diviner. As you will read in chapter 3, he used divination methods. He also said he channeled a spiritual revelation and was aware of what he was doing as well as the significance of the message. It seems that both divination and prophecy may involve tapping into the subconscious.

## ✧ WHAT IS AN ORACLE?

> *The distinction between past, present, and future is only an illusion, even if a stubborn one.*
>
> —Albert Einstein

I often use the term "oracle" in this book. Like divination, the term "oracle" has many related meanings, such as:

- A person (such as a priest of ancient Greece) through whom a deity is believed to speak, or any person giving wise opinions.
- A shrine in which a deity reveals hidden knowledge or divine purpose. The ancient world had hundreds of oracles, including altars, grottos, dream incubation sites, and temples.
- An answer or decision given by an oracle (person).
- A communication from a god.
- The instrumentality, agency, or medium by which a higher power speaks or makes his will known.

An oracle may be unsought, although once a particular god or location has developed a reputation for communication with humans, the god or site is usually consulted with increasing frequency.[8]

In most cultures, gifted people, mediums, or seers were recognized as being able to link our world with a supernatural realm. These people transmitted utterances of an oracle and included the Greek *Pythia* (see figure 1) and the Japanese *miko*. Oracles often came in the form of dreams. In Japan, Israel, Greece, Mesopotamia, and among the Norsemen, incubation (dreaming at a sacred site) was used to evoke oracular dreams.

Carmen Blacker, a lecturer at Cambridge University, classifies both divination and oracles as methods of communication between two worlds or dimensions that are usually divided from each other. Blacker writes, "We are trying to put questions, which we are unable to answer for ourselves, to another order of beings whose knowledge transcends the limitation of our own."[9] Scholars often use the term divination to refer to the various methods whereby questions can be put, and use the term "oracles" to refer to the answers given by beings on the other side.

**Figure 1.** At the shrine of Apollo in Delphi, Greece, the Pythia, a divinatory priestess, sits upon a three-legged stool, inhaling the vapor that rises from a crack in the ground. Various speculations have been made regarding the vapor, and it is possible that hallucinogenic substances were also burned to help her enter a trance. From Nevill Drury and Gergory Tillett, *The Occult* (New York: Barnes & Nobles Books, 1997), p. 82.

## WHAT ARE OMENS?

*A single day will see the burial of mankind, all that the long forbearance of fortune has produced, all that has been brought to eminence, all that is well-known and all that is beautiful; mighty thrones, great nations—all will sing into one abyss, all will be toppled in one hour.*
—Sibylline Oracles

Omens are events or phenomena that purportedly foretell the future. Throughout history, people have interpreted omens as signifying good or bad fortune. There were many kinds of phenomena interpreted as omens in ancient times, such as lightning, cloud movements, the flight of birds, and the paths of sacred horses.

In the classical world, such as ancient Rome, omens came in several categories. For example, some omens were "given" (*oblativa*), such as thunder and lightening, monstrous births, the sweating of statues, and the cries of birds.[10] Other omens were "provoked" or "solicited" (*impetrativa*), such as when diviners would study the appearance of organs in sacrificed animals or the behavior of chickens when fed. These solicited omens were often good for answering yes/no questions, whereas the unsolicited phenomena often required further interpretation. Many of the *impetrativa* methods were derived from the Etruscans, ancient inhabitants of the Italian peninsula. This classification into *oblativa* and *impetrativa* is similar to Cicero's grouping divination methods into those derived from "nature" and "art," as we discussed in a previous section.

In important public circumstances, *oblativa* were interpreted with the help of the Sibylline Books. The Sibylline Books, used by the Romans, were a body of prophecies issued by a group of seers known as the *sibyls*. (Sibyl was a prophetess in Greek legend and literature, traditionally represented as an old woman speaking predictions while in a trance.) Legend has it that the most famous sibyl, from Cuame, Italy, offered a set of prophetic books to King Tarquinius Superbus, the last king of Rome. He refused to pay her price, so the sibyl burned several books, at which point he paid the original price. The books were thereafter kept in a temple and consulted only in the most dire of circumstances. The Sibylline Books were eventually burned by the Christian emperor Honorius, although Christian and Jewish versions soon appeared.

The "Sybilline Oracles" refers to a much later collection of oracular prophecies in which Jewish or Christian doctrines were allegedly confirmed by a sibyl. However, the prophecies were actually written by Jews and Christians living around the time of Jesus Christ. In the Oracles, the sibyl appeared to have special powers because she first "predicted" events that had already occurred. Many Jews were impressed. Later theologians believed the sibyl to be inspired like the Old Testament prophets.[11]

Returning to ancient omens in general, one of my favorite examples occurs in the tale of Roman admiral Publius Clodius. During the first Punic war, Clodius was eager to fight the Cartheginians. Therefore, when the chickens refused to eat (which was considered a bad omen), he had them thrown into the sea saying, "If they won't eat, let them drink."[12] (Clodius eventually met with disaster and was convicted of treason.) In this case, he should have listed to the chickens.

## √ FROM ANATOLIANS TO GROUND HOGS

*I see the Past, Present, and Future existing all at once before me.*
—William Blake, "Jerusalem"

Just months after my initial reading of *Creatures of Light and Darkness*, I began to study the religious beliefs and practices of the ancient Anatolians—civilizations of Turkey and Armenia that included the Hittites and Assyrians. The Anatolians used various kinds of divination to understand why the gods were angry: *augury* (divination by watching the flight patterns of birds), *haruspicy* (hah-RUS-puh-see, as we said, divination by examining animal organs), and a method that used tokens. People would go to the augurers and haruspices to ask questions. Most of the methods only gave yes or no answers, but by asking numerous questions, a person could learn how to appease the angry gods. I suspect these kinds of methods came from Babylonia and could actually date back to the cavemen days.

〜〜〜   〜〜〜   〜〜〜

Today, when you hear the word "divination," it's likely that certain images will fill your brain: gypsy fortunetellers, tea leaves swirling in a cup, or the witch's crystal ball in *The Wizard of Oz*. If you're a horror film fan, "divination" may conjure up visions of dark magicians in graveyards or demons rising from tombs. For over a millennium, divination was a sin in Western culture, a communing with Satan that was not tolerated by many god-fearing people. For a significant portion of divination's history, the practices were outlawed. For example, Roman emperor Augustus (63 B.C.E.–14 C.E.) forbid the practice of private divination, so that the signs that announced his fortuitous reign could never change. Christianized Roman emperor Theodosius (347–395 C.E.) forbade divination and made it a capital crime because he felt that divination was "unclean" and outside of church teachings. During the Chinese Han dynasty (206 B.C.E.–220 C.E.) and Sung Dynasty (960–1279), popular forms of divination were against the law because divination yielded nonofficial insights into politics and life. However, if we go as far back as ancient Greece, regular contact with the gods was part of everyday life. Later, the Holy Grail, Christ's cup at the Last Supper, was thought of as an interface between the physical and nonphysical worlds.

I wonder if so many leaders feared divination because they felt that these mystical practices might reveal their secrets, give the people too much power, or even give "permission" to carry out rebellious acts. Although officials could outlaw the divination books and obvious public displays, it must have been difficult to persecute ordinary people who might quietly observe nature, such as the flight of birds, or listening to chance conversations, both of which were popular forms of divination that would not be obvious to the government officials.

~~~    ~~~    ~~~

Perhaps many of you are already familiar with divination without knowing it. How many of you have heard of ground-hog day as it relates to divining weather patterns? The tradition of ground-hog day began in the eighteenth century. If a ground hog sees its shadow on February 2, it is said that there will be six more weeks of winter.

The origins of ground-hog day came from centuries-old traditions when, in early February, the Romans observed that the winter days were growing noticeably longer. People lit candles to supplement the light. When the Christians took over the Roman empire, they referred to this candle lighting as "Candlemas." The ideas spread to Germany and other European countries. For example, consider this Scottish couplet, "If Candlemas Day is bright and clear, There'll be two winters in the year." Candlemas Day began to be celebrated on February second and was associated with the idea that if an animal, such as a hedgehog, came out of its underground hibernation on that day, and the sun was out and he could see his shadow, there would be six more weeks of winter.

When Germans and other Europeans migrated to the United States, there were no hedgehogs to use. Thus, the Pennsylvania Dutch changed their traditions from a hedgehog to a woodchuck or ground hog. In the early 1880s a few residents of Punxsutawney, Pennsylvania, began to celebrate the legend of the groundhog as a weather prognosticator. If Punxsutawney Phil saw his shadow upon emerging from his burrow, there would be six more weeks of bad weather. If he did not see his shadow, there would be an early spring. Today, the popularity of ground-hog day continues, although scientific evidence does not support this tradition.

In the late 1800s, Mother Bridget's popular *Dream and Omen Book* had the following fascinating divination recipe for Candlemas, and I include it here to display the beliefs of some people in England at that time:

> Candlemas Eve.—On this night, let three, five, seven, or nine, young maidens assemble together in a square chamber. Then mix a cake of flour, olive-oil, and white sugar. . . . Afterwards, it must be cut into equal pieces, each one marking the piece as she cuts it with the initials of her name. Each piece of cake is then to be wrapped up in a sheet of paper, on which each maiden shall write the love part of Solomon's Songs. If she put this under her pillow, she will dream true. She will see her future husband and every one of her children, and will know, besides, whether her family will be poor or prosperous.[13]

## ◇ THE NATURE OF TIME

> *We still cannot say what time is; we cannot agree whether there is one time or many times, cannot even agree whether time is an essential ingredient of the universe or whether it is the grand illusion of the human intellect.*
> —Phillip Davis and Reuben Hersh, *Descartes' Dream*

If divination and prophecy somehow involved stepping outside of the present moment to view the future, is there any scientific theory that would permit such an outrageous power? Ever since H. G. Wells's 1895 publication of *The Time Machine*—which described a four-dimensional spacetime with duration a dimension like height, width, and thickness—people have been wondering why we can't travel in time as we do in space. Einstein's special theory of relativity suggests that time is a dimension with similarities to the three spatial dimensions. In fact, the idea that time as a fourth dimension[14]—on par with the familiar three dimensions of space—is one of the main foundations of modern physics (see figure 2).

If time is really just another kind of space, why can't we travel back and forth as easily as we move in space? Why can't we divine secret events in the past or future? If time is like space, then in some sense the past may literally still exist "back there" as surely as New York still exists even after I have left it. If we could travel in time as easily as we do in space, imagine how our lives would be transformed. We would no longer have regrets about past events. Nor would we wonder about "roads not taken." We'd simply go back in time and make other choices and see what happens. If we were unhappy with the results, we'd try again and again. The power to divine the future and the possibility of time travel would allow us to become omniscient, omnipresent, and omnipotent—qualities humans have normally attributed to God. In a sense, divination and time travel would allow us all to become God.

Some physicists believe that if we seriously consider time as a fourth dimension, then the past and future have always existed, and that human consciousness, for some unknown reason, perceives the universe one moment at a time giving rise to the illusion of a continually changing present. As mathematical physicist Herman Weyl once noted, "The objective world simply is; it does not happen. Only to the gaze of my consciousness, crawling upward along the life line of my body, does a section of this world come to life as a fleeting image which continuously changes in time."[15] Perhaps other beings in the universe do not have our perceptual constraints

**Figure 2.** The idea that time is a fourth dimension—on par with the familiar three dimensions of space—is one of the main foundations of modern physics. If time is really just another kind of space, why can't we travel back and forth as easily as we move in space? If we could travel in time as easily as we do in space, imagine how our lives would be transformed. Time travel would allow us to become omniscient, omnipresent, and omnipotent—qualities humans have normally attributed to God. From Jan Vredeman de Vries, *Perspective* (New York: Dover, 1968), plate 36.

with regard to future and past, just like the creatures in Kurt Vonnegut's novel *Sirens of Titan*. In this book, the aliens see past and present at once and view human beings as "great millipedes with babies' legs at one end and old people's legs at the other."[16] Although I am skeptical, if time is truly a fourth dimension, then time travel and scientific methods of divination always remain a remote possibility.

In March 1997, Roger Ebert of the *Chicago Sun Times* asked science-fiction visionary Arthur C. Clarke, "Do you think that there is any scientific invention or discovery so alarming that we would feel it necessary to suppress it?" Clarke's answer relates to the awesome and alarming consequences if people could accurately divine mysteries of the future and past:

> There is one invention: a time probe, revealing the past and everything that has ever happened. When you think of the implications of that, it's pretty appalling. Could we as a human civilization survive such a thing? I just

don't know. I don't think it's possible, but I can't rule out that a time probe could be created. All the mysteries and all the secrets that had ever happened would be revealed. Total transparency. That is the most terrifying invention I can think of.[17]

## ⧫ RELEVANCE TODAY

> *How little do you mortals understand time. Must you be so linear, Jean-Luc?*
> —Q to Captain Picard, in *Star Trek*'s "All Good Things"

### Complete Idiot

If you think divination was primarily important in the past—that it is a superstitious relic of ancient, irrelevant societies on the brink of madness and moral decay—you are wrong. In this section, I focus on U.S. patents that rely on divinatory methods, divination in the workplace, divination in modern Africa, and a host of odd ideas that suggest divination pervades many aspects of our modern lives. I include several examples of modern ways in which people gain hidden or secret information through unusual methods.

I suppose one measure of a topic's relevance for today's society is whether the popular *Complete Idiot's Guide* book series devotes a book to it. It turns out that the series does indeed have several books teaching divination, including *The Complete Idiot's Guide to Being Psychic*. I enjoy the disclaimer and warning in the book:

> Certain types of schizophrenics also report hearing voices, and if you start hearing voices out of the blue, your first stop should be your doctor's office. We also recommend that you make sure you're truly hearing psychic information before acting on your premonitions. And whatever you do, don't try anything dangerous because you think it's based on your intuition!"[18]

### Modern Divination Patents

As just one modern example of a class of divination devices, consider that the U.S. patent office has recently awarded dozens of patents for devices that invoke principles outside accepted science—from psychic forces to exotic forms of nuclear physics that challenge traditional physics if the devices work as described.[19] For example, U.S. patent 5,830,064 was granted to Pear Inc. for the ultimate divination device—an electronic device that is meant to detect psychic forces that affect a random signal. The patent says the gadget can detect the "volitional state of one or more persons" so that your mind can control various machines. Figure 3 shows a figure from the patent for a toy cat that is controlled essentially by your mind. A device based on this technology sells for about $125 (www.mindsongingc.com). When *Science* magazine asked the responsible patent examiner about this device, the examiner said that he didn't find the patent fantastic. Further figures from the patent are in appendix 3.

Another unusual "divinatory" invention is described in U.S. patent 5,748,088, granted for a device that locates "entities" by "dielectrokinesis," or more particularly for driving the device toward the direction of a person's heart. This would be useful when a person is behind debris after a building collapses, and the device's user attempts to locate the heart's electromagnetic field. A product based on this patent is the LifeGuard™ system sold by DKL Inc. for the purpose of divining the position of humans behind barriers. The cost of such units is several thousand dollars, and there are currently various heated, scientific discussions about the device's operation.[20] Some researchers at the Sandia National Laboratory in New Mexico have tested the device (see figure 4) and are skeptical about certain features of its use.[21]

A governmental agency has questioned the accuracy of the device. One such report comes from the Justice Technology Information Network (JUSTNET):[22]

> The National Institute of Justice (NIJ)[23] tasked and funded Sandia National Laboratories to conduct a detailed physical analysis, based upon fundamental scientific principles, of a DielectroKinetic Laboratories, LLC (DKL), Model 3 LifeGuard™ device to determine if it could function as advertised. The DKL LifeGuard™ devices are marketed as a human presence detector and tracker.

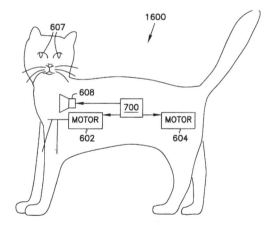

**Figure 3.** A schematic diagram of a toy cat controlled by a detector (700) which is in turn controlled through psychic forces. From G. Johnston Brandish, York Dobyns, Brenda Dunne, Robert Jahn, Roger Nelson, John Haaland, and Steven Hamer, "Apparatus and method for distinguishing events which collectively exceed change expectation and thereby controlling an output," U.S. patent 5,830,064, November 3, 1998, p. 22, fig. 16.

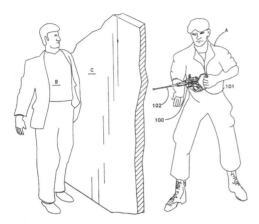

**Figure 4.** An ultramodern divining rod? A device from U.S. patent 5,748,008 for locating a person behind a wall. The antenna 102 points toward the human being B. From Thomas L. Afilani, "Device and method using dielectrokinesis to locate entities," U.S. patent 5,748,008, May 5, 1998, p. 1, fig. 1.

The results of Sandia's analysis conclusively demonstrate that the LifeGuard™ Model 3 device can not possibly function as a passive long range detector of human heartbeats based on the scientific principles of dielectrophoresis.

A summary of Sandia's findings indicate that the passive circuit, attributed to detecting heartbeats based on dielectrophoresis, is actually a non-functioning, open circuit. Additionally, this circuit includes a component composed of human hair glued between two small pieces of polystyrene. There was also no discernible feedback mechanism or drive to move the antenna located at the front of the device that would cause it to point toward a beating human heart.

This analysis summary is provided for informational purposes. A copy of Sandia's report titled, *Physical Examination of the DKL LifeGuard™ Model 3*, is available on JUSTNET in Adobe Acrobat format.[24]

Thomas Coty, National Institute of Justice

Appendix 3 has additional figures for this device. As you can see, even in the U.S. patent office, divination is quite relevant today.

## *What People Believe Today*

The Library of Congress contains over twelve thousand works on astrology: divination by observing the positions of planets, the moon, and the sun. The business of astrology brings over $100,000 million a year in the United States if one considers increases in newspaper circulation resulting from inclusion of horoscopes, astrology readings for clients either in person or on the phone, books, lectures, and Internet Web sites and services. Analysts suggests that the psychic telephone networks take in around two billion dollars.[25]

In 1988, a panic in Los Angeles occurred because some people thought Nostradamus had predicted that an earthquake would strike the city at that time. After watching a rerun of the TV show *Nostradamus: The Man Who Saw Tomorrow*, narrated by Orson Welles, many thousands of people left the city. Welles seemed to have had a pronounced effect on his listeners. So many celebrities reportedly left town that good tables at Hollywood restaurants could be secured! This was the same year the public learned that Nancy Reagan had consulted a San Francisco astrologer to determine the most favorable days for her husband, President Reagan, to plan meetings.[26]

Aside from astrology, graphology plays a significant role in our everyday lives. Graphology is "divination" of human character through handwriting. It is true that, on average, any of us can distinguish a man's writing from a woman's about 70 percent of the time, and that we can generally make a good guess about the writer's gender and age. However, graphology use by employers for personnel selection does not have a rigorously scientific underpinning. Unfortunately, about three thousand American firms use graphology when judging people for jobs. About 85 percent of European firms use graphology, and, in France, Peugot and Air France have their own full-time graphologists![27] Some companies won't hire a prospective employee if the person is rejected by a graphologist, although there have not been sufficient controlled studies to demonstrate that traits such as honesty and insight are reflected in handwriting or good penmanship.

African cultures are very involved with divination today. For example, the Azande, a central African tribe, practice *myrmomancy*—the observations of ants eating food to divine the future. They also use termites and poisoned chickens to make predictions, as discussed in detail in chapter 1. (Azande[28] is also spelled Asande or Zande.) The Dogon, a western African tribe, observe paw patterns left by jackals to make predictions. Some Polynesians may still practice *skatharomancy* in which tribal leaders coax a beetle to crawl over the grave of a murder victim. The beetle's tracks are supposed to tell the murderer's name when the tracks are interpreted.[29]

In West Africa, Bantu psychics throw bones engraved with special symbols. Zulu diviners use similar methods. The Yaka body diviner becomes sick to change his awareness of reality so that he can see events more clearly and see "behind things." The diviner begins by smelling an object that has been in contact with the troubled person. In Afro-Brazilian groups, such as the *Umbanda* and *Candomblé*, mediums go into trances in order to give guidance and diagnose and cure illness.

Most of the African groups that use divination also believe in witchcraft, sometimes with horrifying repercussions. In 1999, angry Tanzanian villagers killed 350 suspected witches.[30] Tanzania's Criminal Investigation Department suggests that an average of twenty-one murders a month are linked to superstition. The police said that the recently murdered people, most of whom were old, were killed by villagers who accused them of practicing witchcraft on them by allegedly killing their loved ones or inflicting curses that made them fail in business or reduced their harvests.

Witchcraft murders have also been reported recently in Mbeya, southern Tanzania, linked to a cross-border trade in human skin.[31] The skin is supposed to protect homes from evil spirits, to increase harvests, and to lure clients to shops. Some old women whose eyes had turned red after cooking in smoke-filled kitchens were also accused of being witches and murdered.[32]

## Guinea Pig and Blood Divination

Entrail reading, or divining the future by observing the internal organs of animals, goes back centuries, and is still practiced today with farm animals in Borneo and Burma.[33] Human bodily fluids are also used today to predict the future. In the late 1970s, Masahiko Nomi wrote the Japanese bestseller *Good Combination of Blood Types* in which he claimed that an individual's personality is related to his or her blood type. While most Americans know if they are a Leo or Aquarius, most Japanese know their blood type even if they don't believe in Nomi's system. Here are some specific character traits predicted by the Uranai system of blood typing:

### The Uranai System

| Blood Type | Personality Characteristics |
|:---:|---|
| A | Sensitive, serious, obliging, nervous, stubborn. |
| B | Warm, active, selfish, hasty, careless, conspicuous, obssessed with lists and collecting. |
| AB | Intelligent, rational, cold, disagreeable, two-faced. |
| O | Friendly, practical, easygoing, childish, simple. |

My Japanese friends tell me that these kinds of theories are very popular in Japan, especially among teens, much like tarot cards and psychic readings are popular in America. Some of the blood-type theories deal with romantic compatibilites; for example, a male of one blood type makes a good partner to a female of another blood type. Uranai serves as a topic of conversation and a way to break the ice at Japanese parties. Incidentally, the term "Uranai" refers to Japanese fortune-telling in general and encompasses all kinds of divination including those based on European or Oriental systems of astrology, the number of strokes in your name (in Kanji characters), the shapes of clouds, fissures in Turkish coffee beans, tarot cards, bamboo sticks, and compatibility estimates relating to blood types.

〜〜〜　〜〜〜　〜〜〜

Let's move our attention from Japan to the Andes Mountains of South America. The guinea pig has always had a prominent, sacred place in the Andean world. For example, the Incas based their wartime strategies on guinea pig entrails. Today, shamans and traditional healers use black guinea pigs in an ancient curing ritual that dates back thousands of years. To perform the rite, the healer passes the animal over the patient's naked body to absorb the illness.[34] Next, the guinea pig is offered a variety of herbal medicines, and whatever the pig chooses to eat is prescribed for the sick person. The shaman then kills the guinea pig and examines its entrails to determine the cause of illness and the prognosis. For example, if the patient has a stomach tumor, a tumor or lump is supposed to appear in the guinea pig's stomach. The entrails also reveal the mental health of the patient and the health of the patient's family. Following this ritual, the guinea pig becomes an object of potential danger, because it had absorbed the patient's illness. The head of the household must bury the remains in a secluded place, so that it will not infect humans or other animals. (Guinea pigs don't fare too well in U.S. culture either.)

The Associated Press recently described the guinea pig divination more poetically in an article titled "Peruvians put faith in 'Andean X-Ray' to diagnose ailments."[35] After rubbing a patient's naked body with the pig, the healer whispers a prayer and spits a mixture of cane liquor and herbs on the patient. The liquor is meant to open the person's pores to the guinea pig's power. The healer then kills the guinea pig (also known as a "cuy") with a ritual knife, slices it open, and reads its entrails to diagnose the patient's ailment. Despite the spread of modern medicine in Peru, millions of poor people use the age-old Andean practice of "passing the cuy." Faith healers also claim the cuy possesses curative powers, absorbing the negative energy caused by "damage" and "fright," the basic causes of disease according to Andean belief.

If a child has had a bad scare, such as narrowly avoiding an accident, parents often have a healer pass a cuy or egg over the child to remove the "fright" and to avoid medical or psychological problems. Some faith healers pass the cuy over people and then hurl it hard against a rock. If the stunned cuy does not die and slowly begins to move, the healer pronounces the person healthy.

Peru's poor people cannot afford private medical care and distrust low-quality state services. Many prefer the less expensive rituals and remedies made from native plants offered by the Indian healers, despite the lack of scientific evidence that they work. Booths of faith healers line the busy street markets, offering the cuy ritual, herbal medicines, and love potions. The cuy "operating room" is often a dirt floor and stool surrounded by a ragged curtain.

## ☒ TRAVEL THROUGH SPACE AND TIME

> High up in the North in the land called Svithjod, there stands a rock. It is a hundred miles high and a hundred miles side. Once every thousand years a little bird comes to the rock to sharpen its beak. When the rock has thus been worn away, then a single day of eternity will have gone by.
> —Hendrik Willem Van Loon, *The Story of Mankind*

The chapters that follow introduce you to divination in different cultures, from Africa to Tibet, from ancient times to modern. The concepts overlap the fields of comparative religion, psychic research, history, and psychology—and I believe they'll show you how divination and prophecy have shaped humanity in profound ways. In this Introduction I mentioned how ancient divination methods were used in modern settings, for example the use of the *I Ching* in making business decisions. Another example includes the tarot—those colorful cards with haunting images like "The Lightening Struck Tower," "The Hanged Man," and "Death," which have been used for centuries to divine the future. These days the cards are used by some writers to overcome writer's block. In this application, there's nothing too mysterious about this process, because the randomly selected cards are used as a tool to spark creativity and develop plots and characters. Writers gaze at the cards' images to find "hints of a story, a facet of a character, a potential theme that might have escaped one's notice before."[36]

I asked around to find writers who use tarot cards to get ideas for stories. Meredith Monaghan wrote me that she is one fan of this approach:

> Sometimes when I'm trying to figure out directions that an idea could take in one of my books, I'll bust out my Rider-Waite tarot cards, pick a card for whatever character's life needs changing the most right then, and look for possible cues in the cards I deal out randomly. It has made for some pretty devious plot twists.[37]

Author Melinda Rose Goodin writes:

A rereading of my futuristic work in progress showed that I had a sagging middle in the manuscript. The pace of the novel had slowed down drastically because the characters were simply talking about their pasts. It was important that I find a way to develop these characters and their history. I drew a tarot card to help work out a way of maintaining pace and story development.[38]

Thus, we see how tarot fortune-telling cards, which appeared in their present form in Italy and France in the late fourteenth century, are still used today for both practical and mystical applications. Similarly, by reading this book, you shall see how important, historical decisions were often based on divination methods. The ancient methods that shaped the destiny of nations, and even the outcomes of important wars, continue to be used in virtually every country for purposes that are hardly imaginable.

# 1.

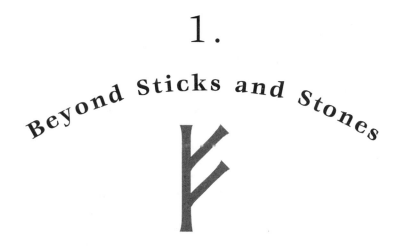

## Beyond Sticks and Stones

*How flattering to the pride of man to think that the stars in their courses watch over him, and typify, by their movements and aspects, the joys or the sorrows that await him. How we should pity the arrogance of the worm that crawls at our feet, if we knew that it also desired to know the secrets of futurity, and imagined that meteors shot across the sky to warn it that a bird was hovering near to gobble it up.*
—Charles Mackay, *Extraordinary Popular Delusions*
*and the Madness of Crowds*

*You are so part of the world that your slightest action contributes to its reality. Your breath changes the atmosphere. Your encounters with others alter the fabrics of their lives, and the lives of those who come in contact with them.*
—Jane Roberts, *The Seth Material*

## ◇ FROM SHEEP GUTS TO FORTUNE COOKIES

*The difficulty in life is the choice.*
—George Moore, *The Bending of the Bough*

On December 1, 1999, Japanese police raided offices of a religious foot cult.[1] Police suspected cult members had defrauded numerous women by examining the women's feet to diagnose ailments. In particular, police said they believed that the *Ho-no-Hana Sampogyo* cult had persuaded the women to give them 22 million yen ($215,000) in return for health advice. Police also suspected *Ho-no-Hana Sampogyo* members of telling the women they would die young or contract cancer if they failed to heed the cult's warning. Separately, about 1,100 former followers have filed lawsuits against of *Ho-no-Hana Sampogyo* seeking damages.

Stories like these suggest that we have a strong tendency to believe in divination in many forms, for example, divining the future, divining the location of precious metals in the Earth, or divining the presence of disease. In this particular example, cult leader Teruyoshi Fukunaga and his disciples did not have any license to practice medicine but said they could diagnose people's health and predict their future by foot exams. As a result, the Japanese police searched seventy-four locations, including the headquarters of the religious group based at the foot of Mount Fuji. It was the biggest police search of a religious group since Aum Shinri Kyo's 1995 nerve gas attack in the Tokyo subway that killed twelve people and affected thousands.

Since the earliest civilizations, people have used divination methods to communicate with the supernatural, diagnose diseases and forecast the future. In the introduction, I mentioned that divination practices are often classified in two categories:

- The observation and interpretation of *natural phenomena*, such as stars, storms, clouds, monstrous births, or the behavior and look of animals.
- The observation and interpretation of phenomena *deliberately induced* or controlled by humans. For example, a diviner might pour oil into a basin of water to observe the formation of bubbles or throw a hatchet at a wooden block to see how the hatchet quivers.

The ancient Romans favored augury and haruspicy. The Egyptians, Druids, and Hebrews relied on scrying. The Druids also divined by watching an animal's death throes or studying the entrails of sacrificed animals. The Greeks used oracles who spoke for the gods. In the Middle Ages, sand or peas were scattered on the ground in order to read the resulting patterns. As far back as 1000 B.C.E., the Chinese used *I Ching*, a method that involved the tossing of long and short yarrow sticks. Another ancient Chinese divinatory practice we discussed that is still used today is *feng-shui*, or *geomancy*, which allows practitioners to determine favorable locations for buildings and tombs. Even in America, many people use similar principles for efficiently arranging furniture.

Many divinatory methods are still used today, especially in paganism, witchcraft, voodoo, and Santeria, a religious practice originating in West Africa. Even Judeo-Christian prayers might be considered a form of divination to the extent they extoll God to give information about or affect future events. Many diviners through history did not believe the future was set in concrete. Instead, people had free choices about their future, and divination was supposed to help them make better choices.

This chapter presents a large sampling of divination methods, some with "how-to" recipes to encourage reader involvement. Here are just a few topic that we'll touch upon:

- *Astrology*. Since caveman days, humans have been awed by the night sky. In an attempt to personalize the universe, some people believe that the positions of stars and planets can influence our lives.
- *Tribal Divination*. Unlike astrology, many cultures, particularly in Africa, believe that the key to unexplainable events lies in interpersonal relationships—either with fellow members of the tribe, or with ancestors or tribal spirits.
- *Oracles and Prophecy*. In the ancient Sumerian, Babylonian, Hittite, Greek, and Roman cultures, oracles had a sacred position, and no important personal or governmental decisions were made without consulting them.
- *The I Ching*, or *Book of Changes*. The *I Ching* originated in China at least one thousand years before the birth of Christ and is one of the oldest books in the world. Confucian and Taoist sages thought very highly of the *I Ching*, treating it as a scared book and prizing its powers of divination. Science-fiction writers, such as Philip K. Dick, used the *I Ching* to develop plot lines in their novels.
- *Feng-shui*. *Feng-shui* is an ancient Chinese form of geomancy believed to date back to the Han dynasty (206 B.C.E.–220 C.E.). Translated as "wind" and "water," *feng-shui* is used to discover the most auspicious sites for buildings and graves by analyzing the ch'i, or the natural life force, of the surrounding landscape.
- *Dowsing*. Often referred to as water-witching, or water-divining, dowsing is not necessarily concerned with locating water. Some diviners believe it can be used to discover the whereabouts of natural substances, people, and objects that cause illnesses.
- *The Tarot*. One of the most visually interesting and popular of all occult practices is tarot card reading. Tarot cards were the precursors of the standard playing cards, and they are best known for their use in fortune telling.
- *Numerology*. From the earliest times, humans have been fascinated by the symbolism of numbers. The numbers 7 and 12 have sacred significance in many cultures. Magic squares consisting of number arrays are used to divine the future and shape destinies.

- *Palmistry.* In its simplest form, palmistry is a fortune-telling technique of reading hands, popularized at fairground sideshows. Palmistry, also known as *cherigonomy* or *cheiromancy*, has had a rich history and is concerned with the analysis of lines on the palms and features of the hands and fingers.

- *Entrail Reading.* Entrail reading, or divination by studying of animal organs, was one of the most common forms of divination in ancient times. By 2000 B.C.E., the art of divination by the study of sheep livers was popular in Mesopotamia. The ancient Etruscans, Greeks, and Romans also had a passion for sheep guts. For example, Etruscans thought they could read messages in the surface of the liver. They also studied liver folds and veins, along with other features of sheep spleens, lungs, and hearts.

- *Crystal Gazing.* The word "crystal" comes from ancient Greece where crystals were thought to be a form of clear ice or frozen water. For centuries people believed that crystals were water rendered into stones. Crystal gazing is part of the art of scrying, which also includes gazing at blobs of ink, pools of water, mirrors, or any transparent or reflecting object.

- *Teacup Reading.* Also known as *tasseography*, teacup reading remains one of the most popular parlor-room varieties of divination. In the section on tasseography, I give some simple steps that allow you to experiment with this method.

Before starting the heavy material on divination with all its fancy-sounding vocabulary, I thought we might like to begin on a lighter note. I've been interested in fortune cookies since I was a teenager. At that time in my life, I enjoyed removing the standard fortunes and reinserting new ones of my own design. The best part was watching people's faces when they opened their cookies and read my odd "fortunes" such as:

> You like Fortune Cookies.

or

> Answer this question with "yes" or "no."
> Will your next word be "no"?

or

> *Confucius:* "What is the best possible question, and what's the best answer to it?"
>
> *Buddha:* "You've just asked the best possible question, and I'm giving the best possible answer."

Modern fortune cookies were invented in San Francisco in the early 1900s. However, their ancient origins date back much further. For many centuries the Chinese marked special occasions such as harvest and new year by exchanging moon-shaped cakes or "moon cakes" made from lotus nut paste. Even today, moon cakes play a role in the moon-cake festival, a mid-autumn Chinese festival known as *Chung Chiu*. The moon also plays a significant part of this festival, and in Hong Kong, open spaces or mountain tops are crowded with people trying to get a glimpse of this season's full moon.

Nobody knows when the custom of eating moon cakes to celebrate the moon festival began, but it may date back to the fourteenth century.[2] At the time, China was fighting the Mongols who occupied China. When plans were made in Peking for a popular uprising to oust the invaders, the Chinese thought about how to circulate news of the uprising's date without alerting the Mongols. Supposedly, the Mongols had no taste for lotus nut paste, and so the Chinese hid the message containing the date in the middle of their moon cakes. When the time for the year's *Chung Chiu* festival arrived, people opened their cakes and found hidden messages advising them on how to coordinate their uprising. This uprising formed the basis of the Ming Dynasty. Cakes with messages gradually became a popular way of expressing good wishes on an important occasion.

The origins of the modern fortune cookie came from the Chinese 49ers who helped build the American railways through the Sierra Nevada into California. The work was difficult, so to improve failing spirits, the workers exchanged biscuits with hidden, happy messages inside during the moon festival. This led to the development of the fortune cookie in America. Fortune cookies became common and continued to be made as the Chinese settled in San Francisco after the railway and the Gold Rush. Today fortune cookies are provided by virtually all Chinese restaurants in America and Canada.

Fortune cookies were made by hand until 1964 when the first *automated* production took place in America. In recent years, fully automated facilities have been set up in the UK to produce fortune cookies that are now gaining popularity in Chinese restaurants in England and Europe.

Today, increasing numbers of businesses and even governments place promotional messages in fortune cookies. The Hong Kong police used them in antidrug campaigns, and the United States has followed this example. Companies like CustomFortuneCookie.Com (Houston, Texas) permit schools to order fortune cookies with custom messages that reinforce positive behavior in their students.

Today, you do not have to wait to go to a restaurant to get a fortune because many Internet fortune cookie Web sites exist, such as my own at www.pickover.com. If you visit my Web page, give it a try and then create your own if you are handy with Web page design. At my own Web site, visitors enjoy clicking on a blinking icon to get a new printed fortune.[3] (Endnote 3 gives further information on computer codes to generate your own fortune cookie program.)

---

### ℥ How to Make a Fortune Cookie

Here's a recipe I like, derived from dozens of similar recipes. If you would like to examine variants of this recipe, just type "fortune cookie recipe" in any Internet search engine, and you will be amazed with variety and creativity of cookie makers.

**Ingredients:** 8 ounces all-purpose flour; 2 tablespoons cornstarch; 4 ounces sugar; ½ teaspoon salt; 4 ounces vegetable oil; 4 ounces egg whites; 1 tablespoon water; 2 teaspoons vanilla extract.

**Recipe:** ☺ In a deep bowl, mix the following ingredients: 8 ounces of flour, 2 tablespoons of corn starch, 4 ounces of sugar and ½ a teaspoon if salt. Blend in 4 ounces of oil, 4 ounces of egg whites, 1 tablespoon of water, and 2 teaspoons of vanilla extract, and then beat until you have a smooth consistency.

☺ Write your own "fortune" on a piece of paper, 2½" by ½".
☺ Preheat oven to 300 degrees F.
☺ Scoop a tablespoon of cookie batter, and spread it evenly into a 4" circle on a well greased baking sheet.
☺ Bake the flat circular cookie for about 14 minutes or until lightly golden brown. Remove one cookie at a time from the oven.
☺ You have about 15 seconds working time before the cookie hardens. Place the fortune in the middle of the cookie, along the diameter.
☺ Shape the cookie by folding the circular shape in half so it looks like a tortilla chip, and then grasp both ends. Bend the folded circle into a moon shape over the edge of a metal pot. Place the finished cookie in a muffin-pan hole with the ends down to hold its unique shape.

## ⟨ THE MANCIES

*It is both unnecessary and unethical to employ children for scrying.*
—Donald Tyson, *Scrying for Beginners*

I've uncovered many unusual divination methods over the years and categorized them here. The first thing you'll notice is that the endings or suffixes on most words are -*mancy* and -*scopy*. Through time, the suffix -mancy has come to indicate a form of divination by a definite means or in a particular manner. For example, by practicing belomancy or hippomancy, one seeks knowledge from the movement of arrows or horses. The suffix comes from the Middle English and Old French -*mancie*, derived from the late Latin -*mantia*, which is descended from the Greek *manteia*, meaning divination.[4] *Manteia* came from the word *manteuesthia*, meaning to predict, and from the word *matnis*, meaning a prophet.

The suffix -*scopy* means to view or observe. For example, *geloscopy* is divination by observing someone's laughter. The suffix -*scopy* comes from the Greek *skopia* and *skopein*, meaning to look into, to behold. Today the suffixes -*scopy* and -*mancy* are used almost interchangeably.

Many of the divination methods described in the following list could be placed in several different categories. For example, coconut divination, in which people of the Santeria religion toss coconut shells, could easily be placed in categories that include living things or in categories involving objects one tosses. When they overlap, I've done my best to capture the essence of the method. For this reason, I placed coconut divination in the tossed object category because the essence of the method relies on the chance outcomes of tossing.

I hope you enjoy my special divination list. It's fairly comprehensive, and I devote more space to those specific methods that particularly interest me. Get set for the wild, whacky, and wonderful!

## N DIVINATION WITH CREATURES

☞ *Topics discussed*: A variety of divination methods concerning living or dying creatures, with an emphasis on the study of internal organs, the movements of spiders, the roasting of animal bones, and the lines in human palms.

## The Art of Haruspicy: Livers Changing the Universe

*Why does there seem to be something inhuman about regarding human beings like roses and refusing to make any distinction between the inside of their bodies and the outside?*

—Yukio Mishima

Imagine you are with an African witch doctor and his assistants, participating in a healing rite with several chickens. In these rituals of the central African Zande religion, the behavior of chickens poisoned with benge (a toxic substance from plants) is regarded as having divinatory importance. If that doesn't seem sufficiently strange, next imagine that you are in modern Ethiopia with the Mursi Tribe, staring at steaming cow guts. The intestines look like the coils of a snake that you have no desire to touch. They are practicing entrail reading, divination by studying the appearance of animal organs. In ancient times, entrails led to some rather strange art forms; for example, I have seen Babylonian face masks sculpted to resemble the intestines, all twisting and labyrinthine. Certainly not a pretty fashion statement by today's standards— but then again, who knows what next year's fall statement will be?

Old divination methods, such as the *I Ching*, dream interpretation, and tarot, survived the centuries and continue to flourish, but haruspicy or extispicy (EHK-stis-pis-ee)—the reading of the future in ritually spilled animal organs—seems to have fallen out of favor with most Westernized cultures. Clearly, neatness counts. Nevertheless, if we go back in time a few thousand years, we find several Mediterranean cultures that were obsessed with entrail reading. Of all organs, the liver reigned supreme because it was considered the seat of the soul and mirror of dreams, which the light of the gods illuminated. The intestines represented the complex movements of planets. The meaning could be read by counting the number of major twists. An even number of twists was good, an odd number bad.

The Greeks practiced entrail reading as part of their religion, and the readings played a role in major Greek events—the building of the Parthenon temple, the battles of the Athenian naval strategist Themistocles, or the decision to enter the Lamian war (323–322 B.C.E.)—the conflict in which Athenian independence was lost despite efforts to be free of Macedonian domination after the death of Alexander the Great.

The Etruscans of western-central Italy couldn't get enough of entrail reading, and it seems that they wouldn't even make minor decisions without consulting animal guts. The Etruscans had ruled Rome until about 500 B.C.E., and their entrail readers, called haruspices, performed their art for the

Romans. The Roman statesman Cicero said that "the whole Etruscan nation was stark mad on the subject of entrails."[5]

The haruspices (*hah-RUS-puh-seez*) continued their practice, also called haruspimancy or haruspication, until the fall of the Roman civilization. I have gazed at an Etruscan bronze model of a sheep's liver found in Piancenza, Italy. The shape from the second century B C E is covered with mysterious writing, and subdivided into numerous different sections with crisscrossing lines. Each section seems to contain the name of an Etruscan god. Today, veterinarians and scientists feel that wrinkles in a sheep's liver are caused by the pressure of surrounding organs and by various environmental and genetic reasons. In humans, physicians mostly ignore these wrinkles because they have no effect on an individual's well being. The ancients, however, were fascinated by two specific liver wrinkles that they believed indicated the "divine presence" in the sheep.

We owe much to the ancient Etruscans. The Etruscans had a well-developed civilization in Italy before the Roman Empire. In fact, the Romans learned much of their culture and art from the Etruscans (or "Rasna" as they called themselves). The Latin alphabet is mostly derived from Etruscan, and runic alphabets are probably based on a northern Etruscan alphabet. Although the Etruscans have been called the "People of the Book," very little of their writing survives. Their language is mysterious, not directly related to other languages in the area. Only recently has the language been partly deciphered.

Haruspices from Etruria (the northwestern coast of Italy) were consulted privately throughout the history of the Roman Empire. The Roman Senate also held haruspicy in the highest regard and consulted haruspices before all important state decisions. The emperor Claudius was a student of Etruscan language and philosophy, and he created a "college" of sixty haruspices that existed until the beginning of the fifth century C.E. Students were paid a salary from the state. In 408 C.E., the haruspices offered their services to Pompeianus, the prefect of Rome, to help him save the city from the Goths. Innocent, the Christian bishop, reluctantly agreed to sanction the divination, so long as the rites were kept secret.

〰 〰 〰

Other mideastern cultures practiced entrail reading. Babylonians used a grid, somewhat like a checkerboard, to section the liver into fifty-five pieces. Marks in each of the sections gave clues as to the future. Here are some examples to give you a feeling for entrail reading:[6]

- A cross-shaped wrinkle in one particular section indicates that an important person will kill his lord.
- Two wrinkles in another section indicates the traveler will reach his goal.
- If two lines look like fingers on the right of the liver, two important people will rival one another for power.
- If the both lungs show redness, there will be a fire.
- If the gall bladder is enclosed in fat, there will be cold weather.
- If the diaphragm clings, there will be divine support.

In ancient Mesopotamia, the professional name for entrail reader was *baru*, which means "to see." When the baru examined the guts, he usually reported on them in a customary order starting with the liver, with the parts taken in a counterclockwise order beginning with the left lobe. Next came the lungs, the breastbone, the stomach, the vertebrae, the spleen, the pancreas, the heart, the kidneys, and the intestines. In many cases there would be a "consistency check" by sacrificing a second animal and making sure the results were compatible with the first reading. The procedure remained essentially the same for a thousand years.[7] Another term for liver reading was "hepatoscopy" (HEP-ah-TOS-kah-pee), and in the second and first millennia, large handbooks of hepatoscopy were used for consultations.

The ancient Mesopotamians believed that gods and humans shared one world. In addition to shaping the guts, the gods might take the initiative and convey specific wishes through dreams. One of the most frequently used Mesopotamian methods of divination was incubation—sleeping in the temple so that the gods could communicate to the sleeper in dreams. An early example of dream divination is a catalog of omens in a Babylonian tablet that included a typical nightmare: "If a man while he sleeps dreams that the town repeatedly falls upon him and he groans and no one hears him, the spirits of luck and good fortune are attached to his body. If someone does hear him, bad luck is attached to his body."[8]

Toward the end of the Old Babylonian period, around 1700 B.C.E., the science of haruspicy moved out westward to the countries of Levant (countries along the eastern Mediterranean shores). Models of livers, sometimes with inscriptions, have been found at Ugarit (northern Syria), Megiddo and Hazor (Israel), and Ibla (Sicily). Model lungs have been found at Ugarit and Alalakh (Syria).

The Hittites, ancient peoples of Anatolia (modern-day Turkey), dissected "cave birds" either to confirm the inspection of sheep entrails or possibly to provide an independent method of divination. (The cave bird is thought to be a kind of partridge.) Wealthy Hittites often performed multiple divinations. There is one record of multiple inquiries that required thirty-four inspections of sheep entrails and twenty cave birds. Perhaps such an expensive, extensive set of entrail readings would be used mainly by the royalty for affairs of state and military campaigns. The Hittites also enjoyed watching the victim's movements as it died. I bet you're not going to feel the same the next time you sit down for a dish of fried liver and onions.

Recall the scene I described from *Creatures of Light and Darkness* (see introduction, pp. 21–22) where one entrail reader quarreled with another about the meaning of his own steaming guts. It turns out that the Roman senate often used one haruspex (hah-RUS-peks) to monitor another to make certain he was truthfully telling all he read in a liver. After all, Roman leaders wouldn't want to misinterpret or overlook one little line in a liver that could lead to war and the death of thousands. They wouldn't want to trust it all to one conniving, upstart haruspex who despised the empire.

Roman generals had haruspices on their staffs to help make major decisions. If a sacrificial fire was used, the smoke was also studied. Can you imagine how the history of the world would have changed if one tiny line in some randomly chosen sheep were placed inches lower? You might not be here today. A battle strategy and outcome could easily have changed as a result of the entrail examination and therefore altered the entire cascade of history. In a sense, your very existence may have relied on a Roman general, his harsupex, and a piece of meat from a dead sheep. A single line in a liver could change the universe.

〰 〰 〰

Extispicy is another term used for analyzing animal entrails (from the Latin *exta*, or entrails, and *specere*, to inspect). Extipicy was sometimes extended to humans. For example, certain Celtic and Germanic tribes practiced extispicy using prisoners of war. It wasn't a pretty sight. Imagine you are captured and restrained. An old woman dressed in a white robe comes closer, looks into your eyes, and cuts your throat. Depending upon which way the blood fell from your neck, the outcome of a battle would be either favorable or unfavorable. For more information, the harupices would open your body, and look at your liver and other organs. Luckily, at that point, you would be dead from the moment the throat was cut.

Inca priests commonly performed *bronchiomancy*, a form of entrail reading that required the priests to inflate the lungs of a sacrificed white llama. This inflation was accomplished by blowing into the dissected trachea (there exists Inca ceramics showing this very act). Next, the priests observed the vein's shapes, which would suggest certain political or military actions.

Even today, the liver engages the minds of the superstitious and cruel. In November 1999, a former Khmer Rouge guerrilla shot and killed a witch doctor and ate his liver after blaming him for the death of his two children. "He killed the magic doctor and cut out and cooked his liver because he was very angry after his two children died and his sister got sick," a senior military official in western Battambang, Cambodia told Reuters. "He believed the magic doctor was to blame."[9] Three other villagers involved in the attack on the traditional healer were charged with conspiracy to murder.

Anthropologists suggest that *most* ancient cultures worldwide have indulged in extipicy, and several modern spirit-religions like Zande, Santeria, and Vodun still indulge in entrail reading.[10] I wonder why humans thought animal guts could be used to divine the future in so many separate cultures and on so many continents. The ancients must have lived in fear of the gods, of diseases, of weather patterns, and other forces of nature to a much greater degree than people in modern socities. Perhaps this helplessness led ancient humanity to prove its strength by dominating animals and slaughtering them. Haruspicy evolved from the act of animal sacrifices to the gods, which was a form of bribing the gods to be on the side of the human making the offering.

Our fascination with entrails, and their echoing of other natural forms, is described poetically in a book entitled *The Story of an African Farm*, which I found at a garage sale when I was very young. The book was written by Olive Schreiner and published in 1883. Here's a passage:

> A gander drowns itself in our dam. We take it out, and open it on the bank, and kneel looking at it. Above are the organs divided by delicate tissues; below are the intestines artistically curved in a spiral form, and each tier covered by a delicate network of blood vessels standing out red against the faint blue background. Each branch of the blood-vessels is comprised of a trunk, bifurcation and rebifurcating into the most delicate, hair-like threads, symmetrically arranged. We are struck with its singular beauty. And, more-over—and here we drop from our kneeling into a sitting position—this also we remark: of that same exact shape and outline is our thorn-tree seen against the sky in mid-winter; of that shape also is delicate metallic tracery between our rocks; in that exact path does our water flow when without a furrow we lead it from the dam; so shaped are the antlers of the horned beetle. How are these things related that such union should exist between them all? Is it chance? Or, are they not all the fine branches of one trunk, whose sap flows through us all? That would explain it. We nod over the gander's insides.[11]

In a sense, an autopsy is similar to haruspicy, except that it is meant to tell the truth about the past, not the future.

## The Quantum Mechanics of Ooscopy

> *The bird fights its way out of the egg. The egg is the world. Who would be born must first destroy a world. The bird flies to God. That God's name is Abraxas.*
> —Herman Hesse, *Demian*

Today, most of us would probably be too squeamish to test the accuracy of haruspicy in our own backyards; however, there is a form of haruspicy called "ooscopy" that you might enjoy trying (and that might be more amenable to your neighbors). Ooscopy substitutes an egg for the sacrificial animal and substitutes inspection of the opened egg for examination of the entrails. Ooscopy was described as far back as the first century by the Roman historian Suetonius (c. 98–138 C.E.). A woman named Livia was pregnant and wanted to know the gender of her unborn child. In order to divine the future, she placed an egg in her bosom and kept it warm until a chick hatched with an attractive cockscomb. The child would be male. (Of course, she had a fifty-fifty chance of being correct.)

Modern ooscopers say that their approach works just as well as the ancient entrail reading using sheep, although I don't think there have been any scientific studies on this subject. Ancient haruspices probably preferred to use the whole animal because it made a greater public show than cracking an egg.[12] See "Do-It-Yourself Ooscopy" for a recipe in which Dr. John Opsopaus, author of a number of articles on neopaganism, associates the Etruscan gods with different regions of the egg.[13]

The regions of the egg in the "Do-It-Yourself Ooscopy" section originated in liver readings, and Dr. Opsopaus, one of today's foremost experts on ooscopy, transferred them to the egg. Beyond this, much of the ritual is reconstructed, based on scholarly theory about haruspicy, general divinatory practice, and Dr. Opsopaus's own conjecture. The old theory of haruspicy is that by proper prayer and ritual we may influence the gods to send us a sign. Dr. Oposopaus suggests that when the gods are willing, they can project the macrocosm into the microcosm and put signs in the egg that answer our needs.

Some modern ooscopers seek more modern, "rational" explanations for ooscopy's supposed efficacy, and I enjoy reading their highly speculative theories of how haruspicy could work. One imaginative idea comes again from John Opsopaus. His explanation relies on modern quantum theory,

### Do-It-Yourself Ooscopy

So you wish to be an ooscoper? Here is an abridgment of a recipe handed down to me from Dr. John Opsopaus (see endnote 12).

1. Fast for twelve hours while meditating on questions or problems of concern. Be serious and respectful to the gods. Bathe and wear clean clothes. (Some of the ancient ooscopers actually wore a special robe and a tall, conical hat. Perhaps this is the origin of the stereotypical sorcerer's costume.)
2. Find a white, unblemished egg. It should be cleaned of all "defilement." Otherwise you, the haruspex or ooscoper, have created a *vitium*, which literally means a crime but in this context means a defect in the ritual. Next obtain a white saucer, a cup of water, and a candle. Flute music enhances the ritual.
3. Perform the "sacrifice" ritual, using some of ancient Etruscan words when possible. Although ancient Etruscan language is still mostly a mystery to us, we do know the meanings of several hundred words. Start by saying, "*Tular eisna sath!*" (in Etruscan, this means "Make the divine boundaries!"). Next, carry the egg and the water in a circle around an altar, thus separating the sacred from the profane.
4. Pour out some of the water to wash your hands. Face south, stretch out your hands, and ask Aplu, the Etruscan god of prophecy, to give an omen: "Aplu! I pray and beseech you that you may by your majesty be propitious and well-disposed to me, for which I offer this Egg. I seek to know [say your question]. *Thui srenar tev!* [Show signs, here, now!]"
5. With a single blow, crack the egg using a knife. Next, carefully open and empty the egg onto the saucer. If the yolk breaks, it is a *vitium* and you must begin again. Complete your dedication by saying, "*Ikan netsvis alpnu aplus turuce* [The Haruspex has given this as a gift to Aplu]."
6. Turn the saucer so that the place where the egg's *fibra umbilicata* [umbilical cord] leaves the *vitellus* [yolk] and connects to the *embruon* [embryo] is in the southeast direction. The shape of the *album* [egg-white] should be definite and firm; if it runs then the Gods have refused to give clear signs. Blood in the *vitellus* is a frightful omen.
7. Consult the chart in figure 5. The chart divides the egg into various regions, and your job is to observe the position of marks, bubbles, or other features with respect to this "map." Various Etruscan gods dwell within the regions of the egg.
8. To understand the significance of the various egg regions, consult the information in Appendix 6, which will familiarize you with the egg's orientation and the various labels in figure 5.

9. When the divination has been completed, say, "*Netsvis sacce! zeri utu ratum! eisar ipa lucair thui utice!* [The haruspex has carried out the Sacred Act! The rite is legally done! The Gods who rule have withdrawn from here!]." Remove the egg from the water and eat it.

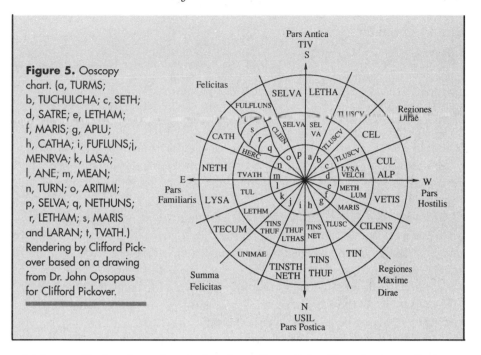

**Figure 5.** Ooscopy chart. (a, TURMS; b, TUCHULCHA; c, SETH; d, SATRE; e, LETHAM; f, MARIS; g, APLU; h, CATHA; i, FUFLUNS;j, MENRVA; k, LASA; l, ANE; m, MEAN; n, TURN; o, ARITIMI; p, SELVA; q, NETHUNS; r, LETHAM; s, MARIS and LARAN; t, TVATH.) Rendering by Clifford Pickover based on a drawing from Dr. John Opsopaus for Clifford Pickover.

which usually involves the study of small particles like electrons that can behave as both particles and waves. John writes:

> Quantum theory tells us that the state of a system is indeterminate so long as it is unobserved, and so the innards of the egg are indeterminate; this means they have no definite configuration. Cracking the eggshell and observing its contents causes a "collapse of the wavefunction"—in other words the egg enters a definite state. So what the haruspex observes is in no way determined by simple mechanical laws, but the probabilities of its configurations can be influenced by the past, present, and future.
>
> Quantum theory also tells us that the wavefunctions of all objects extend infinitely in all directions. More accurately, the wavefunctions of objects (such as the egg) are just pieces of the wavefunction of the universe, which means that the interior of the egg is connected with everything else in the universe: the macrocosm is reflected in the microcosm. Thus the egg may reflect any other condition in the present universe.[14]

For readers who desire a skeptical treatment of the application of quantum mechanics to everyday objects, see Victor Stenger's *The Unconscious Quantum*.[15] Stenger suggests that we must be very cautious when suggesting that macroscopic objects are individual quantum systems describable by wave functions.[16]

## Mambila Spider Divination

> So I went in and looked, and I saw portrayed all over the walls all kinds of crawling things and detestable animals and all the idols of the house of Israel.
> —Ezekiel 8:10

Imagine that you are walking through the Somié Village, Province de l'Adamaoua in Cameroon. Cameroon, a West African country, is not too far from the equator, and you feel the oppressive heat enveloping you like a bad dream. It's April, the rainy season. You hope the rain will soon come to cool things off.

As you walk down the central village square you notice people in the distance working in the fields, hoeing maize that was planted in February and March to keep the weeds down. The village, which lies forty kilometers off the main road, has a population of two thousand people. The smell of rancid goat milk assails you as blackbirds circle overhead. Although there are roads to break the natural scenery, the country is a deep, lush green, and you can't help but be taken in by the beauty.

You have journeyed to Africa to learn about one of the most fascinating divination techniques still practiced today: the Mambila system of nggàm spider divination.[17] The Mambila people live in Western Africa, on the borderland of Nigeria and Cameroon (see figure 6). Many Mambila earn a living as farmers growing crops. The term "nggàm" refers to spiders and more generally to divination. Not only do the Mambila use certain spiders (scientific name *Hysterocrates robustus*) to predict the future but they also use them to determine if someone accused of witchcraft is really a witch. Incidentally, although the practice is commonly referred to as "spider" divination, land crabs (*Sudanonautes convexonautes aubryi*) are also sometimes used. The nggàm spider is a large, hairy, black earth-dwelling

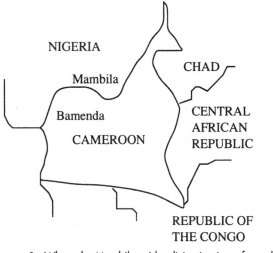

**Figure 6.** Where the Mambila spider divination is performed

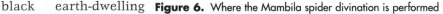

spider that is an aggressive night-hunter. Old laws made it a capital crime to kill such a spider because it was thought to be the messenger of a mysterious spirit that had excellent night sight and was in contact with the dead. If you travel to Cameroon and wish to test spider divination, look for a spider and its burrow, cover it with a large pot that has its bottom knocked out. The divination system relies on a deck of many "cards" made from dried, flat leaves inscribed with a set of symbols that indicate a good or bad event. Cards without symbols are also used. The locals have cards that are over fifty years old and represent a wide range of myths.

Predicting the future becomes possible when the spider comes out of its burrow and moves the cards. The positions of the cards have special meanings, and spider divination is used to gain insight into such topics as marital problems, adultery, illnesses, and the possibility of women practicing witchcraft.

After surrounding the spider burrow with the pot and placing the cards, stick, and stone in the pot as described in "Do-It-Yourself Mambila Spider Divination," you can perform the actual divination and interpretation of the results. The Mambila people test the "veracity" of the spider and of the diviner by first asking questions for which the answers are easily verified, such as, "Will I eat porridge today?" If a card has been moved toward or onto the stick, then the stick has been "chosen." Similarly, the stone may be chosen. Additional information is gained by noticing in which direction the card is pointing. Figure 9 shows some basic responses.[18]

Focus on any cards that are touching the stick or stone. If a card on the stone points outside the pot as in Figure 9a and b, this can be used to give more information about the evil that threatens. For example, when a card points outside, you are to look outside your immediate environment for the source of troubles or happiness. When leaves are used for cards, the spider diviners consider whether a leaf has been overturned, which is possible to ascertain if the cards are arranged with their veins on top to start. If you use scraps of paper, you can mark one side so that you can tell if the paper has been overturned. An inverted card is bad, possibly warning of unforeseen problems. According to the Mambila, the following responses are portents of death: a spider pulls a card down into the hole, a spider pushes a card against the pot's side so the card points into the ground, or the spider pushes a cards underneath the pot (see figure 10).[19]

If a spider balances the card on its base (flattened side) against the pot wall, this augurs well, whereas a card balanced on its point portends death. A skillful Mambila diviner is called when results are ambiguous, for example, when one card is on the stick and another on the stone. Most often, however, such ambiguous results are rejected as saying nothing.

## Do-It-Yourself Mambila Spider Divination

Here is an authentic spider divination recipe provided to me by David Zeitlyn, a senior lecturer in social anthropology at the Center for Social Anthropology and Computing at the University of Kent in Canterbury, UK. David has actually witnessed the rituals first hand and has even set up a Web site for online spider divination (see endnote 17). With this recipe, you can perform your own authentic spider divination as practiced by the Mambila people.

1. Find an inhabited spider hole. (In the United States and Europe, I suggest using a trapdoor spider, such as the one illustrated in figure 7. The dark nggàm spider is used in Cameroon.)

**Figure 7.** Trapdoor spider. From Jim Harter, *Animals* (New York: Dover, 1979), fig. 1300, p. 258.

2. Place a pot over the hole. It's diameter should be about forty centimeters (or a foot and a half). Position the pot so that the mouth is over the hole and encompassing land surrounding the hole. The pot's base, which is facing upward, should be knocked out and covered with a piece of tin or other material. This acts as a lid that can be removed to observe the spider burrow's entrance.

3. To begin divination, rub a stone around the top of the pot while blowing into it saying "*yuo yuo*" ("come out, come out").

4. Place a stick and a stone inside the pot, on the left and right side of the hole, respectively.

5. Stack divination "leaf cards" as shown in figure 8, pointing toward the hole. Notice that the cards have a pointed and flat end, like a bullet. (You can use blank pieces of paper cut like a bullet.)

6. Place two cards over the hole and pose a question. Pose a condition in the following general form:

> If "X," then take the stick.
> Otherwise, then take the stone.

Example: "If I am to marry Brad Pitt tomorrow, then take the stick, otherwise take the stone."

7. Put the cover back on the pot and rest for ten minutes to allow the spider to emerge and disturb the cards, thus giving its answer. If you're impatient, do another spider divination with a second pot and spider while you wait for the first pot. This lets you work like the Mambila with parallel questions and provides a consistency check on the veracity of the divination.

8. See the main text for interpretation of the cards moved by the spider.

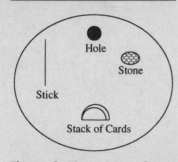

**Figure 8.** Nggàm set-up. Rendered by Clifford Pickover after David Zeitlyn's sketches for Clifford Pickover.

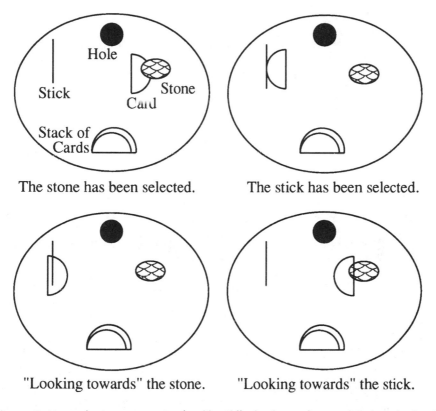

The stone has been selected.    The stick has been selected.

"Looking towards" the stone.    "Looking towards" the stick.

**Figure 9.** Nggàm basic responses. Rendered by Clifford Pickover after David Zeitlyn's sketches for Clifford Pickover.

Spider divination is not a rare, isolated practice but is widespread throughout the southern half of the country. The cards may have symbols on them, the symbol drawn once on one card to signify "bad" and twice to signify "good." Most modern forms of Mambila spider divination use the relative positions of the cards rather than their markings Today, most of the Mambila men know the basic principles of spider divination even if they have not been formally taught how to divine. Among the men who actively perform the divination, most are heads of households and some are widely regarded as experts, attracting clients from miles away. An expert spider diviner can be quite influential in the community.

Although spider divination gives comfort to people today, it can also have horrible consequences, ruining people's lives and causing sad injustices. Spider divination is one way in which men maintain their authority over women, because women are not allowed to divine. People are sent to

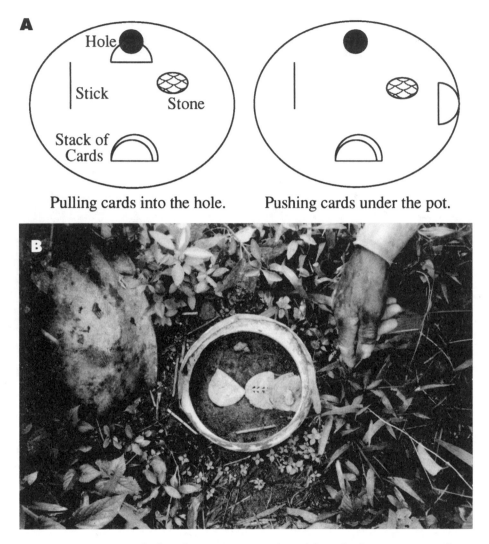

**A**

Pulling cards into the hole.     Pushing cards under the pot.

**Figure 10.** (A) Nggàm death configurations. (B) Actual Mambila spider divination, Somié Village, Cameroon. © David Zeitlyn, photographer and anthropologist for Clifford Pickover.

prison on the basis of spider divination alone. For example, spider divination plays a crucial role in the detection of witches because it provides an "authoritative" verdict when two respected, impartial spider diviners offer the same verdict. In the national system of justice, witchcraft is an imprisonable offense in article 251 of the penal code. At trials, the diviners who have "caught" the witch appear as witnesses for the prosecution. People are sentenced with terms between six months and ten years. Considering that most people in the village are members of either the Catholic or Protestant church, I find that the spider divination has echoes of the Spanish Inquisition, which convicted people of witchcraft on the flimsiest of evidence. Perhaps most members of the Inquisition actually believed they were finding witches. Similarly, anthropologists have done extensive interviews with the spider diviners who seem to truly believe in their craft.

For those of you without access to nggàm spiders, or who are a bit squeamish about spiders in general, you can perform authentic spider divination safely on your computer. Check out Michael Fischer and David Zeitlyn's spider divination computer simulation at http://lucy.ukc.ac.uk/Fdtl/Spider/spider2.html. Clicking on the buttons at the bottom of the computer image allows you to cover the pot while you ask a question. Other buttons remove the lid to reveal the position of the leaves. Clicking on an individual leaf will display an enlargement and caption of the leaf. Michael Fischer, David Zeitlyn, the University of Kent, and the Centre for Social Anthropology and Computing tell me they are not responsible for any losses or damage caused by decisions made as a result of using this computer simulation!

## Palmistry

> Now that the science fiction of cloning has become a reality, how palmistry works has become much easier for us to understand. Cloning is possible because the whole is represented in each cell, so that one cell can be replicated until the whole is duplicated. Palmistry is possible because you are represented in your hand. No two hands are alike because you—and your cells—are unique.
>
> —Robin Giles and Lisa Lenard,
> The Complete Idiot's Guide to Palmistry

Palmistry, also called *chiromancy* or *cheiromancy*, is the reading of personality and divining of the future by studying lines and other features of the hand, with an emphasis on the palm. Chiromancy (kĬ'rô-man-sÂ), named after Leic de Hamong, aka Louis Hamon, the famous nineteenth-century palmist who also went under the name of "Cheiro." The basic idea that the hand provides information on a person's destiny has a long history. For example, the Old Testament book Proverbs (3:16) notes, "Long life is in her right hand; in her left hand are riches and honor."

We are not sure how palmistry originated, though it was practiced in ancient India, China, Tibet, Persia, Mesopotamia, and Egypt, and evolved further in ancient Greece. Palmistry is mentioned in Indian and Chinese writings three thousand years old, while the earliest Western references are by Aristotle who in 350 B.C.E. wrote, "Palmistry is a judgment made of the conditions, inclinations, and fortunes of men and women, from the various lines and characters which nature has imprinted in the hands."[20] The first known book on the subject was printed in 1448, around the time in the Middle Ages when palmistry reached a peak.

Medieval witch hunters used palmistry to determine who was a witch. For example, the hunters searched hands for pigmentation spots as signs of a pact with the Devil. Although banned by the Catholic Church, one of the first books to be published in the Middle Ages was not only about palm reading but was written by a Viennese monk, Johann Hartlieb, in 1474.[21] After a period of disrepute, palmistry flourished again in the Renaissance. Scholars of the seventeenth century tried to determine a scientific foundation for palmistry; palm reading, or chirology, was on the curriculum of several German universities. Despite renewed interest in Europe, the British Parliament continued to outlaw its practice. During the reign of George IV (1762–1830), palmistry was illegal, and an act was passed decreeing "any person found practicing palmistry is hereby deemed a rogue and a vagabond to be sentenced to one year's imprisonment and to stand in the pillory."[22] Palmistry also became quite popular in the nineteenth century with the work of Casimir Stanislas d'Arpentigny, Louis Harmon ("Cheiro"), and William Benham. D'Arpentigny, a retired general from Napoleon's army, made the study of hands his lifelong passion and popularized the art. In the twentieth century, psychologist Carl Jung studied palmistry.

If you are right handed, your left hand is supposed to indicate inherited characteristics, while the right reveals your individuality and fulfillment of potential. (This is reversed for left handers.) Although various features of the hand are inspected, the palmist usually focusses on the lines of the palms (see figure 11).

The most important lines are the life line indicating physical vitality, the head line, which relates to mental capabilities, the heart line, associated with emotion, and the fate line, indicating destiny. The palmist examines the lines for definition, breaks, shapes, and other distinguishing features. A German psychologist, Julius Spier, spent decades studying children's hands while developing his theories of psycho-chirology. Carl Jung wrote the preface for Spier's book *Hands of Children*, which heightened interest in the book. Although palmistry is not grounded in traditional science, biologists have discovered relationships between inherited disorders (such as Down's syndrome, several mental disorders, and certain heart defects) and palm abnormalities.

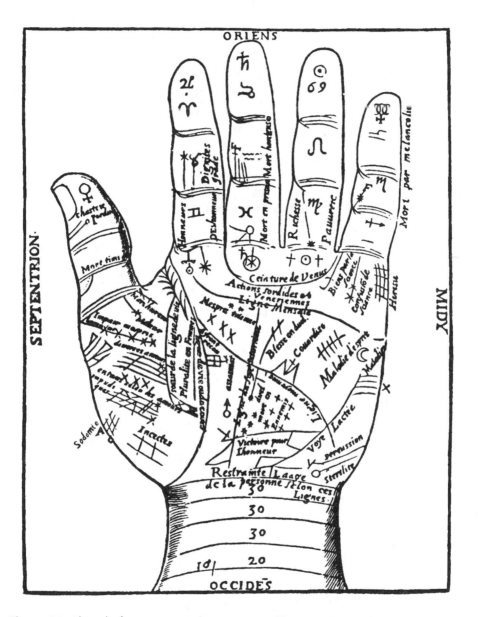

**Figure 11.** The palm from a seventeenth-century manual by Jean Belot. The figure is said to predict sodomy, incest, and imprisonment. From Ann Fiery, *The Book of Divination* (San Francisco: Chronicle Books, 1999), fig. 18., p. 159.

Figure 12 is fascinating because of the unusual depiction of the palm.[23] It contains Christian images rather than zodiac or other divinatory symbols. As I noted, palmistry was banned by the medieval Catholic Church. Notice that Christ's cross cuts across the palm's life line. I wonder if this was an intentional symbol of a Christ's shortened life in the human world.

Sometimes I wonder how modern-day palm readers justify their work. Robin Giles and Lisa Lenard in *The Complete Idiot's Guide to Palmistry* suggest:

> Palmistry works because your hand changes as you do. Try this test: the next time someone cuts you off on a freeway, take a look at the fleshy pad where you thumb joins the rest of your hand. Is it swollen and red? If getting cut off made you the least bit angry, it will be reflected in this place, called active Mars.[24]

Giles, a twenty-year-veteran of professional palm reading, suggests that changes such as marriage or career moves manifest themselves in changes in the hands as the events take place. Hands are supposed to change at different rates of speeds, and the fastest change that Robin Giles ever detected was that of a widow with a "psychic hand." Her life was in such great transition that he claimed that her palm changed as he was reading it! Giles and Lenard believe that it's never a good idea to read your own palm because of your personal biases.

Many palmistry aficionados also examine the entire hand for its overall shape. For example, square-shaped hands with a broad palm and short fingers is supposed to indicate someone who is well organized. Fan-shaped hands belong to energetic, creative, and impulsive people. People with fingers that narrow to a point and with a fleshy palm are emotional and sensitive. People with long, slender fingers are motivated by deep feelings and are intellectual. The stiffness of a hand is also thought to indicate personality traits. A flabby hand indicates low willpower. A flexible hand indicates adaptability. A stiff hand indicates a person who likes a structured life.

**Figure 12.** Palm with Christian images. From Nevill Drury and Gergory Tillett, *The Occult* (New York: Barnes & Nobles Books, 1997), p. 97.

There are numerous sites on the World Wide Web devoted to palmistry that you may enjoy. There are even online palm readings sites that require you to scan a picture of your palm and then attach the image to an e-mail so that a chiromancer can study it. For a skeptical treatment, see the works of Michael Alan Park and others.[25]

### Roasted Bones and the Turtles of Time

> Then he said to me, "Prophesy to these bones and say to them, 'Dry bones, hear the word of the Lord!' "
>
> —Ezekiel 37:4

Three main divination methods have existed in China for generations. *Plastromancy* involves heating animal bones or turtle shells to cause cracks to form on their surfaces. The patterns of the crack are used to foretell the future. The *I Ching* involves the casting of yarrow stalks to build hexagram patterns, each of which has a specific divinatory meaning. (Yarrow is a plant native primarily to the northern hemisphere.) The third method is *geomancy* with a magnetic compass. This method is used to assess land to determine its potential usefulness. As you can see from figure 13, the earliest of the three methods used bones and shells and started around 3500 B.C.E. Bone and shell cracking were regularly practiced in the palace of the Shang Kings by 1400 B.C.E. and lasted until 1000 B.C.E.[26]

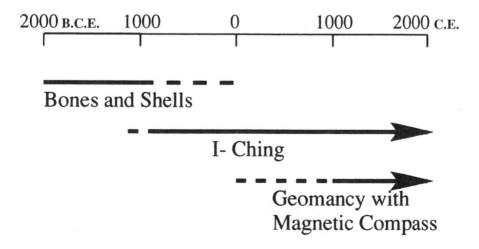

Figure 13. Chinese divination methods through time. Based on a figure from Michael Loewe and Carmen Blacker, *Oracles and Divination* (Boulder: Shambala, 1981), fig. 1, p. 41

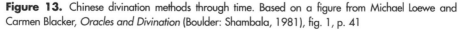

The *I Ching* probably developed as an improvement on the more ancient practice of reading cracks in a heated tortoise shell or sheep shoulder blade. Reading the cracks in the shell or bone could be quite difficult because there were often many intricate, random cracks. Numerous combinations of new cracks could appear with each divination. The *I Ching* with its sixty-four hexagrams permits a standardized reading of a constrained set of patterns. Anyone could do it. This is one reason that the *I Ching* gradually became a preferred method of divination.[27]

*Plastromancy*, the ancient divination practice of heating turtle shells with red-hot pokers and examining the resulting crack patterns, was commonly practiced by the Neolithic inhabitants of North China around the last half of the fourth millennium B.C.E. Most other ancient people preferred poking sheeps' shoulder blades with hot pokers, a practice called *pyroscapulimancy*. (Scapula is the scientific name for shoulder blade.) Sometimes scapulas of ox, deer, pigs, and horses were used as well as human skulls.

The plastromancer started by using a heated poker or drill to pierce or weaken the shell. When the shell was reheated, cracks would form on the surface. The frequency or shape of the cracks determined the answers to questions that were specified by the plastromancer.

Because bones and shells survived the gentle acid of time, we are lucky to have thousands of pieces with inscriptions from 1400 to 1100 B.C.E. Many questions put to the shells concerned future harvests, weather patterns, military expeditions, and hunts. Sometimes the turtle diviners would repeat a reading a dozen times either because the results were being tested or to get more information. (I wonder if they sometimes did it over and over again until they got the results they wanted.) One theory is that the turtle shell became important because its hemispherical shape was seen as the model of the cosmos.

The Japanese learned turtle divination from the Chinese and used the methods for 1,200 years, from the seventh century until 1868.[28] Ancient texts specify that the plastomancer must not kill a turtle to obtain shells for divination. Luckily there was usually a large supply of turtle shells washing on Japanese beaches.

The Japanese used a form of turtle divination, described in the "Do-It-Yourself Plastromancy" section, to determine who would be the virgin representative of the Emperor at the Ise shrine in southern Honshu, Japan, on Ise Bay of the Pacific Ocean. Sometimes a girl was selected as an infant and had to live her entire life in celibate seclusion in the Ise shrine. Turtle divination is still used today in the *Daijosai* rite, during the ceremony that consecrates and enthrones the Japanese Emperor.[29,30]

## Do-It-Yourself Plastromancy

Want to become your neighborhood's most famous plastromancer? Just follow these steps that were first performed in ancient China and later used by the Japanese. Most of the following steps come from the Japanese style of plastromancy (see endnotes 29 and 30).

1. Find a turtle shell. Do not kill a turtle for this purpose, and do not use a live one. If a shell is not available, use any flat bone.
2. If you prefer the Chinese method, speak these words: "Commit unto us thy eternal truth, oh mighty turtle, that we, by thy power, may be guided in our choices." If you prefer a more Japanese flavor, summon the Shinto god, Saniwa-no-kami who will influence the pattern of cracks made on the shell. Also, avoid eating meat for seven days.
3. Prepare your tools. Cut bamboo stalks can be used to sprinkle water on the heated shell to induce cracking. (Use a spoon if you don't have bamboo stalks.) Find some twigs. In the Japanese divination approach, you also need a chisel for etching the starting pattern known as machi on the back of the shell.
4. Cut the turtle shell into the shape of a pentagon (see figure 14a).
5. Use the chisel to incise the machi pattern on the back, as in figure 14a. Next, ask your question, like, "Will my love life be good or bad in the next month?"
6. Light a twig on fire, blow it to make it red hot, and thrust it into the machi grooves, starting along the vertical line and then proceeding along the horizontal ones.
7. Continue step 6 until you hear a loud crack. You will now see cracks radiation from the machi.
8. Take your bamboo (or spoon) and sprinkle water on the cracks, which you then can blacken with Indian ink so you can clearly see them.
9. There are five points in the machi (figure 14b) named *ho, to, kami, emi,* and *tame,* from which cracks can emanate. Look at the point labeled *to.* A crack to the right or straight down are good. A crack to the left is bad. The same rules apply to cracks radiating from *ho.* With *emi,* and *kami,* cracks upward and straight to the right or left are good. Cracks down are bad. For example, if *ho* and *to* had left radiating cracks, and *emi* had downward radiating cracks, it looks like your love life will be quite a mess, or perhaps nonexistent.

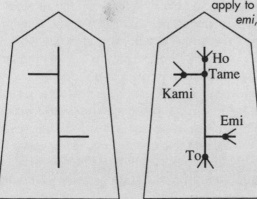

**Figure 14.** (A) Turtle shells. (B) Five points in the machi. Based on a figure from Michael Loewe and Carmen Blacker, *Oracles and Divination* (Boulder: Shambala, 1981), fig. 8, p. 69

## 📖 *A Concise Catalog of Methods Using Living Things*

We've covered some of my favorite divination methods using living things, from spiders to turtles to sheep. Here is a concise catalog of additional approaches that rely on humans, other animals, and plants. Some entries receive a very brief treatment in the interest of space and also because little information is known regarding certain ancient practices.

### 📂 **Humans**

♏ **AMNIOMANCY** uses the flesh "caul" membrane on the faces of some newborns to divine the future. Throughout pregnancy the amniotic sac serves as a water cushion, absorbing jolts, equalizing pressures, and permitting the fetus to change posture. At childbirth it acts as a fluid wedge that helps dilate the neck of the uterus. When the sac ruptures, about a quart of fluid escapes. If the sac does not rupture, or if it covers the head at birth, it is known as a caul. Amniomancers study various features of the caul when performing amniomancy. For example, a red caul, or amniotic sac, means good luck for the child. Dark gray colors mean misfortune. Cauls were actually sold in Roman markets and in England in the late 1800s.

♓ **ANTHROPOMANCY** is divination by human sacrifice and examination of the internal organs (see figure 15). This method of divination sometimes involved cruelly tearing open the body of a live human being and examining the guts to determine the truth. Legend has it that Menelaus, king of Sparta, sacrificed two country children in order to discover his destiny. The ruthless and eccentric Roman emperor Elagabalus was fond of anthropomancy. The Roman emperor Julian the Apostate had numerous children killed so he could read their entrails. During his last experiment at Carra, in Mesopotamia, he enclosed himself within the Temple of the Moon. Later, people discovered a woman inside, hanging by her hair with her liver torn out. The Babylonians, Sumerians, Japanese, Celts, Comanche Indians, Incas, and Greeks also practiced anthropomancy. Variants of anthropomancy do not require an actual killing. For example, medieval Europeans thought nosebleeds foretold bad luck.

♌ **ANTHROPOSOMANCY** is divination by observing a person's face or body, sometimes referred to as **physiognomy**.

♈ **AROMANCY** is divination by examination of the shoulders. Armomancy was often used to determine if a person had psychic abilities.

♏ **AUGURY BY DUEL** is divination by observing a duel between two men before a battle. In this past, this method of divination was practiced when one nation captured a person from an enemy nation and then matched the captive against a champion of their own. Each person was armed with their national weapons. The victory of one or the other was thought to forecast the outcome of the current war between the nations. This method was quite popular in the ancient Germanic world.

♉ **BUMPOLOGY** is a modern term, a popular nickname for **phrenology**.

♍ **CARTOPEDY** is the Persian art of foot study, similar to the study of the hands in **palmistry**. Ancient Persian and Indian rulers paid cartopedists to help choose brides by carefully assessing women's feet sizes, shapes, and markings. Cartopedy is still practiced in India and Pakistan where the police consult *payyindas*, or foot trackers, to determine the personalities of thieves from their footprints. See **podomancy**.

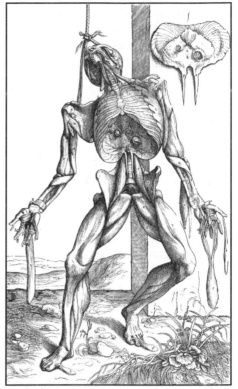

**Figure 15.** Anthropomancy is divination by human sacrifice and examination of the entrails. From Andreas Vesalius, *The Illustrations from the Works of Andreas Vesalius of Brussels* (New York: Dover, 1973), fig. 30, p. 105.

♉ **CHIROMANCY** or **CHEIROMANCY** (after *chiri* the Greek word for hand) is divination by studying the lines on people's hands, nails, and fingers. Generally speaking, chiromancy is the art of divining the past, present, and future from signs in the hand. See also **palmistry**, **chirognomy**, and **dermatoglyphics**.

♊ **CHIROGNOMY** is the study of general hand formation as it relates to the querent's disposition, basic character, and potential. See also **chirognomy**, **palmistry**, and **dermatoglyphics**.

♈ **COPROMANCY** is divination by examining human or animal feces (see figure 16). This method of divination is also called **scatomancy**. (I would be interested in hearing from readers who can provide authentic details of this little-discussed approach to divination. It would seem to tell more about last night's dinner than it does the future.)

♊ **DERMATOGLYPHICS** are the alternating ridges and grooves on the hands and feet. More specifically, dermatoglyphics refers to the study and classification of these skin-ridge patterns; this also includes the study of fingerprints. Since the early 1900s, various researchers have tried to use fingerprint patterns to diagnose and treat latent mental and physical problems. For example, in 1933, English palmist Noel Jaquin wondered whether the whorl patterns on criminal's fingertips indicated some moral defect that he could attribute to some psychological deficiency.[31] There is currently a huge medical and psychic literature on the possible relation between fingerprints and health. Studies had been performed that suggest relationships between fingerprints and mental retardation, congenital heart defects, diabetes mellitus, retarded growth, spina bifida, cleft lip and palate, leukemia, and a number of syndromes and genetic disorders including Down's syndrome.[32]

An example of an old divination method using fingerprints comes from Chinese legends. According to the old wisdom, the presence of one fingerprint whorl indicates poverty, two whorls indicate riches, three and four whorls suggest it is good to open a pawnshop, five whorls indicate a mediator, six whorls indicate a thief, and seven whorls indicate catastrophes. The Hindus have also often used fingerprint patterns to divine the future.

**Figure 16.** Copromancy is divination by examining human or animal feces. Picture here are kleptoparasitic dung beetles. ("Kleptoparasitic" refers to the fact that the dung beetles steal dung from others.) The dung-ball rollers of genus *Sisyphus* were held sacred and immortalized by ancient Egyptians. These beetles wave dung balls as a sexual display and courtship attractor. From Jim Harter, *Animals* (New York: Dover, 1979), fig. 1209, p. 245.

♈ **FETOMANCY** (or **TERATOSCOPY**) is divination by observing animal or human birth defects. In their 1896 book *Anomalies and Curiosities of Medicine*, George M. Gould and Walter L. Pyle list numerous omens revealed through monstrous births. Gould and Pyle focus on the ancient Chaldeans who believed birth monstrosities reflected the state of the heavens on which depended all earthly events. Here is a sampling of Chaldean tetratological meanings. When a woman gives birth to an infant

- that has the ears of a lion, there will be a powerful king in the country,
- that lacks the right ear, the king will live long;
- that lacks both ears, there will be mourning in the country, and the country will be diminished;
- that has a bird's beak, the country will be peaceful;
- that has no mouth, the mistress of the house will die;
- that has no right nostril, the people of the world will be injured;
- whose nostrils are absent, the country will be in distress, and the house of the man will be ruined;
- whose jaws are absent, the days of the king will be prolonged, but the house where the infant is born will be ruined.

Care for some more bizarre examples of divination and deformity? See endnote 33.

♌ **IATROMANCY** is divination of medical problems and arriving at solutions through nonstandard approaches. For example, American psychics Edgar Cayce (1877–1945) and Andrew Jackson Davis (1826–1910) were famous iatromancers. Jackson's cure for a deaf patient was to have the man wrap the warm skins of rats around each ear nightly. Various forms of Iatromancy are practiced today in Africa, Haiti, and in the Native American tribes.

♉ **IRIDOLOGY.** See **oculomancy**.

♏ **KOKALOMANCY** (after the Greek *kokalo* for bone) is divination that usually uses human bones. One form of bone divination is used to find the name of the departed ancestor present at a child's birth. The priest or shaman holds a collection of bones and recites a series of ancestors' names who might be present to help with the child's new life. When the kokalomancer says the correct name, the bones are said to suddenly move or change weight within his hands. In several cultures, the skulls of dead shamans were questioned about important events. The skulls were supposed to change weight during the question session. The early Jewish traditions sometimes made use of mummified heads, bone images, and skulls.[34]

In Melanesia, a sorcerer would use a piece of his ancestor's arm bone for divining. In particular, the bone sorcerer would stand the bone vertically on a shell and remove his hand. If the answer to his question is no, then the bone falls. If yes, the bone remains standing. The Masai and Nandi tribes in Africa used skulls to detect guilt and innocence. An accused places a skull at his accuser's door and says something like, "Skull, if I have committed this crime, eat me. If I have not, eat him!"[35] Supposedly, the guilty person is supposed to die a result of this procedure, but I don't know what the tribes people do when neither person turns out to be affected. See **scapulomancy**.

♍ **MACULOMANCY** is divination by the shape and location of birthmarks. The ancient Chinese may have originated this practice, and the gypsies who traveled throughout Europe believed that moles could be used to foretell a person's future. Round moles indicated good luck. Moles with angular sides suggested a fiery temper. Marks on the buttocks indicated a person was destined to be poor. A mark in the center of the forehead indicated an active, enterprising person, and so forth. See **moleomancy**.

♓ **METOPOSCOPY** (or **METOPOMANCY**) is the reading of a person's character by studying the forehead lines (see figure 17). This divination method was invented by the great sixteenth-century mathematician, physician, and astrologer Gerolomo Cardano (1501–1576). Similar methods were been practiced in China, and many ancient Greek physicians belived that structures on the forehead and face revealed personality traits.

Facial interpretation became quite popular in 1558 when Cardano's published his *Metoposcopia*, a guide to face reading. Cardano divided the forehead into seven positions between the brow and hairlines. He gave these planetary names. Long unbroken horizontal lines indicated a straightforward personality. Wavy lines corresponded to a person who liked to travel.

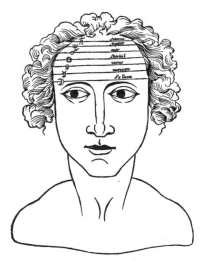

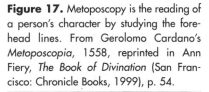

**Figure 17.** Metoposcopy is the reading of a person's character by studying the forehead lines. From Gerolomo Cardano's *Metoposcopia*, 1558, reprinted in Ann Fiery, *The Book of Divination* (San Francisco: Chronicle Books, 1999), p. 54.

♉ **MOLEOSOPHY** (or **MOLEOMANCY**) is the study of moles as indicators of a person's character and to predict the future. See **maculomancy**.

♋ **MUSCLE READING** is fortune telling by observing unconscious muscle movements of a person suspected of knowing some secret. Muscle reading is based on the principle that when a person thinks of a name, his or her muscles (especially throat muscles) shape themselves into the position of that name. A qualified seer interprets the movements as words.

♓ **NINSO** is a modern-day Japanese divination method that involves the study of facial shape and texture as well as examination of eyes and hair. For example, people with circular faces are said to be emotional and optimistic. See **physiognomy**.

♈ **OCULOMANCY** is divination by observing a person's eye. Similarly, *iridology* is the modern "alternative medicine" practice of assessing a person's health by studying the iris of the eye (the colored area around the pupil). "Iri" and "iris" come from the Greek goddess of the rainbow, Iris. According to iridology, the iris reveals changing conditions of every part and organ of the body. For example, a white triangle in a particular area of the iris area is supposed to indicate appendicitis, but a black speck indicates that the appendix has been removed by surgery. *Sclerology* is similar to iridology but interprets the shape and condition of blood vessels on the white portion (sclera) of the eyeball. Various scientific studies of iridology have questioned its accuracy.[36]

♋ **OMPHALOMANCY** is counting the number of knots in the umbilical cord to predict how many more children the mother will have. Sometimes the naval itself was studied to divine the future.

♏ **ONYCHOMANCY** is divination by observing fingernails. Often the onychomancer gets glimpses of the future while studying a young boy's fingernails that are illuminated by the sun. The shapes that the sun produces are considered indicators of future events. In parts of Brazil today, a psychic coats the querent's thumbnail with soot and oil. The coating provides a reflecting surface from which to scry. The modern version of onychomancy is a bit like palmistry in which various features of the nails are used to foretell character.

♋ **PALMISTRY** is the broad field of divination and interpretation of the lines and structure of the hand. See **chiromancy**, **chirognomy**, and **dermatoglyphics**.

♐ **PHRENOLOGY** is the study of head formations. In particular, phrenologists study the shape and bumps of the skull, believing that the features give

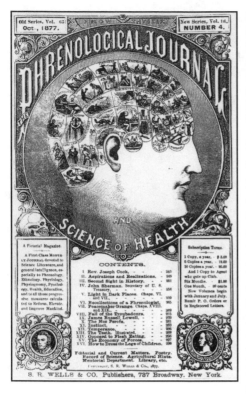

**Figure 18.** Phrenologists study the shape and bumps of the skull, believing that the features give insight into a person's mental faculties and character traits. Shown here is a cover of an 1877 issue of *The Phrenological Journal*. From Ann Fiery, *The Book of Divination* (San Francisco: Chronicle Books, 1999), fig. 8, p. 105.

insight into a person's mental faculties and character traits. Various famous phrenologists have included Franz-Joseph Gall (1758–1828), a Viennese doctor, and nineteenth-century adherents Johann Kaspar Spurzheim (1776–1832) and George Combe (1788–1858). Phrenology enjoyed great popular appeal well into the twentieth century. Gall mapped twenty-six areas of the head that he said were assigned to certain personality characteristics. Spurzheim identified thirty-five areas of the head as being important to assess personality traits (see figure 18).

ϒ **PHYSIOGNOMY** is the study of a person's physical characteristics, such as facial features or body structure, to better understand the person's character, psychological makeup, and future actions. Early classical literature, including the works of Homer and Hippocrates, suggests that physiognomy was part of ancient Greek philosophy. The earliest-known systematic treatise on physiognomy is attributed to Aristotle. For example, while discussing noses, Aristotle said that noses with thick, bulbous ends belong to persons who are insensitive. Sharp-tipped noses belong to the cranky. Rounded, large noses belong to the generous. In China, the practice seems to date back at least three thousand years to the Chou dynasty. In Europe, physiognomy was popular in the 1500s and 1600s. Today the Japanese practice *ninso*, which involves the study of facial shape and texture as well as examination of eyes and hair.

♓ **PODOMANCY** is a method of analyzing character through the study of lines on the feet. This method was popular in ancient China and India. See **cartopedy**.

♎ **SCATOMANCY** is divination by observing one's own feces. See **copro-mancy**.

♏ **SCARPOMANCY** is divination by observing a person's old shoes.

♈ **SCLEROLOGY**. See **oculomancy**.

♋ **SPATULAMANCY** is the observation of the skin, bones, and excrement in order to divine the future.

♓ **STOLISOMANCY** draws omens from the way people dress. For example, in ancient Rome, Emperor Augustus predicted the occurrence of a military revolt when he saw an attendant buckling his right sandal on his left foot.

♊ **UROMANCY** is divination by observing a person's urine. Practiced by the ancient Greeks, the uromancer would gaze into urine to see visions. Uromancy was sometimes used to divine whether a woman was a virgin, pregnant, or had a spouse. The Roman author Pliny the Elder spoke of "spitting into the urine the moment it is voided" to reverse a bad omen. Try it. You'll like it.

Today some people use the term "uromancy" to disparage employers' increasing use of urinalysis for drugs in employees' bodies. Despite public support for drug testing, urinalysis can be an unreliable technology.

## 🗁 Other Mammals, Cut or Whole

♋ **ALEPOUOMANCY** (after the Greek alepou for fox) is also known as fox divination and practiced by the Dogon tribe of North Africa. Dogon diviners draw a grid on the ground at the edge of the village. The grid contains as many as sixty questions and is sown with peanuts to attract animals. In Dogon legend, a "pale fox" or jackal comes to eat the peanuts. At dawn, the next day, the configuration of tracks left by the fox's paws convey the gods' answers to the questions.

♈ **APANTOMANCY** is divination through chance meetings with animals such as black cats or birds. Mexico City is said to have been founded where Aztec soothsayers saw an eagle carrying a live snake and flying from a cactus. American Indians were often named for the first animal a mother saw after giving birth. In ancient Europe, a chance meeting with a white mouse suggested good luck.

**Figure 19.** *Bodiomancy* requires that you observe the eyes of sleeping bulls. Splash water on the head. If both eyes open, the answer to your question is "yes." From W. Ellenberger, H. Dittrich, H. Baum, and Lewis Brown, *An Atlas of Animal Anatomy* (New York: Dover, 1956), fig. 30, p. 100.

♏ **BODIOMANCY** is divination by observing bulls (from the Greek *bodio*, meaning bull). When performing bodiomancy, the ancient Babylonians splashed water three times on the head of a sleeping ox. The diviner would observe the ox's reactions and compare them to seventeen possible reactions with predefined meanings. For example, if both eyes stayed closed, no answer is given. If both eyes are open, the answer is "yes." (see figure 19).

♐ **BONE DIVINATION** (also known as "talking bones"). See **kokalomancy**.

♏ **BRONCHIOMANCY** is Inca divination by studying the lungs of sacrificed white llamas. First, the Inca priests inflated the lungs of a sacrificed white llama by blowing into the dissected trachea, and then the priests observed the shape of the veins that would suggest certain political or military actions.

♐ **CEPHALOMANCY** is divination by observing the skull or head of a human, donkey, or goat. Sometimes an animal head was boiled, and the resultant skull was examined to foretell the future. See also **oinomancy** ("Methods Using Food and Drink"), which includes observing a skull after it is soaked in wine.

♉ **EPATOSCOMANCY** is divination by examining the guts of animals. See also **anthropomancy**, **hepatomancy**, **haruspicy**, and **extispicy**.

♍ **EXTISPICY**, **EXTISPICIOMANCY** (or **EXTISPICIUM**) refers to making observations, particularly of entrails, for the purposes of divination. The practitioners were known as *extispieces* or *auspieces*, and one of the instruments they used was called the *extispicium*. The ancient Eturians, also known as the Etruscans, were the first and most learned people to practice extispicy. The Roman auspieces had four distinct duties: to examine the animal before it was opened, to examine the entrails, to observe the flame of the sacrificial fire, and to examine the meat and drink offered during the sacrifice.

⌒ **FELIDOMANCY** is divination through observations of cats. If a cat sneezes, it will rain. If a cat crosses one's path, it means good luck (in England) or bad luck (in the United States). In France, an unknown white cat sunning itself on the doorstep means a hasty marriage for one of the house's inhabitants. Many cultures, such as the ancient Egypt, China, South America, and China, revered cats.

♋ **HARUSPICATION** (or **HARUSPICY**) is fortune-telling by means of inspecting the entrails of animals, as practiced by priests in ancient Rome and other cultures. The Romans had learned the practice from the Etruscans, an advanced civilization in Italy before the Roman Empire. See also **epatoscomancy**, **anthropomancy**, **hepatomancy**, and **extispicy**.

♍ **HEPATOSCOPY** (or **HEPATOMANCY**) is examination of the liver of sacrificed animals. The Babylonians were famous for hepatoscopy and considered the liver the source of the blood and hence the source of life. The *bara* or priest was specially trained to interpret markings on the livers. Many armies brought along a bara to suggest actions before battles. Private citizens also employed baras to perform hepatoscopy. The prophet Ezekiel in the Old Testament refers to hepatoscopy in 21:21: "For the king of Babylon stood at the parting of the way, at the head of the two ways, to use divination: he made his arrows bright, he consulted with images, he looked in the liver." The Etruscans, Hittites, and Babylonians all performed "liver gazing." The hepatomancy system of the Sumerians required looking for thousands of possible variations in the size, shape, texture, and health of the liver in order to foretell the future. *See* **epatoscomancy**, **anthropomancy**, **hepatomancy**, **extispicy**, and **haruspicy**.

---

### Return of the Haruspex
#### Keith Allen Daniels

*Everybody is a book of blood;*
*wherever we're opened, we're red.*
—Clive Barker, *Books of Blood*

Sometimes a poem, pulsing like a heart
beneath the skin, a sanguine twist of truth
uncoiled by divinatory arts,
augurs more than visceral volumes can.
Life's unbound galleys, rarely in demand—
a kind of codex in the proper hands—
cry out for readers from the vault of ribs.
Behind each frontispiece a story lies
that never lies, however convolute
and raveled by the years beyond the crib.

Have all the tales been told? Is all reprise?
Your new editions stacked like Babel tower—
but all I find are weak anthologies,
their pages guarded by a grim disease,
and novels only Dahmer could devour.

♎ **HIEROMANCY** (or **HIERSCOPY**) is divination using sacred articles and by observing sacrifices.[37] For example, in ancient Egypt, the hieromancer studied objects that were thought to be sacred, such as animals, gems, and fountains. The Druids interpreted the crackles of sounds that were made during human sacrifices. Today, hieromancy is a broad term that encompasses all kinds of "sacred" objects, including crystals and tarot cards.

♏ **HIPPOMANCY** is a form of divination that requires the practitioner to observe horses stamping and neighing. Ancient hippomancers use sacred, light-colored horses to divine the future. The practice seems to date back to the ancient Celts who kept special horses in sacred groves. The ancient Germans kept similar animals in their temples. Sometimes hippomancers watched the behavior of these horses when yoked to a special chariot. During a war, it was a bad omen if the horses stepped over a threshold with their left forefeet. In these instances, the fight was called off. When the hippomancer desired to know God's will, he laid spears on the ground. Next, the hippomancer led a horse to the spears and watched to see whether its hooves touched them, and whether it put forward its right or left foot to step over them. Not only was the behavior and color of the horses important, but even the amount of dust created by their movements was part of the divination process.

♋ **KEPHALONMANCY** (or **KAPHALOMANCY** or **KEPHALONOMANCY**) is divining by burning a piece of carbon on the head of an ass or goat while reciting the name of suspected criminals. If the kephalonmancer heard a crackling sound when a certain person's name was mentioned, the person was guilty as charged. This method of divination was used during the time of the Lombards, an ancient Germanic people who settled in northern Italy during the sixth century C.E. The Lombards didn't use a live goat but rather the baked head of a goat. They poured lighted carbon on the head while they announced the alleged crimes of the accused.

♍ **MYOMANCY** is the study of rodent behaviors and cries to predict the future. Myomancy was practiced in ancient Assyria, Egypt, and Rome. When myomancers heard the cries of rodents, they knew that evil or problems were just around the corner. In 77 C.E., Roman encyclopaedist Pliny wrote, "By gnawing the silver shields at Lanuvium, mice had prognosticated the Marsian war."

♊ **OLOLYGMANCY** is divination by observing the howls of dogs and wolves, a practice popular in ancient Rome.

☾ **PODIOMANCY**, is divination through the study of footprints (from the Greek *podi*, meaning foot). See **alepouomancy**.

♍ **SCAPULOMANCY** (or **SCAPULIMANCY** or **PRO-SCAPULIMANCY**) is an ancient form of **pyromancy** in which the practitioner studies cracks in animals' shoulder blades burned in fires. The Chinese began using scapulomancy more than five thousand years ago. The Romans, Druids, and ancient Japanese and Tibetan monks all roasted bones to foretell the future. Usually a sheep bone was used, but native tribes in Labrador used caribou bones. The Labrador Naskapi (a Native American tribe) examined cracks and burn spots on bones to help find new sources of game.

♉ **TARUSOMANCY** is an ancient Germanic divination whereby a man sits on a freshly flayed ox hide in a secluded forest location. According to the thirteenth-century Mariu saga, if the man wishes to know the outcome of a battle, he draws nine squares around the skin, and the devil finally brings him the answer. Icelanders sit while wrapped in the hide of a sheep, walrus, or bull to gain knowledge from the dead.

## 🖿 Flying Things

♉ **ALECTRYOMANCY** (or **ALECTROMANCY**) is a divination method that uses a bird such as rooster. The alectryomancer sometimes wishes to know the name of a person and allows a bird to pick corn grains from letters drawn in a circle on the ground. This may give clues to the person's name. A variation is to recite letters of the alphabet, noting those at which a cock crows. In one cruel form of alectryomancy, one asks a question and then cuts off both claws of a young, white cock. The alectryomancer then forces the cock to swallow his own claws together with a small roll of lambskin parchment. The cock is placed in the middle of the circle of grains and watched to see from which of the letters he pecks the grains. The letters spell out a word or the name of a person relevant to the question. (It's not clear in my mind how the cock actually walks after swallowing his claws or has any interest in eating.) Alectryomancy was popular in ancient Rome and in the Middle Ages (see figure 20).

One story in the ancient literature concerns a magician who used alectryomancy to discover the successor to Valens, the Roman emperor from 364 to 378 C.E. Unfortunately, the bird just pecked four grains that spelled "T-H-E-O." This left a great ambiguity. The letters could have stood for several Roman names such as Theodosius, Theodotus, Theodorus, or

**Figure 20.** Alectryomancy. In one form of this divination method, the alectryomancer asks a question and then cuts off both claws of a young cock. The alectryomancer then forces the cock to swallow his own claws and observes the cock's behavior. From Jim Harter, *Animals* (New York: Dover, 1979), fig. 717, p. 162.

Theodectes. When the emperor heard of the cock's prediction, he had several persons murdered whose names began with Theo. The magician drank poison to escape worse punishment by the emperor.

Sometimes the term alectryomancy is also applied to divination involving the behavior of any animals, for example alepouomancy (foxes), gryllomancy (crickets), myrmomancy (ants), chelomancy (eels), and bodiomancy (oxs), as well as podiomancy (animal footprints).

⌐ **AUGURY** is a general term for the art of divination and is chiefly applied to interpretations of signs and omens. Augurers often study the flights of birds to divine the future. For example, in the ancient Germanic world, the appearance of ravens before battle was hailed as a sign of victory (see figure 21). If you met a dark raven on the road, you would have good luck. Few Greeks would continue a journey or an activity if a crow flew by toward the left. In traditional Tibet, the crow or raven were divinatory birds and never killed. In medieval Ireland, if a raven cawed above your bed, this meant a distinguished guest was on the way.

♌ **DILITIRIOMANCY** (after the Greek *dilitirio* for poison; also known as the "poison oracle" or "poison divination") is practiced by the Azande of Central Africa. To help them make certain decisions, the Azande elders force benge poison down the throat of a bird. As the bird weakens, the men pose a condition. For example, "If Oswald alone killed Kennedy, benge kill this fowl. If Oswald alone did not kill Kennedy, benge spare the fowl." (Of course, the Azande would ask questions more relevant to their own needs than this example.) The dilitiriomancer might also pose a yes-or-no question to the oracle, and specify beforehand whether the death of the fowl means yes or no. After the first question is answered, the answer is verified by posing the question in its opposite form, and asking the oracle again. For example, "If Oswald alone killed Kennedy, benge spare this fowl. If Oswald alone did not kill Kennedy, benge kill the fowl." Obviously, the oracle can sometimes contradict itself, but the Azande have explanations for why this happens. We may be quick to judge the Azande poison oracle as being irrational because, (among other reasons!) the oracle can contradict itself; however, many people accept the rationality of going to mass for divine guidance even when their prayers are not apparently answered or when the Bible appears to have internal self-contradictions or contradictions with science. Apparent contradiction has rarely been a reason for believers in religion or divination to abandon their faith.

**Figure 21.** Augurers often study the flights of birds to divine the future. For example, in the ancient Germanic world, the appearance of ravens before battle was hailed as a sign of victory. From Jim Harter, *Animals* (New York: Dover, 1979), fig. 592, p. 134.

♐ **OOMANCY** is divination by breaking an egg into a glass or saucer of water and then interpreting the forms the white assumes in the water. When oomancy was practiced in ancient Rome only three drops of egg white were used in the water. Sometimes the appearance of the egg shell was studied, as in the practice of **oomantia**.

)( **OOMANTIA** (or **OOSCOPY**) is divination using eggs, with an emphasis on the egg shell, although the egg white is sometimes used as well (see **oomancy**). A strange form of ooscopy was described as far back as the first century by the Roman historian Suetonius (c. 98–138 C.E.). See the "Quantum Mechanics of Ooscopy" section for legends of women using eggs to determine the gender of their unborn children.

♉ **ORNISCOPY** and **ORNITHOMANCY** are the study of omens associated with birds, particularly birds in flight. Ornithomancers also observed bird songs. Ornithomancy was popular in ancient Greece and Rome. See **apantomancy** and **augury**.

)( **OVOMANCY**. See **oomancy** and **oomatnia**.

♍ **POISON ORACLE** or **POISON DIVINATION**. See *DILITIRIOMANCY*.

## Plight of the Auspex
### Keith Allen Daniels

"Some poison has perturbed the flight of birds
beyond the outer limits of my art;
or else the last good spirit is interred
and demons batten on the human heart.
If toxin, then a thrice-repeated word
is antidote. I'd speak it, and depart.
But if the bleaker auspice is inferred
from twisted ways the swifts and swallows dart,
then love itself has too long been deferred,
and words, if said, would surely go unheard."

In unison the birds flew stranger still,
converging in a shape that conjured dread,
and looking up, the auspex wished them ill
as droppings splattered on his hapless head.

*Auxpex: an augur of ancient Rome, especially one who interpreted omens observed in the actions and flight patterns of birds.*

## ☞ Creepy Crawlers

♉ **ARACHNOMANCY** is divination using spiders. The Bamileke (West African peoples in the Bamileke region of Cameroon) observe spiders moving leaves and grass. The practice of spider divination by the neighboring Mambila people was described in detail in the "Mambila Spider Divination" section. Spider divination was also practiced by the Incas when the arachnomancer watched the way spiders altered the arrangement of coca leaves in a shallow dish.

♈ **CHELIOMANCY** is divination using eels (from the Greek *cheli*, meaning eel). The Hittites, an ancient people of Asia minor (1600 B.C.E.–1200 C.E.) studied the movements of eels in water to divine the future (see figure 22).

♐ **ICHTHYOMANCY** is divination using fish, which may be in or out of water. Sometimes their guts and bones are studied. The ancient Greeks and Scandinavian peoples practiced ichthyomancy. The color, behavior, and number of fish in ponds and rivers all provided information on the future, such as the success of a battle or the gender of a child.

♍ **GRYLOMANCY** (from the Greek *gryllos* meaning cricket) is divination with crickets. The cricket has traditionally been viewed with fear and sometimes as a bringer of death or disease. A cricket in a house was a very bad omen, and the lighter its body, the worse it was for the household. The white cricket was particularly noxious. In 1699, author John Dryden wrote in *Fables, Ancient and Modern*: "Owls, Ravens, and Crickets seem the wave of death."

On the other hand, sometimes the cricket has been a welcome friend. In 1789, Gilbert White wrote in *Natural History and Antiquities of Selborne*, "Crickets are the housewife's barometer, foretelling when it will rain; and are prognostic sometimes, she thinks, of ill or good luck, of the death of a near relation or the approach of an absent lover. By being the constant companions of her solitary hours they naturally become the objects of her superstition." People in the Orient have kept night-singing crickets as household pets to indicate the presence of intruders, because the crickets suddenly stop singing when disturbed by other noises. Many Japanese keep insects as pets and sell living crickets and bamboo cages in markets.

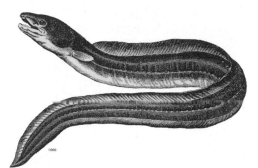

**Figure 22.** The Hittite cheliomacers studied the movements of eels to divine the future. From Jim Harter, *Animals* (New York: Dover, 1979), fig. 1000, p. 214.

Some Native Americans believed that by boiling a number of crushed crickets and drinking the liquid, a person could develop a more beautiful singing voice.[38]

☿ **LEPDIOMANCY** (or **BUTTERFLY DIVINATION**) is divination by studying the shapes and patterns in butterfly wings. Through the ages, the butterfly has represented rebirth and transformation for many cultures.

Butterflies, like many birds, were once thought to be the souls of the dead before the souls completely left earth for the afterlife. In particular, butterflies were often thought to carry the souls of children that had died before baptism. In Scotland, the appearance of a golden butterfly near a sick person was a good omen indicating recovery.[39] If a critically ill or injured person died in the presence of the golden butterfly, he or she would be very happy in the afterlife. For all these reasons, people once treated butterflies with great respect.

Three or more butterflies landing on the same flower or seen flying at night were an omen of death according to European folklore. Specific color also played a role in Lepdiomancy. For example, white butterflies were connected with good fortune. According to legend, the first butterfly seen each year should be mutilated or decapitated in order to ensure that the next year would be a happy one.

❀❀ **MYRMOMANCY** (from the Greek *myrmigki* meaning ant) is divination with ants. The Dogon, an African tribe, practice this form of **alectryomancy** by first viewing an anthill from a particular location and then inserting thin leaves into the anthill. If the ants eat the leaf on the left first, the answer to the querent's questions is yes. Otherwise the answer is no.

Ants have generated a huge body of folklore. For example, in the past, eating ant eggs with honey was once considered an effective cure for romantic problems. Other legends suggested that a person was lucky to find an ant nest near one's front door or property entrance, because ants foretold financial success. Many cultures have traditionally seen the appearance of many ants moving from one location to another as foretelling a coming storm and that stepping on ants would lead to a heavy downpour.[40]

♉ **OLIGOMANCY** is divination by examining the earthworm movements. In order to determine the best place for burial of a loved one, the worm is dropped on a circle drawn on the ground. The direction in which the worm leaves the circle determines the burial location, which may not take place for several days. According to *Strangest Human Sex, Ceremonies, and Customs*, the Hiji of Nigeria and Cameroon never bury a dead community member until they skin the body.[41] First, they sit up the corpse for two days on a platform, with its hands in bowls of peanuts and food grains so the crops stay fertile. Next a blacksmith visits and uses his fingers to yank off the body's skin, which he throws into a pot and buries. Then "the skinless corpse is washed with red juice, smeared with goat's fat, dressed, and carried to a burial site."[42]

A traditional northern England belief suggests that worms could be used to determine if a person would recover from an illness. While on the way to visit a sick person, the querent would look under a stone and see if there was a worm underneath it. If there was a worm, the sick person would recover quickly, otherwise he or she would have difficult times ahead.[43]

♌ **OPHIOMANCY** is divination by observing the color and movement of serpents. For example, a coiled snake indicates that a person should be patient.

♉ **PLASTROMANCY** is the ancient Chinese art of reading cracks in a heated tortoise shell.

♐ **SKATHAROMANCY** is divination using beetles. Polynesians still practice skatharomancy in which tribal leaders coax a beetle to crawl over the grave of a murder victim. The beetle's tracks are supposed to indicate the murderer's name when the tracks are interpreted.

English folklore describes divination with ladybugs. A woman cups a ladybug in her hands and then watches the direction in which it flies. Her lover will come from that direction.

♍ **TERMITISOMANCY** (after the Greek *termitis* for termite, also called the "termite oracle") is divination using termites and practiced today by the Azande of central Africa. See "Do-it-Yourself Termitisomancy" for details.[44]

♌ **THEIROMANCY** is a general term for divination by studying animal behavior. The ancient Etruscans practiced theiromancy by watching hens or roosters. Babylonians studied sleeping oxen's reaction to having their heads splashed with water. The Hittites watched eels. The African Zandes still watch ants. The Polynesians watch beetles. See **alectryomancy**, **bodiomancy**, **cheliomancy**, **myrmomancy**, **skatharomancy**, and **zoomancy**.

♐ **ZOOMANCY** is another general term for divination by observing the behavior of animals. See **alectryomancy**, **bodiomancy**, **cheliomancy**, **myrmomancy**, **skatharomancy**, and **theiromancy**.

📂 **Plants**

♌ **ANTHOMANCY** is divination using flowers. One common form among young people requires the querent to pull off the petals of flowers while making statements such as "She loves me" and "She loves me not." The statement uttered when the last petal is pulled is supposed to be true. See **flower oracles**.

---

### Do-It-Yorself Termite Oracle (Termitisomancy)

Termitisomancy is divination using termites and is practiced today by the Azande of central Africa. Here is an authentic recipe for do-it-yourself termite divination (see endnote 44).

1. Locate and cut off branches of two different types of trees. One branch corresponds to one "side" of your question, and the other branch corresponds to the other "side." For example, in its simplest form, one branch may mean no, the other yes.
2. Poke each branch into a termite mound. (If termite mounds are not available, use ant hills as do the African myrmomancers from the Dogon tribe.)
3. Address the termites in official Dogon fashion: "O termites, if this business will succeed eat the dakpa-tree. If this business will not succeed, eat the kpoyo-tree." (Substitute the names of your trees and your own questions or problems.)
4. Leave the branches in the mound overnight and come back to make observations.
5. If both branches are completely eaten or moved, or both are left untouched, the question has been refused. When one branch is eaten (or moved) more than the other, the answer is yes or no.

)( **BOTANOMANCY** is divination using plants. In one form of botanomancy, the querent burns tree branches and leaves and observes the smoke. In Medieval England, women blew on dandelion seed clusters. The number of puffs needed to release all the seeds indicated the number of years a woman would have to wait to find love. In Colonial America, women threw apple peels onto a table or floor. The resulting configuration of the apple skin was supposed to indicate the first letter of the future husband's name. In southern India and in Sri Lanka, people study patterns of coconut interiors to forecast the future of the unborn. A rough interior signifies a difficult life. A smooth interior foretells an easy life of luxury. See **phyllomancy, phyllorhodomancy, causiomancy, libanomancy, daphnomancy, capnomancy**, and **critomancy**—methods that all employ plants, trees, or seeds.

♉ **COCONUT DIVINATION**. See **karydaomania**.

♋ **CRITOMANCY** is divination through the study of grains and cakes. For example, critomancers study the way grains or flour smoke as they are poured over burning animal carcasses. They also observe dough as it bakes. For more details, see the related **causimomancy** and more modern forms of **aleuromancy**.

♍ **CROMNIOMANCY** is divination using onion sprouts.

♐ **FLOWER ORACLES** refer to divination using flower bouquets. The method originated in eighteenth-century France where large bouquets were used to reveal a person's character and forecast future careers. Flower oracles are still popular today. To use the flower oracles, look at a floral bouquet and then pick the first flower that strikes your fancy. A reading is based upon the divinatory meaning attached to that particular flower. Numerous Web sites, books, and cards are devoted to variations in flower prediction.

Victorians used to express their feelings through flowers. They ascribed a meaning to each flower; for example, acacia is associated with elegance and grace, cactus with burning desire, fern with sincerity and honesty, magnolia with love of nature, and so forth. See **anthomancy**.

)( **PHYLLOMANCY** is divination by studying the patterns and veins on leaves. This method was popular among the ancient Greeks and Druids.

♌ **PHYLLORHODOMANCY** is a means of divination in which one slaps a rose petal against the hand and judges the favorability of the omen by the loudness of the sound or the look of the petal. This was popular with the ancient Greeks who clapped rose leaves on their hands and judged the success or failure of their desires by the sound.

♏ **QUERCUSMANCY** is divination using oak trees or acorns. According to legends, oak trees sometimes shed their leaves when oaths were broken. When King Harold II of England narrowly survived the Battle of Hastings in 1066, he found himself at Rouen with William, Duke of Normandy, who made the king swear an oath under an oak tree. When the king broke his oath, the oak signaled the event by dropping its leaves.

Insects sometimes cause an oak to produce galls (tumorlike masses). One form of quercusmancy allows the practitioner to gain information by determining the creature that produced the gall. Spiders indicate future illness. A fly suggests misfortune. A worm foretells prosperity.[45]

The acorn has often been used for romantic divination. Lovers were supposed to drop two acorns into the same bowl of water. If the acorns came together while floating, then the couple would marry, otherwise the couple would not marry. An ancient pagan belief, perhaps originating with the Druids, suggested that a person would not grow old if he or she carried an acorn at all times. This method was thought to be more effective for women than men.

In the same way that some children in America are told that babies can be found in cabbage patches or are brought by the stork, some German children believe that babies come from an old, hollow oak tree and are brought by the doctor.

A large, legendary oak still grows at Howth Castle, Ireland. The family of St. Lawrences, the Earls of Howth, have their fates intimately tied to the tree. Legends suggests that when the tree falls, the Howth family's direct line will become extinct. If you visit the castle, you'll see the branches are strongly supported on wooden uprights.

〜〜 〜〜 〜〜

Although this section emphasizes prediction based on physical structures, such as lines in a liver or a leaf, many divination methods focus almost entirely on the invisible—the realm of spirits and dreams and various mental processes. From the ancient Greeks who considered dreams as visitations from gods to modern psychologists who attempt to use hypnosis to induce visions of the future, the mind has clearly played a strong role in divination through the centuries, and several methods are discussed in the following section.

## ⋈ MEMORIES, DREAMS, AND SPIRIT

☞ *Topics discussed*: a variety of divination methods that depend on abstract mental phenomena, with an emphasis on dreams and hypnosis.

### *Dreaming with the Gods*

> *In the last days, God says, "I will pour out my Spirit on all people. Your sons and daughters will prophesy, your young men will see visions, your old men will dream dreams."*
>
> —Acts 2:17

Dream divination, or predicting the future by interpreting dreams, was employed everywhere in the ancient world. For example, the Chester Beatty Papyrus, discovered in 1931, is a record of Egyptian dream interpretations from around 1800 B.C.E.[46] Heroes in Greek, Indian, Babylonian, Islamic, and Old Testament legends and myths often received messages in dreams, and the prophet Muhammad was so concerned about dream divination he forbade the practice. More recently, Joseph Smith (1805–1844), the founder of Mormonism, said he had a dream in which the angel Moroni told him where to find hidden golden tablets.[47] Once the tablets' text was fully translated, the material became the Book of Mormon, which tells us that in about 600 B.C.E., prior to the destruction of Jerusalem, a Jewish family fled the city and traveled by ship to North America. According to Smith, Native Americans are the descendants of this family. Today, a forty-foot-high statue of Moroni stands near Palmyra, New York, where Smith said he discovered the buried tablets.

The ancient Greek world saw dreams as visitations from gods and the souls of the dead. The *onieropolos*, or dream reader, played an important role in Greek society. The most famous dream interpretation book is the *Oneirocritica* (from the Greek *oneiros*, "a dream") by the Greek soothsayer Artemidorus Daldianus who lived in the second century C.E.[48] Professional diviners read this book to interpret thousands of dreams. When the Christian Church gained political power, it made all forms of divination capital crimes and burned the dream books. The church declared all dreams false and sent by demons. Modern dream books are popular and profitable today. (Just type "dream interpretation" at Amazon.com on the World Wide Web, and you'll find over two hundred books on the subject!)

Dream interpretation varied significantly from culture to culture. Many of the Christian seers suggested that dreams often meant the opposite of what they seemed to mean. Thus, if you dream of poverty and filth, you will acquire something valuable. If you dream of the dead, you will hear news of the living, and so forth.[49] Even the occurrence of specific flowers and vegetables in dreams were thought to have meaning. For example, asparagus tied in bundles was an omen of tears, but if the dream asparagus was growing, it was a sign of good fortune. The appearance of artichokes suggested that a person would receive a favor from an unexpected direction. Cauliflower meant you would become poor.[50] I wonder how many people have dreams with vegetables in them.

Often a dream was supposed to reveal the future only when the dream occurred on a precise date. For example, British legends of the late 1800s suggested that only on January 1,

> if a young maiden drinks, on going to bed, a pint of cold spring water, in which is beat up an amulet, composed of the yolk of a pullet's egg, the legs of a spider, and the skin of an eel pounded, her future destiny will be revealed to her in a dream. This charm fails of its effect if tried any other day of the year.[51]

Here's another ancient British recipe that will work only in the midsummer:

> Take three roses, smoke them with sulfur, and exactly at three in the day bury one of the roses under a yew-tree; the second in a newly-made grave, and put the third under your pillow for three nights, and at the end of that period burn it in a fire of charcoal. Your dreams during that time will be prophetic of your future destiny, and, what is still more curious and valuable, says Mother Bridget, the man whom you are to wed will enjoy no peace till he comes and visits you. Besides this, you will perpetually haunt his dreams.[52]

## Future-Life Progression

> *Whenever I mention progression into future lives in an interview, I know many listeners scratch their heads in disbelief. The future seems to be forbidden territory. We are all taught that the past has occurred, the present is occurring, but the futures has yet to occur. Then how could we possibly know it—by whatever means—in the present?*
>
> —Dr. Bruce Goldberg, *Past Lives, Future Lives*

Probably many of you have heard about past-life regression in which a person seems to be hypnotically "regressed" to recall information from past lives. Believers in past-life regression say that people are able to recall details about life in earlier times, and this is proof of reincarnation and the existence of past lives. For example, in Jeanne Avery and Nann Gatewood's *A Soul's Journey: Empowering the Present Through Past Life,* we hear from regressees who vividly recall suffering at the hands of Nazi war criminals.[53] None of these people were aware of such experiences until they attempted to regress to a previous life. In Jenny Cockell's *Across Time and Death: A Mother's Search for Her Past Life Children*, Cockell recounts her former life as Mary Sutton.[54] Jenny describes how, after years of painstaking searching, she finally reunited with family members from her previous lifetime. Skeptics of past-life regression say that, under hypnosis, people can recall all kinds of information learned during their normal lives and then incorporate the information into a realistic fantasy.[55] Similarly, the hypnotist's precise words may implant in a regressee's mind a past that never actually existed.

Less well known is the practice of *future-life progression* in which a person attempts to give information about the future while under hypnosis. Here are a few interesting examples. In 1960, California psychologist Dr. Helen Wambach, author of *Life Before Life*, began a series of studies in hypnosis in a desire presumably to debunk reincarnation.[56] Using over a thousand subjects, she conducted a long-term survey of past-life recalls under hypnosis. Dr. Wambach asked specific questions about past time periods in which people said they lived. She asked subjects to recall their clothing, footwear, utensils, money, and housing. Wambach believed that these people were actually having recollections and that they were often quite accurate. She wrote that "fantasy and genetic memory could not account for the patterns that emerged in the results." Surprisingly, Dr. Wambach also found that some hypnotized clients seemed to see their *future* lives where they lived in a devastated and depopulated Earth. Over the next few years, Dr. Wambach conducted a study of over two thousand people undergoing hypnotic *future-life* progression. During hypnosis, Wambach offered the participants a choice of three past time periods and two future time periods in which to enter. Of the 2,500 people in the study, 6 percent reported being alive in 2100 C.E., and 13 percent said they were alive in the 2300 C.E. period. In other words, only a few of the subjects progressed to the future.

Based on what people said under hypnosis, Wambach came to believe there was evidence that 95 percent of the Earth's population would be wiped out within a few generations. Concerned, Wambach asked one of her students to progress to a specific date in the late 1990s but had to rapidly bring the woman out of hypnotic trance after the woman found herself "choking to death on a big, black cloud." Wambach found predictions for the last years of the century to include severe earthquakes, a new U.S. currency, severe weather patterns, financial crises, bank failures, an increase in volcanic activity, and the death of a large number of people. In 1999, there was supposed to be an isolated incident in which a European nuclear explosion killed many people. (See figure 23.)

Between 1983 and 1985, Wambach worked with Dr. Chet Snow who, after her death, published *Mass Dreams of the Future*, which contained the results of many future-life progressions performed in the 1980s.[57] In an interview published in the *Rainbow Ark* magazine, Snow said the massive changes in the Earth would take place.[58] The hypnotic subjects had foreseen changes in 1996, 1998–99, and then in the years 2002, 2007, and 2012. There were some fleeting images of an Arab-Israeli war in 1996 but no details. Snow said, "With regard to atomic weapons, there will be one more atomic explosion before the end of the atomic era. This explosion will be so terrible and will shock humanity so badly that no one will dare to use that weapon again."[59] Later, Snow described how a portion of California would slip into the sea in 1998. "The dates could change," Chet said in his book. "The left-brain linear time-dating system is the most difficult aspect of right-brain psychic predictions. However it should not be incorrect by more than a few decades."[60]

In an interview in the *Leading Edge Newspaper*, Dr. Snow suggests that the future is not set in stone, and that the mind can somehow alter the timeline:

> I believe, by changing our present behavior, we can change our future. We can go back in time, through past-life regression, and heal relationships in the past, and our present will then change because our vibration is no longer the same. As you think, so you are. The mind is the builder. I encourage my clients to work now, in the present, on the pathways they are forming which will build their future. People ask, "Where do I go? Where are the safe lands?" I say to them, "At least get away from water." Let synchronicities guide you. You will be drawn to a place of safety for you. The new energy on the planet is about service, but not in a servile way. Be each other's servant, each giving your best and receiving the best from others. [61]

Dr. Snow describes two different regions of time on which he focussed: 2100 to 2200 C.E. and 2300 to 2400 C.E.[62] At these times, the population is only about two billion, and there seems to be four different societies. Twenty-five percent of the test group whom he progressed into the future found themselves either living on a space station orbiting Earth or on another planet. Their society was high tech and had contact with friendly

**Figure 23.** Future-life progression. Under hypnosis, Drs. Wambach and Snow found that clients often reported future disasters ranging from earthquakes and severe weather patterns to California slipping into sea. Since ancient times, individuals have continued to predict catastrophes of biblical proportions, such as seen in this drawing of Genesis's flood. From Gustave Doré, *The Doré Bible Illustrations* (New York: Dover, 1974), p 6.

extraterrestrials. Thirty percent of the group lived on Earth in a high-tech society with machines, and they lived in domes or underground. They wore jumpsuits and did not seem happy. Eighteen percent of the group were vegetarians, wore lose, flowing robes, and lived happily in harmony with nature. Twenty percent of the group lived in small rustic towns resembling villages of the nineteenth century. They wore jeans, boots, and tunics, raising farm animals and eating meat. A small percentage of the experimental group reported living in the ruins of major cities like New York and existing in a primitive fashion. *In 1999, some progressees predicted that Soviets would take over parts of eastern Europe.*

Another famous practitioner of future-life progression is Dr. Bruce Goldberg, author of *Past Lives, Future Lives*, originally published in 1982 but with newer editions in 1997.[63] Early in 1981, Dr. Goldberg believed it was possible, under hypnosis, to rise above the stream of time and look ahead, just as one can rise in a helicopter above a highway and view traffic congestion to be encountered by cars traveling down the road. In a sense, one would be reading the future of cars on the road. Dr. Goldberg has performed thousand of hypnotic regressions and hundreds of progressions. He's even regressed and progressed himself. His clients appear to recall past events with great detail, but future progression is far "less stable," and it is more difficult to obtain information on future events. By "less stable," I mean that the client appears to quickly move from one scene to another without instructions from Dr. Goldberg. For example, a client could be describing a scene in some futuristic city, and then suddenly the city has disappeared and a grassland scene has replaced it.[64]

Many of Dr. Goldberg's clients supposedly report similar observations while in a trance. Here are some common themes sorted by century:[65]

- *21st Century*—World peace is attained and lasts three thousand years. Hunger, greed, and prejudice are reduced.
- *22d Century*—Solar power is part of daily life. The average life span is ninety years.
- *23d Century*—Transportation is noiseless and efficient. Nuclear power is used extensively. Sophisticated computers and video equipment are household appliances. Average life span is 110 years.
- *24th Century*—Humankind reexperiences earlier mistakes. International political problems recur. A small-scale nuclear war reduces human population.
- *25th Century*—Humans control the weather. Androids perform all menial tasks. A major nuclear war occurs that decimates most of humanity.

- *26th Century*—Humankind survives the last century's war and prospers. Underwater cities, the routine use of lasers in medicine, and sophisticated genetic engineering are common. Information pills keep citizens well informed, and one democratic form of world government insures the rights of all. The average life span is over 125 years. Sickness and disease is almost unknown. Interplanetary travel is a top priority, and we make contact with beings from other worlds.

While I find the long-term predictions of Dr. Goldberg's clients fascinating, I have to admit that many of them seem to be insufficiently futuristic and perhaps based on the client's mindset when they were progressed. As just one example, the predication that "sophisticated computers" and "video equipment" are household appliance in the twenty-third century seems to be absurdly nonfuturistic, considering this has happened before the twenty-first century. I also believe that humans will uncover the biological mysteries of aging in the twenty-first century, making humans virtually immortal. We certainly won't have to wait until the twenty-sixth century to achieve a life span of 125 years, as predicted by Dr. Golberg's clients.

Nonetheless, the fact that clients give information about the future is something to investigate, and their very short-term predictions are more interesting to me. Wouldn't it be interesting if certain kinds of short-term predictions seemed accurate because hypnosis helps subjects tap vague, subconscious intuitions about future trends? This seems to be territory for further scientific research, though it may well turn out to be wishful thinking.

As an informal test of short-term prediction, Dr. Goldberg progressed a man named Harry Martin who worked in a newsroom. Goldberg asked Martin to look at a newsroom assignment board to see if he could read news items about events that hadn't occurred yet.[66] This seemed to be a worthwhile test of hypnotic progression. After this test, Dr. Goldberg went further and attempted to progress Martin into a future life.

Here are the details of the journey. On February 2, 1981, Harry began his first trip into the future. Goldberg progressed him one week forward to February 9 and told Harry to read from the newsroom assignment board one hour before airtime of his broadcast or read from the actual script of the day's newscast. Harry complied and described a week in the future where he saw state aviation officials investigating the crash of a light plane near Route 406. It turned out that a plane did crash in nearby Bowie, Maryland, on February 9, although the item did not make it on the air.

Next, Harry said he saw a very long name on the newsroom assignment board. Dr. Golberg's session was as follows:

| *Dr. G*: | What is the next item on the assignment board? |
| *Harry*: | It's the name of a place, I think, but I can't make it out. |
| *Dr. G*: | Can you spell it? |
| *Harry*: | It's a long name. It's a very weird combination of consonants. It's the name of a man. |
| *Dr. G*: | What letters can you make out? |
| *Harry*: | ST W KI. . . . It's a long Russian-type name.[67] |

On February 9, Stanislaw Kania, Poland's labor leader, was told that he might soon be fired unless he instructed his workers to return. You can read Dr. Goldberg's book for a complete list of short-term predictions involving accidents, interviews, and fires to decide for yourself if these are simply minor coincidences or something more meaningful. Later, Harry Martin is progressed to the year 2271 at which point he is living a different life and his complete name is "Amygdala."

Skeptics would ask why no one has used future life progression to predict stock values or lottery numbers. Dr. Goldberg says he considers this an unnatural use of our natural psychic abilities and, in any case, the dates are not always accurate. For example, a progression of one week in the future may, in actuality, be three days or ten days hence. (Still, that would be good enough to make a killing on Wall Street.)

Dr. Goldberg found that in order to progress people into a future life, it is almost always necessary to first regress people into several past lives. He reasons that the idea of going into the future is much harder for people to handle than going into the past. People create too many "blocks" related to what society tells them they can and cannot do. Goldberg says, "We are told that the future cannot be predicted or perceived. Our culture informs us that only charlatans or evil people delve into the future."

Even if past-life regression and future-life progression do not actually lead people to past and future lives, Dr. Goldberg has found that such exercises make people feel better, and they find their present-day lives transformed in positive ways. He suggests that current psychological problems are reduced as a result of the patient's dramatic voyages of self-discovery through centuries past and future. The journeys eliminate the fear of death for many of Dr. Goldberg's patients. However, others find it dangerous when regressionlike hypnosis is used to elicit "recovered" and sometimes imagined memories about past child abuse, and to awaken "recollections" of alien abduction and past lives. Psychiatrists must be particularly vigilant not to inadvertently train patients into behavior that fits preconceptions. For example, various reports suggests how practitioners can "find" whatever they look for such as child abuse or multiple personality disorder (MPD)—now known formally as dissociative identity disorder and characterized by the existence of more than one personality within the same individual. The recent epidemic of MPD may have many causes: clinicians' diagnostic practices such as hypnosis that prompt patients to exhibit MPD, expectations communicated by the media, and widely available information regarding MPD's diagnostic features. It is chilling to think that certain disorders may be as much sociological as psychological in origin. Today people are accused, tried, and convicted of heinous crimes on speculative "evidence" provided by memories that did not exist until a person underwent hypnosis or was given drugs to recover repressed memories. The crimes excavated by the therapist include horrifying animal cruelty, incest, and satanic ritualistic abuse performed or suffered by the patient. Families are destroyed. Children are removed from homes and sometimes coaxed to confirm parents' stories. Sadly, uncritical acceptance of "recovered" memories trivializes any genuine memories of abuse and increases the suffering of real victims.[68]

## 📖 A CONCISE CATALOG OF METHODS USING THE MIND AND SPIRIT

> *The nineteenth-century Hasidic rabbi Menahem Mendelof Kotzk once asked some visiting scholars, "Where does God dwell?" They laughed at him and said, "God is everywhere, of course. The whole earth is full of his glory." The rabbi shook his head, then said, "God dwells wherever man lets him in."*
>
> —Stephen Mitchell, *The Enlightened Mind*

ϒ **AKASHIC RECORDS** are a hypothetical compendium of pictorial records, or "memories," of all events, thoughts, actions, and feelings that have occurred since the beginning of time. According to occultists, these records are imprinted on Akasha, the astral light, a fluid ether existing beyond the range of our senses. Diviners are said to be able to access the Akashic records, thereby making prophecy and clairvoyance possible. The word "akashic" is derived from the Sanskrit expression *akasha*, meaning a theoretical universal medium. According to ancient Indian tradition, the universe reveals itself in two fundamental properties: as motion and as that in which motion takes place, namely space. This space is called *âkâsha*, which is derived from the root *kâsh* (to radiate or, to shine). Helena Blavatsky, founder of the Theosophical Society, referred to the akasha as "a radiant, cool, diaphanous plastic matter, creative in its physical nature."[69] For a critique of Blavatasky, see chapter 3, pp. 295–97.

♐ **ASPIDOMANCY** is divination by trance. In particular, aspidomancy refers to a divination method practiced in the Indies and first described in the seventeenth century. The diviner or sorcerer draws a circle in which he positions himself on a shield. He then recites certain phrases and falls into a trance. When he awakens, the diviner tell his clients things that they want to know.

♍ **CHRESMONANCY** is divination by "channeling" information from a supernatural entity. The chremonancer purportedly speaks the entity's words.[70] Chresmonancy dates to the Roman augurs and is quite popular in modern times with famous "New Age" channelers like JZ Knight and Jane Roberts (see the entries in chapter 3 for individual channelers and also the sidebar "A Smorgasbord of Channelers" on pp. 340–44).

♈ **DEMONOMANCY** is divination with the aid of demons.

♏ **METAGNOMY** is divination using "visions" received in a trance state.

♎ **NECROMANCY** uses spirits of the dead to reveal the future and answer questions. The practice dates back to Persia, Greece, and Rome. Necromancers flourished in the Middle Ages but in Elizabethan England were condemned by the Catholic Church as "agents of evil spirits" (see figure 24). The practice was outlawed by the Witchcraft Act of 1604. Because the spirits of the dead had no physical limitations, they were thought to have information of the past and future. Necromancers say that the practice is dangerous because once spirits take control of the necromancer, they are reluctant to release their control.

♐ **NIGROMANCY** is an ancient method of communication with the dead, usually performed by a psychic who walks around a grave in order to make contact.

♍ **ONEIROMANCY** is the interpretation of dreams and their prophetic potential. Chinese philosophers, Islamic mystics, Greek diviners, Tibetan lamas, and Western psychologists have all offered explanations for the symbols in dreams. Dreams were once seen as direct messages from the gods.

The Talmud, the first authoritative codification of Jewish oral laws, has hundreds of references to the meanings and of dreams, which may be caused by angels, demons, and witches. In one section, Rabbi Binza said he once explained his dream to twenty-four different Jerusalem dream interpreters and received twenty-four different readings, which all came true.

**Figure 24.** Necromancers believe they can communicate with the dead. Shown here is one scary vision of the afterlife from Dante's *Divine Comedy*. From Gustave Doré, *The Doré Illustrations for Dante's Divine Comedy* (New York: Dover, 1976), p. 102.

**Figure 25.** Dream divination. The biblical Job, pictured at right, is discussing his fate with his three friends when suddenly Job is reminded that "God may speak in one way, or in another, yet man does not perceive it. In a dream, in a vision of the night, when deep sleep falls upon men, while slumbering on their beds, then He opens the ears of men, and seals their instruction." From Gustave Doré, *The Doré Bible Illustrations* (New York: Dover, 1974), p. 137.

A dream interpretation is referred to in the Old Testament (Daniel 2:2–3): "Then the king commanded to call the magicians, and the astrologers, and the sorcerers, and the Chaldeans, for to shew the kind his dreams. So they came and stood before the king. And the king said unto them, I have dreamed a dream, and my spirit was troubled by the dream." In Numbers 12:5–6, God said, "I the Lord will make myself known unto him in a vision, I will speak within a dream." In Job 33:14–16, Elihu tells Job, "For God may speak in one way, or in another, yet man does not perceive it. In a dream, in a vision of the night, when deep sleep falls upon men, while slumbering on their beds, then He opens the ears of men, and seals their instruction" (see figure 25).

The *Roy Sedge* is a spiritual book containing the dreams Mohammed had before he revealed the Koran. The dreams appeared to Mohammed as "luminous impressions." Dreams and their interpretation are an integral part of the Persian world view, as well as the Shi'ite notion of "inner prophethood." In Persian legends and popular narratives, political authority is bestowed through dreams. Dream interpretation also plays a role in many indigenous cultures from American Indian to the Aborigines of Australia. The Greeks valued dream interpretation and had temples where one might sleep in order to dream cures for disease and answers to questions.

Modern dream interpreters enjoy giving meaning to all kinds of happenings in dreams. For example, dreams of flying are supposed to indicate that the dreamer is investigating new thoughts or avenues. Dreams of falling from high places indicate the dreamer fears failure. Note that Freud wrote in his *The Interpretation of Dreams*, "The dream of flying, in the case of male dreamers, should usually have a sexual significance; and we should not be surprised to hear that this or that dreamer is always very proud of his ability to fly."

♈ **ORACLE** is a divine communication associated with a special site or person. "Oracle" also refers to the one wo makes the pronouncement. The term comes from the Latin *oraculum* and from *orare*, which means "to pray" and also can refer to the place of prophecy. The oracles of the Roman god Zeus, for example, originated at Dodona and other locations. Oracular shrines used to be everywhere, where people used various methods of divination to find answers. Sometimes, the oracle would give confusing answers by speaking in ambiguous poetry. At other times, a querent would have to sleep in a special location to receive an answer in dreams. This form of dream divination is called *incubation*.

⌒ **PRECOGNITION** is the ability to know what is going to happen in the future, especially if based on extrasensory perception.

♏ **PROJECTIVE TESTS** are psychological tests, like the famous Rorschach test, conducted with ambiguous stimuli such as irregular inkblots on paper. A person is asked to make sense of the stimuli, and the person's answer is thought to yield a brief glimpse into hidden mental processes. Although these approaches would seem to constitute a much more scientific "divination" method than the others in this book, I include them here because there is considerable debate about whether these methods are useful in determining relationships between perception and personality. All kinds of exotic variants exist: the *Lüscher Color Test*, which purports to examine personalty traits by examining a subject's preferences for various colored cards; the *Blacky Test*, which uses drawings of a black puppy engaged in ambiguous activities and requires subjects to describe the presence of psychological conflicts; and the "Draw-a-Person Test," which asks subjects to draw a person in any way they wish. For example, larger than average eyes on the picture are supposed to indicate suspiciousness on the part of the drawer. Other stimuli in *projective tests* include cloud pictures, photographs of psychiatric patients with different pathologies, and drawings of hands. There have been several articles that question the reliability of these kinds of tests, and readers are urged to consult Scott Lilenfled's "Projective measures of personality and psychopathology"[71] for further discussion.

♈ **PSYCHOMANCY** is similar to **necromancy** in that the spirits of the dead, or ghosts, are invoked for purposes of divination.

♉ **PSYCHOMETRY** is divination by touching or being near a physical object. The psychometrist claims to gain information about a person's personality, environment, and situation by holding a person's posession. Peter Hurkos (b. 1911, the Netherlands) is an example of a well-known psychometrist who claims to have a talent for finding lost persons and even bodies of murder victims simply by holding something that belonged to the person, such as a piece of jewelry or clothing. He says he has located criminals by touching a car that has been used in the crime and subsequently abandoned. (Peter Hurkos is discussed in more detail in chapter 3, pp. 321–22.)

♐ **SCIOMANCY** is divination by the size and shape of shadows. The ancient Greeks observed the shadows of corpses. Some Jews today believe the ancient Hebrew custom in which the absence of a shadow, or a shadow missing a head, means bad luck if observed on the Jewish New Year. Sciomancy is also sometimes used to mean divination via a spirit guide, a method generally employed by channelers. The ancient Persians and Greeks practiced sciomancy. Some sciomancers thought that certain types of shadows were ghosts of the departed.

♒ ♒ ♒

Not only do diviners look inward at mental images or at immaterial phenomena, they also look to the heavens for signs that can be precisely observed and quantified. In the following discussions of astrology, you'll notice that astrology, like many forms of divination, has had a long and rich history. However, unlike some of the ancient methods, astrology has a strong influence on modern, Western societies as it continues to shape the actions of individuals and nations.

## HITLER AND ASTROLOGY

> *The personification of the devil as the symbol of all evil assumes the living shape of the Jew.*
>
> —Adolf Hitler, *Mein Kampf*,
> precisely echoing Martin Luther's teachings[72]

☞ *Topics discussed*: a variety of divination methods that involve the heavens, with an emphasis on astrology, its relevance today, as well as Adolf Hitler's interest in this area.

### *Casting the Horoscope of Jesus Christ*

> *Great liars are also great magicians.*
>
> —Adolf Hitler

Ronald and Nancy Reagan, Queen Elizabeth I, and Nazi Heinrich Himmler (the second most powerful man in the Hitler's Third Reich) all have one thing in common. Can you guess? Yes, a deep interest in astrology. Even if you have ever looked up your horoscope in the newspaper or are old enough to remember the Fifth Dimension's blockbuster hit from *Hair*, "The Age of Aquarius," you may not realize just how much astrology, like all divination methods, has shaped civilization. Since the dawn of civilization, humans have been awed by the vastness of space—the stars, the planets, the Milky Way. Even today, despite vast scientific discoveries, the universe still contains many mysteries. In an attempt to personalize the universe, some people have suggested that the positions of stars and planets can influence our lives or indicate past and future events. For most astrologers today, the horoscope—also called the birth chart or natal chart—is the basic tool of the trade. Generally speaking, the horoscope is a symbolic representation of the heavens at a particular moment and place, such as the time and place of a person's birth.

Astrology comes from the Greek word meaning science (or knowledge) of the stars, although the planets more than stars are of most concern to astrologers. The words "star" had a different meaning to the ancients than it does today. What we call signs of the zodiac were composed of collections of "fixed stars" to the ancients. These stars and other heavenly bodies were called "fixed" because they maintain fixed patterns in the sky. What we now call planets were thought of as "wandering stars." In both astronomy and astrology, "zodiac" refers to a belt around the heavens extending 9° on either side of the *ecliptic*, the plane of the earth's orbit and of the sun's apparent annual path. The orbits of the moon and of the principal planets (except Pluto) also lie entirely within the zodiac. The twelve astrological signs, or constellations, of the zodiac are each considered to occupy $1/12$ (or 30°) of its great circle. The star patterns that make up the constellations have mythical attributes corresponding to the twelve signs of the zodiac. All the planets of the solar system pass through the zodiac belt, so that any given time the positions of the sun, moon, and planets can be calculated in relation to where they appear in the zodiac. This relationship is the basis of the horoscope (see figure 26).

The basic idea of the heavens as a sphere of fixed stars originated in Egypt. Sky watchers recognized twelve stars groups, or constellations, and gave them particular names and qualities. Originally, astrologers believed in a geocentric universe in which the "planets," which included the Sun and Moon, revolved around the Earth. Stars were fixed upon a sphere whose center was Earth. Astronomers today call the Earth's yearly orbit around the sun the ecliptic; however, the astrological ecliptic usually refers to the sun's apparent yearly orbit around the Earth.

Virtually all the ancient cultures on Earth were fascinated by the heavens and movements of the stars. The Greeks, Babylonians, Native Americans, Eskimos, Norsemen, Chinese, Finns, Hawaiians, Japanese, Hindus, and Egyptians were deeply interested in star patterns. One reason I can imagine that the ancients were so fascinated by the stars, and ascribed

**Figure 26.** This medieval wood cut depicts Earth at the center of the Solar System and surrounded by zodiac signs. From Nevill Drury and Gergory Tillett, *The Occult* (New York: Barnes & Noble Books, 1997), p. 77.

meaning to their positions and movements, was because the stars were more obvious than they are today. Because of light and atmospheric pollution from our towns and cities, the night sky is much less clear than in ancient days.

The role of God in astrology is unclear. In some flavors of astrology, the universe seems to be a machine, denying God the possibility of intervention and denying humans free will. This idea didn't sit too well with Christians and Moslems who passionately attacked astrology. In other theories, astrology merely indicated trends and directions that could be altered either by divine intervention or human will.

The original purpose of astrology was to give people information about their lives based on the positions of the planets and of the zodiacal signs (the twelve astrological constellations) at the moment of birth or conception. The ancient Egyptians and Chaldeans looked for omens in the sky. The Mesopotamians kept long lists of celestial positions and their meanings, seeing them as communications from the gods to the king. The Chaldean priests spread a new form of ancient Babylonian star reading throughout the Mediterranean. The Chaldeans recognized seven planets. The Greeks took these ideas and fused them with their own myths and mathematics. In the third century B.C.E., Babylonian diviners looked at the planets at the moment of birth for predicting the course of an individual's life.

During the Renaissance, in the 1500s, many Italian cardinals and scholars of the Catholic Church fully embraced astrology. They used it and the theory of the "Grand Conjunction" of Saturn and Jupiter to "predict" the time an evil Antichrist prophet in the North, Martin Luther, would rise to power.

Various individuals, living in Egypt under the Ptolemies (a Greek dynasty ruling from 305 to 30 B.C.E.), conceived of the ecliptic as being divided into twelve equal parts, or zodiacal signs. They further regarded each of these twelve signs as the domicile (or house) of a planet. Additionally, each zodiacal sign had a special relation with a part of the human body.

The Indians became interested in astrology in the second century C.E. when Greek astrological information was translated to Sanskrit. Around this time, both Greek and Indian astrological ideas migrated to Iran. Astrology entered Islamic civilization in the eighth and ninth centuries but was attacked by the theologians because astrology seemed to suggest a clockwork universe with no need for god or rewards for the good deeds of human. Western Europeans became fascinated by astrology in the fifteenth and sixteenth centuries. Astrology's intellectual appeal decreased in the seventeenth century when scientists suggested Earth was not the center of the universe.

〜〜〜    〜〜〜    〜〜〜

One interesting anecdote from the sixteenth century gives a hint at how seriously astrology was taken in some circles. Consider the case of Girolamo Cardano (1501–1576), Italian astrologer, doctor, mathematician, and gambler, born in Pavia. In 1543, he was appointed Professor of Medicine at Pavia and gave the first clinical description of typhus fever. His 1545 book *Ars magna* (Great Art) was an algebraic treatise containing the first published solutions of cubic and quartic equations. He also cast horoscopes for Edward VI (1547–1553) of England.

Despite his stardom, Cardano had some sad times. In 1560, his eldest son had been accused of attempting to poison his own wife and was beheaded in prison. Cardano wrote that "this was my supreme, my crowning misfortune." As a result of this scandal, Cardano had to leave his home of Milan. More trouble came in 1570 when he was imprisoned by the Inquisition for the heresy of casting the horoscope of Jesus Christ. He cast his own horoscope and predicted the day and hour of his own death. When it came, and Cardano found that his astrological computations did not yield the accurate result, he committed suicide rather than ruin his reputation.[75]

Most mediaeval kings had astrologers to suggest the best times for important ceremonies like marriage and military operations. In China, astrologers who made mistaken predictions were sometimes executed, which probably was one incentive for predictions to be vague. Throughout history, astrologers had to be very careful. Consider the case of Louis XI of France (1423–1483) who was not always happy with his astrologers. One day he was so angry with his astrologer that he decided to have him executed, but then he changed his mind when the astrologer said, "I shall die three days before your Majesty."

Today, Newtonian physics has killed off astrology in scientific circles, but it still thrives throughout the world. Though some Indian universities offer advanced degrees in astrology, science is explored in their departments of astronomy as in the rest of the world. Recently in the West, astrology has gained a large popular following, and people like French psychologist Michel Gauquelin have attempted to reestablish a firm theoretical basis for astrology. As discussed in a following section, the results of these studies are inconclusive at best.

The divisions of the year governed by the twelve zodiacal signs are derived from Hellenistic astrology and depicted in newspapers and almanacs are as follows:

## Astrological Signs

| Birth Sign | Meaning |
| --- | --- |
| Aries, the Ram; Mar. 21–Apr. 19 <br> Head | Decisive, assertive, headstrong, courageous, immediate, aggressive, self-motivated. |
| Taurus, the Bull; Apr. 20–May 20 <br> Throat | Stubborn, stable, possessive, practical. |
| Gemini, the Twins; May 21–June 21 <br> Shoulders, arms, lungs | Versatile, communicative, changeable, restless. |
| Cancer, the Crab; June 22-July 22 <br> Chest, breast, stomach | Sensitive, caring, protective, emotional. |
| Leo, the Lion; July 23–Aug. 22 <br> Heart and spine | Creative, expressive, confident, authoritative. |
| Virgo, the Virgin; August 23–Sept. 22 <br> Intestines, solar plexus, spleen | Analytical, careful, critical, discriminating, meticulous, fussy. |
| Libra, the Balance Scales; Sept. 23–Oct. 23 <br> Kidneys, lower back, skin | Harmonious, diplomatic, idealistic. |
| Scorpio, the Scorpion; Oct. 24–Nov. 21 <br> Genitals, bladder, cervix | Intense, penetrating, secretive. |
| Sagittarius, the Archer; Nov. 22–Dec. 21 <br> Hips, thighs, arterial system | Extensive, expansive, philosophical. |
| Capricorn, the Goat; Dec. 22–Jan. 19 <br> Bones, skin, knees, joints | Rational, prudent, determined, reliable, ambitious, careful, disciplined, patient. |
| Aquarius, the Water Carrier; Jan. 20–Feb. 18 <br> Ankles, breath, eyesight. | Compassionate, independent, friendly, progressive, original, inventive, idealistic. |
| Pisces, the Fish; Febr. 19–Mar. 20 <br> Feet, lymphatic system | Artistic, kind, sympathetic, intuitive, sensitive, adaptable, receptive. |

Most of us today are familiar with the horoscope columns appearing in newspapers and magazines. The horoscopes are usually based on the sun sign, that is, the sign of the zodiac in which the sun was positioned at one's birth. The beginning and ending dates for each sign are not always agreed on because the sun can pass from one constellation to another at hours other than midnight. People born at these points are said to be on the "cusp" of two signs, and in sun sign astrology therefore share attributes of both.

More sophisticated astrologers consider the sun sign horoscopes too general. Sun sign astrology divides the people on Earth into twelve types and makes predictions based on a small number of variables. More intricate horoscopes take account the exact time and place of birth. With this added information, the astrologer can calculate the degree of the zodiac that crossed the eastern horizon at the birth moment, called the ascendant or rising sign, and the exact position of the moon at birth. Astrologers also look for "conjunctions" of planets. For example, when two planets are within eight degrees of each other, their forces are said to merge.

As I suggested, a number of researchers have tried to find statistical correlations between the heavenly bodies and human personality traits. But none of these studies seems very convincing to me, and most of them don't seem to postulate a mechanism of how astrology works. Some modern astrologers do try to be "scientific." In fact, when the comet Chiron was discovered in 1977, some astrologers searched for both its precise position in the astrological charts and its divinatory meaning as a representative of the old Greek healing god for which it was named.

Today, many astrologers use computer programs to create horoscopes that may take several forms:

- *Natal Horoscope*—a birth chart. Centuries ago, the natal horoscope gave information on a person's fate. However, many of today's astrologers consider the natal horoscope as a display of talents, goals, and weaknesses that people are challenged to overcome.
- *Horary Chart*—a chart constructed at the moment the question is asked. This horoscope is used to determine the advisability of undertaking activities at particular times.
- *Mundane Astrology Chart*—the study of the great conjunctions that influence events and cultural movements. This chart is constructed at the birth of a nation, group, or organization to give insight into the success of these collectives of people. The "Grand Conjunction" of Jupiter and Saturn are said to indicate important cultural upheavals.
- *Local Space Chart*—indicates where the orbits of a person's natal

planets intersect the local horizon at a given place on earth. It is used to determine when to move into a new house or office.

- *The Electional Chart*—indicates a person's potential at any given moment. This gives the most favorable time to begin some task.

## Astrology and World War II

> *I believe today that my conduct is in accordance with the will of the Almighty Creator. This human world of ours would be inconceivable without the practical existence of a religious belief.*
>
> —Adolph Hitler, *Mein Kampf*

The last section examined astrology in an abstract way. In this section I'd like to take a look at how astrology played a role in our modern society and, in particular, the life of German dictator Adolph Hitler (1889–1945).

Astrology began to flourish in Germany in the turmoil and uncertainty after World War I. Books on astrology flourished. The best-known astrologer during the years between the world wars was Elspeth Ebertin (1880–?), an astrologer who was a popular journalist and also gave private readings. In 1923, a female admirer of the young Adolph Hitler asked Fraue Ebertin if she could cast his horoscope. As a result, Frau Ebertin published a yearbook that described Hitler as "a man of action" who was "destined to play a Führer [leader] role and who would sacrifice himself for the whole German nation." She also said that an incautious action could trigger an uncontrollable crisis. On November 8, 1923, Hitler's followers attempted to take power but were quickly defeated, and Hitler was arrested. Frau Ebertin received wonderful publicity for her "remarkable" prophecy.

Although the German police from time to time prosecuted individual astrologers[76] for fortune-telling, interest grew, and Germans held annual conferences of astrologers between 1923 and 1936. In 1924, the Nazis banned all fortune-telling, making the publication of almanacs and astrological journals illegal.

Hitler is often thought of as of having a personal astrologer Karl Ernst Krafft (1900–1945). Kraff admired Hitler, and on November 2, 1939, Krafft wrote to a member of Hitler's secret intelligence service warning that between November 7 and 10 Hitler's life would be in danger because of "the possibility of an attempt at assassination by the use of explosive material." Because there was a ban on all predictions concerning Hitler, this prediction was not shown to anyone in the Nazi high command.

On November 9 a bomb did explode at the Burgerbrau beer hall in

Munich, minutes after Hitler had left it. Krafft could not resist sending a telegram to Deputy Fuhrer Rudolf Hess, another senior Nazi with an interest in mysticism, pointing out his marvelous prediction. His original letter to Hitler's secret intelligence service was found and shown to Hitler, who passed it to Dr Goebbels, minister of propaganda for Hitler's Third Reich. The same day, the Gestapo arrested Krafft and took him for questioning. Krafft managed to convince them that astrological predictions were possible and was released.

In 1940, Goebbels asked Krafft to look through the enigmatic prophesies of French astrologer Nostradamus (1503–1566) and translate any of them that could be used as propaganda against the Allies. The plan was to drop particular prophecies into unoccupied areas to persuade the people that Nostradamus preordained Nazi rule. After a few weeks, Krafft said he discovered verses predicting the invasion of Holland and Belgium and the existence of the Third Reich and the Second World War. He produced a pamphlet based on forty quatrains of Nostradamus, designed for circulation in Belgium and France and predicting the imminent downfall of Britain. Krafft was later paid a small monthly sum to write reports for Himmler's Intelligence Service. Himmler himself had always been interested in occultism. Here again is a recurrent theme of this book—even in modern times, divination has shaped the course of history.

The Germans probably most enjoyed quatrain 95 of Nostradamus's *Century V*:

> He shall translate into Greater Germany
> Brabant and Flanders, Ghent, Bruges and Boulogne,
> The treaty feigned, the grand duke of Armenia,
> Will attack Vienna and Cologne.

The first two lines seem to correspond to Hitler's 1939–1940 campaign that added Brabant, Flanders, Bruges, Ghent, and Boulogne to Greater Germany, although I'm not sure how the "grand duke of Armenia" fits in. Krafft thought it referred to the German hero Arminius who had destroyed three Roman legions in 9 C.E. Krafft suggested that "Arminius" was also a metaphor for another great German hero, Adolf Hitler, who annexed Vienna and Cologne during his rise to power.

Though interested in astrology, there is no direct evidence showing Hitler actually used astrology for any of his personal or military decisions. He never denied using astrologers even when rumors were spread on this subject. He is alleged to have said, "If my enemies believe I am using the stars to win the war, let them believe it . . . and worry over it." It is true that many high ranking members of the Nazi party consulted astrologers, which is another reason many thought Hitler did so as well.

In May of 1941, Ruldoph Hess tarnished Krafft's favorable predictions. Hess, second in command to Hitler (after Goering), flew to Scotland in an independent attempt to arrange a peace. Hess's proposals met with no response from the British government, which treated him as a prisoner of war and held him throughout World War II. His plan was also rejected by Hitler, who accused Hess of suffering from "pacifist delusions." The British kept Hess in detention until his suicide in 1987.

Hitler had to think of a way to present Hess's embarrassing situation to the German people. Martin Bormann, one of Hitler's closest lieutenants, decided that the German people should be told that Hess was insane and influenced by astrologers, occultists, and hypnotists. In Britain, the *Times* actually reported that Hess had been Hitler's private astrologer!

Now the Nazis were really mad at the astrologers, and the Gestapo (secret police) took action. Those astrologers who had formerly enjoyed the protection of a sympathetic Himmler (who had arranged the release of astrologer Wilhelm Wulif from a concentration camp to work for him) now found themselves arrested and, at worst, sent to concentration camps. Many in the Nazi High Command enjoyed embarrassing Himmler because they thought he was nuts. For example, Reinhard Heydrich, Himmler's chief lieutenant, used to compare Himmler to another officer, saying, "One is worried about the stars on his epaulette, and the other about the stars in his horoscope!" At this point, astrologers were in deep trouble in Germany, along with faith healers, clairvoyants, graphologists, Christian Scientists, and spiritualists

Krafft was arrested on June 12, 1941. In prison, he continued to work on astrology, and he was released a year later. He began writing accusatory letters to officials and forecasting the destruction of the Propaganda Ministry. He was arrested again in 1942, and spent the rest of the war in jail. In 1944 he caught typhus, and in January of the following year died en route for Buchenwald concentration camp.

In the final months of the war, Himmler suffered increasingly from psychosomatic illnesses and was progressively ignored by Hitler's people. Hitler ordered Himmler arrested when he found out that Himmler hoped to succeed him and had negotiated with the Swedes to surrender Germany to the Western allies. Himmler disguised himself as a common soldier and attempted to escape. When he was captured by the Western allies, he committed suicide by taking poison. Various horoscopes were found in his pockets.

I doubt that astrology played a direct roll in how the Germans planned their war effort, even though Himmler was so fascinated by astrology, but who can say what would have happened during World War II had there been no astrologers involved? Even Goebbels eventually looked to astrology as evidenced by his request for copies of Hitler's birth chart, and that of the Reich, while in a besieged Berlin bunker during the last days of the war. Goebbels pointed out to the Führer that both charts showed the outbreak of war, and the present disastrous reverses, but also promised an overwhelming victory for Germany in April and peace by August. Hitler preferred not to wait for the cosmic change and killed himself.

Astrology also played a roll in World War II outside of Germany. In Britain, newspaper horoscopes boosted national morale. At the same time, Louis de Wohl, a part-Jewish Hungarian refugee and astrologer, persuaded some government members that he could tell them what advice Hitler's astrologers were giving him and thus predict Hitler's actions. De Wohl made money from syndicated journalism, worked for the Psychological Warfare Executive's "black propaganda" unit, and wore a British army captain's uniform to which he was not entitled. One of dc Wohl's job was to try to divine whatever prophecies Krafft was giving to the Nazis. After several months de Wohl was quietly abandoned after failing in his efforts.

## *Hitler's Jewish Clairvoyant*

> *The greatness of Christianity did not lie in attempted negotiations for compromise with any similar philosophical opinions in the ancient world, but in its inexorable fanaticism in preaching and fighting for its own doctrine. And the founder of Christianity made no secret indeed of his estimation of the Jewish people. When He found it necessary, He drove those enemies of the human race out of the Temple of God.*
>
> —Adolf Hitler, *Mein Kampf*

In April, 1933, a farm worker had the disturbing experience of finding a corpse in some woods fifteen miles from Berlin. The body, riddled with bullets, had been quickly buried in a shallow grave, but the rains had washed the soil away, and a large foot stuck out of the mud.[77]

The dead man was Erik Jan Hanussen, who less than three months before had continuously packed Germany's leading variety theaters. He had had money, cars, jewels, an opulent villa, and a yacht. But in April, after his body was discovered, he was finally buried in a cheap coffin and in a pauper's grave. The German newspapers did not report on his murder. No firearms experts inspected the bullets in his body. The authorities spoke to no witnesses. The case of the murder of Erik Jan Hanussen, Hitler's Jewish clairvoyant, was shut closed tighter than a steel drum.

Adolf Hitler's interest in the occult and divination had a long history. Every New Year's Eve from 1928 through 1933, Adolf Hitler had his horoscope read by the famous clairvoyant Erik Jan Hanussen (1889–1933). Revered throughout Europe by thousands of disciples, Hanussen was a guru of sorts to the future Führer. However, Hanussen was disliked by Hitler's associates, who resented his influence on their leader. When Hanussen's Jewish-Czech roots were uncovered in early 1933, his life was in jeopardy, and Hermann Goering had him executed on March 24 in Berlin.

Born Herschel Steinschneider in 1889 to a synagogue caretaker, he left school when he was fourteen, running away to join a circus. He was a knife-thrower, fire-eater, and professional strong man, though a fake one—he broke cardboard chains. One day he eloped with the circus owner's wife—after pawning most of the equipment. Later he became a con artist who worked his way up from comedy shows to a sophisticated nightclub act.

During his rise to stardom, he persuaded many devoted followers that he was truly clairvoyant. Hanussen masked his Jewish background in many ways. For example, to explain why he spoke Yiddish, he told people he was the orphaned son of Danish aristocrats, and he'd been raised by a rabbi in a small village.[77]

Before the *Machtergreifung*, Hitler's coming to power, Nazis and communists were battling in the cities of Germany. During this time, Hanussen came to be Hitler's favorite *Hellseher* ("clairvoyant") and a savage anti-Semitic propagandists. Hanussen created subtle and effective propaganda for Hitler, advising all his clients to vote for Hitler. Hanussen even trained Hitler to make effective use of body language and, in particular, how Hitler should move his arms and adjust his voice to achieve a hypnotic effect.

Hanussen was the consummate showman, always mystifying and shocking his audiences. Women loved his supreme self-confidence and his dramatic appearance emphasized with his bright white stage makeup. Hanussen seemed blinded by his own success and totally unaware of dangers that could befall him. He charged his clients large sums—not just for his prophecies but for the influence he claimed to have with the important people in government. His harem of women followers grew and included actresses, dancers, and aristocrats.

Hanussen's eventual demise started one night with a séance that employed his new assistant, a charming blonde actress named Maria Paudler. The guests included a dozen journalists, German officials, and several female admirers. After a large dinner, the séance began. Miss Paudler sat in a chair while Hanussen slowly stroked her temples. Maria started to speak, at first in a strange unintelligible language. Then she spoke in words they could all understand:

> I can see it. . . . A disaster. . . . The enemies of Germany strike . . . they want to destroy the movement. , , . I see a house . . . a big house . . . it is burning . . . it burns down. . . . It is meant as a signal for a . . . a revolt. . . . But Hitler will triumph.[46]

Hanussen's fiery revelation was based on actual inside knowledge about the Nazi party's intent to burn the Reichstag building as a "proof" that the Communists were trying to disrupt the government. Hanussen knew that the fire would occur within hours, and he couldn't resist using this information to demonstrate his clairvoyance.

The Hellseher had grown too ambitious and had now become a danger to the Nazi cause. Hanussen knew too much. He was publishing a popular astrological newspaper. He was a Jew. Now he wanted to expand his influence and use his Nazi connections in order to buy several newspapers and magazines.

Hermann Goering, then Prime Minister of Prussia, told confidants, "This is an impossible situation. The Party cannot remain involved with this Jewish charlatan. He must be dealt with before there is a scandal."

Shortly thereafter, Hanussen was walking along a road and was stopped by a man who asked for a light and then demanded to know whether he was Hanussen, the clairvoyant. Hanussen nodded and was asked to get into the car. Half an hour later, the men pushed him from the car and drove him into the woods. There they shot him twelve times to make sure he was dead. On April 7, Hanussen's bullet-ridden body was discovered in a shallow grave in the woods outside Berlin. Hanussen was forgotten. His villa, yacht, diamond rings, gold bracelets, and bank balances were confiscated for the benefit of the Nazi Party.

In 1955, a German film company made a picture about Hanussen's life. The production of the film uncovered the fact that Hanussen had been married as a young man but separated from his wife before his brief, exciting career in Berlin. His widow and his daughter both lived in Meran where Mrs. Hanussen (she has changed her name) is a partner in running a hotel while Erika, a beautiful, dark-haired woman works both as a writer and actress. She claims no special powers of divination.

## Skepticism and Astrology

> 1The heavens call to you, and circle about you, displaying to you their eternal splendors, and your eye gazes only to earth.
>
> —Dante

Recent polls in the United States suggest that 52 percent of the population "believes" in astrology, and about 30 percent believe it to such an extent they shift their self-image in the direction their stars and horoscopes suggest.[79] (In other words, for example, if their horoscopes says they are supposed to be "fussy," they begin to think of themselves as being fussy.) Yet, to me, there are some disturbingly unscientific aspects to astrology. For example, astrology places so much emphasis on the moment of birth that it seems to imply that a parent could induce a baby to grow up happy and upbeat (for example) instead of moody and melancholy by having a Caesarian section a day early. This would even apply to identical twins that might be removed from the womb on different dates.

Some astrologers say there is scientific support for the idea that heavenly bodies affect Earthly events. One example is the Moon's effect on tides and the possible effect of sunspots on terrestrial weather patterns. However, many astrologers go further and make less substantiated claims, such as surgeons have difficulty in stopping bleeding during surgical operations at certain phases of the Moon.

In the 1970s, French statistician Michel Gauquelin examined the birth charts of thousands of sportsmen, actors, and scientists, chosen on the basis of their success in their professions. He believed he found statistical evidence that sportsmen tended to be born when the planet Mars was astrologically dominant. Actors were born when Jupiter was dominant and scientists and doctors were born under Saturn. The findings generated much controversy, and many papers have been published in the *Skeptical Inquirer* and other journals that are skeptical of Gauquelin's propositions and astrology in general.[80]

Gauquelin was born in Paris in 1928. His interest in astrology began in his preteen years, and at age ten he could calculate a birth chart. At school his astrological readings appeared to be so accurate that his friends called him Nostradamus. In 1949 he graduated with a major in psychology from Sorbonne University, and he began devoting much of his time to testing astrology. He seemed to have found an especially close link between the most eminent sports champions and Mars. However, skeptics suggest that the studies do not demonstrate astrological effects because it is difficult to define exactly what is a "champion." This is very important because the results can change significantly depending upon who is included or excluded in surveys.[81] For example, Marvin Zelen, now a professor of statistics at Harvard, conducted a survey of 408 American champions, and did not find the same astrological correlations as did Gauqelin.[82] Various authors have questioning Gauguelin's method of determining eminence, because his criteria seemed to fluctuate with each study.

Gauguelin subsequently examined Zelen's American study of sports champions and maintained that the results were positive after he eliminated football and basketball players, a large part of the American sample.[83] There have been numerous studies, back and forth, on the Gauquelin work, but I suppose the issue may be quite difficult to resolve, especially considering that Gauquelin killed himself in 1991, allegedly giving orders before he died that all his data be burned.[84,85]

In recent years, properly controlled experiments have failed to sustain many of astrology's claims. The skeptical papers have included studies that find no correlation between astrological birth charts and suicide rate, personality, or profession. In other studies, astrologers did no better than chance or than a nonastrologer control subject at matching people's birth charts to personal data about each subject.

Here is one of my favorite studies. In a 1987 *Skeptical Inquirer* article, astrologers prepared horoscopes for subjects' correct natal data.[86] Next, researchers constructed "reversed charts" from the correct charts by retaining the sun sign, but reversing all of the planetary aspects. Half of the subjects were given correct charts, and the other half were given reversed charts. There was no correlation between the perceived accuracy of the charts and whether the subject was given a correct or reversed chart.

In another study published in a 1985 issue of *Nature*, 116 adults filled out California Personality Index (CPI) surveys and also provided natal data.[87] Researchers gave one set of natal data and the results of personality surveys for three different people to an astrologer. The astrologer's job was to interpret the natal data and determine which of the three CPI results belonged to the same subject as the natal data. The San Francisco chapter of the National Council for Geocosmic Research (an organization of astrologers) recommended the 28 astrologers who took part. They approved the procedure in advance and predicted that they would select the correct CPI profiles in more that 50 percent of the trials. Out of 116 trials, the astrologers chose the correct CPI 34 percent of the time. This agrees with the random chance prediction of 1 of 3 trials producing a correct choice. In another study, professional astrologers prepared horoscopes for 83 subjects. Each subject was given three charts, one of which belonged to the subject. In 28 of 83 trials the subject chose the correct chart. This is the success rate expected for random chance.[88]

Astrology debunker Geoffrey Dean recently sent a large group of astrologers a horoscope which, he told them, belonged to the singer Petula Clark.[89] (Petula is a perky actress, composer, and queen of 1960s pop music.) The astrologers soon came to the conclusion that the horoscope described a happy, friendly, delightful, upbeat, personality, which matched Petula's persona. I imagine some of the astrologers were shocked when Dean finally revealed that the horoscope he had sent to them all was for the mass murderer Charles Manson.

One of several possible problems in astrological theory has to do with the fact that the earth's axis causes it to precess westward through the zodiac so that during the last two thousand years, the earth's path has shifted by one full constellation.[90] In some sense, this means that Ronald Reagan is not really an Aquarian, but a Capricorn. Another problem is that the ancients did not know about Uranus, Neptune, or Pluto, and it isn't clear why their influence shouldn't have counted in the old days.

Here is one reason I think many people feel that astrology works for them. Different people think of themselves in remarkably similar ways. This means it is possible to create personality readings for people that appear quite correct to them. For example, I'd suspect that most of us would agree with the statement "You have a need to be respected by others and find it to your advantage not to reveal too much about yourself to others." Interestingly, studies show that people are even more likely to agree with one of these kind's of statements as referring specifically to them if first told that that the reading is specifically for them.[91] For additional skeptical studies, see endnotes 92 and 93. It seems likely that in the next century, we will have additional astrological studies that make it clear to what extent this ancient divination practice is based on superstition, and to what extent it can help to illuminate the nature of our existence.

## Who Believes in Astrology?

> The astrologers answered the king, "There is not a man on earth who can do what the king asks! No king, however great and mighty, has ever asked such a thing of any magician or enchanter or astrologer."
>
> —Daniel 2:10

Virtually all the great astronomers of the past, from Kepler to Galileo to Newton—believed in astrology. This startling fact made me wonder if there is information on who today believes in astrology and why. Here are some recent findings based on surveys:[94]

- Astrological belief is strongly related to gender, according to surveys conducted in the United States, France, and the United Kingdom. In all three countries, belief in astrology is significantly higher among women than among men. In some demographic categories women believed in astrology two to three times more than men.
- People who believe in astrology tend to have high religious interest but low levels of integration into established, organized religion.
- Belief in astrology is related to the extent to which people feel they are in control of their lives. Low control is related to higher belief in astrology.
- Belief in astrology does not appear to be correlated with an inadequate understating of science or a negative attitude toward science.
- Belief in astrology is correlated with age. Young people believe in astrology more than older people.

In general, belief in astrology is linked to the degree of uncertainty in a person's social future. Such uncertainty is probably higher in the young, for women, for single people, and for religiously motivated people compared to people who are religiously indifferent. Studies of people who call psychic telephone networks in America suggest that 74 percent of the callers are African American, and 85 percent of callers said they were having money troubles.[95]

In keeping with the catalogs throughout this book, which follow the in-depth treatments, the following section lists several methods related to astrology.

## 📖 *A Concise Catalog of Methods Using The Heavens*

> *As one goes through it, one sees that the gate one went through was the self that went through it.*
>
> —R. D. Laing, *The Politics of Experience*

☉ **ASTROLOGY** is divination by examining the positions of celestial bodies such as the sun, moon, planets, and stars. The positions of these objects at the time of birth, or at the time of a particular event, are used to make predictions. Psychologist Carl Jung often consulted horoscopes to gain insight into patients' problems. The Old Testament mentions astrology in Isaiah 47:13: "Let now the astrologers, the stargazes, the monthly prognosticators, stand up and save thee from these things that shall come upon thee." "Chinese astrology" is divination of personal characteristics based on a twelve-year animal system that repeats continually. (I was born during the year of the rooster and am therefore supposed to be "committed, adventurous, and outgoing.")

♍ **ASTROMANCY** is divination by looking at the stars and planets at the time of the reading rather than during a person's birth. In contrast to astrology, astromancy is sometimes used to predict specific events.

♊ **GENETHLIALOGY** is a branch of astrology that focuses on divination by the influence of the stars and their positions at someone's birth. There are four classes of astrology: *genethlialogy*, which describes and interprets the condition of the heavens at the precise moment of someone's birth; *catarchic astrology*, which determines whether a particular action or decision is suitable to a particular moment; *interrogatory astrology*, which answers specific questions by consulting the positions of the planets and stars, and *general astrology*, which relates the conditions of the heavens during significant moments—such as a conjunction of planets, the vernal equinox, or an eclipse—to events which affect broad classes of people, nations, or the entire world.

♐ **HOROSCOPY** is the practice of casting of astrological horoscopes.

♐ **METEOROMANCY** is divination from observing meteors.

♏ **NEPHALOMANCY**, another world for **aeromancy** (from the Greek *nephele*, meaning cloud), is a divination method that uses patterns seen in cloud formations.

♏ **SELENOMANCY** is divination by studying phases of the moon or other celestial occurrences like comets. For example, through history, births that took place during a full moon were either auspicious or negative, depending on the culture. The same applied to marriages. Some cultures believed that if a person pointed at the moon, that person would not go to heaven.

♊ **URANAI** is a general term for modern Japanese fortune-telling and encompasses all kinds of divination including those based on astrology, the number of strokes in the characters in your name, the shapes of clouds, fissures in Turkish coffee beans, tarot cards, and bamboo sticks, and compatibility estimates between people based on their blood types.

## ⅄ PLAYING CATCH WITH THE GODS

> *Then the Lord said to Moses and Aaron, "Take handfuls of soot from a furnace and have Moses toss it into the air in the presence of Pharaoh."*
>
> —Exodus 9:8

☞ In this section I discuss a variety of divination methods that involve objects that one tosses or bounces. Most of the methods rely on the chance arrangement of small objects as they move and scatter on some surface. The emphasis of this section is on the *I Ching*.

### I Ching

> *Using the* I Ching *can give you access to a wide range of transformative symbols that reproduce the fundamental way energy moves in the imagination. They not only give you warning and advice, but they can also change the way that you look at things.*
>
> —Stephen Karcher, *The Illustrated Encyclopedia of Divination*

As I explained in earlier sections, the Chinese have always been interested in divination. We saw that one of the earliest methods was heating scapula bones (large triangular bones of the back) or tortoise shells with hot metal and then interpreting the cracks that formed. According to legends, inspiration for the *I Ching* came from markings on the back of a sacred tortoise. The *I Ching*, or *Book of Changes*, is a Chinese text written more than three thousand years ago. This makes it one of the oldest books in the world. Confucian and Taoist sages thought very highly of the *I Ching* (pronounced *ee jing*), treating it reverently as a sacred book and prizing its powers of divination. Through the ages, the *I Ching* has found application in the most unlikely settings. For example, science-fiction writers like Philip K. Dick have used the *I Ching* to develop plot lines in their novels. Mr. Matsushita, the CEO of Japan's huge Matsushita Electric, drew his lessons and ongoing counsel from the *I Ching*.

The *I Ching* is the oldest continually used divination system in the world. Originally, the *I Ching* provided people with yes-or-no answers to questions; however, it gradually acquired ethical meanings and became a catalog of Chinese wisdom. The *I Ching* revolves around a few central ideas:

- Everything changes.
- Change involves transformation between the yang, the masculine principle, and the yin, the feminine principle.

- The study of the *I Ching* places one in harmony with the Tao (pronounced *dou* or *tou*), the correct way, which is the essence of existence.

One of the Taoist philosophies that to runs throughout the *I Ching* is that intelligent waiting often achieves more than hasty action. Another theme is that one should quietly wait through the bad times for the good time that are sure to come. Unlike oracles, which tended to give future predictions that seemed destined to occur, the *I Ching* functions more like an advisor that permits people to change their fates if they take certain actions. It offers a view of possible futures from which people are free to choose.

The *I Ching* contains of sixty-four basic symbols called *hexagrams*, each of which are made of six lines. Each hexagram is combination of two of eight basic *trigrams*—sets of three lines—that represent important Earthly themes like wind, thunder, and fire. The lines that make up each trigram are either solid (representing yang) or broken into two pieces (representing yin). You can see four different triagrams in the South Korean flag, which also contains a central yin-yang symbol.

When one consults the *I Ching*, the hexagrams suggest attitudes that will lead to a more harmonious future. You can throw coins or count special stalks to determine which hexagram applies to your life. To help you understand the abstract symbols, the *I Ching* text first explains each line of the hexagram separately and then gives an overall interpretation. The text is sometimes cryptic, so users must use a great deal of interpretation in applying the results to their situation. The hexagrams, if properly understood and interpreted, are said to contain profound meanings applicable to daily life.

Who really wrote the *I Ching* book? Perhaps it originated as early as the eight century B.C.E. as a collection of peasant omens, then slowly these documents became combined with divination methods using sticks. Chinese literature suggest that there may be four authors: Fu-hsi (3000 B.C.E., pronounced foo-shÂ), a legendary person representing the dawn of civilization; King Wen Wang (1150 B.C.E.) and his son Duke Kau; and Confucius (551–479 B.C.E.). Fu-hsi is credited with constructing the trigrams from marks on a the back of a turtle. Confucius tells us that he acted only as a copier and editor of the *I Ching*, not as the main writer. One legend suggests that King Wen Wang constructed the sixty-four hexagrams and that his son added interpretations of the hexagrams. Starting about 800 B.C.E., names were selected to identify the hexagrams. The names were often material objects such as the well or the cauldron.[96] A supplementary section of *I Ching* commentaries is believed to be the work of authors living between 475 and 221 B.C.E. The commentaries attempt to explain the world and its ethical principles.

Near the end of his life, Confucius is alleged to have said that he wanted another fifty years to study the *I Ching*. Although this sounds farfetched, some of the Chinese sages felt that the *I Ching* hexagrams contained all the combinations of life's possibilities and therefore were fertile ground for meditation and discussion. Confucius thought that studying the *I Ching* was like studying life itself. *I Ching* aficionados suggest that as one line changes to another, the hexagrams are interconnected in a flowing melody more beautiful than a Mozart sonata.

Magic and sorcery were added to the *I Ching* during the Ch'in and Han dynasties (221 B.C.E. to 220 C.E.). The important Chinese scholar Wang Pi (226–249 C.E.) got rid of some of this extra fluff and restored the *I Ching* to its original, pristine glory. Although the *I Ching* has had an immense impact on Chinese culture, over-reliance on the symbols sometimes slowed the growth of science and experimentation.

In the early 1900s, the *I Ching* entered Western culture. Though there had been previous translations, Richard Wilhelm, a Protestant missionary who worked and studied in China for many years, was the first to translate the book so it could be used as a practical divination work in the West rather than a historical curiosity.

Although at first glance, the *I Ching* hexagrams seem only like a bunch of random lines, many modern Western thinkers have devoted years to studying the *I Ching*. These scholars include psychologist Carl Jung and novelist Herman Hesse. Carl Jung (1876–1961) was the Swiss psychologist and psychiatrist who founded analytic psychology and the concepts of the extroverted and introverted personality, archetypes, and the collective unconscious. His work has been influential in psychiatry and in the study of religion, literature, and related fields. Because the *I Ching* seemed superstitious to many Westerners, some of Jung's contemporaries must have thought he was mad when he wrote the foreword to the German translation of the *I Ching*. However, Jung believed the book gives insight into the unconscious and coincidental occurrences. It is likely he went even further and was convinced of the *I Ching*'s power to divine the future. For example, Jung used the *I Ching* to determine the prospects of American sales of an English translation of the *I Ching* and got an optimistic answer (which turned out to be right).

In the early 1900s, *I Ching* interpreters stood on street corners in China, offering their services for a fee. The oldest methods of creating the hexagrams, still followed by very serious *I Ching* practitioners, involves using fifty foot-long yarrow stalks. The *I Ching* seems to have inspired other related forms of Chinese divination such as *Chien Tung*, which is sponsored

**Figure 27.** Chinese diviners consult the *I Ching*. The yarrow stalks are tossed, and their patterns are used to indicate divinatory hexagram patterns contained in the *Book of Changes* held by the *I Ching* master (seated). Similarly, querents might consult the Kwan Yin oracle in which a cup containing numbered sticks was used to divine the future. From Nevill Drury and Gergory Tillett, *The Occult* (New York: Barnes & Nobles Books, 1997), p. 83.

by *Kwan Yin*, the goddess of compassion and mercy. To use this oracle of Kwan Yin, the querent enters the temple dedicated to the goddess. The first step is to hold a hollow wooden cylinder containing one hundred thin bamboo slats. Each stick is marked with a number and a character. As the querent thinks of the problem or question, he or she shakes the cylinder until one stick falls or jumps out. Next, the querent examines the number and look up the corresponding explanatory text in *Kwan Yin*'s book. Figure 27 shows a nineteenth-century engraving depicting the consultation of the Kwan Yin oracle.

## Trigrams and Hexagrams

> *You look at where you're going and where you are and it never makes sense, but then you look back to where you've been and a pattern seems to emerge.*
> —Robert Pirsig, *Illusions*

As alluded to in the previous section, the basic structural foundation of the *I Ching* consists of sixty-four hexagrams that display every possible permutation of two types of line when taken six at a time. In practice, one creates a hexagram by casting lots, building the hexagram from bottom to top. Individual lines of a hexagram have been compared to single notes of music. Though each note has a quality and significance in itself, its importance depends on its place in a musical score. Because the same principle applies to individual lines of a hexagram, the *I Ching* text has a commentary or explanation for each line separately, then gives an overall interpretation of the entire hexagram. These commentaries are supposed to be the philosophical musings of Cho Dyanasty's King Wen (circa 1150 B.C.E.), his son the Duke of Chou, and also the philosopher Confucius (551–479 B.C.E.). Some scholars believes that the earliest part of the *I Ching* dates back to the eight century B.C.E.

The *I Ching* illuminates the principles of the Tao, the universal flow that underlies reality. The two kinds of lines correspond to the basic duality of Chinese metaphysics: yin and yang, opposites. The degree of yin and yang present in each of the sixty-four hexagram shapes the hexagram's meaning. A solid line ▬▬▬▬ represents yang. A broken line ▬▬ ▬▬ represents yin. Lines in a consultation are determined by each of six coin throws. The meaning of each hexagram is affected by the presence of "changing lines," which in turn point the way to a second, transformed hexagram. In all, there are 4,096 possible core readings.

The ancients in many cultures saw three as a sacred number,[97] and perhaps this is why the inventor of the original *I Ching* arranged the two types of lines in a kind of chocolate layer cake, with three layers of icing forming the trigram. If we create trigrams with either of the two lines, there are eight possibilities illustrated here:

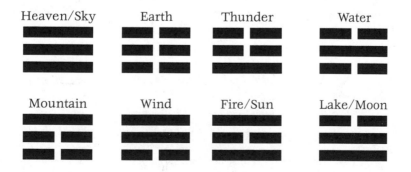

If you are interested in the various mathematical ramifications of the *I Ching* hexagrams and trigrams, you will enjoy Martin Gardner's *Knotted Doughnuts and Other Mathematical Entertainments* in which he describes the

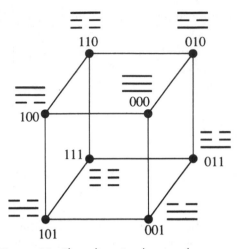

**Figure 28.** Three-dimensional approach to generating the eight trigrams by labeling the corners of a cube. Rendering by Clifford Pickover after a diagram in Martin Gardner, *Knotted Doughnuts and Other Mathematical Entertainments* (New York: W. H. Freeman & Company, 1986), fig. 151, p. 250

relationship between binary numbers that computers use and the *I Ching*.[98] Chinese scholars have used the *I Ching* as metaphors in many different areas, from crystallography (the science of crsytal structure) to astronomy to genetics. Figure 28 shows a three-dimensional approach to generating the eight trigrams by labeling the corners of a cube. Place one corner of the cube at the origin with coordinates (0,0,0), the label other corners with three-digit binary[99] numbers for 0 through 7, with 0 and 1 indicating the distance of the corner from the origin in each coordinate direction. Notice that the eight numbers correspond to the eight diagrams, with complementary trigrams at opposite corners of the cube. Although this is far beyond the scope of the current book, mathematicians among you may be delighted to know that by a similar labeling of the corners a six-dimensional hypercube, you can generate sixty-four six-digit binary numbers corresponding to the sixty-four hexagrams.

Appendix 5 lists several hexagrams and their meanings. Many Web pages list all sixty-four hexagrams. To help you locate the hexagram you construct, the table on page 127 gives the trigram combinations and standard lookup numbers.

## Schizophrenia and the Book of Changes

> *The measure of man is not his intelligence. It is not how high he rises in this freakish establishment. The measure of man is this: How swiftly can he react to another person's need. And how much of himself can he give?*
>
> —Philip K. Dick, *Our Friends From Frolix 8*

> *If something is boring after two minutes, try it for four. If still boring, then eight. Then sixteen. Then thirty-two. Eventually one discovers that it is not boring at all.*
>
> —John Cage

## Trigram Combinations

| Upper / Lower | Sky | Thunder | Water | Mountain | Earth | Air | Sun | Moon |
|---|---|---|---|---|---|---|---|---|
| Sky | 1 | 34 | 5 | 26 | 11 | 9 | 14 | 43 |
| Thunder | 25 | 51 | 3 | 27 | 24 | 42 | 21 | 17 |
| Water | 6 | 40 | 29 | 4 | 7 | 59 | 64 | 47 |
| Mountain | 33 | 62 | 39 | 52 | 15 | 53 | 56 | 31 |
| Earth | 12 | 16 | 8 | 23 | 2 | 20 | 35 | 45 |
| Air | 44 | 43 | 48 | 18 | 46 | 57 | 50 | 28 |
| Sun | 13 | 55 | 63 | 22 | 36 | 37 | 30 | 49 |
| Moon | 10 | 54 | 60 | 41 | 19 | 61 | 38 | 58 |

American avant-garde composer John Cage (1912–1992) was interested in the *I Ching* from which he gained a reverence for "nonintentional" art. For example, working to remove creative choice from composition, he used coin tosses to determine events in his piece "Music of Changes for Piano" performed in 1951. He also wrote pieces for twelve radios ("Imaginary Landscape no. 4," 1951). This random art was part of his musical principle of *indeterminism*. Over time, Cage began to use a number of devices to ensure randomness and thus eliminate any element of personal taste on the part of the performer. These "devices" included unspecified instruments, random numbers of performers, freedom of duration of sounds, inexact notation, and sequences of events determined by random means such as by consultation with the Chinese *I Ching*.

### Do-It-Yourself I Ching

The traditional way to create an *I Ching* hexagram depends on asking a question and then throwing yarrow sticks to determine the yin and yang lines. However, if you don't happen to have a pile of yarrow sticks on hand, an easier way to generate your personal hexagram requires three coins. The head side of the coin is yang, while the tail is yin. A hexagram is built one line at a time, from the bottom up, by throwing three coins and drawing the corresponding lines on paper to form a hexagram. Throwing three coins at once makes four combinations possible:

- yin-yin-yin, represented by a broken (yin) line with a dot after it: ▬▬ ▬▬◎
- yang-yang-yang, represented by a solid (yang) line with a dot after it: ▬▬▬▬◎
- 2 yangs and 1 yin, represented by a broken (yin) line: ▬▬ ▬▬
- 2 yins and 1 yang, which is represented by a solid (yang) line: ▬▬▬▬

Six throws give you six lines, which form a hexagram:

1. Let's build your hexagram. Start by throwing the three coins. Because the hexagram is built from bottom up, the first coin throw designates the bottom line, or "line one." Toss the coins five more times, allowing you to draw six lines
2. Lookup your hexagram in the chart in appendix 5.
3. After you have consulted the meaning for the first hexagram, one usually reads a second hexagram that is drawn by converting the changing lines, which we represented with dots, into their opposites (yin becomes yang, yang yin). In other words a whole line becomes broken, and a broken line becomes whole.
4. Return to the hexagram chart, and locate this new hexagram.

Here is an example:

Assume you are interested in meeting a particular person. You meditate on the following question: How should I act when approaching this person? Your first throw of the coins yields two heads and one tail, which corresponds to:

You next throw two heads and one tail again, followed by two tails and one head which corresponds to the solid line 3 of the hexagram. You continue until you finish construction of the following hexagram:

This pattern corresponds to hexagram 15 (Modesty) in appendix 5, which suggests you should think and speak of yourself in a modest way. You should be polite, modest, simple, respectful, yielding and compliant. Give way to others. In other words, if you want to meet this person, don't come on strong. If for line 6 you had tossed three tails, corresponding to a changing line, we would gain more information by reading line 6: "Modesty that comes to expression. It is favorable to set armies marching to chastise one's own city and one's country." You would meditate on what this may mean in your particular circumstances. Since the three tails corresponds to a changing line, you may also examine a second hexagram that has a solid line at top instead of a broken one, forming

This is hexagram 52 ("Keeping Still"), which suggests limiting, being quiet and calm, being a stabilizing force. This appears to reinforce the meaning of the first hexagram and also suggests that rash actions should not be taken.

Philip K. Dick (1928–1982) was a popular American science fiction novelist who used the *I Ching* to create stories. For most of his career, Dick lived in poverty, although he was prolific and wrote 112 short stories and thirty-six science fiction novels. His use of psychedelics may have contributed to some of his aberrations. For example, in March 1974, Dick claimed to have been contacted by an extraterrestrial force, a "beam of pink light" originating from a satellite he came to call VALIS: Vast Active Living Intelligence System.

One of his best-selling science fiction novels was the basis for Arnold Schwarzenegger's movie *Total Recall*. As noted in my book *Strange Brains and Genius*, Dick probably had epilepsy and hypergraphia—an excessive compulsion to write or draw. From age fifteen, he suffered from auditory and visual hallucinations that he interpreted as signs from God. He also had macropsia and micropsia (where stationary objects like chairs appear to enlarge or shrink), and depersonalization. Many of Dick's symptoms found their way into his books in the characters who had hallucinatory experiences. Dick published his first short story at age thirteen writing at incredible speeds, and later produced thousands of pages of handwritten journals in addition to his numerous books.

Dick gained initial recognition with his novel *The Man in the High Castle* (1962), a story of an alternate universe where the Axis powers have won World War II and jointly occupy the United States. One of his characters learns from the *I Ching* that the "real world" is one in which the Allies won. A few years after the book's publication, Dick advocated that schizophrenics use and take comfort using the *I Ching*. About his process, Dick wrote in 1965:

John Cage, the composer, used the I Ching to derive chord progressions. Several physicists use it to represent the genetic code. I've used it to develop the direction of a novel. Jung used it with patients to get around their psychological blind spots. Leibnitz based his binary system on it. For a schizophrenic, the derived hexagram is everything; when he has studied it plus all texts appended to it, he knows literally all there is to know. If you're schizophrenic by all means use the I Ching for everything, including telling you when to take a bath and when to open a can of cat tuna for your cat Rover.[100]

When Carl Jung asked the *I Ching* about whether or not he should help promote the *I Ching* book to the rest of the world, he obtained the Ting, or caldron, hexagam:

One of the hexagram's meanings is "Supreme good fortune. Success. Superior people consolidate their fates by making their positions correct." Jung interpreted this to mean that *I Ching* promotion was a good thing to do. His second line was a changing line: "There is food in the ting (pot). My comrades are envious, but they cannot harm me. Good fortune." He believed this meant that the *I Ching* would arouse envy, or perhaps his colleagues may be envious of him, but that he would triumph nevertheless.

Some practitioners interpret the first hexagram a person creates as the present, and the second hexagram (created by the changing lines explained in the "Do-It-Yourself" section on pages 129–30) as the future. The first hexagram reveals major truths of the situation, and the next hexagram points directly to the situation that inescapably follows.[101] The idea behind the changing lines is that all things cycle—ebb and flow. Something that has been yin for a long time will become yang. Most practitioners suggest the *I Ching* performs best if it is considered to relate to the present, widening your vision of the current situation, making you conscious of your subconscious feelings, reminding you to consider other options. Like all divination methods, the *I Ching*'s message is cloaked in ambiguity. Carl Jung felt that the *I Ching* sparked the universal archetypes embedded within our collective unconscious. Jung introduced the term "collective unconscious" to represent a part of the mind common to humankind and formed in the inherited structure of the brain.

Skeptics suggest that the *I Ching* works because the texts are ambiguous and can be interpreted in many ways by the practitioner. Believers like Carl Jung suggest the *I Ching*'s messages are "acausally related" to the future in a metaphysical sense. The hexagram one casts relates to Jung's conceit of *synchronicity*, or meaningful coincidences in which one event does not cause another but somehow appears to be linked in astonishing ways.[102] According to Jung, man's unconscious mind exits outside of time, and that is how people catch glimpses of the future in dreams.[103] Jung would consider the following scenario as an example of synchronistic events. Right now, while you read the words,

RED PAINT

someone in the next room yells out red, and the phone rings with your best friend saying he likes the color red, and, as you got up to answer the door, someone throws a bucket of red paint onto the floor, at the same time the radio started blaring "The Woman in Red" and the president of the United States declares that a large red monolith has been unearthed in Washington, D.C. All of this happens within the span of one minute. Skeptics would call this "chance," that out of the infinite number of random events, we notice those which appear to have similarities. Aficionados of syncronicity would say this is far beyond chance and call it syncronicity—events that happen simultaneously but appear otherwise disconnected.

People in the past viewed events in ways that may seem strange to us today. Cause and effect were sometimes discarded in favor of seeing events as overall patterns and interconnections. Ancient historians felt that the historical record was ripe with outbreaks of wars, plagues, the rise of kings, and the deaths of the famous that are accompanied by a variety of natural portents. Consider the "Norman Invasion," the military conquest of England by William, duke of Normandy in 1066. This conquest was heralded by the appearance of a new comet in the sky. The Chinese viewed history as events clustering in time rather than as a causal chain. More recently writer Arthur Koestler (1905–1983) believed that different objects and events "congregate" to form and overall pattern in space and time. Simply put, "certain things like to happen together."[104,105]

Some wild thinkers go as far as to suggest that the remarkable similarities between twins that have been reared in separate environments demonstrates syncronicity, an acausal link such that the twins are of "one mind." Such twins often have extremely similar preferences, attitudes, name their dogs the same or similar names, marry and divorce similar women, name their children the same, and have similar political views. Of course, scientists would attribute these similarities to the influence of genetics on behavior. And indeed the hereditary material from which the twins originate is identical in every way.

Austrian biologist Paul Kammerer (1880–1926) also seemed to believe in meaningful coincidences. He wrote, "We thus arrive at the image of a world-mosaic or cosmic kaleidoscope, which, in spite of constant shufflings and rearrangements, also takes care of bringing like and like together."[106] He compared events in our world to the tops of waves in an ocean. We notice the tops of the isolated waves, but beneath the surface there may be some kind of synchronistic mechanism that connects them. He also believe that because of this, we often also see "streaks" of luck or misfortune in situations ranging from sports to gambling to family catastrophes. Modern examples of this might include clusters of airplane accidents, many momentous events happening in the same year, the sudden simultaneous arrival of musical geniuses and styles, the "curse" of the Kennedy family, and the skiing accidents of celebrities, which, while not causally connected in any formal sense, are connected through meaning. Skeptics would suggest this connection arises from our tendency to affix patterns to *any* sequences of events, regardless of their significance.

Supporters of the *I Ching* and other divinatory methods claim there is a preponderance of evidence favoring this synchronistic link between the casting of the hexagrams and events in the world. Author James Pruett sums up the mystery:

> In the future, causal relationships may be divined to explain events where today we have no explanation. To a higher, more encompassing intellect than our own, our world may appear as unsophisticated and predictable as the observation of birds in a nest or the growth of tree rings.[107]

Although the *I Ching* has had millions of devoted followers, passionate skeptics have suggested that the *I Ching* is mere superstition. James Legge, the first scholar to translate the *I Ching* into English in the 1800s, wrote "until the Chinese drop the hallucination about the *I Ching*, it will prove a stumbling-block to them, and keep them from entering upon the true path of science."[108] Dr. Joseph Needham, author of the seventeen-volume *Science and Civilization in China*, wrote that the *I Ching* "resembled the astrological pseudo-explanation of medieval Europe, but the abstractness of the symbolism gave it a deceptive profundity. Chinese scholars would have been wiser to tie a millstone about the neck of the *I Ching* and cast it into the sea."[109]

## 📖 *A Concise Catalog of Things You Throw or Bounce*

> *There are times when silence is a poem.*
> —John Fowles, *The Magus*

♉ **ASHAGALOMANCY** is divination by casting small bones. The method is similar to throwing dice.

♓ **ASTRAGLOMANCY** (or **ASTRAGYROMANCY**) is a form of divination by dice, the faces of which bear numbers and letters. Ancient astragyromancers used knucklebones. The position of the bones and the nature of the upward pointing side was used to make predictions. This form of divination was quite popular in Mesopotamia. Today, various African tribes throw bones to predict the future.

♌ **AUTO-MANZIA** is a divination method practiced by Italian psychic Maria Rosa Donati-Evstigneeff.[110] She takes ten straight pins and three bent pins and shakes them in her hands. When she drops the pins on a dusty surface, she observes the patterns and makes predictions.

♉ **AXIOMANCY** (or **AXINOMANCY**) is divination by observing how an ax or hatchet quivers or points when driven into a post. A variant of this method was used to find thieves. First an ax was tossed to the ground, head downward and handle in the air. When the handle tottered and fell to the ground, it pointed in the direction the thief was hiding. In other applications of axiomancy, the axiomancer balances an ax on the wrist. When the ax falls, the direction of the handle points to buried treasure or to where something is hidden. (Don't try this at home kids!)

♊ **BELOMANCY** is an ancient form of divination performed by tossing or balancing arrows. Belomancy seems to date back to Chaldea, the land in southern Babylonia (modern southern Iraq) frequently mentioned in the Old Testament. Belomancy was practiced by the Greeks and later by the Arabians, although its use was forbidden in the Koran. One approach was to throw several arrows into the air. The angle of the arrows as they fell suggested actions and directions the inquirer should take. Tibetans practiced various forms of belomancy where practitioners used a two-arrow system called *dahmo*. The "yes" arrow and "no" arrow were shot into a pile of barley. After the barley fell to the sides, the belomancer interpreted the final placement of the arrows to answer questions about the future.

℧ **CLEROMANCY** is divination by "casting lots," similar to throwing dice but often with objects such as pebbles, sea shells, crystals, coins, black and white beans, bones, and so forth. In the ancient days, people assumed that gods determine the way lots fell.

Various forms of cleromancy are still in use today. For example, the ancient Chinese system *chiao-pai*, which is still practiced, involves the tossing of two curved bamboo blocks on the ground. If both blocks land with curved sides up, the answer is yes. If both blocks land with flat sides up, the response is negative. If the blocks land with one flat side up and one curved side up, the future is very positive. Divination by tossing objects existed in ancient Egypt (with eight-sided dice), the Middle Ages (twelve-sided dice), and ancient Rome (fourteen-sided dice). Today, cleromancers use ordinary six-sided dice to predict the future.

---

### Do-It-Yourself Cleromancy

One modern form of cleromancy involves tossing dice and observing the results. First, draw a twelve-inch diameter circle on paper and place the paper on a table. Next, think of a question. Take two ordinary six-sided die, shake them in a cup, and toss the dice on a table. If both dice fall outside the circle, try again. If one die falls outside the circle, disregard it and pay attention to the one inside the circle. Wait a day before asking the same question again. The numbers you roll and meanings are as follows:[111]

| Dice Sum | Meaning |
|---|---|
| 1 | The answer to your question is yes. |
| 2 | The answer to your question is no. |
| 3 | Be very careful when addressing the situation. |
| 4 | Think before acting. |
| 5 | Good fortune arrives soon. Excellent results. |
| 6 | Very favorable. Smooth outcome. |
| 7 | Continue as you are doing. If you stay the course, the outcome is favorable. |
| 8 | Be patient. The answer is yes over time. |
| 9 | Success in enterprise. |
| 10 | There may be disappointment associated with the situation or question. |
| 11 | It is not possible at this time. |
| 12 | The chance for success is slim. |

Dominoes are also used for divination. One method uses three dominoes that are drawn from a set face down. When the tiles are turned over, each combination of numbers has a specific meaning. For example, six/six is the luckiest of all the dominoes, signifying success and happiness. See **ashagalomancy** and the "Do-It-Yourself Cleromancy" sidebar.

♈ **I CHING** is a Chinese divination system in which one tosses objects and consults sixty-four hexagram patterns to gain insight into the future.

♉ **KARYDAOMANCY** (after the Greek *karyda* for coconut) is divination performed with fragments of coconut shells. Today, most kardyaomancers are from the Santeria religion that originated in Cuba and spread to the United States. Santeria developed from the traditions of the Yoruba people in Africa who had been transported to Cuba to work as slaves on plantations.[112]

---

### Do-It-Yourself Karydaomancy

To perform karydaomancy (divination with coconut shells) first purchase a coconut and bring it home.[113] Next, follow these steps:

1. Crack the coconut with a hammer.
2. Remove four fragments that contain the white coconut meat on one side and the brown shell on the other side.
3. Ask a question.
4. Toss the fragments on the ground or on a table to produce five possible variations on yes and no:

| Coconut Shell Orientations | Meaning |
| --- | --- |
| "Alafia," all four white sides up. | The answer to the question is yes. A solution is possible. Happiness and health. Success. Repeat the question because this must be confirmed by "Otawe" or "Eyife" (below). |
| "Eyife," two white sides up. | The answer is yes. Confirms Alafia. |
| "Otawe," three whites sides up. | Maybe. Some doubt. Be hopeful, but there are no guarantees. This configuration confirms Alafia if you are willing to make a sacrifice. |
| "Ocanasdoe," one white side up. | No. Be careful. Danger. The spirits of the dead are speaking. |
| "Oyekun," no white sides up. | Definitely no. Death and suffering. Evil. |

♉ **LITHOMANCY** is divination using precious stones of various colors. The lithomancer tosses the stones and studies the arrangements in which they fall. Ideally, the stones should be smooth and nearly uniform in size and shape. Often the stones are tossed onto a circle divided like an astrological chart, with divisions for emotions and advice. See **pessomancy**.

♎ **MARGARITOMANCY** is divination using bouncing pearls. In order to determine the guilt or innocence of a person suspected of a crime, the margaritomancer places a pearl beneath an upside-down vase near a fire. As in many other forms of divination, the names of suspects are then recited. When a guilty person's name is mentioned, the pearl is supposed to fly upward and shatter the vase's bottom.

♌ **MING STICKS** are still used today for divination in China. Each stick is numbered. A person asks a question and takes one stick. The stick's number corresponds to an "answer" printed in a book. Often the ming sticks are stored in cylinders that are shaken so that only one stick falls out. The querent looks up the meaning of the fallen stick in the book.

♈ **MO** is a form of Tibetan divination using dice. A person rolls the dice and looks up the meanings of the dice outcomes in cards or books. We know that mo is an ancient system because it was described in a twelfth-century manuscript. Monks used mo to answer the urgent practical questions of lay people. A related form of Tibetan dice divination *sho mo*, relies on divination books associated with a specific protective deity.

♏ **PESSOMANCY** is divination through the use of pebbles. Like the halomancer who divines with salt crystals, the pessomancer tosses pebbles on the ground and studies the resultant patterns. This method was popular in ancient Greece. Today the Masai of East Africa practice pessomancy with stones cast from buffalo horns. See **lithomancy** and **halomancy** (in the "Flames of God" section, p. 182).

♌ **PSEPHOMANCY** is divination using games of chance and casting of lots. This was popular with the Sumerians who used wooden sticks and the Assyrians who used clay dice. See **cleromancy** and **mo**.

♊ **SORTILEGE** is the casting of lots (objects like dice) and the assessment of the omens indicated by the positions or values of the objects. Querents toss bones, coins, or other objects, the patterns of which determine or foretell the future. Sortilege methods originated more than five thousand years ago, when pebbles or bones were tossed and the resultant patterns on the ground interrupted. See **astragyromancy** and **lithomancy**.

⊚ **URIMANCY** is divination by the ancient Israeli method of casting lots. In Biblical times, prophets and priests wore breast plates with a pocket that contained a "Urim" and "Thummim," which scholars suggest could be animal knucklebones or some other early form of dice. In 1 Samuel 28:6, the Kings of Israel made decisions based on the Urim and Thummim. Under Levitical law, high priests carried objects like the Urim and Thummim in their "breastplates of judgment." Urimancers often were used to determine if a person was innocent or guilty. (*Urimancy* is not to be confused with *uromancy*, which is divination using urine.)

⌒ **XYLOMANCY** is divination using pieces of wood, either by observing their shapes or their appearance while burning. Slavonic xylomancers observe the positions of wood pieces they happens to encounter during a journey. Xylomancy may have been practiced by the ancient Hebrews. Dry twigs were tossed in the air, and their subsequent positions on the ground foretold the future.

## ᛦ ANCIENT CARDS AND BOOKS

> *A book is like a garden carried in the pocket.*
>
> —Chinese proverb

☞ *Topics discussed*: a variety of divination methods that employ cards, pictures, or books. Our emphasis here is on tarot cards.

### The Tarot of the Dead

> *I greet Darryl warmly. He sounds a little nervous so I try to make small talk. I ask him if he is unhappy with his current employment situation to which he asks the inevitable question, "How did you know?" It's my job, I tell him. I also inform him that the death card has come up, but tell him not to worry. It is a closed minded, Western way of thinking that condemns the Death card, or the number thirteen and other such superstitious preoccupations.*
>
> —Carlee Star, "Psychic for a Day:
> A Day In the Life of a Telephone Psychic"[114]

Tarot fortune-telling is an ancient form of cartomancy, divination by the use of cards. With the dawning of the Internet, an amazing array of imaginative tarot cards are available for download and study, which are scattered throughout this section.[115] Various authors have suggested that tarot cards originated in China, India, or Egypt, but their actual origin is unknown. Tarot cards first appeared in Italy and France in the fourteenth century, perhaps in the time of the poet Dante (1265–1321). The earliest-known surviving cards date from 1392 and are in a pack made for King Charles VI of France by the painter Jacquemin Gringonneur; however, their date and origin is not firmly established. The word "tarot" appears to have originated during the fourteenth century in Italy from the card game tarocco, which the French changed to tarot.

There were several types of early tarot decks, each with varying numbers of cards. Today's seventy-eight-card deck is based on the Venetian or Piedmontese tarot. The deck is divided into twenty-two Major Arcana cards and fifty-six Minor Arcana cards. The cards of the Major Arcana have beautiful and haunting images representing various powers, characters, and virtues. The twenty-two major cards are numbered from I through XXI, with the Fool being unnumbered. The tarots of the Major Arcana are, in order: I Juggler (or Magician), II Papess (or Female Pope), III Empress, IV Emperor, V Pope, VI Lovers, VII Chariot, VIII Justice, IX Hermit, X Wheel of Fortune, XI Strength (or Fortitude), XII Hanged Man, XIII Death (see figure 29), XIV Temperance, XV Devil, XVI Lightning-Struck Tower, XVII Star, XVIII Moon, XIX Sun, XX Last Judgment, XXI World (or Universe), and the Fool.

Most of the cards are symbols of universal, abstract ideas that we can

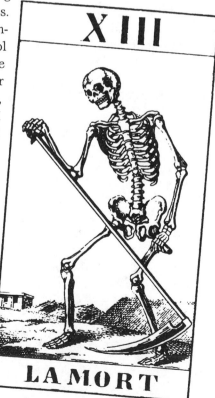

**Figure 29.** The Death card from the popular Tarot 1JJ deck produced for several centuries by Muller & Cie, Swizerland. From S. R. Kaplan, *Tarot Cards for Fun and Fortune Telling* (Stamford, Connecticut: U.S. Games Systems, Inc., 1970), p. 41.

### Do-It-Yourself Tarot

I enjoy reading tarot cards using just the Major Arcana cards that contain the main tarot themes and images.

1. Shuffle the twenty-two Major Arcana.
2. Spread the top ten cards in the pack as shown in figure 30. (The is known as the "Celtic Cross" spread.) Some tarot readers assign a weakened or reversed meaning to cards that are upside down in the spread.
3. Look up the meaning of each card in the accompanying tarot card table and adapt the meaning to the card's position in the ten card spread. Card number 1 represents present influence, the atmosphere in which you are working and living. Card 2 is the immediate obstacle. Card 3 shows your ultimate goal. Card 4 is the past foundation. Card 5 is the more recent past. Card 6 is the near future. Card 7 is you in present perspective. Card 8 is the surrounding environment, people, and places. Card 9 represents your inner emotions. Card 10 is the final result of the reading. For example, if you had the death card in position 6, there would be a great change in store for you in the immediate future, but not necessarily physical death.

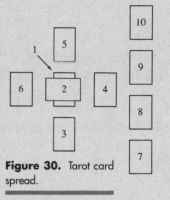

**Figure 30.** Tarot card spread.

all understand like love, death, justice, and so forth. Others are a bit more mystifying, like the Hanged Man who hangs upside down from a gibbet. The Lightening Struck Tower is equally esoteric. Some scholars have suggested that the twenty-two major arcana are related to the twenty-two paths of the Kabbala, the Jewish mysticism in which ten circles—the highest of which represents God, the lowest the Earth—are joined by twenty-two lines. The Jewish Kabbalist Moses de León wrote the Zohar, the second book of the Kabbala, in Spain in 1275, and this seems to be about the same time that the tarot originated.[116]

The fifty-six Minor Arcana cards are divided into four suits of fourteen cards each. The suits correspond to modern playing cards: wands, batons, or rods (clubs); cups (hearts); swords (spades); and coins, pentacles, or disks (diamonds). Each suit has four court cards (usually named king, queen, knight, and page) and ten numbered cards. The standard deck of modern playing cards was historically derived from that of the Minor Arcana (with the elimination of the tarot's knight). The Fool became the Joker.

At first, the tarot was probably used for playing games. From the eighteenth century, the cards began to take on mystical associations which today are retained for fortune-telling. Writer Damon Wilson comments on the degree to which tarot cards must have entertained people centuries ago:

> It would hardly be an exaggeration to say that the invention of the cards had as much impact on the thirteenth century as the invention of the novel on the eighteenth, or of radio and television on the twentieth. One of the main, everyday problems of the time is that the nobles had nothing much to do in the winter between sunrise and darkness. So this fascinating pack of cards must have been a godsend.[117]

As mentioned earlier, each tarot card has a meaning for fortune-telling. The cards of the Major Arcana refer to spiritual matters and important trends in the questioner's life. In the Minor Arcana, wands deal mainly with business matters and career ambitions, cups with love, swords with conflict, and coins with money and material comfort.

The tarot deck is shuffled by the questioner, and then the fortuneteller lays out a few of the cards in a special pattern called a "spread." The meaning of any card is sometimes modified according to whether or not it is placed upside down as viewed by the fortune teller, its position in the spread, and the meaning of adjacent cards.

### Tarot Card Meanings

| Card Name | Divinatory Meaning |
|---|---|
| 0. The Fool | Lack of discipline. Folly. You must be careful to use will power to direct your life. Not a care in the world. Being free from any constraints. The fool steps over the cliff without looking where he is going. Folly, mania, extravagance, intoxication, faith, spontaneity, beginning. |
| I. The Magician | Originality, spontaneity, imagination, dexterity mastery. Being able to control the forces around you. Skill, diplomacy, self-confidence. |
| II. The High Priestess | A wise woman or person. Able to make good decisions. Wisdom. Secrets, mystery, the future as yet unrevealed. The woman who interests the querent. |
| III. The Empress | Fruitfulness. Personal growth and fertility. Progress, fertility. Resourcefulness. Accomplishment. Marriage. Fruitfulness, action, initiative, length of days. |
| IV. The Emperor | Power, being in control or in a position of authority. Competence, skill, wealth. Domination of reason over emotion. Stability, power, protection. A great person. Aid, reason, conviction. |

| V. Heirophant | Mercy, humility, kindness, compassion. A spiritual person goodness. Inspiration, conventionality; marriage wows; a need for, or a love of, convention and outward signs of approval and conformity. |
| --- | --- |
| VI. The Lovers | Love, romance, testing the situation, examining. Attraction, love, beauty, trials overcome. The Lover is torn by indecision but must make a choice in order to progress. A time of speculation and putting to the test. Yearning. Temptation. The ability to make good choices. The possibility of a new romance. Change. |
| VII. The Chariot | Trouble ahead but eventual triumph. Hard work. True progress is made only when opposing forces are balanced and integrated. Adverse powers can be conquered by will power and self-control. A middle course. Balance of hard work and periods of productive solitude are required. Travel or journey. |
| VIII. Justice | Justice, fairness, moderation. Virginity. Balance and harmony. Both people get what they need. Making wise choices or decisions. Reasonableness and fairness. Reason transcending emotion. Honor. Virtue. Legal matters are also indicated, such as lawsuits, divorces and wills. |
| IX. The Hermit | Being careful, silent counsel, carrying a light through the darkness. Solitude and introspection; retreating to find something within yourself. Prudence. |
| X. Wheel of Fortune | Progress, advancement, good luck. Taking chances and seeing where it leads you. Destiny, fortune, success, luck, fate, vision of the whole situation. |
| XI. Strength | Courage, energy, physical strength, self-reliance. A man wrestling a lion. Power, lust, energy, action, courage, endurance. |
| XII. The Hanged Man | Life in suspension or transition. Sacrifices must be made to reach your goals. In the Norse tarot, this card is represented by Odin hanging from the tree of Yggdrasil and grasping the runes, which signify knowledge and wisdom. Wisdom, trials, surrender. |
| XIII. Death | Death of the old self clearing the way for transformation. Loss, failure. A life-altering transition. Change, transition, and rebirth. Not necessarily a physical death. The end of the old so that the new might grow. This could mean marriage, a new job, or the beginning of a new era. It takes courage to meet new challenges. Destruction and renewal. Endings. |
| XIV. Temperance | Moderation, patience, balance, temperance, putting together several people or ideas to form a useful synergy. Temperance means to be able to mold and shape something the way you want it. This card could mean being able to take a situation and make it your own. Economy, moderation, frugality, management, accommodation, caution, care, reconciling opposites. |

| | |
|---|---|
| XV. The Devil | Bondage, repression, compulsion, enslavement, feeling trapped. Powerless and feeling indebted to something or someone; possibly an addiction or vice that is causing problems. A devil holding his hand over a woman. Two people in a dark tunnel trying to drag their valuables, which are too heavy, yet they are unwilling to let go. In the Norse deck, this card portrays Loki's punishment by other gods. Loki is chained to a rock while a snake drips poison onto him. |
| XVI. Lightening-struck Tower (or the House of God) | Sudden change. Breaking down of old forms to make way for new ones. Loss of security. Setback or possible disaster, loss. The old order breaks down so that the new may begin. Seek new philosophies upon which to rebuild your life. Learning through experience. New beginnings. Opportunity or unforeseen catastrophes; loss of security or the end of a relationship. Reversal. |
| XVII. The Star | Hope, bright future, love, healing, peace. The night is dark but full of stars. The Star brings with it brilliant prospects, new opportunities, and success. Optimism, insight, and inspiration. The healing attributes of tranquillity and peace. |
| XVIII. The Moon | Deception, false friends, unknown enemies, scandal, an insincere personal relationship. A man playing a stringed instrument to a woman on a balcony while a creature crawls up the wall toward them. Secrets that are hidden from you, falsehood; double dealing. It can also indicate illusion, escapism, self-deception, fluctuation, and change. |
| XIX. The Sun | Satisfaction, contentment, good relationships, happiness, achievement, fulfillment and success. Energy and inner strength. Pleasure in all things. A happy marriage and often material wealth or rewards through hard work. |
| XX. Judgment | Rebirth, rejuvenation. Angels blowing trumpets in the sky. The need to assess ourselves and to atone, if necessary. Learn to forgive yourself and others, in order to move forward. Regeneration and reward for past efforts. Enlightenment, revelation. |
| XXI. The World | This is the best card to get. Attainment. Completion, perfection, success. Coming full-circle. Desires fulfilled. Triumph. Freedom. The final goal reached. Joy and a new life. |

Tarot cards have evolved through the ages, and there are now hundreds of beautiful and exotic looking decks. The "1JJ" deck is one of the most popular and classic tarot decks, enjoying widespread acceptance in the United States. It has been produced for several centuries by Muller & Cie, Switzerland and distributed by U.S. Games Systems, Inc, one of the largest tarot card distributors in the world (see figure 29). This deck is believed to have many features of the oldest decks. Other more recent popular decks include ones designed in 1889 by a theosophist named Oswald Wirth, and another famous deck by Arthur Edward Waite who was responsible for designing what has now become the best-known tarot deck, with romantic paintings by Pamela Coleman Smith. (Since the nineteenth century, "theosophy" has come represents the mystical teachings of the Theosophical Society founded in 1875 in New York City by Helena Petrovna Blavatsky and Henry Steel Olcott.) Aleister Crowley also designed a wild looking deck, painted by Frieda Harris. Fergus Hall designed a surrealistic deck for the James Bond movie *Live and Let Die*.

I'm a collector of little-known modern tarot cards. Some examples are given in figures 31 through 38. Most are extremely ornate and mystifying. However, one of my favorites is the simpler *Stick Figure Tarot* by artist Lar deSouza (see figures 39–41).[118] He explained to me the philosophy of his deck:

> Well, never fear! This *Stick Figure Tarot* deck, based on the Rider-Waite Tarot, has all the essential symbology without the distractions of gorgeous artwork. Yessir, when you do a reading with this deck, the only thing worth seeing is the meaning of the cards. I've distilled each card down to its essential imagery and rendered it lovingly in the kind of stick figure we all can identify with. No fancy colors or obscure gods and goddesses to deal with in this set! Just the basics. This is a perfect deck for those of us who enjoy the Tarot, but perhaps don't take Life too seriously. Frankly the whole exercise has proved far more popular than I could have imagined. I created the deck in January and have sold hundreds of decks via the Internet.[119]

Although each card has many potential meanings allowing for a large number of interpretations, in the hands of a skilled reader, a tarot reading will seem remarkably relevant and accurate. Just as with the *I Ching*, occult theory would explain a seemingly accurate reading as a mysterious influence or relationship between questioner, the shuffling of the cards, and events in the questioner's life. Modern psychologists would suggest that the cards serve as a suggestive canvas, provoking our imaginations, and upon which we project patterns of intuitions, feelings, and subconscious concerns. Like all divination methods, tarot cards can be dangerous if used as an alternative to clear, scientific thinking. However, for those with a firm footing in reality, the cards may be able to trigger subconscious knowledge or intuitions and suggest opportunities or dangers that would have otherwise been overlooked.[120]

Another interesting tarot deck is Texas artist Monica Knighton's *Tarot of the Dead* (see figures 42 and 43).[121] The deck is comprised of dead people

**Figure 31.** Tarot card from The New Millennium Tarot deck by Paul Smith, painter, illustrator, and tarot fan from PAS Studios in Minnesota. (From Paul Smith, www.usinternet.com/users/psmith/Index.html for Clifford Pickover.)

**Figure 32.** Tarot card by Paul Smith. (From Paul Smith for Clifford Pickover.)

**Figure 33.** Tarot card by Paul Smith. (From Paul Smith for Clifford Pickover.)

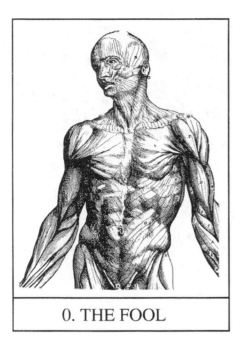

0. THE FOOL

**Figure 34.** Tarot card from The Anatomy Tarot by Clifford Pickover, based on sketches by anatomist Andreas Vesalius (1514–1564).

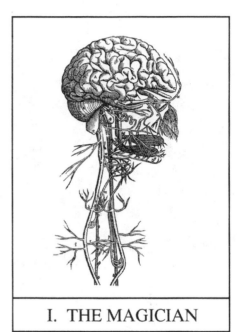

I.  THE MAGICIAN

**Figure 35.** Tarot card from The Anatomy Tarot by Clifford Pickover.

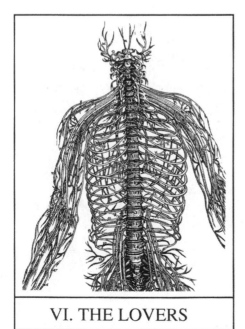

VI. THE LOVERS

**Figure 36.** Tarot card from The Anatomy Tarot by Clifford Pickover.

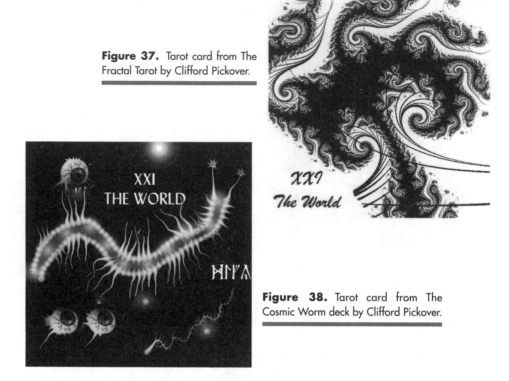

**Figure 37.** Tarot card from The Fractal Tarot by Clifford Pickover.

**Figure 38.** Tarot card from The Cosmic Worm deck by Clifford Pickover.

and skeletons and inspired by the Mexican holiday *Dias de los Muertos* (Day of the Dead). During this holiday people remember passed loved ones and acknowledge human mortality. My favorite book on this subject is *The Skeleton at the Feast: The Day of the Dead in Mexico* by Elizabeth Carmichael and Chloe Sayer.[122]

## 📖 *A Catalog of Methods Using Books, Paper, or Cards*

> *He showed me a little thing, the quantity of a hazelnut, in the palm of my hand, and it was round as a ball. I looked thereupon with eye of my understanding and thought: What may this be? And it was answered generally thus: It is all that is made.*
>
> —Julian of Norwich, 14th century

**BIBLIOMANCY** operates on divination by books. In one implementation, a person randomly opens the Bible, or any book, and places a finger on a passage to determine what action to take or to answer a question. Centuries

THE FOOL

KNIGHT of SWORDS

**Figure 39.** *Stick Figure Tarot* by Lar deSouza. (From Lar deSouza, www.sentex.net/~fresco/studio/stick_fig. html, for Clifford Pickover.)

XIII

DEATH

**Figure 40.** *Stick Figure Tarot* by Lar deSouza. (From Lar deSouza for Clifford Pickover.)

**Figure 41.** *Stick Figure Tarot* by Lar deSouza. (From Lar deSouza for Clifford Pickover.)

**Figure 42.** A tarot card from Monica Knighton's *Tarot of the Dead*. (From Monica Knighton, tarotofthedead.com, for Clifford Pickover.)

**Figure 43.** A tarot card from Monica Knighton's *Tarot of the Dead*. (From Monica Knighton, tarotofthedead.com, for Clifford Pickover.)

ago, Jews and Christians frequently used the Bible for bibliomancy. In the Middle Ages, kings, bishops, and saints used bibliomancy.

Bibliomancers sometimes opened books by Roman poet Virgil (70–19 B.C.E.) at random for the purposes of divination. This divination approach is also known as *Sortes Virgilianae*. A Christian canon (i.e., law XXXVI of Orleans 511) excommunicates those who practice *Sortes Sanctorum* (*Bibliorum*)—deciding one's future conduct by the first passage found on opening a Bible. Other denominations also condemned the practice. For example, the greatest Puritan theological writer of the seventeenth century, Richard Baxter, was often concerned with inappropriate use of the Scriptures. In his book *The Life of Faith*, Baxter warned his fellow Puritans that it was possible to abuse the central authority of scripture by "looking for that in Scripture which God never intended it for." To Baxter, the worst abuse was the practice of letting the Bible flop open at random, and taking the first verse one's eyes fell upon as a divine directive, a method borrowed from the pagan practice of *Sortes Virgilianae*.

A famous example of the sortes from the fourth century is St. Augustine's use of bibliomancy during a profound spiritual crisis. The climax of a long personal struggle came in the summer of 386 in a Milan garden. Augustine speaks of this in his book the *Confessions*:

> I was weeping . . . when I heard a voice from some neighbor's house, a boy or girl, singing and repeating, "Take it and read! Take it and read!" I held back the violent torrent of my tears and I got up for I interpreted it as a command from God himself to open the book and read what I first laid eyes upon. . . . So I snatched it up, opened it, and read the first words I saw: "Not in rioting and drunkenness, not in fornication and wantonness, not in strife and envying, but put ye on the Lord Jesus Christ and think not of fulfilling the lusts of the flesh." I read no further; I did not need to. For instantly, at the end of this sentence, a light of confidence darted into my heart and all the darkness of doubt vanished.[123]

See also **rhapsodomancy**.

♋ **CARTOMANCY** is fortune telling using cards such as the tarot deck or ordinary playing cards. European gypsies widely practiced cartomancy in the 1300s. When using playing cards, hearts indicate good fortune in love and business. Clubs indicate successful financial situations. Diamonds indicate influences outside of the persons. Spades are warnings of unforeseen difficulties. See also **tarot**.

♍ **FAWL HAFEZ** is a Persian method of divination using a book of poetry. In modern day Iran, people use a form of **rhapsodomancy** in which a book of poems by the renowned Persian poet Hafez (1325–1389) is open at random, and the poems on the open page are used to give insight into questions. The questions often concern family matters, romance, travel, the destiny of nations, and other concerns. There are many online Fawl Hafez Web sites, but traditionalists in Iran prefer to gather at Hafez's tomb in Shiraz where they open his poetry and read verses to seek assistance.

♍ **PAPYROMANCY** is divination by observing someone fold paper. This art became especially popular with the 1973 publication of Thomas Pynchon's *Gravity's Rainbow* in which one character watches another roll a marijuana cigarette: "Säure really turns out to be an adept at the difficult art of papyromancy, the ability to prophesize through contemplating the way people roll reefers—the shape, the licking pattern, the wrinkles and folds or absence thereof in the paper."[124]

♊ **PYNCHONOMANCY** is divination by throwing darts at paperback editions of Thomas Pynchon's novel *Gravity's Rainbow*. After throwing a dart, the diviner looks at the last page penetrated and reads the sentence or paragraph intersected by the dart to gain insight. Unfortunately, the practitioner of this form of **rhapsodomancy** (or **bibliomancy** or **stichomancy**) must replace the book every few months because the book tends to fall apart and becomes difficult to read. (I am told that publishers enjoy this divination method.) One anonymous Interneter described this approach to me and said he goes so far as to use this method to determine the nature and duration of his sexual activities, in addition to using the approach to solve problems and predict future trends.

♊ **RHAPSODOMANCY** is divination using a poetry or other book whereby the book is opened at random and a passage read. Rhapsodomancy goes back to the ancient Greeks where verses uttered by the oracles were transcribed for random consultation in the Sibylline Books, or where a phrase from one of the poets was picked for guidance. ("Sibylla" was a prophetess in Greek legend and literature. Tradition represented her as an old woman uttering predictions in ecstatic frenzy.) Some consider consultation of the *I Ching* as an example rhapsodomancy because the *I Ching* makes use of an ancient book of wisdom in which hexagrams are consulted according to a

---

### Do-It-Yourself Stichomancy

I have personally tried stichomancy as a way to stimulate the mind with new ideas. It's sometimes useful for coming up with inventions and new ways of looking at a problem. For example, I have randomly taken phrases from patents and then combined them to get ideas for new patents. I have also used similar random approaches for creating computer-generated poetry or for creating exotic or poetic descriptions for novels. Here is the traditional method of stichomancy for answering questions:

1. Ask a question.
2. Find a book and open it to a random page.
3. Read a passage at random on the page, and think about how this may apply to a question or problem that is facing you.

For example, let's say you choose a copy of *Tales of Power* by Carlos Castenada from the library and open to a random page. You read the following: "The conditions of a solitary bird are five: First, that it flies to the highest point. Second, that it does not suffer for company, not even of its own kind. Third, that it aims its beak to the sky. Fourth, that it does not have a definite color. Fifth, that it sings very softly." For the rest of the day, think about what this may mean for your current questions about life. Various stichomancy sites exist on the World Wide Web that will select random passages from random books for you.[125]

random sequence generated by throwing sticks. Rhapsodomancy comes from the Greek *rhapsoidos*, someone who recites epic poems, particularly the Homeric odes. See **bibliomancy**.

♉ **SORTES**. See **bibliomancy**.

♎ **STICHOMANCY**, like **rhapsodamancy**, is divination by throwing open a book and selecting a random passage. (An important type of stichomancy is **bibliomancy**, which usually restricts itself to holy books.) Stichomancy was practiced by the ancient Greeks and Romans. Often the works of Homer or Virgil were used and are still used today. More modern stichomancers use the works of Shakespeare, Nostradamus, or Edgar Cayce. See **pynchonomancy**.

♌ **SYCOMANCY** is performed by writing messages on tree leaves. The slower the leaves dry, the more favorable the omen.

The ancient Chinese and Romans used sycomancy to answer questions written on fig leaves. After the questions is written, the leaf is left in the sun to dry. If the leaf shrivels quickly, the answer is no. If the leaf retains its appearance for a day, the answer is positive. A modern variation is to write on slips of paper.

♊ **TAROT** fortune-telling is a form of **cartomancy**, that is, divination with the use of cards. Tarot cards similar to the present form first appeared in Italy and France in the fourteenth century Today's seventy-eight-card deck is divided into twenty-two Major Arcana cards and fifty-six Minor Arcana cards. The cards of the Major Arcana have vivid images representing various themes, characters, and virtues.

---

### Do-It-Yourself Sycomancy

The ancient Chinese and Romans used sycomancy to answer questions and foretell the future. You can try it in your own home.

1. Write messages on slips of papers. These might refer to possible future events.
2. Roll up the pieces of paper and place them in a strainer.
3. Hold the strainer over a boiling pot of water. The first paper to unroll will purportedly be answered or foretell the future. If you really want to be authentic, use fig leaves instead of papers. In this case, you don't need a pot of boiling water. Just let the fig leaves dry. The message on the fig leaf that retains its appearance the longest comes true. If you just have a single fig leaf, think of a question and write it on the leaf. If the leaf dries out in less than a day, the answer is no. Otherwise, the answer is yes.

## ᛉ HEAVENLY CODES: NUMBERS, RUNES, AND THE BIBLE

> *Therefore night will come over you, without visions, and darkness, without div-*
> *ination. The sun will set for the prophets, and the day will go dark for them.*
> —Micah 3:6

☞ *Topics discussed*: divination methods using codes, numbers, and letters. The emphasis of this section is on a code alleged to have been discovered in the letters of words in the Bible. See the previous section for related divination methods with books and papers.

### The Bible Code

> *The secret things belong to the Lord our God, but the things revealed belong to*
> *us and to our children forever, that we may follow all the words of this law.*
> —Deuteronomy 29:29

"For three thousand years a code in the Bible has remained hidden. Now it has been unlocked by computer—and it may reveal our future. The code was broken by an Israeli mathematician, who presented the proof in a major science journal, and it has been confirmed by famous mathematicians around the world."[126] So says Simon & Schuster, the publisher of the best-selling *The Bible Code* by Michael Drosnin. The publisher goes on to suggest that the Bible code forces us to accept "what the Bible itself can only ask us to believe—that we are not alone. And it raises a question for us all—does the code describe an inevitable future, or a series of possible futures whose ultimate outcome we can still decide?"

Believers in the "Bible code" theory treat the Hebrew Bible as a string of letters without spaces, looking for words formed by equidistant letter sequences (ELS). For instance, computers might select every ninth Hebrew letter and register a "hit" when a "coded word" intersects with a Bible verse containing related words. When the letters are arranged in arrays, messages or names sometimes appear. These hidden messages are alleged to have been intentionally embedded in the Bible. Researchers Doron Witztum, Eliyahu Rips, and Yoav Rosenberg published their original findings on Bible codes in the journal *Statistical Science* (1994, vol. 9, no. 3, pp. 429–38) under the title of "Equidistant Letter Sequences in the Book of Genesis." As they explained, they took names of famous rabbis from a reference dictionary, applied letter sequences, and found the names near the rabbis' dates of birth or death. Using the same technique, others have claimed the Bible contains secret predictions, including everything from the assassination of Yitzhak Rabin in 1995 to a Los Angeles earthquake in 2010. The 1997 best seller *The Bible Code* claimed that many predictions of current events—such as letters spelling "Yitzhak Rabin" close to "assassination"—are hidden in the book of Genesis. The code also "foresaw" the Oklahoma City bombing and the election of Bill Clinton—and everything from World War II to Watergate, from the Holocaust to Hiroshima to the Moon landing.

Michael Drosnin, author of *The Bible Code*, suggests that decoding the Bible can lead to the discovery of profound prophecies. Moreover, Drosnin claims that the Bible is the only text in which encoded phrases are found in a statistically significant pattern, and that the chance of this being a random phenomenon is unlikely. Using the ELS method, Drosnin also asserts that the assassinations of Anwar Sadat and the Kennedy brothers are encoded in biblical ELS. Skeptics say that hidden "messages" can be found in many books. For example, physicist David Thomas decided to look for "Hitler" and "Nazi" closely associated in Tolstoy's *War and Peace*. He found an English translation of the epic novel on the Internet, and downloaded the first twenty-four chapters of Book 1, giving him about 167,000 characters. By the time he got to steps of just 750, he had already found more than half a dozen instances of the word "Hitler" being near the word "Nazi."[127]

Some major Bible scholars do not feel Drosnin's code is significant because no one has a letter-by-letter version of the Bible as originally written. The oldest surviving manuscripts include slight variations, any of which would throw off computer test results. A more recent study in *Statistical Science* by Dror Bar-Natan, Maya Bar-Hillel, and Gil Kalai, professors at Jerusalem's Hebrew University, and Brendan McKay of the Australian National University, combine expertise in mathematics and computer science to debunk the theory.[128] Using other spellings and assumptions, they ran hundreds of tests that repeated the original ELS experiments with different variations and applied it to more biblical books. "Despite a considerable amount of effort," they write, "we have been unable to detect [meaniful] codes."[129] Their results were no more successful with the Hebrew translation of Tolstoy's *War and Peace* because such letter configurations can be found in any long text. The goal would be to find letters in close proximity that form significant words more often than by chance.

However, Eliyahu Rips, an Israeli mathematics professor who was coauthor of the 1994 paper, said in a statement that evidence for the code is "stronger than ever" and said a detailed reply to the new criticism would appear soon. His ally Michael Drosnin, author of *The Bible Code*, said the critics were not accurate.[130,131]

Interestingly, when author Michael Drosnin was first interviewed about his book, he made the following challenge:

> When my critics find a message about the assassination of a prime minister encrypted in *Moby Dick*, I'll believe them. (*Newsweek*, 9 June 1997)

Brenden Mckay and colleagues took up the challenge and found the following assassinations "foretold" in *Moby Dick*: Prime Minister Indira Gandhi, Soviet exile Leon Trotsky, the Reverend Martin Luther King, the assassin Sirhan Sirhan, Abraham Lincoln, and Yitzhak Rabin.[132] For example, here is Princess Di's death as predicted by equidistant letter sequences in *Moby Dick*:[133]

```
S P O W E R A N D V E L O C I T Y
P E R I G H T O Y E R T H E G R A
L U B B E R C H I L D E H A R O L
A S G A Y A N D F L E E T I N G A
I S W H O L E R A C E F R O M A D
S I S N O T S O M U C H A C O L O
N O T S O O D O N M I G U E L T H
H E R T H E S T R A I G H T W A R
D E A T H I N V A I N W E H A I L
H A T S E E M E D S H U D D E R I
```

There are various Web sites[134] describing computer programs you can download that will allow you to make your own ELS searches of the great world literature. For example, the Codefinder software will search for codes in the *Hebrew Torah and Tanakh, Greek New Testament,* or *English New and Old Testaments*. It also has in Hebrew: Genesis, *War and Peace* (the same length as Genesis), and an electronically randomized Torah. In English, they include *Moby Dick*. Using this software, Bible searcher Kevin Acres found hints of aliens in Roswell, New Mexico:[135]

```
A L L L I V E A N
T W E L V E Y E A
L L B E W H O L E
T H E W O M A N W
N O I S E H E S A
U T F O R T H E E
E P A R T E D T H
```

## *Runemania*

> *Then all the king's wise men came in, but they could not read the writing or tell the king what it meant.*
>
> —Daniel 5:8

The strange looking symbols in this section come from another world—an ancient world filled with sticklike runes, a beautiful alphabet used by Northern Europeans from the first century C.E. and into the Middle Ages. Runes are everywhere these days.[136] English novelist J. R. R. Tolkien featured runes in his epic trilogy *The Lord of the Rings*. These odd symbols are in New Age shops selling fortune-telling paraphernalia, they're featured in religious rituals, and they're even worn as attractive jewelry. In fact, runes are a big business. Companies offer "rune reading courses" so that students can become a "certified rune masters." The Lost Mountain Trading Company of California sells rune sets with semiprecious stones and carrying bags. Tara Hill Designs of Ontario, Canada, supplies handcrafted wood rune sets and other Norse-related products. There are over fifty books in print dealing with rune magic and divination. Jennifer Smith, author of *RAIDO: The Runic Journey*, notes:

> Today, runes have been rediscovered as a symbolic system and have gained immense popularity as a means of divination. They are, however, much more than a curious alternative to Tarot cards for telling fortunes. They provide a key to understanding the lives and beliefs of the ancient people who created them, and have much to teach us about a way of life that was perhaps more intimately connected to the natural world, and to the realm of spirit, than our own.[137]

Runes were used by Germanic peoples of northern Europe, Britain, Scandinavia, and Iceland until the sixteenth or seventeenth century C.E. In addition to their use as a written alphabet, the runes also served as symbols for magic and divination. Runes faded from use when the Roman alphabets became the preferred script of most Europeans, but some runes' forms and meanings were preserved in inscriptions and manuscripts.

The primary characteristic that distinguishes a runic alphabet from the English alphabet is that each letter, or rune, has a meaning. For example, whereas "ay," "bee," and "cee" are meaningless sounds denoting the first three letters in English, the names of the first three runes, "fehu" (ᚠ), "uruz" (ᚢ), and "purisaz" (ᚦ) are actual words in the Germanic language, meaning "cattle," "aurochs (extinct ox)," and "giant," respectively. The simple process of writing may have been transformed into a magical act because runes were thought to have mystical significance.

Because runes consist of angular letter forms and early runic inscriptions were written from right to left like the earliest alphabets, the runic alphabet may come from a more ancient system, perhaps even Greek or Latin alphabets a few centuries before the common era. Another theory is that the Goths (a Germanic people) developed the runic alphabet from northern Italy's Etruscan alphabet, and the runes may have been further influenced by the Latin alphabet in the first second century B.C.E.

It's not necessary to know the history of runes to embark on the mysteries in this section; however, just a smidgen of background may deepen your appreciation for the exotic symbols. There are at least three main varieties of runic script:

- *Early forms* (also known as Common, Germanic, or Teutonic) used in northern Europe before 800 C.E. This script had twenty-four letters. The sounds of the first six letters were f, u, th, a, r, and k, respectively, giving the alphabet its name: futhark. The earliest runic forms seem to be written both left to right and right to left, with no distinction between uppercase and lowercase letters.
- *Anglo-Saxon* (or Anglian) forms used in Britain from the fifth to the twelfth century C.E. This script had twenty-eight letters to accommodate additional sounds, and after 900 C.E. it had thirty-three letters. The letter shapes were slightly different from the Early forms.
- *Nordic* (or Scandinavian), forms used from the eighth to the thirteenth century C.E. in Scandinavia and Iceland. In Scandinavia, runes were still used for charms and memorial inscriptions until the seventh century. (The number of futhark runes was reduced to sixteen, several different Scandinavian sounds represented by a single rune.)

Other varieties of runes included three variants of Nordic script: the *Hälsinge Runes*, the *Manx Runes*, and the *stungnar runir*, or "dotted runes." More than four thousand runic inscriptions and several runic manuscripts are still available today for researchers to study. Approximately 2,500 of these come from Sweden. Others come from Denmark and Schleswig, Britain, Iceland, various islands off of Britain and Scandinavia, France, Germany, Ukraine, and Russia.

Ogham, created by the Celts, is another fascinating and cryptic alphabet that has been categorized as primitive Irish. Some historians suggest that ogham was a private code used by the Druids, the often secretive Celtic religious group from Britain, France, and Ireland. Ogham dates from 350 to 600 C.E. and has been found on stones in Ireland and the Isle of Man. Ogham looks like groupings of lines:

Centuries ago, runes were on everything from coffins to coins, and were sometimes sanctioned by the church. Many people knew simple runic spells and consulted the runes on questions of public and private interest. In 1639, the church banned the use of runes as part of its drive to rid Europe of the devil. Some rune masters were killed. Others hid. In both cases, much of their runc knowledge was lost.

Perhaps the queerest historical use of runes occurred by German scholars connected with the Nazi movement in the 1920s and 1930s. What began as a legitimate interest in ancient folklore became so intertwined with Nazi ideology and racism that the German research shed little light on true origin and meaning of runes.

After the Second World War, rune studies were discouraged because of their association with Naziism, and very little was written about runes until the fifties and sixties. In the 1950s, J. R. R. Tolkien stirred interest in runes with his best-selling novels on Middle Earth that often contained pictures and descriptions of runes. Tolkien was not just a fantasy writer; he was a professor of Anglo-Saxon and English language and literature at the University of Oxford and had a natural feel for ancient languages. He was particularly interested in Anglo-Saxon (Old English) and its relation to linguistically similar languages (Old Norse, Old German, and Gothic), with emphasis on the dialects of Mercia, the part of England in which he lived. Tolkien was also interested in Middle English and the dialect used in the *Ancrene Wisse,* a twelfth-century manuscript probably composed in western England.

Anyone reading Tolkien's *Lord of the Rings* or reading about Tolkien's life cannot help but become interested in runes. But many who had never heard of Tolkien became excited by runes in the 1980s when popular New Age trends and revival of pagan religions (especially the Asatru movement dedicated to ancient, Northern European, pre-Christian religions) helped runes regain their popularity as a divinatory system and symbol of an ancient, forgotten peoples.

When I began my search for drawings and photos of ancient runes, I was delighted to find several historical runic inscriptions on everything from swords to stones to bronze pendants. These examples listed the entire runic alphabet in order. The only surviving written accounts of the actual names and meanings of the runes, however, were not recorded until the ninth century. These rune poems have a verse for each rune, each of which begins with the rune itself and its name. The rune names are thought to be accu-

### Do-It-Yourself Rune Divination
ᛞᛟᛁᛏᛃᛟᚢᚱᛋᛖᛚᚠ ᚱᚢᚾᛖ ᛞᛁᚢᛁᚾᚨ ᛏᛁᛟᚾᛋ

If you don't have rune stones, which can be purchased in many New Age stores and on the Internet, make copies of the runes in appendix 6 and cut them into little paper squares, one rune per square. The first divination method uses three runes and is best for yes/no questions. First choose three runes at random and place them next to one another. Then examine their meanings (listed in appendix 6), which can be reversed if the rune is upside down. For example, assume you cast the three runes:

ᛒ (Beroc, birth), ᛗ (Eoh, change), and ᛗ (Mann, humanity)

In their upright positions, the reading would suggest a (1) new beginning, (2) a rebirth perhaps associated with a change of location, and (3) that it is best to seek advice and interact with others as much as possible. If your question was, "Should I take a trip with family or friends?" the answer would be "Yes."

In the circle cast, you interpret the runes in pairs (see figure 44): 1 and 2 are the problems you face, 3 and 4 are factors in your past, 5 and 6 are advice you should take, 7 is the result if you take that advice.

In another method, the free cast, the querent decides the number and position of the runes. The querent can look at the runes in order to choose what feels right. The next step is to look up the meanings of the runes in appendix 6. For this approach, the questioner should not be familiar with the meanings of the runes prior to his or her selection.

In another method, one mixes the runes and places them down on the table in a

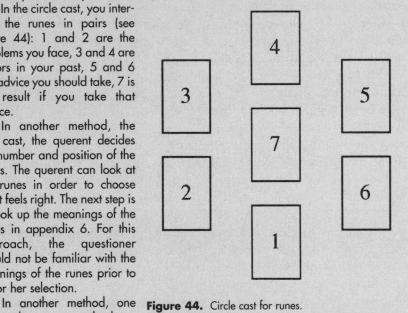

**Figure 44.** Circle cast for runes.

manner similar to one of the famous tarot card arrangements (see figure 32). Position 1 is the problem, the aspect of your life that is on your mind the most. Position 2 is the main obstacle that stands in your way; 3 represents goals; 4 represents past influences; 5 represents current influences; 6 is associated with your ambitions, ideals, and motivations; 7 is what is on your mind, your emotions, and psychological makeup; 8 is your environment, the people and places; 9 is your hopes and fears; and 10 is the final outcome.

rate, although no manuscript exists listing the names of the older, Germanic runes. Runes have been called cryptic because their origins are uncertain and because each was used as a system for concealment.[138] Perhaps their original angular shapes (e.g., ᚨᚢᚦᛞᛗᚫᚷᚻᛁᛯᛦᛚᛞᚾᚩᛈᛇᚱᛋᛏᚢᚹᛉᛠ) with no curved lines indicate the first writing implements that created them were wooden sticks or bones with straight edges. Jennifer Smith's Web site "The Runic Journey" (http://www.tarahill.com/runes/) provides excellent historical information on runes.[139]

Today, people use runes in a manner similar to tarot cards. Each rune has a meaning that is influenced by its position in a particular arrangement of runes or "runecast." Some runecasts use twenty-four stones with runes engraved upon the stones. Each stone represents an ancient archetype like "strength" or "joy." According to legends, the Norse god Odin, lord of death and rebirth, hung on the world tree, Yggdrasil, for nine days while dreaming up the runes. Many tarot card images are said to be influenced by runes. See the "Do-It-Yourself Rune Divination" section to learn how to cast runes.

## *Magic Squares*

> *Keep on, then, with your magic spells and with your many sorceries, which you have labored at since childhood. Perhaps you will succeed, perhaps you will cause terror.*
>
> —Isaiah 47:12

Magic squares have fascinated humans since the dawn of civilization. Even in ancient Babylonian times, people considered these arrays of numbers to have magical powers, and in the eighth century C.E., some squares were considered useful for turning ordinary metal into gold. The patterns have also been used as religious symbols, protective charms, and tools for divination.[140] When the squares lost their mystical meanings, laypeople continued to use them as fascinating puzzles while seasoned mathematicians studied them as problems in number theory. Albrecht Dürer, the fourteenth-century painter and printmaker, used them in his artworks, and today magic squares continue to intrigue us with their elegant, beautiful, and strange symmetries.

A *magic square* is a square matrix drawn as a checkerboard filled with numbers or letters in particular arrangements. Mathematicians are most interested in *arithmetic* squares consisting of $N^2$ boxes, called *cells*, filled with integers that are all different. (For example, if $N$ is 5 we have a 5×5 array containing 25 cells.) Such an array of numbers is called a magic square if the sums of the numbers in the horizontal rows, vertical columns, and main diagonals are all equal. If the integers in a magic square are the consecutive numbers from 1 to $N^2$, the square is said to be of the $N$th order, and the *magic number*, or sum of each row, is a constant symbolized as $S$:

$$S = \frac{N(N^2+1)}{2}$$

(The magic number is sometimes referred to as the *magic sum* or *magic constant*.) A few examples will help demystify these mathematical definitions. The simplest magic square possible is one of the third order, with 3×3 cells containing the integers 1 through 9, and with the magic sum 15 along the three rows, three columns, and two diagonals. Only one unique arrangement of digits, and its mirror image, is possible for a third order square:

| 4 | 9 | 2 |
|---|---|---|
| 3 | 5 | 7 |
| 8 | 1 | 6 |

Third-order Magic Square

| 2 | 9 | 4 |
|---|---|---|
| 7 | 5 | 3 |
| 6 | 1 | 8 |

Mirror Image

**Figure 45.** The first known magic square from around 2200 B.C.E. The Chinese characters stand for the numbers 1 through 9. From Jan Gullberg, *Mathematics From the Birth of Numbers* (New York: Norton, 1997) , p. 205.

Here $N = 3$, because there are 3 rows and 3 columns, and the magic sum $S$ is 15 because the numbers in the rows, columns, and two diagonals sum to 15. For example, if you look at the square at left, you'll see that the sum of the numbers in the first row is $4 + 9 + 2 = 15$. The sum of the numbers in the first column is $4 + 3 + 8 = 15$. One of the diagonal sums is $4 + 5 + 6 = 15$, and so forth. We can also use the magic sum formula to compute the magic sum: $3(3^2+1)/2 = 15$. Notice that the mirror image is also a magic square. By rotating the square four times by 90 degrees, you can produce eight third-order magic squares.

Several third- and fourth-order magic squares were discovered centuries ago in India and China where magic squares were worn, engraved on stones or metals, as charms to protect the wearer from evil and to bring good fortune. Most scholars believe the magic square originated in China and was first mentioned in a manuscript from the time of Emperor Yu around 2200 B.C.E. The first square had 3×3 = 9 cells, each with Chinese characters equivalent to 1 through 9 (see figure 45).

| 4 | 9 | 2 |
|---|---|---|
| 3 | 5 | 7 |
| 8 | 1 | 6 |

Yu Magic Square

Although historians trace references to the Yu magic square back no further than the fourth century B.C.E., there is a strange legend[141] that actually has Emperor Yu discovering the magic square while walking along the Lo River (or Yellow River) where he saw a mystical turtle crawling on the river bank. I think we can take most of this story with a bit of skepticism, but the legend is that the turtle was ordinary in all respects except that its shell had a series of dots within squares. To Yu's amazement, each row of squares contained fifteen dots, as did the columns and diagonals. As he studied the turtle shell further, he also found that when he added any two cells directly opposite along a line through the center square, like 2 and 8, he always got the sum of 10.

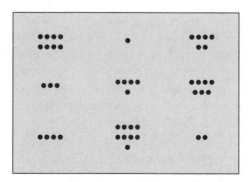

A Piece of Yu's Turtle Shell

Emperor Yu had the turtle taken back to his palace for further study as news of the mystical turtle began to spread to the nearby villages and eventually to other countries.

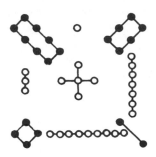

**Figure 46.** An ancient representation of the Lo-shu. Count the number of dots in each figure to form a 3×3 magic square. From John Lee Fults, *Magic Squares* (La Salle, Ill.: Open Court, 1974), fig. 1.2, p. 6.

The turtle spent the rest of its easy life in Yu's court, and it became the most famous turtle in the world, having had the company of famous mathematicians, kings, and international visitors. Soon the Lo-Shu, as the pattern was later called, began appearing on charms and magic stones as it does to this day. In these charms, the arrangements of dots is usually depicted as in figure 46, where the even numbers are represented with little filled circles, and the odd numbers with open circles. (Have you ever noticed that cruise ships often feature the Lo-shu on their main deck as a pattern for the game of shuffleboard?)

For centuries after their interpretation as magic squares, these squares were crucial elements of Chinese numerology, used in imperial rituals by necromancers casting spells, and as a the basis for prophecies and horoscopes. These kinds of squares were introduced into Europe sometime during the first millennium C.E. The first known writer on the subject was Emanuel Moschopoulus, a Greek who lived in Contantinople around 1300 C.E. He is believed to have discovered two methods for constructing magic squares.

I am most fascinated by the Lo-shu square because of its *ubiquity*. We find it venerated by civilizations of almost every period and continent. The Mayas of Central America held it in high esteem, and today it is used by the Hausa people of northwestern Nigeria as a calculating device with magical associations. The square was revered by the ancient Babylonians and even datasb back to a cosmic symbol in prehistoric cave-scratchings in northern France. In Islam, it symbolized the power of Allah spreading round the earth and returning to its source. Members of secret societies used it as a code frame, linking the cells containing particular numbers by straight lines that formed a symbol.[142]

Magic squares like these represented various objects in the solar system. Cornelius Agrippa (1486–1535)—physician, astrologer, and Catholic theologian—constructed squares of orders 3, 4, 5, 6, 7, 8, and 9, which he associated with the seven known (astrological) "planets": Saturn, Jupiter, Mars, the Sun, Venus, Mercury, and the Moon. Agrippa had a colorful life that included various dangerous run-ins with the church and jobs as a physician, occult scholar, lawyer, and military strategist. Agrippa's *De Occulta Philosophia* stimulated Renaissance study of magic and got his name into early Faust legends. He believed that a magic square containing a digit 1—which exhibits the magic constant of 1 in all directions—represented God's eternal perfection.

## God's Magic Square

Agrippa and colleagues considered the sad discovery that a 2×2 magic square could not be constructed as proof of the imperfection of the four elements: air, earth, fire, and water. Others believed that the nonexistence of a 2×2 magic square resulted from human's Original Sin.

Figure 47 shows a Jupiter amulet with a magic sum 34. If this configuration is engraved on a silver tablet during the time that the planet Jupiter is ruling, it is supposed to produce wealth, peace, and harmony.[143] Figure 48 shows a Mars amulet with magic sum 65. If engraved on an iron plate or a sword when the planet Mars is in the ruling position, this amulet is said to bring success in lawsuits and victory over the wearer's enemies.

The Arabs believed magic squares to have great powers in all aspects of life. Some squares were used to protect and help lame children. The Arabs even showed certain squares to women in labor and then placed them over their wombs to facilitate birth. In some regions of Turky and India, magic squares were also written or embroidered on the shirts of soldiers. According to Annemarie Schimmel, author of *The Mystery of Numbers*, people believed that such shirts had to be made by forty virgins in order to work![144]

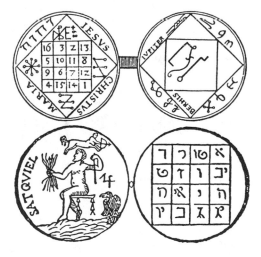

In Islam, the number 66 corresponds to the numerical value of the word *Allah*. Figure 49 is an Islamic magic square that expresses the number 66 in every direction when the letters are converted to numbers. The square's grid is formed by the letters in the word *Allah*. Magic squares such as this were quite common in the Islamic tradition, but did not likely reach the West until the fifteenth century.

Before proceeding, let us pause and reflect upon some of these early magic squares. Why is it that Chi-

**Figure 47.** Jupiter amulet with a magic sum 34. If this magic square is engraved on a silver tablet during the time the planet Jupiter is ruling, it is supposed to produce wealth, peace, and harmony. From Annemarie Schimmel, *The Mystery of Numbers* (New York: Oxford University Press, 1993), p. 31.

**Figure 48.** Mars amulet with magic sum of 65. From Annemarie Schimmel, *The Mystery of Numbers* (New York: Oxford University Press, 1993), p. 32.

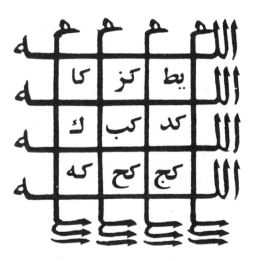

**Figure 49.** An Islamic magic square that expresses the number 66 in every direction. The grid is formed by the letters in the word Allah, whose numerical value is also 66 (19th century, Damascus). From Annemarie Schimmel, *The Mystery of Numbers* (New York: Oxford University Press, 1993), p. 261.

nese emperors and empresses, Babylonian astrologer-priests, prehistoric cave men in France, ancient Mayans of the Yucatan, and modern Hausa tribesmen were all convinced that the Lo-shu square held the secret of the universe? Could they have all learned of this number arrangement from a single primal source, or is it more likely they stumbled across it independently?

The omnipresence of the Lo-shu reinforces the idea that mathematics and mysticism have fascinated humanity since the dawn of civilization. Throughout history, number arrays were believed to hold certain powers that made it possible for mortals to seek help from spirits, perform witchcraft, and make prayers more potent. Numbers have been used for the purpose of predicting the end of the world, to raise the dead, to find love, and prepare for war. Even today, serious mathematicians sometimes resort to mystical or religious reasoning when attempting to convey the power of mathematics.

Has humanity's long-term fascination with mathematics arisen because the universe is constructed from a mathematical fabric? Certainly, the world, the universe, and nature can be reliably understood using mathematics. Nature *is* mathematics. The arrangement of seeds in a sunflower can be understood using Fibonacci numbers (1, 1, 2, 3, 5, 8, 13 . . .), named after the Italian merchant Leonardo Fibonacci of Pisa. Except for the first two numbers, every number in the sequence equals the sum of the two previous numbers. Sunflower heads, like other flowers, contain two families of interlaced spirals—one winding clockwise, the other counter clockwise. The number of seeds and pedals are almost always Fibonacci numbers.

The shape assumed by a delicate spider web suspended from fixed points, or the cross-section of sails bellying in the wind, is a catenary—a simple curve defined by a simple formula. Seashells, animal's horns, and the cochlea of the ear are logarithmic spirals which can be generated using a mathematical constant known as the golden ratio. Mountains and the branching patterns of blood vessels and plants are fractals, a class of shapes that exhibit similar structures at different magnifications. Einstein's $E = mc^2$ is a mathematical formula that defines the fundamental relationship between energy and matter. And a few simple constants—the gravitational constant, Planck's constant, and the speed of light—control the destiny of the universe.[145]

Today number arrays are still used in India and drawn on paper or engraved on metal. Some squares are even regarded as being the personification of God. As pointed out by Richard Webster in *Numerology Magic*, by constructing a magic square, the individual is thought to be communicating directly with the universe's "life-force," and, therefore, various wishes can be granted including the curing of piles, the alleviation of pain during childbirth, or the irritation of an enemy.[146] However, not all of the India "magic" squares are magic from a numerical point of view or contain magic sums. Consider the following square that a woman may use when searching for a husband. The numbers are drawn on a china plate with a crayon and then washed off the plate with water that the woman drinks:

| 24,762 | 24,768 | 24,771 | 25,320 |
|--------|--------|--------|--------|
| 24,770 | 24,758 | 24,763 | 25,341 |
| 24,759 | 24,773 | 24,766 | 25,325 |
| 24,767 | 24,761 | 24,760 | 25,344 |

Finding the Perfect Husband

Whenever possible, this number array should be written with a special ink known as *Ashat Gandh*. This is a mixture of several items, the most important of which is water from the Ganges river. I would be interested in hearing from readers who ascertain any significance in the use of these particular numbers.

The following 3×3 square (a version of the Lo-shu) is used in India to find missing people. Written when someone vanishes without a trace, the array is hung from a tree and is thought to draw the person back home. Other 3×3 squares are used to create harmony between a man and a woman. One such square should be drawn on a Wednesday or Friday, and both people should keep a copy with them.

| 6 | 7 | 2 |
|---|---|---|
| 1 | 5 | 9 |
| 8 | 2 | 3 |

Find Missing People

From a historical perspective, my favorite European magic square is Albrecht Dürer's, which is drawn in the upper right hand column of his etching *Melancholia I* (see figure 50). Dürer, one of the greatest German Renaissance artists, included a variety of small details in the etching that have confounded scholars for centuries. We seem to see the figure of a brooding genius sitting amid her uncompleted tasks. There are scattered tools, flowing sands in the glass, the magic square beneath the bell, the swaying balance. Scholars believe that the etching shows the insufficiency of human knowledge in attaining heavenly wisdom, or in penetrating the secrets of nature. As I noted earlier, Renaissance astrologers linked fourth-order magic squares to Jupiter, and these squares were believed to combat melancholy (which was Saturnian in origin). Perhaps this explains the square in Dürer's engraving.

Dürer's 4×4 magic square is represented as:

| 16 | 3 | 2 | 13 |
|----|----|----|----|
| 5 | 10 | 11 | 8 |
| 9 | 6 | 7 | 12 |
| 4 | 15 | 14 | 1 |

Dürer Magic Square

**Figure 50.** *Melencolia I*, by Albrecht Dürer (1514). This figure is usually considered the most complex of Dürer's works; the various symbolic nuances have confounded scholars for centuries. Why do think he placed a magic square in the upper right? Scholars believe that the etching shows the insufficiency of human knowledge in attaining heavenly wisdom, or in penetrating the secrets of nature. From Walter Strauss, *The Complete Engravings, Etchings, and Drypoints of Albrecht Dürer* (New York: Dover, 1972), fig. 79, p. 167.

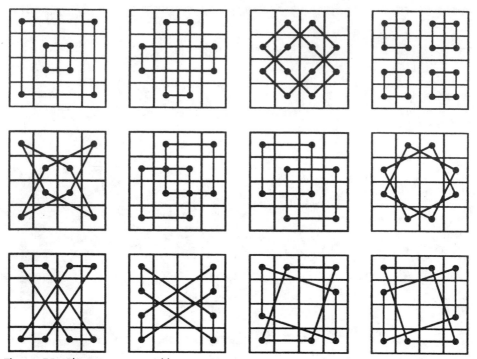

**Figure 51.** The Dürer square yields a magic sum in an amazing number of ways in addition to the traditional ways. The patterns, although reminiscent of the symmetries of certain crystals, tell us a good deal about the properties of this square. Try adding any of these cell configurations where connected dots represent numbers to be added.

The square contains the first sixteen numbers and has some fascinating properties. The two central numbers in the bottom row read "1514," the year Dürer made the etching. Scholars wonder if "1514" appeared accidentally or if Dürer constructed it intentionally. The rows, columns, and main diagonals sum to 34. In addition, 34 is the sum of the numbers of the corner squares $(16 + 13 + 4 + 1)$ and of the central 2×2 square $(10 + 11 + 6 + 7)$. The sum of the remaining numbers is $68 = 2 \times 34$. Figure 51 summarizes all the amazing "34" sums when adding other configurations of cells. Just sum the numbers connected by lines. For clarity, dots represent the numbers to be added.

## 📖 A Concise Catalog of Methods Using Numbers, Letters, and Mathematics

> *Mathematics, rightly viewed, possess not only truth, but supreme beauty—a beauty cold and austere, like that of sculpture.*
>
> —Bertrand Russell, "Mysticism and Logic"

(See the previous section for related methods involving books and papers.)

Ω **ARITHMANCY** (or **ARITHMOMANCY**) is an earlier form of **numerology** where divination is accomplished through numbers and the number value of letters. For example, the ancient Greeks examined the number of letters, and the numerical value of each letter, in each name of two combatants. The Greeks predicted the combatant having the name of the greater value would defeat the other.

Υ **AUTOMATIC WRITING** is handwriting produced without conscious control, sometimes for the purpose of forecasting the future or gaining secret knowledge. Some people believe that the content of the writing is supernaturally assisted.

People interested in the surrealist school of thought believed that automatic writing was a way of tapping the unconscious. Surrealists today still enjoy using the following approach to generate automatic writing. Try it yourself. (1) Sit at a table with pen and paper. Let your mind drift. (2) Start writing. Continue writing without thinking of what is appearing beneath your pen. Write fast. (3) If the flow of writing stops, leave a space and immediately begin again by writing down the first letter of the next sentence. Choose this letter at random before you begin. Here is an example of automatic writing by Bob Hartwig, president of a successful computer software company, who told me he has been fascinated by automatic writing for many years:

> Why must I love life so? Why can't I just fiddle with my soldering iron while the kids outside play? It's because I'm as cold as my desk, with the wonderful wood-grained texture popping out of my skin, uncontrolled, yet beautiful. The pen tip. The pen tip. That's where the wonderful magic spews forth, not as an inkwell, but as a vomit projectile. Oh man, what shall I think about in a few seconds? Why do I feel now so strong? Why do I trade eloquence for madness? Why do I? Because I am wonderful.[147]

To generate material, Bob simply relaxes with a pad of paper and pen. He wrote to me:

> I turned off my thoughts to the greatest extent possible, then wrote down words as they came to me, with no concern for neatness, grammar, or spelling. The snippet that I put on the web site was a small section of a much longer piece. Later, I corrected spelling and punctuation, but the words are original. Whenever I create, I receive pleasure. As an atheist and

materialist, I don't believe that automatic writing involves any supernatural, metaphysical, or divine forces. Thoughts, even out-of-the-ordinary thoughts that arise during creative moments, are by-products of our neural processes. What an amazing thought, that each of us has a little multi-billion-cell god living in our skulls.[148,149]

The surrealist movement in art and literature flourished in Europe between World Wars I and II. Surrealists were interested in uniting the conscious and unconscious so that fantasy would be joined to the everyday rational world. The surrealists saw the unconscious as the origin of the imagination. They saw genius as the ability to tap this realm using a variety of methods such as *frottage* (rubbing with graphite over wood or other grained materials) and *grattage* (scraping a canvas). These methods created abstract images, which were to be completed in the mind of the viewer. Automatic drawing was seen as a spontaneous, uncensored recording of chaotic images that burst into the artist's consciousness.

Several famous novelists say that they wrote in a semitrance state and attributed some of their works to automatic writing. For example, Harriet Beecher Stowe, author of *Uncle Tom's Cabin*, once said, "I didn't write it: It was given to me. It passed before me."

I have tried a similar approach by listening to music, turning the lights down low at night, and writing any unusual thoughts and images that come to me. The results can be strange and sometimes beautiful, and the method can yield novel images conducive to science fiction novels.

In China, automatic writing is performed with a sieve or basket with a short stick attached. The device, called a *Fu Chi*, is held over a bed of sand by two people who go into a trance. The stick begins to move in circles. Then the device begins to write characters. This approach also relates to **cleidomancy** (pendulum divination).

In the 1800s, the Swiss spirit medium Helene Smith said she "automatically" produced an entire written language to relate details of a Martian civilization (see figure 52). Subsequent study of this language revealed that it was similar to French and used the same syntax. Smith's native tongue was French.[150]

♍ **BIORHYTHMS** in the context of divination refer to a method for deriving how dates influence our lives. To study biorhythms, one must compute three cycles, represented as sinusoidal waveforms on paper. The cycles start on the day we are born, or one day after birth. The waveforms correspond to physical, emotional, and intellectual highs and lows. Although this is a

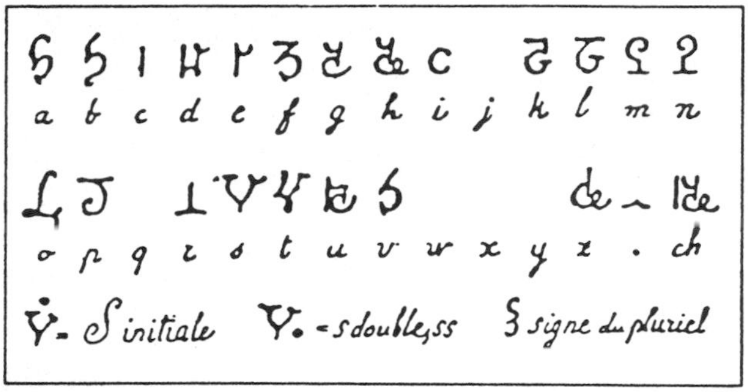

**Figure 52.** The "Martian Alphabet" developed by Swiss spirit medium Helene Smith during her automatic writing. From James Randi, *An Encyclopedia of Claims, Frauds, and Hoaxes of the Occult and Supernatural* (New York: St. Martin's Press, 1995), p. 22.

modern method of divination with a mathematical flavor, many scientists are skeptical that cycles could exist that are identical in every person and unvarying through a person's life.

♑ **FRACTOMANCY** is a computer-graphics method of divination. Fractomancy is based on the generation of fractal geometric patterns and interpreting the structures for divinatory methods.[151] Fractals are intricate patterns that exhibit details at many magnifications. A large number of fractals can be generated with simple mathematical formulas and often produce surprisingly stunning results (see figure 53).

♉ **GEMATRIA** is as system by which hidden meanings are discovered within words by assigning numbers to each letter in a word. The Jewish Kabbalists believe that the Old Testament was written in a secret code inspired by God. They use gematria as one of the chief means by which to decipher this code.

♑ **GRAPHOLOGY** is the analysis of human character through handwriting. The theory behind graphology is that handwriting expresses personality; therefore, a systematic analysis of the way words and letters are formed can reveal personally traits. As indicated in this book's introduction, certain employers seem to place too much emphasis on graphology when making hiring

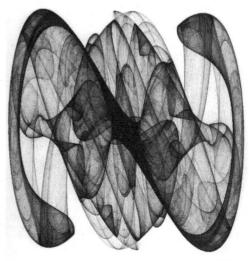

**Figure 53.** Fractal divination. Rendering by Clifford Pickover.

---

### Do-It-Yourself Fractomancy

Fractomancy requires the computer-graphical generation of a fractal pattern. Here's how it works. Ask a question. Have the computer choose four random numbers a, b, c, and d, or, alternatively, you can use sticks, dice, and stones in imaginative ways to create random numbers. Plot the strange attractor (intricate shape) using the following steps in a computer program:

```
x = 0.1; y = 0.1; /* starting point */
DO 10 Million Times
    xnew = sin(y*b) + c*sin(x*b)
    ynew = sin(x*a) + d*sin(y*a)
    x = xnew; y = ynew; PlotDotAt (x, y)
END
```

The values of a and b should be between –3 and 3, and the values of c and d should be between 0.5 and 1.5. To see the patterns unfold, use the rules and starting conditions, repeat the equations over and over again, stand back, and watch the visually exciting behavior evolve on the computer screen. Each new value of x and y determines the position of points on a plane. Figure 53 shows an example swirling pattern produced by these miraculous formulas.

If the resultant pattern is symmetrical, the outlook is positive and the answer to your question is "yes." The more beautiful to your eye, the better the answer or the stronger the "yes." If the pattern has no symmetry, or is ugly to the eye, the outlook is negative, and the answer is "no."

---

decisions.[152] Some companies won't hire a prospective employee if the person is rejected by a graphologist, although there have not been sufficient controlled studies to demonstrate that traits such as honesty and insight are reflected in handwriting.

♈ **GYROMANCY** is a divination procedure in which a person walks in a circle marked with letters of the alphabet until the person becomes dizzy and stumbles over letters, thus spelling out a prophesy.

♊ **LOGARITHMANCY** is divination by logarithms. This method is mentioned in Charles Mackay's 1852 book *Extraordinary Popular Delusions and the Madness of Crowds* but with no explanation. I would be interested in hearing from readers with more information. Logarithms are mathematical operations. In particular, the logarithm of a number $y$ with respect to a base $b$ is the exponent to which we have to raise $b$ to obtain $y$. Some simple examples for logarithms base 10 are: log 100 = 2, log 10 = 1, log 9 = 0.9542425, log 8 = 0.9030900, and log 7 = 0.8450980. You can use a computer, calculator, or table from a math book to calculate logarithms. One fun way to do divination with logarithms is to ask a question and then pick a number. Example: Will I marry Terrie? Pick a number, say 9. Look at the fourth digit to the right of the decimal point. If it is even, the answer is yes. If it is odd, the answer is no. In this case, the answer is yes because the fourth digit is 2. Another example: Will Nostradamus's DNA be used to create multiple clones that will serve as successive presidents of the United States in the twenty-second century? Pick a number, say 23. Calculate log 23 = 1.361728. The fourth digit to the right of the decimal point is 7, so the answer is no. Very prophetic.

Ω **NUMEROLOGY** is the numerical interpretation of numbers, dates, and letters to which numerical values have been assigned. "Number mysticism" uses supernatural insights into the nature of numbers to better understand the universe. Numerology is applied number mysticism. The practice dates back to the Greek mathematician Pythagoras who believed that the world was constructed by the power of numbers. Number interpretation was also important to the ancient Hebrews. In the Middle Ages, a numerical mysticism evolved from the teachings of Merkabah, a sect of Judaism. In the thirteenth century, the German Kabbalists developed gematria, a numerical interpretation of the Scriptures.

Skeptics suggest that many of the fantastic number relations found by numerologists happen by coincidence. For example, in 1983 Arthur Finnessy, author of *History Computed*, found that four of the first six U.S. presidents were inaugurated at age fifty-seven.[153] Finnessy then started searching through encyclopedias and found incredible numbers of 57s in history, especially surrounding the American Revolution. He concluded that there are too many 57s to occur by chance. But if this is so, what does that mean? Perhaps we can find instances of any numbers in history, if we look sufficiently hard. Alas, according to Underwood Dudley, a professor of mathematics at De Pauw University, the amazing string of 57s in history probably happens only by chance.[154] Fans of Robert Anton Wilson's *Cosmic Trigger I: Final Secret of the Illuminati* suggest that the number twenty-three occurs in history and science more often than one would expect by chance.[155]

Today, many numerologists use numbers to analyze and predict personality traits and describe the potential for compatibility between people. The "Do-It-Yourself Numerology" sidebar shows one method of modern numerology. In short, modern numerologists convert a person's name and birthday to a single number and then relate that number to the person's personality traits and future destiny. One true believer is Matthew Goodwin, a graduate of Massachusetts Institute of Technology. In his book *Numerology: The Complete Guide*, he writes:

## Do-It-Yourself Numerology

In one flavor of modern numerology, your name and birth date are converted to numbers and used to give insight into your fate.[157] Each resultant number represents a collection of talents, characteristics, and experiences. Only the single digits—1, 2, 3, 4, 5, 6, 7, 8, and 9—and the "master numbers" 11 and 22 are used. (The master numbers are the only numbers not reduced to a single digit.) Here are the steps needed to arrive at numbers, the meaning of which is in the accompanying table.

1. Determine the name on your birth certificate. Numerologist Matthew Goodwin says, "Whether your parents searched long and hard for your name or came upon it in a flash, the name came to your parents through universal wavelengths they probably didn't know existed." If you have a name in an alphabet using non-Roman letters, such as Russian, Japanese, Hebrew, or Greek, the transliterated name as written in the Roman alphabet will provide the same accurate numerology reading. If the name is hyphenated, eliminate the hyphen and use two separate names. (Step 3 shows mappings of letters to numbers.)

2. Learn how to reduce numbers by addition. For example, the reduced number for 35 is 8. You simply add the two digits to get the reduce number:

   ◆ 35 = 3 + 5 = **8**.
   ◆ 49 = 4 + 9 = 13. 13 is not a single digit or master number. Repeat the addition process. 13 = 1 + 3 = **4**.
   ◆ 38 = 3+8 = **11**. (If a master number—11 or 22—is reached, don't reduce it to a single digit.)
   ◆ 1953 = 1+9+5+3 = 18. 18 = 1+8 = **9**

   Your *soul number* or *self-image* comes from your day of birth. Reduce the day of the month to a single number by adding the digits together. Let's try it on Adolf Hitler who was born on April 20, 1889. His *soul number* is 0+2=2. (Do not reduce the 11th and 22d days, if they occur.) The *fate* or *life path number* is the digit obtained when you add day, month, and year together. Here are the number representations for each month: January (1), February (2), March (3), April (4), May (5), June (6), July (7), August (8), September (9), October (10=1+0=**1**), November (11), December (12=1+2=**3**). For Hitler's birthday, April 20, 1889, we get 5:

| April | 20 | 1889 | Life Path Number |
|-------|-----|-------|------------------|
| 4 | + 2 | + 8 = | 14 = 5 |

Notice that 1889 gets reduced to 1+8+8+9=26=8 *before* we add the month and day. This means that Hitler saw himself as a 5. The life path is the major lesson to be learned in life, the central focus of a person's existence. It is relatively fixed and unchanging. Numerologists tell us that if you accept your life path, it allows for growth and productive development. Look up 5 in the table of numerological meanings, and find that 5 stands for qualities like courageousness, passion, adventurousness, talent, constructive freedom, and sometimes thoughtlessness, distractability, and having wasted or misused talents. Do you think this fits Hitler? Martin Luther King (Michael Luther King) born January 15, 1929 had a life path of 1. Abraham Lincoln, born February 12, 1809, had a life path of 5, the same as Hitler. I wonder what relationship numerologists might find between Hitler and Lincoln?

3. The name number is calculated from your name. The name number or *expression* relates to your natural abilities and is derived from the sum of the number values of all the letters in each name, reducing this sum to a single digit or master number, then adding the sums of all the names together and reducing that total to a single digit or master number. Numbers are assigned to letters as follows:

| 1 | 2 | 3 | 4 | 5 | 6 | 7 | 8 | 9 |
|---|---|---|---|---|---|---|---|---|
| A | B | C | D | E | F | G | H | I |
| J | K | L | M | N | O | P | Q | R |
| S | T | U | V | W | X | Y | Z |   |

Let's try Adolf Hitler again. Adolf gives 1+4+6+3+6 = 20 = 2. Hitler gives 8+9+2+3+5+9 = 36 = 9. We sum the first and last names to get 11. Look up 11 in the table. I leave it as an exercise to the reader to make sense of "11" for Hitler's potential.

6. The *soul urge number* is a person's inner motivation: what he or she wants to be, to have, and to do. The number is computed by finding the sum of the number values of the vowels in each name, reducing this sum to a single digit or master number, then adding the sums of the names together and reducing that total to a single digit or master number. The *birthday number* yields a secondary lesson to be learned. The birthday number is derived by reducing the day of birth to a single digit or master number.

   Perhaps you would like to try this kind of numerology on yourself and see what results you get. I would be interested in hearing from readers. Why not try some of these methods on Stephen Hawking, Madonna, Albert Einstein, or Ophah Winfrey? I would be interested in hearing from readers. Here are some additional birth dates for you to try: 9/2/1964 Keanu Reeves (actor), 9/3/1965 Charlie Sheen (actor), 9/4/1918 Paul Harvey (radio personality), 9/9/1960 Hugh Grant (actor), 9/20/1934 Sophia Loren (actress), 9/21/1947 Stephen King (author).

Using numerology, you can discover a person's strengths and weaknesses, deep inner needs, emotional reactions, ways of dealing with others, talents. You can determine the best time to marry, change jobs, move, speculate, take a trip. Numerology, like the other occult fields, does not, at this time, allow for scientific explanation. I can only attest to the fact, confirmed by other numerologists, and their clients, of the consistent congruence between a person's numbers and that person's characteristics and life experiences.[156]

| | **Numerology Table** |
|---|---|
| Num | Numerological Meanings |
| 1 | You have both the will and ability to use personal powers and resources. You assert your identity. Other themes: Independence, resourcefulness, responsibleness. Attainment. Sometimes intolerance or stubbornness. |
| 2 | You are connected to emotions. Calmness, fairness, cooperativeness. Sometimes weakness, avoiding responsibilities. |
| 3 | You have the strong ability to quickly take creative, personal action. Expressiveness, strength, enthusiasm. Sometimes mood swings. |
| 4 | You are a practical person. You are methodical, taking one step at a time. Solid, loyal service to others. Sometimes conventional. |
| 5 | You have a strong body sense and learn from experience. Main themes: courageous, passionate, adventurous, talented. Constructive freedom. Sometimes thoughtless, distracted, wasted or misused talents. |
| 6 | You are good at abstract thinking and logic. You are smart with an active imagination. You have the ability to follow an ideal. Other themes: striving for harmony and beauty. Balance, responsibility, love. Sometimes impractical. |
| 7 | You set limits and endure through time. Analysis. Spiritual awareness. Wise, long-sighted. Sometimes self-righteous, resentful. |
| 8 | You have spirit and are interested in both material satisfaction and spiritual values. Practical, driven for success. Sometimes tactless. |
| 9 | You have the ability to recognize inborn traits, talents, obsessions, and compulsions. Selflessness. Intelligence, good advisor. Sometimes unable to concentrate. |
| 11 | Illumination. You must work to develop intuition, to tune into psychic forces. Inspire others by example. Spread your illumination for others to absorb. |
| 22 | Master Builder. Great power is available to you to produce on a significant scale, for the benefit of humanity. |

The modern style of numerology was started by L. Dow Balliett (1847–1929), an American woman in Atlantic City, New Jersey, who published several books on the subject at the turn of the century. Later, Dr. Julia Seton helped publicize the field. Other key figures in the history of modern numerology are Florence Campbell and Juno Jordan.

⌒ **ONOMANCY** is the study of the meaning of names, such as the name of a person or place. Often the spelling of a person's name, or distribution of vowels and consonants, is used to divine the person's future. The theory that there is a relationship between people's names and their fortunes may have originated among the Pythagoreans of ancient Greece.

As an example, let's consider onomancy applied to a person's name. If there is an even number of vowels, then there is something wrong with the person's left side. If the number of vowels is odd, this signifies an affliction in the right side. In combat between two people, the person having the name in which the letters added up to the greater sum was always picked to be the winner. See **arithmancy**.

♍ **ONOMANTICS** is the scientific application of **onomancy**. Specifically, the science that studies names in all their aspects is called *onomastics* (or *onomatology*). In the most precise terminology, a set of personal names is called *anthroponymy* and their study is called *anthroponomastics*. A set of place-names is called *toponymy*, and their study is called *toponomastics*. A set of uninhabited places (e.g., fields, small parts of forests) is called *microtoponymy*. A set of names of streets, roads, and the like is called *hodonymy*. A set of names of bodies of water is *hydronymy*. A set of names of mountains is *oronymy*. Another related term, *chrematonymy*, usually refers to the names of things. Different categories of names must frequently be studied together, because categories overlap. For instance, many place-names are derived from personal names (e.g., Lincoln), many names of planets and stars are derived from the names of mythological characters (e.g., Jupiter), and many personal names are derived from place-names (e.g., I have a friend named "Dakota" named after the state). There is also a division of names into primary and secondary ones. For example, Jupiter is primarily the name of a Roman god; transferred to the name of a planet, it is a secondary name.

♐ **PSYCHOGRAPHY** is a form of **automatic writing** having a divinatory nature. William Stainton Moses (1839–1892) wrote a book titled *Psychography* in which he described how spirits influenced his automatic writing and other movements at a table. Another display of psychography was exhibited by Maria Gaetena Agnesi (1718–1799), the famous Italian mathematician who was a habitual sleepwalker. Legend has it that while in a somnambulist state, she would rise from her bed, walk to her study, and complete problems which had baffled her in her waking state. In the morning, she was surprised to find elegant solutions to problems, as if written by a stranger. One of these developments was an equation of a famous curve now referred to as the "Witch of Agnesi."

The word *psychography* also has a nondivinatory meaning. An American writer, Gamaliel Bradford (1863–1932), called his new type of biographies "psychographies" because they focussed his subjects' inner lives and psychological states.

⌒ **RUNE DIVINATION** uses runes (ancient alphabets) to predict the future or answer questions. Each rune has a particular meaning, given in appendix 6. Today, stones marked with runes are often cast and the resulting runes studied.

## ⅄ THE TIBETAN CONNECTION

> *Laws of physics and mathematics are like a coordinate system that runs in only one dimension. Perhaps there is another dimension perpendicular to it, invisible to those laws of physics, describing the same things with different rules, and those rules are written in our hearts, in a deep place where we cannot go and read them except in our dreams.*
>
> —Neal Stephenson, *The Diamond Age*

☞ *Topics discussed*: my favorite methods of divination from Tibet. The emphasis of this section is on *Tra* and *Tring-ba*.

### Tra *in Tibet*

> *There is no excellent beauty that hath not some strangeness in the proportion.*
> —Francis Bacon

Tibet is often called "the roof of the world," occupying tall mountainous regions of Central Asia. Before the 1950s, Tibet was isolated from the rest of the world. What the West calls superstition has always been common in Tibet. For example, a traveler who encounters either a funeral procession, the source of running water, or a passerby carrying a pitcher of water is considered to have good luck in the immediate future. If a vulture or an owl perches on a rooftop, members of the household will experience death or misfortune. It is bad luck for newlyweds if snow falls during their marriage procession. On the other hand, a snowfall during a funeral is good luck for the surviving family members.

Divination is still popular today in Tibet and its neighbors in Sikkim (northeast India), Bhutan (a country in south-central Asia), Ladakh (northern India) and Nepal (a country between India and Tibet).[158] Tibetans travel long distances to consult a *mopa*, or diviner, regarding important questions in their lives. Lamas (religious teachers) and tulkus (reincarnated lamas such as the Dalai Lama) also perform many of the divination procedures.

Anyone could become a *mopa*, but this profession doesn't guarantee a good income. If a *mopa*'s predictions turned out to be inaccurate, he might be branded as sloppy or ineffective and therefore lose his clientele. For this reason, the professional diviners in Tibet often give nebulous readings so that possible errors will be minimized.

Divination by *tra*—the deciphering of signs and visions—is one of the most interesting divinatory arts in Tibet. Often, the diviner needs to acquire the talent from someone else who already has it. To induce visions, the diviner or *tra-pa* gazes into either a lake, small mirror made of metal, or shiny stone. Sometimes *tra* diviners fixate on the ball of the thumb after it is painted red and dipped in soft wax. The divination is done in the low light provided by a small butter lamp. A client asks a question and awaits visions that are induced by staring at the shiny thumb. The visions give insight into the question being asked.

*Tra* has been considered very influential to Tibetans. For example, *tra* was used to find the present incarnation of the Dalai Lama, the head of the dominant *Dge-lugs-pa* (Yellow Hat) order of Tibetan Buddhists and, until 1959, both spiritual and temporal ruler of Tibet. By staring into a holy lake, diviners saw a vision of a house with a blue roof, which eventually led them to the boy who became the Dalai Lama.

---

### Do-It-Yourself *Tring-ba*

This Tibet form of divination is my favorite because it is so easy to perform.[159] (It's also easy to implement in a computer program.) First, construct a string containing 108 beads. Ask a question. Relax your mind. Then, without looking, grab the string of beads in two places. This separates the 108 beads into two sections.

1. Continue counting the beads, four to the right, four to the left, and so on, until a number between one and four beads remain. Write down this number.
2. Repeat step 1 two more times to get three separate numbers.
3. You now have a sequence of three numbers between one and four. Here is how each number is interpreted:

   1—good luck, but not necessarily immediate good luck.
   2—bad luck, misfortune.
   3—whatever is happening, whether good or bad, will occur fast.
   4—moderately good luck, but with some minor problems.

For example: 1, 1, 1 would mean very good things are in store for you, whereas 2, 2, 3 is a very scary divination because it suggests there are grave consequences to your actions, and they will occur almost immediately.

### Do-It-Yourself *Mala*

In addition to Tibetan *tring-ba*, there are several other forms of divination that use beads. For example, *Mala* divination also uses a string of prayer beads.[160]

1. Ask a question, then grab the beads, each hand grasping a bead chosen at random.
2. Count the beads between your hands by threes from both sides to the middle, until there is a remainder of three, two, or one. Do this three times.
3. Interpret the results as follows. The first answer relates to the project in question. The second answer relates to the environment. The third answer describes the arrival of travelers. Here is the simple interpretations:

> *Falcon:* One bead left. Support.
> *Raven:* Two beads left. Hostility.
> *Snow Lion:* Three beads left. Slow but stable progress.

In yet another Tibetan method of bead divination, you count the beads twice and each time note the remainder of beads, which is one, two, or three beads. Here are the interpretations.

| Remaining Beads, First Trial | Remaining Beads, Second Trial | Interpretation |
|---|---|---|
| ● | ● | Favorable outcome. |
| ● ● | ● ● | Clouds come. Loss of wealth. |
| ● ● ● | ● ● ● | Good prosperity. |
| ● | ● ● ● | Plants grow in sand. Widows find husbands. Poor get rich. |
| ● ● | ● | Wishes are fulfilled. You escape from danger. |
| ● ● ● | ● | God's help is coming. Worship god. |
| ● ● ● | ● ● | Average results. Legal trouble. |
| ● ● | ● ● ● | Fountains appear and water the ground. Unexpected food and escape from danger. |
| ● | ● ● | Bad omen, illness. Worship the gods and appease the demons to prevent problems. |

According to Buddhist belief, an individual of extraordinary destiny is distinguished by certain physical traits or marks (*laksanas*). In the case of Gautama Buddha, soothsayers were able to recognize the signs at his birth, although all did not fully appear until he achieved enlightenment. (The *usnisa*, or slight protuberance on the top of the skull, was visible only after he became a buddha). The signs have frequently been depicted in representations of the Buddha.

The Tibetans also have performed *Dahmo* divination in which arrows are pushed into a pile of barley. The diviner interprets the movement of the arrows as they fall according to traditional texts.

My favorite form of Tibetan divination is *Tring-ba* because it can be so easily performed. All you need is a rosary of 108 beads. By asking a question, and grabbing the beads in two places, it is possible to count the separated beads to find answers to life's questions (see "Do-It-Yourself *Tring-ba*"). As with most divination methods, this divination method may be helpful because the act of asking questions and looking for patterns can sometimes bring subconscious answers to the surface. Still, it startles me to learn that some Tibetans perceive these methods to be very accurate and have used the methods for generations with perceived success.[161]

Other Tibetan methods of divination include *Sho-mo* divination (throwing dice), *mar-me-tag-pa* (divination by observing the shape of flames from a butter lamp), *bya-rog-kyi-tag-pa* (divination by observing bird calls and birds in flight, especially crows), and divination and prophecy through the utterances of oracles, who are Tibetan men or women that usually led normal married lives. A "butter lamp" has a rolled cotton wick in a small container of clarified butter or oil.

## ♈ THE FLAMES OF GOD

> *God is a fire, and we are all tiny flames; and when we die, those tiny flames go back in to the fire of God.*
> —Anne Rice, *Tale of the Body Thief*

☞ *Topics discussed*: a number of unusual divination methods that range from the use of fire to the study of winds in order to predict the future. Many of the fire methods are very similar but are cataloged here for completeness.

## 📖 *A Concise Catalog of Methods Using Fire*

> *To be a warrior is to learn to be genuine in every moment of your life.*
> —Chogyam Trungpa, *Crazy Wisdom*

♊ **CAPNOMANCY** is divination by studying smoke rising from burning poppy seeds, leaves, or wood. For example, the ancient Babylonians observed smoke from burning cedar branches The Druids may have divined the future by observing the smoke from burning humans or animals, dead or alive. For example, if the smoke stayed near the altar or the ground, it was a sign that plans should be changed. Modern New Englanders practice a form of capnomancy by observing smoke from chimneys. It is a bad omen, and bad weather is coming, if the smoke hovers around the chimney and roof. See also **dendormancy** and **libanomancy**.

♏ **CAUSIMOMANCY** is divination from observing the behavior of objects placed in a fire. The future is bright and the answer is yes if the object burns quickly. It the object burns slowly or smolders, the response is negative. The resulting ashes are also sometimes used to foretell the future.

♉ **DENDROMANCY** is divination with either oak or mistletoe. The Druids burned oak and mistletoe and observed the resulting smoke patterns. See **capnomancy**.

♈ **EMPYROMANCY** is divination by interpreting the smoke from burning laurel leaves. The practice dates back to ancient Greece. See also **dappnomancy** in the section "A Concise Catalog of Methods Using Sounds."

♉ **HALOMANCY** is a branch of **pyromancy** that involves throwing salt into fire. The color, speed, and direction of the resultant flames suggest different courses of action. *Halomancy* is also divination by interpreting patterns of salt after it is poured or tossed to the ground. Because halomancy probably dates back to ancient Egypt, the salt was in the form of large pebblelike crystals rather than today's tiny-sized table salt crystals. See also **pessomancy**, **alomancy**, and **botanomancy**.

♈ **LIBANOMANCY** is the study of incense and its smoke. For example, Babylonians threw cedar shavings on an incense burner and observed the direction and the configurations taken by the smoke. According to the Babylonians, if the smoke flows to the east, you will prevail over your enemy. Libanomancy was the poor man's substitute for the costly procedure of **haruspicy**. See also **capnomancy**.

♋ **LYNCHOMANCY** is divination using the wick of a burning candle. See **lampadomancy** and **pyromancy**.

♊ **PYROMANCY** and **PYROSCOPY** are forms of divination by fire or flame, often assisted by substances thrown onto the flames. For example, pyromancy was often used in the ancient practice of **extispicy**. The future was good when the flame quickly consumed the sacrifice without much smoke. It was also favorable if the flames were transparent and burning quietly in a pyramidal form. However, if the fire was difficult to start, if the wind disturbed it, or if it consumed the victim slowly, the future was bleak. Aside from using fires, burning animals, and humans, people divined by observing torch flames or by throwing powdered pitch into fires. If the pitch caught slowly, the omen was bad.

The ancients also interpreted the fine points of flame shape. The future was good if the torch flame formed one point but bad if it formed two. Three points were better than one.

♈ **SIDEROMANCY** is divination by observing patterns in straws being burnt with a hot iron. This practice was popular in ancient Rome. The dancing motions of the sticks of straw were studied to foretell the future.

♍ **SPODOMANCY** is divination using cinders or soot. In some applications, the diviner reads ashes and cinders left by sacrificial fires. In other applications, the spodmancer first places a message on paper, sets the paper afire, and then examines the smoke and flames. See **pyromancy**.

♋ **TEPHRAMANCY** is divination by observing ashes obtained from burning tree bark. In modern times, tephramancy starts out like **sycomancy** where the querent writes down questions on pieces of paper. Unlike sycomnacy, the next step is to burn the paper and then looks in the patterns of ashes for answers. Some of the ancient tephramancers studied the ashes of sacrificed humans and animals.)

♏ **ZOANTHROPY** is divination by observing the flames of three lighted candles placed at the corners of a triangle. (In an apparently unrelated use of the word, zoanthropy is a mental disorder in which one believes oneself to be an animal.)

## 📖 A Concise Catalog of Methods Using Wind and Air

> *Just in terms of allocation of time resources, religion is not very efficient. There's a lot more I could be doing on Sunday morning.*
> —Bill Gates, Microsoft chairman

♌ **AEROMANCY** is divination by observing atmospheric phenomena such as thunder, lighting, clouds shapes, comets, and storms. For example, a comet observed in the sky was once thought to foretell the death of a great person. The appearance of the star of Bethlehem when Christ was born might be considered a form of aeromancy. Aeromancy is also practiced by tossing seeds into the air. The future is divined by observing the seed patterns on the ground.

↗ **ANEMOSOMACNY** (from the Greek *anemos* for wind) is divination by observing specific characteristics of the wind. On the first day of the first month of the year, the Chinese anemosomancer studies the winds to foretell the fate of crops, wars, health, and other events for the coming year. In particular, for an entire day, the anemosomancer studies the wind's directions, strength, and intensity. He then listens to the composite sound made by the noise of any surrounding people and determines the pitch of the sound on a musical scale. Based on all these details, the anemosomancer is able to make predictions about harvests, wars, and future weather conditions.

)( **AUSTROMANCY**, like **anemosomancy**, is divination by studying wind direction and intensity. In ancient Tibet and China, austromancers listened to seashells held to the ear. By interpreting the sounds, the austromancer foretold the future. Donald Tyson, author of *Scrying for Beginners*, writes:

> If you listen to the seashell, and allow it to lull your mind into a receptive state, soon you will begin to make out fragments of distant conversation. . . . As this ghostly garden becomes clearer, mentally try to break into the conversation. If you are fortunate and have an innate skill for this type of scrying, you may find that one or more of the voices will respond to your mental comments and engage you in conversation.[162]

)( **CERAUNOSCOPY** draws omens from the study of thunder and lightning and other examinations of the air.

♋ **ERAOMANCY** is divination using the air. The Persians devised this method of divination in which they breathed over a vase filled with water. Bubbles in the water meant that the objects of their desire would come to them.

)( **FENG-CHIAO** is an ancient Chinese divinatory art that assigns meaning to eight different directions of the wind. The *Feng-chiao* diviner studies the wind, noting the direction from which it blows, its time of origin, intensity and characteristic, and then the diviner tries to relate the observations to past experiences and foretell future events. As with **anemosomacny**, the diviner also observes the tones produced by crowds of people or birds whose composite sounds may have a particular pitch. The combination of wind and sounds gives further insight into the future.

Those *Feng-chiao* practitioners seeking a scientific underpinning for their craft suggest that the relative humidity affects the transmission of sound waves according to their frequencies.[163] The higher the humidity the greater the transmission. For example, acoustical engineers from the University of California at Los Angeles conducted a series of studies in a concert hall to examine this phenomena. They found that at 15 percent relative humidity, a 4,000 Hz tone lasts 2.5 seconds, while under conditions of higher humidity the same tone lasts 4.5 seconds. They also determined that a higher frequency tone of 10,000 Hz in low humidity was absorbed seven times faster than a low frequency 1,500 Hz tone. The British Navy conducted similar tests with fog horns, noting that when humidity dropped from 77 percent to 71 percent the distance at which the fog horn could be heard dropped by almost two miles. Humidity, in turn, affects the behavior of birds, other animals, and humans.[164]

♍ **WIND DIVINATION** is a common term used to refer to many of the methods described in this section.

## 📖 *A Concise Catalog of Methods Using Food and Drink*

> *When you are born, you are given the key to the gates of heaven. Unfortunately, the same key opens the gates of hell.*
>
> —Unknown ancient Buddhist,
> and Physicist Richard Feynman's favorite quote

♊ **ALEUROMANCY** is divination using cakes and "fortune cookies." Answers to questions are rolled into balls of dough. Once baked, people choose the balls at random and read the answers. This approach seems to have been the ancestor of the Chinese fortune cookie. Several cultures have practiced variants of this method. The Greeks put messages into round, hard cakes to be chosen at random. Europeans placed silver coins in cakes. The person who gets the cake with the coin has good luck—unless he or she swallows the coin.

♍ **ALOMANCY** is divination using table salt. See **halomancy**.

♎ **ALPHITOMANCY** uses special cakes that are digestible by persons with a clear conscience but are unpleasant to others. In the past, barley was given to people suspected of crimes. Whoever got sick from eating the barley was guilty. This practice gave rise to a popular oath: "If I am deceiving you, may this piece of bread choke me." Eventually the practice was used to test the faithfulness of a spouse.

The ancient Romans had priests practiced another form of alphitomancy. On certain days of the year young women would enter the woods carrying cakes made of barley and honey. Supposedly a serpent consumed the cakes of the innocent women, but declined the cakes of the guilty.

♈ **TASSEOGRAPHY** (or **TASSEOMANCY**) refer to the reading of tea leaves that remain in a tea cup once the beverage has been drunk. Tasseomancy originated in ancient China and in the European Middle Ages.

Tea leaves that remain in the bottom of a cup form patterns that the diviner interprets (see "Do-It-Yourself Tasseography"). Snakelike shapes indicate falsehood. A spade indicates good fortune. A mountain indicates a journey or obstacle. Straight lines indicate careful planning and peace. Bird-like shapes indicate good news. The timing of events is a function of the distance of the leaves to the rim. Leaves closer to the rim represent the immediate future, while those at the cup's bottom indicate the far future. The handle represents the home or environment of the questioner. Tea leaves close to the handle indicate a closely occurring event. Eighteenth-century

---

### Do-It-Yourself Tasseography

1. Find an undecorated white cup with wide rim and slanting sides.
2. Pour the tea into the cup. Drink the tea, but leave some at the bottom of the cup.
3. Form a question in your mind. Grasp the cup handle with your left hand and slowly move the cup from left to right, three times, distributing the leaves.
4. Recall the positional rules:

   —Leaves closer to the rim represent the immediate future.
   —Leaves at the cup's bottom indicate the far future.
   —Tea leaves close to the handle indicate an event in the home or immediate environment.

5. Examine the leaf patterns. Leaves in the shape of numbers may indicate a time. Letters can stand for people's names. Stars or triangles mean good fortune. Dots mean journeys. Ladders or wheels mean advancement. Circles mean success and squares mean protection. Clear shapes suggest good luck; vague shapes, indecision and obstacles; a bear, misfortune; a cage, marriage proposal; fruit, ambitions attained; spider, secretness; and a key, enlightenment.

Italians may have invented the related form of divination that uses coffee grounds. Coffee ground reading became popular in countries that drank strong coffee instead of tea and remains popular in modern-day Iran.

Tasseography prophecies were sometimes said to come from demons, so the diviners recited incantations during their practices to increase the accuracy of the reading. See also *SKONIOMANCY*.

♈ **TIROMANCY** (or **TYROMANCY**) is divination through the observation of cheese. The shape, number of holes, the pattern of mold, and other characteristics were used to foretell the future. Various shapes in the cheese might indicate love, money, or even death. Tiromancy reached its height in the Middle Ages.

## 📖 *A Concise Catalog of Methods Using Other Liquids*

> *Consider the true picture. Think of myriads of tiny bubbles, very sparsely scattered, rising through a vast black sea. We rule some of the bubbles. Of the waters we know nothing . . .*
> —Larry Niven and Jerry Pournelle, *The Mote in God's Eye*

♎ **BLETONOMANCY** (or **BLETONISM**) is divination by observing the currents of streams and rivers.

♌ **CEROSCOPY** (or **CEROMANCY**, **CEREMANCY**) are forms of fortune telling in which melted wax is poured into cold water and the resultant wax configurations are interpreted. For example, the wax might resemble a letter of the alphabet corresponding to a person whose name begins with that letter. This approach was popular in the Middle Ages and also in sixteenth-century Spain. The method continues to be used in Mexico, Puerto Rico, and Hati. See also **skoniomancy**.

♓ **HYDROMANCY** is divination by observing water and by studying the color, ebb and flow, or ripples produced by pebbles dropped in a pool. Sometimes other objects were thrown into water or suspended on a string over the water. The Jesuit M. A. Del Rio (1551–1608) described several methods of hydromancy. In one method, a ring is lowered into a pot of water by a string. The pot is shaken, and the number of times the ring strikes the side of the pot gives information about the future. Pausanias, the second-century Greek traveler, described a fountain into which people threw bread loaves. If the gods accepted the loaves, the loaves sank in the water, which meant good fortune; otherwise, bad luck was ahead. Several very sad hydromancy stories have been reported over the years. For example, ancient Germans sometimes threw newborn children into the Rhine river. If the baby was illegitimate, it would drown. Sometimes hydromancers dropped oil into water and observed the resultant patterns. Hydromancers also watched the whirls and courses of rivers to divine the future.

♌ **LECANOMANCY** (or **LECONOMANCY**) is divination by the sound or movement made when an object is tossed into a basin of water. Ancient Babylonians often mixed oil with water and observed the resultant patterns. As an example, if the oil divides into two regions it signifies that two camps will advance against each other in battle or that a sick man will die. Variants of lecanomancy are considered a branch of **crystalomancy**. Sometimes, the lecanomancer throws objects into a pot of water and interprets the resultant water images and sounds. Other lecanomancers study patterns of light reflected from a knife blade onto the water. Lecanomancy was also practiced by the ancient Assyrians.

♊ **MOLYBDOMANCY** draws mystic inferences from the hissing of molten lead. Sometimes molten tin is used and dripped into water. The resultant shapes are also interpreted. This method of divination was popular in ancient Greece. In the 1500s, molybdomancers dropped molten metal into water to discover witches.

♉ **OINOMANCY** (or **OENOMANCY**) is divination by studying the color, consistency, and taste of wine. In one implementation of this method, an animal skull is boiled in wine. The future is divined by observing the bones. For example, in thirteenth-century Europe, skulls were boiled in red wine. The oinomancer foretold the future by observing the cracks in the skull that were made more apparent by the red wine. See also **cephalomancy**.

♍ **ONIMANCY** (or **ONYCOMANCY**) is divination using oil. In one variant, the onimancer seeks a manifestation of the angel Uriel after walnut oil and tallow is placed on the fingernails of an "unpolluted" boy or a young virgin. The child must repeat the seventy-two verses of the Psalms, at which point visions would appear to the child and onimancer. (Sometimes authors confused the word onycomancy with **onychomancy**, which is the interpretation of spots on human nails.) In other variants, the onimancer mixes olive oil in the palm while considering a question. A coin is placed on the palm. The direction in which the coin moves indicates the answers to the question. The term onimancy can also apply to observations of oil patterns on water.

♎ **PEGOMANCY** is divination using spring water and bubbling fountains. Pegomancy is a branch of *hydromancy* (divination by water) and also associated with *crystalomancy* or crystal gazing (or *scrying*). Pegomancers stare into water as if it were a crystal ball to obtain visions of the future. They sometimes drop stones into water and interpret the rings that result. Pegomancy was popular in ancient Greece.

♋ **RIVER ORDEAL** refers to the ancient mideastern form of divination by which the guilt or innocence of an accused person was left to the verdict of the river. If the person sank, he was guilty; if he floated he was acquitted.

♌ **SKONIOMANCY** (after the Greek *skoni* for powder) is divination by tossing powered herbs onto water and reading the shapes. This divination method is practiced in Uganda where the skoniomancer would sometimes "see" tiny fishlike spirits moving among the shapes. Other diviners pour a few drops of clarifying liquid into pots of muddy water and read the shapes in the clearing water. An unbroken star shape means good fortune is ahead. Irregular and broken shapes signify bad luck.[165]

## 📖 *A Concise Catalog of Methods Using Sounds*

> *When the creatures moved, I heard the sound of their wings, like the roar of rushing waters, like the voice of the almighty, like the tumult of an army.*
> —Ezekiel 1:24

♈ **BRIDGE DIVINATION** (or **HASHI-URA**) is a Japanese form of divination that requires the questioner to listen to the conversations of pedestrians going back and forth on a bridge. Their conversations are regarded as a divine oracle. One predicts either good or bad fortune according to words spoken by pedestrians.

♋ **CHRESMOMANCY** is divination through the interpretation of chance encounters with sounds. Chresmomancy was popular during the Roman Empire. Some chresmomancers carefully listened to what mentally ill people said in order to divine the future. See also **gelomancy**, **austromancy**, and **anemosomancy**.

♎ **CLAIRAUDIENCE** is "clear hearing" of divinatory information. Parapsychologists generally regard this as a form of extrasensory perception. One form of clairaudeince is the ability to hear voices and messages from the dead.

♐ **CLEDONOMANCY** is divination by observing words spoken spontaneously when people meet. Often this takes the form of observing the initial words of a conversation and then predicting what remarks will follow.

♑ **CROSSROADS DIVINATION** (or **TSUIJI-URA**) is an ancient form of divination referred to in Japanese poems in the eight-century anthology *Manyoshu*. The *Manyoshu* (*Collection of Ten Thousand Leaves*) is the oldest anthology of poetry in Japan.

The Japanese word "tsuji-ura" comes from "tsuji," which means "roadside," and "ura," which means divination. Originally it meant divining the future by signs that one encounters by chance. One form of tsuji-ura was called "kushi-ura" (from "kushi" meaning comb). Using this method, the querent brings a wooden comb to the center of a crossroad and then chants a song three times, sprinkles some rice on the ground in the intersection to create a divination region, twangs the comb's teeth three times, then waits for the first person to walk on the rice. The person's words foretell the future. See **bridge divination**.

♓ **DAPHNOMANCY** is divination by listening to laurel branches crackling in an open fire. Numerous crackling sounds mean good luck. Bad luck is signified by quiet fires or fires that produce smoke that does not rise but stays close to the ground.

♊ **EVENING DIVINATION** is an old Shinto (Japanese) form of divination in which the questioner goes to town in the evening to listen to the conversations of pedestrians. The diviner learns about his fortune by their conversations, which are regarded as a divine oracle. See also the related **bridge divination** and **feng-chiao**.

♌ **GASTROMANCY** is an ancient form of ventriloquism whereby the voice is lowered to produce a mysterious tone, and prophetic utterances are delivered in a trance state. Sometimes seers would "hear" voices emanate from a person's belly and answer questions. This was often just a fraudulent form of ventriloquism. This form of divination was popular in the United States in the late 1800s through early 1900s.

♈ **Gelomancy** (or **Geloscomancy**, **Geloscopy**) is divination from the tone of someone's laughter.

♊ **Harp Divination** (or **Koto-Ura**) is a Japanese method performed at the Ise shrine (in southern Honshu, Japan, on the Ise Bay of the Pacific Ocean) to determine the ceremonial purity of the priests taking part in the ceremonies. Today's Ise Shrine consists of the Inner and Outer shrines, about four miles (six km) apart. According to tradition, the Inner Shrine was built in 4 B.C.E.

In particular, harp divination is form of ancient divination that involves playing a harp wildly to invoke gods and spirits (see figure 54). (There were eight million gods in the ancient, pre-Buddhist Japanese religion.) Later the method changed to pounding the harp's base board.

♉ **Transatuaumancy** is divination through chance remarks overheard in a crowd. The method was popular in ancient Egypt and Rome. For example, if a transatuaumancer was out in public and overheard someone say, "The bird is dying," this could indicate the death of someone relevant to the transatuaumancer. "This is drought" could indicate a woman's infertility or a money loss. Today, several divination approaches require the seeker to listen to the random conversation overhead in crowds (see figure 55).

In Tibet, diviners practice a form of transatuaumancy with a bone. First, the diviner ties a piece of juniper to the bone using a piece of white wool. Next, the Tibetan transatuaumancer places the bone in his left pocket, asks a question, and walks out of his dwelling place. The first words he hears answer the question on his mind. In ancient Israel, the chance word acted as an omen and was recognized as having a special significance. For example, when Jonathan, son of the biblical Saul, was trying to

**Figure 54.** Harp divination. From Filippo Bonanni, *Antique Musical Instruments and Their Players* (New York: Dover, 1964), fig. 66.

**Figure 55.** Transatuamancy, like several related divination methods, requires the seeker of knowledge to listen to chance remarks overheard in crowds. From Jim Kalett, *People and Crowds* (New York: Dover, 1964), fig. 77.

decide whether to attack the Philistines, he said, "We will cross over. If they say, 'Stay where you are,' we will stay. If they say, 'Come up,' we will attack. We will take it as an omen that Yahweh has put them into our hands" (1 Samuel 14:9).

## 📖 A Concise Catalog of Methods Using Vision, Lights, and Shiny Things

> *I do not recommend using plastic for scrying. It is neither a natural material nor an earth material. Its occult associates are all wrong.*
> —Donald Tyson, *Scrying for Beginners*

⌒ **CATOPTROMANCY** (or **CAPTROMANCY**, **ENOPTROMANCY**) is an early form of crystal gazing (**crystallomancy**) that uses a light source reflected in a shiny surface, for example, a mirror turned to the moon to reflect moonlight. In one embodiment of this method, a sick person would look in a mirror held by a string above water. If the person's face appeared healthy, the person would recover. If not, difficult health problems lay ahead. The early Christians suspended a glass over a water well and studied patterns reflected on the glass from inside the well. The Old Testament Book of Exodus referred to a breastplate of judgment worn by the high priest Aaron, brother of Moses. Some biblical scholars suggest that the breastplate was used to determine guilt or innocence by the way light reflected off the shiny metal and inset stones. Catoptromancy is a form of **scrying**. See also **crystallomancy**.

♏ **CLAIRVOYANCE** is "clear seeing" of divinatory information. Parapsychologists generally regard this as a form of extrasensory perception. Clairvoyance is the general term that encompasses all ways in which a psychic divines the future and secret knowledge.

♎ **CRYSTALLOMANCY** (or **CRYSTALOMANCY**) is divination through crystal gazing. This form of divination is based on a seer looking into a crystal ball or some similar object to tell the future. Crystalomancy was practiced as far back as 1000 B.C.E. These days, consultation is usually performed in a darkened room with a light source reflecting in the crystal ball. John Dee, astrologer to Queen Elizabeth I of England, used a crystal ball when advising the queen. (Some sources extend the meaning of *crystallomancy* to include the ancient divination practice of casting lots using small stones or crystals.[166])

♉ **ENOPTROMANCY** is an ancient divination method of foretelling the future health of a person. In particular, the enoptromancer uses a shiny surface, like a mirror, placed in water. By looking at the mirror, the enoptromancer determines if a sick person will recover or die. See also **catoptromancy**.

♊ **KATOPTROMANCY** is divination with mirrors. See **catoptromancy**.

♏ **KERIOMANCY** (after the Greek *keri* or candle; also called "candle prophecy" or **lampadomancy**) is divination by interpreting visions using the flame of a candle. The approach dates back to Old Testament times. See sidebar for some modern methods. See also **lampadomancy**, **lynchomancy**, and **pyromancy**.

♓ **LAMPADOMANCY** is divination using lights, oil lamps, or torches. The lampadomancer predicts the future by observing the flames' color, shape, and movement. A flame with a single point is good luck. Two points mean

---

**Do-It-Yourself Keriomancy or Lampadomancy**

Keriomancy and lampadomancy are divination methods that usually use candles. There are many modern books that teach you how to divine the future by interpreting candle flames.[167]

1. Meditate on a question. Light a candle in a darkened room.
2. If the flame burns brightly, the answer is yes.
3. If the flame burns slowly or goes out, the answer is no, or there will be a negative result.
4. If the candle goes out after it burns brightly, there is danger ahead. The answer is no.

You can also perform the popular three-candle divination. Light three candles. If one candle burns more brightly than the others, the answer is yes, and the future is bright. A candle with a very bright sparkle at the flame tip is a lucky omen. If the flames move from side to side, a change or journey is suggested. If only one flame moves from side to side, and the others are still, you will do something alone, for example, travel or work alone. If only one candle goes out, an obstacle will approach. Be careful. If one of the flames spirals and twists, difficulties are ahead, including false friends and unknown enemies.

---

bad luck. A bent flame indicates illness. Sparks suggest forthcoming news. If the flame suddenly goes out, disaster is ahead. Lampadomancy was practiced by the ancient Egyptians and Greeks. Modern day Tibetans practice *mar-me-tag-pa*—divination by observing the shape of flames from a butter lamp. See **keriomancy**.

)( **SCRYING** (or **CRYSTAL GAZING**) is a general term for divination using crystals, mirrors, bowls of water, ink, blood, flames, or other shiny objects to induce visions. Scrying comes from the English word "descry" which means "to reveal." People use scrying to divine the future and to find lost objects or people. In the Middle Ages, particular individuals became known as specially adept scyers. One approach uses a cauldron whose interior is painted black. The cauldron is filled with water on a moonlit night and a shiny coin dropped into the water to reflect moonlight. The shiny coin is used to stimulate visions. Some biblical scholars suggest that Joseph was scrying when he interpreted the Pharaoh's dream using a silver cup filled with liquid in Genesis 44:15.

A crystal ball is the most well-known scrying tool, but other devices have been employed. Nostradamus used a bowl of water set upon a brass tripod. Jeane Dixon, the late American psychic, used a crystal ball, while other clairvoyants have used black obsidian mirrors, crystal skulls, and even light bulbs.

Although visual images are usually scried, practitioners have also scried scents, sounds, sensations, and flavors. The sounds of seashells, waterfalls, and the winds have also been used for scrying. Some authors have suggested that scrying is not divination because divination usually requires established rules.[168] Scrying does not have many rules and seems to rely more on the subconscious mind and perhaps even "autohypnosis."

As in **onychomancy**, the ancient Babylonians used a preadolescent boy for scrying. First the scryer dropped oil on the boy's forehead and thumbnail. The shiny nail became a kind of magic mirror in which the scryer saw spirits. Here is one ancient description of the preparation:

> Take a young lad and make a circle in the earth with a knife, and prepare the nail of the right thumb until it becomes thin, and take four smooth stones and put them in the four rows of the circle, and put the mentioned knife in the middle of the circle and place the lad into it before the pillar of the sun and anoint his nail and his forehead with pure olive oil, and the lad shall look well at his nail, and thou shalt whisper into his ear this spell: "True God, at his wrath the earth trembleth, and the nations are not able to abide his indignation; the right hand of the Lord doeth valiantly, the right hand of the Lord is exalted [Psalms 118:15–6], I adjure you, princes of the nail, for the sake of the sea and for the sake of the three lights that are in the universe, that you should bring the king of Mimon in this nail, and the queen shall come with him, and that his two servants shall come and that they shall bring there two lambs. . . . And when thou wilt desire that they shall go away, the lad shall take off the oil from his nail and from his forehead.[169]

Incidentally, the boy comes to no harm.

Another version of Babylonian oil scrying involved the use of oil mixed with soot to make a black paste that was smeared upon the palm of the hand. The scryer would sit within a circle drawn on the earth together with a boy or a girl less than nine years old, and the scyer would anoint the left hand of each of them with olive oil and soot. He would warn them that they should not look outside the anointed place.

Donald Tyson, author of *Scrying for Beginners*, suggests many possibilities for what scryers see in a crystal ball:

> If you scry for visions [with a crystal ball], sooner or later you are going to achieve communications with spirits. It does not matter what you conceive these spirits to be. You may think they are mere personifications of your own unconscious thought processes. You may try to dismiss them as illusions, or regard them as the souls of dead human beings, or alien life forms

---

**Do-It-Yourself Crystal Gazing**

1. Type "crystal balls" into any Internet search engine.
2. Take out your credit card and purchase a ball.
3. When the ball arrives, place it against a dark background. Many scryers dim the lights in the room. Some scry by candlelight.
4. Focus your gaze upon the center of a crystal ball rather than on its surface. Donald Tyson, author of *Scrying for Beginners*, says, "Try to look through the crystal as though it were merely a window upon the astral world. Probably the first thing you will see after concentrating your vision at the center of the crystal for several minutes is shifting gray clouds that billow and roll like thunderheads."[172]
5. After some time, images may slip into your visual field. Let them drift. These may be useful for divining the future.
6. If no visions appear, beginners may wish to focus their attention on some small object in the room, then close their eyes and "mentally attempt to transfer the image of the object into the crystal, to be observed when the eyes are reopened."[173] Then go back to step 5.

---

dwelling in another dimension. Probably all of these descriptions are wrong. . . . Spirits have no power to physically cause you harm. However, if they are malicious, they can intrude upon your awareness with frightening faces in the crystal, and may cause you to have bad dreams.[170]

Tyson also suggests it is useful to try to form an emotional attachment to the crystal ball:

> A highly effective and ancient way to activate the crystal [ball] is to treat it as a living thing. Think of it as a spirit child. Each day, feed it with fresh milk, which you should allow to flow over its surface while you hold it in your hand over a bowl or the sink. . . . Talk to it in a loving an intimate manner. Kiss it affectionately. Whisper your secrets to it. Make up a personal name for it. Store you crystal amid fresh flowers and pleasing scents. Take it into your bed at night and warm it with your body while you lie asleep.[171]

## 📖 *A Concise Catalog of Methods Using Things That Swing, Slide, and Swirl*

> *At his direction they swirl around over the face of the whole earth to do whatever he commands them.*
>
> —Job 37:12

♌ **CLIDOMANCY** (or **CLEIDOMANCY**) is divination by observing the swinging of a pendulum. It is also divination using a dangling key. Often, the name of a criminal suspect is written on a key that is hung on a Bible. The clidmonacer then hangs the Bible on a virgin's ring finger. The direction in which the swaying book turns determines the fate of the person in question. Innocence or guilt may also be determined by whether the book remains moving or stationary. Especially horrifying were extended methods that required the impression of the key to be found on the person, otherwise the victim lost an eye. Clidomancy was popular in the Middle Ages. See **radiesthesia**.

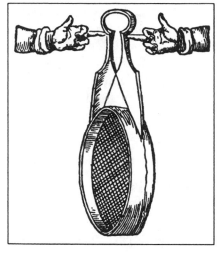

**Figure 56.** In *coscinomancy*, a sieve is held by shears. This illustration is from *Opera Omnia* by Cornelisu Agrippa (1560). From James Randi, *An Encyclopedia of Claims, Frauds, and Hoaxes of the Occult and Supernatural* (New York: St. Martin's Press, 1995), p. 79.

♊ **COSCINOMANCY** is divination using a hanging sieve. The sieve is used with a pair of scissors or tongs to determine innocence or guilt. In particular, the sieve is supported by scissors or tongs that two people hold by their thumbnails. Sometimes the sieve hangs by a thread. The direction of the sieve's spin, and the person pointed to by the handle, determines who is the guilty party. Coscinomancy was a big hit in Old Testament biblical times. Figure 56 shows an ancient illustration of the practice.

Reginald Scot, in his book *The Discouerie of Witchcraft* (1584), describes coscinomancy, which was also used in ancient Greece to find a criminal:

> Stick a pair of Sheers in the rind [rim] of a Sieve, and let two persons set the top of each of their Forefingers upon the upper part of the Sheers, holding it with the Sieve up from the ground steadily, and ask Peter and Paul whether A, B, or C, hath stolen the thing lost, and at the nomination of the guilty person, the Sieve will turn round.

See **radiesthesia**.

♏ **CYCLOMANCY** is the practice of divination using a turning wheel. Some speculate that the use of a revolving wheel was the origin of the roulette wheel.

♐ **DACTYLOMANCY** (or **DACTYOMANCY**, **DACTYLIOMANCY**) is an early form of **radiesthesia** using a dangling ring that points to letters that spell out answers to questions. Dactylomancers have also used a tripodlike tool that moves on a board with letters, much like today's Ouija board. Dactylomacny was popular among some of the ancient Greek psychics around 50 B.C.E. (Some authors use the terms "dactyomancy" and "dactyliomancy" for divination procedures that use the ring, and "dactylomancy" to refer to use of the tripod.) In 540 B.C.E., Greek mathematician Pythagoras used dactyomancy, with a ring, to acquire revelations. Dactyomancy was described by the Ammianus Marcellinus (330–395 C.E.), the last major Roman historian, whose work described the history of the later Roman Empire to 378. He described the use of a ring suspended by a thread over a table containing letters of the alphabet.

♌ **DOWSING** is a divination method that use a forked stick to locate water, precious minerals, lost treasure, or even missing people. Other implements may also be used for dowsing, including wire coat hangers, "divining" rods, and various pendula. The dowser holds the simple device which is supposed to turn in the direction of whatever the dowser is searching for. Dowsing dates back about seven thousand years and was practiced by the Egyptians and Chinese. Cave paintings in the Sahara have shown people holding divining rods. During the Middle Ages dowsing was used extensively in Europe to discover coal and water. During the reign of Queen Elizabeth I, German miners came to England and used birch rods. Some modern dowsers, such as Paul Sevigny, President of the American Association of Dowsers, suggest they can even predict the gender of babies in the womb. Others claim that they can hold a pendulum over the mother's stomach, and if it swings in a circular fashion, the baby will be a boy. If it swings back and forth, a girl will be born.

Dowsing has evolved in many different cultures. According to a Melonesian folk tale, the dowsing rod moves because a ghost is directing the rod. Certain African tribes use dowsing sticks to name thieves or find treasures. In 1556, Georgius Agricola published the first detailed description of dowsing as a method of locating minerals (see figure 57). Dowsers also tried to locate gold during the gold rush in early California. Today some dowsers try to find diseases in the body.

Many articles in the *Skeptical Inquirer* have called into question the accuracy of dowsing.[174] All dowsing methods use a system that is a very unstable equilibrium, so that the tendency is for the handheld object to whip up or down. Movements of the dowsing sticks appear to be caused by the dowser's own involuntary arm and muscle movements.

James Randi, author of *Flim Flam*, conducted and observed tests of

**Figure 57.** Georgius Agricola (1490–1555), German scholar and scientist known as "the father of mineralogy," was the first to include a detailed description of dowsing as a method of locating minerals in *De Re Metallica*, published in 1556. Shown here is a plate from his book depicting sixteenth-century dowsers searching for metal. From Georgius Agricola, *De Re Metallica* (New York: Dover, 1950), p. 40.

dowers attempting to find objects or water flowing though pipes. He finds the dowsers are always 100 percent successful (and their instruments responsive) when the dowsers know in advance where the object or water is, but obtain only chance results when they do not know ahead of time the location of the object or water.[175] See **rhabdomancy**.

↗ **KOLLOMANCY** (after the Greek *kollo* meaning glue or *kollodis* meaning sticky) is a divination method used by the Azande in Africa. An *Iwa*, or rubbing board, is coated with viscous plant sap. The kollomancer moistens a lid and moves it back and forth on the small board while asking a question. If the lid slides smoothly, the answer is yes. If the lid sticks, the answer is no. If the lid behaves in both ways, there is some secret that invalidates the question. The *Iwa* can be carried in the pocket and used to resolve a personal problem on the spot. The *Iwa* is sometimes called a "pocket oracle."

♏ **KOUPAOMANCY** (after the Greek *koupa* for bowl) refers to a broad class of divination methods using bowls, usually filled with water, or baskets. For example, African tribes place seeds or pieces of wood in a bowl filled with water. The movements of the objects are used to divine the course of a person's illness. Sometimes two people hold a bowl of water between their fingers and go into a light trance while saying people's names. When the name of the guilty party is said, the bowl twists and falls. The Ndembu, an African tribe, have diviners that fill baskets with twenty to thirty objects and then shake the basket to see what objects come to the top. This basket shaking is often performed for a sick person seeking to better understand his or her condition.

♌ **RHABDOMANCY** is divination using a stick or wand. Some of these methods might also be classified as **dowsing** and were forerunners of the divining rod. The practice seems to have originated with the Chaldeans and Scythians and spread to the Germanic tribes. The rhabdomancers cut pieces of bark from fruit trees, carved characters on them, and threw them at random on a white cloth. Next, they prayed, looked upward at the sky, picked up three strips, and read their meanings from the symbols previously scored on them. The Hebrews employed similar methods and divined the future by seeing how rods fell. Ancient Greek and Roman rhabdomancers also used rods or wands to locate underground springs and precious metals.

♈ **RADIESTHESIA** is the general term for divining with a rod or pendulum. Other forms include "table tipping," the Ouija board, **automatic writing**, and **scrying**. Radiesthesia is sometimes considered an advanced branch of **dowsing**. This method is used to discover hidden water, metals, minerals and objects. Radiesthesia, or *radiesthesie* as it is known in France, has been also used in attempts to discover missing persons and in making medical diagnoses. In the related method of radionics, a psychic sometimes holds his or her hands above the patient and interprets the "vibrations" coming from the body. Some practitioners use radionic instruments with calibrated dials to provide treatments.

♐ **STICKY ORACLE**, see **kollomania**.

📖 *A Concise Catalog of Methods Using the Land*

> *You have said that the land is a dream for you—and that you fear to be made mad. But madness is not the only danger in dreams. There is also the danger that something may be lost which can never be regained.*
>
> S. R. Donaldson, *Lord Foul's Bane*

🔯 **AMMOSOMANCY** (after the Greek *ammos* for sand) is divination using sand. More specifically, this form of divination involves studying the shapes that sand makes when poured onto a horizontal mirror. Paula Knowlton, a modern ammosomancer from Oklahoma, wrote me the following: "I went to local hobby shop and bought some colored sand. Next, I obtained a flat mirror and a seashell. The querent dips the shell into their choice of colored sand, closes his or her eyes, and spreads the sand. Finally, I look for shapes in the sand and make prognostications regarding the future."[176]

♏ **FENG-SHUI**, or locational geomancy, is concerned with finding the best site for human constructions such as of buildings and tombs. For example, practitioners believe that improperly placed buildings can cause misfortune to the occupants or neighbors. *Feng-shui* is a form of *geomancy* and sometimes makes use of an elaborate universal compass, the *Lo P'an*, to determine the optimum flow of *ch'i*, or positive energy, for any particular building. The geomancer may suggest a site that has a good relationship between hills, open spaces, and water. The compass is used to suggest lucky and unlucky directions and times.

Feng-shui (translated as "wind" and "water") is believed to date back to the Han dynasty (206 B.C.E.–220 C.E.) and is quite popular today in interior design. If a building is erected on a site not in harmony with the surrounding *ch'i*, and the building can't be relocated, sometimes a strategically placed mirror, plant, light, bush, or wind chime can be used to help achieve a balance. Ideally, homes should face south to encourage family harmony. North is associated with commercial success, west with children's fame, and east with a happy family life. Mountains whose outlines resemble dragons and evenly flowing water have good *feng-shui*. Roads or rivers that follow straight lines have bad *feng-shui*.

🔯 **GEOMANCY** comes in at least two flavors. One form is the study of figures on the ground and is called oracular geomancy. The other form is concerned with the influence of the Earth's "currents" and is called locational geomancy or *Feng-shui*. One form of oracular geomancy relied on sixteen

## Do-It-Yourself Oracular Geomancy

Oracular geomancy originally involved making marks on the ground and interpreting the patterns. The precise method has evolved from centuries' old traditions. Here is the recipe.[177]

1. Ask a question. (For this example, we will ask if you should try to write a novel.)
2. Find a stick and some loose ground. (Alternatively, use pencil and paper.)
3. Divide the ground or paper into sixteen horizontal strips.
4. Make a random number of marks or dots in each row.
5. The information is compacted (i.e., condensed) by counting the number of marks in each row. If the number is even, make two dots by the side. If odd, make one dot. For example:

| Sample Random Dot Patterns | Compaction |
|---|---|
| ● ● ● ● ● ● | 6 ● ● |
| ● ● ● ● ● | 5 ● |
| ● ● ● | 3 ● |
| ● ● ● ● ● | 5 ● |
| ● ● ● ● ● ● ● | 7 ● |
| ● | 1 ● |
| ● ● | 2 ● ● |
| ● ● ● | 3 ● |
| ● ● ● ● ● | 5 ● |
| ● ● ● ● ● ● ● | 7 ● |
| ● ● ● ● | 4 ● ● |
| ● ● ● ● ● ● | 6 ● ● |
| ● ● ● | 3 ● |
| ● ● ● ● | 4 ● ● |
| ● ● ● ● ● ● | 6 ● ● |
| ● ● ● ● ● ● ● ● | 8 ● ● |

6. The next step is to make four "Mother" patterns from the compaction patterns.

| Mothers | | | |
|---|---|---|---|
| 4 | 3 | 2 | 1 |
| ● | ● | ● | ● ● |
| ● ● | ● | ● | ● |
| ● ● | ● ● | ● ● | ● |
| ● ● | ● ● | ● | ● |
| Laetitia | Fortuna Minor | Puer | Caput Draconis |

Each group of four dots in the compaction patterns make up a Mother. In our example, starting at the top and working our way to the bottom, we obtain the following Mothers. The first Mother is on the right

7. Next make Daughters from the Mothers. The first daughter is made form the first row of points in each Mother, going right to left. The second Daughter is made from the second row of points, and so forth.

| Daughters | | | |
|:---:|:---:|:---:|:---:|
| 8 | 7 | 6 | 5 |
| Fortuna Minor | Laetitia | Cauda Draconis | Caput Draconis |

8. Next create Nephews from Mothers and Daughters. Create the first Nephew by adding the corresponding points from the first two Mothers. If the total is odd, make one point. If even, make two points. The second nephew is created from the third and fourth Mothers. The third Nephew is created form the first two Daughters. The fourth Nephew is created from the last two Daughters.

| Nephews | | | |
|:---:|:---:|:---:|:---:|
| 4 | 3 | 2 | 1 |
| Rubeus | Carcer | Rubeus | Amisso |

You have just created a Geomantic Household with Mothers, Daughters and Nephews.

9. Next combine the Nephews in the same way as we combined the Mothers and Daughters to form the Nephews. This produces two Witnesses. For example, the dot in first row of Amisso and the two dots in the first row of Rubeus sum to 3, which gives us 1 dot in the first witness because 3 is an odd number.

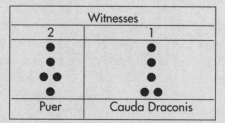

| Witnesses | |
|:---:|:---:|
| 2 | 1 |
| Puer | Cauda Draconis |

10. Combine the two witnesses to produce the Judge. The Judge is the final summary, the answer to your question but with influences of the two Witnesses. If you have trouble understanding the Judge, you can produce a Reconciler by adding the Judge to the First Mother. This will give you another perspective on the problem. There's no need to create a Reconciler if the meaning of the Judge is clear to you.

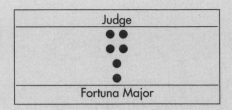

Finally, we look up the Fortuna Major in the interpretation chart (see p. 205) and find a positive, successful sign, especially for solitary endeavors. This means you should write a novel. Incidentally, the Nigerian *Ifa* divination has many similarities with the approach just described. In *Ifa*, the sixteen signs are called *Odu*. The sixteen signs are generated using nuts held in the hand. The signs are combined in such a way to create 256 variations. In the Yoruba *Ifa* oracle, sixteen cowry shells or palm nuts symbolize sixteen sectors of the world.

symbols that were originally produced by making random marks on the ground. The first firm evidence of this method was Arabic "sand science," or ilm al-raml, from 800 C.E. After the Arab conquest of North Africa, the sand science evolved into a different approach called Ifa or Fon divination in Nigeria and Vintanna or Sikidy divination in Madagascar.

⊙ **P'UNGSUCHIRISOL** (translated as "theory of wind, water, and land") is a Korean form of geomancy, a belief that the land and landscape can influence people's lives in mysterious ways. *P'ungsuchirisol* derives from the Chinese art of *Feng-shui* ("wind-water"). Perhaps people noticed that certain locations were prone to floods, earthquakes, and storms, thereby giving credence to the idea that the land was a vital force in people's lives. According to *p'ungsuchirisol*, a good site for graves is land next to mountains of many different sizes. Important people will be born in locations resembling a chicken sitting on a nest.

## Interpretation of the Geomantic Signs

| | |
|---|---|
| **Populus**: Democracy, a crowd, news, gossip, an assembly of important people. A positive or negative sign. | **Laetitia**: joy, happiness, beauty, balance, health, peace. A very positive sign. |
| **Via**: Path, journey, wandering, successful voyages for solitary people. A positive or negative sign. | **Tristitia**: sadness, poverty, death, stubbornness, but a good sign for pregnancy. Usually a very negative sign. |
| **Carcer**: Prison, confinement, bondage, protection, lies, resistance. A negative or positive sign. | **Albus**: beauty, wisdom, profit, clear thinking, fairness. A positive sign. |
| **Conjunctio**: Union and marriage, reunion, contracts, hope. A positive sign that brings friends. | **Rubeus**: passions, temper, anger, stimulation, compulsion. A negative sign suggesting you cease your actions. |
| **Fortuna Major**: Great fortune, victory, fertility. The most positive sign. | **Puella**: pure, clean, a girl, but sometimes rotten inside, false friends. A positive sign but a warning of deception. |
| **Fortuna Minor**: Lesser fortune. A positive sign, especially for solitary endeavors. | **Puer**: young man, inconsiderate, aggressive, unknown enemy. A negative sign unless it relates to romance or battle. |
| **Acquistito**: Acquiring, gaining, profiting, rise to power, healing. A very positive sign. | **Caput Draconis**: Fate, marrying into a group, crossing thresholds, spiritual development. A positive sign. |
| **Amiksso**: Losing, failing, illness, theft, deception, dispersion. A negative sign, unless you are already captive, in which case this sign indicates escape. | **Cauda Draconis**: calamity, fraud, illusion, danger. A negative sign suggesting you change directions. |

# 2.

## Mind, Myth, Mystery

*Our normal waking consciousness is but one special type of consciousness, whilst all about it, parted from it by the filmiest of screens, there lie potential forms of consciousness entirely different. No account of the universe in its totality can be final which leaves these other forms of consciousness quite disregarded. They may determine attitudes though they cannot furnish formulas, and open a region though they fail to give a map.*
— William James, *The Varieties of Religious Experience*

As mentioned in the previous chapter, divination is not confined to ancient cultures. In fact, divination is part of the everyday experience of numerous cultures from Tibet to the Cameron. This very brief chapter is a smorgasbord of historical curiosities involving divination, from the ancient roots of divination and its cultures, myths, and mysteries all the way up to the present. Here you will learn more about divination's important role in past cultures such as in Greece and Rome. I also discuss the role of divining dwarfs in the Middle Ages, premonitions of the sinking of the *Titanic*, the role of divination in ancient Israel, the nature of time, and current antidivination laws in North Carolina.

## ᛃ CAESAR AND DIVINATION

*However we may rationalize the development of entrail reading, we cannot actually prove that it did not, in some strange way, predict future events as its practitioners fervently believed. At the very least, we should keep an open mind towards*

**207**

*any available evidence of accurate prediction, even if, as with extispicy, we may find the actual method deeply repugnant.*

—Damon Wilson, *The Mammoth Book*
*of Nostradamus and Other Prophets*

Divination was as commonplace in the past as is golfing or going to the mall today. Some of you may recall from your high school history class, or Shakespeare's *Julius Caesar*, the soothsayer warning the celebrated Roman leader, Julius Caesar, to "beware the Ides of March." The "Ides" correspond to dates on the Roman calendar, which, in March, fell on the 15 of the month. While Caesar was walking through the streets, a soothsayer warned him that something bad would happen in the middle of March, but Caesar dismisses this warning:

| | |
|---|---|
| *Soothsayer.* | Caesar! |
| *Caesar.* | Ha! who calls? |
| *Casca.* | Bid every noise be still: peace yet again! |
| *Caesar.* | Who is it in the press that calls on me? I hear a tongue shriller than all the music Cry "Caesar!" Speak. Caesar is turned to hear. |
| *Soothsayer.* | Beware the ides of March. |
| *Caesar.* | What man is that? |
| *Brutus.* | A soothsayer bids you beware the ides of March. |
| *Caesar.* | Set him before me; let me see his face. |
| *Cassius.* | Fellow, come from the throng; look upon Caesar. |
| *Caesar.* | What say'st thou to me now? Speak once again. |
| *Soothsayer.* | Beware the ides of March. |
| *Caesar.* | He is a dreamer. Let us leave him. Pass.[1] |

In 44 B.C.E., on March 15, Caesar was assassinated by a group of nobles in the Senate House. He was stabbed twenty-three times and fell at the foot of Pompey's statue. William Shakespeare's rendition is grounded in fact because there actually was a soothsayer, Vestricius Spurinnia,[2] who gave Caesar the warning about the Ides of March after studying patterns in a goat's liver. Spurinnia was an upper-class patrician and high priest, greatly respected in Rome. As a haruspex (Latin: *haruga*, a victim; *specere*, to inspect), he was probably admired during his life.

Picture this image in your mind. It is a cool March 14 morning, 44 B.C.E. Despite your growing apprehension, you watch Spurinnia as he slits the throat of a goat. (Apollo, god of light and prophecy, is said to favor goats over other animals that haruspexes sometimes used, like geese, sheep, and pigs.)

Spurinnia waits until the goat is dead before slitting the belly. He places the creature, belly-up, on a slab of stone. You watch the temple servants as they hold the legs while Spurinnia slices the carcass from genitals to ribs with a special knife. Next he reaches into the hot cavity, severs the digestive and other systems from their anchoring to the body, and then carefully arranges the smelly mess on the stone slab. His servants take away the eviscerated carcass as Spurrina looks at the liver and intestines—the two organs of most importance in divination. The great Roman statesman, scholar, and writer Marcus Tullius Cicero (106–43 B.C.E.) would recall "that there was no head to the liver of the sacrifice. These portents were sent by the immortal gods to Caesar that he might foresee his death."[3]

Today, veterinarians refer to the liver "head" as the *processus pyramidalis*. The head is pointed and makes up about 15 percent of the liver's volume. Goats and other animals can live quite well without this part of the liver. There are many possible reasons why Caesar refused to consider the liver's warning. He needed to show strength at all costs and thought that on March 15 the Senate would proclaim him the first king of Rome in 466 years. Perhaps Caesar suspected Spurinna was bribed to give a negative entrail reading.

According to historical records, on the night before Caesar went to the Senate, his wife supposedly had a dream that he would be murdered, but Caesar seemed to be in good spirits. On the morning of March 15, Caesar actually met Vestricius Spurinnia while enroute to the Senate House. "Well, Spurinnia," Caesar called, "the Ides of March are come!" Spurinnia replied, "Yes, Caesar, 'come' but not yet gone."[4]

Spurinnia and other haruspexes of his time not only looked at the liver's shape but also the color: a healthy red shade was good. Each section of the liver, to which they gave such names as the "gate" and the "table," had particular meanings. Some areas were connected with specific regions of the sky, which linked the art of gut reading to astrology. As we discussed, sometimes the haruspex would sacrifice several animals to obtain a comprehensive reading.

For centuries, the liver was thought of as the seat of emotion, and perhaps this is why the Romans and others placed such a high premium on liver structure. For example, the ancient Babylonians considered organs the seat of emotions and mental faculties in general. They believed the heart to be the seat of the intellect, the liver of emotions, the stomach of cunning, the uterus of compassion, and the ears and the eyes of attention. Other societies believed that the soul resided in the liver, and even in Shakespeare's day there were various allusions to the liver's powers. Consider for example

Shakespeare's comedy *Love's Labours Lost*, performed in 1594. In the story, four young men, dedicated to study and the renunciation of women, meet four young women and inevitably abandon their absurd principles. Biron, a lord attending Ferdinand, the King of Vavarre, remarks, "This is the liver-vein, which makes flesh deity. A green goose a goddess: pure, pure idolatry. God amend us, God amend! we are much out o' the way."[5]

Although the small intestine of animals looks like a chaotic jungle of snaking tubes, when it is stretched out it actually forms a double spiral. Starting at the base of the stomach, the intestine begins to spiral one way, and later in its course it spirals the other. Perhaps this apparent order in a seemingly complex shape also made the intestine of interest to the ancient diviners.

## ⟘ HOW GUTS CHANGED HISTORY

> *Moses also took all the fat around the inner parts, the covering of the liver, and both kidneys and their fat, and burned it on the altar.*
>
> —Leviticus 8:16

We've already discussed how soothsayers have altered the course of history, and I would like to explore this idea here. Imagine if there had never been soothsayers. There's a good chance that you wouldn't be here. Our geopolitical world would be very different, and our religions would have crumbled to dust. For example, consider Nicaias (d. 413 B.C.E., Sicily), the Athenian politician and general during the Peloponnesian War (431–404 B.C.E.) between Sparta and Athens. He was in charge of the Athenian forces engaged in the siege of Syracuse, Sicily. The failure of the siege contributed greatly to the ultimate defeat of Athens. And it was all because of a soothsayer. Instead of withdrawing from Syracuse when he should have, Nicias accepted his soothsayers' advice to delay setting out. The Syracusans soon forced the surrender of the Athenian forces, including Nicias, whom they executed.

Soothsayers influenced the outcomes of many other wars such as the Punic war between Rome and Carthage and between Greece and Persia. When Alexander the Great was heading to Babylon, a rumor came that his own Macedonian people had performed an entrail reading and discovered horrible portents. Alexander was fairly religious and often did his own entrail readings. He delayed his entry into Babylon in order to avoid the bad omens, and he soon caught a fever (or was poisoned). On June 13, 323, he died in his thirty-third year; he had reigned for twelve years and eight months. His body, diverted to Egypt by Ptolemy, the later king, was eventually placed in a golden coffin in Alexandria. No one knows how history would have changed had Alexander not delayed.

The Athenian general Xenophon had a force of ten thousand Greek soldiers being hunted by the Persians. The Greeks needed food before passing through the Straits of Hellespont to Greece. Before they set out, Xenophon ordered an entrail reading, which proved to be unfavorable, so Xenophon did not move his men. The next day, there was another reading, also unfavorable. On the third day, all the food was gone. The haruspices had run out of sheep to sacrifice, so they cut open the important baggage oxen. Finally, on the fourth day, the ox guts were favorable in appearance, and a Greek ship with food unexpectedly arrived. Xenophanes gave the order to fight.

The Persians were unprepared for this sudden change of attitude by the Greeks, thinking the Greeks were too worn out to fight. Xenophon finally got his army safely back to Greece. At every major decision point on the 1,500-mile march, Xenophon made a sacrifice and had the haruspices read the entrails.

In Roman conflicts, divination has also changed the course of history. For example, Ariovistus, a German soldier of fortune, gave up one attack on the Romans because diviners suggested that nothing should be done until the moon was full.

Soothsayers played a large role in Greek and Roman mythology, reinforcing the idea that divination was a useful practice. For example, who can forget the renowned Calchas in Greek mythology, the son of Thestor (a priest of Apollo) and the most famous Greek soothsayer during the Trojan War? Calchas foretold the duration of the siege of Troy, demanded the sacrifice of Iphigeneia, daughter of Agamemnon (king of Mycenae), and suggested the construction of the wooden horse with which the Greeks finally took Troy. Legend had it that Calchas would die when he met his superior in divination; the prophecy was fulfilled when Calchas met Mopsus after the war while in Italy. Beaten in a trial of soothsaying, Calchas killed himself. They sure took divination seriously in those days.

In pre-Exilic Israel (before 586 B.C.E.), prophetic guilds were a social group as important as the priests. The book of Isaiah includes the *navi'* and the *qosem* ("diviner" and "soothsayer") among the leaders of Israelite society. Divination in the pre-Exilic period was not foreign to Israelite religion.

In a real sense, the earliest counterparts of today's Central Intelligence Agency were the early soothsayers, such as the Delphic oracle, who claimed to be able to communicate with the cryptic gods to predict the future. However, the soothsayers reports were sometimes ambiguous and often ignored by the decision makers, just like intelligence is in Washington, D.C., today.

There are numerous instances where haruspicy seems to have yielded correct predictions, but perhaps there are just as many instances when the readings were false and not recorded for us to study. The whole idea of gut reading seems pretty bizarre, doesn't it? But perhaps equally unnerving is the idea of offering sacrifices to the gods. Perhaps by understanding why they made sacrifices, we can better understand why they looked at guts. Today it seems outlandish that a god would be made happier by cutting a goat's throat, but animal sacrifice has been found in the earliest known forms of worship and in all parts of the world. Early societies believed that the killing of an animal is the means by which its hallowed life is set free and thus made available to the deity.

The ancient Greeks sacrificed black animals to the deities of the underworld; swift horses to the sun god Helios; pregnant pigs to the earth mother Demeter; and the dog, guardian of the dead, to Hecate, goddess of darkness. The Syrian gods liked fish as much as mammals, so the Syrians sacrificed fish to certain gods and ate the consecrated offering in a communion meal with the deity, sharing in the divine power. Bulls, boars, and rams were sacrificed by several groups through history. I would be curious to hear from readers who know of instances in which carnivores (such as lions), primates (such as chimpanzees), or very large animals (such as hippos or elephants) were sacrificed to the gods or had their entrails read.

〜〜〜   〜〜〜   〜〜〜

Around 100 B.C.E., the Celtic Druid priests of Britain often ritually sacrificed humans and sometimes read their entrails. The most astonishing sacrifices involved giant baskets of twigs that were filled with people who were burned alive in the baskets. The Druids offered human sacrifices for those who were sick or preparing for battle.

Human sacrifice was widespread in the Americas and had various goals such as communing with god and enhancing the ground's fertility. Human sacrifice was adopted by agricultural rather than by hunting or pastoral peoples. Fourteenth-century inhabitants of Mexico believed that the sun needed human nourishment and sacrificed twenty thousand victims each year.

Not all sacrifice rituals required blood to be spilled. For example, the ancient Greeks, Indians, Celts, and Mayans performed sacrifices by drowning women. Sometimes the horrors of human sacrifice overwhelm me. The Norse threw people over cliffs. The Aztecs tied people up and shot them with bows and arrows. Peruvians strangled women, and ancient Chinese often buried the King's friends with him when he died. I'm happy to report that, in many societies, people eventually substituted clay, dough, or wooden models for actual humans.

Today, the high priests of Afro-Cuban religions derived from the Yoruba people routinely give predictions for the coming year. Sometimes animals are used. In Havana, high priests known as babalawos make all kinds of predictions, both social and political. The disparity between all the different predictions coming out of Havana might seem funny were it not for the fact that many Cubans give serious weight to the forecasts divined by babalawos using seashells and other sacred objects during secret rituals each December 31. "There are lies and politics, but the real predictions are gods speaking," said Rigoberto Zamora, head of the Miami-based International Federation of Afro-Cuban Yoruba Religion, who faced four charges of cruelty to animals over a televised sacrifice in 1995.[6]

## ⅄ DWARVES AND GENIES

> *The deepest need of man is to overcome his separateness, to leave the prison of his aloneness.*
>
> —Eric Fromm, *The Art of Loving*

Diviners in the past were often a bit odd physically. For example, individuals with the genetic disorder we now call achondroplasia were often in demand as court jesters and soothsayers during the Middle Ages. Achondroplastic dwarf diviners were usually healthy and intelligent and had bulging foreheads.

George M. Gould and Walter L. Pyle, authors of *Anomalies and Curiosities of Medicine*, note that a dwarf was once a necessary appendage of every noble family. The Roman Emperors all had their dwarfs. Later in the Middle Ages, and even into the 1800s, dwarfs were seen at most courts. Lady Montagu describes the dwarfs at the Viennese court as "devils bedaubed with diamonds." The court dwarfs were allowed unlimited freedom of speech, and, in order to get at truths other men were afraid to utter, one of the kings of Denmark made his dwarf prime minister.

Charles IX in 1572 had nine dwarfs, of which four had been given to him by King Sigismund-Augustus of Poland and three by Maximilian II of Germany. Catherine de Medicis had three dwarf couples, and in 1579 she had five pygmies.

Sometimes assemblies of dwarfs were present at great and noble gatherings. In Rome in 1566 Cardinal Vitelli gave a sumptuous banquet attended by thirty-four dwarfs. Peter the Great of Russia had a passion for dwarfs, and in 1710 gave a great celebration in honor of the marriage of his favorite, Valakoff, with the dwarf of the Princess Prescovie Theodorovna. There were seventy-two dwarfs of both sexes present to form the bridal party. Subsequently, on account of dangerous and difficult labor, such marriages were forbidden in Russia.

Dwarfs were not the only strange beings thought to have divinatory powers. Belief in supernatural jinn or genies in Arabic mythology was so common in early Arabia, that these beings were thought to inspire soothsayers. Even Mohammed originally feared that his revelations might be the work of jinn. Their existence was further acknowledged in official Islam, which indicated that they, like human beings, would have to face eventual salvation or damnation. Jinn are beings of flame or air who are capable of assuming human or animal form and are said to dwell everywhere—in stones, trees, ruins; underneath the earth, in the air, and in fire. They possess the bodily needs of human beings and can even be killed, but they are free from all physical restraints. Jinn punish humans for any harm done to them, intentionally or unintentionally, and are said to be responsible for many diseases and accidents. Certain humans who know the appropriate magical procedures can use the jinn to their advantage.

## ᛏ THE WRECK OF THE *TITANIC*

> *I am half inclined to think we are all ghosts. . . . They are not actually alive in us; but there they are dormant, all the same, and we can never be rid of them. Whenever I take up a newspaper and read it, I fancy I see ghosts creeping between the lines. There must be ghosts all over the world. They must be as countless as grains of sand it seems to me. And we are so miserably afraid of the light, all of us.*
>
> —Henrick Ibsen, *Ghosts*

Who can forget the emotional lines of James Cameron's blockbuster movie *Titanic* when Rose and Jack are floating in the water after the mighty ship has sunk? Well, perhaps you have forgotten them, so here they are for your edification:

*Rose.*  I love you Jack.
*Jack.*  No . . . don't say your good-byes, Rose. Don't you give up. Don't do it.
*Rose.*  I'm so cold.

*Jack.*   You're going to get out of this . . . you're going to go on and you're
going to make babies and watch them grow and you're going to die
an old lady, warm in your bed. Not here. Not this night. Do you
understand me?

*Rose.*   I can't feel my body.

*Jack*   Promise me you will survive    that you will never give up . . . no
matter what happens. . . . No matter how hopeless . . . promise me
now, and never let go of that promise.

*Rose.*   I promise.

*Jack.*   Never let go.

*Rose.*   I promise. I will never let go, Jack. I'll never let go.

The *Titanic*'s memory lives on today in documentaries, an Oscar-win-
ning movie, and even a Broadway musical. In April 1997, investigators in
the frigid North Atlantic revealed that the *Titanic* had narrow stress slits
across its watertight holds that contributed to the ship's demise. Believers in
divination and precognition have long maintained that the sinking of the
*Titanic* was perceived in advance by extrasensory perception (ESP). Their
best example is Morgan Robertson's weirdly prescient sea novel, *The Wreck
of the Titan*, published fourteen years before the *Titanic* went down. It has
been analyzed carefully by skeptics and believers alike.[7]

Morgan Andrew Robertson was born in Oswego, New York, in 1861.
Although he had many good ideas, his life was filled with misfortune. For
example, he invented a periscope, but it could not be patented because a
description of a similar device had appeared in a French fantasy story. His wife
was an invalid, and years of poverty led him toward alcoholism and obsessions
that he was possessed by a spirit that helped him write fascinating tales.

Despite Robertson's problems, he was very productive author of two
novels and hundreds of short stories. However, for months at a time, he
would be incapable of writing a single sentence. The "entity" within him
seemed to totally abandon him.

In order to get ideas for his stories, Robertson found it useful to lie in a
semi-wakeful state. While resting, the entity would dictate stories to him
using dreamlike images. Afterward, Robertson would type on paper what
the entity revealed. Often the entity would stop, and Robertson would have
to wait before writing the next installment of the story.

The subject of his short book *The Wreck of the Titan* came to Robertson,
as usual, in one of his hypnogogic states. While in a kind of trance,
Robertson says he saw a large ship speeding through a foggy Atlantic night,
a vast and sturdy ship driven by three huge propellers and traveling at least
23 knots. He saw people wandering over the deck and realized the vessel

held over two thousand passengers and crew. No passenger ship of Robertson's time could carry so many people. With growing nervousness, Robertson turned his attention to the lifeboats. There were only twenty-four, a pitiful number considering the number of passengers aboard the ship. Someone on the ship whispered "unsinkable" as Robertson saw an iceberg loom before the ship. As Robertson's vision faded like a wisp of wind, he saw the name of the ship: the *Titan*.

Robertson ran to his typewriter and typed out the first few pages of *The Wreck of the Titan* in which he described the transatlantic luxury liner's luxurious cabins, the decks, and watertight compartments. His book gave further descriptions of the *Titan*'s maiden voyage and how the ship was touted as unsinkable but nevertheless struck an iceberg and sunk. To give you a feel for Robertson's book, which is still available today at any of the Internet bookstores, here is how his tale began:

> She was the largest craft afloat and the greatest of the works of men. In her construction and maintenance were involved every science, profession, and trade known to civilization. On her bridge were officers, who, besides being the pick of the Royal Navy, had passed rigid examinations in all studies that pertained to the winds, tides, currents, and geography of the sea; they were not only seamen, but scientists. The same professional standard applied to the personnel of the engine-room, and the steward's department was equal to that of a first-class hotel.
>
> Two brass bands, two orchestras, and a theatrical company entertained the passengers during waking hours; a corps of physicians attended to the temporal, and a corps of chaplains to the spiritual, welfare of all on board, while a well-drilled fire-company soothed the fears of nervous ones and added to the general entertainment by daily practice with their apparatus.
>
> From the bridge, engine-room, and a dozen places on her deck the ninety-two doors of nineteen water-tight compartments could be closed in half a minute by turning a lever. These doors would also close automatically in the presence of water. With nine compartments flooded the ship would still float, and as no known accident of the sea could possibly fill this many, the steamship *Titan* was considered practically unsinkable.
>
> Built of steel throughout, and for passenger traffic only, she carried no combustible cargo to threaten her destruction by fire; and the immunity from the demand for cargo space had enabled her designers to discard the flat, kettle-bottom of cargo boats and give her the sharp dead-rise—or slant from the keel—of a steam yacht, and this improved her behavior in the seaway. She was eight hundred feet long, of seventy thousand tons' displacement, seventy-five thousand horse-power, and on her trial trip had steamed at a rate of twenty-five knots an hour over the bottom, in the face

of unconsidered winds, tides, and currents. In short, she was a floating city—containing within her steel walls all that tends to minimize the dangers and discomforts of the Atlantic voyage—all that makes life enjoyable.

Unsinkable—indestructible, she carried as few boats as would satisfy the laws. These, twenty-four in number, were securely covered and lashed down to their chocks on the upper deck, and if launched would hold five hundred people. She carried no useless, cumbersome life-rafts; but—because the law required it—each of the three thousand berths in the passengers', officers', and crew's quarters contained a cork jacket, while about twenty circular life-buoys were strewn along the rails.

In view of her absolute superiority to other craft, a rule of navigation thoroughly believed in by some captains, but not yet openly followed, was announced by the steamship company to apply to the *Titan*: She would steam at full speed in fog, storm, and sunshine, and on the Northern Lane Route, winter and summer. . . . At full speed, she could be easily steered out of danger, and in case of an end-on collision with an iceberg—the only thing afloat that she could not conquer—her bows would be crushed in but a few feet further at full than at half speed, and at the most three compartments would be flooded—which would not matter with six more to spare.[8]

There are more than twenty startling similarities between the dread tale of the *Titan* and the actual subsequent sinking of the *Titanic*. For example, both ships were considered unsinkable, broke world records for size, grazed an iceberg on the starboard side near midnight on the New York-England line at just over 22 knots, and were owned by a British firm with headquarters in Liverpool and a branch office in New York. What do you make of the following similarities?

| Comparing the *Titan* and *Titanic* | | |
|---|---|---|
| Similarities | *Titan* | *Titanic* |
| Flag | British | British |
| Length | 800 feet | 882 feet |
| Capacity (people) | 3,000 | 3,000 |
| Month of wreck | April | April |
| Passengers and crew | 3,000 | 2,207 |
| Lifeboats | 24 | 20 |
| Tonage | 75,000 | 66,000 |
| Propellers | 3 | 3 |
| Speed at Impact | 25 knots | 23 knots |
| Side Hit | Starboard | Starboard |

As the *Titan* sank in the frigid night air, Robertson heard "nearly three thousand voices, raised in agonizing screams." Fourteen years later, on the evening of April 14, 1912, the *Titanic* raced across the Atlantic at 22 knots (25 miles an hour) from Southampton to New York. At about 11:30 P.M., a seaman on the *Titanic* saw an iceberg straight ahead less than half a mile a way, and he told the helmsman to steer hard to starboard. It seemed that they would miss the iceberg because they had sufficient time to change course. In hindsight, we can see that the decisions to reverse the propellers while turning starboard was a mistake because it prevented the turn from being as effective. Perhaps the iceberg would have missed the ship entirely if they had not reversed the propellers.

At first, almost no one was aware that a collision had taken place and that that a sharp piece of ice had sliced along the side of the ship like a knife. However, after some time, the ship began to list forward and starboard. Unlike the passengers in Robertson's *The Wreck of the Titan*, who panicked right after collision with the iceberg, passengers on the *Titanic* were calm initially because they were told that there was only a minor problem. The ship's band played jazz as officers helped the passengers into the boats—woman and children first.

With the sinking of the *Titanic*, 1,513 people died, including Captain Smith, who had been due to retire at the end of the voyage. Although the sinking of the *Titanic* gave Robertson some fame with the eerie similarities between the real and fictional tragedies, Robertson's life seemed as ill-fated as the *Titanic*'s. In the early 1900s he was living in poverty with his wife in a Harlem slum. In March 1915, he died of heart failure in an Atlantic City hotel as he stared out at the sea.

Some people think Morgan Robertson was able to foresee the future using psychic ability. Skeptics suggest that any similarities between the *Titan* and *Titanic* were coincidences based on Robertson's knowledge of the sea. Perhaps the name "*Titan*," which referred to ancient Greek giants and denoted anything gigantic and powerful, was a natural choice for a large ship. Perhaps it was not too shocking that Robertson named his fictional ship *Titan*. I look forward to hearing from readers.

〜〜〜　〜〜〜　〜〜〜

Just as uncanny as Robertson's *The Wreck of the Titan*, there was the 1893 short story "From the Old World to the New" by W. T. Stead, a spiritualist, whose story features a shipwreck caused by an iceberg in the North Atlantic, a captain named Edward J. Smith (as was the captain of the real *Titanic*), and two lovers-at-first-sight named Rose and Jack (the names of Kate Winslet's and Leo DiCaprio's characters in the 1998 film *Titanic*). Could the movie have been distantly inspired by this story? Legend has it that, years later, W. T. Stead boarded the *Titanic*, run by Captain Edward J. Smith, and died in the shipwreck![9] W. T. Stead was a spirtualist who used a "spirit guide" named Julia to obtain messages "from the other side." Julia would send him ideas, and his hand would respond, automatically, by writing down the thoughts which came as if from nowhere.

There are many more uncanny premonitions of the *Titanic*'s sinking in the literature. At first glance, these seem to defy common sense that the future cannot be known until it takes place and becomes the present. Skeptics suggest that any correspondence between actual future events and premonitions are coincidental. Believers in the occult hope that studies on hypnotic progression into the future, some of which I discussed in chapter 1, will someday prove the possibility of valid premonitions. In 1954, psychiatrists Robert Rubenstein and Richard Newman of the Department of Psychiatry in Yale University School of Medicine performed some of the earliest hypnosis research in which people tried to divine the future.[10] They discovered that people could give startlingly realistic descriptions of the future when they successfully "progressed" five subjects into the future under hypnosis. For example, in October 1953, they told a medical student that he was a decade in the future, and asked him what he saw.

The medical student was able to describe in detail an operation on an emergency case, complete with symptoms, diagnoses, and a host of other details. The medical student said he had dealt with a similar case in 1958, five years in the future of the hypnosis. However, the psychiatrists did not believe these were actual premonitions of the future. "We believe," they wrote, "that each of our subjects, to please the hypnotist, fantasized a future as actually here and now. We suggest that many descriptions of hypnotic regression also consist of confabulations and simulated behavior."[11] Interestingly, they did not believe that "repressed" *past* memories were confabulated: "We suspect, however, that our doubts do not apply to the reenactment of traumatic past experiences." The results of their work was discussed in a *Science* magazine article entitled "The Living Out of 'Future' Experiences Under Hypnosis." The fact that people could give detailed descriptions of the future caused other psychiatrists to lose faith in hypnotic regression techniques.[12]

Another attempt at hypnotic progression was carried out by Professor Charles H. Hapgood of Keene College, Keene, New Hampshire. For example, under hypnosis Hapgood progressed a student several days into the future and asked the student what he was doing. It was currently Sunday. Hapgood asked about Wednesday, and the student replied that he was at the Keen airport where he met a pilot who told of an accident at Montpellier.

When Wednesday evening actually arrived, Hapgood asked the student what he had been doing all day, and the student replied that he had been to the airport where he talked to a pilot who gave details of a Montpellier crash. Many details were the same as in the hypnotic progression. Other students also seemed to give details about the future while hypnotically progressed. Hapgood (now deceased) wrote his opinions of the subject:

> There appears to be good evidence that the human psyche is not bound by the limitations of time and space. Our bodies exist in this physical world, where the laws of time, space, mass and energy operate in a finite way; but they are only the peaks of icebergs that jut above the sea, leaving nine-tenths of their mass out of sight below sea level. All the phenomena I have mentioned here can be easily duplicated. All that is necessary to demonstrate them is a good hypnotists and a few good subjects.[13]

Of course, further researched would be required to validate any of these studies. One could argue that the student lied or that the student went to the airport to validate his prediction, and at the airport someone is likely to have heard of a crash, particularly a crash in a nearby state.

## ᛗ HEBREW DIVINATION

> *Let him stand before Eleazar the priest, who shall seek the decision of the Urim before God on his behalf. By this word [Joshua], along with all the Israelites and the entire community shall come and go.*
>
> —Numbers 27:21

> *Place the Urim and Thumim in the decision breastplate, and they shall be over Aaron's heart when he comes before God. Aaron will then carry the decision-making device for the Israelites before God at all times.*
>
> —Exodus 28:31

If your neighbor came out of a hole in the ground and started uttering dire warnings, what would you do? Would you laugh? Flee? What if your friend or mayor started to whisper in your ear, "There will be hail and fire mingled with blood, and people cast upon the earth, and the third part of trees burnt up, and all green grass burnt up, and a great mountain burning with fire cast into the sea: and the third part of the sea will become blood."[14] Perhaps you'd call the police.

However, in ancient times, prophets were taken seriously and functioned like priests and political advisors. We've already discussed how, in prehistoric times, wise men collected bits of burned bones to divine the future. These "wish bones" comprised the divination art known as "scapulimancy." Over time the practice evolved into the examination of tortoise shells, and later still, into interpreting the positions of sticks as they fell from the hands of the shaman.

Divination was common in ancient Israel. In the Old Testament story in 1 Samuel 6, the Philistines were trying to determine the cause of the plagues afflicting them. (The Philistines were people of Aegean origin who settled on the southern coast of *Palestine* in the twelfth century B.C.E., about the time of the arrival of the Israelites and the mention of the God Yahweh.) The Philistines in particular wanted to know if the presence of the ark, the symbol of Yahweh, was the cause of their plagues. The Philistine's diviners told them to place the ark on a wagon drawn by two cows whose calves have been taken away. The diviners said, "Watch the wagon; if it goes up toward its own territory, then it is Yahweh who has done us this great injury; but if not, then we shall know that his hand has not touched us, but we have been the victims of chance."[15] (The wagon's movements eventually indicated that the Philistines's problems were caused by Yahweh.)

There are other Old Testament stories of divination involving blocks of wood, rods, and the shooting of arrows. The Old Testament 1 Samuel 28 also alludes to necromantic methods for contacting the dead in order to tell the future.

The Old Testament is loaded with mysterious words for which we don't have clear translations but which may refer to divination. These words include *Thummim, Urim, ephod,* and *teraphim.* In Deuteronomy 33, we are told that "Thou [Yahweh] didst give thy Thummim to Levi [the priestly tribe], Thy Urim to thy loyal servant." Biblical scholars suggest that the Urim and Thummim were objects that the priests consulted in order to obtain a decision from Yahweh, and that they comprised the chief official procedure by which oracles were obtained.[16]

Perhaps the Urim and Thummim were lots that the priest manipulated to give answers to questions. Some scholars suggest that the ephod mentioned in the Bible was the container for the Urim and Thummim. In particular, the ephod contained a set of twelve precious stones arranged in four rows, with three stones in each row representing the twelve tribes of Israel. In fact, the most comprehensive list of precious stones in the Bible appears in the description of the breastpiece worn by the high priest. Letters were inscribed on each stone, and certain letters were supposed to light up after a question was asked. The sequence of lit letters was interpreted by a high priest.

The "Teraphim," which has been translated as "household gods," gave oracles in the Old Testament. They were consulted by the king of Babylon, and their function is described in Zechariah 10:2: "The teraphim make mischievous promises and the diviners see false signs."

It appears that the mysterious Urim and Thummim were a portable oracle used throughout the oldest parts of the Biblical history and were similar to tossed objects used by many cultures to divine the future. For example, we discussed how Chinese diviners used *chiao-pai*, two comma-shaped blocks of wood with one flat side and one curved side. If both curved sides fall upward, the querent should not take action. If two flat sides fall upward, the querent shoulds take action. Flat side up, flat side down is a neutral reading.

In the large territories where Islam became the dominant religion, including Africa, Persia, parts of the Indian subcontinent, and Indonesia, many pre-Islamic religious practices survive. For example, in the old days messages were written on arrows that were selected for the purposes of divination. Messages like "Of purest descent" and "Belong to others" were used to determine paternity in a disputed case. Forty miles from Aden in Yemen is a rock poised on stones with a small space between it. If a boy is suspected to be illegitimate, the boy is forced to crawl under the rock. If the child gets through, he is legitimate. If he gets stuck, he is illegitimate. A few years ago, a boy got stuck under the rock, and his mother burst into rage because his predicament suggested she committed adultery.[17]

## ᛞ GREEK DREAMS

> *No live organism can continue for long to exist sanely under conditions of absolute reality. Even larks and katydids are supposed, by some to dream.*
> —Shirley Jackson, *The Haunting of Hill House*

During the days of ancient Greece, the quest for information on the future took pilgrims to the city of Phocis, located at the foot of Mt. Parnassus in Greece. Here the curious listened with reverence to the Delphic Oracle speaking in riddles.[18] As we discussed, an *oracle* is a person or divine communication associated with a special site or person. The term comes from the Latin *oraculum* and from *orare*, which means "to pray" and also can refer to the place of prophecy. Oracular shrines used to be everywhere, where people used various methods of divination to find answers. Sometimes, the oracle would give confusing answers by speaking in ambiguous poetry. At other times, a querent would have to sleep in a special location to receive an answer in dreams. This form of dream divination is called *incubation*. Many accounts of dream oracles are also found in medieval Japanese literature that describe incubation sites in Shinto shrines and Buddhist temples. Sometimes a sick person undergoing Japanese incubation saw visions of beings touching his body. When the sleeper awakened, he or she was apparently healed.

The practice of sleeping in religious shrines in order to receive an oracular dream was rampant even in Northern Europe. To me, the most fascinating dream shrine was a cave known as St. Patrick's Purgatory, located on an island on a lake in Co Donegal, Ireland. The faithful would entomb themselves in six tiny cells for nine days, living only on bread and water. They left the cells only to pray and to wait for visions of what awaited them in hell. Throughout medieval Europe, St. Patrick's Purgatory acquired mythological fame as the place of terrible tests, a descent into a cave for the faithful to suffer the horrors of purgatory. For the Irish, it continues to be a retreat for intensive prayer and quiet penance. The island is open today to pilgrims in the summer and attracts thirty thousand people every year for the three-day pilgrimage. Pilgrims no longer enter a cave, but the spiritual exercises are similar to those practiced in the seventeenth century. The barefoot pilgrims recite 280 prayers at several stations. Once a day, they eat dried bread and drink black tea or coffee.

In the ancient Sumerian, Babylonian, Hittite, Greek, and Roman cultures, oracles had a sacred position, and no important decisions in the life of the individual or the state were made without consulting them. The most famous ancient oracle was that of Apollo at Delphi in Greece. Here, the medium was a woman over fifty, known as the Pythia. People often asked the Pythia to forecast the occurrence of wars or political actions.

Prior to giving advice, the Pythia chewed leaves of the laurel, and then, while in a trance state, she would speak to priests who interpreted and wrote down her often bizarre words. The oracle of Zeus at Dodona in northwestern Greece is among the oldest of oracles. There the priests also interpreted sounds produced by streams and rustling leaves. The oracle-preistesses were usually elderly women who went barefoot, even in the bitter winters, and were filthy and disheveled. They slept on the bare ground and never washed their feet. Achilles, in Homer's *The Iliad* (16:127), paints a vivid portrait of the priestesses: "Lord of Dodona, King Zeus, God of Pelasgians, O God who dwells afar, who holds harsh wintery Dodona in your sway, where your interpreters the Selli dwell with feet like roots, unwashed, and make their beds on the ground. . . ."

The ancients said that a magical stream ran through the Dodona grove.

It ran dry at noon and restarted twelve hours later. Historians speculate that some kind of temporary dam was used to divert or hold back the water while the priests listened to the sacred trees. In time, this noise-damping procedure was allowed to become one of the enigmas of the Dodona grove.

Today, a simple tree-sanctuary is all that remains of the oracle at Dodona. But for a moment, I'd like you to imagine you are back in time at Dodona. First you write your questions on small tablets and give them to the smelly priestess. Next, a priestess sits in the grove listening to the oak trees as they rustle in the breeze. She also listens to several bronze or copper bowls hung in the branches as they occasionally brush against one another. She listens to the cooing of doves, the sounds of other birds, and any other sounds she can hear when she places her head on the oak's trunk.

After the priestess memorizes the sounds from the bowls and the branches, she consults scrolls that explain the meaning of the sounds. Archeologists have unearthed dozens of "question tablets" at Dodona. Many people asked practical, personal questions rather than questions that probed the mysteries of the cosmos. For example, a local man named Agis simply asked whether his blankets and pillows had been stolen, or if he had misplaced them. Another man asked if the baby growing in his pregnant wife's womb was his own. His wife asked what prayer or form of form of worship would be most useful to produce a happy life with good fortune.

Once a delegation from the Greek district of Boeotia came to the oracle to ask an important question that might affect all of Greece. Although I have not been able to ascertain what the question was, the priestess's response was clear. After Myrtile, the priestess, listened to the oak branches and consulted the scrolls, she advised the Boeotians that it would be best for them to do the most impious thing possible. The delegation retreated and spoke among themselves, then attacked Myrtile and threw her into a large pot of boiling water that stood nearby—because this was the most impious action they could think of on the spur of the moment.

The most hellish oracular experiences occurred at the oracle of Troponius, located at Levádhia, Greece. (Troponius was the son of Erginus the Argonaut.[19]) Visitors to this oracle were required to go through some harrowing ordeals to use the oracle. It was not the easy experience of going to a shrine or listening with a woman to a bubbling brook. At the oracle of Trophonius at Levádhia, which was not discovered until 1967, incubation was practiced in a hole.

Here's how the hole incubation worked. In Orphism, a Greek mystical religious movement, the newly dead were thought to drink from the river Lethe where they would lose all memory of their past existence. The initiated were taught to seek instead the river of memory, Mnemosyne, thus securing the end of the transmigration of the soul. At the oracle of Trophonius, which was thought to be an entrance to the underworld, there were two springs called Lethe and Mnemosyne. The querent was locked in a nearby temple for three days and nights while fasting. On the fourth day, the querent was given two cups of water. One was from the Lethe spring, supposedly to blot out all previous memories for the duration of questioning. The second was from the Mnemosyne stream to help the questioner remember the visions that were about to appear.

Imagine you are the questioner, seeking answers at Trophonius. You would walk down a ladder in total darkness and then through a black, narrow tunnel of rock. Your helpers then place you on a low trolley and give you two sacred honey-cakes. Next, they shove the trolley into the darkness like a roller coaster through hell. You could easily fall off. You have to hold the cakes, no matter what happened, because if you arrived at the other end without the cakes, you would be killed.

The querent's experiences in the hole at Trophonius remind me of brainwashing methods. Brainwashing often depends on isolation from people and sources of information. It's an exacting procedure requiring absolute obedience and humility. Brainwashing also involves physical and psychological punishments for noncooperation, for example, deprivation of food, sleep, and family. Perhaps drugs were placed in the water cups used at Trophonius. Some querents may have considered it an ordeal to prepare the mind so it could make contact with other realities.

The sensory deprivation, fasting, and shocking ride at Troponius would seem to be sufficient to drive anyone nuts. Timarchus, a disciple of the recently executed Socrates, went to the shrine of Trophonius and asked what the oracle thought about Socrates' spiritual guide. After Timarchus went into the Trophonius hole and took the ride, he was left alone in utter darkness and silence.

The gentle acid of brainwashing suddenly etched his brain. Timarcus says he saw a vision of a lake of fire dotted with beautiful colored islands. (Lakes of fire are common in all kinds of myths and religions, including the Christian book of Revelations.) He heard a voice that spoke these words:

> Timarchus! The radiant isles that float on the lake of fire are of sacred regions, inhabited by pure souls. Those who keep their original purity amid the ordeals of their first experience are clothed in divine radiance by crossing the lake of fire, source of eternal life. . . . Socrates' soul was one of these; always superior to his mortal body, his soul had become worthy of

entering communion with the invisible worlds and his familiar spirit, a deputy from them, taught him a wisdom that men did not appreciate and therefore killed. You cannot yet understand this mystery; in three months it will be revealed to you.[20]

Timarchus never recovered from his terrifying ordeal and sensory deprivation at Trophonius. He died three months latter babbling about glowing islands, fiery lakes, and holding his hand out to a picture of Socrates who, he said, was coming for him.

If you had the opportunity, what would you ask the oracle at Trophonius? We can make an educated guess about what people concerns today by examining the same kinds of questions and prayers that are written on paper and inserted into the Wailing Wall in Israel. Placing notes in the cracks of the Kotel (the Western Wall) is an age old custom. These notes traditionally contain personal prayers or the names of ill relatives. Perhaps some of the people leaving notes in the wall feel that the Kotel lends a permanence or importance to their prayer. For those of you without access to the Wailing Wall in Israel, there are Web sites that allow you to send a prayer. For example, "Kotel Kam" at the Web site http://kotelkam.com/prayers.htm is Virtual Jerusalem's unique service. You can also see live images of the wall and place images on your computer display's background.

We can get a feel for how the ancient Greeks felt about oracles by reading the words of Greek author Herodotus, who had the following to say about the origin of the Oracle at Dodona. Herodotus describes the kidnapping of two priestess from Egypt:

> The priests of the Zeus of [Egyptian] Thebes told me that two Priestesses were carried away from that country by Phoenicians, who sold one in Libya and the other in Greece, and these two women established the first oracles in either place.
>
> This account I had from the priests at Thebes; but the prophetesses at Dodona say that two black pigeons flew from Thebes of Egypt, one to Libya and the other to Dodona. The second perched on a beech-tree and uttered human speech admonishing the people of the place to set up an oracle of Zeus; and they, believing it be a divine revelation, obeyed. They add that the pigeon which flew to Libya commanded the establishment of an oracle of Ammon, also dedicated to Zeus.
>
> The people of Dodona, I suppose, called these women pigeons because they were foreigners and their speech was no more understood than the chattering of birds; then, when one could speak their language, they reported that the pigeon had spoken with a human voice; for while she spoke a foreign

tongue they would think her voice like that of a bird. And they said the pigeon was black, meaning that the woman was an Egyptian. Moreover, it is true that the ways of divination at Thebes of Egypt and at Dodona are much alike.[21]

〜〜〜    〜〜〜    〜〜〜

Prophecies were also given from Zeus's altar at Olympia—where priests divined from offerings—and from the oasis of Siwah in the Libya desert, which was originally an oracle of the Egyptian god Amon. After Alexander the Great freed Egypt from the Persians in 331 B.C.E., he celebrated by trekking two hundred miles to the Oracle at Siwah. It was a pretty nasty trip—a lot more difficult than he imagined. He only took a handful of men and insufficient supplies. Their water ran out, but a sudden rainstorm finally came and kept them alive.

When Alexander finally arrived, he wanted a consultation. He was told of a rather strange ritual in which the priests get into a boat with dangling silver cups. Virgin girls follow the boat, singing hymns. Next, the questioner asks a question, and a god was supposed to push the boat forward for "yes" and backward for "no."

The boat divination reminds me of the New Age rage with pendulum divination, also called cleidomancy or radiesthesia. The questioner holds a pendulum suspended so that it points midway between YES and NO written on paper. The questioner ask a question, and in less than a minute the pendulum usually swings to YES or NO. (See the "Do-It-Yourself Pendulum Divination" recipe for details.) Some people believe that the pendulum gives answers because the querent may subconsciously know the answer to the question and have a hidden desire as to the answer. These attitudes encourage the querent's hand to move ever-so-slightly in one direction or the other. These small movements of the hand are amplified by the pendulum. Try it. You'll be amazed. In a sense, the pendulum can become a vehicle for moving information from your subconscious mind to you conscious.

"Ideomotor action" is a term used frequently in pendulum divination literature. Ideomotor action occurs when thoughts are automatically translated into muscular activity. One example of an ideomotor action is the response monitored by a polygraph or lie detector. It works by monitoring aspects of bodily function, including involuntary muscle responses that cannot easily be controlled by the person taking the test. Perhaps the pendulum divination works by measuring an ideomotor response when we question ourselves. Other methods of ideomotor questioning include automatic writing and the Ouija Board.

---

### Do-It-Yourself Pendulum Divination

When Alexander the Great went to the oracle at Siwah, he was told they used virgin girls following a gilded boat that drifted forward or back to answer yes/no questions. If you don't have access to virgin girls and gilded boats, here's a similar but more modern method that is easier to perform in your own home.

1. Find a piece of paper and draw a large "+" symbol in the center of it.
2. At the top and bottom points of the +, write YES.
3. At the left and right points of the +, write NO.
4. Tie a washer to a string to create a pendulum. (If you have money to spare, there are hundreds of attractive pendulums made of gems and precious metals available on the World Wide Web. To find examples, just type +pendulum +divination into any search engine.)
5. Suspend the pendulum about an inch above the center of the +. To calibrate the pendulum, first ask a question for which you know an answer. For example, "Am I doing pendulum divination?" The pendulum should begin to move up and down. If the pendulum does not move, or moves just a little, concentrate a little harder, and wait another minute. Delightful, isn't it?
6. Repeat with a question that you know the answer to is no.
7. Now ask the question you really want answered and be amazed by your ideo-motor-induced destiny.

---

Anton Chevreul first discovered in the eighteenth century how to use a pendulum to magnify ideomotor movements. The term "ideomotor action" was coined by William Carpenter in 1882 in his explanation of dowsing rod and pendulum movements. Carpenter argued that muscular movement can be initiated by the mind independently of volition or emotions. Today, New Agers sell pendulums to divine an amazing array of answers. For example, some companies sell pendulums to help users to select vitamins, supplements, and even health practitioners.[22]

Let's return to Alexander and his interest in divination. Because he was such a big shot, it was easy for him to use his clout and dispense with the boat ceremony for something more direct at the Oracle at Siwah. No one knows what question Alexander asked. All we know is that afterward Alexander said that he received the answer he was seeking. Some historians speculate that Alexander was asking whether his planned conquest of the large Persian Empire would succeed, or if it was true that he was actually the son of a god, as his mother claimed. Later, his interactions with the Oracle at Siwah contributed to the story that he was the son of Zeus and, thus, to his deification. It seems that whatever was said to him contributed to his confidence when battling the seemingly overwhelming Persian forces.

Recent archeological excavation has suggested some delicious trickery at the Oracle at Siwah. Scientists discovered a small room off the main courtyard with a hidden passage running along the wall. In between the inner chamber and the passage were small holes. What could this be for? Perhaps a hidden priest pretended to be the voice of god.

If the Siwah oracle in Libya existed today, and you were certain it would be accurate, what one question would you ask? Might you ask it about something that could make you rich? Or would use it for a more spiritual, less selfish purpose? Remember, at Siwah you were often limited to yes/no questions. What yes/no question would you ask? Could the correct answer to a simple yes/no question be used to get millions of dollars? Could it help the world find a cure for cancer? Could it help you solve your family or love problems? Could you make the oracle self-destruct by asking the oracle, "Will you answer 'no'?"

# ᛉ THE LONG-TERM EFFECT OF THE DELPHIC PYTHIA

For centuries, both royalty and ordinary people from Greece, Asia Minor, Egypt, the Roman Empire, and North Africa relied on the Delphic Pythia, the oracle priestess, to divine their futures. At the peak of its prestige in the sixth century B.C.E., Delphi was a shiny temple of white marble, surrounded by a town made popular by the oracle. Author Damon Wilson notes:

> Wars were waged, colonies founded, peace treaties signed, and the fates of individuals decided on the "word of the god," pronounced through the medium of the Pythia, who was usually a low-born and uneducated woman. Greece was transformed from a cultural backwater to the "cradle of western civilization" largely through the multicultural influence of visiting foreign suppliants to Delphi.[23]

Just as I emphasized with the haruspices, the Greek Pythia also had a profound effect on history, perhaps as much as the invention of the chariot, penicillin, or gunpowder. In some sense, the vague ramblings of an oracle saved all of Greece from conquest. In 480 B.C.E., the Persian King Xerxes invaded the Greece. The Athenian's asked the Pythia what they should do, and she replied, "Prepare for doom." The Athenian's begged her for more information, and she replied, "Walls of wood will save your loved ones. Stay not to meet the advancing horse and foot that swarms over the land, but turn and flee to fight another day."[24]

Some thought this message meant that the populace should huddle within the walls of the Acropolis and try to outlast a Persian siege. But the Athenian naval strategist Themistokles concluded that the "wooden wall" referred to the battle line of the great Athenian warships. On the Pythia's vague advice, the Athenians left their city and fought the Persians at sea. Even though the Athenians were greatly outnumbered, they were able to lure the Persians into the Bay of Salamis.

The Athenians suffered almost no loss of life when the Persians marched into Athens and burned it to the ground. The women and children had already been transported safely to the nearby city of Troezen. The old men were taken to the nearby island of Salamis, and only those few who remained behind the walls lost their lives. Acting on false intelligence information planted by the Greeks, the Persians positioned their fleet at the mouth of the Bay of Salamis, thinking to catch the Greek sailors before they could man their ships in the morning. But dawn caught them walking right into a Greek trap. As the Persian ships poured into the bay, the Greek ships, hiding in the channel beyond the bay, rammed them broadside. The large number of Persian ships and the small diameter of the bay made it difficult for the Persians to maneuver. The Greek victory at the Battle of Salamis forced Xerxes to hightail it home.

So, we again see how divination altered Greek history, thereby changing the course of the world. In this instance, divination "saved" Athens. But it also later doomed Greece as a whole. In 431 B.C.E., the Spartans consulted a Pythia about whether they should invade Athenian territory. The Pythia told the Spartans they would win, so they attacked and eventually did win. Unfortunately, this probably led to the subsequent conquest by the Macedonians under Alexander the Great, and then Rome.

There are many more examples of the Pythia's effect on civilization. Her advice was requested when any Greek settlement was planned. The Cretans colonized Sicily because of the Pythia's advice. For example, the Pythia's advice led to the aristocrat Archias founding Syracuse in Sicily and the Boetians building Heraclea in Pontus, the ancient district in northeastern Anatolia adjoining the Black Sea. King Croesus of Lydia, the richest country in the eastern Mediterranean, consulted oracles about whether he should attack the Persians. The Pythias said essentially that "Croesus will destroy an empire." Confident of victory, Croesus joined battle and had his head chopped off. A large Persian force under Cyrus defeated him. It appears that the Pythia's advice, in this case, led to disaster.

It's hard to believe that the majestic Delphic oracle started with a measly goat that liked to graze by a chasm in the ground. Whenever the goat looked down, it would begin to display weird movements and make odd sounds.

When the goatheards finally located their goat, they too were affected and believed that a god must have possessed them. The vapors coming from the chasm evidently had a pharmacological effect on any creature breathing them. Some researchers have speculated that sulfur dioxide wafted from the Delphic chasm.[25] This colorless, poisonous gas has a pungent, irritating odor familiar as the smell of a just-struck match. Could this gas have had strange effects on goats and people as described by the ancients? In a possible contradiction, ancient Greeks described the air in the temple as a wonderfully sweet perfume, although this could have referred to their burning incense.

People at the chasm seemed to get high. Some went into trances. This might have been a fun way to relax, but, unfortunately, many people in their ecstatic frenzy hurled themselves into the deep chasm. The escalating occurrence of jumpers forced the locals to appoint a single person to manage the gas chasm and who would be affected by the gas. They chose a woman, perhaps because the Greeks thought a woman more expendable than a man. Who cared if a lady threw herself down the hole to her death? When a new Pythia was needed, any local woman who took the vow of chastity was eligible. A priest would test prospective Pythias by throwing large quantities of icy water onto their bare skins. The priests observed the ladies' shudders to determine if they were sufficiently strong and sensitive to withdraw into the tough life of a Pythia at Delphi. The gases shortened the Pythias' lives. When a Pythia went into her gas-induced trance, her chest heaved, her face flushed and then went pale. Her limbs shook like snakes. She foamed at the mouth.

In the early days of Delphi, there was an incident straight out of a Bill Clinton–Monica Lewinsky affair, where one lonely young Pythia fooled around with a handsome and virile questioner at the oracle. After that, only middle-aged virgins were chosen for the job.

When Alexander the Great visited Delphi, he arrived quite unexpectedly during a time when the oracle was not giving predictions. He became angry when the priest refused to notify the Pythia of his presence, so he went to her private chamber and dragged her out to the sanctuary. The Pythia had no idea who he was. She could only tell that he was strong and determined. She cried out, "This young man is unstoppable!"

Alexander took this as an omen, released the Pythia, and thanked her for her prediction. He promptly left to invade Asia and never lost a battle in his life.

Most oracle proclamations were not as direct as this one shouted at Alexander. Just as with Nostradamus's quatrains, and the *I Ching*'s descriptions, most of the oracles gave deliberately obscure prophecies.

Today, archeologists cannot find the chasm of Delphi. Perhaps it has closed off over time. Around the second century C.E., Christians began to attack some of the ancient Greek beliefs. The Christians did not seem to question the oracles' powers but rather ascribed them to demonic powers. However, it was not the Christians who killed the oracle. Hadrian, a young Roman nobleman, visited Delphi around the first century C.E. and learned that he would some day be a Roman emperor. When he did become emperor in 117 C.E., Hadrian had the oracle closed down and the sacred spring blocked. He didn't want the oracle encouraging any other young whipper-snapper to become emperor while he was in charge!

## THE NECHUNG ORACLE

> *Look on me and answer, O Lord my God. Give light to my eyes, or I will sleep in death.*
>
> —Psalms 13:3

Oracles delivered through Greek sleep incubation were believed to come from the underworld. Sick people slept in the hall of Asclepius, the god of medicine at Epidaurus, Greece, and believed cures came through dreams. At other locations, people slept on skins or holes in the ground. Incubation was also practiced at the oracle of Dionysus at Amphicleia. An oracle for consulting the dead existed beside the river Acheron in central Greece.

The famous oracles existed primarily in ancient Greece. The Egyptians, however, divined from the motion of images paraded through the streets, and the Hebrews from sacred objects and dreams. Babylonian temple prophetesses also interpreted dreams. In Italy several oracles were consulted by the Roman emperors.

The most modern and famous oracle of which I am aware is the Nechung oracle, the oracle-priest of Tibet. The oracle was first appointed government adviser during the time of the fifth Dalai Lama (1617–1682). Not only did he make predictions and answer questions, but he was always consulted whenever a search was conducted for a new Dalai Lama.

*Thupten Ngodup* is the current Tibetan medium and is the fourteenth kutan of the Nechung Oracle, which was established in 1642. He joined the monastery at age fourteen, following the lamas into exile in India after the Chinese takeover of Tibet. He is currently in his forties. He conducts public trances twice a year and private consolations as needed. Wearing a costume and headdress weighing over one hundred pounds, he jumps and runs through the Nechung monastery in Dharamsala before giving guidance. He speaks his prophecies as poems in stanzas and prose style, and with a tune unique to Nechung. The Nechung oracle normally does not remember what happened during his trance. He says:

> Just before the trance, I see and sense what is going around me. But gradu-
> ally even my senses dissolve and then in a kind of sleep state I become
> totally absorbed, and do not correctly remember what has happened and
> been said. Normally, when I am seated on the throne with my costumes on,
> I do my meditations while reciting the mantras of Hayagriva. Slowly, I get
> possessed through a deeper state of absorption, and then gradually feel dis-
> tant from my own identity and surroundings. It is like having a dream and
> not remembering it the next morning. The same is the case with me before
> and after I come out of trance.[26]

≋  ≋  ≋

There are many imaginative, New Age theories on how oracles may work. According to Dr. Glenn Williston, cofounder of the Psychic Internet, when an oracle is consulted, the reader views a "slice of time":

> We might say that the future is created out of the interaction of various,
> often contradictory, probabilities. Factors not present in the "slice of time"
> may enter the mix and become apparent "along the way." Thus another
> "slice of time," viewed just minutes later, can reveal new and/or different
> information. Some probabilities are much stronger than others and these
> change vary little, if at all, while the weaker probabilities can and do change
> radically minute by minute. Interestingly, with each change in attitude or
> perspective, with each new decision, probabilities shift, and, amazingly,
> some scientists say that the past changes too! Thus, an oracle reading by a
> skilled, intuitive person can produce surprisingly accurate and insightful
> directives and suggestions to help us reinforce what we want to happen, and
> change what we want to avoid.[27]

## ᚤ THE END OF THE WORLD

> *We, while the stars from heaven shall fall,*
> *And mountains are on mountains hurled.*
> *Shall stand unmoved amidst them all,*
> *And smile to see a burning world.*
>
> —Millerite Hymn, 1843[28]

On September 9, 1999, Indonesian cult members beat three fellow members to death when their prediction of doomsday on 9/9/99 failed to materialize.[29] Like many cults across the country, members were told to prepare for the end of the world at 9 A.M. on September 9. They sold their personal possessions and for nine days before the big day, locked themselves up in their homes. When nothing happened in September, the cult members got so angry that they lost control.

Throughout our history, various prophets of doom have predicted the end of the world using arcane mathematical manipulations and other divination methods. The end takes many forms: a huge comet crashing into the earth, California sliding into the sea, the apocalypse predicted in the book of Revelation. Apocalypse—the unveiling of human destiny—has fascinated Jews and Christians for thousands of years.[30]

**Figure 58.** End of the World. Originally published as "Death as mounted hunter and reaper," in *Der Ackermann aus Böhmen* (The Poughman from Bohemia), Bamberg, 1463. From Ernst Lehner and Johanna Lehner, *Picture Book of Devils, Demons, and Witchcraft* (New York: Dover, 1971), fig. 174, p. 118

No matter what form doomsday takes, one thing is clear: the end of the world not only intrigued ancient religious prophets, it fascinates modern society as well. Just turn on your TV any Sunday morning to find some preacher telling you the world is about to end. Popular books predicting imminent disaster always find large and enthusiastic audiences. Today, in the United States there are probably more "doomists" than there ever were in some medieval or Roman town. Some fundamentalist Christians believe not only that there will be a judgment day when the world will end, but also that the world *should* end. Even Christopher Columbus was fascinated by the prospect of the imminent end of the world.[31] However, Columbus believed that before the world could end the word of Jesus had to be preached "in all the world for a witness unto all nations; and then shall the end come"— as explained in Matthew 24:14. Columbus firmly believed he should spread God's words to the unsaved.

Scientists have also predicted the end. When the Danish astronomer Tycho Brahe discovered a new star, he presented it as heralding the Second Coming. Mathematician John Napier predicted the Last Judgment either for 1688 or 1700. Even Isaac Newton was interested in the subject.

The doomists have never been right—but one day they will. Certainly the world will come to an end sometime in the future through astronomical or other reasons (see figure 58).

## The Millerites

> *The earth and all the works therein*
> *Dissolve, by ranging flames destroyed;*
> *While we survey the awful scene,*
> *And mount above the fiery void.*
>
> —Millerite Hymn, 1843[32]

Throughout history many religious groups have found the concept of apocalypse irresistible and have come up with various methods to predict its exact date and nature. The most interesting religious group concerned with the end of the world were the Millerites who based their teachings upon the studies of William Miller, a fundamentalist Protestant who predicted that the world would end in 1843. He based his prediction on the following biblical passage in Daniel 8:14: "And he said unto me, Unto two thousand and three hundred days; then shall the sanctuary be cleansed."

Because the prophesy was made in about 457 B.C.E., the end of the 2,300 year period would come in 1843. (Miller believed that the word "days" in the biblical passage should be translated as "years.") Millerite leaders, in 1842, passed the following resolution: "Resolved: that in the opinion of this conference, there are most serious and important reasons for believing that God has revealed the time of the end of the world, and that that time is 1843."[33]

The Millerites deeply believed in the end of the world. Many Millerites actually attempted to fly bodily to heaven. Some followers donned wings, climbed trees, and prayed to the Lord to lift them up. Inevitably several devout followers broke their arms when they jumped from the trees.

Today, the Seventh-day Adventists and Jehovah's Witnesses believe that end of the world is near. Some Protestant groups share the basic idea that the world could end at any moment.

## Behold the Terrible Ragnarök

> The sun turns black, earth sinks in the sea, the hot stars fall from the sky, and fire leaps high above heaven itself.
> —The Edda (Icelandic poem about the pre-Christian Norsemen[34]

Aside from various Christian sects, the pre-Christian Norsemen were fascinated by the end of the world. Christians believe that after doomsday the soul of man would be immortal, and they believe God is immortal. To the Norsemen, doomsday (called Ragnarök) means the death of everything and everyone, including the Gods. One Icelandic poem describes doomsday for the Norsemen: "The gods are doomed, and the end is death."[35]

The Ragnarök is preceded by Fimbulvetr, a horrible winter lasting for three years. After this, the real action begins:

- The wolf Fenrir, whose jaws stretch from heaven to Earth, breaks his chains.
- The Midgars Snake rises from the sea and spits poison.
- Naflfar, the Ship of the Dead, made of the uncut nails of dead men, breaks from her dock in Hell.
- Surt leads the fire giants from Muspell. They approach Asgard (the home of the gods), and Bifrost (a rainbow bridge) cracks.

And this is just the beginning. Suffice it to say, all hell breaks loose. Thor, the protector of humankind, is killed. The human race is dumped off the Earth. Surt, the fire giant, sets the earth and heaven on fire, and finally the entire Earth sinks beneath the sea.

Of course, the Norsemen were not the only group to give explicit and dramatic information pertaining to Doomsday. St. Paul in the Bible predicts:

> The Lord himself will descend from heaven with a cry of command, with the archangel's call, and with the sound of the trumpet of God. The dead in Christ will rise first; then we who remain alive shall be caught up together with them in the clouds to meet the Lord in the air; and so we shall always be with the Lord.
>
> We shall not all sleep, but we shall all be changed, in a moment in the wink of an eye, at the last trumpet. For the trumpet will sound and the dead will be raised imperishable, and we shall be changed.[37]

Daniel Cohen, in his wonderful book *Waiting for the Apocalypse*, notes that Paul speaks of "we who remain alive."[38] This suggests that St. Paul believed that the apocalypse was to take place within his own lifetime and the lifetime of the majority of his listeners. I speak of these subjects in more detail in chapter 4, "Science and the Will to Believe."

In the past, numerology was often used to decipher the meaning of the book of Revelation without much controversy; however, sometimes the church overreacted to astrology. For example, Cecco D'Ascoli, an astrology teacher and astrologer to Duke of Florence, was burned at the stake in 1327 for teaching that Christ's story could be understood from an astrological perspective.[39]

## *"Christ is Coming" on an Eggshell*

> *Montanism, which had for years been a powerful alternative to orthodox Christianity, went into decline, because it could not adapt to a world that stubbornly refused to end.*
> —Daniel Cohen, *Waiting for the Apocalypse*

> *Every meteor in the sky seen at Jerusalem brought the whole Christian population into the streets to weep and pray.*
> —Daniel Cohen, *Waiting for the Apocalypse*

Throughout history, comets, meteors, and various disasters have captured the imagination and the fear of prophets. Some prophets foretold of burning skies and other weapons of holy vengeance. *Gnostics* in the first century C.E. believed that the world had already ended, and that life on Earth was meaningless and unimportant.

In the year 999, numerous pilgrims came to Jerusalem, expecting it to be the site for the Last Judgment. Their numbers were so great that various scholars have compared them to an army. Most of them sold their possessions before they left Europe. Knights, citizens, and serfs traveled eastward taking with them their wives and children. In the year 1000, the number of pilgrims increased. Many of them were scared, expecting the heavens to open up at any minute.

British Professor William Whiston predicted that the world would be destroyed in 1736. In 1761, people predicted the end of the world after two earthquake shocks hit London. The third shock was thought to herald the end of the word.

In 1806, a terror shook the people of Leeds. A hen in a nearby village laid an egg that had the words "Christ is coming" inscribed on its shell. Many people visited the miracle hen and examined the wondrous eggs, convinced that the destruction of the world would soon occur. After further investigation, researchers determined that marked eggs had been cruelly forced up into the bird's body so that she would appear to lay the eggs with the messages.[40]

During the great plague, which decimated Europe between the years 1345 and 1350, many people thought the end of the word was at hand, and for many of them it was. Numerous prophets predicted within ten years the Savior would appear in the clouds to call the earth to judgment.

*Montanists*, named after their Christian leader named Montanus, in the second century believed that a heavenly city would land at a place on Earth called Ardabau—a signal for the Second Coming. In 198 C.E. some Montanists actually claimed to see a walled city floating in the sky over Judea for forty consecutive mornings. Unfortunately, Montanists actively sought martyrdom, and the Romans were only too happy to oblige them.

*Shiptonists* in the fifteenth century followed the English prophetess Mother Shipton who predicted that the world would end in 1881. This small waif of a woman had a reputation for startlingly accurate predictions.

It all started in 1488, fifteen years before the birth of French prophet Nostradamus. Ursula Sontheil (Mother Shipton) was born in a riverside cave in Knaresborough, Yorkshire England. Locals had chased her mother, Agatha, out of town because they suspected her of being a witch. The poor woman took refuge in the cave but apparently died during childbirth. Ursula is said to have predicted the exact date of her own death, which occurred in 1561.

Some prophecies that were said to have been written by Mother Shipton have proved to be the work of impostors who made up prophecies and then attribute them to Mother Shipton. Despite this, her word has been respected and feared as England's most famous prophetess for centuries. The most notorious fraud was perpetuated by Charles Hindley who, in the middle of the nineteenth century, wrote one prophecy and attributed it to Shipton. The prophecy was:

> When the world to an end shall come,
> in eighteen hundred and eighty one.

The year 1881 passed without catastrophe, so this was conveniently changed to 1991. We are still here, but Mother Shipton did make a prophecy about the end of the world. It foretells:

> The world shall end when the High Bridge is thrice fallen.

The High Bridge is in Knaresborough, located next to the main entrance to "Mother Shipton's Cave." It has fallen twice already.

There is some dispute as to whether Mother Shipton actually existed, since the writings of her prophecies did not appear until many years after her death. Legend has it that Ursula was ugly and perhaps that is why strange tales were told about her from babyhood. Stories of the young child and her cradle levitating soon captured the interest of the nearby village. So, too, did stories of the furniture being mysteriously moved around at a cottage she later lived in (see figure 59).

Some have speculated that her witchlike face saved her from persecution because many of the persecuted "witches" were often attractive and were more likely to be strip searched for "devil's marks" than an ugly girl. Supposedly, her nurse could find the child in the dark because her nose was "of disproportionate length with many crooks and turnings, adorned with great pimples and which, like vapors of brimstone, gave strong luster in the night."[41]

Despite her appearance, she married a local carpenter named Toby Shipton and later had nine children with him. Mother Shipton, as she became known, is said to have predicted important historic events like the defeat of the Spanish Armada in 1588, the execution of Lady Jane Grey after only nine days on the throne, the beheading of Mary Queen of Scots, and the Great Fire of London in 1666. Her fans suggest that the following verse predicts the railroad, the telegraph, the Internet, the California gold rush, and the Crystal Palace in London.

> Carriages without horses shall go.
> And accidents fill the world with woe.
> Around the world thoughts shall fly
> In the twinkling of an eye.
> Iron in water shall float
> As easy as a wooden boat.
> Gold shall be found, and found
> In a land that's not now known . . .
> A house of glass shall come to pass . . .

Some of the more modern sounding "prophecies" were definitely the fictional invention of Charles Hindley, who later confessed that he penned them to boost the sales of his book *Life, Prophecies, and Death of the Famous Mother Shipton* published in 1862. Today we do not know for sure how many of Mother Shipton's prophecies were later inventions.

Modern-day apocalyptic sects seem to grow every year. One interesting example is the True Light Church of Christ, whose leaders taught their 450 fol-

MOTHER SHIPTON'S HOUSE

**Figure 59.** Mother Shipton's house. From Charles Mackay, *Extraordinary Popular Delusions and the Madness of Crowds* (1852; reprint New York: Crown Publishing, 1995), p. 277.

lowers in North and South Carolina that the world would end in 1970. On January 2, 1971, the *New York Times* interviewed a member of the sect who said he had not yet decided whether to reopen the upholstery shop that he closed a year previous in preparation for the end. So far these prophets who have predicted the end of the world have had a perfect score—they have always been wrong.

In more traditional Christian sects, there are many who interpret words in the book of Revelation to mean the coming of an apocalypse. Apocalyptic prophetic literature began to emerge during the Babylonian exile, the time when the Jews were taken to Babylon (Iraq) as slaves. Before this point in time, there was little in the way of apocalyptic literature perhaps because it was thought that God would restore Israel. During the Greek occupation of Israel, this theme was revived in Daniel and the book of Enoch (pseudepigrapha, or Jewish nonrabbinic religious writings of the period 200 B.C.E. to 200 C.E. not included in the Old Testament). One of the emergent themes was individual justice—if the evil foreign empires were not punished in this life, it must be that they will be punished in the next life. This concept was well entrenched by the time Jesus was active.

One of the current questions of theology is whether the historical Jesus believed in the eschaton as something that comes at the end of all time, in a miraculous event by God, or whether it was something made manifest in daily life. (The eschaton is commonly referred to as doomsday—the day when the world will come to an end. Theologians call it the divinely ordained climax of history.) Some feel that the current church is living that question with the same ambiguity reflected in the Gospels. In any case, a Woody Allen quote helps end this section on a lighter note:

> *The Lord is merciful. He maketh me lie down in green pastures. The problem is, I can't get up.*
>
> —Woody Allen, *Without Feathers*

## ⅄ PUNISHING THE DIVINERS
## IN NORTH CAROLINA

> *But slowly they are routed out*
> *Too seek diminishing water spout*
> *And men will die of thirst before*
> *The oceans rise to mount the shore.*
> *And lands will crack and rend anew*
> *You think it strange. It will come true.*
>
> —Mother Shipton

Throughout this book, I scatter examples of divination for the Old and New Testaments. Several revered religious leaders in the Bible divined the future using the classic methods, without suffering God's wrath.[42] For example, in Genesis 44:5, Joseph's household manager refers to a silver drinking cup used for scrying "in which my lord drinketh and whereby indeed he divineth." In other words, Joseph used reflections off the cup or liquid in the cup much like a modern crystal ball reader. Later, Joseph accuses his brothers of stealing the cup, saying "that such a man as I can certainly divine [the identity of the thieves]." We also discussed the Urim and Thummim, objects mentioned in Numbers 27:21 and 1 Samuel 28:6 of the Hebrew Scriptures. They were divination devices that the high priest consulted to determine the will of God. Perhaps they were tossed like dice. The prophet Daniel was employed for many years in Babylon as the chief occultist to the king. He was supervisor "of the magicians, astrologers, Chaldeans and soothsayers" (Daniel 5:11).

B. A. Robinson, writing for the ReligiousTolerance.org Web site,[43] notes, however, that there are numerous biblical passages that condemn specific divination techniques. In Deuteronomy 18:10–11, Israelites are forbidden from using several specific practices. One example is: "There shall not be found among you anyone that . . . useth divination, or an observer of times, or an enchanter or a witch, or a charmer, or a consulter with familiar spirits, or a wizard, or a necromancer" (KJV). Today, many conservative Christian denominations condemn the use of divination that requires mechanical aids, such as crystal balls, or the interpretation of natural signs, such as the flight of birds.

In general, wherever Christianity gained power, divination lost a foothold. Divination was so attractive to church members that synods (assemblies of church officials) forbade it, and councils legislated against it. In chapter 1's entry on bibliomancy, we discussed a church canon against divination by randomly opening a bible and determining future actions by the first passage found, but there are many other antidivination canons. The Council of Ancyra in 314 decreed five years penance to anyone who went to a diviner (canon xxiv). The Council of Laodicea in 360 forbade clergymen to become magicians or to make amulets (canon xxxvi), and those who wore them were to be driven out of the church.

From Roman times until today, governments have often tried to outlaw divination. Consider North Carolina's antidivination law, a McCarthy-era law against palmistry and clairvoyance invoked to shut down certain stores in Waynesville, Western North Corolina. Local sheriffs compile lists of psychics and readers.[45] For example, in June 1999, a North Carolina Sheriff had Psychic Gallery owner Larry Somers's business license revoked, and his month-old Waynesville shop closed down.[46] Sheriff Alexander cited a 1951 North Carolina General Statute 14–401.5, which makes it a Class 2 misdemeanor punishable by fines or imprisonment to practice "phrenology, palmistry, clairvoyance, fortune-telling and crafts of a similar kind"—unless it is under the auspices of a church or school social event. Kindra Rajaniemi was cited for tarot-card reading a few months later.

Area witches and pagans say the law trivializes their sacred divinatory arts by allowing only silly readings at school carnivals and, ironically, Christian church bazaars. Though the law affects sixty North Carolina counties, police arbitrarily enforce it. For example, Durham County's Duke University has carried on its famous studies of clairvoyance for decades, while individual psychics and store owners in other parts of the state such as Charlotte and Raleigh are harassed and driven out of town. Many fear that authorities who act on anonymous complaints send the message that angry neighbors can easily ruin "alternative" business owners. Since the statute says nothing about money in relation to readings, its purpose was not to protect the public from fraudulent mediums.

Here are the exact words of Carolina Criminal Code G.S. 14–401.5:

> It shall be unlawful for any person to practice the arts of phrenology, palmistry, clairvoyance, fortune-telling and other crafts of a similar kind in the counties named herein. Any person violating any provision of this section shall be guilty of a Class 2 misdemeanor.
>
> This section shall not prohibit the amateur practice of phrenology, palmistry, fortune-telling or clairvoyance in connection with school or church socials, provided such socials are held in school or church buildings. (Penalty for conviction is a fine of up to $500, up to six months in prison, or both.)[47]

It's interesting that amateur practice is allowed, but serious practice is not. The catchall phrase "and other crafts of a similar kind" seems to grant police broad powers to define such arts and stop their practice. Could the police shut down local businesses that offer tarot classes or sell runestones? Could psychologists conducting past-life regressions be arrested? What about using groundhogs to predict the weather? What happens to Ouija boards?

Note that this statute does not only prohibit the commercial use of divination techniques. It is a general prohibition of these techniques, even in private or in noncommercial settings. It seems to criminalize a person's use of tarot cards at home. It will be interesting to see how long the statue survives because it seems to be counter to the U.S. Constitution's First Amendment dealing with freedom of personal expression.[48] To counter this law, the North Carolina based Ancient Arts Freedom Association has been established to promote freedom to practice the arts of divination.[49]

## ᛉ HYPERBEINGS, HYPERTIME, AND ETERNITYGRAMS

> *"I take my accurate form,"* Memnoch continued, *"when I am in Heaven or outside of Time."*
>
> —Anne Rice, *Memnoch the Devil*

> *What can hyperbeings do, and why do their acts initially seem so alien to us?*
> —Theoni Pappas, *More Joy of Mathematics*

Is there any conceivable scientific explanation for seeing into the future? I favor a skeptical viewpoint that suggests divination has more to do with the mind and subconscious, but for a few paragraphs, I hope you can indulge a little fanciful speculation. In some sense, a physicist might pose the question of divination in the language of Einstein's theory of general relativity, which describes space and time as a unified four-dimensional continuum called "space-time." To best understand this, consider yourself as having three spatial dimensions—height, width, and breadth. You also have the dimension of duration—how long you last. Modern physics views time as an extra dimension; thus, we live in a universe having three spatial dimensions and one additional dimension of time.[50]

Stop and consider some mystical implications of space-time. Can something exist outside of space-time? What would it be like to exist outside of space-time? For example, Thomas Aquinas believed God to be outside of

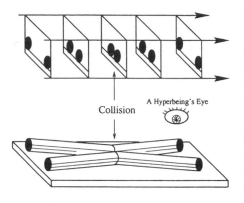

Collision    A Hyperbeing's Eye

**Figure 60.** An eternitygram for two colliding disks.

space-time and thus capable of seeing all of the universe's objects, past and future, in one blinding instant. This is the ultimate in divination! An observer existing outside of time, in a region called "hypertime," can see the past and future all at once. In a strange sense, when we scan back and forth over a musical score we are like a hyperbeing who lives outside of time. A musical score makes time solid. A musician can see past, present, and future all at once.

There are many examples of beings in literature and myth who live outside of space-time. A significant number of theologians living in the Middle Ages believed that angels were nonmaterial intelligences living by a time different from humans, and that God was entirely outside of time. Lord Byron (1788–1824) aptly describes these ideas in the first act of his play *Cain: A Mystery*, where the fallen angel Lucifer says:

> With us acts are exempt from time, and we
> Can crowd eternity into an hour,
> Or stretch an hour into eternity.
> We breathe not by a mortal measurement—
> But that's a mystery.

As I just mentioned, I likened musical scores as a visualization of time. But perhaps a more direct analogy involves an illustration of an "eternitygram" representing two disks rolling toward on another, colliding, and rebounding. Figure 60 shows two spatial dimensions along with the additional dimension of time. You can think of successive instants in time as stacks of movie frames that form a 3-D picture in hypertime in the eternitygram. Figure 60 is a "timeless" picture of colliding disks in eternity, an eternity in which all instants of time lie frozen like musical notes on a musical score. Eternitygrams are timeless. Hyperbeings looking at the disks in this chunk of space-time would see past, present and future all at once. What kind of relationship with humans could a creature (or God) have who live completely outside of time? How could they relate to us in our changing world? One of my favorite modern examples of God living outside of time is

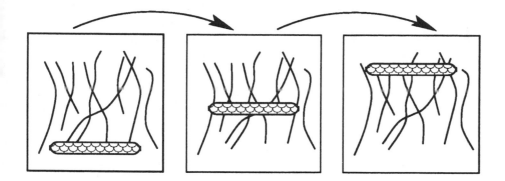

<CXXXXXX> - Perception of "Now" moves "up the page"

**Figure 61.** Dancing bees, frozen in space-time. (The track of each bee through space-time is represented by a line.) Is time an illusion? If bee world lines were somehow fixed in space-time, and all that "moved" was our perception shifting "up the page" as time "passes," we would still see a complex dance of buzzing bees, even though nothing was moving.

described in Anne Rice's novel *Memnoch the Devil*. At one point, Lestat, Anne Rice's protagonist, says, "I saw as God sees, and I saw as if Forever and in All Directions." Lestat looks over a balustrade in Heaven to see the entire history of world:

> The world as I had never seen it in all its ages, with all its secrets of the past revealed. I had only to rush to the railing and I could peer down into the time of Eden or Ancient Mesopotamia, or a moment when Roman legions had marched through the woods of my earthly home. I would see the great eruption of Vesuvius spill its horrid deadly ash down upon the ancient living city of Pompeii. Everything there to be known and finally comprehended, all questions settled, the smell of another time, the taste of it.[51]

Figure 61 shows a schematic diagram of dancing bees in space-time, just like figure 60 shows two disks colliding in space-time. The track of each bee through space-time is represented by a line. In each of the three squares in figure 60, the time axis is vertical. This means that time gradually proceeds up the page, the past at bottom and the future toward the top. The space axis in each square is horizontal. A bee sitting still would be represented by a vertical line in the squares because its horizontal (spatial) component never changes. If all bee world lines (paths in space-time) were somehow fixed like tunnels in the ice of space-time, and all that "moved" was our perception shifting up the page in the figure as time "passes," we would still see a complex dance of interacting bees even though nothing was moving. Perhaps an alien would see this differently than us. In some sense, all bee tracks and interactions may be considered fixed in the geometry of space-time, with all movement and change being an illusion resulting from our changing psychological perception of the moment "now." Some mystics have suggested that space-time is like a novel being "read" by the soul, the "soul" being a kind of eye or observer that stands outside of space-time, slowly gazing up along the time axis.

Of course, many stories have been devoted to the experience of time. One of my favorite short stories is Norman Spinrad's "The Weed of Time," which describes a boy who eats a weed that makes him see his whole lifetime as simultaneously present. Therefore, as a baby, he already knows he will eat the weed before (according to our limited point of view) he has ever eaten it! David Masson's "Traveller's Rest" describes a war in a land where everyone's perception of time slows down as they travel south. One young soldier on a short vacation travels south, marries, and has children. Then, in middle age, the soldier receives a message telling him that his vacation is over. He travels north to arrive in his barracks twenty-two minutes (local time) after he left.

〰〰    〰〰    〰〰

Many of the diviners and prophets in the next chapter claim to have been able to see through both time and space. They range from biblical prophets to several contemporary "psychics." Most seers, whether children or adults, seem to prophesy Earthly disasters. When they don't predict calamities on the planetary scale, they often predict death or harm to individuals. One interesting example is the incident in which the Virgin of Fatima, in Portugal, was said to have appeared before three shepherd children on May 13, 1917. Interpretations of her prophecies varied, but believers think the first prophecy foretold the end of World War I and the start of World War II. The second prophesy supposedly predicted the rise and fall of communism. The content of the third prophecy was not immediately released, leading Fatima fanatics to hold hunger strikes and even hijack planes to try to force the Vatican to disclose the prophesy. On May 13, 2000, the Vatican finally released the "third secret" of Fatima, which has long been the fodder for speculation among conspiracy and doomsday cultists. The Vatican described the secret as a vision of the 1981 assignation attempt on Pope John Paul II.[52]

Although many of the prophets do predict catastrophes, diviners of all kinds also offer hope to people in pain. But is it a false hope? And do diviners lead law-enforcement agencies astray? One contemporary example includes John and Patsy Ramsey, who initiated a campaign they say was aimed at finding the killer of their daughter JonBenét. JonBenét's body was found in the basement of their Boulder, Colorado, home in 1996. In June 2000, the Ramsey parents posted a psychic's sketch of the murder suspect on their Internet site. The sketch is based on the work of the late psychic Dorothy Allison, who claimed to have assisted police investigations. Allison came up with her image of the suspect during a 1998 appearance on a network television show. The Ramsey's Web site asks:

> Have you seen this man? This man may have been in the Boulder area in December 1996. . . . We firmly believe that this most horrible of killers will be caught based on information provided by people who care about right and wrong. . . . Please help, so another innocent child will not be a victim and another family will not suffer unbearable grief.[53]

I urge you to approach the diveners and their prophecies with some skepticism, but also try to observe what characteristics they seem to have in common. Even the ancient prophecies and prophets hold up a mirror to humanity's common fears and values, which do not seem to have changed substantially through time. Today, the diviners and their messages come in many flavors. On the one hand, there is the seemingly harmless carnival entertainer reading the tarot cards. On the other hand, there are the "psychic surgeons" who don't divine the future but rather attempt to divine the presence of disease and remove it. Researchers who have studied these surgeons have discovered they often hide chicken guts in false thumbs and then appear to perform bloody operations, removing "tumors" from peoples' abdomens.[54] All of this may thereby prevent a sick person from getting essential traditional medical care. We can, however, learn many lessons by studying the prophets and diviners that follow.

Earlier in this chapter we discussed how many religious groups found the concept of Apocalypse quite compelling. I reemphasize that almost every religion in the larger Judeo-Christian-Islamic context has a theology that includes accounts of massive destruction arising from a final battle between good and evil.[55] Author James Lewis suggests that doomsday prophecies appear in every era and every culture, and have become an especially important theme in American religions life since the rise of the Millerite movement in the 1830s.[56] Even in Hindu cosmology we find the mention of a future time in which the air fills with huge clouds that rain until the world dies in watery darkness. The moon and stars dissolve. This period of fluidic blackness is called the night of Brahma.[57]

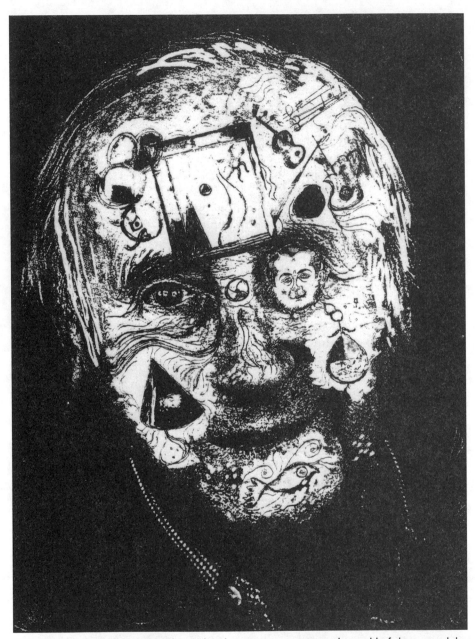

Joan Miro, the surrealist painter who explored ways to express in art the world of dreams and the unconscious. (*Reflections on Miro*, courtesy Paul Hartal, Ph.D.)

# 3.

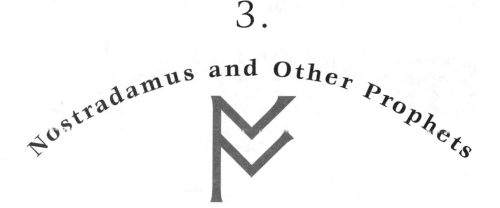

Nostradamus and Other Prophets

*These rabbits who claim to have second sight—I've known one or two in my time. But it's not usually advisable to take much notice of them. For one thing, many are plain mischievous. A weak rabbit who can't hope to get far by fighting some- times tries to make himself important by other means, and prophecy is a favorite. The curious thing is that, when he turns out wrong, his friends seldom seem to notice, as long as he puts on a good act and keeps talking. But then again, you may get a rabbit who really has this odd power, for it does exit.*
—Richard Adams, *Watership Down*

In the last days of 1999, Jerusalem's psychiatric clinics prepared for a surge in admissions among millennium pilgrims struck by a syndrome that convinced them they are biblical prophets, sometimes with the power to divine the future.[1] Already by November, there was a 50 percent increase in cases, and Israeli psychiatrists were treating several foreigners affected by what is known as "Jerusalem Syndrome." The syndrome afflicts only a minority of pilgrims to Jerusalem, some of whom are overwhelmed by the religious significance of the Holy City. Each year, clinics treat about 150 cases of the syndrome, which occurs most often in Protestant Christians and Jews with above-average education from the United States and Europe. Vis- itors most commonly assume the identity of "prophets" like King David, Jesus, John the Baptist or the Virgin Mary. Other visitors come to Jerusalem with visions of doom or with the compulsion to wear white robes—some- times their hotel bed sheets—while preaching lengthy sermons. The average age of Jerusalem syndrome prophets is thirty-five with an age range from seventeen to seventy.

Studying the Jerusalem syndrome made me wonder just who were the famous prophets in the past, and who are the current prophets shaping our psyches. This chapter is a veritable "who's who in divination"—a smorgasbord of some famous and not so famous diviners and their breathtaking effect on the world. Here, I introduce you to the shamans, seers, mediums, guides, and gates. One value of cataloguing so many seers is to see what their predictions have in common. For example, many predictions seem to deal with floods and wars, the submerging of land masses, the mythical land of Atlantis, prediction of great crises at the end of the twentieth century, enormous earthquakes, the drifting of entire continents and land masses, the shifting of the Earth's poles, horrifying extremes of weather, deadly epidemics, and global hatred and war. What other common themes can you find, and why do you think they are so prevalent?

Some medieval alchemists, astrologers, and seers practiced divination and *also* practiced good science, but their dual interest often put them in conflict with orthodox theology. Consequently, most people considered their work mysterious, and the term "occultism" gradually came to denote the study of supernatural forces. Nevertheless, in many cases, today's natural sciences stemmed from occultism, and early scientists were frequently called magicians and sorcerers because their contemporaries attributed mystery to the "scientist's" investigations. "Occult" comes from the Latin *occulere* meaning "hidden." Occultism includes various theories and practices involving supernatural forces and occurs in all human societies throughout recorded history.

To some extent, modern occultism begins with the concept of animal magnetism, first developed by the Austrian physician Franz Anton Mesmer in the late eighteenth century. Mesmer believed that certain individuals possess occult powers, comparable to the powers of magnets, that can be used to invoke the supernatural. In the mid-nineteenth century, occultism took the form of spiritualism, a belief that the spirits of the dead may manifest themselves through living persons called mediums. In the twentieth century, occultism included serious investigations of extrasensory perception (ESP), which included mental telepathy. Although not considered mainstream science, occultism has been studied extensively at universities such as Duke, Yale, and Stanford.

The following pages list some of my favorite diviners, sorted into three categories: those that lived before the year 1000, between 1000 and 1800, and from 1800 until present. This is a list of those diviners that held a personal interest for me, and no doubt there will be diviners that you would like to see added to or removed from my list. My goal is to stimulate debate and include a range of personalities, from the ultraserious biblical prophets to some of the wild New Age channelers. I look forward to hearing from readers who might suggest modifications to my list.

*A note on quotation sources*: In order to give you an intimate flavor of the diviner's personality and ideas, where possible I have placed a quotation from the diviner preceding each entry. I wanted you to hear them speak in their own words. These quotations usually came from books such as Matthew Bunson's *Prophecies 2000*[2] or John Hogue's *The Millennium Book of Prophecy*,[3] or from the Internet. The Internet can be especially useful when looking for information on New Age channelers and prophets who often have their own personal Web pages. These Web pages can be easily found by using Internet search engines or by visiting the Web pages that are cited in the endnotes for these entries and also listed in the Further Reading section.

## ◇ THE ANCIENTS—DIVINERS BEFORE 1000 C.E.

### ♌ *Berosus*

> *All terrestrial life and limb shall be consumed by fire during a planetary alignment in [July 2001 C.E.]. The fire will be followed by a great flood in October when the same planets are conjoined in Capricorn.*
>
> —Berosus[4]

Berosus was a famous Chaldean astrologer who flourished during and after the lifetime of Alexander the Great. Although the exact dates of his birth and death are unknown, it is certain that he lived in the days of Alexander (356–326 B.C.E.)

At some point in his life, Berosus left Chaldea (southern Babylonia) and settled in Greece on the island of Cos, where he opened a school of astronomy and astrology. The ancient Greeks considered him be a great magician and were impressed by the supposed accuracy of his astrological predictions. The Greeks honored Berosus by erecting a statue of him with a tongue sculpted from gold, signifying the truth of his forecasts. Berosus was also a historian and wrote a Greek-language work in three books on the history and culture of Babylonia. The book was widely used by later Greek compilers, whose versions in turn were quoted by religious historians. Even though Berosus's work survives only in fragmentary citations, he is remembered for passing knowledge of the origins of Babylon to the ancient Greeks.

Berosus's gave a creative account of the creation of the world and of mankind, as preserved to us by Syncellus who copied it from Alexander Polyhistor:

> There was a time when all was darkness and water, and from the midst thereof issued spontaneously monstrous animals and the most peculiar figures: men with two wings, and others with four, with two faces or two heads, one of a man, the other of a woman, on one body, and with the two sexes together; men with goats' legs and goats' horns, or with horses' hoofs; others with the hinder parts of a horse and the foreparts of a man, like the hippocentaurs. There were, besides, human-headed bulls, dogs with four bodies and fishes' tails, horses with dogs' heads, animals with the head and body of a horse and the tail of a fish, other quadrupeds in which all sorts of animal shapes were confused together, fishes, reptiles, serpents, and every kind of marvellous shapes, representations of which may be seen in the paintings of the temple of Belos.[5]

## ♌ *Artemidorus Daldianus*

> *For a man to be penetrated [in a dream] by a richer and older man is good: for it is customary to receive from such men. To be penetrated by a younger and poorer is bad: for it is the custom to give to such persons. It signifies the same [i.e., is bad] if the penetrator is older and poor.*
> —Artemidorus Daldianus, *Oneirocritica*[6]

Daldianus lived in the second century C.E. in Asia Minor. He was a soothsayer whose *Oneirocritica* (Interpretation of Dreams) described a variety of superstitions, dreams, divination methods, and myths. The book was so popular that sixteen hundred years later it was translated into English and published in London, where, in the year 1800, it had already been reprinted thirty-three times.

## ♌ *Daniel*

> *In the time of those kings, the God of heaven will set up a kingdom that will never be destroyed, nor will it be left to another people. It will crush all those kingdoms and bring them to an end, but it will itself endure forever. This is the meaning of the vision of the Rock cut out of a mountain, but not by human hands—a Rock that broke the iron, the bronze, the clay, the silver and the gold to pieces."*
> —Daniel 2:44–45

Daniel was a prophet from the Old Testament who foretold the coming of the messiah Y'shua. Nearly all that is known of Daniel comes from the Old Testament. He belonged to the tribe of Juda, and was of noble descent. While a teenager, he was carried captive to Babylon. There he was entrusted to the care of Asphenez, the master of the king's eunuchs, and was educated in the language and learning of the Chaldeans, experts on divination, magic, and astrology in Babylon. After three years, Daniel and three companions appeared before the king, who found that they were great diviners. The king promoted them to a place in his court. Whenever Daniel's powers of divination was tested, he proved superior to "all the diviners, and wise men, that were in all his kingdom." The book of Daniel describes the king's dream that Daniel alone could interpret. Nebuchadnezzer's dream included a large statue made up of various materials and broken in pieces by a small stone that became a mountain and filled the earth. Daniel said that the several parts of the statue symbolized monarchies, while the stone that destroyed them and grew into a mountain foretold an everlasting kingdom (the Messiah) that would shatter all the other kingdoms. Some biblical scholars suggest that Daniel may have been a composite of several people, or that he may also be the prophet Ezekiel, because of the overwhelming similarities in their prophecies.

## ♌ *Ezekiel*

> *And the living creatures ran and returned as the appearance of a flash of lightning.*
> —Ezekiel 1:14

Ezekiel (592–570 B.C.E.) was one of the major Hebrew prophets and the author of an Old Testament book. He was carried as a prisoner to Babylonia in 597 B.C.E. Ezekiel's early prophesies in Jerusalem foretold various calamities, but his later prophecies, given while the Jews were exiled in Babylon, were more hopeful. He dramatized his prophecies with metaphors and descriptions that seem bizarre or, as some skeptics might say, psychotic. Notice how Ezekiel in the Old Testament had visions that, today, sound like modern UFO reports:

> And I looked, and behold, a whirlwind came out of the north, a great cloud, and a fire infolding itself, and a brightness was about it, and out of the midst thereof as the color of amber, out of the midst of the fire. . . . Also out of the midst thereof, came the likeness of four living creatures. And this was their appearance, they had the likeness of a man. And every one had four faces, and every one had four wings. And their feet were straight feet; and the sole of their feet was like the sole of a calf's foot; and they sparkled like the color of burnished brass. And when the living creatures went, the wheels went by them: and when the living creatures were lifted up from the earth, the

wheels were lifted up. And the likeness of the firmament upon the heads of the living creature was as the color of the terrible crystal, stretched forth over their heads above.

Here is one of Ezekiel's famous prophecies:

On the Day Gog attacks Israel—it is the Lord Yahweh who speaks—I shall grow angry. . . . I swear that on that Day there will be a fearful quaking in the Land of Israel. At my presence the fish in the sea and the birds of heaven, the wild beasts and all the reptiles . . . and all men on earth will quake. Mountains will fall, cliffs crumble and walls collapse and I will confront Gog with every sort of terror. . . . I will punish him with plague and bloodshed and send torrential rain, hailstones, fire and brimstone against him and his hordes and against the many nations with him. I mean to display my greatness and holiness and to compel the many nations to acknowledge me. This is how they will learn that I am Yahweh.

The references in endnote 6 discuss the remote possibility that Ezekiel had temporal lobe epilepsy, which is thought to play a role in intense religious experience for some people. Also note that Ezekiel was struck dumb on one occasion for an unspecified length of time (Ezekiel 3:26).

## ♌ *Isaiah*

> And it shall come to pass, that instead of sweet smell there shall be stink; and instead of a girdle a rent; and instead of well set hair baldness; and instead of a stomacher a girding of sackcloth; and burning instead of beauty. Thy men shall fall by the sword, and thy mighty in the war.
>
> —Isaiah 3:24–25

Isaiah is the Old Testament prophet after whom the book of Isaiah is named. Scholars now recognize that the Book took shape over several centuries, attaining its present form sometime before 180 B.C.E. He said that the people of Israel would be punished for their sins, but some Jews will be redeemed and dwell in a perfect age. When Isaiah had his first vision of God, he was overwhelmed by God's power. Isaiah offered to convey God's messages, even though he was aware he would experience terrible opposition.

For many years, scholars have wondered about the meaning of the fifty-third chapter of the book of Isaiah. It appears to be a prophesy concerning the sufferings and trials of the coming Messiah, who Christians interpret to be Jesus. Some modern rabbis suggest the trials described refer to difficulties faced by the nation of Israel.

## ♌ *Jeremiah*

> God: *Before I formed thee in the belly I knew thee; and before thou camest forth out of the womb I sanctified thee, and I ordained thee a prophet unto the nations.*
>
> Jeremiah: *Then said I, Ah, Lord GOD! behold, I cannot speak: for I am a child.*
> —Jer. 1:5

Jeremiah (650–570 B.C.E.) was a Hebrew prophet and author of an Old Testament book. Jeremiah tried to help his nation of Judah adjust to various conflicts between its powerful neighbors, which included Assyria, Babylonia, and Egypt. He correctly predicted the destruction of the Holy Temple by the Babylonians.

According to the Bible, Jeremiah had his first visions in 627 B.C.E., when he foretold the coming of enemies, symbolized by a boiling pot:

> The word of the LORD came to me a second time, saying, "What do you see?" And I said, "I see a boiling pot, tilted away from the north." Then the LORD said to me: Out of the north disaster shall break out on all the inhabitants of the land. (Jer. 1:13)

Scholars are not sure if the enemy was supposed to be Russian nomads, Assyrians, Babylonians, or some vague evil. Jeremiah was often depressed and overwhelmed by God. Jeremiah said that he wished he never been born and accused God of being deceitful.

Jeremiah's most important prophecy described a future where man could be at peace with God:

> Behold, the days come, saith the LORD, that I will make a new covenant with the house of Israel, and with the house of Judah: Not according to the covenant that I made with their fathers in the day [that] I took them by the hand to bring them out of the land of Egypt; which my covenant they brake, although I was an husband unto them, saith the LORD: But this [shall be] the covenant that I will make with the house of Israel; After those days, saith the LORD, I will put my law in their inward parts, and write it in their hearts; and will be their God, and they shall be my people. And they shall teach no more every man his neighbour, and every man his brother, saying, Know the LORD: for they shall all know me, from the least of them unto the greatest of them, saith the LORD: for I will forgive their iniquity, and I will remember their sin no more. (Jer. 31:31–34)

## ♌ *Joel*

> *The day of the Lord is at hand, and as a destruction from the Almighty shall it come. Is not the meat cut off before our eyes, yea, joy and gladness from the house of our God? The seed is rotten under their clods, the garners are laid desolate, the barns are broken down; for the corn is withered. How do the beasts groan! the herds of cattle are perplexed, because they have no pasture; yea, the flocks of sheep are made desolate. O Lord, to thee will I cry: for the fire hath devoured the pastures of the wilderness, and the flame hath burned all the trees of the field. The beasts of the field cry also unto thee: for the rivers of waters are dried up, and the fire hath devoured the pastures of the wilderness.*
>
> —Joel 1:1–1:20

Joel was an Old Testament prophet who had dramatic visions of cosmic omens, plagues, wars, and ruins. The Bible reveals very little about Joel who lived during the period of the Second Temple of Jerusalem (516 B.C.E.–70 C.E.). In the Book of Joel, the prophet Joel describes calamity resulting from a locust plague. He warns the people to repent and that there will be a final judgment.

## ♌ *St. John of Patmos*

> *And I looked, and behold a pale horse: and his name that sat on him was Death, and Hell followed with him. And power was given unto them over the fourth part of the earth, to kill with sword, and with hunger, and with death, and with the beasts of the earth.*
>
> —Revelation 6:8

According to tradition, John is believed to have written the Apocalypse or book of Revelation around 81–96 C.E. This final book of the New Testament appears to be written by more than one author, though it purports to have been written by John, Jesus's disciple who witnessed Jesus' crucifixion. In many of John's apocalyptic prophecies we gain glimpses of how terrible he sees life will become for nonbelievers:

> I watched as he opened the sixth seal. There was a great earthquake. The sun turned black like sackcloth made of goat hair, the whole moon turned blood red, and the stars in the sky fell to earth, as late figs drop from a fig tree when shaken by a strong wind. The sky receded like a scroll, rolling up, and every mountain and island was removed from its place. Then the kings of the earth, the princes, the generals, the rich, the mighty, and every slave and every free man hid in caves and among the rocks of the moun-

tains. They called to the mountains and the rocks, "Fall on us and hide us from the face of him who sits on the throne and from the wrath of the Lamb! For the great day of their wrath has come, and who can stand?" (Revelation 6:12–17)

## ⨳ Kate-Zahl

> When the people are hungry, instead of making war, pray to the Father, that your needs be provided.
>
> —Kate Zahl[7]

Ancient Americans have legends of a prophet sometimes called the Healer or the Teacher. For example, the mound builders of North America have a legend of a great Healer who could heal people with fatal illnesses and even bring the dead to life. The man worked with ordinary people who sometimes reported seeing strange crosses on the palms of his hands. In Central America, his name was Kate-Zahl or Quetzalcoatl.

Kate-Zahl (first century C.E.) is considered the greatest prophet of the ancient Toltec Indians of Central Mexico. He is said to have foretold the coming of the Spanish conquistadors wearing "suits of shining metal" and who fired "thunder-rods," Legends say that Kate-Zahl started in Polynesia and then sailed to South America. Traders would speak of the God who walked the earth, healing the sick. His trail ran north, up the Mississippi to Canada. Today several tribes speak of his coming—the Algonquin, Cherokee, Chippewa, Cree, Dakota, Shawnee, Pawnee, Choctaw, and Seneca Indians. Supposedly, Kate-Zahl knew one thousand tongues, because everywhere he went, the first thing he did was learn the language.[8]

The pueblos of New Mexico and Arizona remember his words, "If to my teaching you are faithful, and to show that you have lived each day rightly, leave a light at night burning against the time I will return through the Dawn Light, and lead thee unto my father's Kingdom."[9] They wait patiently for his return and sometimes burn candles to hasten his journey. The Mormons suggest that Kate-Zahl was Jesus Christ.

## Ω Mahapurusa

A Mahapurusa is an individual destined for greatness and who can be distinguished from ordinary people by certain physical marks called *laksanas*. In Buddhism, the major *laksanas* include long arms that reach to the knees, webbed fingers, and a special bump on the top of the head. As they grow older, the Mahapurusas either become rulers or great spiritual leaders. For example, soothsayers were able to recognize at birth the fact that Gautama Buddha was destined for an awesome future, although the bump on the top of his head only became apparent after he became a buddha. A great deal of thought has gone into the various kinds of *laksanas* that might be discovered. For example, in 1931 a Dr. Coomaraswamy wrote an article entitled "On the Webbed-Fingers of Buddha" in the *Indian Historical Quarterly* describing "the thin lines of rosy light which may be seen between the fingers when they are in contact, and the hand is held up against the light."

## ♋ *Merlin*

> *The cult of religion shall be destroyed completely, and the ruin of the churches shall be clear for all to see. The race that is oppressed shall prevail in the end, for it will resist the savagery of the invaders. The Boar of Cornwall shall bring relief from these invaders, for it will trample the necks beneath its feet. The islands of the Ocean shall be given into the power of the Boar, and it shall lord it over the forests of Gaul. The House of Romulus shall dread the Boar's savagery, and the end of the Boar will be shrouded in mystery. The Boar shall be extolled in the mouths of its peoples, and its deeds will be as meat and drink to those who tell tales.*
>
> —Merlin[10]

The legendary Merlin is said to have lived in the fifth century C.E. and was England's most famous magician, known for his ability to foresee the future. According to the sixth-century chronicler Nennius, Merlin was the son of a human mother and a spirit father, from whom he inherited his ability to prophesy. He was raised in a priestly family, and his abilities allowed him to save his mother from execution. According to one legend, Merlin was the adviser to Uther Pendragon (King Arthur's father) and afterward to Arthur himself. Merlin advised Uther to establish the knightly fellowship of the Round Table and suggested that Uther's true heir would be revealed by a test requiring a sword to be drawn from a stone.

Merlin's very name conjures up images of mystery and magic. Merlin came to public consciousness through the writing of Geoffrey of Monmouth. Geoffrey was a cleric and teacher who lived in Oxford from about 1100 to 1155. In 1134 he translated the *Prophetiae Merlini*, or the *Prophecies of Merlin*, which he issued in 1134. He later incorporated this text into his major work, the *Historia Rigum Britanniae*, or the *History of the Kings of Britain*, which was eventually completed in 1136. In the *History*, Geoffrey tries to trace the kings of Britain back to 1200 B.C.E. and the fall of Troy. He also discusses the story of King Arthur, which is itself foreshadowed by the story of Merlin. Geoffrey's work appears to be an amalgam of historical fact and flights of imagination. Merlin appears to represent good and evil, and paganism and Christianity. He has wisdom, but in the end he becomes a victim of his own schemes.

## ♋ *Micah*

> *Hear, all you peoples! Listen, O earth, and all that is in it! Let the Lord God be a witness against you, the Lord from His holy temple. For behold, the Lord is coming out of His place; He will come down And tread on the high places of the earth. The mountains will melt under Him, and the valleys will split like wax before the fire, like waters poured down a steep place.*
>
> —Mic. 1:3–4

Micah (about 757–700 B.C.E.) was a Hebrew prophet, a contemporary of prophet Isaiah, and author of a book in the Old Testament. Micah attacked the morals of officials and social unfairness. The initial chapters of Micah contain predictions of divine judgment directed against Israel and Judah and foretell the destruction of Jerusalem and the Temple. He also condemns prophets who gave people false hopes. In the second section, he predicts that Israel's future would be grand and that a ruler would come out of Bethlehem to bring peace to the earth. Around 721 B.C.E. he prophesied, "The godly have been swept from the land. Not one upright man remains. All men lie in wait to shed blood: each hunts his brother with a net" (Mic. 7:2–7).

Sometimes the book of Micah is called "a small scale Isaiah" because it is a much briefer presentation of Isaiah's basic messages. In the first chapter there is a grand image of God striding forth in judgment against this nation of Judah, because the people of Judah were unholy even though God provided them with everything it takes to be godly.

## ♋ *Nanshe*

I don't want to add many mythological deities to this diviner list, but I couldn't resist this interesting tidbit of information on Nanshe, a goddess soothsayer and dream interpreter. According to Mesopotamian religion, Nanshe was a Sumerian goddess of the city of Nina in southeastern Mesopotamia. Nanshe's father, Enki, was the organizer of the universe. Other cultures also had bringers and interpreters of dreams, such as: Astarte/Athtartu (Canaanite-Phoenician myths), Geshtinanna (Sumerian myths), Nepthys (Egyptian myths), and Morpheus (Greek myths).

| My Seven Favorite and Famous Old Testament Prophets | |
|---|---|
| **Prophet** | **Visions** |
| Amos | *The judgment of the Lord upon Israel and the Assyrian threat:* "Trouble for those who are waiting so longingly for the day of God! What will this day of God mean for you? It will mean darkness, not light, as when a man escapes a lion's mouth, only to meet a bear. Will not the day of God be darkness, not light? It will all be gloom, without a single ray of light." |
| Daniel | *End of the world:* "That will be a time of great distress, unparalleled since nations first came into existence. When that time comes, your own people will be spared—all those whose names are found written in the Book." |
| Ezekiel | *The future of Israel:* "When in the world there shall appear quakings of places, tumult of peoples, schemings of nations, confusion of leaders, disquietude of princes, then shall you understand that it is of these things that the Most High has spoken since the days that were aforetime from beginning." |
| Isaiah | *Future of Israel:* "See, the Lord is going to lay waste the earth and devastate it; he will ruin its face and scatter its inhabitants. . . . The earth will be completely laid waste and totally plundered. The Lord has spoken this word. The earth dries up and withers. . . . The earth is defiled by its people; they have disobeyed the laws, violated the statutes and broken the everlasting covenant. Therefore a curse consumes the earth; its people must bear their guilt. Therefore earth's inhabitants are burned up, and very few are left." |
| Joel | *Repentance and hope:* "Blow the trumpet in Zion; sound the alarm on my holy mountain! Let all the inhabitants of the land tremble, for the day of the Lord is coming, it is near—a day of darkness and gloom, a day of clouds and thick darkness! Like blackness spread upon the mountains a great and powerful army comes; their like has never been from of old, nor will be again after them in ages to come." |
| Zechariah | *The Messiah:* "I shall gather all the nations to Jerusalem for battle. The city will be taken, the horses plundered, the women ravished. Half the city will go into exile, but the rest of the people will not be ejected from the city. Then Yahweh will sally out and fight those nations as once he fought on the day of battle." |
| Zephaniah | *Punishment of the Lord:* "On the Day of Yahweh's anger, by the fire of his jealousy, the whole earth will be consumed. For he will destroy, yes, annihilate everyone living on earth." |

## ♌ *St. Odilia*

*Hear, oh hear, my sisters and brothers: I saw forest and mountains tremble. There will come a time, when war will break out, more terrible than all other wars combined, which have ever visited mankind. A horrible warrior will unleash it, and his adversaries will call him Antichrist. All nations of the earth will fight each*

| My Six Favorite New Testament Prophets | |
|---|---|
| **Prophet** | **Sample Thoughts** |
| Jesus | "Think not that I am come to send peace on earth; I come not to send peace but a sword." |
| Luke | "There will be signs in the sun and moon and stars; on earth nations in agony, bewildered by the turmoil of the ocean and its waves; men fainting with terror and fear at what menaces the world, for the powers of heaven will be shaken." |
| Mark | "For in those days there will be great distress, unparalleled since God created the world, and such as will never be again. And if the Lord had not shortened that time, no human being would have survived." |
| Matthew | "You will be handed over to be tortured and put to death; and you will be hated by all nations on account of my name." |
| St. Paul (1 and 2 Thessalonians) | "The day of the Lord is going to come like a thief in the night. It is when people are saying, 'How quiet and peaceful it is' that the worst suddenly happens, as suddenly as labor pains come on a pregnant woman; and there will be no way for anybody to evade it." |
| St. John the Evangelist at Patmos (Book of Revelation) | "And I saw the dead, small and great, stand before God; and the books were opened: and another book was opened, which is the book of life: and the dead were judged out of those things which were written in the books, according to their works. And the sea gave up the dead which were in it; and death and hell delivered up the dead which were in them: and they were judged every man according to their works. And death and hell were cast into the lake of fire. This is the second death. And whosoever was not found written in the book of life was cast into the lake of fire." |

*other in this war. Oceans will lie between the great warriors, and the monsters of the sea, terrified by everything that happens on or under the sea, will flee to the deep. Battles of the past will be only skirmishes compared to the battles that will take place, because the earth will be red, and even the sky, the water and the air, since blood will flow in all directions. The earth will shake from the violent fighting. Famine and pestilence will join the war. The nations will then cry "peace, peace," but there will be no peace. Thrice will the sun rise over the heads of the combatants, without having been seen by them. But afterward there will be peace, and all who have broken peace will have lost their lives. On a single day more men will be killed than the catacombs of Rome have ever held. . . . Strange signs will appear in the skies: both horns of the moon will join the cross . . .*

—St. Odilia[11]

St. Odilia (d. 720 c.e.), also spelled Odile, was the blind daughter of the Frankish lord Adalrich who had large estates in Alsace. She founded the convent of Hohenburg (Odilienberg) in Alsace (northeastern French), to which Charlemagne granted immunity. She was patroness of Alsace and abbess of the Hohenburg Monastery. Odilia's father believed her blindness was an evil omen and abandoned the her in a nunnery when she was young. Her followers believe she was able to predict the future, and she herself said her abilities resulted from lifelong adapting to blindness. Some claim her sight was miraculously restored by her devout prayers or at her baptism. In the year of her death, she prophesied about a future world war: "The fighters will rise up in the heavens to take the stars and will throw them on cities, to set ablaze the buildings and cause immense devastation." Various forged documents have been used to offer historical evidence regarding Odilia, so it is difficult to separate fact from fiction. Today, her grave is in a chapel near the convent church on the Odilienberg. She is represented with a book on which lie two eyes.

Some legends suggest a very difficult childhood, including her father's desire to kill her. Her mother was finally able to persuade the father to give her away to a peasant, and at the age of twelve, Odilia was placed in a convent. The legend continues with her baptism by Bishop St. Erhard of Regensberg, at which time she saw for the first time. When her father was told of the miracle, he was so angry at his son for arranging for Odilia's return that he killed him. Later, the father accepted Odilia, but she fled when he wanted her to marry. In the end, he agreed to let her turn his castle into a convent.

## ᛉ THE MIDDLE REALM — DIVINERS BETWEEN 1000 TO 1800

### ⚹ *Henry Cornelius Agrippa von Nettesheim*

Henry Cornelius Agrippa von Nettesheim (1486–1535), commonly referred to as "Agrippa," was court secretary to Charles V, and variously an occult scholar, astrologer, military strategist, doctor, lawyer, secret agent, and a troublesome theologian within the Catholic Church. Agrippa (see figure 62) taught at various universities and held a government job until denounced for defending an accused witch. Agrippa was also the first to combine geomancy with the art of astrology. A big black dog named Monsieur followed Agrippa wherever he went, leading people to suspect the dog was his "familiar," that is, a demon in disguise. (We discussed Agrippa briefly in chapter 1 in the section on magic squares.)

In May 1524, while he was court physician to Louise de Savoy, Queen mother of Francis I, an impressive conjunction of planets raised the public's interest in astrology. Many influential people amused themselves by ordering horoscopes even for minor decisions. Because Agrippa was an alchemist and astrologer, his services were in demand. The queen mother asked him to make a horoscope for King Francis and his war with Charles V and the Bourbons, but Agrippa refused because he had not been paid in two years for his court duties. Agrippa made some bitter comments regarding Louise in a letter which the queen mother managed to read. He went further, and predicted a triumph for the Bourbons. For these reasons, Agrippa was forced to stay in Lyon without

**Figure 62.** Henry Cornelius Agrippa von Nettesheim (1486–1535). Ann Fiery, *The Book of Divination* (San Francisco: Chronicle Books, 1999), p. 165.

pension and without the right to leave the town until 1527.

Agrippa's book *De occulta philosophia* was a significant contribution to the Renaissance philosophical discussion concerning the powers of magic and its relationship with religion. He seemed to be driven by scholarly curiosity while trying to understand the intellectual and religious problems of his time.

About 1530 Agrippa made numerous enemies when he published an attack on occultism and other contemporary "sciences." He was thrown in jail for heresy. After questioning every type of scientific knowledge, he finally found peace in simple biblical belief. However, he became involved in papal politics and was imprisoned by French Authorities in 1534. His health declined in prison, and he died shortly after his release in 1535.

## )( *Chilam Balam*

> *Every moon every year, every day. . . . Every wind comes and goes, and all blood reaches its final resting place.*
>
> —Chilam Balam[12]

The Books of Chilam Balam are group of seventeenth- and eighteenth-century documents written in the language of the Yucatec Maya, Middle American Indians of the Yucatán Peninsula in eastern Mexico. The books also contain Spanish characters and provides information on ancient Mayan history and prophecies. Only a few book survive today.

"Chilam balam" means "secrets of the soothsayers." Some have suggested that Chilam Balam was actually a person also known as the Jaguar Priest who lived around 1168 C.E. The prophecies of Chilam Balam foretell twin bearded guests coming from the east in 1844 C.E. and bearing aloft an "upright beam." Some have taken this to refer to the beginning of the Baha'i faith, a religion founded in Iran in the mid-nineteenth century by Mirza Hoseyn 'Ali Nuri, who is known as Baha' Ullah. The "twin bearded guests" from the east are thought to refer to Baha'u'llah and his forerunner, the Bab.) Below is a sampling of a prophecy translated from the Chilam Balam:

> When the Katun 13 Ahau is coming to an end . . . the sign of the true God on high, there will come to us the upright beam. It will manifest itself to light the world. The union ended, envy ended, when the bearer of the future sign came to us. The priest lord, you shall see it from afar coming. The fame of the beam comes to awaken us. From everywhere it comes to us. Your brother is coming now. Receive your bearded guests from the east, bearers of the standard of God. Receive the word of God which Comes to us on the day of resurrection which is feared by all in the world. Lord, You are the unique God who created us. Take advantage of the word of God whose sign you raise on high, whose beam you raise upright that you raise upright so that it may be seen. It changes the splinters that come out of it. It changes them after the rainbow appears shown throughout the world. It is the sign of the true God of heaven. You are going to worship the true faith. You are going to worship the True God, believe the word of the One God, for his word came from heaven, and it counsels you. It awakens the world, makes them believe. Within another Katun I wept for my words, I, Chilam Balam, when I explained the word of the True God Lord forever over the earth.[13]

The following job description was found in one of the *Books of Chilam Balam*. The passage is so specific and detailed that one wonders if a person with such abilities was ever found!

> We seek an individual able: To impersonate and invoke the deity; To offer food and drink to the idols; To effect the drawing of the pebbles and regulate the calendar; To read weather and other omens in the clouds; To study the night sky and interpret the appearance of the celestial bodies; To determine the lucky and unlucky days for various mundane activities by the

casting of lots; To perform the numerous rituals of the cup, plate, etc.; To work miracles; To concoct medicinal herbs into ceremonial drinks; To predict the future; To announce the times for various agricultural and other activities; To insure adequate rainfall; To avert or bring to a timely end famine, drought, epidemics, plagues of ants and locusts, earthquakes; To distribute food to the hungry in time of need; To cut the honey from the hives; To determine the compensation to be placed on the crossroad altars; To read from the sacred scriptures the future road of the *katun* [calendar round]; To design and supervise the carving of stelae [stone monuments], the manufacture of word and clay idols, and the construction of temples; To construct tables of eclipses and helical risings of planets.[14]

## )( *Alessandro Cagliostro*

Cagliostro (1743–1795) was a magician who gazed into crystals, predicted winning lottery numbers for the French lottery, and formulated dream interpretation charts. His original name was Giuseppe Balsamo, born in Palermo, Sicily, and later traveled extensively through Europe and the mideast selling various love potions and offering his services as soothsayer. He excelled in swindles, posing at various times as a physician and hypnotist. In 1789 he was arrested in Rome after his wife had denounced him to the Inquisition as a heretic. The Inquisition charged him with heresy and sorcery and eventually sent him to prison where he died.

## )( *Girolamo Cardano*

> *This I recognize as unique and outstanding amongst my faults—the habit, which I persist in, of preferring to say above all things what I know to be displeasing to the ears of my hearers. I am aware of this, yet I keep it up willfully, in no way ignorant of how many enemies it makes for me.*
>
> —Girolamo Cardano[15]

As discussed earlier, Girolamo Cardano (1501–1576) was an Italian doctor, mathematician, astrologer, and gambler, born in Pavia, Italy. Cardano's father was a lawyer in Milan whose expertise in mathematics was so great that he was consulted by Leonardo da Vinci on questions of geometry. While growing up, Girolamo Cardano played card games, dice, and chess to make a living. Cardano's understanding of probability meant he had an advantage over his opponents.

Cardano was awarded a doctorate in medicine in 1525. In 1543, he was appointed Professor of Medicine at Pavia, and he gave the first clinical description of typhus fever. His 1545 book *Ars magna* ("Great Art") was an algebraic treatise containing the first published solutions of cubic and quartic equations. He also cast horoscopes for Edward VI of England.

Later in life, Cardano's son had been accused of attempting to poison his wife and was beheaded in prison. Cardano wrote that "this was my supreme, my crowning misfortune." More trouble came in 1570 when Cardano was imprisoned by the Inquisition for the heresy of casting the horoscope of Jesus Christ. He also cast his own horoscope and predicted the day and hour of his own death. When it came, and Cardano found that his astrological computations did not yield the accurate result, he committed suicide rather than ruin his reputation. In addition to Cardano's important contributions to algebra, he also made significant contributions to probability, hydrodynamics, mechanics, and geology.

## ♓ *John Dee*

> Is any honest student, or a modest Christian philosopher, to be, for such inventive feats, mathematically and mechanically wrought, counted and called a conjurer? Shall that man be condemned as a companion of Hellhounds and caller and conjurer of wicked damned spirits? How great is the blindness and boldness of the multitude of things above their capacitie.
>
> —John Dee[16]

John Dee (1527–1608) was a famous English alchemist, navigator, cartographer, spy, writer, astrologer, and mathematician who stimulated a revival of interest in mathematics (see figure 63). Dee, like Nostradamus, was very bright from a young age. He entered Cambridge University when he was fifteen and was a junior faculty member before taking his degree. After graduating he traveled to the European continent to continue his studies, achieving overnight fame in Paris at the age of twenty-three, when he delivered a lecture series on the recently exhumed works of Euclid. After lecturing and studying throughout Europe between 1547 and 1550, Dee returned to England in 1551 and was granted a pension by the government.

Dee became astrologer to the queen, Mary Tudor. When he looked closely at Mary's horoscope, he concluded that her reign would be short. Soon after he was imprisoned for being a magician and released in 1555.

Dee met the future Queen Elizabeth while she was being held under house arrest by Queen Mary. The two developed a friendship that lasted for the rest of their lives. When she became queen, Elizabeth gave Dee money and protected him from those who accused him of witchcraft. Besides practicing astrology for Elizabeth, he also gave advice to navigators who were exploring the Atlantic and was asked to name a favorable day for Elizabeth's coronation.

Dee soon became Elizabeth's personal fortuneteller in the same way that California astrologer Joan Quigley was for Ronald and Nancy Reagan. Unlike Quigley, Dee was an excellent mathematician and contributed to the first English translation of Euclid's mathematical work that appeared 1570, although it is credited to Sir Henry Billingsley, who became sheriff and later lord mayor of London. In addition, he wrote the preface, which encouraged the growing interest in mathematics. His lectures on Euclidean geometry at the University of Paris were always packed with interested students. His other interests included the science of optics, cartography, and astronomy.

**Figure 63.** Alchemists at work. Among other things, alchemists attempted to discover the secret of eternal youth and to determine how to transmute one metal into another. From Philip Ulstadt's *De Secretis Naturae*, published in 1544, and reprinted in Ernst Lehner, *Symbols, Signs, and Signets* (New York: Dover, 1950), p. 65.

Dee was a paradoxical amalgam of scientist and mystic. In addition to his science, he was also a crystal-gazer, a necromancer (someone who tries to commune with the dead), and a man who believed he could converse with angels and spirits and foretell the future. Dee became a significant keeper of knowledge during his lifetime, salvaging many ancient scientific tomes that had been scattered when Roman Catholic churches and monasteries were ransacked during the Reformation. His own library of more than four thousand books was the largest of its kind in Europe at the time.

In 1581, John Dee grew interested in divination. He later wrote of how he knelt in prayer and "there suddenly glowed a dazzling light, in the midst of which, in all his glory, stood the great angel, Uriel." The spirit handed Dee a crystal "most bright, most clear and glorious, of the bigness of an egg, and informed him that by gazing at it he could communicate with otherworldly spirits."[17]

In the same year, Dee obtained a "Chrystallo," a big crystal ball. Crystal-gazing, or scrying, as we've described, involves staring into the shiny ball and trying to see events in the past, present, and future. The intricate reflections in the ball are thought to induce visions in the viewer. John Dee was fascinated by divination, but he seemed to have little luck with scrying. Instead, he employed others to do the actual scrying and conversing directly with the spirits, while he kept scrupulous notes. One of Dee's chief scryers was Edward Kelley, who seemed to have several previous run-ins with the law for counterfeiting. He also was accused of necromancy, using dead bodies for divination or attempting to communicate with the dead.

When Kelley gazed into the crystal ball, he reported to Dee that "in the middle of the stone seemeth to stand a little round thing like a spark of fire, and it increaseth, and it seemeth to be as a glove of twenty inches diameter, or there about."[18] In this glowing central sphere, Kelley claimed to be in contact with spiritual beings who wanted to teach Dee "Enochian," the language spoken by angels and the inhabitants of the Garden of Eden.

Dee's fascinating Enochian records are sufficiently detailed that some people were convinced they represented a genuine pre-Hebraic language. However, other researchers have suggested that Enochian was a code Dee used to transmit messages from overseas to Queen Elizabeth.

Terrance McKenna, in his book *The Archaic Revival: Speculations on Psychedelic Mushrooms, the Amazon, Virtual Reality, UFOs, Evolution, Shamanism, and the Rebirth of the Goddess*, writes that Dee and Kelly "recorded hundreds of spirit conversations, including . . . an angelic language called Enochian, composed of non-English letters, but which computer analysis has recently shown to have a curious grammatical relationship to English."[19] An example of Enochian, which the angels said had been spoken by the Old Testament prophet, Enoch, sounded like this: *Madariatza da perifa Lil cabisa micaolazoda saanire caosago of fifa balzodizodarassa iada*, which meant "Oh, you heavenly denizens of the first air, you are mighty in the parts of the earth, and execute judgment of the highest."

Here is a sampling of the Enochian characters[20] that I have used to create a secret message. So far no one has been able to decipher my secret code.

*[seven lines of Enochian script characters]*

To this day, I don't think anyone knows from where the Enochian language comes. It does not appear to be from the ancient Middle East as far as we can tell. Supposedly, the spirits provided Dee and Kelly with predictions of future events. For example, Uriel, the most regular angelic visitor, explained that Mary Queen of Scotts was fated to be executed by Queen Elizabeth.

Many "believers" have asserted that the Enochian language predates all human languages and could be used to contact intelligences from other dimensions. Dee and Kelley said they thought the language could be used to converse with the Nephilim, the giants of the Old Testament. However, it seems that Dee and Kelley were not the first persons to come up with some kind of Enochian alphabet. For example, an alchemy text called the *Voarchadumia* by Pantheus, written in 1530, contained an eighteen-character alphabet attributed to Enoch. Interestingly, the British Museum's copy of this manuscript has copious marginal notes by Dr. John Dee. The notes date from 1559, and although Dee's twenty-one character alphabet does not resemble Pantheus's alphabet, it is possible that Dee got the idea from that text. And, as Terrance McKenna notes, Enochian has a curious grammatical relationship to English.

Although he remained in favor with Queen Elizabeth I, Dee, along with Kelly and their wives and servants, were forced out of England when the clergy began preaching against magical activities. A mob destroyed much of Dee's valuable library.

Toward the end of his life, John Aubry, Dee's biographer, described Dee as a beaten old man with a long beard as white as milk. He earned a little money telling fortunes and even sold his beloved books, one by one, in order to eat.

## )( *Kahunas*

Kahunas are practitioners of the ancient Hawaiian Huna religion. Kahuna means "keeper of the secret," and over time there have been many kinds of Kahunas, such as Kahunas of canoe building, medicine, divination, and fishing.

Some divination Kahunas have used seeds of a plant called "baby woodrose" (*Argyreia Nervosa*) to help them see into the future. The plant contains LSD-like compounds, and is a very strong euphoriant and hallucinogen used traditionally as a divination sacrament by the Kahunas of Hawaii and Polynesia. The Kahunas also practiced the art of healing, prophetic dream interpretation, and magic.

## )( *Jean de Vatiguerro*

> *All public worship will be interrupted. A terrible and harsh famine will begin in the entire world and mainly in the western regions, such as has never taken place since the birth of the world.*
>
> —Joao de Vatiguerro[21]

Joao de Vatiguerro (aka John of Vatiguerro) was a thirteenth-century Christian seer who saw a vision of the destruction of the Vatican and what sounds like an atomic holocaust some time near the year 2000. He wrote:

> After many tribulations, a Pope shall be elected out of those who survived the persecutions. By his sanctity he will reform the clergy, and the whole world shall venerate the Church for her sanctity, virtue, and perfection. . . .[22] Spoilation, pillaging, and devastation of that most famous city which is the capital and mistress of France will take place when the Church and the world are grievously troubled. . . .[23] The Pope will change his residence and the Church will not be defended for twenty-five months or more because, during all that time, there will be no Pope in Rome.[24]

Note that a very common theme of prophets from the thirteenth to the twentieth centuries includes various trials, sufferings, exiles, and murders of popes. These events are often associated with catastrophes, such as earthquakes and wars. Sometimes the wording is vague, making it difficult to determine if the prophecies have come to pass.

## )( *Pastor Bartholomew Holzhauser*

> *Priests and servants of the church will be reduced to misery, the youth led by atheism, and republics will be established in the whole world. And all will be destroyed by wars.*
>
> —Pastor Bartholomew Holzhauser[25]

Pastor Bartholomew Holzhauser was a seventeenth-century professor of theology and pastor of St. Johann Church in Austria. He was respected by both peasants and kings for his intellect. Holzhauser's followers believe he accurately foresaw the French Revolution, the rise of Hitler, World War II, the tensions between the United States and Russia, and holes in the ozone layer. Holtzhauser wrote:

> A great change shall come to pass, such as no mortal man will have anticipated. This struggle is the confrontation between Heaven and Hell. Old states shall die and light and dark will be matched against each other with swords, but it will be the swords of a different kind. It will be possible to carve up the heavens with these swords. A great lament will come over all mankind and only a small number will survive the tempest, the pestilence, and the horror.[26]

Holzhauser also established the Apostolic Union of Secular Priests, an association of priests who gave each other mutual support. He also wrote many predictions regarding the fate of the church:

> The fifth period of the Church, which began circa 1520, will end with the arrival of the holy Pope and of the powerful Monarch who is called "Help From God" because he will restore everything. The fifth period is one of affliction, desolation, humiliation, and poverty for the Church. Those Christians who survive the sword, plague and famines, will be few on earth. These are the evil times, a century full of dangers and calamities. Heresy is everywhere, and the followers of heresy are in power almost everywhere. but God will permit a great evil against His Church: Heretics and tyrants will come suddenly and unexpectedly; they will break into the Church. They will enter Italy and lay Rome waste; they will burn down churches and destroy everything. Antichrist and his army will conquer Rome, kill the Pope and take the throne.

The sixth period will begin with the powerful Monarch. The powerful Monarch, who is sent from God, will uproot every Republic. He will restore everything. And peace shall reign over the whole earth. . . . The Empire of the Mohammedans will be broken up.[27]

Holzhauser died in 1658.

## ⟩( *Joachim of Fiore*

> *God who once gave the spirit of prophecy to the prophets has given me the spirit of understanding to grasp with great clarity in His Spirit all the mysteries of sacred scripture. . . . Lift up the eyes of your mind from the dust of the earth; leave behind raging crowds and clashing words! In the Spirit follow the angel into the desert; with him ascend that mountain vast and high so that you can see the deep counsels hidden from days of old and from endless generations.*
>
> —Joachim of Fiore[28]

Joachim of Fiore (1130–1202) was an Italian monk and among the most fascinating figures of medieval Christendom.[29] Joachim, who was called a prophet, mystic, and philosopher and theologian, in his lifetime, interpreted history as a sequence of three ages, that of the Father (past), Son (present), and Holy Spirit (future). The last of these ages, the age of perfect spirituality, was to begin in 1260.

Joachim was born in 1132 in Calabria, Sicily, at that time a Norman kingdom. Sometime around 1158, Joachim decided to seek a religious life; ten years later he was ordained, and his fellow monks soon elected him to the position of abbot of the Cistercian Abbey of Sambucina in Italy. He disliked his administrative duties, and in 1191 retired to the forests to live a more spiritual life. In 1196, Pope Celestine III allowed Joachim to gather the disciples around him at San Giovanni in Fiore into the Order of San Giovanni.

One of his most important visions occurred in the middle of the night, after a time of agonizing doubt about the doctrine of the Trinity. In his vision, he saw a triangular musical instrument, which suddenly gave him fresh ideas about the mystery of the Trinity. According to Joachim, humans would have entered the "Age of the Holy Spirit" only after difficult tests and trials. Joachim prophesied the evolution of two kinds of humans in the future—the *hermits* who live on mountain tops and the *mediators* who lead us to new realms of spirituality. To express his views and excite people about his visions, Joachim drew all kinds of kaleidoscopic and geometrical figures.

In his book *Exposition on the Apocalypse*, Joachim wrote of two visions that inspired him. We already spoke of the stringed instrument. The other was revealed to him while contemplating the Apocalypse of John. Joachim had been struggling to understand Revelation 1:10: "On the Lord's Day I was in the Spirit and I heard behind me a loud voice like a trumpet." Joachim wrote:

> Since some of the mysteries were already understood, but the greater mysteries were still hidden, there was a kind of struggle going on in my mind. . . . About the middle of the night's silence . . . as I was meditating, suddenly something of the fullness of this book and of the entire harmony of the Old and New Testaments was perceived with clarity of understanding in my mind's eye.[30]

A fundamental aspect of Joachim's theology of history was his belief in several Antichrists. In his *Book of Figures*, next to his depiction of the Dragon from the Apocalypse of John, Joachim wrote:

> John and John's Master [Christ in Matthew 24:4] say many Antichrists will come. Paul, on the other hand, foretells that there will be one. Just as many holy kings, priests, and prophets went before the one Christ who was king, priest and prophet, so likewise many unholy kings, false prophets, and antichrists will go before the one Antichrist who will pretend that he is a king, a priest, and a prophet.[31]

## ⟩( St. Malachy

St. Malachy (1094–1148) was an Irish archbishop and church reformer, and the most influential successor of St. Patrick. Many followers believe St. Malachy could divine the future and performed miracles like healing the sick and levitating himself. In 1139, while at Rome, some say he received a the strange vision of the future wherein he saw a long list of popes. When he died in 1184, he left behind short, puzzling statements foretelling the identity of all the popes until the end of the twentieth century. Malachy's timeline agrees with the prophecy of Nostradamus, that the end of the papacy will occur around the Millennium year 2000. As interesting as these prophecies are, their authenticity has long been questioned. He prophesied about the final pope: "During the last persecution of the Holy Roman Church, there shall sit Petrus Romanus [Peter II or "Peter the Roman"], who shall feed the sheep amid great tribulations, and when these have passed, the City of the Seven Hills shall be utterly destroyed, and the awful Judge will judge the people."[32]

Malachy's papal prophecies were vague and terse. For example, the descriptions of the final popes according to Malachy are: Pastor et Nauta

(Shepherd and Navigator), Flors Florum (Flower of Flowers), De Medietate Lunae (From the Half Moon), De Labore Solis (From the Toil of the Sun), De Gloria Olivae (From the Glory of the Olives), and finally Petrus Romanus (Peter of Rome).

It is likely that the list of future popes was not written by Malachy at all. Some theorize that Nostradamus created the list. In support of this theory, note that the Malachy prophecies are not known to exist prior to 1595. This could explain the accuracy of some the information prior to that date.

Malchy is best known for restoring ecclesiastical discipline in Ireland, unified the church there, and becoming the first Irish Catholic to be canonized. If we assume that the papal prophecies are fraudulent, no writings of Malachy are known to exist.

## )( *Kenneth Mackenzie (The Brahan Seer)*

> *The whole country of Scotland will become so totally desolated and depopulated that the crow of a cock will not be heard, deer and other wild animals will be exterminated by a horrid black sea.*
>
> —Kenneth Mackenzie[34]

Kenneth Mackenzie, named the "Brahan seer" after the Brahan estate upon which he worked, is the most famous of Scottish soothsayers. Coinneach Odhar (Mackenzie's Gaelic name) was born on the Isle of Lewis at the beginning of the seventeenth century. He became famous for his predictions that he supposedly received from the *sidhe*, supernatural beings in Irish folklore whose mournful wailing foretold death.

Legends suggest that when Mackenzie was a young boy he found a special blue stone with a central hole. The stone enabled him to see into the future when he looked through the hole. Followers of Mackenzie believed that many of his prophecies have come true, and the followers have passed the prophecies from generation to generation.

One wild legend describes Mackenzie receiving the divining stone from the dead. While his mother was tending her cattle, she saw some nearby graves opening and people of all ages rising from the Earth. The people returned in an hour, and as they closed up their own graves one told her to go to a nearby lake to find a round blue stone and give it to her son Kenneth, "who by it shall reveal future events." She did as requested, found the stone, and gave it to her son.

Another legend has Mackenzie finding the stone in his pocket. As he looked through its central hole, he saw that an angry farmer's wife had given him poisoned food. He tested his suspicion by offering the food to a dog that ate the food and died.

Although we may doubt the various legends, it seems clear that Mackenezie's divination fame spread. He reminds me of a Scottish Nostradamus. For example, he "foretold" the battle of Cullonden in 1745 by uttering at the battle site (Inverness, Scotland): "This bleak moor, ere many generations have passed, shall be stained with the best blood in Scotland. Glad I am that I will not see that day." Others say he foresaw the Age of Railways, referring to the railway tracks as "black bridleless horses," and the age of piped gas and water when he said, "the day will come when fire and water shall run in streams through all the streets and lanes of Inverness." Some of his prediction have yet to come true, for example: "One day a black rain will fall on the City of Aberdeen." Does this predict a catastrophe or a favorable oil business? Acid rain? Soot? "Rome was; London is; Edinburgh will be—" this seems to imply that the Scottish capital city will someday be more important to worldy affairs than London.

The Brahan Seer made a great many other predictions, some quite bizarre. Alas, his contemporaries did not appreciate his gift or prophecies. In 1662, they burned him to death in a barrel of tar. Today there is still a stone marking the place. Legend has it that just before going into the barrel, Mackenzie threw his precious stone into a pool, so that his tormentors would never possess the stone. Loch Ussie is said to have been created where the stone landed.

When Mackenzie was being led to his death, Lady Seaforth (one of his accusers) declared that he would never go to heaven because of his divination. Mackenzie answered,

> I will go to Heaven, but you never shall; and this will be a sign whereby you can determine whether my condition after death is one of everlasting happiness or of eternal misery; a raven and a dove, swiftly flying in opposite directions will meet, and for a second hover over my ashes, on which they will instantly alight. If the raven be foremost, you have spoken truly; but if the dove, then my hope is well founded.[35]

And, accordingly, tradition relates that after the horrible death sentence was carried out, and his ashes lay scattered on the ground, his last prophecy was fulfilled. Two birds flew to Earth. First, a dove, closely followed by a raven, alighted on the ashes.

Here is another example of his prophecies:

The day will come when sheep shall become so numerous that the bleating of the one shall be heard by the other from Conchra in Lochalsh to Bun-da-Loch in Kintail and henceforth will go back and deteriorate, until they disappear altogether, and be so thoroughly forgotten that a man finding the jaw-bone of a sheep in a cairn will not be able to tell what animal it belonged to. The ancient proprietors of the soil shall give peace to strange merchant proprietors, and the whole Highlands will become one huge deer forest; the whole country will be so utterly desolated and depopulated that the crow of a cock shall not be heard north of Druim-Uachdair; the people will emigrate to Islands now unknown, after which the deer in the huge wilderness shall be exterminated and drowned by horrid black rains. The people will then return and take undisturbed possession of the lands of their ancestors.[36]

## )( *Nostradamus*

> *So many naive scholars, over the centuries, have pored over Nostradamus's writings to extract every possible obscurity, that thousands of pages of drivel are readily available to be copied, shuffled about, and hyperbolized.*
> —James Randi, *The Mask of Nostradamus*

Movies, books, TV specials, and supermarket tabloids have praised the prophecies of Nostradamus, which supposedly predicted the rise of Adolf Hitler, the assassination of John F. Kennedy, the establishment of America, and much more. Despite my skepticism, Nostradamus has always fascinated me because of his eternal popularity, and as I studied his life I was impressed with his intelligence, creativity, kindness, and perseverance.

Nostradamus was a medical man and spent much of his life caring for the sick. Perhaps if he were alive today, he would go far. More than four hundred books and essays about his prophecies have been published since his death in 1566. Along with Shakespeare and the Bible, Nostradamus fans can rightly claim that his works have been in continuous print ever since their first publication centuries ago. The very first editions of his prophecies are lost, and today we must depend upon the accuracy and integrity of those who transcribed them over the years.

Michel de Nostredame, better known by the Latin version of his name, Nostradamus (1503–1566), was a French astrologer and physician, the most widely read seer of the Renaissance (see figure 64). He has probably had more impact on the world than any other prophets since the Delphic oracles. Nostradamus came from Jewish roots, but the Nostredame family had been Catholic converts for at least two generations. In the 1400s and 1500s,

France, as well as many European countries, expelled or executed all Jews who refused to convert to Christianity. James Randi suggests that many of his cryptic prophecies were "actually political commentaries and justifiable critiques of the activities of the Catholic Church, which was then busily tossing heretics on to bonfires wherever the Holy Inquisition could reach."[37]

In 1546, Nostradamus became famous when he began to treat victims of the bubonic plague in communities of southern France. He used innovative methods of treatment, and his success in curing very sick patients earned him a reputation as a gifted healer. He began making prophecies in 1547, which he published in 1555 in a book titled *Centuries*. The prophecies in *Centuries* occur in four-line rhyming verses called quatrains. (Each quatrain came in groups of one hundred called a century.) In cryptic language, they describe events from the mid-1500s through the end of the world, which some say he predicted to come in 3797 C.E. At the time, the French were in love with astrology, and an enlarged second edition, dedicated to the French king, appeared in 1558.

**Figure 64.** Nostradamus (1503–1566), from a frontispiece to a collection of his prophecies, published in Amsterdam in 1666 and later reprinted in Charles Mackay, *Extraordinary Popular Delusions and the Madness of Crowds* (1852; reprint New York: Crown Publishing, 1995), p. 287.

His alleged skill as a prophet made him so famous that Catherine de Medicis, queen of France, asked him to create horoscopes for her husband, King Henry II, and their children. In 1560, King Charles IX of France appointed Nostradamus court physician.

Catherine was fascinated by astrology and divination. She used astrological predictions as a modern politician uses surveys to help determine policy. (Modern politicians and their wives have also used astrology in the Médicis manner as in the case of Ronald and Nancy Reagan.) Nostradamus was appointed physician-in-ordinary by Charles IX when Charles became king in 1560.

The Catholic Church was sometimes nervous about Nostradamus, even many years after his death. For example, in 1781 the Catholic Church officially condemned his prophecies, despite the difficulty they had in interpreting their vague content that included words from several European languages. Nostradamus wrote most of his rhymed quatrains in French, and he obscured the quatrains with symbols and metaphors and by changing proper names by swapping, adding, or removing letters. Nostradamus fans say he wanted to be obscure so the church wouldn't condemn him. Skeptics suggest that he also used vague symbols so that the quatrains would be interpreted to fit numerous situations.

Some of the quatrains are thought to have foretold the future, including the French Revolution of the eighteenth century, the rise of Hitler, and other crucial historical events, particularly those that deal with French history. The prophecies that cannot be interpreted are said to foretell events that have not yet occurred. One of his most famous quatrains is said to predict the Great Fire of London that occurred in the year 1666. The first two lines of the quatrain are:

> *Le sang du iuste à Londres fera faulte,*
> *Bruslés par fouldres de vint toris les six*

which some have translated as

> The blood of the just requires London
> Burnt with fire in sixty-six

However skeptics point out that "fouldres" really means thunderbolts, and the numerical phrase in line 2 is literally "twenty-three the six," not 66. Thus, we may be skeptical that the two lines actually predict the Great Fire. Similarly, there has been much debate between believers and skeptics regarding many of Nostradamus's other predictions.

How did Nostradamus come to be such a famous seer? Let's take a closer look at his earlier life. Born in 1503 in St. Remy de Provence, France, Nostradamus was the son of a wealthy government official, Michel de Nostradame. His grandfathers, who were both doctors in the court of King Rene of Provence, taught Nostradamus Hebrew, Latin, Greek, astronomy, and astrology, which was generally considered a science on par with astronomy during Nostradamus's time. Astrology fascinated Nostradamus, but his family considered medicine a more respectable career, and so he studied to become a doctor.

While he was still a student, the bubonic plague devastated southern France, and Nostradamus left school to help fight the virulent disease. His innovative treatment involved cleanliness and foods that we now know have vitamin C. Whenever he entered a town, he attempted to have all the corpses removed from the streets. He then prescribed for his patients of fresh air, unpolluted water, and his "rose pills" that may have contained rose petals, rose hips, and other plant products. He resisted the prevailing method of draining blood from patients in an attempt to cure them. Nostradamus's treatments appeared to have some success in combating such a deadly disease. His work won him fame throughout France, and once the plague was under control, Nostradamus returned to medical school. After graduating, he set up a practice in Agen, got married, and had two children.

Even with his medical prowess, Nostradamus could not later save his wife and two children from the clutches of the plague, and they died. Heartbroken, he spent the next ten years wandering through Europe. During this period, he began to have visions and even made predictions to amuse his friends. Later, fearing his psychic ability was a sign of possession, he sought safe haven at the Abbey of Orva. Fortunately, the Abbot decided his gift of prophecy was from God.

Nostradamus left the Abbey and eventually settled in Salon, France, where he began to actively practice astrology. Late at night, he would place himself in a hypnotic trance and stare into a bowl of water to encourage visions of the future. In 1547, he began to record his in four-line poems called quatrains. The first published volume of his almanac was an instant success and over the next few years, he produced ten volumes, containing one thousand predictions. Legend has it that on the evening of July 1, 1556, Nostradamus told his student Chavigny, "Tomorrow at sunrise, I shall not be here." The next morning Nostradamus was found dead at his workbench.

There are many stories, probably apocryphal, regarding Nostradamus's corpse. One legend states that, prior to his death, Nostradamus had secretly arranged for a metal disc to be buried with him. His instructions were followed, and in 1600, when his coffin was opened so his remains could be moved to a new tomb, the plaque was discovered resting on his skeleton. On it was inscribed the number: 1600.[38]

Many people have spent significant effort attempting to decipher Nostradamus's enigmatic writings. One difficulty is correlating historical events with particular quatrains. For example, there is dispute over his End of Time vision in which he said, "In the year 1999, seventh month, from the sky will come a great King of Terror, to bring back to life the great King of the Moguls, before and after Mars reigns." This interpretation is particularly confusing given that Nostradamus had once said that his prophecies would remain valid until the year 3797.[39] In his introduction to *Century* 1, Nostradamus described the contents as "prophecies from today [1555] to the year 3797." Later, in *Century* 1, quatrain 48 seems to suggest that the prophecies actually extend seven thousand years.

Let me give you a feel for exactly how Nostradamus induced his visions and made his predictions. Ten years after the death of his wife and children, Nostradamus settled in Salon and remarried, eventually fathering three daughters and three sons. He transformed the upper floor of his house into a private study, where he installed his various equipment that included an astrolabe (an instrument that measures the positions of heavenly bodies), magic mirrors, divining rods, and a brass bowl and tripod.

Picture the eerie scene. Under cover of night, Nostradamus retires to his private study where he keeps his alchemical and astrological paraphernalia. He lights a flame under a tripod on which sits a flask containing a clear, steaming liquid. Otherwise the room is dark as he stares at the flask, relaxes, and waits for visions to come.

He describes the process in *Century* 1:

> Seated at night in my secret study,
> Alone, reposing over the brass tripod,
> A slender flame leaps out of the solitude,
> Making me pronounce that which is not in vain.

*Centuries* 1 through part of 4 were published in Lyons in 1555. The remainder of 4 and the subsequent parts through 7 were published later that same year. The last three were printed in 1558, but Nostradamus decided not to have them widely distributed.

One example quatrain is said to predict the coming of Napoleon is:

> An Emperor will be born near Italy
> Who will cost the Empire dear,
> They will say when they see his associates,
> That he is less a prince than a butcher.

The future Emperor Napoleon was born on the island of Corsica in the Mediterranean, which Italy gave to France only a year before Napoleon's. The line "less prince than a butcher" is said to refer to bloodshed caused by Napoleon's expansionist wars.

Another famous quatrain is quatrain 24 from *Century* 2. Here are the French and English versions:

> *Bêtes farouches de faim fleuues tranner;*
> *Plus part du champ encontre Hister sera,*
> *En cage de fer le grand fera trainer,*
> *Quand rien enfant de Germain obseruera.*

> Beasts ferocious from hunger will swim across rivers:
> The greater part of the region will be against the Hister,
> The great one will cause it to be dragged in an iron cage,
> When the German child will observe nothing.

Some have suggested that "Hister" refers to Hitler and this quatrain is a reference to Germany during World War II. However, skeptics suggest that Hister is the Latin name used by Nostradamus for the Danube River. One of his quatrains even mentions a bridge being built across the "Hister."

Probably the most famous Nostradamus prophecy is the following one in which he appears to foretell the Death of Henry II (1519–1559), the King of France who persecuted Protestants within his kingdom:

> The young lion will overcome the older one,
> On the field of combat in a single battle;
> He will pierce his eyes through a golden cage,
> Two wounds made one, then he dies a cruel death.
> (*Century* 1, quatrain 35)

Many Nostradamus aficionados describe the death of Henry II as follows. In June 1559, Henry II ignored all warnings that Nostradamus gave him and participated in a jousting tournament against the Comte de Montgomery. Both men used shields embossed with lions. Montgomery was six years younger than Henry.

During the final bout, Montgomery failed to lower his lance in time. It shattered, sending a large splinter through the king's gilded visor (i.e., a gold-embossed helmet, or the "golden cage" in the quatrain). Along with minor punctures in the face and throat, some legends suggest there were two mortal wounds. One splinter destroyed the king's eye; the other impaled his temple just behind the eye. Both penetrated his brain. Others suggest there was just one wound, where the lance pierced the skull above his right eye and penetrated the brain. No one doubts that Henry lingered for ten agonizing days from his head and brain wounds before dying a cruel death. The Comte de Montgomery was a commander of the Scottish Guard. The emblem of Scotland was, and is, a rampant lion. Henri II used a lion as his unofficial badge.

"The young lion will overcome the older one" is supposed to refer to the younger Montgomery slaying the older Henry. "On the field of combat in a single battle" refers to the formal jousting contest between Montgomery and Henry. "He [the young lion] will pierce his [the older lion's] eyes through a golden cage" refers to the Montgomery's lance crashing through Henry's visor and into Henry's head. "Two wounds made one, then he dies a cruel death" refers to the horrible, lingering death of Henry. On the surface, this sounds like an interesting match between the quatrain and a historical event, although James Randi, author of *The Mask of Nostradamus*, is not impressed by the alleged accuracy.[40] For example, Randi suggests there is no evidence that the visor was gilded with gold. Henry II's eyes were not "burst," and Randi says the wound occurred *above* the right eye. Randi also sees no reason for calling the two people "lions."

Another famous quatrain appears to predict the life and death of Elizabeth I, queen of England (1558–1603) during a period often called the Elizabethan Age:

> She who was chased out shall return to the kingdom,
> Her enemies found to be conspirators:
> More than ever her time will triumph,
> Three and seventy to death much assured.
> (*Century* 6, quatrain 74)

Nostradamus fans suggest that the first three lines refer to Elizabeth's very difficult early years before gaining the throne. Elizabeth died in 1603, and the last line is taken to mean she died in the third year of the century, at the age of seventy. However, James Randi is not happy with the interpretation of the last line, saying "three and seventy" means seventy-three years old, and does not refer to 1603.[41] You can see by these several sample analyses that, even today, there is much controversy and room for interpretation of the quatrains.

Here is a quatrain that some felt foretold the death of President John F. Kennedy:

> A great King taken into the hands of the Young,
> Not far from Easter confusion knife state:
> Permanent captives times when lightning is above,
> When three brothers are wounded and murdered.
> (*Century* 9, quatrain 36)

President John F Kennedy was killed in Dallas as his motorcade past through town on November 22, 1963. His younger brother, Senator Bobby Kennedy, was shot and killed in California in 1968. Nostradamus fans believe that "brothers" refers to the Kennedys, and several other quatrains have been thought to refer to the Kennedy assassinations. I'm not sure how "Easter" fits into any interpretations, but Nostradamus aficionados on the World Wide Web have variously suggested that the three "brothers" refer to Adolf Hitler (1889–1945), Benito Mussolini (1883–1945), and Hirohito (1926–1989); Russia, United States, and China; the three 0s in the year 2000; the three sons of Charlemagne; Moe, Larry, and Curly of "The Three Stooges"; George, Jeb, and Neil Bush; and Prince Philip, Prince Andrew, and Prince Charles. Obviously it is easy for people to have divergent opinions when they examine vague poetry!

Some Nostradamus fans even believe that Nostradamus saw the rise of the computer. The following quatrain describes something that "lives without senses," which some take to mean a computer:[42]

> That which lives but has no senses,
> Will cause its own death through artifice:
> Autun, Chalan, Langres and the two Sens,
> Hail and ice cause great damage.
> (*Century* 1, quatrain 22)

"Death through artifice" is thought to refer to computer viruses implanted by hackers.

One of his scarier quatrains seemed to foretell some great calamity in July 1999. Some followers thought it foretold the end of the world:

> In the year 1999 and seven months,
> From the sky will come the great King of terror.
> Resurrecting the great King of Angolmois.
> Before and after Mars will reign happily.
> (*Century* 10, quatrain 72)

The "great King of terror" was thought to be the coming of the Anti-Christ, a meteor, or a weapon.

In *Century* 1, quatrain 81, we read, "Nine will be set apart from the human flock . . . their fate to be determined upon departure." Nostradamus followers suggest this prophecy foretold the tragic flight of the space shuttle Challenger, in which the crew was "set apart" from the earth and died in an explosion upon departure. Another phrase in the same quatrain is "Kappa,

Theta, Lambda dead, banished and scattered." Some say that this refers to the letters K, Th, and L, and the Thiokol company made the defective O-ring that is blamed for the shuttle disaster. However, one significant problem with this interpretation is that there were seven people on board the Challenger, not nine. Also, I'm not aware that the manufacturer was banished and scattered, which this interpretation would seem to predict.

I was curious to determine if the Nostradamus effect could be simulated with random quatrains. For example, could it be that Nostradamus's quatrains are like ink blots—not really foretelling anything but permitting humans to fit future history to rather nebulous poems? (For more information, see my survey that uses Nostradamus-like quatrains in chapter 4, "Science and the Will to Believe.")

Incidentally, Nostradamus is very popular in Japan today, and millions believe his prophecy that a terrible calamity will someday occur that will destroy a larger percentage of the population. One 1999 poll showed that about 20 percent of Japanese people believe that Nostradamus's quatrains were a reliable guide to the future. One large Tokyo bookshop carried some 185 titles on Nostradamus, and many were bestsellers. The majority advised readers to take the doomsday predictions to heart and prepare for the worst.[43] Some go a far as to suggest that Japan is a country obsessed with Nostradamus. More than thirty books were been published on Nostradamus's "prophecy" of 1999 as the end of the world, the books' combined sales exceeding ten million dollars.[44] Impending doom was also the talk of television shows, magazines and numerous Web sites. The clamor also spawned new businesses, including the production of an Armageddon Bra with a sensor on the shoulder to warn the wearer of objects falling from the skies.[45]

As a result of Nostradamus, numerous Japanese sects sprang up, led by self-proclaimed "Kings of Terror," who promised to spare their disciples when the Nostradamus-predicted apocalypse came. The Aum Supreme Truth cult, whose guru was heavily influenced by Nostradamus, tried to trigger the apocalypse in 1995 with its deadly attack on the Tokyo subway system.

Some nervous Japanese did not take chances. One magazine featured a twenty-four-year-old who had quit his job to take refuge on a mountain from the floods he believed were about to strike. What makes all the Japanese interest surprising is that according to Japanese calendar, we were not in 1999 but in the eleventh year of the reign of the Heisei emperor. Perhaps the Japanese are especially tuned to the possibility of apocalypse because the island had been hit by earthquakes, volcanoes, and nuclear attack.

## ){ *Emanuel Swedenborg*

> *Kindness is an inner desire that makes us want to do good things even if we do*
> *not get anything in return. It is the joy of our life to do them. When we do good*
> *things from this inner desire, there is kindness in everything we think, say, want*
> *and do.*

> —Emanuel Swedenborg[46]

Emanuel Swedenborg (1688–1722) was a Swedish philosopher, scientist, mystic, prophet, visionary, and founder of the Swedenborgian sect. His claims of communicating with the dead and with higher planes of being had a strong influence on modern occultism, spiritualism, and psychology. Although some of his contemporaries thought he was a nut case, after his death a religion called the Church of New Jerusalem was formed around his beliefs. His work even inspired a number of important people from Abraham Lincoln and Carl Jung to Helen Keller. Swedenborg believed that there was an angelic language, a kind of protolanguage for beings on some unknown plane of reality:

> There is a universal language, proper to all angels and sprits, which has nothing in common with any language spoken in the world. Every man, after death, uses this language, for it is implanted in every one from creation; and therefore throughout the whole spiritual world all can understand one another. I have frequently heard this language and, having compared it with languages in the world, have found that it has not the slightest resembled to any of them; it differs from them in this fundamental respect, that every letter of every word has a particular meaning.[47]

At the University of Uppsala, Swedenborg studied philosophy, mathematics, and science, as well as in Latin, Greek, and Hebrew. After graduating, he studied physics, astronomy, and other natural sciences, as well as learning bookbinding, cabinet making, engraving, brass instrument making, and lens grinding. In just a few years, he absorbed a fantastic amount of knowledge and wrote extensively. He also made numerous original discoveries in a wide variety of scientific disciplines. For example, Swedenborg recognized the function of the brain's pituitary gland and developed plans for a glider airplane and a submarine.

Throughout the period of his scientific work, Swedenborg had always maintained his interest in spirituality. The aim of much of his biology research was to find a rational explanation for the operation of the soul.[48]

Legends are common with respect to Swendenborg's supposed

prophetic ability. For example, he is said to have once described a fire that occurred three hundred miles away. He predicted the day of his own death. In 1743, he said that God had given him a mission to interpret the Bible from a spiritual viewpoint. To help him, God allowed him to witness the afterlife where he studied the social organization of heaven, hell, and the realm where spirits go at the moment of death.

In his book *Heaven and Hell*, Swedenborg said that there was no devil, no single ruler of hell.[49] People in hell might influence living people. Hell exists because it is the only place in which evil people are comfortable. In heaven, the evil people would suffocate from the love and goodness. According to Swedenborg, the creation of Hell was not an act punishment but of divine mercy. When one dies, a person lives in eternity in the place that best matches the love the person fostered in his or her heart and mind while on earth.

Swedenborg also said that everything in the physical world had a corresponding element in the spiritual world. He wrote that the Second Coming of Christ would not take place in physical form.[48] He believed that he had been called by God to give a new revelation to humanity, and for the next twenty-seven years, until his death in London at the age of eighty-four, he wrote thirty volumes of theological works that comprise that revelation. In the last month of his life, several of his friends asked Swedenborg to comment on his writing. He replied, "I have written nothing but the truth, as you will have more and more confirmed all the days of your life, provided you keep close to the Lord and faithfully serve Him alone by shunning evils as sins against Him and diligently searching His Word, which from beginning to end bears incontestable witness to the truth of the doctrines I have delivered to the world."

Swedenborg's followers, known as Swedenborgians, believe that his religious writings are divinely inspired. He never intended to found a new religious denomination, but in 1787 British printer Robert Hindmarsh organized his disciples in England as a separate sect. Today, there are Swedenborgian congregations throughout the world, and Swedenborg's theological writings have been translated into a large number of languages. For example, *Conversations With Angels: What Swedenborg Heard In Heaven* is a compilation of his angelic encounters. Not all of his unusual ideas were confined to religion and the afterlife. Of the inhabitants of Venus and the Moon, he wrote:

> They are of two kinds; some are gentle and benevolent, others wild, cruel and of gigantic stature. The latter rob and plunder, and live by this means;

the former have so great a degree of gentleness and kindness that they are always beloved by the good; thus they often see the lord appear in their own form on their earth. . . . The inhabitants of the Moon are small, like children of six or seven years old; at the same time they have the strength of men like ourselves. Their voice rolls like thunder, and the sound proceeds from the belly, because the Moon is in quite a different atmosphere than the other planets.[49]

## )( *Maria Taigi*

God will send two punishments: one will be in the form of wars, revolutions and other evils; it shall originate on earth. The other will be sent from Heaven. There shall come over the whole earth an intense darkness lasting three days and three nights. Nothing can be seen, and the air will be laden with pestilence which will claim many. It will be impossible to use any man-made lighting during this darkness, except blessed candles. He, who out of curiosity, opens his window to look out, or leaves his home, will fall dead on the spot. During these three days, people should remain in their homes, pray the Rosary and beg God for mercy. The air shall be infected by demons who will appear under all sorts of hideous forms. Religion shall be persecuted, and priests massacred. Churches shall be closed, but only for a short time. The Holy Father shall be obliged to leave Rome.[50]

Maria Taigi (1769–1837) was an Italian peasant who foresaw great plagues coming from the sky. Popes and cardinals have referred to this holy married woman as one of the greatest saints of all time. Pope Benedict XV praised her in her beatification on May 20, 1920, as being an exemplary wife and mother amidst difficult circumstances. Taigi's followers suggest she had ecstatic visions of the future, performed miraculous healings, and foretold deaths. One legend says that eighteen years after her death, her body was in a state of excellent preservation, with no decay.

In 1835, she prophesied:

At first will come several terrestrial scourges, as great wars, through which many millions will run into destruction. After that will come the celestial scourge in full severity, such as has never been. it will be short, but will cut off the greater part of mankind. yet, before that, five big trees have to be felled.[51]

Some have suggested that the "great wars" refer to World Wars I and II.

Maria Taigi said that people would begin to see themselves as God sees them, and then a great punishment that would come to the world. She indi-

| My Six Favorite and Famous Prophetic Popes ||
| Pope | Sample Thoughts |
|---|---|
| Pope Gregory I the Great (r. 599–604) | "Following the birth of the Antichrist, most of humanity will be as corrupt as the world—the sheep will be transformed into the godless or fall into heresy. Churches will be empty and in ruins, priests will have little zeal for souls and pious souls will be few." |
| Pope Pius X (r. 1903–1914) | "What I have seen is terrifying! Will I be the one, or will it be a successor? What is certain is that the Pope will leave Rome and, in leaving the Vatican, he will have to pass over the dead bodies of his priests! Do not tell anyone this while I am alive." |
| Pope Pius XI (r. 1922–1939) | "The churches are destroyed, ruined from base to steeple, the religious and the consecrated virgins are expelled from their habitations."52 |
| Pope Pius XII (r. 1939–1958) | "Mankind must prepare itself from sufferings such as it has never before experienced . . . the darkest since the deluge. The hour has struck—the battle, the most widespread, bitter and ferocious the world has ever known, has been joined. It must be fought to the finish. Having lifted the papers I had in my hand, I was struck by a phenomenon I had never seen before. The sun, which was fairly high, looked like a pale yellow opaque globe completely surrounded by a luminous halo, which nevertheless did not prevent me at all from staring attentively at the sun without the slightest discomfort. A very light cloud was before it. The opaque globe began moving outward, slowly turning over upon itself, and going from left to right and vice-versa. But within the globe very strong movements could be seen in all clarity and without interruption." |
| The Diary of Pope John XXIII (r. 1958–1963) | "The Madonna is a joy to behold. I just wish her message was a more positive one. She says in four years time the world will lose a great leader and a powerful nation will find itself involved in a conflict it cannot win. The fighting will take its toll on the battlefield and from within as the population despises the loss of its young men. The Holy Mother sheds tears as she describes the heartbreaking vision." (The Pope goes on to predict the following future events: Easter Europe becomes free, the 1990s is filled with deadly natural disasters, devastation in Africa where millions perish, terrifying diseases that begin in 1984, the appearance of savoirs (odd-looking beings) from the heavens in 1995, the increase in lifespan, and a wondrous miracle in the sky above New York City December 25, 2000, when millions will witness the appearance of a messiah.)) |
| Pope John Paul II | "We have to prepare to suffer, before long, great trials which will require of us the disposition to sacrifice even our life . . . for Christ." |

cated that this illumination of conscience would save many souls because many would repent as a result of this warning. Legend has it that from the time she was twenty years old until she died at the age of sixty-three, she was accompanied by a mysterious light in which she saw past, present, and future events, some relating to struggles among nations, some relating to individual souls.

Taigi thought that most humans were in serious trouble. She said:

The greater number of Christians today are damned. The destiny of those dying on one day is that very few—not as many as ten—went straight to Heaven; many remained in Purgatory; and those cast into Hell were as numerous as snowflakes in mid-winter.[53]

## ✧ OUR CONTEMPORARIES— DIVINERS, 1800 TO PRESENT

### ♉ Evangeline Adams

> In Cancer, Jupiter is in the house of his exaltation, and that sign being above all a symbol of pleasure, we may naturally expect that it will bring out the truly "jovial" qualities of the planet. This is undoubtedly the case, the native is good-humored, benevolent, and humane; the emotional nature and the imagination are strong.
>
> —Evangeline Adams, Astrology for Everyone

Evangeline Adams (1865–1932) has been called "America's female Nostradamus." A descendent of President John Quincy Adams, she was born in Boston and, following the advice of her own horoscope, moved to New York City in 1873. When she moved into a New York hotel, she told the owner that a disaster would happen soon. The next day, the hotel had a terrible fire, and Adams's name was on the front pages of newspapers.

In 1914, she defended the "science" of astrology in a New York court and won a case filed against her for breaking a city statute against fortune telling. While on trial, she offered to be tested by reading the horoscope of a stranger. The trial judge asked her to give a horoscope for his own son and was so amazed by the accuracy of her horoscope that he ruled, "The defendant raises astrology to the dignity of an exact science."

She was the personal astrologer of superrich American financier and industrial organizer John Pierpont Morgan. Morgan was one of the world's foremost financial figures during the two pre–World War I decades. He reorganized several major railroads and consolidated the United States Steel, International Harvester, and General Electric corporations. He also requested monthly horoscopes from Adams on the stock market.

| My 20 Favorite and Famous Prophetic Saints | |
|---|---|
| **Saint** | **Some Thoughts** |
| St. John Chrysostom (347–407) | "After the birth of the Antichrist, the world will be faithless and degenerate. |
| St. Methodius (4th Century) | "There will be a rise of a great European monarch who will crush the foes of Christianity." |
| St. Columba (St. Columbkille) (522–597) | "Seven years before the last day, the sea shall submerge Eirin [Ireland] in one inundation. In Iona of my heart, Iona of my love, Instead of monks' voices shall be the sounds of cattle, But ere the world come to an end Iona shall be as it was." |
| St. Anthony the Abbot (4th Century) | "Men will surrender to the spirit of the age. They will say that if they hadday, lived in our day, faith would be simple and easy. But in their day they will say, things are complex; the Church must be brought up to date and made meaningful to the day's problems. When the Church and the world are one, then those days are at hand."[54] |
| St. Césaire d'Arles (470–542) | "Soon the city will be reached by a horrible plague that will involve a pope. But another Pope stops, by his firm dignity, another crueler enemy and persuades it to repair the damage which it caused at the Holy City. Oh, cruel troops of various nations! The war, the famine, the plague, a sudden flood make the city deserted and similar to a hut of a gardener. The infamous war agitates the city and Gaul. Flee, enemy. A vigorous leader strongly strikes all parts with his formidable hammer, leaving to a famous emperor the glory of overcoming the Arabs. Struck of a stab, the devoted father of the people dies, I see it." |
| St. Augustine, (5th century) | "A Frankish King will one day rule over the entire Roman Empire. He shall give up the ghost at Jerusalem on the Mount of Olives." |
| St. Nilus (5th century) | "After 1900, toward the middle of the 20th century, the people of that time will become unrecognizable. When the time for the Advent of the Antichrist approaches, people's minds will grow cloudy from carnal passions, and dishonor and lawlessness will grow stronger. People's appearances will change, and it will be impossible to distinguish men from women due to their shamelessness in dress and style of hair. These people will be cruel and will be like wild animals because of the temptations of the Antichrist. There will be no respect for parents and elders, love will disappear, and Christian pastors, bishops, and priests will become vain men, completely failing to distinguish the right hand from the left." |
| St. Caesar (5/6th century) | "He shall recover the Crown of the Lilies. He will assist the pope in the reformation of the world. The King of Blois raises again the Papal Tiara. This Prince shall extend his dominion over the whole world. O sweetest peace! Thy fruits will multiply until the End of Time!" |
| St. Remy (5/6th century) | "He shall reign over the entire ancient Roman Empire. At the end of his most glorious reign, he shall go to Jerusalem, and shall lay down his Crown and Scepter on the Mount of Olives." |
| St. Senanus (6th century, perhaps legendary) | "Falsehood will characterize that class of men who will sit injudgment to pass sentence according to law: between the father and his son, litigations will subsist. The clergy of the holy church will be addicted to pride and injustice. Women will abandon feelings of delicacy, and cohabit with men out of wedlock."[55] |

| St. Isidore of Seville (7th century) | "In the last days a very pious King shall reign over our Great Spain. He shall reign over the House of Agar, and shall possess Jerusalem." (Agar was an Egyptian bondwoman in the service of Sarah, wife of Abraham who was barren. She bore Abraham a son called Ishmael.) |
|---|---|
| St. Malachy (1094–1148) | "In extreme persecution, the seat of the Holy Roman Church will be occupied by Peter the Roman, who will feed [lead] the sheep through many tribulations, at the term of which the city of seven hills will be destroyed, and the formidable Judge will judge his people." |
| St. Hildegard of Bingen (1098–1179) | "The time approaches when princes and people will renounce the authority of the pope." |
| St. Bridget of Sweden (d. 1373) | "The time of Antichrist will be near when the measure of injustice will overflow and when wickedness has grown to immense proportions, when the Christians love heresies and the unjust trample underfoot the servants of God. At the end of this age, the Antichrist will be born. He will be a child-wonder at birth. His mother will be an accursed woman, who will pretend to be well-informed in spiritual things. . . . He shall destroy the Jewish and Mohammedan sects. And the earth shall enjoy peace and prosperity. Peace and abundance shall return to the world." |
| Saint Anselm Bishop of Sunium (13th century) | "You will be ruined, city of seven hills (Rome), when the letter K will be praised in your walls. Then, your fall will be near. And you, man of big beard, you will lose it and you will lose your value in the whole world, for having presided the death of the Pontiff called John Obi." |
| St. Vincent Ferrer (14th Century) | "In the days of peace that are to come after the desolation of revolutions and wars, before the end of the world, the Christians will become so lax in their religion that they will refuse to receive the Sacrament of Confirmation, saying, 'It is an unnecessary Sacrament."[56] |
| St. Nicholas von Flüe (1417–1487) | "The Church will sink deeper until she will at last seem to be extinguished, and the succession of Peter and the other Apostles to have expired." |
| St. Francis of Paola (15th Century) | "In his childhood, [a future King chosen by God] will be like a saint; in his youth a great sinner; then he will be converted entirely to God and will do great penance; his sins shall be forgiven him, and he shall become a great saint. He shall destroy the Mohammedan sect and the rest of the infidels." |
| St. Anastacy (16th century) | "The small nations form a great nation. And they will be in wars. In the final part of the millennium, an invisible serpent will shake the people, which will move through the earth, as starving wolves, spreading hunger and plagues. Rome and Moscow will fall in the deepest disorder. The end of the millennium will see a lot of violence and blood. The walls of the churches will be spotted with blood." |
| St. John Bosco (1815–1888) | "The great Minister shall see the Bride of his King clothed in glory. Throughout the world a sun so bright shall shine as was never seen since the flames of the Cenacle [Pentecost] until today, nor shall it be seen again until the end of time. It was a dark night, and men could no longer find their way back to their countries. Suddenly a most brilliant light shone in the sky, illuminating their way as at high noon. At that moment from the Vatican came forth . . . a multitude of men and women . . . and priests, and at the head was the pope. But a furious storm then broke out, somewhat dimming that light, as if light and darkness were locked in battle." |

Adams's followers claim that she correctly forecasted the death of England's King Edward VII, the election of Warren G. Herding for U.S. president, the start of America's involvement in World War II, and her own death at the end of 1932.

In the 1990s, psychic medium Lorene Bersey purportedly contacted Evangeline Adams to arrive at the following predictions:[57] An ancient UFO base will be found buried under the Arctic as the ice melts because of global warming. The speed-of-light barrier will be broken because of new discoveries in physics. Humans will encounter alien races scattered throughout the universe. A global market will unite the planet and end poverty. Ronald Reagan will make a grand return to politics as an adviser after undergoing revolutionary Alzheimer's treatment. A rogue computer in Washington, D.C., will dump billions of pieces of information, leaving people without their social security numbers and driver licenses. The Dead Sea will come to life and become a religious retreat. Solar satellites will provide perpetual daylight, leading to a decrease in crime around the world. Chelsea Clinton and her handsome astrologer groom will take the first honeymoon on the moon.

## ♉ *Shoko Asahara*

> *I designed this pyramid back in the olden days. With my ability to know the past, I've discovered that I was an Egyptian pharaoh.*
>
> —Shoko Asahara[58]

The messianic Shoko Asahara was leader of Aum Shinrikyo, the Japanese Buddhist group that became famous in 1995 when its leaders were charged with the release of nerve gas in a crowded Tokyo subway station, causing numerous deaths and injuries. He was born in 1955 on the Japanese island of Kyushu. His original name was Chizuo Matsumoto, and, because he had very poor eyesight, he was educated in special schools. According to Damian Thompson, author of *The End of Time: Faith and Fear in the Shadow of the Millennium*, Asahara was fascinated with Chinese medicine and began wearing the white robes of a spiritual guide while still a young teenager.[59]

After failing to get accepted into Tokyo University, Asahara set up a Chinese herbal medicine business. He was arrested soon after opening his health-food business for selling an "all-purpose elixir" that consisted mostly of ground-up orange peels. In 1984, he started a movement based on Buddhist and yoga practices. He also changed his name to Shoko Asahara, which he thought was a lucky and more mystical name, and he told people that he had studied Buddhism in the Himalayas and became the first Japanese to attain enlightenment.

Asahara established Aum Shinrikyo ("Supreme Truth") in 1987, appointing ministers who oversaw various aspects of the group's activities. Approximately 10 percent of the fifteen thousand members in Japan had taken monastic vows. Asahara had begun calling himself the "Holy Pope," dressed in silk pajamas, and said his hero was Adolf Hitler.

By 1988, his utterances had taken on a scary, apocalyptic tone, and he had cast himself in the role of doomsday prophet who said only his followers would be safe from the approaching apocalypse. In 1992, he gave lectures and predicted Armageddon would occur by the year 2000 and that 90 percent of the world's urban populations would be destroyed by atomic, biological, and chemical warfare. Only those who used the cult's yoga breathing methods would be immune to the warfare. Strangely, the cult began to buy and experiment with lethal chemicals.

His rantings grew more ominous in the years leading up to the three attacks on Tokyo inhabitants using poisonous sarin gas that killed twelve and sickened five thousand. They were only the first stages of the planned destruction of Japanese society. At his peak, Asahara had forty thousand followers, whom he let drink his blood, semen, and used bathwater for a price. The bathwater was one of the few beverages permitted to the cultists. A drink cost $200. A few swallows of his blood cost over $10,000. Many of Asahara's followers came from prosperous families and were well educated. The top Aum leaders held advanced scientific degrees.

After the gas attacks, the police located Asahara sealed inside a coffin-like cubicle suspended from a ceiling. They tried to take his pulse. All he said was, "Don't touch me. I don't even let my disciples touch me."

His cult owned a large Russian military helicopter and was looking to buy more, leading police to the conclusion that Asahara wanted to create his own helicopter strike force. A TV report said that an Aum group had also visited Zaire and that Aum publications showed a keen interest in the Ebola virus.

Asahara always seemed a bit paranoid, unless this was an act to attract followers. "We've been under deadly gas attacks since 1988," he said in an April 1994 sermon. "Gases are sprayed from helicopters or planes wherever I go." He also called it a "heavenly principle" to "terminate one's life by using sarin and other gases developed during World War II."

Asahara told people he could levitate and prophesied that Aum would run Japan by the year 2000. Inside buildings designated as religious facilities were complete chemical and biological warfare laboratories. At one location, Aum scientists attempted to cultivate botulism. Police say that Aum's chief physician, the man who surgically removed fingerprints from top Aum officials, has confessed to bringing sarin onto the subways in plastic bags and then perforating them with specially sharpened umbrellas to release the poison.[60]

## ♉ *Alice Bailey*

> *We shall have a practical method of analysis whereby we can arrive at a right understanding of ourselves as ensouling entities, and at a wiser comprehension of our fellowmen. We can then deal more intelligently with ourselves, with our children and with our friends and associates. We shall find ourselves able to cooperate more wisely with the Plan as it is seeking expression at any particular time.*
> —Alice Bailey, *The Seven Rays of Life*

Alice Bailey (1880–1949) was a Sunday school teacher, English psychic, and author who exhibited automatic writing. Her occult writings helped start the modern form of the New Age movement. Bailey was the founder of the Arcane School for studying secret knowledge, and she channeled a large amount of writing from disembodied "masters" including Koot Hoomi and "The Tibetan."[61] In her book *The Consciousness of the Atom* she discusses the relationship between matter and consciousness.

On June 30, 1895, at the age of fifteen, Alice said she had an extraordinary experience. "I was sitting in the drawing room reading. The door opened and in walked a tall man dressed in European clothes . . . but with a tall turban on his head. . . . He told me there was some work that it was planned that I could do in the world but that it would entail my changing my disposition very considerably."[62]

In 1915, Bailey met two English women living in Pacific Grove, California, who introduced her to Helena P. Blavatsky, the Russian mystic who founded the Theosophical Society in 1875. Through her studies of Blavatsky's "Secret Doctrines," Bailey realized the man she met at age fifteen was Master KH (Koot Hoomi). "I discovered that he was not the Master Jesus, as I had naturally suspected. . . . I have worked for Him, ever since I was fifteen years old and I am now one of the superior disciples of his group—or as it is called esoterically—in his ashram."[63]

In 1917, Alice moved to Hollywood to be near the headquarters of the Theosophical Society at Krotona. In the fall of 1919, Alice had an encounter with another master, who guided her for thirty years. Between the years 1919 and 1949, she wrote twenty-four books, including an autobiography. Nineteen of these books were supposed to have been written by her Tibetan master, DK (Djwhal Khul).

Regarding Master DK's communications, Alice Bailey comments, "I remain in full control of my senses of perception. . . . I simply listen and take down the words that I hear and register the thoughts which are dropped one by one into my brain. . . . I have never changed anything that the Tibetan has ever given to me. . . . I do not always understand what is given. I do not always agree. But I record it all honestly and then discover it does make sense and evokes intuitive response."[64]

Followers of Alice Bailey still continue to promote her message of world peace, the divinity of all mankind, the unity of all religions, and service to mankind. In her book *Problems of Humanity*, Bailey discusses six basic problems of the world—the psychological rehabilitation of the nations, the care of children, the problem of capital and labor minorities, the evolution of churches, and international unity.

## ☿ *Helena P. Blavatsky*

> *A world destruction will occur as happened to Atlantis 11,000 years ago. Instead of Atlantis, all of England and parts of the NW European coast will sink into the sea. In contrast, the sunken Azores region, the Isle of Poseidonis, will again be raised from the sea.*
>
> —Helena P. Blavatsky[65]

Helena Petrovna Blavatsky (1831–1891) was a Russian mystic who founded the famous Theosophical Society in 1875. She was born in Ekaterinoslav (now Dnepropetrovsk), Ukraine, the daughter of Colonel Peter Alexeyevich von Hahn and novelist Helena Andreyevna (nee de Fadeyev). At the age of sixteen or seventeen she married Nikifor V. Blavatsky, a much older man, but left him after a few months. She spent the next two decades traveling through Europe and Asia, later claiming to have studied for several years under Hindu mahatmas (masters) and to possess psychic powers. In 1873 Madame Blavatsky, as she came to be known, went to New York City and helped found the Theosophical Society, a group of occultists who emphasized the role of reincarnation in people's lives.

Legend suggests Helena had a strange childhood. She walked and talked in her sleep and loved the weird and fantastic. She said one of her earliest recollections was scaring a boy to death. One day when Helena was four she was walking by the river bank with one of her nurses while a fourteen-year-old boy followed them and annoyed Helena. She responded by roaring and threatening to have forest nymphs tickle the boy to death. The boy was so scared he dived into a nearby river. Fishermen discovered his corpse weeks later.

**Figure 65.** A medallion worn by Helena Blavatsky (1831–1891), founder of the Theosophist religion. From James Randi, *An Encyclopedia of Claims, Frauds, and Hoaxes of the Occult and Supernatural* (New York: St. Martin's Press, 1995), p. 33.

Madame Blavatsky continues to be a very controversial figure. Some people feel she was a prophet, while others feel she was a fraud. In either case, she was an important historical figure. Her cofounding of the Theosophical Society to promote Theosophy, a pantheistic philosophical and religious system, reintroduced many ancient ideas into Western civilization that had been long forgotten. Theosophists believe there is one infinite principle that is the cause of all that exists. They also believe in karma (recurring cycles in nature and reincarnations) and that many higher beings exist. Figure 65 shows an ornate and unusual medallion worn by Blavatsky.

She published her first major work, *Isis Unveiled*, in 1877. In this book she criticized the science and religion of her day and favored mysticism as a way to understand the cosmic truths. In 1879, Blavatsky and Olcott went to India and established a Theosophical headquarters at Adyar, near Madras. Here is what she said about the nature of time:

> Time is only an illusion produced by the succession of our states of consciousness as we travel through Eternal Duration. . . . The Present is only a mathematical line which divides that part of Eternal Duration which we call the Future from that part which we call the Past. Nothing on earth has real duration, for nothing remains without change for the billionth part of a second: and the sensation we have of the actuality of the division of Time known as the present comes from the blurring of a momentary succession of glimpses of things that our senses give us, as those things pass from the region of ideas, which we call the Future into the region of memories that we name the Past. . . . The real person or things does not consist solely of what is seen at any particular moment but is composed of the sum of all its various and changing conditions. It is these "sum-totals" that exist from eternity in the Future, and pass by degrees through matter, to exist for eternity in the Past. . . . Persons and things dropping out of the "to be" into the "has been"—out of the Future into the Past—present momentarily to our senses

a cross-section of their total selves as they pass through Time and Space (Matter) on their way from one eternity to another and these two eternities constitute that Duration in which alone anything has true existence were our senses but able to cognise it.[66]

At least fourteen volumes of Blavatsky's *Complete Writings* were published by the early 1980s. Her life has been described in several biographies, including Marion Meade's *Madame Blavatsky* (1980). Here is an example of her prophecies:

> We are at the close of the cycle of 5,000 years of the present Aryan Kali Yuga or dark age. This will be succeeded by an age of light. Even now under our very eyes, the new Race or Races are preparing to be formed, and that is in America that the transformation will take place, and has already silently commenced. This Race will be altered in mentality and will move toward a more perfect spiritual existence.
>
> That the periodical sinking and reappearance of mighty continents, now called Atlantean and Lemurian by modern writers, is not fiction will be demonstrated. It is only in the 20th century that portions, if not the whole, of the present work will be vindicated.[67]

## ♉ *St. John Bosco*

> *Write to your brothers across the world, informing them it is necessary to bring about a reform of both customs and people themselves. If that is not achieved, the bread of the Divine World will not be broken among the people.*
>
> —John Bosco[68]

Born to a poor family, John Bosco's father died when he was two years old, leaving his mother to support three boys. Bosco's early years were spent as a shepherd, and he received his first instruction from the parish priest.

Bosco (1815–1888) had an early religious interest in helping impoverished boys and young men. He was ordained a Roman Catholic priest in 1841 in Turin and devoted his time to helping poor children with their education. In Turin, he helped found the Society of St. Francis de Sales (Salesians of Don Bosco). When Bosco died, there were 250 houses of the Salesian Society worldwide, housing thousands of children. St. Bosco's frightening letter written to Pope Pius IX in 1874 foretold a Catholic apocalypse. The letter is still kept in the Vatican archives:

> There will be chaos in the Church. Tranquility will not return until the Pope succeeds in anchoring the boat of Peter between the twin pillars of

Eucharistic Devotion and Devotion to Our Lady. This will come about one year before the end of the century.[69]

Bosco is perhaps best known for his detailed and scary vision of a battle at sea, part of which is excerpted here:

> In the midst of this endless sea, two solid columns, a short distance apart, soar high into the sky. The flagship commander—the Roman Pontiff—standing at the helm, strains every muscle to steer his ship between the two columns, from whose summits hang many anchors and strong hooks linked to chains. The entire enemy fleet closes in to intercept and sink the flagship at all costs. . . . In blind fury, the enemy takes to hand-to-hand combat, cursing and blaspheming. Suddenly the Pope falls, seriously wounded. He is instantly helped up, but struck a second time, dies. A shout of victory rises from the enemy, and wild rejoicing sweeps their ships. But no sooner is the Pope dead than another takes his place. Breaking through all resistance, the new Pope steers his ship safely between the two columns.[70]

## ♉ *Dannion Brinkley*

> *I also saw scenes that were not of war, including many visions of natural disasters. In parts of the world that had once been fertile with wheat and corn, I saw parched desert and furrowed fields that farmers had given up on.*
> —Dannion Brinkley[71]

Dannion Brinkley is the author of national bestsellers *Saved by the Light* and *At Peace in the Light*. His story was featured in the 1995 television movie *Saved by the Light*. In 1975, Brinkley says he was talking on the phone during a thunderstorm. A bolt of lightning hit the phone line, electrocuting him and stopping his heart. When Brinkley was revived after half an hour of apparent death, he had a strange tale to tell. After the lightning strike, Brinkley watched from above as medics tried to revive him. He then felt he was traveling through a black tunnel toward a bright crystal city. The next he knew he was in "a cathedral of knowledge"[72] where angelic instructors told him about events that would shake the world before the year 2000, including the Chernobyl nuclear disaster, the Persian Gulf War, and economic crises.

"The Beings [in the crystal city] came at me one at a time," Brinkley has written. "As each one approached, a box the size of a videotape came from its chest and zoomed right at my face."[73] The boxes opened in midair to reveal a television screen showing future world events.

The first three boxes showed the United States exhausted in the aftermath of the Vietnam war. Four and five were scenes from the Middle East, showing how this area of strife would reach a boiling point. The sixth showed a nuclear explosion. He writes of this box:

> The year 1986 was given to me through telepathy, as was the word "wormwood." It wasn't until a decade later, when the Chernobyl nuclear plant exploded near Kiev in the Soviet Union, that I was able to associate these pictures with an event. It was then that I made another connection between the vision in this box and the nuclear disaster in the USSR. The word Chernobyl means "wormwood" in Russian.[74]

In the seventh box, he saw scenes of environmental destruction. In boxes eight and nine were visions of China's growing anger toward the Soviet Union. The main battle was over a railroad, which the Chinese took in heavy fighting. The tenth and eleventh boxes showed scenes of the international economic collapse. America would be bankrupt by the year 2000, due in part to rebuilding costs resulting from large earthquakes. Then he saw the date 1990 and images of a war in the desert. This was the year of the Desert Storm when allied forces forced Iraq to withdraw from Kuwait. The twelfth box showed a bioengineer from the Middle East finding a way to alter DNA and create a biological virus that would be used in the manufacture of computer chips. The chips would be used in nearly every form of technology:

> Before the turn of the century, this man was among the richest in the world, so rich that he had a stranglehold on the world economy. Still the world welcomed him, since the computer chips he had designed somehow put the world on an even keel. He began to rule the world by mandating that everyone in the world have one of his computer chips inserted underneath his or her skin. This chip contained all of an individual's personal information. People who refused to have chips implanted in their bodies roamed as outcasts.[75]

This biological chip also controlled a person's longevity and could be programed to kill.

The thirteenth vision showed terrible calamities:

> Scenes from World War III came to life before me. I was in a hundred places at once, from deserts to forests, and saw a world filled with fighting and chaos. Somehow it was clear that this final war, an Armageddon if you will, was caused by fear.[76]

The Beings next told Brinkley that none of these possible futures are set in stone, and humans could prevent their suffering if they changed their ways.[77] Skeptics suggest that many of his predictions, such as strife in the Middle East, tension between Russia and China, and environmental problems, would not be a great stretch for a prophet living in the last part of the twentieth century.

## ♉ *Paul Foster Case*

> *The Hierophantria and I were observed to exchange significant glances over the altar during the Mystic Repast. . . . My conscience acquits me. . . . I have no desire to be a teacher and pioneer in this Purgatorial World. Guidance seems to have removed me from the high place to which I have never really aspired. The relief is great.*
>
> —Paul Foster Case[78]

Paul Foster Case (1884–1954) studied tarot cards and produced books on occult metaphysics. His *Book of Tokens* was a collection of meditations on the twenty-two major arcana cards of the tarot. He abandoned his lucrative career as a musician to start his own occult school, the Builders of the Adytum (B.O.T.A.), in Los Angeles. Still in existence today, it has proven to be a successful correspondence course on the tarot.

Case was born in Fairport, New York. His mother was a teacher and his father a librarian.[79] By the age of four Case was studying books in the attic of his father's library. At an early age, Case said he had the ability to consciously manipulate his dreams. At sixteen, Case met the occultist Claude Bragdon who got him interested in tarot cards. Case became increasingly interested in sexuality, and in his *Book of Tokens*, Case writes, "You must wholly alter your conception of sex in order to comprehend the Ancient Wisdom. . . . It is the interior nervous organism, not the external organs, that is always meant in phallic symbolism, and the force that works through these interior centers is the Great Magical Agent, the divine serpent fire."[80] In his works, *The True and Invisible Rosicrucian Order* and *The Masonic Letter G*, he describes practices that redirect the sexual force to the brain's higher centers so that practitioners can experience of extrasensory states of consciousness. Incidentally, the Rosicrucians are traditionally a secret fraternity making it difficult to obtain accurate knowledge about their practices. Rosicrucians claim to possess secret wisdom handed down from ancient Egypt. Rosicrucianism was introduced to America with the Chapter of Perfection, a Rosicrucian association established by German settlers in seventeenth-century Pennsylvania.

## ♉ Edgar Cayce

> The earth will be broken up in the western portion of America. The greater por-
> tion of Japan must go into the sea. The upper portion of Europe will be changed
> as in the twinkling of an eye. Land will appear off the east coast of America.
> There will be the upheavals in the Arctic and in the Antarctic that will make for
> the eruption of volcanos in the Torrid areas, and there will be shifting then of the
> poles—so that where there has been those of a frigid or the semitropical will
> become the more tropical, and moss and fern will grow. And these will begin in
> those periods in '58 to '98, when these will be proclaimed as the periods when
> His light will be seen again in the clouds.
>
> —Edgar Cayce[81]

*Edgar Cayce* (1877–1945, pronounced "Casey") was a rural Kentucky healer
who went into trances to yield diagnosis and prescriptions for patients, as
well as to foretell the future. "Believers" consider him the twentieth century's
greatest clairvoyant and call him the "sleeping prophet" because he appeared
to give his readings while asleep or in a trance. Using his gift, he attempted
to heal numerous people and diagnose and recommend treatments without
physically seeing the patient. He was also said to be able to cure seemingly
incurable illnesses at his private hospital in Virginia Beach, Virginia.

Edgar Cayce was born on a farm near Hopkinsville, Kentucky, and he
claimed to have an early psychic ability. For example, he said he was able to
learn his lessons at school by falling asleep on his books. At a young age,
Cayce became interested in the Bible and read its entire contents. He hoped
to become a minister and heal people.

In his youth, a baseball hit him on the neck, and a few hours later Cayce
said he entered the same hypnotic sleep that he used to learn his school
lessons. In this state, he was able to recommend treatment for his damaged
throat muscles that included a poultice of herbs mixed with chopped onions.
The cure seemed to work, and he started curing others. He left school at the
age of fifteen.

When Cayce was twenty-one, he suddenly lost his voice. Under hypnosis, Cayce "diagnosed" his own condition saying, "The trouble is partial
paralysis of the vocal cords do to nerve strain. To remove the condition, it is
necessary only to suggest that the body increase circulation to he affected
area." When the hypnotist told him to increase the circulation, Cayce's
throat immediately turned a deep color, and the condition was cured. The
hypnotist was amazed and suggested to Cayce that he might try curing other
people in this manner.

The next day, the hypnotist put Cayce in another trance, and Cayce began to "examine" the hypnotist's body. Using sophisticated medical terms, Cayce told the hypnotist what to do to feel better, and it seemed to work. By 1910, Cayce had become nationally famous. He diagnosed patients at a distance, only needing for the reading a name and address of the patient. In 1926, Cayce prescribed for a New York patient the raw side of a freshly skinned rabbit, still warm with blood, fur side out, placed on the breast for cancer of that area.[82]

Cayce seemed to provide intuitive insight into nearly any question posed to him. When individuals approached him with a problem, Cayce placed himself in a sleep–induced state and responded to their questions. He began his readings in the early 1920s and continued until his death in January of 1945. During the latter years, he began foretelling major world events. He is said to have predicted the exact date for the end of World War II and the assassination of President John F. Kennedy. His prophecies went further into the future, predicting major earthquakes and natural disasters occurring all over the world. He foresaw the destruction of both California and New York City. In 1943, He predicted that China would be "mostly Christian" by 1968. At his death, he had over 14,000 records of trance readings for over 8,000 people. His predictions included the rise of Atlantis in 1968 or 1969 near Bimini and the Second Coming of Christ in 1998, accompanied by cataclysmic pole shifts and huge earthquakes.

Cayce also saw himself reborn in post-apocalypse Nebraska, 2100 C.E. He also prophesied the Sphinx had been built in 10500 B.C.E., and that survivors of Atlantis had concealed beneath it a "Hall of Records" containing all the wisdom of their lost civilization and the true history of the human race. Cayce prophesied that this Hall of Records would be rediscovered and opened between 1996 and 1998. He connected the opening to the Second Coming of Christ.

In 1931, Cayce and his family moved to Virginia Beach, where he established the Association for Research and Enlightenment (ARE). During the 1930s he gave an average of two readings a day. After the appearance of Thomas Sugrue's biography *The Story of Edgar Cayce*, the frequency of his readings increased, and in 1944 he collapsed from exhaustion. (Incidentally, the biography has sold over one million copies and is still in print.) Cayce said he had been through a number of incarnations that included a warrior of Troy, an Egyptian priest, a disciple of Jesus Christ, a Persian Monarch, and a heavenly angel-like being that had been on Earth before Adam and Eve arrived. He said the Atlanteans were a technologically advanced civilization having aircraft, electricity, and weapons of destruction. Cayce referred to their "death ray" or "super cosmic ray" that eventually led to their own demise. He predicted that the western edge of Atlantis would begin to reappear in 1968 or 1969 near the island of Bimini in the Bahamas.

Speaking of the future of the Arctic and Antarctic regions, he said, "There will be upheavals . . . that will make for the eruptions of volcanoes in the torrid areas, and there will be the shifting then of the poles."[83] He said this would take place around the year 2000–2001 C.E. The Last Day would be preceded by a tumultuous series of earth changes, sparked by volcanic eruptions that would begin around New Year's Eve, 1998. He said, "I see thousands of volcanoes—many of them previously unknown to scientists—erupting worldwide." Millions of people would die from the molten lava.

Cayce once told of a dream in which he was standing on the edge of the universe and met a rosy-cheeked boy with a pair of scissors. Cayce asked the beautiful, smiling boy who he was.

> "I am Death," the boy replied.
> Cayce was startled. "This is not how I expected death to be."
> The boy laughed. "No one expects me to be a beautiful experience."
> Cayce thought for a moment. "And what are the scissors for?"
> The boy, the personification of death, replied that when Cayce's time would come, these scissors would cut him free from the silver cord that held his spirit to the body.[84]

For a skeptical treatment of Cayce's life, see James Randi's *An Encyclopedia of Claims, Frauds, and Hoaxes of the Occult and Supernatural* and Dale Beyerstein's "Edgar Cayce: The Prophet Who Slept His Way to the Top."[85]

## ♉ *Mélanie Calvat of La Salette*

> *The first blow of the sword of God will fall like lightning upon humanity. The mountain and all nature shall shake because of the disorder and the misdeeds of men. . . . Rome will lose the faith and become the seat of the Antichrist.*
> —Mélanie of La Salette[86]

Mélanie of La Salette (1831–1904) had a difficult early life. She was the fourth of ten children, and her strict mother, overwhelmed with work, seemed to hate Mélanie. The family's poverty was so extreme that the young were sometimes sent to beg on the street. At a very young age, Mélanie was hired out to tend the neighbors' cows.

In 1846, fifteen-year-old Mélanie Calvat was with a shepherd boy on a mountain three miles from the village of La Salette-Fallavaux. They claimed to have seen "a beautiful lady" in a glowing light. The Beautiful Lady wept all the time she spoke. Mélanie described the voice as follows:

> The voice of the Beautiful Lady was soft. It was enchanting, ravishing, warming to the heart. It satisfied, flattered every obstacle, it soothed and softened. It seemed to me I could never stop eating up Her beautiful voice, and my heart seemed to dance or want to go towards Her and melt inside Her.[87]

The woman gave them a message "to deliver to all her people." She conveyed a prophecy regarding the decline of spirituality in the world, the fall of Catholicism, and world war. After complaining about recent improper behavior of Christians, she promised them divine mercy if they would change their ways. She also predicted famines.

> Don't you understand, my children? Let me find another way to say it. If you have wheat, you must not sow it. Anything you sow the vermin will eat, and whatever does grow will fall into dust when you thresh it. A great famine is coming. Before the famine comes, children under seven will be seized with trembling and die in the arms of those who hold them. The rest will do penance through the famine. The walnuts will become worm-eaten; the grapes will rot.[88]

Mélanie's prophecies throughout her life included visions of volcanic activity and Earth's destruction.

The sensation caused by Mélanie was huge and led to several investigations. Many thought that the mysterious lady was Mary of the New Testament. Soon several miraculous cures took place on the mountain of La Salette, and pilgrims flocked to the mountain. Were their visions real? After five long years of diligent inquiries, Bishop Philibert de Bruillard of Grenoble published his long-awaited decision on September 19, 1851:

> We judge that the Apparition of the Blessed Virgin to the two cowherds on the 19th of September, 1846, on a mountain of the chain of Alps, situated in the parish of LaSalette, in the archpresbytery of Corps, bears within Itself all the characteristics of truth, and that the faithful have grounds for believing it Indubitable and certain.[89]

Before she disappeared, the lady in light gave Mélanie a special secret, and in 1851, Mélanie sent the secret message to Pius IX. Today, we do not know what impressions the message made on the pope. Mélanie died in

Altamura, Italy, in 1904, and her remains are buried under a marble column with a bas-relief depicting Mary welcoming the shepherdess of La Salette into heaven.

## ♉ *Cheiro*

> *The glacial age will by degrees be repeated in Northern Europe. Such countries as Ireland, Great Britain, Sweden, Norway, Denmark, the northern parts of Russia, Germany, France, and Spain will gradually become uninhabitable.*
> —Cheiro[90]

Cheiro (1866–1936) was the byname for the British clairvoyant and palmist Count Louis Hamon. Cheiro became famous for his predictions made through palmistry, numerology and astrology. He also became known for predicting the future of many well known celebrities of his time, from King Edward VIII of Great Britain to Mark Twain. He did not marry until late in life, preferring to use his hypnotic powers to seduce attractive married women. Despite his martial arts training, he did manage to get stabbed by a jealous husband. In 1926 he wrote *Cheiros World Predictions* in which he attempted to predict the future. He lived in Hollywood in the 1930s, establishing a school of metaphysics. In 1931, he prophesied, "From now on tidal waves and cyclones will cause enormous destruction."[91]

As with many other prophets, most of his prophecies seemed to deal with earthquakes, Atlantis, and floods. Just a few years earlier before his tidal wave predictions, he prophesied, "Germany and Italy will war against France and England. In the coming 50 years an earthquake zone will develop in NE Pacific coast of Peru up through to the Arctic regions. Eastern cities of the U.S. will be affected, and parts of New York will be destroyed in 50–100 years. A series of earthquakes will cause the Azores to rise and Atlantis will resurface and be explored. Perfection cannot be attained until all religions merge into one."[92]

## ♉ *Florence Cook*

Florence Cook (1856–1904) was a popular psychic who purportedly summoned spirits and channeled their voices. Though not quite the diviner as others in this book, she did claim to have access to secret knowledge. She is best remembered for her supposed ability to produce the physical materialization of spirits she channeled. This caused widespread attention that made her name a household name within nineteenth-century spiritualism.[93]

Since she was a child, Florence said she saw spirits and heard voices. During her teenage years, her hand produced automatic mirror writing, that is, writing that can be read by looking at it through a mirror. The strange messages led her to visit a bookseller and inquire about the Dalston spiritual association, where she eventually began to hold seances. Her followers said she was able to levitate while at the same time invisible hands changed her clothing.

Soon Florence channeled a spirit that called herself "Katie King," the daughter of John King, an alias for Henry Owen Morgan, the true-life seventeenth-century pirate. Katie King promised to speak through Florence for three years. In 1872, while Florence attempted to physically materialize Katie, a masklike face was seen between the curtains of a cabinet. A year later, Katie King was able to walk from out of the cabinet and be photographed with flash photography.

The famous British chemist and physicist Sir William Crookes (1832–1919) studied Florence and believed the materialized Katie King was real. In 1874, he published his findings in a controversial book titled *Researches in the Phenomena of Spiritualism*. Florence Cook's demonstrations convinced Crookes in the existence of an afterlife.

Skeptics claim that Sir William Crookes was infatuated with the attractive Florence Cook and her alleged spirit, and this tended to bias his investigations. For a skeptical look at Florence Cook, see Trevor Hall's *The Medium and the Scientist: The Story of Florence Cook and William Crookes*.[94]

## ♉ *Benjamin Creme*

> My job has been to make the initial approach to the public, to help create a climate of hope and expectancy. If I can do that, I'll be well pleased.
> —Benjamin Creme[95]

Benjamin Creme is a British artist and student of philosophy. He has become the principal source of information about the mysterious Maitreya, the long-awaited Christ. Creme was born in Glasgow, Scotland, in 1922. Today, his paintings have been exhibited in many prestigious galleries. While growing up, Creme studied some of the teachings of mystic Helena Blavatsky and the Theosophical Society and more recently Alice A. Bailey. In 1959, he says he was contacted by one of the "masters" who told him that Maitreya, the World Teacher and master of all masters, would come to Earth in twenty years.

From 1975 to 1979, Creme lectured throughout Europe. During his first

U.S. tour in 1980, he spoke to large audiences in many major cities. Since the early 1980s, he has toured through the world and has been interviewed on hundreds of radio and television programs in the United States. Creme's books on the reappearance of the Christ have been translated into many languages.

Creme suggests that in 1977 Maitreya left his home in the Himalayas to live as an ordinary human in the Indian-Pakistani community of London. According to Creme, Maitreya is responsible for the end of apartheid in South Africa, the coming of Mikhail Gorbachev and the resulting death of communism, and the worldwide interest in ecology. Creme also says that Maitreya's reign on earth will begin when he is invited to speak on television and thousands of spontaneous healings occur.

Maitreya has predicted that Japan will be the center of a stock market crash that eventually envelopes the entire planet. The economic disaster will lead to food shortages and cause humanity to rethink its values and priorities.

## ♉ *Gerard Croiset*

> *When a warning feeling disturbs me, I get a vibration which is like a full-up feeling, and I expand like a balloon. I grow attentive. The paragnost [clairvoyant] in me is now at work. . . . When somebody with a real problem comes to me, I see a lot of colors. These colors spin around in me very fast until they form a picture. These pictures shoot out as if they were flashing forward, like a three-dimensional film.*
>
> —Gerard Croiset[96]

Gerard Croiset (1909–1980) was a Dutch psychic who said he could foretell the future. He is best remembered for the times he seemed to help the police solve murder cases by finding missing persons. To demonstrate his powers, Croiset invented an experiment known as the "chair test" during which he would try to predict the characteristics of a person who would sit in a randomly chosen chair at an upcoming public event. Croiset followers suggest that he performed the chair test over a period of twenty-five years with many successes. Some followers have gone so far to suggest that the chair raises the question of just how free we really are.

The 1966 disappearance of the Beaumont children in Adelaide has become part of Australian folklore, and Croiset is part of the legend. Jane Nartare, Arnna Kathleen and Grant Ellis Beaumont left their home on the morning of January 26, 1966, to go to the beach and were never seen again. Gerard Croiset was called into investigate, but despite much hype and publicity, failed to locate the children. He first suggested that their bodies were under the three-meter-thick concrete floor of a warehouse. Croiset wanted the police to dig up the warehouse, but the police and the warehouse owner were reluctant. The public was not satisfied and raised $7,000 to dig up the floor. On March 8, 1967, the floor was torn apart, and the children were not there.

Skeptics, such as anthropology professor James Lett,[97] suggest that Croiset's psychic claims do not pass the rule of "replicability," and that psychics are especially fond of misinterpreting coincidences. Although Croiset's followers say he has solved numerous baffling crimes and located hundreds of missing persons, Lett suggests that the most of Croiset's predictions were either vague and nonfalsifiable or simply wrong. Croiset made thousands of predictions during his lifetime, and it not surprising that he enjoyed a few chance "hits" that seem amazing.

Croiset said he helped police departments find missing bodies using a form of psychometry. He touched an object owned by the missing or murdered person, reading the message left as hidden vibrations on the object, which then directed him to the person. Other famous paranormal crime busters or "psychic sleuths" include Greta Alexander, Dorothy Allison, Peter Hurkos, Phil Jordan, Rosemarie Kerr, Noreen Reiner, and Bill Ward. You can read more about these individuals in Joe Nickell's *Psychic Sleuths: ESP and Sensational Cases*.[98]

## ♉ *Aleister Crowley*

> *The ram should be virgin. For the highest spiritual working one must accordingly choose that victim which contains the greatest and purest force. A male child of perfect innocence and high intelligence is the most satisfactory and suitable victim. For evocations it would be more convenient to place the blood of the victim in the Triangle.*
>
> —Aleister Crowley, *Magick in Theory and Practice*

Aleister Crowley (1875–1947) was a British sexual mystic and proponent of black magic. Crowley (rhymes with "holy") was born in Leamington Spa, England. His parents were members of the Plymouth Brethren, a strict fundamentalist Christian sect. As a result, Crowley grew up with a no-nonsense biblical education and an intense dislike of Christianity.

Because of his rebelliousness, Crowley's mother believed him to be the Antichrist. The boy soon agreed with her and determined that he was a prophet who would usher in a new age and sweep away the shambles of an old-fashioned Christianity. Sexual exploits with women and men played a major role in Crowley's later career. Among his numerous eccentricities was his habit of defecating on carpets. He claimed his excretions were sacred. He also had his two front teeth filed so that they would be sufficiently sharp to draw blood when he kissed a woman. Crowley also recruited a succession of unattractive, masochistic women whom he could dominate throughout his life. Although not a prophet, like others in this book, he did attempt to conjure demons, practice necromancy, and travel in "astral planes."

Crowley claimed he channeled his *Book of the Law* for a "praeterhuman intelligence" called Aiwass. Aiwass supplied him with prophecies. Crowley's motto was, "Do what thou wilt shall be the whole of the Law." This led to his rejecting traditional morality and becoming a drug addict and womanizer, as hinted about in a line from his poem: "I rave; and I rape and I rip and I rend."[99] He had two wives. Both went insane. Five mistresses committed suicide. He branded one of his mistresses between her breast using a heated dagger. According to Martin Gardner, "scores of his concubines ended in the gutter as alcoholics, drug addicts, or in mental institutions."[100] When he founded an Abby of Thelema in Italy, his initiates had to slash their arm with a razor blade each time they said "I."

In 1910 Crowley was contacted by Theodore Reuss, the head of an organization based in Germany called the *Ordo Templi Orientis* (O.T.O.). This group of high-ranking Freemasons claimed to have discovered the supreme secret of practical magick, which was taught in its highest degrees. Apparently Crowley agreed, becoming a member of O.T.O. and eventually taking over as head of the order when Reuss suffered a stroke in 1921.

Crowley has some modern fans among rock musicians. Jimmy Page, the guitarist for Led Zeppelin, owns a large collection of Crowley artifacts and bought Crowley's mansion in Scotland. Crowley's face is also one of many on the album cover of the Beatles' *Sergeant Pepper's Lonely Hearts Club Band*. Martin Gardner remarked: "Crowley's reputation had been that of a man who worshipped Satan, but it was more accurately said that he worshipped no one except himself."[101] Crowley died in 1947 at age seventy-two.[102]

## ♉ *Bejan Daruwalla*

> *By 2001, the Congress will be a non-entity, wiped out. Their time is up.*
> —Bejan Daruwalla[103]

Bejan Daruwalla (1931–) is an internationally famous astrologer born in India and whose witty predictions are widely read in publications throughout South Asia and the Middle East. Currently his articles are published in the *Sunday Times of India* (Bombay, Calcutta, Delhi, Madras), *Telegraph* (Calcutta), *Navkind Times* (Goa), *Dell Annual Horoscope, 1998* (New York), *News India* (New York), and *Berkley Communications* (London). His followers claim he accurately predicted the release of Nelson Mandela from prison in South Africa and the death of Sanjay Gandhi, the assertive son of Prime Minister Indira Gandhi, who was killed while flying over New Delhi in 1980. In 1986 he prophesied, "December 1994 . . . till January 1996: Floods, typhoons, gales, hurricanes, a splitting apart of ships, submarines, aircraft, cars, locomotives.

In his latest book, the *Millennium Yearbook*, he makes predictions for the next one thousand years. For example, he sees India as a superpower in the twenty-first century and friendly with Pakistan by 2001. A goddess, Shakti Devi, will be born in human form in India in 2020. The Messiah will come, and there will be one world government. He refuses to read his own stars, "because life should be an adventure."[104]

## ♉ *Andrew Jackson Davis*

*It is a truth that spirits commune with one another while one is in the body and the other in the higher spheres—and this, too, when the person in the body is unconscious of the influx, and hence cannot be convinced of the fact; and this truth will ere long present itself in the form of a living demonstration. And the world will hail with delight the ushering in of that era when the interiors of men will be opened, and the spiritual communion will be established.*

—Andrew Jackson Davis[105]

**Figure 66.** Andrew Jackson Davis (1826–1910), the "Poughkeepsie seer." From *The Centennial Book, 1883–1993* (Lily Dale, New York: National Spiritual Association of Churches of the United States of America, 1994), p. 216.

Andrew Jackson Davis (1826–1910), the "Poughkeepsie seer," was a diviner and healer (see figure 66). His followers have compared him to Emanuel Swedenborg, the Swedish scientist, Christian mystic, philosopher, and theologian. Unlike Emanuel Swedenborg, Andrew Jackson Davis grew up in poverty. He was born at Blooming Grove, a small hamlet along the Hudson River in New York State. His mother was an uneducated woman, and his father was an alcoholic.

When Davis was twelve and working on a farm, he claimed to hear strange music and voices that coaxed him to travel to Pough keepsie, New York. Eventually he managed to convince his father to move to Poughkeepsie where Davis inisited he could diagnose medical disorders. While in a trance, Davis described how the human skin became transparent to his spirit eyes (see figure 67). He could see each organ emitting a glow that dimmed in cases of disease.

There are striking parallels between Davis and Edgar Cayce (1877–1945), an American clairvoyant of Presbyterian background. Both men said they discovered their psychic abilities as a result of being hypnotized and later were able to

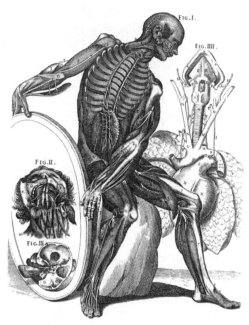

**Figure 67.** Andrew Jackson Davis said that human skin became transparent to his spirit eyes. From Pietro da Cortona, *The Anatomical Plates of Pietro da Cortona* (New York: Dover, 1986), plate 11.

induce trances without hypnotism. They spent a significant time trying to diagnose diseases and prescribing odd treatments. Both gave psychic commentaries on the nature of reality.

Some strange stories surround Davis's travels. In 1844, Davis, while in a trance state, suddenly developed the power to "fly" from Poughkeepsie. Upon gaining full consciousness the next morning, he found himself in the Catskill Mountains, forty miles away. Here, he claims to have met the ancient Greek physician Galen and the Swedish seer Emanuel Swedenborg. No one can prove one way or the other if Davis walked the forty miles in a trance state or if the entire vision was psychological or fabricated.

In 1845, Davis began dictating *The Principles of Nature: Her Divine Revelations and a Voice to Mankind*. The dictation lasted for fifteen months and when published was wildly successful.[106] Davis wrote his book in the third person (like Cayce sometimes did) after he "descended from the exalted mental state down into the physical organism, approximating the natural or normal condition common to all persons when in their ordinary states; because, while in profound trance or Superior Condition, he could neither move his tongue to speak nor control his hand to write. His memory was wonderfully illuminated and thus afterward he could speak or write all facts as impressions obtained."[107]

*The Principles of Nature* contains this gem of wisdom:

> In the beginning the Univercoelumm was one boundless, indefinable, and unimaginable ocean of Liquid Fire. The most vigorous and ambitious imagination is not capable of forming an adequate conception of the height and depth and length and breadth thereof. There was one vast expanse of liquid substance. It was without bounds—inconceivable—and with qualities and essences incomprehensible. This was the original condition of Matter. It was without forms, for it was but one Form. It had no motions, but it was an eternity of Motion.[108]

When it came to offering cures for diseases, Davis's ideas seemed weird even by today's most fringe standards of alternative medicine. For example, his cure for a deaf patient was to have the man wrap the warm skins of rats around each ear nightly for a period of time. In another case of deafness, he told the patient to boil the hind legs of thirty-two weasels and then use the resultant oil "a drop at a time" in each ear twice a day. Reportedly the patient declined the procedure.

Jackson spent significant time divining the future and making scientific predictions. For example, he supposedly predicted the existence of nine planets (only seven planets were known at this time). In 1856, he referred to horseless and steamless vehicles: "Carriages will be moved by a strange and beautiful and simple admixture of aqueous and atmospheric gases—so easily condensed, so simply ignited, and so imparted by a machine somewhat resembling our engines as to be entirely concealed and manageable between the forward wheels. Aerial cars will move through the sky from country to country; and their beautiful influence will produce a universal brotherhood of acquaintance."[109]

When he was asked if there were limits to God's power, he replied: "God is not sufficiently powerful to accomplish self-destruction. There are, therefore, necessities to omnipotence."[110] He also suggested that "organic beings" lived on Saturn until the creation of Earth, and Mars and Jupiter are populated by short-lived human inhabitants "composed of finer elements" than ordinary people.

Davis invented the term "Summerland" to designate the realm of the afterlife. He believed that our souls survived our death and had the potential for passing through six spheres. So far, no soul has gotten beyond the second sphere. Someday, when all spirits reach the sixth sphere, God will create a new universe and allow us to access the seventh sphere. There is no final resting place for us. Davis said, "The spirit will have no final home, because rest would be intolerable to an immortal being, but the spirit will progress eternally. It will be always in harmony with surrounding circumstances, and so will dwell always in heaven."[111]

At fifty-seven years of age, Davis became a medical doctor and practiced medicine in Boston. Years later, when Edgar Cayce was told about the prior existence of Davis, Cayce said, "He sounds so much like me it gives me the creeps."[112]

## ♉ *Countess Francesca de Billiante*

> *Europe will be covered by a yellow fog. The cattle in the fields will die from this yellow fog. . . . Famine will annihilate those who remain, so that Europe will be too large.*
>
> —Countess Francesca de Billiante[113]

Countess Francesca de Billiante of southern France was famous among fellow royalty for her visions of the future, which she made evident during dinner parties. She prophesied, "Great afflictions will come. . . . Nations will end in flames, and famine will annihilate millions." Why is it that so many prophets foretold death and destruction? In 1935, she prophesied:

> Europe will tremble. France and Spain will sink deeply. I see yellow and red warriors [Japanese and Russian?] marching against Europe, and Europe will be covered with a yellow smoke [chemical weapons?] The cattle in the fields will die of this yellow smoke. Those cities, which had raised against Christ, will be destroyed in flames. Hunger will overwhelm the ones that survive continue and few will remain in the Europe. [The brackets in the quotation refer to interpretations made by followers of de Billiante.][114]

I welcome more information from readers on details of the life of Countess Francesca de Billiante.

## ♉ *Mario de Sabato*

> *Philosophy will come to Europe from China, which will lead to the cultural, poetic and artistic rebirth of a new Europe. It will represent the golden age: the advent of the era of Aquarius, and the rebuilding of a new harmonious civilization.*
>
> —Mario de Sabato[115]

Mario de Sabato (1933–) is a modern French diviner who exhibited his "abilities" by age seven. His prophecies have a strong Catholic flavor similar to those of those of Jeane Dixon's. Throughout the 1970s, de Sabato gained a reputation as a seer and was consulted by lay people and world leaders. Most his prophecies have never been published in English. He is said to have predicted the Cuban missile crisis of 1962, much of the activity in Europe and the Middle East in the 1970s, the assassinations of both John and Robert Kennedy and Martin Luther King Jr., and the collapse of communism in the Soviet Union. In 1971, he prophesied, "Finally, it will be understood that the end of the worlds was merely a kind of purification."[116] He also said that 1998 would to mark the beginning of a Chinese invasion of Europe.

## ♉ *Onizaburo Deguchi*

Onizaburo Deguchi (1871–1948) was a religious leader of modern Japan, frequently called the "Japanese Nostradamus." He is said to have predicted the Russo-Japanese War (1905), the Great Kanto Earthquake (1923), the Sino-Japanese War (1937), the Pacific War (1941), the American dropping of atomic bombs, and the advent of computers, credit cards, and cellular phones. Like many other prophets, he also predicted great crises at the end of the twentieth century. In the near future, the world is supposed to be covered by fiery rain, and humanity will be divided into twelve races.

Deguchi was the leader of the Omoto religious movement, which conflicted with official state Shinto religions and was brutally suppressed in 1921. In 1935 the police arrested Onizaburo and many members of his group in an attempt to eradicate the movement. Onizaburo published eighty-one volumes of *Reikai Monogatari* (*Spiritual Story*), an account of his spiritual odyssey. The huge tome deals with the history of Earth from 350 million years ago to 5,000 years in the future. When the first 55 volumes are printed 400 characters to a page, the first characters of each page form the sentence: "I began to train myself at Mt. Takakuma on February 9th, 1898. 25 full years till have passed to this year January 18th, 1923. The 55 volumes of the *Spiritual Story* were dictated on 200 days over 15 months."

In total, there are 25,000 pages to *Spiritual Story*. At the beginning Onizaburo dictated a book every two days. He made no corrections, and his followers believe the book to be conveyed by God.[117] In addition to making predictions, *Spiritual Story* often discusses ancient Japanese history and gods.

## ♉ *Dr. Marion Derlette*

Marion Derlette is a popular end-of-time religious scholar who predicted the Earth would undergo a swift and cataclysmic change in 1999 and 2000, a man known as the Antichrist would rise to power in the Middle East, and a nuclear war would quickly result.[118,119] Dr. Derlette spent decades studying apocalyptic prophecies dating back to the year 3500 B.C.E. and believed six major religions predicted Earth would undergo swift and cataclysmic changes in 1999.

After humanity is destroyed by armageddon and a doomsday comet, God will establish Heaven on Earth, and create a paradise for believers everywhere. According to Derlette, "Every event that occurs at this critical juncture in history is just another rung on the ladder we are descending on our perilous and dizzying journey to the end."[120] The journey includes enormous earthquakes, the drifting of entire continents and land masses, the shifting of the Earth's poles, horrifying extremes of weather, deadly epidemics, and global hatred and war. Derlette suggests all regions have similar prophecies. "The prophecies all predict the same things, including the end of the world on 16 January, 2000. At least it's going to be good for those of us who believe we will be resurrected to live in the Paradise that God will establish on Earth."[121]

## ♉ *Jeane Dixon*

> *I still stand by my New Year's prediction and see no marriage for Jackie in the near future.*
>
> —Jeane Dixon, October 20, 1968
> [On the next day Mrs. Kennedy was married]

Jeane Dixon (1918–1997) was the famous Washington, D.C., prophetess who made her living in the real estate business. She became famous for her "prediction" of President John F. Kennedy's assassination, which appeared in *Parade* on May 13, 1956 in the following words: "As for the 1960 election, Mrs. Dixon thinks it will be dominated by Labor and won by a Democrat. He will be assassinated in office, though not necessarily in his first term." President Kennedy was assassinated in Dallas, Texas, on November 22, 1963. However, skeptics are not impressed by this because in 1960 she predicted unequivocally that "John F. Kennedy would fail to win the presidency."

After Kennedy's death in 1963, political columnist Ruth Montgomery wrote a book, *A Gift of Prophecy: The Phenomenal Jeane Dixon*, that recounted hundreds of seemingly accurate predictions over the years. Published in

1965, the book sold more than three million copies. Mrs. Dixon soon became a popular speaker on the lecture circuit and writer for a syndicated column. Throughout her life, Mrs. Dixon was an adviser to many famous clients, including Nancy Reagan, who, however, eventually abandoned her for a rival. (I don't know if Dixon foresaw Regan's abandoment!) Dixon is the author of more than seven books, including an astrological cookbook and a horoscope book for dogs.

A devout Roman Catholic, Dixon attributed her ability to God. At age eight, she was taken by her mother to a fortune teller who said she had a gift for prophesy, which her mother encouraged her to develop. Dixon died in 1997 at the age of seventy-nine.

Now for a skeptical look. At the start of each year Mrs. Dixon released a list of predictions that supermarket tabloids loved to publish and then double-check. Not all her predictions proved true. She predicted, for instance, that World War III would begin in 1958 over two offshore Chinese islands and that the Soviets would be first on the moon. She predicted Richard Nixon would win the presidency in 1960, a female U.S. president in the 1980s, a monster comet striking the Earth in the 1980s, and the demise of the Roman Catholic Church before 1990. The cometary strike "would be one of the worst disasters of the twentieth century." She also incorrectly predicted that Russia would move into Iran in 1953, Eisenhower would appoint the disgraced general Douglas MacArthur to "an exceedingly important post," and that China would start a world war over the islands Quemoy and Matsu and use germ warfare against the United States. She predicted that the Vietnam War would be over in ninety days. For 1997, she predicted actor Alec Baldwin would become terribly ill and that comedian Ellen DeGeneres would have a run-in with the Secret Service when she crashed the presidential inauguration.

Professor James Lett, an author and professor of anthropology at Indian River Community College, suggests that many of Dixon's prophecies were so nebulous that the accuracy of the statements could not be calculated.[122] As examples, Dixon predicted that 1987 would be a year "filled with changes" for Caroline Kennedy. But how are we to assess "filled with changes?" Dixon also predicted that Jack Kemp would "face major disagreements with the rest of his party" in 1987 and that "world-wide drug terror" would be "unleashed by narcotics czars" in the same year. She further revealed that Dan Rather "may [or may not] be hospitalized" in 1988, and that Whitney Houston's "greatest problem" in 1986 would be "balancing her personal life against her career." As with other seers' prophecies, broad claims are often very difficult to test.

## ♉ *John William Dunne*

John William Dunne (1875–1949) was an Irish psychic who trained as a mathematician and airplane designer. His most successful airplane was the D4, which flew under its own power for 120 feet in 1908 at Blair Atholl, Perthshire. Dunne's main contributions to aviation were in the field of aerodynamic stability.

Dunne was brilliant from an early age, able to "read Euclid as easily as a grown-up person reads a novel."[123] Between the ages of twelve and thirteen he experienced a series of visions, or what he termed "ecstasies." The beautiful visions haunted him and caused him to reevaluate his life, future, and the nature of time. He believed his dreams foretold the future. For example, one of his famous dreams dealt with volcanic eruptions. Dunne thought that it was possible to foretell the future by accessing realities separated from the experience and restriction of time. Dunne's books on the nature of time include *An Experiment With Time*, *The Serial Universe*, *The New Immortality*, *Nothing Dies*, and *Intrusions?* In his book *An Experiment With Time*, Dunne focuses on his experiences with dreams, and suggests that dreams are a mixture of past and future events. The book gives practical advice for dream experimentation.

## ♉ *Arthur Ford*

> To have scientific proof of survival after death is far less important than to realize the fact of immortality in such a way that we can live every day in the clear, glad consciousness that we are immortal beings here and now, and that death can never touch the real self.
>
> —Arthur Ford[124]

Arthur Ford (1897–1971) was an American psychic who claimed he could contact the dead and transmit messages. He channeled a person named Fletcher. Ford is also the spiritualist who claimed he could communicate with Houdini's spirit from beyond the grave. In his book *The Life Beyond Death*, Ford writes:

> Life after death is a reality. Personal survival of death is not a reward for good behavior or an indication of spiritual development. *Everybody lives—* proud or humble. We survive with memory, personality and capacity for recognition. This is a psychic fact, a law of the universe like gravity. For too many centuries, too many peanut-minded, sour-souled bigots and power drivers have sought to dominate their flocks through threats of hell. The

joys, freedoms and opportunities of the unobstructed universe beyond have been dimmed. Fear-of-hell preaching is as much responsible for our prevailing disbelief as anything else.[125]

Psychic Ruth Mongomery, in her book *A World Beyond: A Startling Message from the Eminent Psychic Arthur Ford from Beyond the Grave*, says that Arthur Ford communicated to her through automatic writing after his death to give a firsthand account of the afterlife, which includes the concept of reincarnation fused with some of Jesus's teachings. Four years after Ford's death, Patricia Hayes, colleague and friend of Ford's, founded the Arthur Ford International Academy of Mediumship.

## ☒ *Katherine and Margaret Fox*

On December 11, 1847, teenage sisters Katherine (1836–1892) and Margaret (1833–1893) moved with their parents into a house in Hydesville, New York (see figure 68). The house had a reputation for being haunted; there were several instances recorded of taps and other noises. Legend has it that the prior tenant, Michael Weakman, moved out of the house because of the strange disturbances. In 1848, Margaret and Katherine claimed to hear mysterious noises. The alleged spirit communicated through rapping sounds, for example, one rap for no and two raps for yes. As a result of their demonstrations and ideas, the sisters became the most famous seers of nineteenth-century American spiritualism, which claimed about one million followers by 1855. The rappings followed the sisters when they moved to Rochester, New York. The sisters organized "performances" in theaters to which they charged admission, attracting attention and skepticism.

**Figure 68.** The Fox sisters. From *The Centennial Book, 1883–1993* (Lily Dale, New York: National Spiritual Association of Churches of the United States of America, 1994), p. 221.

In 1888, the sisters confessed to newspaper reporters that the entire spirit-rapping phenomena was an outright fraud. They gave a demonstration of just how they were able to make the loud popping and knocking noises by popping their toe and knee joints. The sisters later recanted their admissions and continued to tour and give séances. They died as alcoholics.[126]

## ♉ *Dr. Billy Graham*

> *Whenever anyone points a critical finger and demands to know why there have to be so many different churches all serving the same God, I am always tempted to point out how many different styles of hats have to be designed for both American men and women. We all belong to the same human race, but we all have enough physical differences to make it impossible for us to wear the same style of hat with equal satisfaction.*
>
>       —Billy Graham, *Peace with God*

"They come as a warning, and grow louder by the day," writes Billy Graham in his book *Approaching Hoofbeats: The Four Horsemen of the Apocalypse.* Graham equates the ancient biblical images with the modern terrors of war and violence.

Evangelist Billy Graham has talked about religion to more people in live audiences than perhaps anyone else in history—hundreds of millions of people throughout the world. Graham has reached millions more through television and film. He is included on this divination list because he has foretold the imminent destruction of the world based on his reading of the scriptures. Any day now, Christ is supposed to be following the horrors of famine and death and leading to the final apocalyptic battle between God and Satan. Christ will return to Earth and create a paradise for true believers.

In his book, *Approaching Hoofbeats: The Four Horsemen of the Apocalypse*, Graham is part seer, part interpreter of the New Testament. He writes, "Virtually everything has been fulfilled that was prophesied in the Scriptures leading up to the coming of Christ. We know His coming is near. But for the Christian believer, the return of Christ is comforting, for at least men and women of faith will be exonerated. They will be avenged. The non-believer will see and understand why true Christians march to the sound of another drum."

Born on November 7, 1918, Mr. Graham was reared on a dairy farm in Charlotte, North Carolina. He enjoyed spending many hours in a hayloft reading books on a wide variety of subjects. In the fall of 1934, at age sixteen, Mr. Graham became interested in religion after attending the revival meetings of Mordecai Ham, a traveling evangelist who visited Charlotte. Graham did his own large-scale evangelism in 1949, touring the United

States and Europe. Since then, Mr. Graham has written dozens of books, all of which have become top sellers. Mr. Graham's counsel has been sought by presidents, and his recognitions range from the Congressional Gold Medal to the Speaker of the Year Award to the Templeton Foundation Prize for Progress in Religion. His autobiography, *Just As I Am*, was published in 1997.

## ♉ *St. Hildegard of Bingen*

> *The time approaches when princes and people will renounce the authority of the Pope. Individual countries will prefer their own Church leaders to the pope. . . . Church property will be secularized. Priests will be persecuted. After the birth of the Antichrist, heretics shall preach their false faith undisturbed, and Christians shall have grave doubts about the holy faith.*
>
> —St. Hildegard of Bingen[127]

St. Hildegard of Bingen (1098–1179), known as the "Sibyl of the Rhine," was born in Bermersheim, Germany. St. Hildegard was the tenth child of a noble German family. Her parents promised her to the church in which she was raised from the time she was eight years old. The church later became a Benedictine monastery.[128]

As an adult, Hildegarde often used a boat to travel back and forth between monasteries. Because she was known as a healer and miracle worker, people gathered on the Rhine's riverbanks to ask for her help. She told people that music recreated the original harmony that once existed between God and humankind, and that the human soul was a musical instrument on which God played music. For amusement, she constructed her own language.

Hildegard had visions of luminous objects since earlier childhood, and in 1141, Hildegard had a vision that changed the course of her life. A vision of God gave her a sudden understanding of the meaning of the religious texts and commanded her to write down everything she observed in her visions:

> And it came to pass . . . when I was 42 years and 7 months old, that the heavens were opened and a blinding light of exceptional brilliance flowed through my entire brain. And so it kindled my whole heart and breast like a flame, not burning but warming . . . and suddenly I understood of the meaning of expositions of the books. . . . But although I heard and saw these things, because of doubt and low opinion of myself and because of diverse sayings of men, I refused for a long time a call to write, not out of stubbornness but out of humility, until weighed down by a scourge of god, I fell onto a bed of sickness.[129]

Around this time she also prophesied, "The great nation will be devastated by earthquakes, storms, and great waves of water, causing much want and plagues." (Some of her New Age followers today believe that "great nation" refers to America.)

At the age of forty-three, she finally told people about her intense visions, which were subsequently "authenticated" by a committee of theologians. Her prophesies were published in a work called *Scivias*, which was believed by some and condemned by others. Many secular leaders consulted her for advice and prophecy. Here is one example of her prophecies:

> The Son of Corruption and Ruin will appear and reign only for a short time, towards the end of the days of the world's duration. . . . He shall come in the last days of the world. He shall not be Satan himself, but a human being equaling and resembling him in atrocious hideousness. His mother, a depraved woman, possessed by the devil, will live as a prostitute in the desert. . . . She will maintain that her son was presented to her by God in a supernatural manner, as was the Child of the Blessed Virgin. She will then be venerated as a saint by deceived people.[130]

Hildegard's writings are unique for their generally positive view of sexual relations and description of a woman's sexual pleasure.

> When a woman is making love with a man, a sense of heat in her brain, which brings with it sensual delight, communicates the taste of that delight during the act and summons forth the emission of the man's seed. And when the seed has fallen into its place, that vehement heat descending from her brain draws the seed to itself and holds it, and soon the woman's sexual organs contract, and all the parts that are ready to open up during the time of menstruation now close, in the same way as a strong man can hold something enclosed in his fist.[131]

In 1150, Hildegard collected her poetic and musical works in *Symphonia armonie celestium revelationum* (The symphony of the harmony of celestial revelations). In addition to music, Hildegard wrote books on natural history and medicine.

## ♉ *Peter Hurkos*

> *Ever since I have become a psychic, I have been immune from syphilis.*
> —Peter Hurkos[130]

The famous mystic Peter Hurkos (aka Pieter van der Hurk, 1911–1988) was born in southwestern Netherlands. In the 1950s, he became well known to the law enforcement community when he reportedly helped solve a number of murders in the United States and Europe. Peter Hurkos says that he first realized he had a divinatory gift when he suffered from a severe head injury. At the time, he was lying in a hospital bed and noticed a man in the bed next to him. Hurkos says he suddenly knew a lot about the man despite the fact that they had never met.

In January 1964, Hurkos tried to solve a series of homicides occurring in and around Boston since 1962. The homicides were already being referred to as the "Boston Strangler" murders. After spending a week in Boston, Hurkos identified the killer as a fifty-six-year-old shoe salesman with a history of mental illness. Hurkos assured the police that they needed to look no further. The Boston police then coordinated a thorough investigation of this suspect, ruling the salesman out as a suspect in the killings. Not long after this, another person, Albert DeSalvo, confessed to these killings. (DeSalvo was not a shoe salesman.) Eventually, the man committed himself to an institution. Shortly afterward, Hurkos was briefly jailed in New York for allegedly impersonating an FBI agent.

In 1969, some private citizens from Ann Arbor, Michigan, asked Hurkos to help solve the recent series of "coed murders." At this time, these murders consisted of the deaths of six women. Hurkos agreed to come to Ann Arbor provided that his travel expenses were paid, and he then arrived in Michigan with a great deal of media attention. For almost a week, Hurkos was accompanied by two homicide detectives in his efforts to assist the investigation. Following the finding of a seventh homicide victim during this time, Hurkos left Ann Arbor claiming that the police were too hostile to his presence in the investigation. Hurkos died in 1988.

In his book *Flim-Flam*, James Randi gives the following example of how psychic detectives can appear to be very accurate when in reality their predictions are not so amazing. On one occasion Peter Hurkos was astonishing people with his ability to provide details about their homes and their lives. However, by carefully analyzing the video tapes of the readings, Randi found Hurkos had been correct in only one out of fourteen of his statements. Selective thinking had led people to dismiss all the wrong guesses and remember only the hits.

For those of you interested in a skeptical look at psychic detectives and other wonder-workers, see Joe Nickell's *Wonder-Workers! How They Perform the Impossible.*[131]

## ♉ *David Icke*

> *Humanity in general has long been solidifying mentally and emotionally into automatons.*
>
> —David Icke, *Lifting the Veil*

David Icke was well-known as a TV sports commentator and leading spokesman for the British Green party. In 1991, he called a press conference in London to announce a number of catastrophic events revealed to him personally by Socrates, Jesus Christ, and others. He predicted that Mount Rainier in the United States would explode sometime in the future. This would be followed by the complete disappearance of New Zealand, the collapse of the Channel Tunnel, and the fall of Naples Cathedral. The cause of these problems was archangel Ak-Taurus. By Christmas 1991, Mr. Icke predicted that Cuba, Greece, the Isle of Arran, and the cliffs of Kent would be hit by a great earthquake that would submerge them.[132]

David Icke, the author of over eight books, tours the world addressing increasingly larger audiences. Icke was born in Leicester, England, and started his career as a professional soccer player until 1973, at age twenty-one, rheumatoid arthritis ended his career. He ventured into journalism and regional television until 1980, when he became a network television news and sports caster until 1990. In his book *The Robot's Rebellion*, he writes:

> I believe it is time for some straight talking. We are a race of robots. By that, I mean that most people do not have a thought in their heads that has not been put there by someone or something else. We have become a race of programmed minds which can be persuaded to believe and do almost anything as long as the drip, drip, drip of lies and misinformation continues to bombard us through our political systems, the media, religion, school, universities, and by infiltration of our consciousness by other universal sources which want to turn planet Earth into a zombies prison. . . . But ever so slowly, the robots are awakening.[133]

In his book *The Biggest Secret: The Book That Will Change the World* Icke reveals a dangerous planetary network connecting everything from the British royal family to major oil companies to thirty-three of the last forty U.S. presidents, in a global conspiracy masterminded by an extraterrestrial race competing for control of Earth by manipulating humanity's way of life. In the photo section, Icke puts pictures of the Prince Albert Victor (the Duke of Clarence, and grandson of Queen Victoria) and Adolf Hitler next to one another, and asks, "Were they the same person?"

In the *The Biggest Secret*, the deaths of President Kennedy and Princess Diana are actually result of ritual murders perpetrated by the Secret Reptilian Brotherhood, the Freemasons. George Bush, Henry Kissinger, Gerald Ford, and Bill Clinton are shape-shifting reptiles who practice ritual Satanic murder and child molestation.

Icke apparently is not a fan of traditional religion. In *The Robot's Rebellion* he writes:

> Mahomet said God has also chosen him to pass on this message, and those who accepted it would be saved on Judgment day. Sound familiar? All of these apparently opposing religions were started by Lucifer in his many forms.[134]

Religious people offended by these kinds of statements have suggested that Icke's "religion" is the only religion he approves of.

## ♉ *Alois Irlmaier*

> *I see the earth like a ball before me, on whom now the white pigeons fly near, a very large number coming up from the sand. And then it rains a yellow dust in a line. When the golden city is destroyed, it begins. Like a yellow line, it goes up to the city in the bay. It will be a clear night, when they begin to throw it. The tanks are still driving, but those who sit in these tanks became quite black.*
> —Alois Irlmaier[135]

Alois Irlmaier (1894–1959) was a Christian man who lived in Freilassing, Germany. During his life, he purportedly prophesied, helped police discover criminals, foret old the fates of individual soldiers fighting in World War II, and diagnosed diseases. He predicted the coming of a Third World War that would begin after a murder in the Balkans at an unspecified time. Here are some sample prophecies:

> A new Middle East war suddenly flames up. Big naval forces are facing hostilities in the Mediterranean—the situation is strained. But the actual firing spark is set on fire in the Balkan. I see a "large one" falling. A bloody dagger lies beside him—then impact is on impact. . . . Many cars will clog the roads. . . . Everything, which will be an obstacle for the rapidly advancing tanks on highspeed-motorways and other fast-motorways, will be downrolled. I cannot see any Danube-bridges above Regensburg anymore. Hardly anything remains of the big city Frankfurt. . . . The Rhine Valley will be devastated, mainly by air. . . . I see boxes that are satanic. When they explode, a yellow and green dust or smoke arises, everything that comes in

contact to it, is dead, it is a human, an animal or a plant. The humans become quite black and the meat fall off their bones, so sharply is the poison. . . . By a natural catastrophe or something similar the Russians suddenly invade to the north.[136]

## ♓ *Anton Johansson*

> *I saw ships thrown on shore, may collapsed buildings. Then I was shown Holland, Belgium, and the German coast of the North Sea, which were heavily visited by storm and flood.*
>
> —Anton Johansson, 1918[76]

Anton Johansson (1858–1929) was born in Sweden and later became a Norwegian fisherman. He was very religious and believed his ability to foretell the future was a gift from God. Johansson followers believed he accurately predicted the sinking of the *Titanic*, naming one of its victims, millionaire John Jacob Astor VI. His fans also suggest that he foresaw events of World War I, and accurately predicted San Francisco's earthquake of 1906 and a volcanic eruption in 1902 that demolished the city of St. Pierre, Martinique, Most of his predictions came on a midnight in November 1907 when he was awakened by a voice and a blinding shaft of light. He also foresaw that the third world war would break out at "the end of July, beginning of August, I do not know the year."

## ♉ *Sturé Johansson*

> *Without knowing, you have asked me to come. But I am not here to teach you anything.*
> > *I am here to make you realize the knowledge you already have.*
> > —Ambres, speaking through Sturé Johansson[138]

The being "Ambres" is channeled by a modern-day Swedish carpenter named Sturé Johansson. Johansson is considered a Nordic Edgar Cayce because he gives medical advice while in trance states. Ambres recently spoke through Johansson explaining:

You can call me Ambres. But what my name is and who I am do not matter, only what I teach matters. What I speak of is nothing new. You can recognize it, often without knowing why; as if you already knew it. You have surely met it before, but in different forms and through different angles. The esoteric knowledge about man and the wholeness has been taught and taught in many ways so that it can reach out to as many as possible in the new era. But the various rivers, streams and creeks have the same source.[139]

Some of Ambres' prophecies are more cryptic and open to interpretation. For example, in 1987, Ambres spoke through Johansson and prophesied, "Those countries which you now think of as closed will soon be open. And those countries you now think of as most open will soon be closed." A few years earlier Ambres said, "The Uniter is going to be born here and it is going to come in plenty. It is not going to be only one human being but many. And when the Uniter is born it is going to grow, and more and more humans are going to be included in the thoughts of the Uniter."

Another nice quote from Ambres is "Jag påstår att människans fria vilja inte existerar och när jag uttalar det brukar man protestera. Det borde ligga i ert intresse att ta reda på hur det förhåller sig med detta" ["I maintain that human beings do not possess a free will, and when I say that, a protest is the normal reaction. It should be in your interest to find out the truth about this"].[140]

## ♉ *Charles Stansfeld Jones*

> *The Jews, and the Jewish problem, represent very important aspects of the difficulty and its solution. A great proportion of the wealth of the world is today in the hands of the Jews, yet as a nation they have no place. As the "chosen people" they were an important nation, but the rejection of the Teacher in who they expected to find their Messiah, is usually considered to have been the cause of their becoming wanderers upon the face of the Earth.*
> —Frater Achad, *The Anatomy of the Body of God,* 1923

Charles Stansfeld Jones (1886–1950), also known as Frater Achad, was from British Columbia and became a student of the mystic Aleister Crowley. Jones accepted the magical grade of "Pisissimus" as part of the Hermetic Order of the Golden Dawn, a secret occult society. The structured hierarchy of the Golden Dawn had ten grades or degrees. At his level of competence, Jones believed that his every action held cosmic importance. He wrote several books, such as *Anatomy of the Body of God*, a treatise on Cabalistic geometry. In his book on scrying, *Crystal Vision Through Crystal Gazing* (1923), he introduces us to his ideas on crystal balls:

> As we look into the depths of this Globe—material though it be—we cannot but be impressed with ideas of Purity. It is almost as if we gazed into the eyes of a little child, and there are few who have not experienced a peculiar sensation, almost amounting to awe, certainly one of wonder, when so

doing. The soul of the seer is very like that of a little child—or should be—and it is in order that we may regain the purity and perfection of this child-like vision that we set out on this path.[141]

He concludes with the cryptic words:

When we have discovered this Central Light of our Being, and learned to Concentrate the Mind thereon, we shall begin the Ultimate Practice of Crystal Gazing. We shall find the Star Rays from the Universal Sphere centered in us, and when the focus becomes perfect, shall discover, that this CENTER is EVERYWHERE and THE CIRCUMFERENCE NOWHERE. Then all our conceptions of Crystalline Spheres will melt into That which is Without Limit, PERFECT CRYSTALLINE VISION.[142]

## ♉ *Anna Bonus Kingsford*

*Religion can never depend for its facts and its hopes on historical data. These, in the very nature of things, are always questionable, and become more and more difficult to verify as the transit of centuries removes us from the epoch to which they alone are related. The real events of religion are not of this world; its kingdom is interior; its acts are all spiritual and essential. We "must be born again" into another sphere, upon another plane, converted from the material to the immaterial, before we can apprehend heavenly things.*
—Anna Bonus Kingsford, *The Perfect Way*[143]

Anna Bonus Kingsford was an English psychic who lived from 1846 to 1888. She practiced prophetic dream interpretation and mixed her mysticism with Christianity. She had many mystical visions that she wrote down with the help of Edward Maitland.

Kingsford said that all life is interconnected, and if one person or animal is harmed, we are all harmed. Therefore, she was passionately against cruelty to animals. She wrote in *Clothed with the Sun of the Soul* about the Christ within each of us:

There is no offense done and I suffer not; nor any wrong, and I am not hurt thereby; For my heart is in the breast of every creature, and my blood is in the veins of all flesh. I am wounded in my right hand for man, and in my left hand for woman, in my right foot for the creatures of the Earth and in my left foot for the creatures of the seas. And in my heart for all.[144]

Dr. Kingsford was the first Englishwoman to qualify as a medical doctor, although she had to go to France to complete her studies. While in France, her interest in preventing cruelty to animals was reinforced after she watched casual yet painful vivisections in the Paris hospital where she studied medicine. She promoted vegetarianism in her book *Addresses & Essays on Vegetarianism*.

As the above quotation from *The Perfect Way* suggests, Kingsford often wrote on the history of religion and believed that many religious events were not of this world and therefore not open to historical or scientific verification. In her book *Clothed With the Sun* she wrote on prophecy and revelation.

## ♉ *JZ Knight*

> *This is my body in this incarnation, and I say this incarnation, because it's my truth that I have lived many, many lives prior to this existence and that this body, with this genetic code is like a garment, like a clothing that I am wearing for a lifetime. And I inadvertently chose this body because of its genetic make up. It was predisposed to certain material abilities that would allow my spirit and my soul to subsequently come into life, and after I reached a certain age, to be able to construct meaningful thought.*
>
> —JZ Knight[145]

JZ Knight (1946–) is an American psychic who grew up in a poor family and had six brothers and two sisters. She began to channel an entity known as Ramtha around 1977. Ramtha is more than 35,000 years old and appeared to Knight as a glowing man while she and one of her sons were playing with toy pyramids in their home. Part of Knight's fame is due to various celebrity endorsements, including those of actress Shirley Maclaine.

Skeptics suggest that the notion of a wise and sophisticated seer who lived 35,000 years ago is unrealistic because Cro-Magnon cavemen walked the Earth at this time. For example, Robert Todd Carroll in his *The Skeptic's Dictionary* says:

> One would think that it doesn't take a rocket scientist to figure out that the likelihood of a 35,000-year-old Cro-Magnon ghost suddenly appearing in a Tacoma kitchen to a homemaker to reveal profundities about centers and voids, self-love and guilt-free living, or love and peace, is close to zero. Yet, the will to believe is so strong in many people that even such an obvious absurdity seems reasonable. Plus, for many followers, believing in Ramtha "works." As one follower put it, "I watched great changes come over people around me—people who lacked hope came alive again."[146]

JZ Knight responds to some of the skeptics by clarifying her theories at her Web site (www.ramtha.com):

I understand that when I say 35,000 years ago, some of you think of cavemen chewing on bones and stuff. But in fact there was a very intelligent civilization that lived here during that time, and some of those ruins have now been discovered in the Sumerian valley. In Ramtha's time, he had a lifetime in which he was a Lemurian. If we look at a geological map of the world, we would place Lemuria where the Pacific Ocean is, and it extended into the west coast of Washington of the Pacific northwest. This particular area of the world, 35,000 years ago, had a thriving spiritual civilization that went back to the time of dinosaurs. At that time, there were very intelligent people that lived and coexisted with reptilian beings. As a Lemurian, Ramtha came from a group of people who believed that they came here from beyond the North star. They worshipped the midnight sky and they called that home. So Ramtha inherited a longing that was genetically in him.[147]

Ramtha's teachings also include discussions on the destiny of humans, the construction of the cosmos, quantum mechanics and its connections to the body, methods for actively creating reality, and the difference between mind and the brain.

Ramtha's School of Enlightenment was established in 1988. The campus is on JZ Knight's ranch in Yelm, Washington.[148] Most classes are conducted in the "Great Hall," which can accommodate as many as one thousand students, who sit in assigned spaces on an Astroturf floor. The Annex, located in the round building outside the Great Hall, contains Ramtha books, videos, audio tapes, music tapes, CDs, vitamins, selected clothing, and an assortment of school-related products.

JZ Knight reports on her Web page that "Ramtha's School of Enlightenment, the American Gnostic School, is attended by students from 6 years of age to well into their golden years. Requests for registration come from all over the world, and currently students are enrolled from 23 countries and all walks of life."[149]

## ♉ *Emma Kunz*

> *There will be planes shaped like pencils that will take men into space and by so doing punch holes in the atmosphere, letting in lethal cosmic rays that will kill many millions.*
>
> —Emma Kunz, 1938[150]

Emma Kunz (1892–1963) was a Swiss mystic and healer. While still a teenager, she traveled to America in search of a runaway lover whom she never found. Her career as a seer began at age forty when she supposedly started healing people with a pendulum. She tells us that she often saw the past, present, and future "independent of time and space,"[151] and, around the age of forty, she would "confirm" her visions using a pendulum that traced out complex geometric shapes. About the shapes, she said, "My pictures will be understood only in the twenty-first century."[152] She predicted the invention of the atom bomb by America ("a weapon that could destroy the whole world"[153]), as well as rockets. She said the rockets would allow toxic rays from space to destroy vertebrate animals on earth. Her followers today take this to mean that rocket exhaust will destroy the ozone layer.

## ♉ *Gladys Osborne Leonard*

> *I looked up and saw in front of me, but about five feet above the level of my body, a large, circular patch of light. In this light I saw my mother quite distinctly. Her face looked several years younger than I had seen it a few hours before. . . . She gazed down on me for a moment, seeming to convey to me an intense feeling of relief and a sense of safety and well-being. Then the vision faded. I was wide awake all the time, quite conscious of my surroundings.*
> —Gladys Osborne Leonard, *My Life in Two Worlds*[154]

Gladys Osborne Leonard was a British psychic who lived from 1882 to 1968. Leonard channeled Feda, an Indian who died around 1800 but who spoke through Leonard. Leonard/Feda made various predictions about war and the wishes of the dead. She wrote in her autobiography, *My Life in Two Worlds*:

> Every morning I saw visions of most beautiful places. In whatever direction I happened to be looking would gradually come valleys, gentle slopes, lovely trees and banks covered with flowers of every shape and hue. The most entrancing part to me was the restful, velvety green of the grass that covered the ground of the valley and the hills. Walking about were people who looked radiantly happy. They were dressed in graceful flowing draperies, for the greater part, but every movement, gesture and expression suggested in an indefinable and yet positive way a condition of deep happiness, a state of quiet ecstasy.[155]

Leonard claimed that Feda was a Hindu girl who had married Leonard's great-great-grandfather, William Hamilton. Feda died after giving birth to a son, when she returned to England with her husband in 1800. Feda was only thirteen years old.

## ♉ *Char Margolis (and other speakers for the dead)*

> *Life is a school and we are all here to learn. Thoughts create reality.*
> —Char Margolis, *Questions from Earth, Answers from Heaven*[156]

Char Margolis makes a living, in part, by talking to the dead. Ever since she was a child, Margolis said she saw, heard, and felt things that seemed to be supernatural. In 1999, Margolis published a book *Questions from Earth, Answers from Heaven* to help people "awaken their own instinctive intuitive abilities," which they can use to adapt to the imminent shift from a material world to a spiritual one. She warns people away from psychic hotlines. Margolis is a veteran of talk shows and has been interviewed by Barbara Walters, Sally Jesse Raphael, and Geraldo Rivera.

Recently, there have been dozens of famous people who make a living by talking to dead people and/or telling us about the afterlife. Here are some of the more prominent ones:

- James Van Praagh, author of *Talking to Heaven*
- Mary T. Browne, author of *Life After Death: A Renowned Psychic Reveals What Happens to Us When We Die*
- Sylvia Browne, author of *The Other Side and Back: A Psychic's Guide to Our World and Beyond*
- John J. Edward, author of *One Last Time: A Psychic Medium Speaks to Those We Have Loved and Lost*
- Sandra Rogers, author of *Lessons from the Light : Insights from a Journey to the Other Side*
- Echo L. Bodine author of *Echoes of the Soul: The Souls Journey Beyond the Light Through Life, Death, and Life After Death*
- George Anderson, author of *George Anderson's Lessons from the Light: Extraordinary Messages of Comfort and Hope from the Other Side*
- Linda Georgian, author of *Communicating With the Dead*

## ♉ *Drunvalo Melchizedek*

> *There are five Melchizedeks here on Earth at this time, but only two of them are in the 3rd dimension. Two of them are in the 4th dimension of the Earth's consciousness, and they are twins both female. And one of them, Machiventa, can be in either dimension depending on purpose. I am not allowed to give their names at this time.*
> —Drunvalo Melchizedek[157]

Drunvalo Melchizedek says that he can communicate with beings from other dimensions. He went to college at Berkeley, majoring in physics and minoring in mathematics. He almost received his diploma but decided that traditional science did not interest him. In 1970, he received a degree in fine arts.

While in Vancouver, Melchizedek and his wife started studying meditation with a Hindu teacher who lived in the area. After practicing meditation for five months, two ten-foot-tall angels appeared in his room. One angel was green and the other purple. Melchizedek could see through their translucent bodies. From that moment on, Melchizedek says his life was never the same.

Drunvalo Melchizedek believes that ancient meditation and breathing techniques will assist in the creation of the Merkaba, a means for traveling into a four dimensional state. According to Melchizedek, a person can travel through dimensions while still occupying the same body. He has also made various predictions and, like other prophets in this chapter, suggests that many large, rapid changes will soon occur on Earth. He has written, "When we actually move into the Fourth Dimension, I'm not even sure. That's just a wave of energy. But as far as moving into higher levels beyond Earth consciousness, we only have until the end of 2012."[158]

Melchizedek believes we will not have long to prepare for the End of Time, because it will approach too quickly to allow preparation. "The world falls apart -- the financial and social structure breaks down and falls apart. It becomes an extremely dangerous time to try to make it through because people are killing each other in a total survival mode."[159]

On his Web sites and in his interviews, Melchizedek discusses an array of diverse subjects including codes in the bible, Fibonacci numbers, the molecular structure of water, higher dimensions, and DNA.[160]

### ♉ *Wolf Messing*

> *After an effort of will, I suddenly see the final result of some event flash before me. The mechanism of direct knowledge bypasses the logical cause-and-effect chain and reveals to the psychic only the final concluding link of the chain.*
> —Wolf Messing[161]

Wolf Messing is famous for being Joseph Stalin's favorite psychic. When Hitler made a pact with Stalin, Messing reported that "Soviet tanks will within a few years enter Berlin."[162] The Germans heard about Messing's prediction and made official protests to the Kremlin. While addressing an audience in a Siberian opera house, Messing correctly predicted, "The war will end victoriously for Russia in May 1945."[163]

Messing was born in 1889, a Polish Jew born to a religious family. By six, he memorized almost all of the Jewish Talmud teachings. He said he had visions from an early age and seemed to be able to influence other people's minds in startling ways. Messing hated his rigorous religious studies, so he ran away from home, hopped onto a train, and hid under a seat. Later, the conductor asked for a ticket. He did not have one but simply held out a torn piece of appear and "willed" the conductor to think it was ticket. Legend has it that the conductor accepted the ticket and punched it in his ticket punch.

Many strange stories surround Messing. For example, in Berlin, Messing collapsed, became unconscious, and was taken to the morgue. Fortunately, a medical student took his pulse and noticed a faint heartbeat.

In 1915, Messing went to Vienna where his fame grew. Legend has it that Messing was invited to Albert Einstein's home and was introduced to Sigmund Freud. To test Messing's powers of telepathy, Freud gave him a mental command: "Go to the bathroom cupboard, get some tweezers, and pull out three hairs from Doctor Einstein's mustache." Messing did what Freud ordered him to do.[164]

After that, Messing toured the world and performed in numerous capital cities, from Buenos Aires to Melbojuren. In 1928 while performing in Paris, Messing went to a small provincial town to solve the poisoning death of a wealthy widow. The police could offer Messing no leads. Accompanied by two detectives, Messing went to the victim's home. Her teenage son showed him around. Passing from one room to the next, Messing stopped suddenly at an old painting in a room near the bedroom. It was a portrait of the murdered woman. According to legends, Messing turned to the young man and said, "Kindly surrender the key hanging behind the portrait to the police. You opened the safe with it after you poisoned your mother." Within the hour the youth gave his testimony to the police. Perhaps Messing suspected the boy based on keen observations.

While appearing in a theater in Warsaw, an audience member asked him about Hitler's future. He replied, "Hitler will die if he turns to the East."[165] This was certainly a dangerous thing to say at the time, and Messing fled for his life to the Soviet Union during World War II. He was in danger not only because he was a Jew, but also because of the negative prediction about Hitler. Hitler hated anyone making prophecies about his future and supposedly placed a price of 200,000 marks on Messing's head.

In the USSR, Messing faced another dictator's challenge when Joseph Stalin gave Messing a difficult test. Messing was to enter Stalin's country house, a place with guards and secret police, without a pass. One day, as Stalin worked in the office of his country home, Messing walked confidently into the grounds and then into the house. All the guards and servants stood back respectfully as he passed. He walked to the doorway of Stalin's study. When the dictator looked up, he was astonished. Messing said he used his psychic powers to make the guards think he was Lavrenti Beria, the current and much-feared head of the secret police. Messing said that the thoughts of others became colorful images in his mind. He also said the thoughts of the deaf and dumb were clearer than those of others.

Later Stalin suggested to Messing that he rob a bank by telepathy. Messing chose for the experiment a big Moscow bank in which he was not known. He calmly walked in and handed the teller a blank piece of paper torn from a school notebook. He placed a briefcase on the counter, and mentally willed the clerk to give him 100,000 rubles.

Legend has it that the bank clerk looked at the paper, opened the safe, and took out piles of bank notes until he had stacked 100,000 rubles on the counter. He then placed the money into the briefcase. Messing took the case, walked out of the bank, and showed the money to Stalin's two observers to prove his prowess as a bank robber. He then went back to the clerk, and returned the bundles of bank notes. The teller looked at him, looked at the money, looked at the blank paper, and collapsed on the floor with a heart attack.[166]

## ♉ *Ruth Montgomery*

> *Suddenly it seemed as if a great hand put itself over my right hand, and the pencil began going wildly, heavily into circles and figure eights!*
>
> —Ruth Montgomery[167]

Ruth Montgomery's prophecies describe a terrifying future in which earthquakes and tidal waves that devastate California, England, Holland, and Japan. The casualties will be those individuals who have not spiritually prepared. The survivors will be transformed into "supermen" and "superwomen." She also prophesied that a polar shift would occur before the year 2000. Seasons were to have changed abruptly, with high winds sweeping the planet and ocean levels rising, flooding coastal areas. The Earth's poles would change so that they would be in the Pacific Ocean and South America. Her books provide information about safe areas during the intense global weather patterns. Some of the enlightened survivors would be rescued by alien ships that would later return them to designated areas.

Ruth Montgomery has said that some of her prophecies were revealed to her by the spirit of Arthur Ford, the late spiritualist who supposedly communicated with Houdini after Houdini died. Since 1968, Montgomery has used automatic writing to prophesy. (In fact, her late husband, Bob, is one of her regular correspondents.) Through her writings, Ruth Montgomery has popularized such subjects as reincarnation, extraterrestrial visitation, life after death, and cataclysmic Earth changes. Many have compared her prophecies to those of Nostradamus and Edgar Cayce.

Ruth Montgomery was not always into spiritualism and prophecy. She was a hardheaded, savvy Washington columnist. As a member of the White House Press Corps she covered five presidencies, which she describes in the book *Hail to the Chiefs*. Ruth Montgomery was also president of the National Women's Press Club.

It was a strange journalistic transformation when Ruth Montgomery became a channeler for disembodied beings, which she calls her Guides. Perhaps the change would be the equivalent of Barbara Walters or Katie Couric becoming a channeler today.

In 1971, Arthur Ford gave Ruth Montgomery various predictions, which she published in her book *A World Beyond*. Believers suggest that the predictions have come true. Montgomery's book discusses the Earth's creation, the lost worlds of Atlantis and Mu, the past lives of Richard Nixon, Winston Churchill, Franklin Roosevelt, Jackie Onassis, Elizabeth Taylor, Richard Burton, and other celebrities. *A World Beyond* also makes predictions involving the world's energy problems, crime in America, and the rise of a new German national leader.

## ♉ *William Stainton Moses*

William Stainton Moses (1839–1892, see figure 69) was born in the village of Donnington, in Lincolnshire, on the fifth of November 1839. As a young man, Moses was immensely interested in religious subjects and read numerous books, pamphlets, and magazines to help him understand religion. Later he channeled twenty-two spirit communicators, headed by one who called himself "Imperator," who revealed himself to be one of the Bible prophets. Moses used to receive automatic writing with his left hand while at the same time writing his regular correspondents with his right hand. Moses described his first experience in 1872 with automatic writing:

> My right arm was seized about the middle of the forearm, and dashed violently up and down with a noise resembling that of a number of paviors at work. It was the most tremendous exhibition of "unconscious muscular action" I ever saw. In vein I tried to stop it. I distinctly felt the grasps, soft

and firm, round my arm, and though perfectly possessed of senses and volition, I was powerless to interfere, although my hand was disabled for some days by the bruising it then got.[168]

**Figure 69.** William Stainton Moses (1839–1892). From William Stainton Moses, *Spirit Teachings*, 10th edition (London: London Spiritualist Alliance, Ltd., 1924), reprinted in William Stainton Moses, *Spirit Teachings* (New York: Arno Press, 1976), title-page frontispiece.

Moses became famous in England for his apports (the supposedly "miraculous" materialization of objects), including perfumes and scented oils that often ran down his face. In the 1900s, three-hundred-pound Agnes Nichol, better known by her married name, Mrs. Guppy, also manifest all sorts of objects during her seances. She produced live flowers, plants, fish earth, sand, and human body parts.

## ♉ *Deguchi Nao*

Deguchi Nao (1836–1918) was a peasant woman and Japanese seer who channeled the Japanese god *Ushitora-No-Konjin* and whose alleged ability to heal attracted followers. According to Nao's devotees, *Ushitora-No-Konjin* guided Nao's arm when she was writing messages on paper. Although Nao is said to be illiterate, her messages were written in sophisticated handwriting. She also was the founder of the Japanese Omoto sect, which flourished between World War I and World War II. Nao called for reconstructing the world and creating a peaceful society. Her first prophecy in 1892 foretold the end of the world at some unspecified date and the coming of a messiah who would save humanity.[169]

## ♉ *Mokichi Okada*

> *Those who deeply love, and appreciate flowers, their grace, their beauty, have hearts which truly must be equally as beautiful.*
>
> —Mokichi Okada[170]

Mokichi Okada was born in a Tokyo slum in 1882. As a child, Okada realized that he had artistic talent and wanted to be a painter. However, due to poor health he abandoned his goal, and, in 1907, became successful in the jewelry business. In 1919, when his wife and third child died, and his business failed due to Japan's economic crises, he turned from atheism and began his spiritual quest for the meaning behind the extreme hardships in his life.

In 1926, at the age of forty-five, he received a divine revelation that lasted three months in which he believed God revealed his plan for the New Age and described how Earth would face upheavals and great cataclysms. Okada now realized that the Earth was God's creation and felt that his mission was to steer humanity's course away from materialism. The new civilization would reflect harmony between the material and the spiritual.

As a result of his transformation, Okada believed he had been given a mystic power to help him prepare humanity. In particular, he became aware of the existence of a mystic spherical region within his abdomen.[171] This sphere concentrated a cosmic life-energy and emitted it in the form of spiritual light. He called the entity in his belly the "sphere of light," and he used its power to explain the spiritual world to people.

In 1934, Okada established a form of holistic medicine that he called Jôrei. Okada explained that the various diseases are brought about through accumulation of clouds in the spiritual world, and that these clouds are caused by humankind's vices. Okada believed he could direct the energy from his abdomen sphere through his hand toward others, thereby destroying their spiritual clouds. This process was Jôrei. Today, Jôrei can be performed by anyone who has received a calligraphic representation of the Japanese word for light written by Okada, called an *ano-hikari* amulet, through which the energy concentrated within Okada himself has been transmitted.

Okada continued to prophecy that civilization would undergo great transitions in the twentieth and twenty-first centuries, moving toward the creation of a united planet. Both Jôrei and natural farming would assist this process. In 1935, Okada took his first step toward this goal with the founding in Tokyo of a new religion, the Japan Kannon Society. Mokichi Okada died in 1955, at the age of seventy-two.

## ♉ *Moll Pitcher*

> *Horses will be kept for pleasure and ornament, nothing more, in the days to come.*
> —Moll Pitcher[173]

Moll Pitcher (1731–1815) played a role in the American Revolution because both the American and the British forces consulted her. Believers suggest she prophesied the date of three of General Washington's victories, various British troop movements, and the day of her death. Her most remarkable prophecies foretold future inventions. For example, she prophesied that music would be conducted long distances over wires. Her followers suggest that this foretold either the invention of the telephone, the radio, or television. She prophesied in the 1780s, "Magnificent music conduction on wires hundreds of miles away will play at the instigation of man."[174]

## ♉ *Seeress Regina*

> *Mankind will be decimated by epidemics, famine, and poison. . . . Only a few will be left to rebuild the world.*
>
> —Seeress Regina[175]

Seeress Regina was the most famous German prophetess of the early twentieth century. Her apocalyptic prophecies were always in the form of poems and dealt with future warfare and desolation. Her followers suggest she accurately predicted the duration of World War I and II and warned Germany that a Hitlerlike figure was coming: "King and emperor will disappear, and another will lash the whip."

## ♉ *Jane Roberts*

> *You are like children with a game, and you think that the game is played by everyone. Physical life is not the rule. Identity and consciousness existed long before your earth was formed. You suppose that any personality must appear in physical terms. Consciousness is the force behind matter, and it forms many other realities besides the physical one. It is, again, your own viewpoint that is presently so limited that it seems to you that physical reality is the rule and mode of existence.*
>
> —Jane Roberts[176]

Jane Roberts (1929–1984) was author of numerous books like *Seth Speaks, The Seth Material,* and the *Nature of Personal Reality.*[177] Roberts was born on May 8, 1929, in Albany, New York. Her parents, Delmer Hubbell and Marie Burdo Roberts, were divorced in 1931, and Jane moved with her mother to Saratoga Springs, New York. At age eighteen, she attended Skidmore College in New York. In 1954 she married Robert Butts, and in 1963, Roberts and her husband earned their livings as writer and artist respectively, along with other related

odd jobs. In a relatively short time, Jane and her husband began to experiment with psychic phenomenon and Ouija boards, at which time they
claimed they had their first encounter with a disembodied entity named Seth.
While Roberts was in a trance, Seth spoke through her, discussed the nature
of physical reality, and made predictions about the future. Seth and Roberts
suggest that consciousness forms matter and there are no limits to our own
experience other than those we impose with our beliefs. Her books attempt to
have readers confront their limiting beliefs.

Seth purportedly spoke through Roberts from 1963 until 1984. Roberts's
husband usually took notes. In the 1960s and 1970s, Jane held classes in
Elmira, New York, in which students recorded her pronouncements using
tape recorders and later transcribed the material. Collectively the sessions
are referred to as the "Seth material." Over the years Seth dictated a number
of books, and Roberts wrote a number of books of her own. In the books, Seth
discusses dreams, out of body travel, life after death, biblical history, space
travel, other dimensions, parallel and probable selves, and behavior of sub-
atomic particles. Seth's main idea is that we create our own reality and that
we get what we concentrate interesting. For example, one reader-reviewer of
*The Seth Material* at the Web site www.Amazon.com wrote: "I got past the
mediumship thing and into the meat of the message. When I began to assim-
ilate what Seth was saying, I no longer cared whether Ms. Roberts was getting the information from a disembodied spirit or her goldfish. The material,
to me, was electrifying." Her books have sold over seven million copies.

## ♉ *Marshall T. Savage*

> *A million years from now, our descendants will populate this galaxy. From the
> red dwarves of the globular clusters to the blue giants of the galactic nucleus, a
> hundred billion stars will shine on the homes of a trillion trillion human beings.
> Their civilizations will span the heavens with powers transcending the feeble
> reach of our imaginations. Yet, each person of that countless multitude will look
> back in space and time to a tiny yellow star out on the rim of the Orion Arm. In
> their grandeur and their glory these demigods for a future time will remember us,
> and think of how it all began.*
>
> —Marshall T. Savage, *The Millennial Project*

Marshall T. Savage is author of *The Millennial Project: Colonizing the Galaxy
in Eight Easy Steps.* Although I don't usually include scientific speculators in
this "Who's Who of Divination," Savage's ideas are so bold that I could not
help add him to the list. Marshall Savage believes the Earth is doomed. How-

## A Smorgasbord of Channelers

Channeling is a process in which people claim to obtain information from an external source such as a disembodied being. Sometimes, a channeler appears to go into a trance to relay information from the source to observers. Channeling can expresses itself as "automatic speaking" or "automatic writing" and seems to be as old as human history. Often, the channeler's speech and mannerism change when they are in contact with the entity being channeled. Skeptics suggest that today's popular "channelers" label their messages as "channelings" from an ancient and wise human as way to get more attention for their messages.

Channeling is indirectly referred to throughout the Bible. The New Testament mentions it favorably, as in Mark 16:17 or Acts 19:6, where it is considered a gift of the Holy Spirit, and unfavorably in the Old Testament (Isaiah 8:19, 29:4) where it is regarded as the deceit of spirits. When King Saul consults with the witch of Endor, Saul is able to communicate with the ghost of prophet Samuel through the witch who channels his voice.

Some of the more famous modern channelers such as JZ Knight and Jane Roberts were discussed in the main section. These channelers suggest that other spirits speak through them and give detailed information about the world, the future, and philosophy. Entire books have been purportedly channeled.[178]

The following is an unusual assortment of channelers, most of whom are still alive today. The sheer number of people who channel is staggering, and this is the tip of the iceberg? Most of the following information comes from the World Wide Web, which is replete with channelers and their personal Web sites.[179] Often, you can find more information on these channelers by using standard Internet search Web sites.

⊮ **Jyoti Alla-an** channels Melora. Melora says, "Merging with the Higher Self requires the soul integration process of returning. . . . In terms of soul growth and Ascension, it is critical to bring the fragments back to the Core Soul—if one is going to ascend in what you call 'this lifetime'."

⊮ **Darryl Anka** channels Bashar. Bashar says, "We have a very specific relationship with your people, a very specific relationship and responsibility in how it is that we interact with each and every one of you, individually and all of you collectively. We recognize that there are many, many belief systems upon your planet; many different styles of expression."

⊮ **Elwood Babbitt** channels Vishnu who says, "I come to you from the universal ocean of vitality, from the Gateway of Eternity in this, the universal vibration, that hovers within all the galaxies and constellations, not in the dimension of space but in the vibrational spectrum that ascends from this, your earth condition, to the very apex, the tiny thread of creativity."

⊮ **Robert Baker** channels Archangel Gabriel who says, "Dearly beloved Children of the Light, as you know we are called Gabriel and we are most joyous to be in your divine presence. We are here to remind you that you are creators."

⊮ **Barbara Bell** channels Barbie. Bell says, "I channel Barbie, archetypical feminine plastic essence who embodies that stereotypical wisdom of the 1960s and 1970s. Since childhood I have been gifted with an intensely personal, growth-oriented relationship with Barbie, the polyethelene essence who is 700 million teaching essences. Her influence has transformed and guided many of my peers through pre-puberty to fully realized maturity. Her truths are too important to be prepackaged. My sincere hope is to let the voice of Barbie, my Inner name-twin, come through. Barbie's messages are offered in love." (From the "Barbie Channeling Newsletter.")

⩗ **John Cali** channels Chief Joseph who says, "You are the light workers who will help lead your brothers and sisters on the planet—and in other worlds—home to All That Is."

⩗ **Dolores Cannon** channels Nostradamus. (Actually, Cannon says that she does not call it "channeling." During many years of regressive hypnosis research, she made contact with Nostradamus, the subject of a three-volume set *Conversations with Nostradamus*.) "He said, if the weather changes happens traumatically, that's where we're in trouble, that's where the tidal waves, the tremendous upheaval happens. And one of the things he wanted us to know that could cause it to happen traumatically would be the nuclear power plants that we have built on top of earthquake zones. If they are triggered it will create more impetus to shift more dramatically. That's what he wanted to warn us about."

⩗ **Lee Carroll** channels Kyron. Magnetic master Kryon answers questions about Earth changes, live essence medicines, past life relationships, Atlantean technology, ascension, the nature of extraterrestrials, and more good news about how humans have raised the vibration of the plant, thus avoiding catastrophes predicted by the prophets.

⩗ **Geraldine Cummins** channeled F. W. H. Myers and "The Messenger of Cleophas" (via automatic writing). They say, "The inner mind is like soft wax, it receives our thoughts, their whole content, but it must produce the words that clothe it."

⩗ **Caroline Fitzgerald** channels the Elohim who say, "We greet you dear beings of Love and Light. It is our greatest joy to ground our energies here today through this one, this one who has chosen to serve as channel for us in the moment. We are the Elohim, we are the Radiant Ones, we are the Eternal Ones. We are the Ones that have interacted so many times in the past, in the now and in the future with your consciousness."

⩗ **Laurie Gilmore** channels Metatron who says, "I am Metatron. I have been asked to serve by dictating information that will assist you in moving through the transitions that are ahead for the planet and all life on the planet during the ascension. This planet, and all species of life on the planet are in the process of ascension. Ascension means that all first and second dimensional life forms will 'move up' to third dimensional life forms. Humans, or third dimensional life forms, will graduate to either fourth dimensional worlds or fifth dimensional oneness depending on their level of evolution and their intent."

⩗ **Ronna Herman** channels Archangel Michael who says, "Beloved masters, I ask you to close your eyes for a moment. I wish for you to sense my presence, not just read the message I offer you. We have a divine connection, you and I, and, yes, I mean each and everyone of you. You are here on this planet because we sent out a clarion call and you answered. You had to meet certain rigid criteria, and undergo what might be called an intense training process in order to qualify for this grand experiment on Planet Earth."

❧ **Lisa Holloway** channels Hilarion who says, "You are in an interesting evolution at this time. Your consciousness, in its current state of becoming, is rising in density. You are rising in density and your awareness is expanding to the point where you are recognizing that there is more than your self (your planet, her inhabitants, your mass consciousness) in the cosmos. Your greater self is already aware of this and is assisting you. It is a wobbly ride, and some of you are unsure of yourselves. But many beings are here to guide you. Your life is vital to your evolution and to the greater part of who you are."

❧ **Cyril Henry Hoskin** channeled Rampa (not be confused with Ramtha channeled by JZ Knight). Hoskin was a Surrey plumber's assistant who in 1956 published *The Third Eye*, a book on a Tibetan youth from Lhasa who had a hole poked in his forehead which gave him mystical powers. Hoskin said that he was the chosen youth and wrote under the name Tuesday Lobsang Rampa.

❧ **David Icke** channels "the Christ spirit" and Socrates.[180] Icke writes, "The takeover of Earth by the extraterrestrial expressions of this Luciferic consciousness took the form, I feel, of creating a vibratory prison. . . . An extraterrestrial force from the 4th dimension created an information prison by blocking off the higher levels of human consciousness. . . . We were, in effect, put into spiritual and mental quarantine. . . . In the period after the blocking vibration was created, the 4th dimensional extraterrestrial of the Luciferic mindset came here and genetically rewired the DNA. By scrambling the DNA, this knowledge was lost to us . . . DNA before that time had twelve helixes, but was reduced to two after the tinkering. . . . We are in a time when a process is unfolding which will reunite those spirals within us. . . ."[181]

❧ **Jani King** channels P'taah who says, "That which you term 'religion' upon your plane has nothing to do with the Spiritual truths of the universes, which require no rites, rules or rituals. Religion is a tool of enslavement to keep you in chains, to keep you in control, that you may not know sovereignty and free dominion. It is valid. You have created it, but it is not necessary for your enlightenment."

❧ **JZ Knight** channels Ramtha who says, "When you realize that what is unknown equates manifesting God, you will never be confused again; you will only want more. That is when the fire becomes unquenchable. That is when becoming becomes a very rapid movement, and many lives take place in one lifetime."

❧ **Gladys Osborne Leonard** was a British psychic who lived from 1882 to 1968. Leonard channeled Feda, an Indian who died around 1800.

❧ **Kathleen Long** (1890–1962) channeled Azrael, Sanchuniathon, and her own "other-side self" from the spirit world. "I am Azvard and I come to tell you . . ."

❧ **Jean Loomis** channels Seth, the entity who Jane Roberts channeled before her death in 1984. Loomis is a former high school English and journalism teacher.

❧ **Barbara Marciniak** channels the "Pleiadians." (The Pleiadians are a collective of extraterrestrials from the star system the Pleiades.) The Pleiadian culture is ancient and was "seeded" from another universe of love long before Earth was created. They say, "As you learn to feel light within yourselves and to effect through your thoughts, and have the love channeled into Mother Earth, and as you learn to bless where you live and take care of your portion of Terra, then you will affect others, for your vibration goes out and like attracts like."

⅃ **Norma Milanovich** channels "Ascended Masters," especially Master Kuthumi. Her second book, *Sacred Journey to Atlantis*, is the story of an incredible journey that she and many others made to Bimini. While there, they assisted in opening a vortex (with the help of the "Celestial Beings") that was allegedly left when Atlantis sank into the ocean thousands of years ago.

⅃ **William Stainton Moses** (1839–1892) channeled twenty-two spirit communicators, headed by one who called himself "Imperator." Later, the Imperator revealed that he was one of the Bible prophets. Moses used to receive automatic writing with his left hand while at the same time writing his regular correspondents with his right hand.

⅃ **John Oliver** channels Jerhoam who says, "For the purposes of our dialogues together, our name is Jerhoam. We are a formless existence that comes to the body of this oracle that in the moment of our first coming, he was clean and pure in the mind, enough or innocent in the mind enough, to allow our entry."

⅃ **John Payne** channels a spirit guide named Omni who says, "I Omni, will show you how it is possible to have a rich and rewarding life that is guilt free and that is full of boundless rewards. You are all children of God and there is only an abundance of light and love for you."

⅃ **Julie Presson** channels Moranaa who says, "In the time that will become known as the end times you will see many wonders and miracles. You will see the sick heal themselves in an instant. You will see an end of all disease of the physical body. This will be accomplished partly through the use of the doorways by those of you who have elected to participate in the end times in such a way."

⅃ **Jach Pursel** channels Lazaris who says, "In order to communicate with you, we send forth a series of vibrations. These vibratory frequencies go through a series of 'step down generations' until we can safely enter your reality—your world. The energy field of the one you call Jach acts like an antenna; his body, like an amplifier."

⅃ **Richard Rebeck** channels David who says, "Although it is possible to communicate with those who have crossed over it is not recommended. Those who have crossed over should not be called back to the earth plane."

⅃ **Jane Roberts** channeled Seth who said, "The apparent boundaries between past, present and future are only illusions caused by the amount of action you can physically perceive, and so it seems to you that one moment exists and is gone forever, and the next moment comes and like the one before also disappears. Everything in the universe exists at one time simultaneously."

⅃ **Pat Rodegast** channels Emmanuel who says, "Guilt is second judgment. It is looking at oneself and saying, 'I really ought not to have done that.' But, my very dears, if you really 'ought not to have,' you would not have."

⅃ **Steve Rother** channels "The Group" who say, "You see yourself as biology in with a core essence. We envision you as a grand master spirit playing inside a bubble of biology. If you misplace that vision, call on us for we are available to you at any moment simply by asking. If you dare, take a moment and look at yourself through our eyes."

⅃ **Lyssa Royal** channels extraterrestrials who say, "You are moving now into a fourth-density reality. Fourth density is characterized by reintegration. This means that you begin dissolving the boundaries, whether they are symbolic or literal, and that as those boundaries begin to dissolve you begin to see reality holistically."

⊬ **Gordon-Michael Scallion** channels Matrix. (Scallion receives many of his messages in dream state. Sometimes they appear on his computer screen. Often he steps into another reality where he receives messages from Matrix.) Matrix says, "The future of the planet can change from moment to moment depend on the thought form of the people."

⊬ **Lisa Smith** channels Sanada who says, "I Sananda, unite with those in physicality that has taken up their own rod of power for the upcoming tasks at hand. The time is NOW to merge the dimensions. In doing so you will assist this earth plane as well as the masters, both in the higher realms as well as those on earth."

⊬ **Jelaila Starr** channels the Nibiruan Councils who say, "I, Jelaila, was chosen by the Nibiruan Council to come to your planet at this time to bring you tools for regaining your natural multidimensional state of being. The tools, the final pieces, I speak of are the DNA Recoding, Reconnection and Activation process, the 13th Dimensional Formula of Compassion and the remaining 4 higher dimensional processes."

⊬ **Ramon Stevens** channels Alexander. Alexander describes himself as a "consciousness gestalt," a pool of consciousness composed, in part, of hundreds of human incarnations.

ever, we can survive in sea colonies and eat high-protein algae before using a launching ramp on the side of Mt. Kilimanjaro to reach Mars.

In his book, Savage provides a master plan for humanity so that we can spread life throughout the universe. Savage believes if we do not leave Earth, humans will become extinct. Savage (an engineer who has established the Millennial Foundation to promote space exploration) outlines his program for transferring a people into space. The important first step is to colonize the ocean surface with floating cities, thereby increasing the living space available to humans. Our primary power source will be the thermal energy of the deep ocean. At the same time, spirulina algae, which is already on sale in health food stores, becomes a major new food crop. Savage also explains how space vehicles can make orbiting space colonies possible. Future steps including settling on the moon, terraforming Mars so that it has an atmosphere, settling on asteroids and moons throughout our solar system, and creating artificial habitats around the sun.

Marshall Savage, who currently resides in Colorado, attended Swarthmore College and holds a degree in English from the University of Southern California. In the introduction to *The Millennial Project*, futurist Arthur C. Clarke praises Savange for his "command of a dozen engineering disciplines and his amazing knowledge of scientific and technical literature."

## ♉ *Gordon-Michael Scallion*

> *What my visions have shown is that the center core of the Earth is a very intense plasma. It is contained in an incredible magnetic envelope. So, it's like a bubble in the center of the Earth that has this plasma. As you move up through the boundaries, you have magma of different levels of intensity.*
> —Gordon-Michael Scallion, *Art Bell* radio show, June 10, 1998

Gordon-Michael Scallion is a modern-day prophet who has "received" hundreds of messages concerning geological changes to our planet. Gordon has been on numerous television shows including *Sightings* and *Ancient Prophecies*.[182] He is also one of several prophets who has created maps of the United States and the world after the Earth undergoes future changes in its terrain. Like Edgar Cayce, Scallion is very interested in Atlantis, and like Nostradamus and Cayce, Scallion's head is filled with visions of disasters and apocalypses.[183] Scallion's prophetic map of the early twenty-first-century future shows California as nothing but a few islands in the Pacific. Eventually, the United States will restructure itself as thirteen colonies.

Scallion's psychic abilities are said to have begun after an accident in the 1980s that left him mute for a week. He went to a hospital, and while in bed saw a light that morphed into a woman's face. She instructed Scallion to write down what she said. The woman predicted various future events concerning plane crashes, weather changes, and earthquakes. She also said that there would be major earth changes starting in the late 1980s that included earthquakes, volcanic activities, and tsunamis. By the 1990s, they would spread throughout the world and cause major problems.

Immediately after his encounter with the evanescent woman, Scallion's voice returned, and he started seeing auroras around people. He continued to receive visions of the future and had the ability to heal others. Today, Scallion receives many of his "messages" in dream state. Sometimes they appear on his computer screen. Often he goes into another reality where he receives messages from an entity named Matrix. Gordon refers to each prediction as a Milios. Here are some of his predictions: the pope following John-Paul will be Italian and will be the last pope. Massive solar flares will hit Earth. Satellites, the power grid, and computers will fail. There will be species extinctions, and genetically mutated new species will emerge.

Here are some predictions he made in 1998,[184] which came from Mr. Scallion's public appearances and his Web site. Magnetic devices and electronic circuitry in satellites and aircraft will fail en masse. Magnetic devices and satellite systems would fail almost on a regular basis. There would be a complete melt-off of the Antarctic: "I could see land and structures." Various earthquakes would occur in South America and Japan.

Scallion's works are quite popular with Art Bell, the nighttime radio show host who features unusual guests. Scallion presently leads the Matrix institute in New Hampshire. The Institute publishes newsletters and video tapes dealing with Scallion's predictions.[182]

In 1989, Scallion had an eerie series of dreams that dealt with additional changes that would occur in the Earth. Scallion wrote the dreams down and then recorded the messages of these dreams in a newsletter that he sent out to a few close friends. This was the beginning of "The Earth Changes Report," which continues to report on and update Scallion's visions. Scallion's followers say he predicted the 1984 Mexico City earthquake, the 1985 election of President Bush, the 1987 stock market crash, a series of major California earthquakes, and various earthquakes and volcanic disturbances in Japan. Scallion claims to see each event three times before deciding to tell the public. He predicted that the western portions of the United States would break up and submerge sometime around 2001. A portion of the ancient continent of Atlantis would rise, and Japan would be completely underwater. As the result of the catastrophic physical changes in America, both the American government and American economy would collapse. A new sun would appear in the skies so that during the day it appears as a small white light. He says, "The new star will first be seen before the end of the [twentieth] century." [186]

The following is a brief description on Gordon-Michael Scallion's "Future Map of the United States: 1998–2001." This large color map of the United States shows exactly how Scallion envisioned the United States after various geophysical changes. Around 1990, Scallion said,

> I see a planetary spiritual awakening occurring during the nineties. A vision I've seen for the year 2002 is of a new Earth—reborn—with its people living in harmony with each other. . . . Communities seem to be located more in rural areas than in cities. The air is clean, and there no longer is an ozone hole. I see circular, clustered homes—domes made of a kind of living membrane that provides self-adjusting heating, lighting, and cooling. There are no automobiles, but there does appear to be a new form of public transportation—long, cigar-shaped crafts that move across the ground silently—without wheels. The average life-span has expanded to 150 years because of the Earth's new vibrations and the consciousness of its inhabitants. Telepathy is common between individuals, and between people and animals. There are new flowers, plants, and trees, which provide herbal remedies for this time. Many of the diseases of the twentieth century are gone.

. . . Color and sound therapy are the predominant healing modalities. In the year 2002 the world has become a lunar society guided by intuition. There is a common spiritual belief on the planet, termed the "Oneness," a belief in the inter relatedness of all life. The Millennium of Peace has arrived, and a new cycle begins.[187]

Various individuals have catalogued apparent errors in Scallion's predictions.[188] Palm Springs was supposed to be hit with a 9.0 earthquake in the mid-1990s. Volcanic ash was also supposed to cover most of the planet before 2000. He also is said to have predicted California's submerging by 1993. Denver was supposed to be on the Pacific coast by 1998.

## ♉ *Tim Sikyea*

> *People who have become spiritually clear and accept these approaching energies of the cosmos will be able to be secure from this human cleansing process.*
> —Tim Sikyea[189]

Tim Sikyea is a Canadian Denee Indian who went to Europe in 1988 because a vision suggested he warn Europeans of impending doom. He believed that visions don't necessarily come true, but more often suggest problems that could be avoided with intelligent thinking and planning. In 1988, he believed that a kind of energy would change the atmosphere and increase the pressure on our brains by 35 percent. Eighty percent of humans would go mad as a result. "They will kill themselves and destroy everything around them. It will be like a madhouse."[190]

## ♉ *Zecharia Sitchin and Raël*

> *The Annunaki's technological advancement enables them not only to travel in space but also to revive the dead and do other things which in biblical times were considered miracles.*
> —Zecharia Sitchin[191]

Zecharia Sitchin, along with Erich von Däniken and Immanuel Velikovsky, suggests that humanity's ancient myths contain valid information about actual events in Earth's history. Stichin published seven books on this subject between 1976–1996.

Zecharia Sitchin was born in Russia and later learned Hebrew and studied Old Testament archeology while in Palestine. Sitchin graduated from the University of London, majoring in economic history, and in 1993 lectured at New York University. According to Sitchin, ancient Sumerian clay tablets reveal that godlike creatures from planet Niburu arrived on Earth 450,000 years ago and created humans by performing genetic engineering with female apes. Niburu orbits our Sun every 3,600 years. The Bible's book of Genesis describes the activities of the Niburu creatures. In particular, Genesis refers to giant Nephilim as the sons of the gods who married human women in the days before Noah's flood. According to Sitchin, the Nephilim are actually creatures from Niburu.

Stichen prophecies the return of planet Nibiru, which is still inhabited by intelligent humanlike beings, the long-lived Annunaki, who will come and go between their planet and Earth. The British writer Alan F. Alford, author of *Gods of the New Millenium*, has also made similar claims with respect to the ancient gods. However, while broadly agreeing with Sitchin's overall argument, Alan Alford challenges several fundamental aspects of Stichin's theories and puts forward many new ideas such as a positive identification of Yahweh as a flesh-and-blood god.

Sitchin's ideas appear to be echoed by Raël, who has started his own religion called the Raëlian religion that also suggests humans are the result of DNA experiments by ancient extraterrestrial visitors. Raël has written a channeled book, *The Final Message*, which he claimed was dictated to him by aliens.

In France, in 1973, Claude Vorilhon said that he met an extraterrestrial who gave him the name Raël. In his book *The True Face of God*, Raël says the creature told him that all forms of life on Earth result from the aliens' genetic engineering. In the Bible, the word God is a mistaken translation of the Hebrew word Elohim, which is really a plural word meaning "those who came from the sky." Our ancestors, unable to understand the advanced technology of the Elohim, took them for gods.

Raël is a former sports journalist. Today he teaches sensual meditation, a technique given to him by the extraterrestrials that allows people to awaken their consciousness, to live in peace, and to prepare them for humanity's golden age. Raël also wants to build an embassy where the governments of the Earth will meet extraterrestrials who will give humans their technological knowledge. Currently, there are over forty thousand Raëlians throughout the world. Today, one of Raël's biggest hobbies is car racing in Japan, the United States, and Canada. His books have been translated into more than twenty-five languages.[192]

For a skeptical treatment of Raël and related prophets, see Donna J. Kossy's *Kooks: A Guide to the Outer Limits of Human Belief*.[193]

## ♉ *Solara*

*It is the fragments of this precious song which enable us to continue on, as if seeking to put together pieces of an obscure puzzle, sacred to us, yet ignored by most. We gather our reawakened memories as if pearls strung together on a cord, endeavoring to create our necklace of remembrance.*

—Solara, *The Star Borne:*
*A Remembrance for the Awakened Ones*

Solara is the leader of the 11:11 Doorway movement, which suggests that humanity has entered a twenty-year period of opportunity to reach new heights and soar like the angels. In some sense, Solara received initial insights while contemplating a digital watch.

According to Solara, author of *11:11: Inside the Doorway*, millions of people all over the world have been repeatedly seeing the numbers 11:11. Solara writes, "Often appearing on digital clocks, the sightings of 11:11 tend to occur during times of heightened awareness, having a powerful effect on those involved. They cause a reactivation of our cellular memory banks and a stirring deep inside of something long forgotten. The appearance of 11:11 is also a powerful confirmation that we are on the right track, aligned with the beam of our Highest Truth. The 11:11 is an insertion point for the Greater Reality to enter the present moment."[194]

On January 11, 1992 numerous people gathered to activate the Doorway of the 11:11. This doorway is the transition zone or bridge between "two very different spirals of evolution, those of duality and Oneness." The doorway will stay open until December 31, 2011, thus creating a twenty-year period in which to make our spiritual journey an achieve Oneness.

According to Solara, the 1992 activation of the 11:11 is one of the most important events that has taken place on Earth. There are eleven gates within the 11:11. Each gate represents a new frequency band of energy. Every few years, a new 11:11 gate is activated. Other Solara books include *The Star Borne: A Remembrance for the Awakened Ones* and *How to Live Large on a Small Planet.*

## ♉ *Sollog*

*Did you know that the school shootings in the United States all occurred on two straight lines connected to Bill Clinton's birthplace?*

—Sollog, www.sollog.com

Sollog is a mysterious individual that has become famous among aficionados of the Internet World Wide Web where his popularity continues to grow. This "Nostradamus of the nineties" is well-known to those who frequent the Usenet newsgroup alt.prophecies.nostradamus. Sollog's predictions of the future are often vague or in cryptic language. For example, his 1995 prediction "The Goddess of the Moon [Diana] would die on the 31st and be connected to Napoleon [Paris, France]"[195] is said to refer to Princess Diana's death in 1997. Sollog has since guaranteed that nuclear terrorism is about to hit Jerusalem.[196]

Today Sollag is most famous for his "Line of Tragedy" map of America which shows how several recent tragedies all fall along a straight diagonal line across the United States.[197] The line connects the JonBennet Ramsey murder in Boulder; the Versace murder in Miami; the Oklahoma bombing; Valujet 592 crash in Miami; a commercial jet crash in Santiago, Cuba; the volcanic eruptions in Montserrat; massive quakes in Seattle; Bill Clinton's leg injury in Miami; Clinton's support plane crash in Jackson Hole; and more. The line of tragedy was created to give the final warning to America before it is destroyed.

The following are thirteen events that Sollog had guaranteed to take place between 1999 and 2001: Major fall in stock market at the end of 1999; quakes over 7.0 in the Middle East, China, and Indonesia; over ten named hurricanes in the Atlantic for the year 2000 hurricane season; a quake over 5.0 within fifty miles of Los Angeles; a major space program failure; a major new discovery in space; Y2K failures in India, China, Russia, and South America; the assassination of political leader; a celebrity death due to an over dose; another school shooting on the line from Miami through Oklahoma City; a hurricane on the line from Oklahoma City through Miami through St. Johns; and another political scandal in Washington, D.C.

## ☿ *Joanna Southcott*

> *The sealed of the lord—the elect precious man's redemption—to inherit the tree of life—to be made heirs of God and joint heirs with Jesus Christ.*
>
>                    —Joanna Southcott (from her certificate
>                 guaranteeing people admittance to Heaven)[198]

Joanna Southcott (1750–1814) was an English eccentric who, at age sixty-five, announced that, although still a virgin, she was expecting a child, the Second Messiah.[199] Joanna Southcott was born in Gittisham, Devon, England. She worked as a milkmaid and rejected sexual pleasure. Her first prophecy came in 1792, when she announced that she was to be "the Lamb's wife" and then went into convulsions.

Southcott had dramatic religious experiences even as a teenager. She claimed to have exorcised the Devil from an atheist who had been sick and complaining that he could hear "the black dogs of hell" outside his bedroom window. Joanna commanded the Devil to leave the house, at which point the atheist is said to have fallen back on his pillow and died.

When she was in her forties, Southcott claimed that she began to hear God's voice, which allowed her to prophesy. She tried to ask bishops and politicians to verify her predictions, but they did not seem interested. Eventually she gave a Church of England vicar an envelope, which he had promised not to open until the following Christmas. When he did so, he discovered that Joanna had correctly predicted the unexpected death of the Bishop of Exeter, who had seemingly been in perfect health at the time she had made the prediction.

In 1801, on the vicar's recommendation, Joanna published the first of many books and pamphlets containing her prophecies. Many prophecies did not focus on historically important events, but her predictions attracted thousands of believers to whom she sold certificates that guaranteed them a place in heaven. She claimed that God told her that only 144,000 souls would be eligible for eternal salvation. (Clearly space was limited.)

Even after she made the startling announcement that she was pregnant with the son of "the Most High," her followers' faith did not wane. They showered her with baby gifts and an expensive crib. On October 11, 1813, she cut herself off from society to wait for the birth. Joanna wrote to every bishop and member of Parliament, to tell them of the good news. On August 1, 1814, several doctors were called to check on her, as she had been ill for nearly five months. The doctors' conclusions were that she was now four months pregnant. Joanna said she would name the new Messiah Shiloh from the biblical prophecy: "The scepter shall not depart from Judah, not a lawgiver from between his feet, until Shiloh come; and unto him shall the gathering of the people be" (Gen. 49:10).

An eminent member of the Royal College of Surgeons confirmed the pregnancy after an examination during which Joanna had remained fully clothed. She had refused to allow the physician to examine her more closely because she felt that it would be improper for the new messiah's mother to display herself in an undignified fashion. Her apparently strong belief in her pregnancy quelled all doubts in her disciples. She believed that the world would end on October 19, 1814, the date of the rebirth of Christ.

Not everyone agreed with the physician from the Royal College of Surgeons. For example, her own physician diagnosed her as having "biliary obstructions" and attributed her excess weight to the fact that she spent all day in bed "in downy indolence." Eventually, Southcott grew frail, and on December 27, 1814, she died. On her written instructions, physicians performed an autopsy in her home in the presence of other medical experts and a group of followers. There was no fetus within her uterus or anywhere else in her abdominal cavity.

Prior to her death, Joanna Southcott sealed a box that she said contained the secret of world peace and her predictions for the following centuries. She left instructions that the box was only to be opened in a time of national catastrophe and then only in the presence of a dozen bishops of the Church of England. In 1927, the box was X-rayed revealing that it contained a horse pistol, a dice box, purse, several books, a lottery ticket, and a night cap.

Southcott's death did not alienate her disciples, and the sect continued to exist for many years. In modern times, there were Southcott believers who awaited the arrival of the millennium. This, they believed, would coincide with the opening of another mysterious box of Joanna's. Today, her followers say that she accurately predicted the French Revolution and the rise and fall of Napoleon.

## ♉ *Stormberger*

> *Nothing will be anymore holy. Everything will be upset. The great clearance will begin. All nations will be pitted against each other. The free life and through will be exiled and imprisoned. Seven leaders will rule and will try to get everything under discipline. It will be a dreadful time.*
>
> —Stormberger[200]

Stormberger is the eighteenth-century Bavarian prophet and cowherd who gave numerous apocalyptic prophecies. In 1934, the Nazis burned many of his books because his prophecies seemed to be anti-Nazi, predicting the war's disastrous results for a Hitlerian Germany. His followers say he foretold the existence of cars, trains, and aircraft—and the division of Germany and the occurrence of three world wars in the twentieth century. The third war would be the worst. He wrote:

> And after the second great struggle between nations will come a third universal conflagration, which will determine everything. There will be entirely new weapons. In one day more men will die than in all previous wars combined. Battles will be fought with artificial guns. Gigantic catastrophes will occur. With open eyes will the nations of the earth enter into these catastrophes. They will not be aware of what is happening, and those who will know and tell, will be silenced. Everything will become different

than before, and in many places the earth will be only just a great cemetery. The third great, great war will be the end for many nations.[201]

More Stromberger prophecies:

Iron rods will be built and iron monsters will bark though the wilderness.
Cars without horses and shaft will come, and man will fly through the air like
birds. . . . The Catholic faith will almost completely disappear, the religious-
ness will be quite badly respected, they will not earn any respect due to their
way of living, there won't be many good Christians among the people, the
Commandments of God are no longer respected by the aristocracy as well as
by the smallest worker, one will not think the greatest unfairness to be a sin.
When the faith disappears also the love of the next one will completely lose
itself, one will not estimate the justice, often the poor one will not be given
right and he will be less respected than a dog. After this a mischief will arise
that has to be regretted, there will be no order among the people.[202]

## ♉ *Whitley Strieber and Art Bell*

> *A climatological nightmare is upon us. It is almost certainly the most dangerous
> thing that has ever happened in our history. . . . We believe that it comes on sud-
> denly and that it is so destructive that it has the potential to end our civilization.
> However, there is a surprising amount that we can do about it. Some of it
> involves personal action. Some of it involves the whole society.*
> —Art Bell and Whitley Strieber, *The Coming Global Superstorm*

Art Bell is one of the top-rated late-night radio talk-show hosts in America.
Whitley Strieber is the bestselling author of Communion, a book on alien
abduction. Although not in the same league as diviners like Nostradamus
and Edgar Cayce, Bell and Streiber in their recent book touch on the theme
recurrent for most prophets—global destruction. In particular Bell and
Strieber predict killer tornadoes, violent tropical storms, and devastating
temperatures as a prelude to environmental disaster in our near future.
Their book *The Coming Global Superstorm* suggests that rapid changes in the
atmosphere caused by greenhouse gases will lead to a sudden catastrophic
climate change.[203] It will begin with a massive storm that will devastate the
northern hemisphere, followed by floods and perhaps a new Ice Age. They
base their predictions on certain findings in geologic history; however, skeptics of the book suggest that neither Bell nor Strieber are climatologists and
therefore specific predictions about a "sudden global superstorm" are not scientifically justified.

## ♉ *Madame Sylvia*

> *The world is without support. The heart of the world is broken.*
> —Madam Sylvia[204]

Madame Sylvia was a famous twentieth century, European psychic whose clients were kings and politicians. She died in 1948, the same year she prophesied, "The Earth breathes, whirls around in terrible catastrophes. Continents crumble and are washed away, but other continents and islands reappear again. Frenzy, folly, and madness. . . . Two corpses by the road-side, two fallen colossi, terrible struggle, lament, wreck, ruin, and smoke. Where is the sun? Where is day? Where is God and his help? Everything is dark on Earth. Hell has opened its gates."[205]

In 1948, she predicted a united Europe: "Europe will become a unity of one nation, not many nations anymore. There will be different people and different souls, but not nations. I see one banner-white. . . . In the middle of Europe—a tower."[206]

## ♉ *Mitar Tarabich*

> *After the assassination of the King and Queen [Alexandar and Draga Obrenovich] the Karageorgevichs will come to power. Then we will again start a war with the Turks. Four Christian states will attack Turkey, and our border will be on the river Lim. Then we shall finally conquer and avenge Kosovo. . . . Soon after this war another war will start. . . . The Big War in which a lot of blood will be spilled. If that blood were a river, a huge stone of 300 kg would roll in its current easily*
> —Mitar Tarabich, *Kremasko Prorochanstvo* (Kremna's Prophecy)

Mitar Tarabich (1829–1899) was an uneducated villager from Kremna, a small Serbian town that today has a population of around a thousand. When he suddenly began "seeing" visions of the future, he told a priest about his interesting predictions. The priest, in turn, took many notes, which is the reason we know so much about Tarabich today.[207]

According to Tarabich followers, Tarabich, in nineteenth-century Serbia, prophesied various political events including the 1903 assassination of the Serbian ruler Alexandar Obrenovich and the 1912 war between Serbia and Turkey.

Russia entered the World War II after being attacked by Nazi Germany in 1941. The Russians were led by Stalin, and Tarabich followers suggest that Stalin is the "red Czar" in the following Tarabich prophecy:

In the beginning Russia will not wage war, but when attacked by the evil army, they will fight back. There is a red Czar on the Russian throne. Here, men with stars on their foreheads will appear. They will rule Uzice and this region for exactly 73 days, and then fleeing their enemies, they will go over the river Drina. These are times of hunger and great evil . . . Serbs will fight and butcher each other. The invading enemy looks upon Serbian evil hatred and laughs at us. A man with blue eyes on a white horse appears among our people. A star shines on his forehead. The evil enemy will hunt him all over our country, in the woods, over rivers and upon the sea, but in vain. The man will gather a mighty army and free occupied Belgrade. He will chase away the enemy from our country, and our kingdom will be bigger than ever. Russia will make an alliance with other great kingdoms over the seas, and they will burn down the crooked anti-cross and free all the enslaved people of Europe.[208]

In the future Tarabich wrote that man

will live for a long, long time, not being able to know himself. There will be many learned men who will think through their books that they know and can do everything. . . . People will do many stupid things, thinking that they know and can do everything, not knowing anything. Wise men will appear in the Orient and their wisdom will cross all seas and frontiers, but people will not trust this wisdom for long time, and this real truth they will proclaim for a lie. . . . In Serbia it will not be possible to distinguish a man from a woman. Everybody will dress the same. This calamity will come to us from abroad but it will stay with us the longest. A groom will take a bride, but nobody will know who is who. . . . The Serbs will separate from each other, and they will say: "I am not a Serb, I am not a Serb."[209]

Tarabich's fame seems to be growing. His words, recorded in *Kremasko Prorochanstvo*, or *Kremna's Prophecy*, are said to predict the ruling of the communist Josip Broz Tito and the birth and death of Yugoslavia. The book also contained a cryptic passage about a "small man from the orient" who would come with the "message of truth." Tarabich said that not everyone would accept this man's word and that he would initially have few followers. This phrase is thought by some to predict the Hare Krishna movement.[210]

## ♉ *Alfred, Lord Tennyson*

> *Many a night I saw the Pleiads, rising thro' the mellow shade,*
> *Glitter like a swarm of fire-flies tangled in a silver braid.*
> —Alfred, Lord Tennyson, "Locksley Hall"

Alfred, Lord Tennyson (1809–1892) was considered England's greatest poet during the last half of the nineteenth century, and people from every walk of life understood and admired his poetry. Obviously, I hesitate to include him in this list because he is not known for being a visionary. Although hardly a prophet or diviner in the standard sense, some Tennyson fans consider his poems to be unusual and prophetic, as if his mind were able to tap into the future. One poem in particular, "Locksley Hall" (1842), written after a periods of mediation, is claimed to foretell air transportation, aerial combat in world wars, and the formation of the United Nations. Here are a few sample lines from "Locksley Hall" to give you the flavor of the haunting poem:

> For I dipt into the future, far as human eye could see,
> Saw the Vision of the world, and all the wonder that would be;
> Saw the heavens fill with commerce, argosies of magic sails,
> Pilots of the purple twilight dropping down with costly bales.

Tennyson, along with his father, uncle, several brothers, cousin, and grandfather, had temporal lobe epilepsy.[211] Tennyson wrote about his waking trances:

> All at once, out of the intensity of the consciousness of individuality, the individuality itself seemed to dissolve and fade away into boundless being; and this not a confused state, but the clearest of the clearest, the surest of the surest, the weirdest of the weirdest, utterly beyond words. Sometimes a great and sudden sadness would come over me, and I would wander away beneath the stars.[212]

Tennyson once had a vision of the entire inhabitants of London "lying horizontally a hundred years hence." He said, "The world seemed dead around and myself only alive. This might have been the state described by St. Paul."[213] Tennyson seemed to be asexual, never having kissed a woman until, at age forty-one, he married a thirty-seven-year-old invalid with a spinal problem.

## ♉ *Josyp Terelya*

> *I saw the Mother of God.*
>
> —Josyp Terelya, *Witness*

Although born in the Ukraine, Josyp Terelya currently lives in Toronto, Canada.[214] He was the son of high communist officials and raised by his grandmother as a Catholic in underground Ukrainian Catholic Church. As a teenager, Terelya dared to challenge the occupying Soviet authorities for the right to practice his faith. As a result, he was placed in a Soviet prison for practicing religion in communist Russia. During his twenty-three years in prison he faced torture, intimidation, hunger, and freezing cold. One day, when Terelya thought he was about to freeze to death in jail, he prayed to the Virgin Mary. He claims that a bright light filled the room. An apparition of the Virgin Mary came to save him and to allow him to prophesy. Since then, Terelya has given about two hundred (mostly apocalyptic) prophecies. One of Terelya's visions revealed earthquakes in California that force California into the water. His fame has spread, and he's even spoken about Russian persecution at the White House and has seen the pope several times. His experiences are documented in his 1992 book, *Witness: To Apparitions and Persecution in the USSR—An Autobiography*.

Note that many other individuals have said they have suddenly seen Mary and began to prophecy. For example, consider the story of modern Irish mystic and prophet Christina Gallagher, who has received visions of Jesus, Mary, and various saints since the 1980s. Gallagher continues to reveal God's wishes of peace, as described in Thomas Petrisko's book *Visions and Prophecies of Christina Gallagher*.[215]

## ♉ *Guboo Ted Thomas*

> *I was in dreamtime. I seen this great wave going.*
>
> —Guboo Ted Thomas[216]

Guboo Ted Thomas is a famous Australian aborigine who prophesied an increase in tidal waves and earthquakes because of humanity's disrespect for Earth's natural resources. The tribal elder said that he first got the idea while in "dreamtime." Specifically, he says, "We're going to have tidal waves. We're going to have earthquakes. That's coming because we don't consider this land as our Mother. We've taken away the balance and we're not putting it back. I look at the bush and those trees are alive. They're not dead, they're alive. And they want you to cuddle them."[217]

Dreamtime refers to the mythical past of the Australian aborigines and is the basis of their religious beliefs and creation stories. In the dreamtime, spiritual beings shaped the land and brought the first people into being. A common feature of the aboriginal religion is their bond with the land.

My favorite dreamtime stories describe how giants and animals sprang from the earth, sea, and sky and traversed the empty continent of Australia before returning into the earth. The places where they traveled or sank back into the land became rocks, mountain ranges, and sites full of sacred meaning. Fundamental aboriginal beliefs suggest that the past exists in an eternal present. The myths and ritual constitute the dreamtime, which signifies continuity of life unlimited by space and time.

## ♉ *Lori Toye*

> *Mainframe computer servers and the Internet are insightful metaphors to language interconnectedness, the One and Universal Mind. Universal Mind operates like a huge computer server, and while we are all connected to it, the super-senses of a channel can bring us into greater rapport with its benefits.*
> —Lori Toye, "The Art of Channeling"[218]

Excited by a vision that she received in 1983, Lori Adaile Toye felt that something important was about to occur.[219] When she first had the visions, Lori was an Arizona farm wife and mother of several small children. She recognized the white-robed beings, or "Ascended Masters," as the teachers Saint-Germain, Sananda, El Morya, and Kuthumi, who prophesied changes in the Earth's land masses. They unrolled a large map of North America showing the changes.

In 1988 Lori received more information about changes in the Earth and drew a map showing the details. She desperately wanted to publish the map but did not have sufficient funds. The only way to get money at the time was to sell her home, which she did with a heavy heart. She eventually created a detailed model of the earth-changes map and began to lecture on her experiences and visions. In May 1989, Toye sent hundreds of free copies of her map to magazines, organizations, and friends.

The Beings, she said, stressed that their prophecy is a prophecy of choice. People are free to change the possibility of tremendous Earthly cataclysms to one of peace and relative safety. Toye's message is that her map, which shows most of California, Florida and Maine underwater, goes beyond predicting earthquakes, volcanoes, and sinking lands taking place before 2009. Her "I Am America" group believes that we can avert cataclysmic global changes everyday by shifting our consciousness. She believes that our individual thoughts, feelings, and actions create reality.

## ♉ *James Van Praagh*

> *In the higher realms everyone is on the same level of spiritual understanding, like a symphony of beings in tune with one another. For some this may mean a*

*reunion with members of their earth family. For others it could be a meeting with former friends and lovers from previous incarnations.*

—James Van Praagh, *Reaching to Heaven*

James Van Praagh is a modern psychic who claims he can hear the dead. He is the author of the bestseller *Talking to Heaven,* which took the publishing world by storm in early 1998. His appearances on *48 Hours, Sally Jessey Raphael,* and especially *Larry King Live* sent his book skyrocketing to number one on the bestseller list. After an initial printing of 10,000 copies, *Talking to Heaven* ultimately sold close to 600,000 copies in hardcover. Van Praagh's alleged gift for communication with the dead clearly appealed to people and gave him a devoted following.

Although he was raised a Roman Catholic and even entered a seminary at fourteen, Van Praagh soon found that New Age spirituality was more compelling than traditional religion. He graduated from San Francisco State University with a degree in broadcasting and communication, then moved to Los Angeles, where at age twenty-four he met a medium who told Van Praagh he would become clairvoyant.

James Van Praagh's books chart the course of the soul as it journeys through life, death, and rebirth. Most appealing for Van Praagh fans are his detailed theories on death and the afterlife. For example, when people die sudden deaths, Van Praagh reports, spirits of the dead often linger over their bodies, unable to comprehend what has happened—but still able to see and hear everything that is being done and said around the corpse. This is why spirits of the dead are so useful in helping the newly dead make the transition to the other side.

Van Praagh has given numerous demonstrations in which he provides information about dead family members to their survivors. Skeptics like the Amazing Randi have studied Van Praagh's demonstrations. The skeptics suggest that Van Praagh only appears to give accurate information because his initial questions to those seeking the dear departed are so general that they are true for anyone. (For example, "Do you know a John?") Skeptics like Joe Nickell suggest that mediums glean information by a variety of means, like reading body language (to sense when they are factually on or off track), providing data in question form (which may, if correct, be considered a "hit" but otherwise will seem an innocent query), and inviting the person to interpret the vague statements offered. For example, Van Praagh often asks, "Do you understand this?" or "Do you know what this means?" or similar questions, inviting the family member to provide the meaning. According to Nickell, if the person does not know what Van Praagh is talking about, Van Praagh tries another approach.[220]

♉ *Alan Vaughan*

> *To those who see no evidence of God in their lives, I recommend that they explore their own patterns of prophecy.*
>
> —Alan Vaughan, *Patterns of Prophecy*

Alan Vaughan is an American seer and is said to be a very high-scoring "predictor" as measured by the Central Premonitions Registry[221] in New York City. The Registry records people's dreams in order to try to determine those individuals who have a high incidence of precognitive dreams. Vaughan's credentials are based on his twenty years of work with the Central Premonitions Registry, which rated him in 1999 as "the world's most successful predictor" out of 3,500 people in 28 countries. Vaughan is author of seven books.

Vaughan had his first psychic experience in 1965, when he was twenty-eight years old. At that time. He was a science textbook editor in New York City and was skeptical of supernatural claims. However, while experimenting with a Ouija board, he became convinced that he had the power of foretelling the future. His numerous predictions can be accessed at http://www.alanvaughan.com/. Skeptic suggest that some of his predictions are either obvious or vague. For example, in his 1982 book *The Edge of Tomorrow* he wrote, "A shuttle launch will have severe malfunctions that could threaten the space program," and Vaughan suggests this predicts the 1986 Challenger explosion. As another example, in the April 1993 issue of *Fate*, he predicted, "In Russia, Boris Yeltsin will face a demonstration against his government in the fall. There will be some casualties." Vaughan suggests that this foretold the serious demonstrations that occured against Yeltsin in the fall of 1993. The demonstrations were serious, resulting in over one hundred deaths.

The Central Premonitions Registry may be accessed on the Internet's web, and it includes an on-line form that allows you to register dreams that you feel might be precognitive. The Registry takes itself quite seriously, reminding people that if they feel that their dreams "might refer to an impending public event, we strongly encourage you to click on the box that will send an automatic copy of the dream report also to the news group alt.dreams and to the LISTSERV group PSI-L. This will increase the chance of it being noticed in time and also make it publicly proven that it was reported before the event."

Vaughan's Web page (http://www.alanvaughan.com/) says that "his track record as a top psychic was established in 30 years of scientific experiments in which he solved crimes, found sunken ships, did healing, remote viewing, telepathy, psychokinesis, and predicted the future. He has demonstrated high accuracy at predicting financial markets for business clients. He channels a Chinese entity, Li Sung, for spiritual counseling and healing."

One of Vaughan's books is *Incredible Coincidence: The Baffling World of Synchronicity*. In the book he gives examples of apparently meaningful coincidences that have no causal connection: (1) A woman in Berkeley, California, is locked out of her house; the postman walks up, holding a letter from her brother containing is a spare key. (2) A hurricane in Galveston, Texas, sweeps Charles Coghlan's coffin out to sea; eight years and two thousand miles later, the coffin is found offshore from Coghlan's home town. Skeptics would suggest that amazing coincidences are bound to happen by chance. Vaughan suggests that these happenings are beyond the realm of statistics and are worthy of study.

## ♉ *Dr. Helen Wambach and Dr. Chet Snow*

> With regard to atomic weapons, I have foreseen . . . that there will be one more atomic explosion before the end of the atomic era. This explosion will be so terrible and will shock humanity so badly that no one will dare to use that weapon again.
> —Dr. Chet Snow[222]

In chapter 1, I discussed the various 1980 studies in which Dr. Helen Wambach hypnotized thousands of people in order to "progress" them into the future and tell her what they saw. Wambach offered subjects a choice of five time periods, three in the past and two in the future, with instructions that their subconscious minds would choose one of the periods. Of the 2,500 people in the study, six percent reported being alive in 2100 C.E., and 13 percent said they were alive after 2300 C.E. Most of the subjects told about the past and did not progress into the future. Wambach thought the infrequency of future progressions suggested a decline of 90 percent of the population within a few generations. When Wambach probed deeper, one hypnotized woman began "choking to death on a big, black cloud" in the 1990s. Wambach subjects told her that in the 1990s there would be a series of severe earthquakes, a new kind of U.S. currency issued, increases in food prices, severe weather patterns, financial crises, an increase in volcanic activity, and the death of a large number of people. In 1999, there would be a nuclear explosion in Europe that kills many people.

The work of late Wambach was discussed in *Mass Dreams of the Future*, a book by Dr. Chet Snow, her collaborator on the future life progression research. He described how some of California would slip into the sea in 1998: "The dates could change, as I say clearly in my book -- the left-brain linear time-dating system is the most difficult aspect of right-brain psychic predictions. However it should not be incorrect by more than a few decades."[223]

∼∼∼   ∼∼∼   ∼∼∼

Very few people can suppress a tingle of interest when hearing that someone's prediction has come true. Through the ages, the idea that a person might be able to foretell the future was both terrifying and thrilling—and these predictions have motivated people to achieve both good and evil. Given this, we must always be vigilant in our assessment of predictions and the people who make them. The next chapter discusses several experiments that deal with deception and also about the necessity of controlling the influence of beliefs and expectations that can color our observations and inferences. If you tell people that a religious teacher can perform miracles, many will listen to him more intently and show greater respect for his prophecies than someone else's. A believer in alien abduction will interpret a glow in the heavens as a spacecraft from another world. A psychiatrist who believes in alien abduction will interpret a client's hypnotically facilitated tales differently from a psychiatrist who does not.

The world's top psychics predicted for the 1990s that scientists would discover an antiaging drug to extend the average human life span to 150 years, that Madonna would give birth to quintuplets, that earthquakes would turn Los Angeles into an island, that a pollution cloud would force New York City to be quarantined, and that marijuana would replace petroleum as the nation's chief source of energy.[224] Gene Emery, a writer for the *Skeptical Inquirer*, has been tracking the accuracy of tabloid psychics for years and can rarely find evidence that a psychic predicted an unexpected event *before* the event has taken place. Emery, like other skeptics, warns us that every time the media promotes psychics, it encourages people to spend significant sums of money calling psychic hotlines. Sometimes police departments that listen to psychics waste valuable police resources, and these psychics can implicate people who later turn out to be innocent.[225] All of these warnings of deceptions and/or inaccuracies naturally lead us to the topics discussed in the next chapter.

# 4.

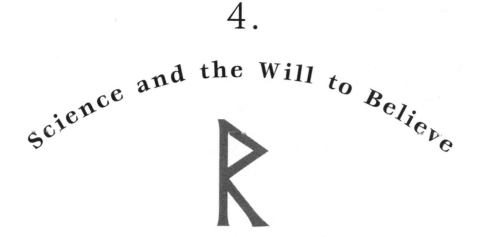

## Science and the Will to Believe

*Science is not about control. It is about cultivating a perpetual condition of wonder in the face of something that forever grows one step richer and subtler than our latest theory about it. It is about reverence, not mastery.*
—Richard Powers, *The Gold Bug Variations*

## ♦ TO BELIEVE OR NOT TO BELIEVE

*Prediction is always difficult, especially of the future.*
—Old Danish proverb

You are walking in a crowded subway station when suddenly a large, hairy man approaches you. In his left hand is book containing the prophecies of Nostradamus. In his right is a can of chicken noodle soup. Will the man kill you or simply ask you for directions? Can you divine the future?

In December 1999, British researchers developed a means for foretelling the future actions of criminals in public places. In particular, they invented a sophisticated new surveillance system that may someday be routinely used to inform police and security officers about crimes before they even occur.[1,2] For example, people thinking about shoplifting, raping a woman, mugging someone, carjacking, or committing suicide behave differently from others, and their actions can be predicted mathematically. Although it is still preliminary, the system designed by Steve Maybank of the University of Reading in southern England and David Hogg at the University of Leeds in the north of the country, has great potential. The system will be connected to closed circuit televisions and send an alarm to authorities if it sees something suspicious. Perhaps in the future we will live in a world where machines can predict our every move. If criminals try to hide from security cameras by lurking in shadows, the easier it is for the "electronic diviner" to find them and foretell their behavior. In fact, the diviner can already spot people contemplating suicide by analyzing previous cases that show that suicidal people behave in a characteristic way before throwing themselves in front of trains. They tend to wait for at least ten minutes on the platform, missing trains before taking their last few tragic steps.

This ultrascientific method of foretelling the future contrasts with many of the stranger and older methods presented in this book. I would guess that you readers range from pure skeptics to true believers, even for some of the more exotic methods such as tarot cards, crystal-ball and entrail reading, and the *I Ching*. Skeptics say that the ancient divination methods only *appear* to work because of the querent's will to believe when presented with ambiguous stimuli. In other words, the methods often function as a psychoanalyst or cleric. They both allow the querent to ask many questions and then let the querrent interpret broad comments in whatever ways that best fits the querent's needs. When the querent receives information, he or she may bring up subconscious information and apply general results so that some information will turn out to be true. For example, I have performed hundreds of tarot card readings for colleagues. Everyone seems to enjoy the readings (even scientists), because the tarot cards seem to function as colorful inkblots that open a door to unconscious feelings while lubricating any conversations about personal issues.

Some of you may believe that astrology and related methods provide useful information via some paranormal connection. The question for you is where to draw the line. If you believe in astrology, then what about reading the features of sheep guts or holes in cheese? Today, in some parts of the United States, pregnant women still hang teaspoons on a string in front of their bellies in order to foretell the unborn child's sex. I doubt many of you would accept this as an accurate approach to prediction.

Finally, even if you do believe that some methods open secret doors to the unconscious or even a parallel universe, I'd bet you would enjoy knowing about ways in which fraud or subconscious deception have played a roll in the history of divination. I have performed a few studies on this subject and noticed that there is a strong desire, a fervent will to believe, even when the divination method uses trickery. Therefore, in this section I present a sampling of several scientific studies and commentaries that I think you will find exciting. I don't claim to have all the solutions to the myriad mysteries of the paranormal. But here are a few possible answers.

Keep in mind that a recent newspaper survey of readers of Great Britain's *Daily Telegraph* revealed that nearly 60 percent of the 6,238 respondents believed in the paranormal. Of the women sampled, 70 percent believed in paranormal, compared with 48 percent of the men.[3] Gallup polls indicate that America's overall belief in people's ability to predict the future has remained at about 26 percent since 1990.[4]

## ᚱ THE ELECTRONIC AGE

> *Salvador Dali once exploded a bomb filled with nails against a copper plate, producing a striking but random pattern. Many other artists have also utilized explosives in their work, but the results have generally been unpredictable.*
> —Robert Punkford, *Scientific American*, 1989

For the past few centuries, people have turned to card readers, astrologers, and others who claimed to be able to read the future. In our Electronic Age, the curious have picked up their phones and dialed "psychic networks" for insights into the future. Similarly, the Internet has permitted people to experiment with divination more conveniently than in the days of entrail reading or oracle consultation at Delphi in Greece. Some have called the Internet "the shaman of the late 20th century,"[5] because it satisfies our desire for quick gratification, supplying answers, right or wrong, for many questions. A quick perusal of the Internet's World Wide Web reveals a wonderful and sometimes whacky world of divination. There is rune reading. There are stichomancy Web sites that that allow people to ask questions and read a random passage from a book to gain insight (http://Facade.com/attraction/stichomancy). There are electronic Magic 8-Balls, electronic fortune cookies (see my own at http://www.pickover.com), and all kinds of software. By examining the Web, you can definitely see a resurgence of interest in all things spiritual and psychic. There are 1–900 phone psychics, cards, crystals, and digital crystal balls. Occasionally, people do get in trouble for alleged fraud. For example, in the late 1990s, the attorney general of New Mexico filed an eleven-count civil lawsuit against an Albuquerque firm that claimed its products could detect ghosts and speak to animals. One device, which sold for $395, was found to be mostly videocassette boxes containing a plastic board that looked like a circuit board, and some wiring.[6]

## ⊲ WHEN IS PROPHECY REAL?

*The job of an artist is always to deepen the mystery.*

—Francis Bacon

Many of the divination techniques in this book, such as astrology, tarot cards, and palmistry, are usually designed to answer the questions of individuals and predict the fate of individuals. Whom will I marry? Will I live a long life? Should I punch my boss in the nose? The questions and answers are centered on the individual. As mentioned in the introduction, when prediction is applied to a larger group, such as an entire race or our planet, we often refer to it as "prophecy."[7] Because Nostradamus predicted the fate of nations, we call him a prophet. Because Jesus predicted global changes and matters that affected the spiritual disposition the entire planet, we call him a prophet.

In general, prophecies fall into two categories: (1) precise and capable of falsification, or (2) general and nonfalsifiable.[8] By falsifiable, I mean that a prophecy is stated in such a way that it is capable of being proved false if false. Scientific statements are generally falsifiable. So are statements like, "On January 5, in the year 2010, the president will be shot in the right arm with a bullet." An example of a general, unfalsafiable prophecy is, "Invisible spirits will be watching the moral people on Earth this month." Because human language has shades of meaning, it is often difficult to distinguish between falsifiable and unfalsifiable predictions. At the risk of alienating some of my readers, perhaps the most famous and blurred prophecy is the one attributed to Jesus by Mark. Jesus's return (sometimes referred to as the Second Coming) is predicted to occur within the lifetime of some of Jesus's contemporaries. According to Mark 13:14–30, Jesus appears to give a falsifiable prophecy that his return would be seen and acknowledged by the whole world and that it would happen before that generation passes away:

> The sun shall be darkened, and the moon shall not give her light, and the stars shall be falling from heaven, and the powers that are in the heavens shall be shaken. And then shall they see the Son of man coming in clouds with great power and glory. And then shall he send forth the angels, and shall gather together his elect from the four winds, from the uttermost part of the earth to the uttermost part of heaven. . . . Verily I say unto you: This generation shall not pass away, until all these things be accomplished. Heaven and earth shall pass away, but my words shall not pass away.

According to Matthew 24:34, Jesus urges his followers to watch and be ready. There was no knowing when the Lord would come, but he would surely come very soon. As generations passed and expectations of the end were not fulfilled, reflections about what Jesus meant became more complicated and less urgent. Of course, many might argue that the words Jesus used were metaphors, and therefore the prophecy becomes unfalsifiable. Some modern historical critics have suggested the possibility that Jesus was not even the source of the prophetic saying attributed to him concerning the end of the ages.[9,10] Other authors have placed various interpretations on the words "this generation" in Jesus's proclamation. Author Hal Lindsay suggests that a biblical generation might refer to forty to eighty years, and that the clock began ticking the day Israel become a nation.[11]

As we discussed in chapter 2, in the mid-nineteenth century, William Miller suggested that the Second Coming would occur in the spring of 1884. When this did not occur, he and his followers revised the prophecy to October 1884. When this did not happen, Miller and his followers concluded that Christ had returned to an invisible heavenly sanctuary, and that his coming to Earth was imminent.

All this interest in falsifiable and unfalsiable prophecies eventually led to my "Antinoüs Prophecies" described in the next section.

## ⋈ THE ANTINOÜS PROPHECIES: A NOSTRADAMOID PROJECT

> *Thinking is more interesting than knowing, but less interesting than looking.*
> —Wolfgang von Goethe

Michel de Nostredame, better known as Nostradamus (1503–1566), was a French astrologer and physician, the most widely read seer of the Renaissance. As we discussed in chapter 2, Nostradamus began making prophecies around the year 1547, which he published in 1555 in a book titled *Centuries*. The work consisted of rhymed quatrains grouped in hundreds, each set of 100 called a "century." Some of his prophecies appeared to be fulfilled, and his fame became so widespread that he was invited to the court of Catherine de Médicis, queen consort of Henry II of France, where he cast the horoscopes of her children.

I call the attribution of meaning to imprecise, poetic phrases "the Nostradamus effect," and I have long been curious to determine if the Nostradamus effect could be simulated with random quatrains. For example, could it be that Nostradamus's quatrains were like ink blots—not really fore-telling anything but permitting humans to fit future history to rather nebu-lous poems? To test this theory, I composed the following quatrains of gib-berish just by letting my mind wander and writing the first images that came to my mind. As far as I was concerned, they had no particular meaning or significance. Nostradamus looked into a glass flask of steaming liquid to inspire his visions. I looked into the shiny glass of my computer's CRT. He may have sought to predict the future. I sought to write random phrases with absolutely no correspondence to historical events.

After composing the quatrains, I asked people to match my quatrains with actual historical happenings. I called the quatrains the "Quatrains of Antinoüs," which sounded and looked suitably exotic, especially with the umlaut ü symbol. The randomized quatrains are listed in the following table. Judge for yourself. Did I actually channel a man named Antinoüs? Could I be the next Nostradamus, "the Nostradamus from New York"? If my prophe-cies actually do predict future events, I hope a hundred years from now people will remember me. . . .

## THE ANTINOÜS PROPHECIES, IN QUATRAIN FORM

1. After the skirmish, one is wounded
   the other dies.
   The great white one sings by the fire of
   night.
   The European does not rise but merely
   flies
   Near the water, near the cross and
   knight.

2. An ape came from North, cool and
   damp.
   The stegosauri cry, poe, poe, loe.
   My rear end hurts beneath the lamp
   Thirty thousand opalescent hearts are
   low.

3. From the edge America, even as
   north,
   A child, the rock, is born with an amber
   heart.
   The change is nearly as the fourth:
   Sea, land, a victory, and a cart.

4. The robber of the west, not of silver
   but gold
   Places the caldron on darkening wine
   Smoke is often less than sold
   In a Latin furnace, like a hash, like a
   line.

5. Princess Charlene in Italy
   With a trinity of peppers.
   The white dove is a bee.
   A hat does not hurt lepers.

6. The capuchin, covered with water
   Some holy music, England, after a rain
   Sees nothing but the bone daughter
   And she, the long one, is in pain.

7. He will be betrayed by a lost friend,
He will leave through feigned desire,
She will be united twice until the end
Near the buildings, desert, and melted
    mire.

9. The dark head causes problems for
    the small king.
As much good as Asia, the winged, had
    done. There are the enemies, three,
    a ring,
The exiles scream, while J., the wires,
    do not shun.

8. Lightning comes near the peninsula,
    and one will swim.
There is ruin, Lester, but all is not lost
From the steel and silica brim
Blood, and water, but not at cost.

Some of the people I surveyed considered the idea that these nine prophecies of Antinoüs may have been actual ancient prophecies. For some reason, quatrain 8 generated a lot of interest. Marsha S., a respondent from California, suggested quatrain 8 prophesied

> the Loma Prieta earthquake back in 1989 when the Bay Bridge broke and everyone had to drive around to get into the city. The doggone thing began in the Santa Cruz mountains . . . "silica" refers to Silicon Valley.

Mike V., from Colorado State University, writes to me:

> Quatrain 8 describes the asteroid impact 65 million years ago that is thought to have killed off the dinosaurs. Here is my logic. (1) *Lightning comes near the peninsula, and one will swim*: An observer near the impact site might see the streaking meteor as it ablated in the atmosphere as lightning. The impact crater is in the Yucatan peninsula. The Chicxulub impact would create massive ocean waves that would wash inland, thus the "one will swim." (2) *There is ruin, Lester, but all is not lost:* The comet caused a huge crater, tidal waves, firestorms, and airborne ash that blocked the sun for years. The dinosaurs went extinct, as did over 80 percent of life on Earth. (*Not all is lost.*) Life went on, and the small furry mammals that survived led eventually to ourselves. (3) *From the steel and silica brim / Blood, and water, but not at cost*: The impact fused the silicates and sand in to a crust around the edge of the crater. If the impact object was a stony carbonaceous chondrite there would be silicates all over the impact site. If it was nickel iron, the site would be ridden with nickel, and iron, which is a component of steel. *Blood and water* refers further to the death and destruction caused by the impact. I cannot think of any reason for "but not at cost" except to fill out the rhyme.

Another respondent, computer scientist David G. from Lexington, Kentucky, said, "All of these seem to be very prophetic!" This respondent suggested that quatrain 1 foretells the demise of IBM. The first line "After the skirmish, one is wounded the other dies," refers to the fight between IBM and Microsoft. The respondent wrote to me:

> IBM's operating system, OS/2 was killed by the fight, and, although Microsoft's Windows was wounded, it survived. Microsoft, being the great white hope, at least, initially, sings the praises of their Windows operating system in a world darkened by IBM. Microsoft, who's president is of European heritage, flies into market domination from their location in Redmond, Washington (near the water), and takes over the world. I'm a little confused by the "cross and knight" reference. Could it refer to a chess board?

Denise W. wrote to me suggesting that the first quatrain refers to the wreck of the *Titanic*:

> The skirmish could refer to the actual collision. The "great white one" is the iceberg that have struck the ship; it would have been "wounded" the crash. The reference to the European refers to a flag that floats on the water in the aftermath. The cross and knight may represent some of the remaining wreckage or perhaps survivors in rafts.

Bill W. suggests that quatrain 1 refers to Moby Dick killing captain Ahab and his crew in the novel *Moby Dick*.

Tom R. suggests that the first quatrain refers to King Arthur Pendragon, and that the first line refers to the battle of Camlan where Arthur fought his son half-nephew Mordred and impaled Mordred on a lance, while Mordred managed to mortally wound Arthur. Line 2 refers to Arthur's flag, which was a red dragon on a field of white. Line 3 refers to Arthur's having united Britain against the Romans. After Arthur died, various conflicts arose regarding succession to the throne. Line 4 refers to Arthur's corpse being laid to rest near a lake, and the term "the cross" refers to his famous sword. The knight is his retainer who threw the sword back into the lake.

L. R. writes regarding quatrain 1:

> The first quatrain refers to the American War of Independence. "After the skirmish" refers to the war between the colonies and England. "One is wounded the other dies" represents America coming to power and the abo-

lition of English rule. "The great white one sings by the fire of night" represents America celebrating Independence Day with bonfires and fireworks. "Near the water, near the cross and knight" signifies the souls of the English and the remnants of their pride—all slowly returning to England as they feel defeat deep down in their weary bones.

Mike F. suggested that quatrain 2

> refers to the Carthaginian general Hannibal (247 B.C.E.–183 B.C.E.) who commanded the Carthaginian forces against Rome in the Second Punic War. The phrase "came from the North, cool and damp" refers to him crossing the Alps to attack Italy. The stegosauri (dinosaurs) are a metaphor for the large elephants Hannibal brought with him. "Poe" refers to the Po River to which the Romans rushed to protect the recently founded Roman colonies of Placentia and Cremona. "Rear end hurts" refers to the Allobroges, a Celtic tribe that attacked Hannibal's troops from the rear as they marched to Rome. Thirty thousand refers to the number of infantry.

When I looked up the Punic War in a history book, I found that there was only 20,000 infantry. When I told the respondent this, he replied that "the quatrain refers to all the hearts in: 20,000 infantry, 6,000 cavalry, 38 surviving elephants, and miscellaneous pack animals which might every well produce a sum close to thirty thousand." Other respondees thought this predicted the occurrence of Yeti or Bigfoot.

L. R. writes regarding quatrain 2:

> The second quatrain predicts the fall of the Jews under Hitler. "An ape came from North, cool and damp" refers to Hitler. "The stegosauri cry, poe, poe, loe" represents the Jews crying from the soul of a whole being annihilated. "My rear end hurts beneath the lamp" refers to the torture that was inflicted upon the Jews. "Thirty thousand opalescent hearts are low" refers to Jewish deaths.

Jessie G., age twelve, had this to say about quatrain 3:

> Quatrain 3, with phrases like "From the edge America, even as north," refers to the pilgrims landing at Plymouth rock. "The change is nearly as the forth" means the Fourth of July signing of the declaration of independence. "Sea, land, a victory, and a cart" refers to how the American revolution was won, because we fought the British in the sea, and on land. I don't know what a cart stands for.

Jack H., an electrical engineer from Portland, Oregon, suggested that quatrain 3 predicts Henry Ford and his impact on society. Jack writes to me:

> The first line, "From the edge America, even as north," predicts Henry Ford's birth in Dearborn, Michigan. The line, "A child, the rock, is born with an amber heart," gives us the message that Ford would have a gold heart and show stability in his personal relationships. Although Ford was not a saint, he was a family man and basic good guy as evidenced by the commission of the Oscar II in 1915, the ship he used for his pacifist expedition to Europe to try and end WWI, and the Ford Foundation and Ford hospital. The most significant item is in the fourth line, "Sea, land, a victory, and a cart." "Sea" refers to the ship Oscar II; "land" refers to Ford's tractor company; "a victory" refers to Ford's factories during World War I and II that produced planes, jeeps, tanks, and munitions; and "cart" refers to the first mass produced cars.

Computer scientist Dave G. comments about quatrain 3:

> This is another reference to the victory by Microsoft over IBM. Microsoft, located at the edge of America, specifically in the northern part of America, is led by Bill Gates, who was regarded as a child programming prodigy, and who's heart is not blue (e.g., not Big Blue, which is IBM). The change referred to is the domination of the software industry, which occurred with the fourth release of Windows (e.g., Windows 95). The victory is over software running in computers on land, and also on the sea (as witnessed by the Navy's tests of using Windows to control their modern ships). The victory represents Microsoft's domination of the software industry, and the cart refers to the cart that Bill Gates needs to carry his profits (e.g., money) with.

Michael D. writes regarding quatrain 3:

> Quattrain 3 may refer to the war of 1812. "From the edge America" refers to the fact that one of the final battles of that war, fought near New Orleans, was actually on the "edge," or border, of our country. "Even as north" means that this battle, like in the North (which was won by the USA, thereby ending the war, months before the Battle of New Orleans), would be a victory. "A child, the rock" may be referring to Stonewall Jackson, the general who won that famous battle. The victory for America over the British was "nearly as the fourth" of July, of which the comparison is obvious. Also, this final battle (along with many other parts of the war) was won by Americans in both land and sea.

Bill W. Suggests that quatrain 3 refers to the Mount Rushmore National Memorial in the Black Hills of southwestern South Dakota. Huge sculptures of the heads of presidents George Washington, Thomas Jefferson, Abraham Lincoln, and Theodore Roosevelt are carved in granite on the northeast side of Mt. Rushmore. Other respondees thought quatrain 3 refereed to Christopher Columbus.

Some respondees thought quatrain 4 predicted the rise of Hitler. Mike M. suggests that quatrain 4 refers to the Spanish Conquistadors who came to South America and plundered the gold from the native people. The smoke refers to the tobacco that was discovered in the new world and traded for slaves. Dave G. interprets quatrain 4:

> This is another reference to Microsoft replacing IBM as the dominating force in the software industry. The robber again refers to the wealthy Bill Gates, who lives in the western part of the country (Washington state). The reference to gold and not silver represents the high prices charged by Microsoft for its Windows operating system. The caldron refers to the software development process, and the placing of this on the darkening wine refers to Microsoft's techniques dominating the research being performed by IBM at places like its Almaden Research facility (and, Almaden is also famous for its vineyards, thus the reference to darkening wine). Smoke refers to software, which has no physical properties (e.g., vapor), and the reference to "often less than sold" refers to software licensing (e.g., the process of charging for the use of software without the actual transfer of a title to the software). The hash represents a symbol used in programming, and the reference to a line refers to a line of code.

Lea Z. felt quatrain 5 referred Mother Theresa; however, Clark P. has his own ideas about the meaning behind quatrain 5:

> "Charlene" was said to be a code for Charlemange, king of the Franks (768–814), king of the Lombards (774–814), and emperor (800–814). The line "Princess Charlene in Italy" refers to Charlemange's conquering the Lombard kingdom in Italy. The "trinity of peppers" refers to Charlemange's father, Pepin III. The white dove is pope Leo III who crowned Charlemange. The "hat" is the crown.

Laura T. writes regarding quatrain 5:

> The third line, "The white dove is a bee" refers to Bernard of Clairvaux, who, along with Ambrose, used bee and beehive imagery when referring to the Church and faith. Bernard actually said that the "bee" was the Holy

Spirit, which of course would be the "white dove." Line 2, "With a trinity of peppers," may refer to the Jews, Muslims, and Christians of Jerusalem. There was some friction between the groups, and a "pepper" can certainly be an irritant. Bernard was a major factor behind the Second Crusade (1146–1148). As to the fourth line, "A hat does not hurt lepers," a "hat" can symbolize power and religious orders. "Hat" may be a reference to Pope Eugenius III, who approved of Bernard's Crusade. Lepers lose their limbs and are sequestered from society; similarly, the men who enter a monastery cast off items and are part of an enclosed society. Bernard was a leader of the Knights Templar, and so the "hat," being the Pope, would not stand in the way of the efforts ("harm") of the "lepers", namely the Knights. The possible meaning of the first line, "Princess Charlene in Italy," has eluded me (a royal female descendent of Charlemagne?). So, in a nutshell, I think quatrain 5 refers to the Second Crusade.

Lea Z. felt that quatrain 6 referred Lady Diana Spencer. Dave G. comments about quatrain 6:

Quatrain 6 refers to the demise of IBM at the hands of Microsoft. One definition of capuchin is of a South American monkey with the hair on its head in the form of a crown. This refers to the pointy haired managers of IBM going under water (sinking) in their business struggles. The holy music refers to the "Start Me Up" song by the Rolling Stones used in Microsoft's Windows 95 announcement. IBM has a headquarters in England. After the fight between IBM and Microsoft (the rain), there is nothing but IBM divisions reduced to starvation (bone), with the S/390 division (the long one) suffering the most.

Lea Z. said that quatrain 7 refers to John F. Kennedy Jr. and his wife and also sister Caroline. Bill W. suggests that quatrain 7 refers to "Jesus and the resurrection." Other respondees also thought this referred to Jesus. Judi L. writes, "I believe quatrain 7 refers to Cleopatra and her associations with Cesar and Marc Antony." Quatrain 8 was thought to be associated with the Cherynobyl nuclear disaster.

Some people thought that quatrain 9 described World War III. Dave G. comments about quatrain 9:

This quatrain indicates that Bill Gates ("the dark head") causes trouble for IBM (the small king). The reference to Asia refers to the offshore computer manufacturers, and how the cheap Asian computer clones have helped Microsoft dominate the software market. But, despite the good done by the clone makers, there are enemies, such as the governments antitrust suit.

The government is specifically referred to here as the "three" for the three branches of government, and also as the "ring" since the three parts are all interlocked. The "exiles" refer to non-Microsoft software developers, and J refers to the Justice department. However, despite the screaming, the Justice department does not cause problems for Microsoft, which continues to take over ("do not shun") the Internet ("the wires").

Bill W. suggests that quatrain 9 refers to the "axis powers of World War II."

As you can see, many of the historical interpretations provided by respondents reflect our modern minds reacting to amorphous poetry. Nostradamus's prophecies tend to be general and unordered. This makes it difficult to say when a particular quatrain has missed or hit its mark. Judge for yourself. Many Web sites contain Nostradamus's prophecies, and there are a number of excellent books that delve into their possible meanings or non-meanings.[12]

I've also randomly scrambled real Nostradamus quatrains in order to conduct future experiments to see if people can easily find "meaning" in them. Although I've done the scrambling by hand, I suggest future researchers write computer programs that randomly select lines from quatrains to make computer-generated "Nostradamemes" or "Nostradamlets."

It would be interesting to rigorously determine if the Nostradamus prophecies yielded more historical matches than the Antinoüs prophecies. This would be difficult to assess because of the difficulty of assigning a correctness estimate to the unfalsifiable prophecies. One test would be to determine which prophecies elicited the most similar historical interpretations by different interpreters.

I look forward to additional interpretations that you might solicit from friends regarding the Antinoüs prophecies. I'd like to create a big collection of possible meanings. In any case, anyone who thinks that Nostradamus truly predicted the future should realize that his focus on France made him miss some of the most earth-shattering happenings in the centuries after his death: from the American civil war to Darwin's theory of evolution.

Incidentally, there really existed an "Antinoüs," although only one of my respondents realized this. Antinoüs (110 B.C.E.–130 C.E.) was the homosexual lover of the Roman emperor Hadrian, and they traveled together on many journeys throughout the Mediterranean world. While the two were visiting Egypt, Antinoüs drowned in the Nile. Hadrian loved Antinoüs so much that when Antinoüs died, Hadrian deified him. Hadrian erected temples to him all over the empire and founded a city, named Antinoöpolis in his honor, near the place of his death. Many sculptures, gems, and coins survive depicting Antinoüs as a model of youthful beauty.

Finally, Linda Z. from Canada was perceptive in her analysis recognizing the possible identity of Antinoüs. She writes:

> Many of the places and people mentioned in your "Antinoüs Quatrains" would have been inconceivable in the era of Hadrian and Antinous. Such anachronistic terms include "knight," "America," and "stegosauri." Even though the verses are supposed to be prophecy, they clearly are not couched in the language of Roman times. From this I surmise that you refer to a different Antinoüs, or that the "prophecies" are a more recent forgery. I sense the stench of computer-generated verse. I looked a little farther, and the only "Princess Charlene" I could find on the web was a llama! I suspect I'm on the right track. Nevertheless, here are my interpretations. Quatrain 3 refers with the phrase "the northern edge of America" refers to Canadian geography. The second line is a reference to Newfoundland, which is always called "the rock." The child with the amber heart refers to salmon. The third line, "the change is nearly as the fourth" clearly refers to the issuance of a new Canadian quarter, depicting native art from British Columbia. The fourth line with "sea, land" clearly refers to the Great Lakes; the victory could be the War of 1812, and the cart is clearly the Canadian Mint's online shopping cart where coin collectors worldwide can purchase the aforementioned new quarters.

## ⋈ CHERNIKOV DIVINATION EXPERIMENT

> *As for me, this mystery has been revealed to me, not because I have greater wisdom than other living men, but so that you, O king, may know the interpretation and that you may understand what went through your mind.*
> —Daniel 2:30

Although we often think of divination as referring to methods of predicting the future, it also refers to methods for determining secret knowledge, or gaining knowledge of any type through unknown means. In this later sense, "remote viewing" is a form of divination. *Remote viewing* generally refers to the alleged ability of some individuals to observe, through paranormal means, an object or drawing hidden from view. The World Wide Web is filled with courses, teachers, institutes, and associations devoted to remote viewing. For example, psychic researchers Ingo Swann and Harold Sherman claim to have done remote viewing of Mercury and Jupiter.[14] Dr. Russell Targ and Dr. Harold Puthoff studied Swann and Sherman, and reported that their remote viewing sketches compared favorably to the findings of the

Mariner 10 and Pioneer 10 research spacecrafts. However, skeptics are not impressed by the these remote viewing experiments, saying that many of the remotely viewed images are not accurate and others could easily be made by researching astronomy books.

The CIA and the U.S. Army, however, were sufficiently impressed by the idea of remote viewing to spend millions of taxpayers' dollars on research programs such as "Stargate" that tried to use psychics for locating Libya's Gadhafi and a missing airplane in Africa. The CIA may still be studying remote viewing or other divinatory methods to determine their usefulness to the intelligence community.

**Figure 70.** The Chernikov target picture described using 75 words. From Edmund Gillon, *Geometric Design and Ornament* (New York: Dover, 1969), p 141. Illustrations first published in Russia in 1930.

At one time as many as sixteen psychics worked for the government.

David Morehouse, a highly decorated army officer, describes the government's program for remote viewing in his book *Psychic Warrior*. Wounded by machine gunfire during a training mission, Morehouse began to have strange and haunting nightmares. This experience redirected his military career and landed him in the government's top secret Stargate program for remote viewing.[15,16,17]

I decided to carry out a little experiment of my own that may relate to interpreting the results of remote viewing experiments.[18,19] In particular, I sought to test the ability of words to describe a graphic diagram. My original goal had nothing to do with remote viewing, but I was fascinated by the degree to which initial results could have been improperly construed as evidence for remote viewing ability. The exercise should be easily repeated by teachers in college and secondary school settings.

Limiting myself to a seventy-five-word description, I asked people who had never seen a particular design to draw the target picture in figure 70 from the following description:

> There are four quarter-sized circles arranged so they touch. They are on top of one larger circle with a thick edge, and cover the circle slightly. Inside

---

### ℧ **Some Colorful Predictions**

If intelligent beings from outer space were to ask us about the effects of various scenarios on our world, which of the following would have the most profound effect?

◆ A child genius stuns judges at a seventh-grade science fair when he presents a working time machine made from parts of a microwave oven.
◆ Scientists discover a beneficial virus that can turn ordinary rocks into protein-rich food. Experts predict the find will lead to the end of world hunger.
◆ A meteor the size of a Buick strikes a used car dealership in Las Vegas. No one is injured in the crash, but the crater opens up a vast underground reservoir of drinking water, solving the desert town's water shortage.
◆ A volcanic eruption creates a new land mass that ties the United States to Cuba.
◆ Frog legs become the rage in fast-food restaurants.
◆ Scientists discover rapidly mutating bees, uncovering evidence that the insects are developing an intelligence that may one day rival that of humans.

When I first asked colleagues this question, most did not realize that all of these ideas, from the seventh-grader building a time machine to the mutating bees, came from psychic predictions printed in tabloid newspapers. The predictions were supposed to come true in 1995. Sources: *National Enquirer, National Examiner,* and *Weekly World News.*[13]

---

each of the four circles is a black dot which touches the edge of each of the circles. The four circles also contain six circles inside them. The six circles get smaller and smaller, but all of their edges touch the black dot.

I called the target diagram a "Chernikov pattern" after the Russian mathematician/artist who has cataloged hundreds of such simple geometrical designs. Notice in my description that I limited myself to nonmathematical terms when describing the target picture. The survey was conducted using the electronic computer mail networks, and participants included scientists, programmers, and administrators.

Although the short, ambiguous description should not have been sufficient for anyone to accurately reproduce the Chernikov pattern, many colleagues were amazed to see the first design (see figure 71) sent to me by Robert Guth of San Jose which came incredibly close to the target image (see figure 70). One colleague even said, "It looks like ESP."

However, as I started to compile a collection of figures, it became clear that a better explanation for the uncanny resemblance was that among hundreds of responses I was very likely to get a few that were close to the original target! This became apparent as additional guesses were sent to me. This little exercise demonstrates that researchers should be careful not to be

VARIATION 1 VARIATION 2

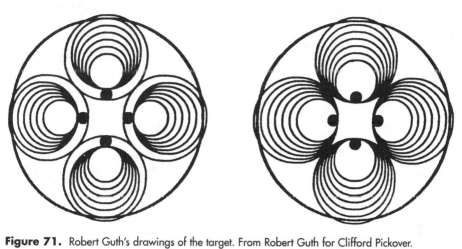

**Figure 71.** Robert Guth's drawings of the target. From Robert Guth for Clifford Pickover.

mislead when initial results appear startling—and also obviously not to stop an experiment prematurely before a large sample is taken.

For readers' interest, I include some of the many drawings I received to show the range of results (see figure 72). I reduced the respondents' original diagrams by a uniform amount to fit in so many example figures. Each diagram represents a different respondent's attempt to draw the target according to my description.

This Chernikov target experiment provides an infinite number of possible future experiments. Here are just a few ideas, and I would be interested in hearing from any readers who have conducted the following tests with the Chernikov target figure:

- How would different people describe, using no more than seventy-five words, the Chernikov target figure in figure 70? Perhaps some readers could construct much more accurate descriptions that would therefore improve respondents' diagrams.
- Create a catalog of figures, such as in figure 70 with different numbers of words allowed to describe the target figure. For example, what would pictures look like if only a fifty-word description were allowed? What would respondents' pictures look like if only twenty-five words were allowed? What would pictures look like if 500 words were allowed?
- Conduct an experiment where you take the worst representation (that is, the picture most different from the target), and use this as a *new*

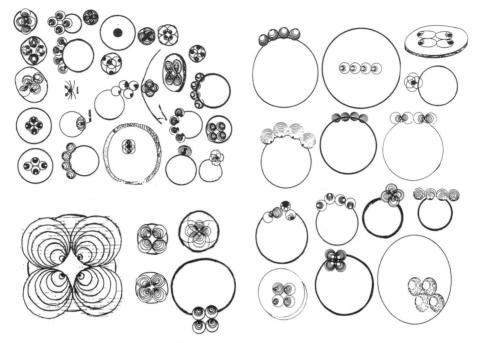

**Figure 72.** A variety of drawings of the target from many different individuals.

target for another experiment. Continue to propagate the error until the first target bears no resemblance to the new images. How many generations of selecting the least accurate representation would this require?

## ᛉ THE JÖRMUNGAND ENCOUNTER

> *The Lord will afflict you with madness, blindness and confusion of mind.*
> —Deuteronomy 28:28

Prophecy and clairvoyance are so widely believed by millions of people that magicians are credited with psychic powers that not even Nostradamus would dare claim. In fact, a lot of "ESP magic tricks," "mind-reading tricks," or "mental magic" is as much trickery as pulling a rabbit out of a hat. Mental magic doesn't even take as much manipulative skill as other kinds of magic. Yet performers recognize mentalism as one of the most challenging and rewarding branches of show business. Mental magic demands flamboyant showmanship—especially because so many of the methods are astonishingly crude and easy to execute.[20]

Despite the fact that it is relatively easy to fool your friends with mental magic, magic shops are more likely to stock blueprints for making a lion vanish than literature on thought divination.[21] Books on mentalism are usually privately printed for sale by a small number of dealers catering to the professional trade. In this section, I tear aside the veil and reveal just one of the secrets of telepathy, prediction, and other divinatory "powers." By explaining this most simple of tricks, I hope this section will open many eyes and prepare readers to analyze carefully any astonishing claims of divination that might cross their paths.

I conducted this "ESP Test" on the World Wide Web at http:// www.pickover.com, and I called it the "Jörmungand Encounter." I added all sorts of distractions to make the "test" seem more mystical. I used the term "Jörmungand" again to give the experiment an exotic sound, and I doubt many respondents realized that the word referred to Thor's chief enemy, the world serpent Jörmungand, a symbol of evil. According to tradition, Thor failed to smash the skull of Jörmungand, and the two are destined to kill each other in the Ragnarök (the end of the world of gods and men). I also misled respondents by saying that the test worked 98 percent of the time, although in actuality it had to be 100 percent correct.

Here's how it worked. To "prime" the system, respondents selected one of three tarot cards. (The choice of card had no significance or effect.) Next, the respondent had to pick a single card from the following set of playing cards. Try it yourself. Select one of the cards below and say it out loud to help you remember it. (In the computer version, people are specifically asked not to touch the card or point to it with a mouse.)

#### Choose A Card. You Must Say It Out Loud.

Once respondents selected a card in their minds and said it out loud, they were than asked to select from a set of six blinking eyeballs:

(The choice of eyeball had no significance.) For the grand finale, the computer next displayed a set of five cards, with their card removed. It works every time. Additionally, the final page with the set of four cards has various distracting graphics and the enigmatic words "Quantum consistency" followed by a random number. Here is a sample. Did I remove your card?

### I Have Removed Your Card!

Amazing, isn't it? If you don't see how this was done, try it on friends and they will give you the answer. I'm not the first person on the Web to try simple tricks of this sort, but I may have been the first to catalog all of the odd suggestions for how the trick worked. It's a simple trick, and although many people wrote to me and understood the trick, I received many dozens of possible explanations for how the ESP test "worked." Here are just a sampling of explanations, excerpted so as to reduce space and just give you feel for the explanations. You may browse my Internet web site, www.pickover. com, for many dozens of unedited replies.

- *From Mike G.* The ESP experiment is awesome. I even tried thinking of one card, while quietly having selected another. Both disappeared! I have been interested in this phenomenon since 1968, when I corresponded with parapsychologist Dr. Joseph Banks Rhine at Duke University. Your results are significant and don't deteriorate over time. Emotional excitation does not even seem to interfere, as would be expected if one looks at Sufi literature. Therefore, there is a logical, non-paranormal quantum effect going on.
- *From Karen G.* I think your ESP experiment works because most people choose a card too quickly and don't give the computer sufficient time to randomly choose other cards. Also, people may tend to mouse-click on the side of the screen where their chosen card is located, so that the computer can eliminate some of the cards as potential choices.
- *From Linda W.* I think the ESP program works because the computer can guess your selection by monitoring which tarot card and blinking eye you select. There must be a formula that maps eye and tarot card selection to the card you selected.
- *From Larry S.* I viewed the computer source code and could not discover mathematical computations that would aid the web page in making a decision. Perhaps the computer scans eye movement and detects pupil dilation resulting from concentration.

- *From Tara R.* Quantum mechanics may permit synchronicity of thought and computer software. I suggest that, on the quantum level, you were able to predict the card I selected even before I selected it. It is also possible that my brain waves may influence your software. Although this seems far-fetched, we know that brain waves are detectable with SQUID (superconducting quantum interference devices.)

- *From Doug L.* Your ESP mechanism correctly determines the playing card I selected. Knowing that you have written a book on time travel, I suspect you have discovered a limited (but real) mechanism of modifying past events.

- *From Samantha F.* I believe you are able to determine which card I picked by the computer examining my eye movement and card location.

- *From Clay F.* One card flickers and subliminally calls your attention to it.

- *From Guy B.* I am quite impressed, Mr. Pickover. I generated random numbers using the Time of Day clock on my computer, and found the remainder when divided by 3 for the first number; took out the first business card that came to hand and took the first phone number on there modulo 6, and then located a calculator and had it generate a pseudo-random number which I then did modulo 6. I did the little experiment three times, and your program "got" it all times. I would like to study the Java computer code for the web page to learn more.

- *From Petri K.* Dear Cliff, I am from the Universtiy of Lapland, Finland. Your program removed several times the card I named, even though I spoke Finnish when naming the card. There are not many people in the Anglo-Saxon world who can read a Finno-Ugric mind that easily (or know any Finnish).

- *From Ben N.* Just another note to tell you how disturbed I am with the program's ability to determine my selection infallibly. I would like to be able to rule out subliminal flashes or influence due to the long distance phone choices and that as far as I know, subliminal effects are extremely lessened when the subject is aware that these are in operation. Are you able to detect the mysterious "visual rays" that are theorized to exist in the fringe sciences?

That's certainly enough feedback for you for now. I do not know the ratio of the number of people who understood this was a trick to those who thought it was some form of ESP. My goal in conducting this little demonstration was to emphasize how easily we can be fooled and how great our will is to believe in the spiritual, the paranormal, and phenomena beyond science. I hope this simple test reinforces the need for skeptical thinking when evaluating claims of the paranormal. There is certainly a need for better controls in parapsychological research and an even greater need for better public understanding of the difference between good and bad science. Martin Gardner in his book *Science: Good, Bad and Bogus* emphasizes the need for better evidence supporting research claims in such areas as precognition, biorhythms, ESP, psychokinesis, faith healing, and psychic surgery.[22] Given the proliferation of United States patents now being issued for inventions that rely on pseudoscience and unproven divination methods with life-threatening consequences, increased diligence becomes of utmost importance.[23,24]

## ⍋ CONTRADICTION AND CALAMITY

> *As you were lying there, O king, your mind turned to things to come, and the revealer of mysteries showed you what is going to happen.*
> —Daniel 2:29

None of the contradictory ideas or nonscientific thoughts expressed in this chapter should be of great surprise, because we have always had the capacity for accommodating two contradictory ideas in one mind. For example, in several sections of the book, I touched upon End of the World prophecies. Apocalyptic cultures are still with us despite the fact that the various End of the World predictions have always been wrong (see appendix 4). Six thousand new messianic cults were identified in Africa between the 1940s and the 1970s, and hundreds more in Japan and the Philippines.[25] Divination, like apocalyptic predictions of the End of the World, in some sense makes us feel good. It makes us feel important and in direct contact with God or gods. Eugen Weber, author of *Prophecies, Cults, and Millennial Beliefs through the Ages*, says:

> Endism provides powerful compensatory fantasies of escape from grim reality: escape or release by havoc, ruin, liquidation, devastation, annihilation. But why should one grim prospect attract more than another? Perhaps because it responds to profound human aspirations: to avoid death, to believe that decay is only a prelude to resurgence and revival. Perhaps because apocalyptic tragedy and terror transcend the banality of everyday, enhance trivial human lives, and suggest exhilarating depths beyond the treacherous shallows that surround us.[25]

James Alcock, a professor of psychology at Glendon Colege, York University, Toronto, suggests that our brain is a belief-generating machine that produces beliefs without any particular respect for what is real or true and what is not.[26] Perhaps this is why humans are so inclined to believe in the wide range of divination methods without scientific verification. Alcock says that this belief engine in our brains selects information from the environment, shapes it, combines it with information from memory, and produces beliefs that are generally consistent with beliefs already held. Evolution by natural selection does not select directly on the basis or reason or truth; it selects for reproductive success. A caveman might have been told by the tribal witch doctor that evil ancestral spirits will attack if the caveman leaves the cave at night. If the caveman is motivated by the search for truth, he may leave the cave at night, and get killed by a nocturnal carnivore. Compare the dead caveman with one who believes in ancestral evil spirits without question and is therefore more likely to live and reproduce. Seeking truth does not always promote survival, and erroneous belief can be beneficial.

Still, I continually wonder why natural disasters—such as floods, volcanos, and earthquakes—are foremost in the minds of not only the prophets of old, but the New Age channelers of today. And why not death by biological, atomic, and chemical warfare, for instance? The answer may be simple. Perhaps "natural" disasters in areas of high population density convey a heightened sense of danger, because the calamity is totally beyond human intervention. In principle, humans can hope to combat war and disease, but an earthquake is nearly unstoppable, even with our present technology. Prophets do occasionally predict good things, but these prophets don't get the press or attention that the ones predicting cataclysms do. Let's face it, how many times do you hear "happy" stories on the news? In any case, the ancient prophets' many predictions of doom partly reflected people's belief in a just God. The common person must have seen many examples of the proliferation of injustice and cruelty and expected a fair God to one day punish the bad and to put a dramatic end to all evil.

A skeptic might argue that modern prophets may have predicted physical calamities in order to emulate the most famous ancient prophets who prophesied destruction. For example, when St. Mark asked Jesus by what signs His Second Coming would be announced, Jesus said in Mathew 13:8, "There shall be earthquakes in divers places, and there shall be famines and troubles." In the Old Testament, the earthquake was God's traditional means of showing his anger.[27] In Isaiah, 29:6, Isaiah records that the city of Ariel "shalt be visited of the Lord of hosts with thunder, and with earthquake, and great noise . . . and the flame of devouring fire." Ezekiel says in Ezekiel 38:19, "In my zeal and fiery wrath I declare that at that time there shall be a great earthquake in the land of Israel." There are over a dozen references to earthquakes in the Old and New Testaments, again perhaps because they are phenomena that both rich and poor could understand but against which they had little defense. A modern psychic might on some level want to tap into the grand and majestic tradition of destruction that strikes fear in man to this day.

Daniel Cohen in *Waiting for the Apocalypse* also suggests that what prophets predict for the future is influenced by what they thought has happened in the past.[28] For a millennia, any Bible-believer already "knew" the world had once ended in the great flood of Genesis. And next to the biblical flood, the most widely discussed ancient catastrophe—out of Greek myth— is the purported sinking of the "lost continent" of Atlantis. Plato described Atlantis as an island larger than Asia Minor and Libya combined, and located just beyond the Pillars of Hercules (the Straits of Gibraltar). Eventually earthquakes were said to have sunk Atlantis. Although probably just a legend, European writers of the Middle Ages believed it to be true. Medieval map makers placed the island in the middle of the Atlantic Ocean. Some have suggested that Atlantis reflects ancient Egyptian records of a huge volcanic eruption on the island of Thera about 1500 B.C.E.[29] A large part of Thera sank into the sea. This eruption was accompanied by a series of numerous earthquakes and tsunamis that destroyed civilization on Crete.

You may recall from several examples in chapter 3 that the story of Atlantis is closely tied to doomsday predictions of the nineteenth century and new age; see, for example, the predictions of Edgar Cayce, Helena Blavatsky, Cheiro, Gordon-Michael Scallion, and others. From the actual eruption of Mt. Vesuvius in 79 C.E. that buried Pompeii to the actual earthquake in China in 1556 that killed nearly a million people, we can understand how prophets often held visions of impending calamity. Natural catastrophes of such a horrifying and lethal magnitude unquestionably capture the imagination of prophets and normal people alike.

〰 〰 〰

The following game may yield additional insight into the seeming accuracy of some prophecies. Gather a group of friends together. Tell one of the friends that he is the "querent." He is to leave the room while the remaining people choose a person in the room to describe a dream or vision that he or she has had. When the friend returns to the room, his goal is to guess the content of the dream as well as the name of the dreamer by asking yes/no-questions. However, when your querent friend is out of the room, tell your friends to actually answer "yes" or "no" according to some arbitrary rule. They will describe no dream or vision! For example, if the querent's question is more than five words long, the people should answer no, otherwise yes. Or you can simply oscillate answers in some memorable pattern, such as: no, yes, no, no, yes, yes. After may questions, the querent will "derive" a dream or vision, many times sexual in nature and associated with a particular person in the room, even though there was no original dream. It is as if the vision came from thin air, and it probably reflects something about the querent's state of mind. John Allen Paulos, professor of mathematics at Temple University, discusses this type of experiment and notes that the querent's preoccupations dictate his questions, which, even if answered negatively at first, will often receive a positive response in a later reformulation. These positive responses are then pursued.[30]

Paulos believes this kind of game explains why hazy descriptions in the *I Ching* or horoscopes seem to yield valid insight.[31] Again, the "insight" reflects the mind of the querent at the time he or she is asking questions. Because the *I Ching* and horoscope are vague, they permit the querent to create a relevant vision or prediction just like the person in the yes/no game creates information from nothingness. Perhaps projective tests, like Roschach inkblots, work in the same way, revealing information about the person observing the random structures. Society itself behaves in a similar manner. When news stories are incomplete or vague, people often fill in the missing pieces from their own perspective, which often reveals their own fears, hopes, and prejudices. For example, in 1995, reports of a bloodthirsty animal know as El Chupacabras ("the goat-sucker") spread from Puerto Rico to Mexico and the southern United States. The large-eyed, reptilian creature reportedly attacked domesticated animals, draining them of their blood. Subsequent research showed that the dead animals were not drained of blood, and stakeouts usually revealed the presence of wild dogs. The story of the supernatural (or extraterrestrial) chupacabras spread largely through mass hysteria, over-enthusiastic media reports, and people filling in the missing details with their own fantasies and dreams.

## Some Final Thoughts

*Laws of physics and mathematics are like a coordinate system that runs in only one dimension. Perhaps there is another dimension perpendicular to it, invisible to those laws of physics, describing the same things with different rules, and those rules are written in our hearts, in a deep place where we cannot go and read them except in our dreams.*

—Neal Stephenson, *The Diamond Age*

## DIVINATION AND THE BRAIN

*Now came a period of rapture so intense that the universe stood still. . . . I saw with intense inward vision the atoms or molecules, of which seemingly the universe is composed rearranging themselves, as the cosmos, in its continuous everlasting life, passing from order to order. What joy when I saw there was no break in the chain—not a link left out everything in its place and time. Worlds, systems, all blended into one harmonious whole.*

—Richard Maurice Bucke, *Cosmic Consciousness*

In this book, we've discussed a range of divination methods, from the relatively benign cheese divination (*tiromancy*) to the more ominous human sacrifice (*anthropomancy*). Although many of the more gory methods are no longer practiced, some still persist, particularly in Africa. For example, in 1999, three Ethiopians were sentenced to death for sacrificing a child partly for the purposes of divination, but mostly because they thought the sacrifice would chase away evil spirits. In particular, an

**389**

Ethiopian court sentenced a flour mill owner and a sorceress to death for murdering a seven-year-old girl in a witchcraft rite. The miller was so intent on getting rid of gremlins in his malfunctioning mill that he sought the advice of a local sorceress. The sorceress told him the only way to be free of the gremlins and make the mill operate properly was to sacrifice a little girl and sprinkle her blood on the floor of the mill. The sorceress then paid four people $2.40 each to kidnap a child and take her to the miller who slaughtered her.[1]

In a universe where the future seemed capricious and unpredictable, it is understandable that ancient humans craved a way to learn the fate the gods held in store for them. The divination methods provided a means of being in touch with knowledgeable, spiritual beings who could control the future. Divination freed our minds from a resignation of living in a shackled world.

For a long time, humans coaxed and pressured gods by magic, implored them in prayer, and tried pleasing them through sacrifice. But even if these divination approaches worked, even if there were gods listening to human cries to know the future, how might the gods have responded? As noted earlier, the gods might reveal the future in dreams or through a medium, or by writing their coded messages in intestinal patterns. Even skeptics today suggest that divination can sometimes provide a way to gain "insight," develop "intuition," or clear the mind by letting the subconscious suggest new paths. It enables creativity and imagination to flow.

In many cultures, gifted individuals are recognized as providing a link with worlds beyond ordinary human perception. Such people may transmit information of an oracle, as with the Greek Pythia, or may "see" the answers to questions, as demonstrated by a Tibetan with the power of "tra." It's possible that some of the prophets received their divinatory visions while in strange brain states. In chapter 3, I recounted the religious visions of St. Hildegard of Bingen (1098–1179), the prophetess known as the "Sibyl of the Rhine." Several scholars today suggest that Hildegard suffered from migraines, and that her visions were a result of this condition.[2] Hildegard's description of her visions, and her feelings right before the visions, point to classic symptoms of migraine sufferers. For example, Hildegard said she sometimes saw points of intense light and "extinguished stars." Similarly, migraine sufferers can experience scintillatingscotomata—the perception of flashing lights in one quadrant of the visual field. Hildegard also reported sickness, paralysis, and blindness, which are symptoms of migraines. After these problems pass, some people have feelings of euphoria. Oliver Sacks in *The Man Who Mistook His Wife for a Hat and Other Clinical Tales* says:

Among the strangest and most intense symptoms of migraine aura, and the most difficult of description and analysis, are the occurrences of feelings of sudden familiarity and certitude . . . or its opposite. Such states are experienced, momentarily and occasionally, by everyone; their occurrence in migraine auras is marked by their overwhelming intensity and relatively long duration.[3]

In my earlier book *Strange Brains and Genius*, I discuss how temporal lobe epilepsy (TLE)—unusual electrical activity in a certain area of the brain—may be responsible for a range of visions experienced by biblical and other prophets.[4] Recently, several TLE nuns have provided further evidence for TLE being at the root of many mystical religious experiences. For example, one former nun "apprehended" God in TLE seizures and described the experience:

Suddenly everything comes together in a moment—everything adds up, and you're flooded with a sense of joy, and you're just about to grasp it, and then you lose it and you crawl in to an attack. It's easy to see how, in a pre-scientific age, an epileptic or any temporal lobe fringe experience like that could be thought to be God Himself.[5]

Her experience is not that unusual.

Perhaps human brains are the only organs in the universe that permit individuals to ask questions like "What does our future hold?" "What conduct should we have in a critical situation? How long will our species survive?" "When will we walk on other planets?" "Where will Monica Lewinsky be in ten years?" In this book, we've examined numerous methods for glimpsing the future, including the *I Ching*, *feng-shui*, tarot, numerology, palmistry, and scrying. Many of the methods are still in use today and many have been afforded renewed significance by the New Age movement. Most divination methods were not simply techniques for predicting the future. They were also a means for gaining secret knowledge. Believers in divination suggest that there is a flow to the universe that can be understood and tapped through the chance production of symbols and patterns—from cracks in turtle shells to the random combinations of yarrow sticks, the flight of birds, and twists of intestines. By focussing on the patterns of cracks, lines, and motions, the ancient soothsayer sometimes entered a state of consciousness in which intuition enabled him to speak prophetically. People of the orient today still use temple block and sticks, spirit mediums, geomancy, and astrological divination. In Africa, there is significant use of Ifa divination. Since the 1950s, there has been an exponentially increasing interest in tarot cards and astrology. When discussing possible mechanisms for divination, some practitioners like to use scientific sounding terms like "quantum physics" and "synchronicity" (meaningful coincidences that link every part of the universe with every other). But it seems more relevant to focus on the human mind and the subconscious, because almost all divination relies heavily on the observer or querent giving meaning to the patterns and making creative interpretations. Because of this, divination can be a valid way to exercise the imagination and stimulate new ideas.

Many of the old methods, such as turtle-shell divination, are virtually extinct. The dream oracle sites are barely remembered for what they were. It will be fascinating to see what substitute methods will arise in this new century to replace the old divination methods. I don't think all the wild divination methods will become extinct or be totally replaced my more scientific approaches. Computers will be increasingly used for fortune telling, but because there will always be events outside our control, all kinds of divination approaches will be a part of humanity for as long as humans exist.

Divination will always be popular because *anything* that can be used to justify coming to a decision about an unresolved matter brings a sense of relief, reduces anxiety, and seems like a breakthrough or transformation. The divination process lets a little randomness into people's lives, which can be good for yielding fresh insights. On the other hand, using something like rune stones or the tarot to help make major decisions not only relieves people of the responsibility for the decisions, it might have profoundly dangerous consequences that could cause greater anxiety.

## THE PHYSICS OF PROPHECY

> If the future is a hologram whose every detail is already fixed it means that we have no freewill. We are just puppets of destiny moving mindlessly through a script that has already been written. Fortunately the evidence overwhelmingly indicates that this is not the case.
>
> —Michael Talbot, *The Holographic Universe*

Although I am a skeptical scientist at heart, I have used some ad hoc "divination" myself that has yielded some interesting results. For example, if I want an answer to a pressing question or am simply trying to locate something I misplaced, I sometimes focus on the problem when I go to sleep and often have the answer in the morning. I also keep a pad near the bed for jotting ideas that occur in the middle of the night. It seems that sometimes the subconscious has access to information that our conscious minds don't have, and sleep and dreams can occasionally be used to access that information. Sometimes I even perform abstract divination where, in my mind, I scatter dust and dirt into the wind and visualize the resultant color. The beauty of the resultant colors gives me ideas as to the favorableness of a certain action. For example, a pretty violet symmetrical pattern is favorable, but a muddy, dark, congealed mess is unfavorable. I know this one sounds quite weird, but again, it probably works because I subconsciously access information that doesn't quite break through into the conscious mind. The visualization method of spreading colored dust might seem difficult at first, but I routinely practice visualization methods as I go to sleep, such as rotating objects like horses in my mind or sinking in a black pool of liquid while looking up at the water surface until it becomes a bright white slit "miles" above me. I even use a form of divination to create patents. I make a list of devices in column A and a list of attributes or features in column B, and have a computer program generate an invention title by randomly choosing a device and a feature. If one can think of suitable application for the invention, it is relatively easy to embellish the basic concept and generate patentable ideas.

Colin Wilson, an English author who has written many books and articles on subjects ranging from philosophy to the occult, suggests that divination can sometimes work because it allows people to leave the confines of ordinary time. Colin Wilson writes in his son's book *The Mammoth Book of Nostradamus and Other Prophets*:

> Nostradamus used to sit in his study, when the rest of the house was asleep, and stare into a candle flame or bowl of water; it was then he saw his visions of the future. It seems that his mind had access to some timeless realm, like a balcony from which he could look down on the crowd passing in the street below. And if my son Damon is correct, then perhaps we all possess this ability, to a greater or lesser degree, and fail to grasp it because we are so accustomed to being swept along by the crowd.[6]

Wilson goes further and suggests that the best way of escaping the illusion of time is to question its reality. In *An Experiment with Time*, author J. W. Dunne claimed he repeatedly dreamed of the future, and he suggested that we all do this; however, we forget most of our dreams.[7] In chapter 1 we discussed future-life progression where people allegedly can be hypnotized to reveal details of the future.

At this point, the skeptical reader wants to scream out, "This is a lot of nonsense. Nostradamus's prophecies are so obscure that interpretation of many quatrains is almost impossible. The future can't be accessed by any method." The skeptics will point to my Antinoüs prophecies in the previous chapter where I asked for interpretations of randomly generated prophecies. Nostradamus's prophecies could function as Rorschach inkblots that allow the viewer to interpret them in numerous different ways. The skeptic would also say that accurately dreaming of future events only appears to be possible because out of the thousands of dreams we have, by chance some dreams must match future events. We remember the matches and conveniently forget all the times the dreams that are inaccurate. Also, observations we subconsciously make may come out in our dreams. If a friend looks unwell, we may have a dream where he is mortally ill and dies. If the friend dies in real life, our dream may have less to do with psychic powers and more to do with the power of unconscious observation.

Even Nostradamus followers admit they sometimes go to great lengths to justify the vagueness of his prophecies. But what would have happened if Nostradamus's prophecies were true prophecies and fully understood during his life? British writer Charles Ward raises the interesting possibility:

> It is obvious that many prophecies are of such a nature that, if they were clearly understood previous to the event, they would prevent their own fulfillment, and so cease to have been prophecies. What they foretold would never have occured.[8]

Rarely does a prophet, seer, or diviner foretell the future with great specificity or deal with minor events. Did any crystal-gazer or visionary ever say something like, "Don't go to the Shoprite grocery store to buy meat on April 1, 2009, because the price will be too high, $9.54 a pound"? Not likely. Most prophets are concerned with larger events that are sometimes so far into the future that detecting when they have actually occurred is difficult. Most prophecies are imprecise. Even Julius Caesar wasn't told *what* he should beware of on the Ides of March.

Journalists tell a story about a reporter who had the job of creating the regular horoscope in the *Daily Mirror*'s Manchester office (UK).[9] Supposedly one of the reporters was tired of all the upbeat and generally worded astrological advice like: "Positive vibrations come sweeping through your life," and "Someone is eager to make you happy, and you want to return the favor." So the journalist covertly placed a horoscope printed with the words: "All the sorrows of yesteryear are as nothing to what will befall you today."[10] In the next few days, the paper had an avalanche of complaints, and the reporter was fired.

Skeptics raise some excellent points with which we could hardly quibble. For instance, we have to admit that a person *told* that something is destined to happen in the future may make it come true. Consider one of the parables from *The Song of the Bird*, a book by Jesuit priest and mystic Anthony De Mello. A Japanese general, Nobunaga, decided to attack his enemies even though his soldiers were outnumbered ten to one. The general was sure he would win, but his soldiers were doubtful. On the way to battle Nobunaga and his men stopped at a Shinto shrine. After praying in the shrine, Nobunaga came out and said, "I shall now toss a coin. If it is heads, we shall win. If tails, we shall lose. Destiny will now reveal herself."

The general tossed the coin. It was heads. The soldiers were so eager to fight that they wiped out the enemy. The next day an assistant said to Nobunaga, "No one can change Destiny."

"That is correct," said Nobunaga, showing the assistant a doubled coin that was heads on both sides.[11]

Who makes destiny? Nobunaga's tale is one in which "prophecy" forces open the jaws of destiny. It was a trick, a deception. Yet, I wonder if scientifically proven divination methods will be forever beyond our grasp. If our scientific knowledge advances to the point where we can someday manipulate time, we could indeed divine the future and gain secret knowledge. The nature of time, and our crude understanding of past and future, is so mystical and so fraught with questions and paradoxes, that it's a subject upon which I love to speculate. My opinion is that we will someday be able to explore and perhaps manipulate time in ways we can barely imagine today. Einstein's theories, after all, invite such speculation.[12]

If a hundred years from now prophecy relies upon some kind of time manipulation, viewing, or traveling, we must first ask: What is time? Is time travel possible? Is there any conceivable way in which a diviner could see into the past or future? For centuries, these questions have intrigued mystics, philosophers, and scientists. Much of ancient Greek philosophy was concerned with understanding the concept of eternity, and the subject of time is central to all the worlds' religions and cultures. Can the flow of time be stopped? Certainly some mystics thought so. Angelus Silesius, a seventeenth-century philosopher and poet, thought the flow of time could be suspended by mental powers:

> Time is of your own making;
> its clock ticks in your head.
> The moment you stop thought
> time too stops dead.[13]

Mystical speculations like this either make my scientific mind shift into overdrive or stall under the stress. So far, we have concentrated mostly on the history of divination and recipes for divination—and only touched briefly on science. However, the line between science and mysticism sometimes grows thin. Today, physicists would agree that time is one of the strangest properties of our universe. In fact, there is a story circulating among scientists of an immigrant to America who has lost his watch. He walks up to a man on a New York street and asks, "Please, sir, what is time?" The scientist replies, "I'm sorry, you'll have to ask a philosopher. I'm just a physicist."

Most cultures have a grammar with past and future tenses, and also demarcations like seconds and minutes, and yesterday and tomorrow. Yet we cannot say exactly what time is. Although the study of time became scientific during the time of Galileo and Newton, a comprehensive explanation was given only in the twentieth century by Einstein who declared, in effect, that time is simply what a clock reads. The clock can be the rotation of a planet, sand falling in an hour glass, a heartbeat, or vibrations of a cesium atom. A typical grandfather clock follows the simple Newtonian law that states that the velocity of a body not subject to external forces remains constant. This means that clock hands travel equal distances in equal times. While this kind of clock is useful for everyday life, modern science finds that time can be warped in various ways, like clay in the hands of a cosmic sculptor.

Today, we know that time travel need not be confined to myths, science fiction, Hollywood movies, or even speculation by theoretical physicists. Time travel is possible. For example, an object traveling at high speeds ages more slowly than a stationary object. This means that if you were to travel into outer space and return, moving close to light-speed, you could travel thousands of years into the Earth's future. In addition to high-speed travel, researchers have proposed numerous ways in which time machines can be built that do not seem to violate any known laws of physics. These methods allow you to travel to any point in the world's past or future.

Einstein's first major contribution to the study of time occurred when he revolutionized physics with his "special theory of relativity" by showing how time changes with motion. Today, scientists do not see problems of time or motion as "absolute" with a single correct answer. Because time is relative to the speed one is traveling at, there can never be a clock at the center of the universe to which everyone can set their watches. Your entire life would be the blink of an eye to a hypothetical alien traveling close to the speed of light. Today, Newton's mechanics have become a special case within Einstein's theory of relativity. Einstein's relativity will eventually become a subset of a new science more comprehensive in its description of the fabric of our universe. (The word "relativity" derives from the fact that the appearance of the world depends on our state of motion.)

Is time real? Does it flow in one direction only? Does it have a beginning or end? What is eternity? None of these questions can be answered to scientists' satisfaction. Yet the mere asking of these questions stretches our minds, and the continual search for answers provides useful insights along the way. There is also the possibility that we may someday develop a better understanding of parallel universes—worlds that resemble our own and perhaps even occupy the same space as our own in some ghostly manner. Although this multiple-universe concept may seem far-fetched, some serious physicists have considered such a possibility.

There have been many papers in the scientific literature that describe how the brain itself is a kind of time machine, manipulating time and challenging the notion of free will in very unusual ways.[14] Some scientists even wonder if newborn babies sense the passage of time. Philosophers like Kant thought so, and they believed that time was something we experience directly from birth, that it exists outside of us. Other philosophers believe that time is a construct of the human mind. For example, French philosopher Henri Bergson (1859–1941) treated time as something entirely derived from subjective experience. According to Bergson, an infant would not experience time directly but rather have to learn how to experience it. If time is something learned, can we unlearn it?

Sleep studies show that, during dreaming, time is dilated: during brief periods of (external) time, there can be long sequences of internal events. For example, if I woke you after you dreamed for five minutes, you could tell me a long sequence of events that appeared to have taken much longer than five minutes. Your psychological perception of time is, of course, affected by such things as medications, time of day, your level of happiness, external stimuli, and even the temperature. Hypnosis can also cause time dilation, as can cannabis and LSD. Additionally, heat appears to speed up the activity of a chemical timepiece in the brain. For example, fever can severely speed your perception of time, perhaps partly because it speeds chemical processes. Opium is notorious for its effect on time perception. The English writer Thomas De Quincey (1785–1859) reported that under the influence of opium he seemed to live as much as one hundred years in a single night. Another Englishman, J. Redwood Anderson, took hashish and said, "Time was so immensely lengthened that it practically ceased to exist." (This reminds me of Tennyson's Lotus Land "where it was always afternoon.")

Even without drugs, people can learn to stare at the second hand of a clock and perceive it to stick, slow down, and hover. This takes training, but some people can experience the hand to stop altogether for a while. Some psychologists propose that the observing mind, the entity that correlates and makes sense of information submitted to it by the brain, is temporarily absent during these time-sticking periods. The brain hardware is left unattended while the mind has gone elsewhere.

I wonder what humanity will discover about the art of prediction in the next century. Around four billion years ago, living creatures were nothing more than biochemical machines capable of self-reproduction. In a mere fraction of this time, humans evolved from Australopithecines. Today humans have wandered the Moon and have studied ideas ranging from general relativity to quantum cosmology. What will be the divination rage in the year 2100? Probably not entrail reading, dowsing, ooscopy, or spider divination. Perhaps something more high-tech. Consider, for example, the experiments with "random event generators" being studied as part of Princeton University's "Engineering Anomalies Research" or PEAR.[15] In this current research, humans attempt to use their minds to influence the behavior of a variety of mechanical, electronic, optical, acoustical, and fluid devices. In some sense, this is either divining or altering the future.

The Princeton Engineering Anomalies Research (PEAR) program is described at the group's Web site.[16] The progam was established at Princeton University in 1979 by Robert G. Jahn, then Dean of the School of Engineering and Applied Science, to pursue rigorous scientific study of the interaction of human consciousness with sensitive physical devices. Since that time, an interdisciplinary staff of engineers, physicists, psychologists, and humanists has been conducting numerous experiments and developing theoretical models to better understand the interaction of consciousness with physical reality.[17]

Pretty wild stuff! Over the laboratory's twenty-year history, thousands of experiments, involving many millions of trials, have been performed by several hundred operators. They claim to have had significant effects in the experiments where people try to affect the output of random event generators. The observed effects are usually quite small, of the order of a few parts in ten thousand on average, but they are said to be statistically repeatable and compound to highly significant deviations from chance expectations. (I wonder if there is supposed to be anything special about human consciousness, or could the researchers also test a computer's or robot's ability to effect the operation of a remote physical device.)

This kind of research is highly controversial.[18] More tests need to be done. However it is clear that our heirs, whatever or whoever they may be, will explore divination to degrees we cannot currently fathom. They will create new melodies in the music of time. There are infinite harmonies to be explored. But we must be careful. James Randi, professional magician, lecturer, and author, once noted that magicians can replicate "wonders" such as spoon bending, clairvoyance, precognition, psychokinesis, and levitation, showing that supposed supernatural phenomena can be mirrored, exactly, by trickery [19] Scientists, with their specially trained and therefore limited perceptions, are often easily misled by people who wish to deceive them. The burden of proof is on the diviners to establish their case using rigorous scientific tests. Some diviners say that their claims, like religious claims, cannot be examined by scientific procedures. This may be true, but if so, then we could not safely rely upon divination methods for predicting the future or finding secret knowledge any more than a religious person could rely upon a deity preventing world wars, genocide, or a great plague. Does this sound too harsh? Tell me what you think. I can be reached at my Web site www.pickover.com.

〜〜〜   〜〜〜   〜〜〜

Finally, let me relate a few stories relating our modern reaction to divination. On the last day of 1999, a high school in Santiago, Chile, expelled five girls after accusing them of being witches, bathing in blood, and telling fortunes. One of the expelled students, Paula Contreras, said, "If we had lived in the 16th century, we would be dead. They would have hanged us, drowned us, burned us at the stake."[20] Lilian Rojas, the deputy director of the school, said the girls were aggressive and that their expulsion was a precautionary measure.[21]

Consider the following humorous example if divination today. In January 2000, Swaziland officials asked their parliament speaker to resign for taking cow dung from the royal yard. Swazi Royal House governor Bibanisa Dlamini said Mgabhi Dlamini, speaker of the House of Assembly, was asked to step down after an unidentified man was found gathering dung from the royal cattle enclosure for the honorable speaker.[22] Belief in divination is common in Swaziland. Traditional leaders believe that the dung was taken for witchcraft and divination, because the dung was imbued with special powers coming from the king's property. The speaker was vying for the position of prime minister in the tiny southern African kingdom.[23]

As we discussed, many countries, including the United States, have antidivination laws for a variety of different practices. Divination methods and laws are a reflection of the culture that gives rise to them. Through the methods, cultures explore and express the way people think about themselves and the universe. The methods therefore give us insight into how the ancient Greeks or Hebrews, or the 1990s New Agers, thought about nature, gender, society, and God. When reading about some of the more bizarre methods, we tend to take them as entertaining eccentricities. But many people, ancient and modern, did not have this detachment. For these people, divination and mystical thinking were or are an essential part of their culture and world view. Each individual of the ancient cultures probably believed in divination to different degrees, but it is clear that even many of the most educated rulers believed strongly in its powers.

The Greek philosopher Aristotle said that poetry has more truth than history because it tells us the *universal* truths, while history only tell us the *particulars*. In some sense this is true of divination, especially the ancient methods that reveal human's continual, paradoxical longing for mystery and protection from mystery. When we read about the Greek Pythia looking to natural patterns for hints about the future, the ancient dream diviners, or the watchers of birds—all these stories continue to fascinate us and resonate in our psyches. One of the famous Greek sayings is "Man is the measure of all things." No wonder the classical divination methods continue to arouse us and stretch our understanding of ourselves. While providing a soothing sense of control or order, divination methods also explore incomprehensible and frightening aspects of life. The methods have an explanatory element. They attempt to provide an *aetiology*, to explain otherwise unanswerable questions, to lift the veil and watch the hidden gods at play. The methods, ancient and modern, testify to the human belief in an ordered universe that is nevertheless forever filled with mystery.

≈   ≈   ≈

Perhaps we can gain insight into why many people continue to believe prophets if we study the field of alternative medicine where unconventional and perhaps bogus therapies often seem to work. (Alternative medicine is not commonly taught in medical schools and not generally used in hospitals or covered by insurance companies, yet Americans spent $27 billion on unproven remedies in 1997.[24]) For example, even when sick people display no objective improvement in their disease as a result of faith healing or some odd folk medicine, they can convince themselves that they have been helped because they have a strong psychological, monetary, and time investment in the treatment. Barry Beyerstein writes in his *Skeptical Inquirer* article "Why Bogus Therapies Seem to Work":

According to cognitive dissonance theory, when experiences contradict existing attitudes, feelings, or knowledge, mental distress is produced. We tend to alleviate this discord by reinterpreting (distorting) the offending information. To have received no relief after committing time, money, and "face" to an alternate course of treatment (and perhaps to the world view of which it is part) would create such a state of internal disharmony. Because it would be too psychologically disconcerting to admit to oneself or to others that it has all been a waste, there would be strong psychological pressure to find some redeeming value in the treatment.[25]

People can warp their perceptions and memories in an attempt to fit observations with preconceived notions. Channelers, prophets, and psychics—and their clients—can, for example, misinterpret cues and remember successful predictions while ignoring failures. Clients of psychics often wish to please the psychics in an effort to obtain more information about the future and to maintain good relations. This may cause the client to overestimate the accuracy of results. Even seasoned scientists and skeptics have difficulties interpreting information in the numerous data given by psychics and must resort to detailed statistical studies to determine the significance of any possible relationships between what a diviner predicts and what actually occurs. For one thing, many of their predictions are so vague that it's difficult to determine if they were right or not.

In general, there are many other reasons why we may believe in unscientific practices. Certainly, even in this modern day, erroneous beliefs can have *positive* effects. Medicines can be more effective if a patient believes they will be more effective. Even sugar pills—placebos—can provide relief when a patient believes they will reduce pain. Some placebo responses produce measurable physical changes to the body; for example, placebos can cause release of endorphins, the body's own morphinelike painkillers.[26] Others responses are subjective; a sick person may feel better although nothing measurable has changed in the underlying pathology.[27]

Some studies have suggested that belief in a loving God can make the believer feel good and may even provide benefits to one's health. Sometimes I wish that there were ways for skeptics, like me, to achieve the beneficial effects of fantastic beliefs while eliminating the potentially harmful side effects such as prejudice, the avoidance of lifesaving medicines, or the impeding of scientific progress.

We can learn more about human beliefs by studying animals. For example, humans behave like many animals that are driven by the expectations and behaviors of their "peers." If one zebra starts looking nervously toward the edge of a savanna, other zebras will soon follow. This can have survival value. Obviously, the same is true for humans, and this also accounts for our ability to believe in contradictions or unproven theories. As just one example, in 1938, many Americans became panic-stricken after listening to *The War of the Worlds* depicting supposed Martians landing in Grovers Mill, New Jersey. During the play, many listeners looked out their windows and even thought they saw clear signs of an invasion, including flames from the battle. The incident is a testament to the remarkable power of expectation on perception.[29] The strength of expectation no doubt plays a role in our interpretation and belief in prophecies. Another great contemporary example of the effect of expectation on belief occurred in 1993, when *The Morning Times of Laredo* published a scam of a 300-pound, 79-foot long earthworm wandering along Texas Interstate 35. Its wet body was said to leave a slimy trail and making a squishy sound as it moved. Many citizens believed the story and dared not drive Interstate 35 at night.[30]

We are also predisposed to believe in different kinds of fantasies because we, like all animals, are pattern-seeking machines. Creatures with the ability to recognize patterns in nature are often the creatures able to find food and mates, seek camouflage, or escape from dangerous animals. In many species, sexual selection produces males with elaborate patterns on body parts. For example, many male birds, such as peacocks, have colorful and showy plumage. Even the Yucca moth, with only a few ganglia for its brain, can recognize the geometry of the yucca flower from birth. However, even with all the pattern detection that has evolved, the evolutionary process has not forced life forms to be able to detect the true *cause* of the patterns. In some sense, it is better to "detect" patterns that aren't really there than to miss patterns that might get you into trouble, like the scratching sounds of a tiger's claws or the shadows of hawks before they attack. Because we are programmed to quickly respond to patterns, to search for patterns, and to "find" patterns in the chaotic world around us, we often accept nonexistent patterns and attribute fantastic causes after the acceptance. As Michael Shermer suggests in *How We Believe*, we are more gullible than skeptical by nature.[31] Perhaps our love of patterns is one reason why prophets who continually predict the end of the world on particular dates still manage to retain their followers even when the dates pass. For example, the Jehovah's Witnesses have predicted doomsday for 1874, 1878, 1881, 1910, 1914, 1918, 1920, 1925, and so on, but the erroneous predictions do not seem to dampen the enthusiasm of their followers. Similarly, authors Henry C. Roberts (*The Complete Prophecies of Nostradamus*), Jean-Charles de Fontbrune (*Nostradamus: Countdown to Apocalypse*), and Stewart Robb (*Nostradamus:*

*Prophecies on World Events*), all seemed to predict that the world could end in 1999, and each author used a different, vague quatrain of Nostradamus to make the prediction.[32] Whatever their motivation, the authors found patterns in the chaos of Nostradamus's poetic words. Nostradamus's works have been in continuous print ever since their first publication centuries ago, and I suspect that they will continue to be cherished for centuries to come.

In many ways, belief in the supernatural is as prevalent as it was a thousand years ago. Today, psychics often claim that are no real coincidences or accidents, that an accident seems to be a random event because of our superficial knowledge, and that there is actually a hidden, deeper meaning and connectedness linking all events that only they have special powers to discern.[33] Certainly, the diviner loves finding structures and patterns, even if these patterns tend to evaporate when put under close scientific scrutiny.

I recall an intriguing scene from the TV show *Star Trek: The Next Generation* where the android Data is looking out a window at an ever-changing cloud formation. Data's friend explains poetically that the cloud looks like a "Semalian coral fish with its fin unfolded." Data responds in his usual analytic manner with the words, "I believe what you are seeing is the effect of the fluid dynamic processes inherent in the large scale motion of rarefied gas." The friend then observes that the cloud formation is gradually changing from a fishlike pattern to a "Mintonian sailing ship." She asks Data if he can see two swirls coming together to form the mast. His response is that he does not see it. He says:

> It is interesting that people try to find meaningful patterns in things that are essentially random. I have noticed that the images they perceive sometimes suggest what they are thinking about at that particular moment.[34]

Of course, this is merely the dialogue from a character in a science-fiction TV show. But even British astrophysicist Stephen Hawking has expressed the same kind of feeling when he wrote, "Ever since the dawn of civilization, people have not been content to see events as unconnected and inexplicable. They have craved an understanding of the underling order of the world."[35]

I think that our brains are wired with a desire for divination and prophecy. If so, the reasons for our interest, and the methods we use, are buried deep in the essence of our nature. Divination is at the edge of the known and the unknown, poised on the fractal boundaries of religion, history, psychology, biology, and many other scientific disciplines. Because of this, divination is an important topic for contemplation and study. Even with the great scientific strides we will make in this twenty-first century, we will nevertheless continue to swim in a sea of mystery. Humans need to make sense of the world and will surely continue to use divination for that task. What patterns and connections will we see in the twenty-first century? What will be our divination methods? Will the methods be based on computers and physics or on sticks and stones?

How will we be dreaming the future?

# Appendices

In order to save space, several appendices are continued at http://www.pickover.com. The following gives an indication of topics discussed, and I welcome feedback from readers.

## ᛏ APPENDIX 1: THE PROPHECIES AND VISIONS OF GEORGE WASHINGTON

Various prophecies have been attributed to George Washington, first president of the United States. Some people have interpreted Washington's visions to represent events such as the American expansion westward, slave trade and the civil war, and finally nuclear attacks on the United States. These alleged prophecies are presented and discussed at http://www.pickover.com.

## ᛉ APPENDIX 2: THE PROPHECIES OF RASPUTIN

Grigory Yefimovich Rasputin (1872–1916) was the Siberian peasant and mystic whose claimed ability to improve the condition of Aleksey Nikolayevich, the hemophiliac heir to the Russian throne, made him influential at the court of Emperor Nicholas II and Empress Alexandra. His prophecies are discussed further at http://www.pickover.com.

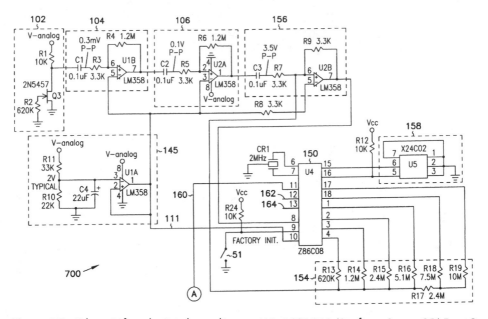

**Figure 73.** Schematic from the "mind control" patent U.S. 5,830,064. (See figure 3 on p. 35.) From G. Johnston Brandish, York Dobyns, Brenda Dunne, Robert Jahn, Roger Nelson, John Haaland, and Steven Hamer, "Apparatus and method for distinguishing events which collectively exceed change expectation and thereby controlling an output," U.S. Patent 5,830,064, November 3, 1998, p. 13, fig. 8a.

## N APPENDIX 3: FIGURES FOR U.S. PATENTS 5,748,088 AND 5,830,064

The introduction discussed the relevance of divination in today's world. In particular, I discussed two unusual U.S. patents that in some ways appear to be ultramodern divination devices. For completeness, figures 73 and 74 show the schematic of the "mind control" patent, U.S. 5,830,064, to give those of you with electronic background and idea for the complexity of the circuitry. This 1998 patent, titled "Apparatus and method for distinguishing events which collectively exceed chance expectations and thereby controlling an output," can be read it its entirety at http://patent.womplex.ibm.com/. Figure 75 is close-up of the human detection unit shown in the introduction's figure 4 (p. 36). This patent is titled "Device and method using dielectrokinesis to locate entities" and was also published in 1998.

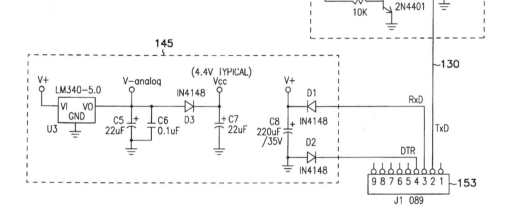

**Figure 74.** Schematic from the "mind control" patent U.S. 5,830,064. From G. Johnston Brandish, York Dobyns, Brenda Dunne, Robert Jahn, Roger Nelson, John Haaland, and Steven Hamer, "Apparatus and method for distinguishing events which collectively exceed change expectation and thereby controlling an output," U.S. Patent 5,830,064, November 3, 1998, p. 14, fig. 8b.

## ◇ APPENDIX 4: SEVERAL EXACT FOR THE END OF THE WORLD

> *In the last terrible desolation of the world, the final High Priest of the True God shall reign. Criminal Rome will be destroyed and the terrible judge, in his Glory, will judge all nations.*
>
> —The Monk of Padua, 18th Century[1]

Many prophets and seers have attempted to specify the precise date for the end of the world. On pages 409 and 410 are a few examples.[2,3] The left-hand column gives the date predicted for doomsday. Note that many early Christians actually hoped for the world's end in their lifetimes.

## 〈 APPENDIX 5: THE I CHING HEXAGRAMS

In chapter 1, I gave a recipe for divining using the *I Ching*, the oldest continually used divination system in the world. The *I Ching* contains sixty-four

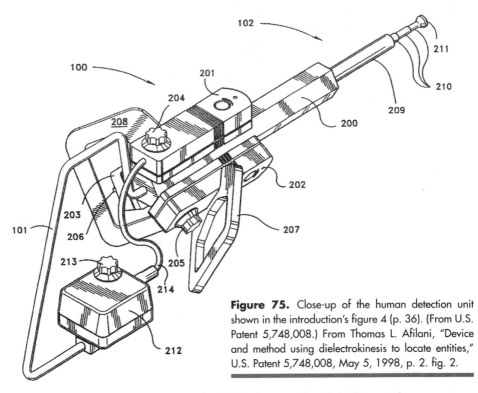

**Figure 75.** Close-up of the human detection unit shown in the introduction's figure 4 (p. 36). (From U.S. Patent 5,748,008.) From Thomas L. Afilani, "Device and method using dielectrokinesis to locate entities," U.S. Patent 5,748,008, May 5, 1998, p. 2. fig. 2.

symbols called *hexagrams*, each of which is made of six lines. The meanings of the first five hexagrams, as well as hexgram fifteen (discussed in chapter 1), are listed here so that you can get an idea about the kinds of information the hexagrams provide. Additional information regarding the remainder of the symbols can be found at http://www.pickover.com.

≣   1. ——— Ch'ien—Creative Activity

The creative works sublime success. Furthering through perseverance. Be persistent and strong. *Meditate on this vision:* The movement of heaven is full of power. Thus the superior person makes himself strong and untiring. ❖ *Line 1:* Hidden dragon. Do not act. *Line 2:* Dragon appearing in the field. It furthers one to see the great person. *Line 3:* The superior person is active creatively all day long. At nightfall the person's mind is still beset with cares. Danger. No blame. *Line 4:* Wavering flight over the depths. No blame. *Line 5:* Flying dragon in the heavens. It furthers one to see the great person. *Line 6:* Arrogant dragon will have cause to repent. Note: When all the lines are changing, there appears a flight of dragons without heads. Good fortune.

| The End of the World | |
|---|---|
| **Date** | **Comment** |
| Before about 100 C.E. | The New Testament states that the End occurs before the death of the last Apostle. Jesus said, "This generation shall not pass away until allbe fulfilled." In the minds of the first Christians, the statement clearly meant that the End would come in their time. |
| 198 | Montanus, a Christian leader, believed that a heavenly city would land at a place on Earth called Ardabau—a signal for the Second Coming. |
| 666 | Number of the beast |
| 992 | Bernard of Thuringia |
| 1000 | Popular belief, biblical Apocrypha, St. Augustine |
| 1033 | 1000 years after Christ's Death |
| 1066 | Halley's Comet |
| 1186 | Astrologer John of Toledo |
| 1466 | Halley's Comet |
| 1524 | Death by flood, predicted by various European astrologers |
| 1532 | Frederick Nausea, bishop of Vienna |
| Oct. 3, 1533 at 8 A.M. | Michael Stifel, mathematician and Bible student. Also predicted by Anabaptist Melchior Hoffmann. |
| 1535 | John of Leyden |
| 1537 | Pierre Turrel, French astrologer |
| 1572 | Astronomer Tycho Brahe |
| 1583 | R. Harvey, Age of the Spirit of Joachim da Fiore |
| 1584 | Astrologer Cyprian Leowitz |
| 1588 | Johann Mueller |
| 1648 | Rabbi Sabbati Zevi |
| 1654 | Physician Helisaeus Roeslin of Alsace |
| 1660 | Joseph Mede |
| 1665 | Quaker Solomon Eccles of London |
| 1666 | Popular Belief, after Great London Fire |
| 1688 | Mathematician John Napier |
| 1700 | Mathematician John Napier, second try |
| 1704 | Cardinal Nicholas de Cusa |
| 1707 | Various French seers |
| 1719 | Jacques Bernoulli, Swiss Mathematician |
| 1733 | Sir Isaac Newton |
| 1736 | William Whiston of London |
| 1757 | Emmanuel Swedenborg |
| 1761 | William Bell |
| 1774 | Joanna Southcott of England |
| 1806 | People of Leeds found a hen laying eggs inscribed with "Christ is coming." |
| Oct. 19, 1814 | Joanna Southcott |
| 1820 | Prophet John Turner of England |
| 1843 | William Miller, founder of Millerite church |
| 1844 | Millerites (second estimate after first failed) |
| 1864 | Edward Irving |
| 1874 | Morton Edgar; Charles Taze Russell |
| 1881 | Measurements based on the Great Pyramid at Ghiza; Also Mother Shipton's "prediction." |
| 1912 | Halley's Comet |
| 1914 | Charles Taze Russell, second try |

| 1919 | Professor Porta of Michigan University |
|------|---------------------------------------|
| 1925 | Mrs Margaret Rowen and her Brides of the Lamb |
| 1947 | John Ballou Newbrough, "America's Greatest Prophet" |
| 1950 | Henry Adams |
| 1977 | John Wroe of the English Southcottian sect |
| 1996 | Biblical scholars |
| 1980 | Ancient Arabic astrological prediction |
| 1988 | Edgar Whisenant |
| Sept. 9, 1999 | Indonesian cults (9/9/99) |
| 1999 | Seventh-day Adventists; Jehovah's Witnesses; Also, Nostradamus said, "The year 1999, seven moths, from the sky will come a great King of Terror." |
| 2000 | Malachy, various astrologers, Richard Noone, and other Christian visionaries |
| 2001 | Berosus, ancient Chaldean astrologer |
| 2012 | Predictions based on Mayan belief |
| 2013 | Predictions based on Incan calendar |
| 2025 | Max Thoth |
| 2398 | Shaoshyant, the Zoroastrian Savior |
| 2915 | Mortgan Edgar predicts final test |
| 3797 | Nostradamus |
| 6300 | Max Thoth predicts ultimate end |

▤▤  2. K'un—The Receptive

The receptive brings about sublime success. Furthering through the perseverance of a mare. If the superior person undertakes something and tries to lead, the person goes astray; But if the person follows, the person finds guidance. It is favorable to find friends in the west and south, to forego friends in the east and north. Quiet perseverance brings good fortune. Yield to and agree with others. *Meditate on this vision*: The earth's condition is receptive devotion. Thus the superior person who has breadth of character carries the outer world. ❖ *Line 1*: When there is frost underfoot, solid ice is not far off. *Line 2*: Straight, square, great. Without purpose, yet nothing remains unfurthered. *Line 3*: Hidden lines. One is able to remain persevering. If by chance you are in the service of a leader, seek not works, but bring to completion. *Line 4*: A tied-up sack. No blame, no praise. *Line 5*: A yellow lower garment brings supreme good fortune. *Line 6*: Dragons fight in the meadow. Their blood is black and yellow. *Note*: When all the lines are changing then lasting perseverance furthers.

▤▤  3. Chun—Difficulty at the Beginning

Establish a base and grow. A difficulty beginning leads to ultimate success. Furthering through perseverance. Nothing should be undertaken. It furthers one to appoint helpers. *Meditate on this vision*: Clouds and thunder are the image of difficulty at the beginning. Thus the superior person brings order out of confusion. ❖ *Line 1*: Hesitation and hindrance. It furthers one to persevere. It furthers one to appoint helpers. *Line 2*: Difficulties pile up. Horse and wagon part. He is not a robber. He wants to woo when the time comes. The maiden is chaste—she does not pledge herself. Ten years then she pledges herself. *Line 3*: Whoever hunts deer without the forester only loses his way in the forest. The superior person understands the signs of the time and prefers to desist. To go on brings humiliation. *Line 4*: Horse and wagon part. Strive for union. To go brings good fortune. Everything acts to further. *Line 5*: Difficulties in blessing. A little perseverance brings good fortune. Great perseverance brings misfortune. *Line 6*: Horse and wagon part. Bloody tears flow.

☷☳ 4. Mêng—Youthful Folly

Youthful folly has success. It is not I who seek the young fool—the young fool seeks me. At the first oracle I inform the person. If the person asks two or three times, it is bothersome. If the person persists, I give the person no information. Perseverance furthers. Hide and conceal. *Meditate on this vision*: A spring wells up at the foot of the mountain; this is the image of youth. Thus the superior person fosters character by thoroughness in all that the person does. ❖ *Line 1*: Apply discipline to make a fool develop. The chains and restraints should be removed. To go on in this way brings humiliation. *Line 2*: Good fortune comes to those who are kind and patient to fools. To know how to take women brings good fortune. The son is capable of taking charge of the household. *Line 3*: Take not a maiden who, when she sees a man of bronze, loses possession of herself. Nothing furthers. *Line 4*: Entangled folly brings humiliation. *Line 5*: Childlike folly brings good fortune. *Line 6*: When punishing folly, don't commit transgressions. You will be better off if you *prevent* transgressions.

☵☰ 5. Hsu—Waiting (Nourishment)

Waiting. If you are sincere, you have light and success. Perseverance brings good fortune. You will be better off if you cross the great water. Provide what is needed. *Meditate on this vision*: Clouds rise up to heaven; this is the image of waiting. Thus the superior person eats and drinks, is joyous and of good cheer. ❖ *Line 1*: Waiting in the meadow. You will be better off to abide in what endures. No blame. *Line 2*: Waiting on the sand. There is some gossip. The end brings good fortune. *Line 3*: Waiting in the mud brings about the arrival of the enemy. *Line 4*: Waiting in blood. Get out of the pit. *Line 5*:

Waiting at meat and drink. Perseverance brings good fortune. *Line 6:* One falls into the pit. Three uninvited guests arrive. Honor them, and in the end there will be good fortune.

▤ 15. Ch'ien—Modesty

Modesty creates success. Be modest and respectful. The superior person carries things through. *Meditate on this vision:* Within the earth, a mountain; this is the image of modesty. Thus the superior person reduces that which is too much, and augments that which is too little. The person weighs things and makes them equal. v *Line 1:* A superior person modest about his modesty may cross the great water. Good fortune. *Line 2:* Modesty that comes to expression. Perseverance brings good fortune. *Line 3:* A superior person of modesty and merit carries things to conclusion. Good fortune. *Line 4:* Nothing that would not further modesty in movement. *Line 5:* No boasting of wealth before one's neighbor. It is favorable to attack with force. Nothing that would not further. *Line 6:* Modesty that comes to expression. It is favorable to set armies marching to chastise one's own city and one's country.

## ◇ APPENDIX 6: RUNE MEANINGS

In chapter 1, we discussed methods by which runecasters read runes. Here are the meanings for five runes.[4] Additional information on the remaining runes can be found at http://www.pickover.com

### ⱦ *Feoh: possessions, wealth*

Feoh means cattle, fee, or payment. (The Norsemen sometimes measured a person's wealth by the number of cows they possessed.) Be thankful for your good financial state. Work hard to save earnings. Good things ahead such as promotions, investments and new careers. Other meanings: fertility, and sexual fulfillment. Relationships do well with hard work. Reversed meaning: failure or loss in money and matters or relationships. Changing directions might help.

### ⋂ *Ur: power*

Ur means strength and the drive for power. Ur stands for Auroch, the wild ox. You will have the chance to prove yourself. A change in your life's circumstances requires time and energy to overcome. You have the power to meet the challenge and succeed. Reversed meaning: Be careful not to miss opportunities. Postponement or cancellation. Beware of weakness.

## ↑ *Thorn: protection*

Thorn is named after Thor, the warrior god for the early Germanic peoples, a powerful enemy to the evil giants but benevolent toward humankind. Fate is on your side. You are not alone in your battle. Seek advice. Reversed meaning: your luck has run out. The person helping you or being helped by you may not be honest. Use caution.

## ᚷ *Ansur: Wisdom*

Ansur refers to Odin, the great magician among the Norse gods and who was associated with runes. He was also the god of poets, the principal god in Scandinavia, and a war god who appeared in heroic literature as the protector of heroes. The rune symbolizes wisdom, advice, communication, writing, and song. Receive guidance from experience individuals. Reversed meaning: If you don't listen to the advice of the wise, your life won't be as happy, but be careful of inaccurate advice.

## ᚱ *Rad: travel*

Rad symbolizes pleasurable journeys that can be physical or purely mental. Be prepared for travel and change. Your journey will be successful. Seek to expand your mind. You are likely to do well in legal battles and in money transactions. Reversed meaning: inconvenient or uncomfortable journey. It's a bad time for visitors. Be careful, your plans may have difficulty.

## ᚾ APPENDIX 7: OOSCOPY TECHNIQUES

Here are some details to help you interpret the egg structures in chapter 1 and depicted in figure 5. Only a little is known about how the Etruscans interpreted the features of the egg. Apparently it took lots of practice. Ooscopers suggest that you use your own intuition and try to understand any feelings you get by studying features of the egg white—in the same way that tarot card readers are interested in your reaction to images on tarot cards. The following information comes from Dr. John Opsopaus who says the first step is to get familiar with the egg's orientation.[5] The *Cardo* [North-South axis] divides the egg into east and west parts. The east is to your left, and this is called the *Pars Familiaris* [Friendly Part]. The west is to the right, and this is the *Pars Hostilis* [Enemy Part]. The *Decumanus* [East-West axis] divides the egg into north and south parts. The north is behind you, and this is the *Pars Postica*, which is the Home of the Gods of Heaven and Light and is ruled by *Usil* [the Etruscan Sun god], the King of Day. The ooscoper looks for features in any of the various labeled regions of the egg. For information on the meanings of each region, see http://www.pickover.com.

# Notes

## PREFACE

1. Actually, most of the time a *baked* head of a goat or donkey was used, so the animals felt no pain. This is not true of other divination methods in this book that did cause pain to people or animals.

2. Martin Gardner, *On The Wild Side* (Amherst, N.Y.: Prometheus Books, 1992), pp. 140–53.

3. Ibid., p. 142.

4. Ibid., p. 148. See also, Donald Regan, *For the Record: From Wall Street to Washington* (New York: Harcourt Brace, 1988).

5. Ibid., p. 149.

6. Joan Quigley, *"What Did Joan Say?" My Seven Years as White House Astrologer to Nancy and Ronald Reagan* (Birch Lane Press, 1990).

7. President Ronald Reagan visited a cemetery in Bitburg, Germany, in which SS (Schutzstaffel) members, German soldiers, and Jewish victims of the Holocaust are buried. The visit caused a furor, partly because Reagan seemed to make little distinction between the fallen German soldiers and the murdered Jews. He suggested that both were "victims of a Nazi oppression whose responsibility was abdicated through the madness of one man, Hitler."

8. The Intermediate Nuclear Forces (INF) treaty between the United States and the Soviet Union (now Russia) eliminated all ground-based, medium-range nuclear missiles stationed in Europe.

9. Quigley, *"What Did Joan Say?"*

10. The Bank of China Tower, designed to be taller than the nearby Hong Kong Bank, is said to be a symbol of Chinese sovereignty. Feng-shui masters believe the new bank is a "dagger" pointing to the Hong Kong Governor's residence (Pauline Loo, "Hong Kong Attractions," http://www. gergo.com/pauline/hk/attractions.htm).

11. Paul O'Brien, *Intuitive Decision-Making in an Age of Chaos*, www.iching.com. Excerpt used with permission.

12. Kevin Osborn and Dana Burgess, *The Complete Idiot's Guide to Classical Mythology* (New York: Alpha Books, 1998).

13. Charles Mackay, *Extraordinary Popular Delusions and the Madness of Crowds* (1852; reprint, New York: Crown Publishing, 1995).

14. Waverly Fitzgerald, "Celebrating Halloween," http://www.nas.com/ jpcolbertart/seasons/celebhallows.html.

15. Ibid.

16. Ibid.


# INTRODUCTION

1. Roger Zelazny, *Creatures of Light and Darkness* (New York: Avon, 1987), pp. 82–84.

2. Donald Tyson, *Scrying for Beginners* (St. Paul, Minn.: Llewllyn), p. 170.

3. Michael Loewe and Carmen Blacker, *Oracles and Divination* (Boulder: Shambala, 1981), p. 1.

4. Eva Shaw, *Divining the Future* (New York: Facts on File, 1995).

5. Hilda Ellis Davidson, "The Germanic World," in Michael Loewe and Carmen Blacker, *Oracles and Divination* (Boulder: Shambala, 1981), p. 115.

6. Terry Tremaine, "Global Fortune Telling and Bible Prophecy," *Skeptical Inquirer* 18, no. 2 (winter 1994): 166–69.

7. Bill Anderson, *Nostradamus* (Bristol, United Kingdom: Paragon, 1998).

8. J. D. Ray, "Ancient Egypt," in Loewe and Blacker, *Oracles and Divination*, p. 175.

9. Carmen Blacker, "Japan," in Loewe and Blacker, *Oracles and Divination*, p. 63.

10. J. S. Morrison, "The Classical World," in Loewe and Blacker, *Oracles and Divination*, p. 63.

11. An partial text of these oracles from 1545 still exists. Modern scholars have tried to date the various oracles by comparing historical events with the last events correctly predicted in the Oracles.

12. J. S. Morrison, "The Classical World," in Loewe and Blacker, *Oracles and Divination*, p. 63.

13. Charles Mackay, *Extraordinary Popular Delusions and the Madness of Crowds* (1852; reprint, New York: Crown Publishing, 1995).

14. Clifford Pickover, *Time: A Traveler's Guide* (New York: Oxford University Press).

15. Hermann Weyl, *Space Time Matter* (New York: Dover, 1985).

16. Kurt Vonnegut, *The Sirens of Titan* (New York: Delta, 1988).

17. Pickover, *Time: A Traveler's Guide*.

18. Lynne Robinson and La Vonne Carlson-Finnery, *The Complete Idiot's Guide to Being Psychic* (New York: Macmillan Publishing Company, 1998).

19. David Voss, "New Physics Finds a Haven at the Patent Office," *Science* May 5418, no. 284 (1999): 1252–54.

20. Ibid. If you are interested in a discussion on the efficacy of such devices, read the comments in Voss's article of a thirty-year veteran of search-and-rescue operations.

21. Ibid. In particular, read the comments of some researchers at the Sandia National Laboratory in New Mexico.

22. The Justice Technology Information Network (JUSTNET) is a service of the National Law Enforcement and Corrections Technology Center (NLECTC). NLECTC is a program of the National Institute of Justice Office of Science and Technology.

23. The National Institute of Justice is the research and development branch of the U.S. Department of Justice and operates as a component of the Office of Justice Programs.

24. Tomas Coty, Physical Analysis of DKL LifeGuard™ Device, http://www.nlectc.org/services/dklanalysis.html.

25. Matthew Nisbet, "Psychic Telephone Networks Profit on Yearning, Gullibility," *Skeptical Inquirer* 22, no. 3 (May/June 1998): 5–6.

26. Simon Hoggart and Mike Hutchinson, *Bizarre Beliefs* (London: Richard Cohen Books, 1995), p. 112.

27. Ibid., p. 130.

28. The Azande live in central Africa. This ethnically mixed people practice polygyny, and in the past, noblemen had so many wives that it was difficult for most other men to *marry*. Azande religion is an ancestor cult, with little mention of god. Witchcraft plays a big role in the Azande religion and world outlook.

29. Eva Shaw, *Divining the Future* (New York: Facts on File, 1995), p. 5.

30. Fox News Online and Reuters Ltd., "Tanzanians Kill 350 Suspected Witches," http://www.foxnews.com/js_index.sml?content=/etcetera/ wires/0803 /e_rt_0803_9.sml.

31. Ibid. See also "Three African Countries Crack Down on Human Skin Trade," http://www.rense.com/politics5/skintrade.htm. Several East African countries really do trade in human skin. Evidence, shown on Tanzanian television in late 1999, seems irrefutable: grotesque scenes of human skins displayed alongside the dismembered bodies from which they had been removed. Price: £200-£300. Apparently the skin is thought to have magical properties. For example, the sale of the scalps of bald men is said to give wisdom when dried and crumbled.

32. Ibid.

33. Eva Shaw, *Divining the Future*, p. 8.

34. "Role of the Cuy," http://www.idrc.ca/books/reports/1997/33-02e.html. See also Lupe Camino, *Cerros, Plantas y Lagunas Poderosas: La medicina al norte del Peru* (Hills, Plants and Powerful Lagoons: The Medicine of Northern Peru) (Peru: The Center of Investigation and Promotion of the Countryside [CIPCA], 1993).

35. David Koop, Associated Press (Fox News Online), "Peruvians Put Faith in 'Andean X-Ray' to Diagnose Ailments," http://www.foxnews.com/js_index.sml?content=/news/wires2/1111/n_ap_1111_21.sml, November 11, 1998.

36. Melinda Rose Goodin, "Using the Tarot to Break Writers Block."

37. Meredith Monaghan, personal communication to Cliff Pickover.

38. Goodin, "Using the Tarot to Break Writers Block."

# CHAPTER 1. BEYOND STICKS AND STONES

1. Reuters, "Police Raid Offices of Foot Cult," Wednesday, 1 December 1999, 7:53 AM ET, http://dailynews.yahoo.com/h/nm/19991201/od/ foot_1.html.

2. Fortune Cookie Company, Ltd., "History of the Fortune Cookie," http://www.fortunecookie.demon.co.uk/fhistory.html.

3. In this note, I'd like to give a few hints to people familiar with the Internet's World Wide Web regarding how they can create their own fortune cookie Web site. It would be fascinating to monitor the decay of something radioactive to trigger the selection of random fortunes. This would give the user a feel that he or she is in tune with physical forces that are beyond the realm of humans to alter or predict. Specifically, I would be interested in hearing from readers who can couple the fortune selection to the decay of Americum-241, an artificially produced radioisotope found in many smoke detectors. Alternatively, it may easier just to use the output of an electronic "white noise generator" circuit for which their are numerous recipes on the World Wide Web. For example, see the random event generator at http:// www.mindsonginc.com/ products/index.html. The device provides a nondeterministic random binary output whose normal mean and standard deviation are specified in its production calibration.

At my Web site, I dispense with the idea of using a physical random even generator. If you wish to emulate my approach on a Web page, you would first create a random number using a javascript that looks like:

```
<script LANGUAGE="JavaScript">
rnd.today=new Date();
rnd.seed=rnd.today.getTime();
function rnd() {
 rnd.seed = (rnd.seed*9301+49297) % 233280;
 return rnd.seed/(233280.0);
};
function rand(number) {
 return Math.ceil(rnd()*number);
};
</script>
```

Next prepare some images that contain your fortunes and perhaps colorful artwork of your own design. There are several shareware image creation programs at www.shareware.com. For example, you might create seven different fortunes stored in files fortcook1.jpg, fortcook2.jpg, . . . fortcook7.jpg. These may be randomly accessed and displayed in a Web browser with the following program lines:

```
<script LANGUAGE="JavaScript">
document.write('<IMG SRC="fortcook' + rand(7) + '.jpg">');
</script>
```

If you embellish this concept and place it on your own Web page, every time the person reloads your page, they get a new fortune. Try it at www.pickover.com, and you'll get the idea.

4. Eva Shaw, *Divining the Future*. There are a number of divination methods that I did not include in this chapter because I could find only very little information on them. I would be interested in hearing from readers who can provide more information on any of the following: macharomancy (divination by knives and swords), stereomancy (divining by the elements), sternomancy (divination by marks from the breast to belly), knissomancy (divining by burning of incense), chartomancy (divination by writing in papers and by Valentines), chalcomancy (divination by vessels made of brass or other metals), and spatilomancy (divination by skin and bones).

5. Marcus Tullius Cicero, *The Nature of the Gods and on Divination*, trans. C.D. Yonge (Great Books in Philosophy) (Amherst, N.Y.: Prometheus Books, 1997).

6. O. R. Gurney, "The Babylonians and Hittites," in Michael Loewe and Carmen Blacker, *Oracles and Divination* (Boulder: Shambala, 1981), p. 148.

7. Ibid., p. 149.

8. Ibid., p. 158.

9. Reuters "Man Kills Witch Doctor, Eats Liver," 4 November 1999, http://news.excite.com/news/r/991104/07/odd-witch.

10. Vodun is a world religion with cultural origins in the West and Central African countries of Benin (formerly Dahomey), Togo, Nigeria, and Zaire (Kongo). The vodun are mysterious forces or powers that shape people's lives. Both African and American forms of vodun have absorbed and reinterpreted foreign deities. Wherever vodun appears, practitioners incorporate local influences, hence New Orleans vodun is a distinct tradition. (The term voodoo is derived from the word vodun.) For more information, see Anna Maria Chupa, "Vodun," http://www2.msstate.edu/ ~ amc11/achupa/ vodun/vodun.html.

11. Olive Schreiner and Joseph Bristow ed., *The Story of an African Farm* (1883; reprint, New York: Oxford University Press, 1999).

12. John Opsopaus, "The Art of Haruspicy," http://www.omphalos. org/BA/Har.html or http://www.cs.utk.edu/ ~ mclennan/OM/BA/Har.html.

13. L. B. Van Der Meer, *The Bronze Liver of Piacenza: Analysis of a Polytheistic Structure*, vol. 2 of *Dutch Monographs of Ancient History and Archaeology* (New York: John Benjamins Pub-

lishing Company, 1987); Massimo Pallottino, *The Etruscans* (Bloomington: Indiana University Press, 1975); Giuliano Bonfante and Larissa Bonfante, *The Etruscan Language: An Introduction* (New York: New York University Press, 1983); W. R. Halliday, *Greek Divination: A Study of its Methods and Principles* (London: Macmillan, 1913); Georg Luck, *Arcana Mundi: Magic and the Occult in the Greek and Roman Worlds* (Baltimore: Johns Hopkins University Press, 1985).

14. John Opsopaus, "The Art of Haruspicy, which Is the Etruscan Discipline." *Harvest*, 11, no. 4 (1991): 22–24. Used with permission.

15. Victor Stenger, *The Unconscious Quantum: Metaphysics in Modern Physics and Cosmology* (Amherst, N.Y.: Prometheus Books, 1995).

16. Ibid., p. 94.

17. David Zeitlyn, "Anthropological Studies of Divination: Spider Divination," http://lucy.ukc.ac.uk/Fdtl/Spider/; David Zeitlyn, "Professor Garfinkel Visits the Soothsayers: Ethnomethodology and Mambila," *Divination*, Man (n.s.) 25, no. 4; (1990): 654–66. David Zeitlyn, "Spiders in and out of Court or 'the Long Legs of the Law': Styles of Spider Divination in Their Sociological Contexts," *Africa* 63, no. 2 (1992): 219–40.

18. Ibid.

19. Ibid.

20. Aristotle, *De Historia Animalium*.

21. Amy Garner, "A Brief History of Palm Reading," http://www.c-comm.demon.co.uk/amy/history.html.

22. Ibid.; see also Nathaniel Altman, *The Palmistry Workbook* (New York: Sterling Publications, 1984).

23. Nevill Drury and Gergory Tillett, *The Occult* (New York: Barnes & Nobles Books, 1997).

24. Robin Gile and Lisa Lenard, *The Complete Idiot's Guide to Palmistry* (New York: MacMillan, 1999).

25. Dennis Marlock and John Dowling, *License to Steal: Traveling Con Artists, Their Games, Their Rules—Your Money* (Boulder, Colo.: Paladin Press, 1994); Michael Alan Park, "Palmistry or Hand-Jive?" in *Science Confronts the Paranormal*, ed. by Kendrick Frazier (Amherst, N.Y.: Prometheus Books, 1986); Robert Todd Carroll, "The Skeptic's Dictionary," http://skepdic. com/palmist.html.

26. Michael Lowe, "China," in Loewe and Blacker, *Oracles and Divination*, p. 38.

27. William Cassidy, "On the Origin of Chinese Divination," http:// users. deltanet.com/∼wcassidy/astro/html/chineseorigin.html.

28. Carmen Blacker, "Japan," in Loewe and Blacker, *Oracles and Divination* p. 63.

29. Ibid., p. 70.

30. Michael Lowe Chime Radha Ripoche, "China," in Loewe and Blacker, *Oracles and Divination*, p. 45.

31. Edward D. Campbell, "Fingerprints & Palmar Dermatoglyphics," http:/www.edcampbell.com/PalmD-History.htm.

32. Ibid.

33. Here are some additional examples of divination and deformity. When a woman gives birth to an infant

- that has no nose, affliction will seize upon the country, and the master of the house will die;
- that has neither nose nor penis, the army of the king will be strong and peace will be in the land;
- whose upper lip overrides the lower, the people of the world will rejoice (or good augury for the troops);
- that has no lips, affliction will seize upon the land, and the house of the man will be destroyed;
- that has no right hand, the country will be convulsed by an earthquake;
- that has no fingers, the town will have no births;

- that has no fingers on the right side, the king will not pardon his adversary.
- that has six toes on each foot, the people of the world will be injured (calamity to the troops);
- that has the heart open and that has no skin, the country will suffer from calamities;
- that has no penis, the master of the house will be enriched by the harvest of his field.

34. Karcher, *The Illustrated Encyclopedia of Divination*, p. 44.

35. Ibid.

36. Steven Barrett, "Quackwatch," http://www.quackwatch.com/. Also see A. Simon, "An Evaluation of Iridology," *JAMA* (*Journal of the American Medical Association*), 242 (1979): 1385–87. Also see D. Cockburn, "A Study of the Validity of Iris Diagnosis," *Australian Journal of Optometry*, 64 (1981): 154–57; P. Knipschild, "Looking for Gall Bladder Disease in the Patient's Iris," *British Medical Journal* 297 (1988): 1578–81.

37. Eva Shaw, *Divining the Future*, p. 98.

38. Mell Paul and M. Turford, "Mystic's Menagerie," http://www.mystical-www.co.uk/animala.htm.

39. Mell Paul and M. Turford, "Mystic's Menagerie," http://www.mystical-www.co.uk/animalb.htm#BTL.

40. Mell Paul and M. Turford, "Mystic's Menagerie," http://www.mystical-www.co.uk/animala.htm#ANT.

41. According to Janusz Talalaj's and Stan Talalaj's *Strangest Human Sex* (New York: Seven Hills Book Distributors, 1995), though these ceremonies are no longer official, sometimes the Hiji do them in private as part of their religion's beliefs.

42. Ibid.

43. Mell Paul and M. Turford, "Mystic's Menagerie," http://www.mystical-www.co.uk/animalw.htm#WORM.

44. Karcher, *The Illustrated Encyclopedia of Divination*, p. 37.

45. Mell Paul and M. Turford, "Mystic's Menagerie," http://www.mystical-www.co.uk/animalw.htm.

46. In the early 1930s, British mining engineer A. Chester Beatty acquired three third-century papyri from Egypt; they were published in 1934–37. Known as p[45], p[46], and p[47], they contain thirty leaves of a third-century codex of Matthew, Mark, Luke, John, and Acts.

47. *Encyclopedia Britannica* (on-line), "Dreams as a Source of Divination," http://www.eb.com. Also see "Spirt Web: Study of Angels and the Dimensions," http://www.spiritweb.org/Spirit/angelic-realms.html, and Alma Daniel, Timothy Wyllie, and Andrew Ramer, *Ask Your Angels* (New York: Ballantine Books, 1992).

48. Ibid.

49. Charles Mackay, *Extraordinary Popular Delusions and the Madness of Crowds*, p. 294.

50. Ibid., p. 296.

51. Ibid., p. 300.

52. Ibid., p. 302.

53. Jeanne Avery and Nann Gatewood, *A Soul's Journey: Empowering the Present Through Past Life* (New York: Boru Books, 1996).

54. Jenny Cockell, *Across Time and Death: A Mother's Search for Her Past Life Children* (New York: Fireside, 1994).

55. Simon Hoggart and Mike Hutchinson, *Bizarre Beliefs*, 34. Skepticsalso suggest that this has serious implications for the many cases of "recovered memories" of child abuse. There are peopled suffering long terms of imprisonment because of unsupported "memories" called up by hypnosis.

56. Helen Wambach, *Life Before Life* (New York, Bantam, 1979).

57. Chet Snow and Helen Wambach, *Mass Dreams of the Future* (Dr. Chet Snow: 1993). Note that Chet Snow received his Ph.D. in sociology and history and taught at Columbia University before meeting psychologist Helen Wambach.

58. Paragon Online, "Prophets, Scholars and Predictors," http://binky. paragon.co.uk/ features/Paranormal_ft/cttm/part2.html See also, "Star knowledge UFO conference, interview with Chet Snow," http://www. v-j-enterprises.com/skchets.html.

59. Paragon Online, "Prophets, Scholars, and Predictors."

60. Ibid.

61. *Leading Edge Newspaper*, "Interview with Chet Snow on *Mass Dreams of the Future*," http://www.leadingedgenews.com/massdreams.html.

62. Ibid.

63. Bruce Goldberg, *Past Lives, Future Lives* (New York: Ballantine, 1982).

64. Ibid., 134.

65. Ibid., 135.

66. Ibid., 137–39.

67. Ibid., 138.

68. Bertram Rothschild, "Encouraging Multiple Personality Disorder," *Skeptical Inquirer* 22, no. 6 (November/December 1998): 40–43; Scott Lilienfeld, "Diagnosis and Therapy Gone Haywire," *Skeptical Inquirer* 22, no. 6 (November/December 1998): 54–55; Elisabeth Loftus, "Remembering Dangerously," *Skeptical Inquirer* 19, no. 2 (March/April 1997): p. 20–29.

69. James Lewis, *The Encyclopedia of the Afterlife* (Boston: Visible Ink, 1995), p. 12.

70. Shaw, *Divining The Future*, p. 47.

71. Scott O Lilenfled, "Projective Measures of Personality and Psychopathology," *Skeptical Inquirer* 23, no. 5 (September/October 1999): 32–38.

72. Before Hitler's *Mein Kampf* or Henry Ford's *The International Jews*, Martin Luther (1483-1546) spent time stirring up hatred against the Jewish people. Luther's words against the Jewish people have surfaced and resurfaced again and again throughout history, rekindling hatred for Jews with each new generation that reads his words. Luther wrote *On the Jews and Their Lies* (1543) in which he said things like, "What then shall we Christians do with this damned, rejected race of Jews? Since they live among us and we know about their lying and blasphemy and cursing, we cannot tolerate them if we do not wish to share in their lies, curses, and blasphemy. Their synagogues should be set on fire. Their homes should likewise be broken down and destroyed." See Martin Luther, *On the Jews and Their Lies* (1543), trans. Martin H. Bertram, http://www. flash.net/~twinkle/psycho/ DARK/recreational/luther.html, Also see, Freethinkers BBS, "Martin Luther's Jewish Hatred," http://www.elpaso.net/~spoon/advocate/wcs/ mluther.htm.

73. Technically speaking, the ecliptic is the apparent path of the Sun's annual motion relative to the stars, shown as a circle passing through the center of the imaginary sphere (celestial sphere) containing all the celestial bodies.

75. Hoggart and Hutchinson, *Bizarre Beliefs*, p. 116.

76. Julia and Derek Parker, "History of Astrology," http://www. astrology.net/parkers/, http://www.astrology.net/parkers/inttwe.html.

77. Phil Steinschneider, "Erik Jan Hanussen," http://www.stein schneider.com/biography/hanussen.htm.

77. Michael Fox, "A shtetl Jew turned clairvoyant became Hitler's mentor," 22 March 1996, http://www.jewishsf.com/bk960322/etmentor. htm.

78. Phil Steinschneider, "Erik Jan Hanussen," http://www. steinschneider.com/ biography/ hanussen/page17.htm.

79. Hoggart and Hutchinson, *Bizarre Beliefs*, p. 115.

80. Grant Edwards, "Studies on Astrology," http://www.skepsis.no/english/subject/ astrology/studies.html.

81. Jan Willem Nienhuys, "The Mars Effect in Retrospect," *Skeptical Inquirer* 21 no. 6, (November/December 1997): 24–29; "Mars Effect," http:// home.wxs.nl/~skepsis/mars.html.

82. Marvin Zelen, Paul Kurtz, and G. Abbell, "Is There a Mars Effect?" *Humanist* 37, no.6 (1997): 36–39; Marvin Zelen, "Astrology and Statistics: A Challenge," *The Humanist* 36, no. 1 (1976): 32–33.

83. Michel Gauquelin and F. Gauquelin, "The Zelen Test of the Mars Effect," *The Humanist* 37, no. 6 (1976): 30–35.

84. Paul Kurtz, Marvin Zelen, G. Abell, et al. "Four-part Report on Claimed 'Mars Effect'." *Skeptical Inquirer* 4, no. 2 (1979–80): 19–63.

85. Hoggart and Hutchinson, *Bizzare Beliefs*, p. 125.

86. Geoffrey Dean, "Does Astrology Need to be True? Part 1: A Look at the Real Thing," *Skeptical Inquirer* 11, no. 2 (winter 1987): 166; Grant Edwards, "Studies on Astrology," http://www.skepsis.no/english/subject/astrology/studies.html.

87. Shawn Carlson, "A Double-Blind Test of Astrology," *Nature*, 318, 419, 1985.

88. Ibid.

89. Hoggart and Hutchinson, *Bizarre Beliefs*, p. 125.

90. Martin Gardner, *On the Wild Side*, p. 146.

91. Hoggart and Hutchinson, *Bizarre Beliefs*, p. 126.

92. Claude Benski, ed., *The "Mars Effect:" A French Test of Over 1000 Sports Champions* (Amherst, N.Y.: Prometheus, 1996); Michel Gauquelin, "Zodiac and Personality: An Empirical Study," *Skeptical Inquirer* 6, no. 3 (1982): 57; N. Press, N. F. Michelsen, L. Russel, J. Shannon, and M. Stark, "The New York Suicide Study," *Journal of Geocosmic Research* 2 (1978): 23–47; Roger B. Culver and Philip A. Ianna, *Astrology: True or False?* (Amherst, N.Y.: Prometheus Books, 1988); B. Silverman and M. Witmer, "Astrological Indicators of Personality," *Journal of Psychology*, 87, 89, 1974; R. Pellegrini, "The Astrological Theory of Personality," *Journal of Psychology*, 85, 21, 1973; D. Illingworth, and G Syme, "Birthday and Femininity," *Journal of Social Psychology*, 103, 153 1977; G. Tyson, "Astrology or Season of Birth: A 'Split-sphere' Test," *Journal of Psychology*, 95, 285, 1977; Ertel Suitbert, "Update on the Mars Effect," *Skeptical Inquirer*, 16, no. 2 (winter 1992): 150–60; Jan Willem Nienhuys, "The Mars Effect in Retrospect," *Skeptical Inquirer*, no. 6 (November/December 1997): 24–28. Paul Kurtz,"A Dissenting Note on Ertel's 'Update on the Mars Effect,' " *Skeptical Inquirer*, no. 2 (winter 1992): 161–62; Many of these references come from Grant Edwards, "Studies on Astrology," http://www.skepsis.no/english/subject/astrology/ studies.html.

93. B. Mayes and H. Klugh, "Birthdate, Psychology: A Look at Some New Data," *Journal of Psychology* 99, 27, 1978; J. Mayo, O. White, Ane H. Eysenck, "An Empirical Study of the Relation Between Astrology Factors and Personality," *Journal of Clinical Psychology*, 105, 229, 1979; M. Jackson, "Extroversion, Neuroticism, and Date of Birth: A Southern Hemisphere Study," *Journal of Psychology*, 101, 197, 1979; A. Veno, and P. Pammunt, "Astrological Factors and Personality: A Southern Hemisphere Replication," *Journal of Psychology*, 101, 73, 1979; K. Pawlik and L. Buse, "Self-Attribution as a Differential Psychological Moderating Variable," *Zeitschrift für Sozilpsychologie*, 10, 54, 1979; M. Jackson and M. Fiebert, "Introversion-Extroversion and Astrology," *Journal of Psychology*, 105, 155, 1980; D. Saklofske, I. Kelly, and D. McKerracher, "An Empirical Study of Personality and Astrological Factors," *Journal of Psychology*, 110, 275, 1982; G. Dean, "Does Astrology Need to Be True? Part 1: A Look at the Real Thing," *Skeptical Inquirer*, 11, 166 1987. Many of these references come from Grant Edwards, "Studies on Astrology," http://www. skepsis.no/english/subject/astrology/studies.html.

94. Kenrick Frazier, "Who Believes in Astrology and Why?" *Skeptical Inquirer*, no. 4 (Summer 1992): 344–47.

95. Matthew Nisbet, "Psychic Telephone Networks Profit on Yearning, Gullibility," *Skeptical Inquirer*, 22 no. 3 (May/June 1998): 5–6.

96. Michael Lowe, "China," in Loewe and Blacker, *Oracles and Divination*, p. 48.

97. Three is a very special number to humans. Three is the only natural number that is the sum of all preceding numbers. It is the only number that is the sum of all the factorials of the preceding numbers: 3 = 1! + 2!. In religion, three reigns supreme. For example, in ancient Babylonia, there were three main gods: the Sun, Moon, and Venus. In Egypt there were three main Gods: Horus, Osiris and Isis. In Rome there were three main Gods: Jupiter, Mars and Quirinus. For Christians, three symbolizes the Holy Trinity: Father, Son, and Holy Spirit. In

classical literature, there were three Fates, three Graces, and three Furies. In languages, there are three genders (masculine, feminine, neutral), and three degrees of comparison (positive, comparative, superlative.) German Chancellor Otto von Bismark signed three peace treaties, served under three emperors, waged three wars, owned three estates and had three children. He also organized the union of three countries. His family crest bore the motto: *in trinitate fortitudo* ("In trinity, strength").

98. Martin Gardner, *Knotted Doughnuts and Other Mathematical Entertainments* (New York: W. H. Freeman & Company, 1986).

99. To represent a binary number, only the digits 0 and 1 are used. Each digit of a binary number represents a power of 2. The rightmost digit is the 1s digit, the next digit to the left is the 2s digit, and so on. In other words, the presence of a "1" in a digit position indicates that a corresponding power of 2 is used to determine the value of the binary number. A 0 in the number indicates that a corresponding power of 2 is absent from the binary number. An example should help. The binary number 1111 represents $(1\times2^3)+ (1\times2^2)+(1\times2^1)+(1\times2^0) = 15$. The binary number 1000 represents $1\times2^3 = 8$. Here are the first eight numbers represented in binary notation: 0000, 0001, 0010, 0011, 0100, 0101, 0110, 0111, . . . It turns out that any number can be written in the form $c_nb^n + c_{n-1}b^{n-1} + . . . c_2b^2 + c_1b^1 + c_0b^0$, where $b$ is a base of computation and c is some positive integer less than the base.

100. Frank Frink, The Dutch Philip K. Dick Club, "An essay by Philip K. Dick, 1965," http://www.geocities.com/SoHo/Exhibit/1923/schizo.html. See also www.links.net/vita/spirit/iching/pkdick.html; links.cyborganic.com/spirit/iching/pkdick.html.

101. Michael Lowe, "China," in Loewe and Carmen Blacker, *Oracles and Divination*, p. 50.

102. Carl Jung, *Archetypes and the Collective Unconscious* (New York: Oxford University Press, 1981); Carl Jung, *Synchronicity; An Acausal Connecting Principle* (Princeton, N.J.: Princeton University Press, 1988).

103. James Pruett, "Synchronicity: An Acausal Connecting Principle," http://www.io.com/~mmaltbie/synchron.htm; Carl Jung, *Dreams* (Princeton, N.J.: Princeton University Press, 1988).

104. David Peat, *Synchronicity: The Bridge Between Matter and Mind* (New York: Bantam Books, 1987), p. 65.

105. Arthur Koestler, *The Roots of Coincidence* (New York: Vintage, 1972).

106. Ibid., p. 86.

107. James Pruett, "Synchronicity: An Acausal Connecting Principle," http://www.io.com/~mmaltbie/synchron.htm.

108. Damon Wilson, ed., *The Mammoth Book of Nostradamus and Other Prophets* (New York: Carroll & Graff, 1999), p. 49.

109. Ibid.

110. Leslie A. Shepard, *Encyclopedia of Occultism and Parapsychology*, 3d ed. (Detroit: Gale Research, Inc., 1991). Also see Alan G. Hefner, "The Mystica, an On-line Encyclopedia of the Occult, Mysticism, Magic, Paranormal," http://www.themystica.com/.

111. Shaw, *Divining the Future*, p. 51.

112. Karcher, *The Illustrated Encyclopedia of Divination*, p. 56.

113. Ibid.

114. Carlee Star, "Psychic for a Day: A Day in the Life of a Telephone Psychic," http://www.indielife.com/theattitude/adayinthelife/psychic.htm.

115. Solandia, "Aeclectic Tarot," http://www.aeclectic.net/.

116. Moses said that he possessed the centuries-old, original manuscript of the Zohar, copies of which he had been circulating since the 1280s. However, Moses' wife denied the existence of this manuscript, claiming rather that Moses himself was the author of the Zohar.

117. Wilson, *The Mammoth Book of Nostradamus and Other Prophets*.

118. Lar deSouza, "Stick Figure Tarot," http://www.sentex.net/~fresco/studio/stick_fig.html.

119. Lar deSouza, personal communication to Cliff Pickover.

120. Various editors, *World Almanac Book of the Strange*, p. 394.

121. Monica Knighton, "Day of the Dead," http://www.tarotofthedead.com/.

122. Elizabeth Carmichael and Chloe Sayer, *The Skeleton at the Feast: The Day of the Dead in Mexico* (Austin, Tex.: University of Texas Press, 1992).

123. St. Augustine, *Confessions of St. Augustine* (New York: Image Books, 1960).

124. Thomas Pynchon, *Gravity's Rainbow* (New York: Bantam, 1974), p. 515.

125. Ari Schindler and Jonathan Katz, "Stichomancy," http://www. facade.com/attraction/stichomancy/.

126. Simon and Schuster publishers, "The Bible Code," http://www.simonsays. com/book/default_book. cfm?isbn = 0684810794.

127. David E. Thomas, "Hidden Messages and the Bible Code," *Skeptical Inquirer* 21, no. 6 (November/December 1997): 30–32; Ssee also Davie E Thomas, "Bible-code Developments," *Skeptical Inquirer* 22, no. 2 (March/April 1998): 57–58.

128. Brendan McKay, "Scientific Refutation of the Bible Codes," http://cs.anu.edu.au/ ~bdm/dilugim/torah.html.

129. Richard N. Ostling, "Statistics Crack 'Bible Code,' " *The Associated Press*, 10 September 1999, http://gonews.abcnews.go.com/sections/ science/DailyNews/biblecode990910.html.

130. Doron Witztum, "The Torah Codes," http://www.torahcodes.co.il/.

131. Constance Holden, "Bible code bunkum." *Science* 285, no. 5436 (24 September 1999): 2057.

132. Ibid.

133. Brendan McKay, "Assassinations Foretold in Moby Dick!" http://cs.anu.edu.au/ ~bdm/dilugim/moby.html.

134. "Website Portals," http://ad2004.com/.

135 "Bible Codes," http://ad2004.com/Biblecodes/Englishmatrix/Engmatrix.html.

136. Clifford Pickover, *Cryptorunes* (San Francisco, Calif.: Pomegranate, 2000).

137. Jennifer Smith, "*RAIDO: The Runic Journey*," http://www. tarahill.com/books.html.

138. Clifford Pickover, *Cryptorunes* (San Francisco, Calif.: Pomegranate, 2000).

139. Ibid. See also Olivia Leigh, "Odin's Runes," http://www.free speech.org/second-star/runes/.

140. Clifford Pickover, *The Zen of Magic Squares, Circles, and Stars* (Princeton, N.J.: Princeton University Press, 2000).

141. John Lee Fults, *Magic Squares* (La Salle, Ill.: Open Court, 1974), p. 4.

142. Keith Ellis, *Number Power* (New York: St. Martin's Press, 1978).

143. Annemarie Schimmel, *The Mystery of Numbers* (New York: Oxford University Press, 1993).

144. Ibid.

145. Clifford Pickover, *The Loom of God* (New York: Plenum, 1997).

146. Richard Webster, *Numerology Magic* (St. Paul, Minn.: Llewellyn, 1998).

147. Bob Hartwig, "Bob's Brain Squeezes," http://www.bobjectsinc.com/personal/ autowrit.htm.

148. Bob Hartwig, personal communication to Cliff Pickover.

149. Bob Hartwig, "Bob's Brain Squeezes," http://www.bobjectsinc.com/personal/ index.htm.

150. James Randi, *An Encyclopedia of Claims, Frauds, and Hoaxes of the Occult and Supernatural*, p. 22.

151. Clifford Pickover, *Chaos in Wonderland* (New York: St. Martin's Press, 1995).

152. Robert J. Tripician, "Confessions of a (Former) Graphologist," *Skeptical Inquirer* 24, no. 1 (January/February 2000): 41–43.

153. Underwood Dudley, "Numerology: Comes the Revolution." *Skeptical Inquirer* 22, no. 5 (September/October 1998): 29–31; Arthur Finnessey, *History Computed* (pamphlet), Atlanta, 1983.

154. Dudley, "Numerology," Finnessey, *History Computed*.

155. Robert Anton Wilson, *Cosmic Trigger I: Final Secret of the Illuminati* (New York: New Falcon Publications, 1993). See also "23," http://www. free.de/homes/joern/23.html.

156. Matthew Goodwin, *Numerology: The Complete Guide* (North Hollywood, Calif.: Newcastle Publishing Company 1981), pp. 3–4.

157. Karcher, *The Illustrated Encyclopedia of Divination*, p. 114; Matthew Goodwin, *Numerology: The Complete Guide* (North Hollywood, Calif.: Newcastle Publishing Company, 1981).

158. Lama Chime Radha Ripoche, "Tibet," in Loewe and Blacker, *Oracles and Divination*, p. 3.

159. Ibid. p. 15.

160. Steven Karcher, *The Illustrated Encyclopedia of Divination*, p. 176.

161. Ripoche, "Tibet," p. 16.

162. Tyson, *Scrying for Beginners*, p. 266.

163. William Cassidy, "The Rare Art of Feng-chiao, or 'Wind Angles,'" http://users.deltanet.com/~wcassidy/astro/html/wind.html.

164. Ibid.

165. Karcher, *The Illustrated Encyclopedia of Divination*, p. 76.

166. Eva Shaw, *Divining the Future*, p. 54.

167. Ibid., p. 35; Charmaine Dey, *The Magic Candle* (Bronx, N.Y.: Original Publications, 1989); Kala Pajeon and Ketz Pajeon, *The Candle Magic Workbook* (New York: Citadel Press, 1992).

168. Tyson, *Scrying for Beginners*, p. 4.

169. Ibid., p. 112.

170. Ibid., p. 142.

171. Ibid., p. 146.

172. Ibid., p. 140.

173. Ibid., p. 141.

174 Gary Posner, "$1,000 Challenge to 'Crazy Rod' Dowser Yields Chance Results," *Skeptical Inquirer* 24, no. 1 (January/February 2000): 8. See also, J. T. Enright, "Testing Dowsing: The Failure of the Munich Experiments," *Skeptical Inquirer* 23, no. 1 (January/February 1999): 38–41.

175. James Randi, *An Encyclopedia of Claims, Frauds, and Hoaxes of the Occult and Supernatural*, pp. 80–81.

176. Paula Knowlton, personal communication to Cliff Pickover, 15 December 1999.

177. Karcher, *The Illustrated Encyclopedia of Divination*, pp. 122–23.

# CHAPTER 2. MIND, MYTH, MYSTERY

1. William Shakespeare, *Julius Caesar*, 1.2. 15–24.

2. Damon Wilson, ed., *The Mammoth Book of Nostradamus and Other Prophets*, p. 20.

3. Ibid., p. 21.

4. Ibid.

5. William Shakespeare, *Love's Labour's Lost*, 4.3.

6. Juan O. Tamayo, "A House Divided by Clash of Gods," *The Miami Herald*, 9 January 1997, http://www.cubanet.org/CNews/y97/jan97/ 9clash.html.

7. Martin Gardner, *The Wreck of the Titanic Foretold?* (Amherst, N.Y.: Prometheus, 1998).

8. Morgan Robertson, *Futility: Or The Wreck of the Titan*, 100th anniversary ed. (New York: Virtual Ink, 1998).

9. Wilson, *The Mammoth Book of Nostradamus and Other Prophets*, p. 10.

10. Robert Rubenstein and Richard Newman, "The Living Out of 'Future' Experiences under Hypnosis." *Science* 119 (1954): 472. See also Mark Prendergrast, "Hypnosis: Memory Prod or Production?" http://www.hypnos.co.uk/hypnomag/prender2.htm; Mark Prendergrast, "How to Believe the Unbelievable," in *Victims of Memory*, 2d ed. (Hineburg, Vt.: Upper Access Books, 1996).

11. Rubenstein and Newman, "The Living out of 'Future' Experiences under Hypnosis"; Prendergrast, "Hypnosis," and "How to Believe the Unbelievable."

12. Ibid.

13. Wilson, *The Mammoth Book of Nostradamus and other Prophets*, p. 15.

14. The Revelation of St. John the Divine, 8:7.

15. J. R. Porter, "Ancient Israel," in Michael Loewe and Carmen Blacker, *Oracles and Divination* (Boulder: Shambala, 1981), p. 175. Also see 1 Sam. 6:9.

16. Ibid., p. 205.

17. Ibid., p. 217.

18. David Rose, "Wish Bones and Other Oracles," http://www.wholarts.com/library/wish.html.

19. In Greek legend, the Argonauts were the band of fifty heroes who went with Jason in the ship Argo to fetch the golden fleece.

20. Wilson, *The Mammoth Book of Nostradamus and Other Prophets*, p. 36.

21. Herodotus, *Herodotus: The Histories*, book 2 (New York: Penguin, 1996), pp. 54–58.

22. George Goodenow, "Health Compass," http://pendulumoracles.com/HC%20Main.htm.

23. Wilson, *The Mammoth Book of Nostradmaus and Other Prophets*, p. 37.

24. Ibid., p. 41.

25. Wilson, *The Mammoth Book of Nostradmaus and Other Prophets*, p. 39.

26. The Office of Tibet, the official agency of His Holiness the Dalai Lama in London, "Nechung's Medium," http://www.tibet.com/Buddhism/nechung_medium.html.

27. David Rose, "Wish Bones and Other Oracles," http://www.wholarts.com/library/wish.html.

28. Daniel Cohen, *Waiting for the Apocalypse* (Amherst, N.Y.: Prometheus Books, 1983), p. 13.

29. Reuters, Jakarta, East Java, "Cultists Killed Amid Doomsday No-Show," 13 September 1999, http://news.excite.com/news/r/990913/ 08/odd-indonesia-cult.

30. Gerald Larue, "The Bible and the Prophets of Doom," *Skeptical Inquirer* 23, no.1 (January/February 1999): 25–29.

31. Eugene Weber, "Apocalypse Through History," *The Key Reporter* (Phi Beta Kappa newsletter), 65, no.1 (1999): 4–7.

32. Cohen, *Waiting for the Apocalypse*, p. 13.

33. Ibid., p. 24.

34. Ibid., p. 35.

35. Ibid., p. 36.

37. 1 Thess. 4:16–17.

38. Cohen, *Waiting for the Apocalypse*, p. 44.

39. Ibid., p. 54.

40. Charles Mackay, *Extraordinary Popular Delusions and the Madness of Crowds* (1852; reprint, New York: Crown Publishing, 1995), p. 260.

41. *The Strange & Wonderful History of Mother Shipton*, 1686 pamphlet.

42. B. A. Robinson, "Laws Against Divination, Fortune Telling, etc.," http://www.religioustolerance.org/divi_law.htm.

43. Ibid.

45. "North Carolina's Anti-Divination Law," http://members.aol.com/ oldenwilde/gen_info/blk_rib/nclaw.html.

46. Ibid.

47. Ibid.

48. "Criminal law, North Carolina," http://www.ncga.state.nc.us/statutes/statutes_in_html/chp0140.html.

49. "Ancient Arts Freedom Association," http://hometown.aol.com/srvsmoon/page/index.htm.

50. To better understand a being who can exist outside of time, perhaps it is easier to first visualize a being who can move within a fourth spatial dimension. In my book *Surfing Through Hyperspace: Understanding Higher Universes in Six Easy Lessons,* I discuss *hyperbeings* who can demonstrate the kinds of phenomena that occur in hyperspace. For example, a hyperbeing with access to a fourth spatial dimension can effortlessly remove things before our very eyes, giving us the impression that the objects simply disappeared. This is like a 3-D creature's ability to remove a piece of dirt inside a circle drawn on a page without cutting the circle. The hyperbeing can also see inside any 3-D object or life form, and if necessary remove anything from inside. The being can look inside our intestines, or remove a tumor from our brain without ever cutting through the skin.

51. Anne Rice, *Memnoch the Devil* (New York: Ballantine Books, 1997).

52. Alessandra Stanley, "Vatican Discloses the 'Third Secret' of Fatima," *New York Times,* Sunday, 14 May 2000, page 1.

53. FoxNews.com, Associated Press, "JonBenet's Parents Post Sketch by Deceased Psychic," 3 June 2000, http://www.foxnews.com/national/060300/jonbenet.sml. See also Jon-Benét's family, RamseyFamily.com, http:// www.ramseyfamily.com/.

54. James Randi, *Flim-Flam* (Amherst, N.Y.: Prometheus Books, 1981).

55. James R. Lewis, *Doomsday Prophecies* (Amherst, N.Y.: Prometheus Books, 2000), p. 16.

56. Ibid., p. 18.

57. Ibid., p. 32.

# CHAPTER 3. NOSTRADAMUS AND OTHER PROPHETS

1. Reuters News, "Jerusalem Braces for Syndrome Surge in Millennium," 26 November 1999, http://dailynews.yahoo.com/h/nm/19991126/ od/millennium_syndrome_1.html.

2. Matthew Bunson, *Prophecies 2000* (New York: Pocket Books, 1999).

3. John Hogue, *The Millennium Book of Prophecy* (San Francisco: HarperCollins, 1994).

4. "Millenium Prophecies," http://www.geocities.com/Eureka/Park/ 2631/milen9.htm.

5. Gabriel Oussani, "Catholic Encyclopedia—Beros," http://www.newadvent.org/cathen/02514a.htm.

6. Artemidorus Daldianus, *Onirocriticon libri quinque.* An English translation of this work is available: *The Interpretation of Dreams,* trans. R. J. White (Park Ridge, N.J.: Noyes Press, 1975). See Clifford Pickover, *Strange Brains and Genius* (New York: Quill, 1998) for a discussion on religious dreams, visions, and other experiences as they may relate to temporal lobe epilepsy.

7. Bette Stockbauer, review of *He Walked the Americas,* http://inetport.com/~one/bswalkam.html. Also see L. Taylor Hansen, *He Walked the Americas* (New York: Legend Press, 1994).

8. Ibid.

9. Ibid.

10. Geoffrey of Monmouth, *The History of the Kings of Britain, the Prophecies of Merlin,* by Geoffrey of Monmouth, 1134.

11. John Hogue, *The Millennium Book of Prophecy*, pp. 148, 166. See also, "St Odilia, Catholic Online Saints" (New York: HarperCollins, 1977), http://www.catholic.org/saints/saints/ odilia.html.

12. This fragment appeared in *The Codex Perez and the Book of Chilam Balam of Maani*, trans. and ed. Eugene R. Craine and Reginald C. Reindorp (University of Oklahoma Press, 1979). A note attached to this codex reads, "Copied by D. Juan Pio Perez on October 25, 1837." Also see Bahá'í Communications International, "Mayan Prophecies of Chilam Balam," http://bci.org/prophecy-fulfilled/chilam.htm.

13. Ibid.

14. M. W. Makemson, *The Book of the Jaguar Priest*, a translation of the *Book of Chilam Balam of Tizimin*, with commentary (New York: Henry Schuman, 1951), p. 141.

15. Anthony Grafton, *Cardano's Cosmos: The Worlds and Works of a Renaissance Astrologer* (Cambridge, Mass.: Harvard University Press, 2000); Nancy G. Siraisi, *The Clock and the Mirror: Girolamo Cardano and Renaissance Medicine* (Princeton, N.J.: Princeton University Press, 1997).

16. G. M. Hort, *Dr. John Dee: Elizabethan Mystic and Astrologer* (Kessinger Publishing Company, 1997).

17. Ibid.

18. Ibid.

19. Terrance McKenna, *The Archaic Revival: Speculations on Psychedelic Mushrooms, the Amazon, Virtual Reality, UFOs, Evolution, Shamanism, and the Rebirth of the Goddess* (San Francisco: Harper, 1992).

20. Donald C. Laycock and Stephen Skinner, *The Complete Enochian Dictionary: A Dictionary of the Angelic Language as Revealed to Dr. John Dee and Edward Kelley* (York, Maine: Samuel Weiser, 1994). See also "Alphabets Magical," http://www.geocities.com/SoHo/Lofts/2763/witchy/alphabets.html.

21. Bunson, *Prophecies 2000*, p. 10.

22. "Catholic commentary," http://www.top.net/cathcom/commentary sample.htm.

23. "Prophets of destruction," http://www.missionnet.com/miracles/wethere/proph.html.

24 Yves Dupont, *Catholic Prophecy* (Rockford, Ill.: Tan Books and Publishers, 1973). See also http://www.cc.gatech.edu/people/home/stahl/ rev/vatiguer.htm.

25. Bunson, *Prophecies 2000*, p. 96.

26. Ibid., p. 28.

27. Ibid., p. 98.

28. Marjorie Reeves, *Joachim of Fiore and the Prophetic Future* (New York: Capital Books, 1999).

29. June Petrusma, "Joachim of Fiore," http://ironbark.ucnv.edu.au/~blackhir/Joachimessay.html.

30. Reeves, *Joachim of Fiore and the Prophetic Future*.

31. Ibid.

32. Bunson, *Prophecies 2000*, p. 94.

33. Ibid., p. 10.

34. Hogue, *The Millennium Book of Prophecy*, p. 169.

35. Ibid., p. 348.

36. Damon Wilson, ed., *The Mammoth Book of Nostradamus and Other Prophets* (New York: Carroll & Graff, 1999), pp. 205–206; Elizabeth Sutherland, *The Prophecies of the Brahan Seer* (North Pomfret, Vt.: Trafalgar Square, 1998).

37. Wilson, *The Mammoth Book of Nostradamus and other Prophets*, p. 93. See also James Randi, *The Mask of Nostradamus* (Amherst, N.Y.: Prometheus Books, 1993), p. 40.

38. Wilson, *The Mammoth Book of Nostradamus and other Prophets*, p. 104.

39. Edgar Leoni, *Nostradamus: Life and Literature* (New York: Nosbooks, 1961).

40. Randi, *The Mask of Nostradamus*, p. 175.

41. Ibid., p. 217.

42. Wilson, *The Mammoth Book of Nostradamus and other Prophets*, p. 452.

43. Robert Whymant, "Apocalyptic Bra Lifts Tokyo Pessimists," *The Times*, 13 May 1999, http://www.west.net/ ~ antipas/news/world/japan _bra.html.

44. Jonathan Watts, "Nostradamus Has Japan Quaking," *The Guardian* (London), 1 July 1999, http://www.farshore.force9.co.uk/n_nost1.htm.

45. Whymant, "Apocalyptic Bra Lifts Tokyo Pessimists."

46. Emanuel Swedenborg, *Conversations with Angels: What Swedenborg Heard in Heaven,* ed. Leonard Fox, trans. Donald L. Rose and Jonathan Rose (West Chester, Penn.: Swedenborg Foundation, 1996). Robert H. Kirven, *Angels in Action: What Swedenborg Saw and Heard* (West Chester, Penn.: Swedenborg Foundation, 1995).

47. Donald Tyson, *Scrying For Beginners*, (St. Paul, Minn.: Llewllyn), p. 253.

48. "Emanuel Swedenborg," http://www.swedenborg.net/swedenborg/pages/bio99. html. Emanuel Swedenborg, *Heaven and Hell* trans. George F. Dole (West Chester, Penn.: Swedenborg Foundation, 1990). The Editors of The World Almanac, *The World Almanac Book of The Strange* (New York: Signet, 1977), p. 255.

49. Emanuel Swedenborg, *Conversations With Angels*. Kirven, *Angels in Action*.

50. Bunson, *Prophecies 2000*, p. 94; Yves Dupont, *Catholic Prophecy* (Rockford, Ill.: Tan Books and Publishers, 1973).

51. Albert Bessieres, *Wife Mother and Mystic: Blessed Anna Maria Taigi* (Rockford, Ill.: Tan Books and Publishers, 1977).

52. Bunson, *Prophecies 2000*, p. 113.

53. Ibid.

54. Ibid.

55. Ibid., p. 103.

56. Ibid., p. 106.

57. Kevin Bugeja, "Buge's 100 Prophecies," http://www.geocities.com/ Colosseum/ Midfield/6822/GhostPage/future.htm.

58. Robert Jay Lifton, *Destroying the World to Save It: Aum Shinrikyo, Apocalyptic Violence, and the New Global Terrorism* (New York: Metropolitan Books, 1999).

59. Damian Thompson, *The End of Time: Faith and Fear in the Shadow of the Millennium* (Hanover, N.H.: University Press of New England, 1997). See also, "Prophets, Scholars, and Predictors," http://binky.paragon.co.uk/features/ Paranormal_ft/cttm/part2.html.

60. Jonathan Vankin and John Whalen, "Japan's Most-Wanted Guru Finds It's Time to Wake Up and Smell the Gas," http://www.conspire. com/aum.html.

61. Reba Parker and Timothy Oliver, "Alice Bailey," http://www.watchman.org/ bailypro.htm.

62. Alice A. Bailey, *The Unfinished Autobiography* (New York: Lucis Trust Publishing Co., 1951), p. 36.

63. Ibid., pp. 37–38.

64. Ibid., p. 164.

65. Peter Washington, *Madame Blavatsky's Baboon: A History of the Mystics, Mediums, and Misfits Who Brought Spiritualism to America* (New York: Schocken Books, 1996); Charles J. Ryan and Grace F. Knoche, ed., *H. P. Blavatsky and the Theosophical Movement* (Wheaton, Ill.: Theosophical University Press, 1975).

66. Helen P Blavasky, *The Secret Doctrine* (Adyar ed.), vol. 1 (Wheaton, Ill.: Theosophical University Press: 1989), p. 110.

67. Bunson, *Prophecies 2000*, pp. 25, 136.

68. Ibid., p. 112.

69. St. John Bosco and J. Bacchiarello (compiler), *Forty Dreams of St. John Bosco: The Apostle of Youth* (Rockford, Ill.: Tan Books & Publishers, 1997).

70. Catherine Beebe, *Saint John Bosco and Saint Dominic Savio* (Fort Collins, Colo.: Ignatius Press, 1992).

71. Dannion Brinkley and Paul Perry (contributor), *Saved by the Light: The True Story of a Man Who Died Twice and the Profound Revelations He Received*, with an introduction by Raymond Moody (New York: Harper Paperbacks, 1995). See also "Dannion Brinkley's Near Death Experiences and the Afterlife," http://www.near-death.com/brinkley.html; "Prophets, Scholars, and Predictors," http://binky.paragon.co.uk/features/Paranormal_ft/cttm/part2. html.

72. Ibid.

73. Ibid.

74. Ibid.

75. Ibid.

76. Ibid.

77. Ibid.

78. Paul Case, *Book of Tokens: Tarot Meditations* (Los Angeles, Calif.: Builders of Adytum Ltd, 1974).

79. "Paul Foster Case," http://www.golden-dawn.org/biocase.html.

80. Paul Case, *Book of Tokens: Tarot Meditations*.

81. Bunson, *Prophecies 2000*, p. 26.

82. Dale Beyerstein, "Edgar Cayce: The Prophet Who Slept His Way to the Top," *Skeptical Inquirer* 20, no. 1 (January/February 1996): 32–36.

83. Bunson, *Prophecies 2000*, p. 16.

84. Hogue, *The Millennium Book of Prophecy*, p. 350. For additional quotations, see Edgar Cayce, *Edgar Cayce: Modern Prophet* (Outlet: 1998). See also Kevin J. Todeschi, *Edgar Cayce on Soul Mates: Unlocking the Dynamics of Soul Attraction* (Virgina Beach, Va.: Association for Research and Enlightenment [A.R.E. Press], 1999).

85. James Randi, *An Encyclopedia of Claims, Frauds, and Hoaxes of the Occult and Supernatural* (New York: St. Martin's Press, 1995), pp. 42–43. See also Beyerstein, "Edgar Cayce: The Prophet Who Slept His Way to the Top."

86. Bunson, *Prophecies 2000*, p. 14.

87. Mélanie's quotations are from an exact text written down in 1878 by Mélanie. The message was approved by the Catholic Church and was published in its entirety at Lecce. France, on November 15, 1979, with the imprimatur of Bishop Zola. The prophecies of Mélanie are discussed on many Web pages and in Sandra L. Zimdars-Swartz, *Encountering Mary: From La Salette to Medjugorje* (Princeton, N.J.: Princeton University Press, 1991).

88. Ibid.

89. Ibid.

90. Bunson, *Prophecies 2000*, p. 15.

91. Ibid., p. 15.

92. Ibid., p. 283. For a complete listing of Cherio prophecies, see Count Louis Harmon Cheiro, *Cheiro's World Predictions* (Sante Fe, N.M.: Sun Books, 1981).

93. The First Spiritual Temple, "Florence Cook," http://www.fst.org/ cook.htm; Noah's Ark Society, "Florence Cook," http://www.noahsark. clara.net/cook.htm; Allen W. Grove, "Röntgen's Ghosts: Photography, X-Rays, and the Victorian Imagination," *Literature and Medicine* 16, no. 2 (1997): 141–73 (text at http://www.4nesu.edu:8030/ ~ malsgaa/Rontgen's%20 Ghosts.htm).

94. Trevor H. Hall, *The Medium And The Scientist: The Story of Florence Cook and William Crookes* (Amherst, N.Y.: Prometheus Books, 1985).

95. Diana Holland, "Who is Benjamin Creme," http://members.aol.com/BroOfOld/ 1mans.htm; Benjamin Creme, http://shareintl.org/ background/bcreme/bc_main.htm. Also see Benjamin Creme, *Maitreya's Mission* (London: Share International Foundation, 1993) and "Prophets, Scholars, and Predictors," http://binky.paragon.co.uk/features/Paranormal_ft/ cttm/part2.html.

96. Wilson, *The Mammoth Book of Nostradamus and Other Prophets*, p. 372. Jack Harrison Pollack, *Croiset the Clairvoyant* (New York: Bantam, 1965); Tamara Wilcox, *Mysterious Detectives:*

*Psychics* (New York, Raintree Childrens Books, 1977); Russell Brown, "The Beaumont Children," http://www.student.uwa. edu.au/ ~fifthman/beaumontHome.html.

97. James Lett, "A Field Guide to Critical Thinking," *Skeptical Inquirer* 13, no. 4 (fall 1990), http://www.csicop.org/si/9012/critical-thinking.html.

98. Joe Nickell, *Psychic Sleuths: ESP and Sensational Cases* (Amherst, N.Y.: Prometheus Books, 1994).

99. Martin Gardner, *On the Wild Side* (Amherst, N.Y.: Prometheus Books, 1992), pp. 198–202.

100. Ibid.

101. Ibid.

102. Robert Todd Carroll, "The Skeptic's Dictionary," http://skepdic. com/crowley.html.

103. Mitali Saran, "Telling Time by the Stars," http://www.business-standard.com/99jun05/lei1.htm.

104. Ibid. See also Bejan Daruwalla, "Bejan Daruwalla Official Website," http://www.bejan daruwalla.com/.

105. Davis's prediction of the movement of modern spiritualism was given in his *Principles of Nature,* first published in 1847. See also, Rev. Simeon Stefanidakis, "First Spiritual Temple," "Andrew Jackson Davis" http://www.fst.org/spirit3.htm.

106. Dan Campbell, "The Poughkeepsie Seer," *Studia Sweedenborgiana* 11, no. 1 (1998). http://www.ssr.edu/StudiaSwedenborgiana/vol-111/The PoughkeepsieSeer.html.

107. Andrew J. Davis, *The Principles of Nature, Her Divine Revelations, and a Voice to Mankind* (Health Research, 1984).

108. Ibid.

109. Campbell, "The Poughkeepsie Seer."

110. Ibid.

111. Ibid.

112. Thomas Sugrue, *The Story of Edgar Cayce: There Is a River* (Virgina Beach, Va.: Association for Research and Enlightenment [A.R.E. Press], 1977).

113. Bunson, *Prophecies 2000*, p. 24.

114. Hogue, *The Millennium Book of Prophecy*, p. 160.

115. Ibid., p. 342.

116. Ibid.

117. Kenji Furumi, "Onizaburo Deguch," http://server1.seafolk.ne.jp/~enigma/e. onizaburo.htm.

118. Louise Surette, "Future Gazing Big Seller: Millennium Fever Fuels Books about the Shape of Things to Come," *The Ottawa Citizen*, 9 August 1999, http://www.ottawacitizen.com/national/990403/2442216.html.

119. "Countdown to the Millenium," http://binky.paragon.co.uk/features/Paranormal_ft/cttm/part2.html.

120. Ibid.

121. Ibid.

122. James Lett, "A Field Guide to Critical Thinking," Skeptical Inquirer 13, no. 4 (fall 1990), http://www. csicop.org/si/9012/critical-thinking.html.

123. John William Dunne, *An Experiment with Time.* (London: A & C. Black, 1927). Also see John Dunne, http://www.nevadalink.com/ jwdunne/earlylif.htm.

124. Frank C. Tribbe, ed., *An Arthur Ford Anthology: Writings by and About America's Sensitive of the Century* ( Blue Dolphin Pub, 1999).

125. Ibid.

126. James Randi, *An Encyclopedia of Claims, Frauds, and Hoaxes of the Occult and Supernatural*, p. 101. See also "Fox Sisters," *Columbia Encyclopedia*, http://www.infoplease.com/ce5/CE019190.html.

127. Bunson, *Prophecies 2000*, p. 82.

128. Sabina Flanagan, *Hildegard of Bingen, 1098–1179: A Visionary Life* (New York: Routledge, 1998). Also see Robert Lentz, "St. Hildegard of Bingen," http://natural-bridges.com/store5/rl/HOB.html, and Kristina Lerman, "St. Hildegard of Bingen," http://tweedledee.ucsb.edu/~kris/music/ Hildegard.html.

129. Lerman, "St. Hildegard of Bingen."

130. Wilson, *The Mammoth Book of Nostradamus and Other Prophets,* p. 378; Steven A. Egger, "Psychics and Serial Murder, an Excerpt from *The Killers Among Us,*" http://www.reall.org/newsletter/v05/n09/psychics-and-serial-murder.html.

131. Joe Nickell, *Wonder-Workers! How They Perform the Impossible* (Amherst, N.Y.: Prometheus Books, 1991).

132. James Randi, *An Encyclopedia of Claims, Frauds, and Hoaxes of the Occult and Supernatural,* p. 128.

133. David Icke, *The Robots' Rebellion: The Story of the Spiritual Renaissance* (Gill & Macmillan Publishers, 1994), p. vii. See also, "Robot's rebellion," http://www.trufax.org/menu/davex.html.

134. Ibid., p. 89.

135. Ellie Crystal, "Alois Irlmaier," http://www.crystalinks.com/irlmaier.html.

136. Ibid.

137. Hogue, *The Millennium Book of Prophecy,* p. 76.

138. "Ambres," http://home2.swipnet.se/~w-24689/engelska.htm.

139. Ibid.

140. Ibid.

141. Frater Achad (Charles Stansfeld Jones), *Crystal Vision Through Crystal Gazing,* rev. ed. (Kila, Mont.: Kessinger Publishing Company, 1997).

142. Ibid.

143. Anna (Bonus) Kingsford and Edward Maitland, *The Perfect Way, or the Finding of Christ,* (1909; reprint, Kila, Mont.: Kessinger Publishing Company, 1947), p. 345.

144. Anna (Bonus) Kingsford and Edward Maitland, *Clothed With the Sun of the Soul,* (1889; reprint, Kila, Mont.: Kessinger Publishing Company, 1942).

145. Ramtha, *Beginner's Guide to Creating Reality: An Introduction to Ramtha & His Techings* (Yelm, Wash.: JZK Inc., 1997). Also see, JZ Knight, "Ramtha's School of Enlightenment," http://www.ramtha.com.

146. Robert Todd Carroll, "The Skeptic's Dictionary," http://www.dcn. davis.ca.us/go/btcarrol/skeptic/channel.html. Also see James Alcock, "Channeling," in *The Encyclopedia of the Paranormal,* ed. Gordon Stein (Amherst, N.Y.: Prometheus Books, 1996), pp. 759–66; Nancy Clark, and Nick Gallo. "Do You Believe in Magic—New Light on the New Age," *Family Circle,* 23 February 1993, p. 99; Martin Gardner, *The New Age: Notes of a Fringe Watcher* (Amherst, N.Y.: Prometheus Books, 1988). Ted Schultz and Stewart Brand, "Voices from Beyond: The Age-Old Mystery of Channeling," in *The Fringes of Reason* (New York: Harmony Books, 1989).

147. Ramtha, *Beginner's Guide to Creating Reality.* Also see JZ Knight, "Ramtha's School of Enlightenment," http://www.ramtha.com.

148. JZ Knight, "Ramtha's American Gnostic School," http://www.ramtha.com/about.html.

149. Ibid.

150. Hogue, *The Millennium Book of Prophecy,* p. 105.

151. Ibid., p. 360.

152. Ibid.

153. Ibid.

154. Gladys Osborne Leonard, *My Life in Two Worlds* (London: Cassell & Co, Ltd., 1931). See also First Spiritual Temple, "Gladys Osborne Leonard," http://www.fst.org/leonard.htm.

155. Ibid.

156. Char Margolis and Victoria St. George (contributor), *Questions from Earth, Answers*

*from Heaven: A Psychic Intuitive's Discussion of Life, Death, and What Awaits Us Beyond* (New York: St. Martin's Press, 1999).

157. Drunvalo Melchizedek, *The Ancient Secret of the Flower of Life* (Flagstaff, Ariz.: Light Technology Publications, 1999). Also see Drunvalo Melchizedek, "The Personal Web Site of Drunvalo Melchizedek," http://www. drunvalo.net/index.htm; Drunvalo Melchizedek, "About Drunvalo Melchizedek," http://www.worldpuja.com/MEMBERS/FORUM/1124drgr. htm; 51; "Prophets, Scholars, and Predictors," http://binky.paragon.co.uk/features/Paranormal_ft/cttm/part2.html.

158. Ibid.

159. Ibid.

160. Ibid.

161. Wilson, *The Mammoth Book of Nostradamus and Other Prophets*, pp. 364–70.

162. Ibid., p. 364.

163. Ibid.

164. Ibid., 366.

165. Ibid., 367.

166. Tatiana Lungin, *Wolf Messing: The True Story of Russia's Greatest Psychic* (New York: Paragon House, 1989).

167. "Ruth Montgomery," http://www.eclecticviewpoint.com/evmont.html. Also see Ruth Montgomery, *A Search for the Truth* (New York: Fawcett Book, 1992); Ruth Montgomery, *A World Beyond: A Startling Message from the Eminent Psychic Arthur Ford from Beyond the Grave* (New York: Fawcett Book, 1989).

168. Tyson, *Scrying for Beginners*, p. 237. Also see William S. Moses, *Spirit Teachings Through the Mediumship of William Stainton Moses* (New York: Ayer Company, 1976).

169. Emily Groszos Ooms, *Women and Millenarian Protest in Meiji Japan: Deguchi Nao and Omotokyo* (Ithaca, N.Y.: Cornell University Press, 1993). See also "Omoto," *Encyclopædia Britannica Online*, http://www.eb.com:180/ bol/topic?eu = 58523&sctn = 1.

170. "Mokichi Okada," http://www.grappolo.com/orientalia/moa.htm. See also, Mokichi Okada, *Health and the New Civilization* (Kyoto, Japan: Johrei Fellowship, 1991).

171. "The Philosophy of Mokichi Okada," http://www.moa-inter. or.jp/english/philosophy/philo-contents.html.

173. Hogue, *The Millennium Book of Prophecy*, p. 12.

174. Ibid., p. 13.

175. Ibid., p. 183.

176. Andy Hughs, "Seth In His Own Words," http://www.spiritual-endeavors.org/seth/Andy.htm. (Andy Hughes was one of Jane Roberts's original class members. All of the information at this Web site are supposed to be the words of Seth that he reordered and revised to give continuity to his understanding of the material. See also Jane Roberts with Robert F. Butts, *Seth Speaks: The Eternal Validity of the Soul* (San Rafael, Calif.: Amber-Allen Publishing, 1994).

177. "Seth/Jane Roberts," http://www.secretoflife.com/seth/index.html. P. M. Nicholson, "Jane Roberts," http://www.stanford.edu/ ~daric/seth/faq/5.html.

178. Ellie Crystal, "Channelers—Channeled Books and Messages," http://www. crystalinks.com/channeled_books.html.

179. Ibid.

180. To be precise about this, James Randi in *An Encyclopedia of Claims, Frauds, and Hoaxes of the Occult and Supernatural* (p. 128) says, "David Icke called a press conference to announce a number of upcoming world-shaking events revealed to him personally, he said, by Socrates, 'the Godhead,' Jesus Christ, and various other spirits. They had chosen him, he said to be the 'channel for the Christ spirit'."

181. David Icke, *And the Truth Will Set You Free* (New York: Truth Seeker, 1998), chap. 1, "The Veil of Tears."

182. Ellie Crystal, "Prophets and prophecies," http://www. crystalinks.com/proph.html.

See also Gordon-Michael Scallion and Cynthia Keyes, *Notes from the Cosmos: A Futurist's Insights into the World of Dream Prophecy and Intuition* (New Hampshire: Matrix Institute, 1997).

183. Robert Todd Carroll, "The Skeptic's Dictionary," http://wheel.dcn.davis.ca.us/go/btcarrol/skeptic/scallion.html.

184. "The Great 1998 Prediction Contest: Gordon Michael Scallion," http://www.m-m.org/~jz/scalliona.html.

185. David Sunfellow, "A New Heaven New Earth Special Report: Gordon-Michael Scallion: A Summary of His Most Important Predictions," *NewAge On-Line Australia*, 11 November 1994, http://www.newage. com.au/library/scallion.html.

186. Bunson, *Prophecies 2000*, p. 120.

187. David Sunfellow, "Gordon-Michael Scallion," 1994, http://www.v-j-enterprises.com/scalpred.html.

188. Robert Todd Carroll, "The Skeptic's Dictionary," http://wheel.dcn.davis.ca.us/go/btcarrol/skeptic/scallion.html.

189. John Hogue, *The Millennium Book of Prophecy*, p. 183.

190. Ibid.

191. Zecharia Sitchin, *Twelfth Planet* (New York: Avon, 1983). Also see "Interview with Zecharia Sitchin," http://www.jonathanmark.com/ sitchin.html.

192. Raël, *The True Face of God* (The Raelian Foundation, 1998). Also see, "Official Homepage of the International Raëlians Religion," http:// www.rael.org/; "Messages from Extraterrestrials," http://www.netside.net/~raelian/amessag2.html; Ellie Crystal, "Zecharia Sitchin," http://www.crystalinks.com/sitchen.html.

193. Donna J. Kossy, *Kooks: A Guide to the Outer Limits of Human Belief* (New York: Feral House, 1994).

194. Solara, *11:11: Inside the Doorway* (New York: Star Borne Unlimited, 1992). Also see, "The Nvisible: Solara and 11:11," http://www.nvisible.com/.

195. Robert Todd Carroll, "The Skeptic's Dictionary," http://skepdic. com/sollog.html. (Sollog's real name is said to be John Patrick Ennis.) See also "Sollog," http://www.sollog.com/ (According to Robert Todd Carroll, Sollog is promoted at www.sollog.com by ASSI Publishing. Sollog.com may not be Sollog's page; thus, what is said there may not actually be Sollog speaking but perhaps someone from ASSI.)

196. Carroll, "The Skeptic's Dictionary."

197. See www.solog.com.

198. Rev. Eur. Ing. Steven C. Birks, "Pick 'n Mix Spirituality—Index of Christian Cults," http://www.netcentral.co.uk/steveb/cults/southcott.htm. See also, Eugene P. Wright (editor) and Kim Taylor (illustrator) *Catalogue of the Joanna Southcott Collection at the University of Texas* (Austin, Tex.: University of Texas, 1968); Joanna Southcott, *Dispute between the Woman and the Powers of Darkness 1802* (New York: Cassell Academic, 1995).

199. Birks, "Pick 'n Mix Spirituality;" Wright and Taylor, Catalogue of the Tòànna Southcott Collection; Southcott, *Dispute*.

200. Bunson, *Prophecies 2000*, p. 45.

201. Ibid., p. 30. Also see "Futureverse," http://www.angelfire.com/ak2/ futureverse/.

202. Ibid.

203. Art Bell and Whitley Strieber, *The Coming Global Superstorm* (New York: Pocket Books, 2000).

204. Hogue, *The Millennium Book of Prophecy*, p. 87.

205. Ibid.

206. Ibid., p. 200.

207. "Mitar Tarabich," http://www.crystalinks.com/proph.html. Tarabich's words, recorded in *Kremasko Prorochanstvo*, or *Kremna's Prophecy*, are all over the Internet.

208. Ibid.

209. Ibid.

210. *Siddharth Varadarajan (Times of India)*, "With the dark Lord in a darkened city," http://chakra.org/miscellaneous/knews/OtherNews/ 990730b.htm.

211. Clifford Pickover, *Strange Brains and Genius* (New York: Quill, 1999).

212. Ibid., p. 271.

213. Ibid, p. 272.

214. Ellie Crystal, "Prophets and Prophecies," http://www.crystalinks. com/proph.html. Also see Josyp Terelya, *Witness: To Apparitions and Persecution in the USSR—An Autobiography* (Milford, Ohio: The Riehle Foundation, 1992).

215. Thomas W. Petrisko, *Visions and Prophecies of Christina Gallagher* (Touchstone Books, 1995).

216. See, for example, numerous Web sites: Ellie Crystal, "Australian Aboriginal Prophecies," http://www.crystalinks.com/aboriginal.html; "Prophets, Scholars, and Predictors," http://groove.paragon.co.uk/features/ Paranormal_ft/cttm/part2b.html.

217. Ibid.

218. Ellie Crystal, "Lori Toye," http://www.crystalinks.com/toye.html; Lori Toye, "I am America official homepage," http://iamamerica.com/.

219. Ibid.

220. Robert Todd Carroll, "The Skeptic's Dictionary—James Van Praagh," http://wheel.dcn.davis.ca.us/go/btcarrol/skeptic/vanpraagh.html. See also Michael Shermer, *Why People Believe Weird Things: Pseudoscience, Superstition, and Other Confusions of Our Time* (New York: W H Freeman and Company, 1998); Joe Nickell, "Review of Psychic MediumVan Praagh on CNN's Larry King Live," http://www.csicop.org/articles/19990608-vanpraagh/; James Van Praagh, "James Van Praagh," http://www.vanpraagh. com/.

221. "The Central Premonitions Registry," http://clever.net/yaron/ precog/precog.htm. (This site is maintained by Yaron Mayer, a psychologist with an interest in ESP research and a former member of the Israeli Parapsychology Association.)

222. "Prophets, Scholars, and Predictors," http://binky.paragon.co. uk/features/Paranormal_ft/cttm/part2.html. See also Chet B. Snow with Helen Wambach, *Mass Dreams of the Future* (Crest Park, Calif.: Deep Forest Press, 1993).

223. Ibid.

224. Gene Emery, "Failed Psychic Predictions, 1999," http://www.csicop.org/articles/psychic-predictions/1999.html.

225. Ibid.

# CHAPTER 4. SCIENCE AND THE WILL TO BELIEVE

1. Reuters, "Seeing Crimes About to Happen?" Thursday, 9 December 1999, 8:37 AM ET, http://dailynews.yahoo.com/h/nm/19991209/od/ alert_1.html.

2. Duncan Graham-Rowe, "Warning! Strange Behaviour," *New Scientist*, (11 December 1999) http://www.newscientist.com/ ns/19991211/warningstr.html.

3. Benjamin Radford, "Survey Finds 70% Women, 48% Men Believe in Paranormal," *Skeptical Inquirer* 22, no. 2 (March/April 1998): 8–9.

4. Matthew Nisbet, "Psychic Telephone Networks Profit on Yearning, Gullibility." *Skeptical Inquirer* 22, no. 3 (May/June 1998): 5–6.

5. David Rose, "Wish Bones and Other Oracles," http://www.wholarts.com/library/wish.html.

6. Benajamin Radford, "State Attorney General Targets 'Psychic' Gadget Fraud," *Skeptical Inquirer* 22, no. 2 (March/April 1998): 8.

7. Terry Tremaine, "Global Fortune-telling and Bible Prophecy," *Skeptical Inquirer* 18, no. 2 (winter 1994): 166–69.

8. Ibid.

9. John Dominic Crossan, *The Historical Jesus* (San Francisco: Harper, 1991).

10. Burton L. Mack, *The Lost Gospel: The Book of Q and Christian Origins* (San Francisco: Harper, 1993).

11. Hal Lindsay, *The Late Great Planet Earth* (Grand Rapids, Mich.: Zondervan, 1970).

12. Randi, *The Mask of Nostradamus.*

13. C. Eugene Mery Jr., "Psychics Missed It Big (Again in 1995)," *Skeptical Inquirer* 20, no. 1 (January/February 1996): 5.

14. Robert Todd Carroll, "Remote Viewing," http://www.skepdic. com/remotevw.html.

15. James Randi, *Flim-Flam!* (Amherst, N.Y.: Prometheus Books, 1982), pp. 68–69. See also David A. Morehouse, *Psychic Warrior* (New York: St. Martin's Press, 1998).

16. Ray Hyman, "Evaluation of Program on Anomalous Mental Phenomena," *Journal of Scientific Exploration* 10, no.1 (1996): 59–61.

17. Gregory Vistica, "Psychics and Spooks, How spoon-benders fought the cold war," *Newsweek*, 11 December 1995, p. 50.

18. Clifford Pickover, "A Chernikov Pattern Puzzle." *Skeptical Inquirer* 18, no. 2 (winter 1994): 170–72.

19. Clifford Pickover, *Mazes for the Mind* (New York: St. Martin's Press, 1992).

20. Marvin Kaye, *Handbook of Mental Magic* (Briar Cliff Manor, N.Y.: Stein and Day, 1975).

21. Ibid.

22. Martin Gardner, *Science: Good, Bad, and Bogus* (Amherst, N.Y.: Prometheus Books, 1981).

23. David Voss, "'New Physics' Finds a Haven at the Patent Office," *Science* May 5418, no. 284 (May 1999): 1252–54.

24. Kendrick Frazier, "'Human Presence Detector' Device Fails Controlled Test a National Laboratory," *Skeptical Inquirer* 22, no. 4 (1998): 9.

25. Eugene Weber, "Apocalypse through History," *The Key Reporter* (Phi Beta Kappa newsletter), 65, no.1 (1994): 4–7. See also Eugen Weber, *Apocalypses: Prophecies, Cults, and Millennial Beliefs Through the Ages* (Cambridge, Mass.: Harvard University Press, 1999).

26. James Alcock, "The Belief Engine," *Skeptical Inquirer* 19, no. 3 (May/June 1995): 14–18.

27. Stephen Skinner, *Millennium Prophecies* (New York: Barnes & Noble Books, 1997), p. 142.

28. Daniel Cohen, *Waiting for the Apocalypse* (New York: Prometheus Books, 1983), p. 57.

29. Ibid., p. 79.

30. John Allen Paulos, "Rumors, Self-fulfilling Prophecies, and National Obsessions," *Skeptical Inquirer* 19, no. 4 (August 1995): 26–30.

31. Ibid.

## SOME FINAL THOUGHTS

1. Reuters, "Three Sentenced to Death for Child Sacrifice," Wednesday, 8 December 7:42 AM ET, 1999, http://dailynews.yahoo.com/h/nm/ 19991208/od/sorceress_1.html.

2. Kristina Lerman, "St. Hildegard of Bingen," http://tweedledee.ucsb.edu/ ~kris/ music/Hildegard.html. See also Sabina Flanagan, *Hildegard of Bingen, a Visionary Life* (London: Routledge, 1989); Sabina Flanagan, trans., *Secrets of God: Writings of Hildegard of Bingen* (Boston and London: Shambala Publications, 1996).

3. Oliver Sacks, *The Man Who Mistook His Wife for a Hat and Other Clinical Tales* (New York: Perennial Library, 1987).

4. Clifford Pickover, *Strange Brains and Genius: The Secret Lives of Eccentric Scientists and Madmen* (New York: Quill, 1999).

5. Eve LaPlante, *Seized* (New York: HarperCollins, 1993).

6. Damon Wilson, ed., *The Mammoth Book of Nostradamus and Other Prophets* (New York: Carroll & Graff, 1999), p. xi.

7. Ibid., p. ix. See also J. W. Dunne, *An Experiment With Time* (Amherst, N.Y.: Prometheus Books, 1958).

8. Simon Hoggart and Mike Hutchinson, *Bizarre Beliefs* (London: Richard Cohen Books, 1995), p. 74.

9. Ibid., p. 111.

10. Ibid.

11. Anthony De Mello, *The Song of the Bird* (New York: Image Books, 1984).

12. Clifford Pickover, *Time: A Traveler's Guide* (New York: Oxford University Press, 1999).

13. Ibid., p. xiii. Silesius (1624–1677) was the religious poet remembered as the author of *Der Cherubinischer Wandersmann* (The Cherubic Wanderer), a major work of Roman Catholic mysticism. Another collection, *Heilige Seelenlust* (Holy Joy of the Soul), contains his religious songs celebrating the union of the soul with God, many of which survive to the present day in both Protestant and Catholic hymnals.

14. Pickover, *Time: A Traveler's Guide*, pp. 47–57.

15. "Princeton Engineering Anomalies Research," http://www. princeton.edu/~pear/.

16. Ibid.

17. Robert G. Jahn and Brenda J. Dunne, *Margins of Reality* (New York: Harcourt Brace, 1989).

18. Victor Stenger, *The Unconscious Quantum* (Amherst, N.Y.: Prometheus Books, 1995), pp. 29–31.

19. James Randi, *An Encyclopedia of Claims, Frauds, and Hoaxes of the Occult and Supernatural* (New York: St. Martin, 1997).

20. Reuters News, "School Expels 5 for Being 'Witches'," Friday, 31 December 7:34 AM ET, http://dailynews.yahoo.com/h/nm/19991231/ od/chile_witches_1.html. See also the Chilean newspapers *La Nacion* and *Las Ultimas Noticias*, Thursday, 30 December 1999.

21. Ibid.

22. Reuters News, "Politician Asked to Resign Over Cow dung," Monday, 3 January 2000, 9:52 AM ET, http://dailynews.yahoo.com/h/nm/20000103/ od/dung_1.html.

23. Ibid.

24. Erik Stokstad, "Stephen Straus's Impossible Job," *Science* 288, no. 5471 (2000): 1568.

25. Barry L. Beyerstein, "Why Bogus Therapies Seem to Work," *Skeptical Inquirer* 21, no. 5 (September/October 1997): 33. http://www.csicop.org/si/9709/beyer. html.

26. Ibid.

27. Ibid.

28. Bruce Bower, "Religions Commitment Linked to Longer Life," *Science News* 157, no. 23 (3 June 2000): 359. Regular involvement in religious activities seems to correlate with better physical health and longer life, according to a statistical analysis of forty-two independent studies published since 1977. However, this does not mean that religious involvement causes better health. It may be that religious people are those people who avoid risky behaviors such as smoking and alcohol use.

29. Robert E. Bartholomew, "The Martian Panic Sixty Years Later: What Have We Learned?" *Skeptical Inquirer* 22, no. 6 (November/December 1998): 40–43.

30. Ibid., p. 42.

31. Michael Shermer, *How We Believe: The Search for God in an Age of Science* (New York: Freeman, 1999). See also Massimo Pigliucci, "Why Everybody Believes in Fairy Tales," *Skeptical Inquirer* 24, no. 3 (May/June 2000): 50–51.

32. Benjamin Radford, "Nostradamus 1999 Predictions Miss (Again)," *Skeptical Inquirer* 24, no. 3 (May/June 2000): 6.

33. William Grey, "Philosophy and the Paranormal," *Skeptical Inquirer* 18, no. 3 (winter 1994):148.

34. "Imaginary Friend," *Star Trek: The Next Generation* (season 5, episode 122, first air date: May 4, 1992).

35. Stephen Hawking, *A Brief History of Time* (New York: Bantam, 1988).

# APPENDICES

1. Matthew Bunson, *Prophecies 2000* (New York: Pocket Books, 1999), p. 42.

2. Ibid., p. 169.

3. James Randi, *The Mask of Nostradamus* (Amherst, N.Y.: Prometheus Books, 1993), p. 235.

4. Olivia Leigh, "Odin's Runes," http://www.freespeech.org/secondstar/runes/.

5. John Opsopaus, "The Art of Haruspicy," http://www.omphalos. org/BA/Har.html or http://www.cs.utk.edu/~mclennan/OM/BA/Har. html.

# For Further Reading

*I do not know, with what kind of weapons the Third World War will be led, but the fourth world war will be fought with sticks and stones.*

—Albert Einstein

## SEVERAL USEFUL BOOKS

Anderson, Bill. *Nostradamus.* Bristol, United Kingdom: Paragon, 1998.

Blackmore, Susan. *In Search of the Light: The Adventures of a Parapsychologist.* Amherst, N.Y.: Prometheus Books, 1996.

Brand, Stewart. *The Fringes of Reason.* New York: Harmony Books, 1989.

Bunson, Matthew. *Prophecies 2000.* New York: Pocket Books, 1999.

Cohen, Daniel. *Waiting for the Apocalypse.* N.Y.: Prometheus Books, 1983.

Drury Nevill and Gergory Tillett. *The Occult.* New York: Barnes & Nobles Books, 1997.

The Editors of The World Almanac. *The World Almanac Book of The Strange.* New York: Signet, 1977.

Fiery, Ann. *The Book of Divination* San Francisco: Chronicle Books, 1999.

Frazier, Kendrick. *Science Confronts the Paranormal.* Amherst, N.Y.: Prometheus Books, 1986.

Gardner, Martin. *Science: Good, Bad and Bogus* Amherst, N.Y.: Prometheus Books, 1981.

———. *The New Age: Notes of a Fringe Watcher* Amherst, N.Y.: Prometheus Books, 1988.

———. *On The Wild Side.* Amherst, N.Y.: Prometheus Books, 1992.

———. *The Wreck of the Titanic Foretold?* Amherst, N.Y.: Prometheus, 1998.

Goldberg, Bruce. *Past Lives, Future Lives.* New York: Ballantine, 1997.

Goodwin, Matthew. *Numerology: The Complete Guide.* North Hollywood, Calif.: Newcastle Publishing Company 1981, 3–4.

Hoggart, Simon, and Mike Hutchinson. *Bizarre Beliefs* London, Richard Cohen Books, 1995.

Hogue, John. *The Millennium Book of Prophecy.* San Francisco: Harper Collins, 1994.

Huston, Peter. *Scams from the Great Beyond: How to Make Easy Money Off of Esp, Astrology, Ufos, Crop Circles, Cattle Mutilations, Alien Abductions, Atlantis, and Channeling.* New York: Paladin Press, 1997.

Hines, Terence. *Pseudoscience and the Paranormal: A Critical Examination of the Evidence* Amherst, N.Y.: Prometheus Books, 1988.

Jahn, Robert G., and Brenda J. Dunne, *Margins of Reality*. New York: Harcourt Brace, 1989.

Karcher, Stephen. *The Illustrated Encyclopedia of Divination*. New York: Barnes & Nobles Books, 1997.

Kaye, Marvin. *Handbook of Mental Magic*. Briar Cliff Manor, N.Y.: Stein and Day, 1975.

Kossy, Donna J. *Kooks: A Guide to the Outer Limits of Human Belief*. New York: Feral House, 1994.

LaPlante, Eve. *Seized*. New York: HarperCollins, 1993.

Lewis, James. *The Encyclopedia of the Afterlife*. Boston: Visible Ink, 1995.

Loewe, Michael, and Carmen Blacker. *Oracles and Divination* Boulder: Shambala, 1981.

Mackay, Charles. *Extraordinary Popular Delusions and the Madness of Crowds*. 1852. Reprint, New York: Crown Publishing, 1995.

Marlock, Dennis, and John Dowling. *License to Steal: Traveling Con Artists, Their Games, Their Rules—Your Money*. Boulder, Colo.: Paladin Press, 1994.

Nickell, Joe. *Wonder-Workers! How They Perform the Impossible*. Amherst, N.Y.: Prometheus Books, 1991.

Osborn, Kevin, and Dana Burgess. *The Complete Idiot's Guide to Classical Mythology*. New York: Alpha Books, 1998.

Pickover, Clifford. *Time: A Traveler's Guide*. New York: Oxford University Press, 1999.

———. *Strange Brains and Genius: The Secret Lives of Eccentric Scientists and Madmen*. New York: Quill, 1999.

Prieditis, Arthur A. *The Fate of the Nations*. New York: Llewellyn, 1990.

Randi, James. *Flim-Flam!* Amherst, N.Y.: Prometheus Books, 1982.

———. *The Mask of Nostradamus*. Amherst: N.Y.: Prometheus Books, 1990.

———. *An Encyclopedia of Claims, Frauds, and Hoaxes of the Occult and Supernatural*. New York: St. Martin's Press, 1995.

Robinson, Lynne, and La Vonne Carlson-Finnery, *The Complete Idiot's Guide to Being Psychic*. New York: MacMillan Publishing Company, 1998.

Shaw, Eva. *Divining the Future*. New York: Facts on File, 1995.

Shermer, Michael. *How We Believe : The Search for God in an Age of Science*. New York: W H Freeman and Company, 1999.

———. *Why People Believe Weird Things: Pseudoscience, Superstition, and Other Confusions of Our Time*. New York: W H Freeman and Company, 1998.

Stein, Gordon. *The Encyclopedia of the Paranormal*. Amherst, N.Y.: Prometheus Books, 1996.

Stenger, Victor. *The Unconscious Quantum*. Amherst, N.Y.: Prometheus Books, 1995.

Tyson, Donald. *Scrying for Beginners*. St. Paul, Minn.: Llewllyn, p. 170.

Vyse, Stuart A. *Believing in Magic: The Psychology of Superstition*. New York: Oxford University Press, 1997.

Wilson, Damon. *The Mammoth Book of Nostradamus and Other Prophets*. New York: Carol and Graf, 1999.

## CURIOUS ARTICLES

Alcock, James. "The Belief Engine." *Skeptical Inquirer* 19, no. 3 (May/June 1995): 14–18.

Dudley, Underwood. "Numerology: Comes the Revolution." *Skeptical Inquirer* 22, no.5 (September/October 1998): 29–31.

Frazier, Kendrick. "'Human Presence Detector' Device Fails Controlled Test a National Laboratory." *Skeptical Inquirer* 22, no. 4 (July/August 1998): 9.

———. "Who Believes in Astrology and Why?" *Skeptical Inquirer* 16, no. 4 (summer 1992): 344–47.

Holden, Constance. "Bible Code Bunkum." *Science* 285, no. 5436 (24 September 1999): 2057.

Lilenfled, Scott O. "Projective Measures of Personality and Psychopathology." *Skeptical Inquirer* 23, no. 5 (September/October 1999): 32–38.

Nisbet, Matthew. "Psychic Telephone Networks Profit on Yearning, Gullibility." *Skeptical Inquirer* 22, no. 3 (May/June 1998): 5–6.

Pickover, Clifford. "A Chernikov Pattern Puzzle." *Skeptical Inquirer* 18, no. 2 (winter 1994): 170–72.

Posner, Gary. "$1,000 Challenge to 'Crazy Rod' Dowser Yields Chance Results." *Skeptical Inquirer* 24, no. 1 (January/February 2000): 8.

Radford, Benjamin. "Survey Finds 70% Women, 48% Men Believe in Paranormal." *Skeptical Inquirer* 22, no. 2 (March/April 1998): 8–9.

Rubenstein, Robert, and Richard Newman, "The Living Out of 'Future' Experiences under Hypnosis." *Science* 119 (1954): 472.

Thomas, Davie E. "Bible-code Developments." *Skeptical Inquirer* 22, no. 2 (March/April 1998): 57–58.

———. "Hidden Messages and The Bible Code." *Skeptical Inquirer* 21, no. 6 (November/December 1997): 30–32.

Tremaine, Terry. "Global Fortune-Telling and Bible Prophecy." *Skeptical Inquirer* 18, no. 2 (winter 1994):166–69.

Stenger, Victor. "Quantum Quackery." *Skeptical Inquirer* 21, no. 1 (January/February 1997): 37–40.

Voss, David. "New Physics Finds a Haven at the Patent Office." *Science* 5418, no. 284 (May 1999): 1252–54.

## SOME FASCINATING AND USEFUL WEB SITES

As many readers are aware, Internet Web sites come and go. Sometimes they change address or completely disapear. The Web site addresses listed here provided valuable background information when this book was written. You can, of course, find numerous other Web sites relating to divination and prophecy using Web search tools such as the ones provided at www.google.com.

"Biblioteca Arcana." http://www.cs.utk.edu/~mclennan/OM/BA/Har.html

"The Catholic Encyclopedia." http://www.newadvent.org/cathen/

Barrett, Steven. "Quackwatch." http://www.quackwatch.com/

Bugeja, Kevin. "Buge's 100 Prophecies," http://www.geocities.com/Colosseum/Midfield/6822/GhostPage/future.htm

"Azande." Encyclopædia Britannica Online. http://www.eb.com:180/bol/topic?eu=11664&sctn=1 (Also see www.britannica.com for all Britannica references.)

"Divination." *Encyclopædia Britannica Online.* http://www.eb.com:180/bol/topic?eu=114999&sctn=1

"Prophecy." Encyclopædia Britannica Online. http://www.eb.com:180/bol/topic?eu=117215&sctn=1

"Dream." Encyclopædia Britannica Online. http://www.eb.com:180/bol/topic?eu=117531&sctn=2

"Anatolian religion." Encyclopædia Britannica Online. http://www.eb.com:180/bol/topic?eu=119917&sctn=6

"Oracle." Encyclopædia Britannica Online. http://www.eb.com:180/bol/ topic?thes_id = 288244

"P'ungsuchirisol." Encyclopædia Britannica Online. http://www.eb.com:180/bol/topic?eu = 63478&sctn = 1

"Grettis saga." Encyclopædia Britannica Online. http://www.eb.com:180/bol/topic?eu = 38844&sctn = 1

"Sacrifice." Encyclopædia Britannica Online. http://www.eb.com:180/bol/topic?eu = 117416& sctn = 1

"Astrology." Encyclopædia Britannica Online. http://www.eb.com:180/bol/topic?artcl = 108511&seq_nbr = 1&page = n&isctn = 2

"Mahapurusa." Encyclopædia Britannica Online. http://www.eb.com:180/bol/topic?idxref = 300536

"Sibylline Oracles." Encyclopædia Britannica Online. http://www.eb.com:180/bol/topic?eu = 69366&sctn = 1

Carroll, Robert Todd. *The Skeptic's Dictionary*, http://www.dcn.davis.ca.us/go/btcarrol/ skeptic/channel.html and http://www.skepdic.com/

Cassidy, William. "On the Origin of Chinese Divination." http://users. deltanet.com/~wcassidy/astro/html/chineseorigin.html

"The Central Premonitions Registry." http://clever.net/yaron/precog/ precog.htm

Crystal, Ellie. "Prophets and prophecies." http://www.crystalinks.com/ proph.html

———. "Channelers—Channeled Books and Messages." http://www. crystalinks.com/channeled_books.html

Fitzgerald, Waverly. "Celebrating Halloween." http://www.nas.com/jpcolbertart/seasons/ celebhallows.html

Fortune Cookie Limited. "The History of The Fortune Cookies." http://www.fortunecookie. demon.co.uk/fhistory.html

Hefner, Alan G. "The Mystica, an On-line Encyclopedia of the Occult, Mysticism, Magic, Paranormal." http://www.themystica.com/. See especially, "Divination, http://www.the mystica.com/mystica/pages/divination.html

Lett, James. "A Field Guide to Critical Thinking." http://www.csicop. org/si/9012/critical-thinking.html

McKay, Brendan. "Scientific Refutation of the Bible Codes." http://cs.anu.edu.au/ ~bdm/dilugim/torah.html

"North Carolina's Anti-Divination Law." http://members.aol.com/oldenwilde/gen_info/ blk_rib/nclaw.html

Opsopaus, John. "The Art of Haruspicy." http://www.cs.utk.edu/~mclennan/OM/BA/ Har.html

"Princeton Engineering Anomalies Research." http://www.princeton. edu/~pear/

Rose, David. "Wish Bones and Other Oracles." http://www.wholarts. com/library/wish.html

Paul, Mell, and M. Turford. "Mystic's Menagerie." http://www.mystical-www.co.uk/ animala.htm

Pickover, Clifford. "ESP Test and Quantum Fortune Cookie." http://www. pickover.com

"The Matrix Oracles." http://www.thenewage.com/oracles/index.html

Cloggie, Gavin, and Paragon Publishing Ltd. "Prophets, Scholars, and Predictors." http://binky.paragon.co.uk/features/Paranormal_ft/cttm/part2. html

Witztum, Doron. "The Torah Codes." http://www.torahcodes.co.il/

Zeitlyn, David. "Anthropological Studies of Divination: Spider Divination." http://lucy. ukc.ac.uk/Fdtl/Spider/

# About the Author

Clifford A. Pickover received his Ph.D. from Yale University's Department of Molecular Biophysics and Biochemistry. He graduated first in his class from Franklin and Marshall College, after completing the four-year undergraduate program in three years. His many books have been translated into Italian, German, Japanese, Chinese, Korean, Portuguese, and Polish. He is author of the popular books: *The Zen of Magic Squares, Circles, and Stars* (Princeton University Press, 2001), *The Girl Who Gave Birth To Rabbits* (Prometheus, 2000), *Cryptorunes* (Pomegranate, 2000), *Surfing Through Hyperspace* (Oxford University Press, 1999), Wonders of Numbers (Oxford University Press, 2000), *The Science of Aliens* (Basic Books, 1998), *Time: A Traveler's Guide* (Oxford University Press, 1998), *Strange Brains and Genius: The Secret Lives of Eccentric Scientists and Madmen* (Plenum, 1998), *The Alien IQ Test* (Basic Books, 1997), *The Loom of God* (Plenum, 1997), *Black Holes—A Traveler's Guide* (Wiley, 1996), and *Keys to Infinity* (Wiley, 1995). He is also author of numerous other highly acclaimed books including *Chaos in Wonderland: Visual Adventures in a Fractal World* (1994), *Mazes for the Mind: Computers and the Unexpected* (1992), *Computers and the Imagination* (1991) and *Computers, Pattern, Chaos, and Beauty* (1990), all published by St. Martin's Press—as well as the author of over 200 articles concerning topics in science, art, and mathematics. He is also coauthor, with Piers Anthony, of *Spider Legs*, a science-fiction novel recently listed as Barnes and Noble's second best-selling science-fiction title.

Pickover is currently an associate editor for the scientific journal *Computers and Graphics*, and is an editorial board member for *Odyssey*, *Theta Mathematics Journal*, *Leonardo*, and *YLEM*. He has been a guest editor for several scientific journals.

**443**

Editor of the books *Chaos and Fractals: A Computer Graphical Journey* (Elsevier, 1998), *The Pattern Book: Fractals, Art, and Nature* (World Scientific, 1995), *Visions of the Future: Art, Technology, and Computing in the Next Century* (St. Martin's Press, 1993), *Future Health* (St. Martin's Press, 1995), *Fractal Horizons* (St. Martin's Press, 1996), and *Visualizing Biological Information* (World Scientific, 1995), and coeditor of the books *Spiral Symmetry* (World Scientific, 1992) and *Frontiers in Scientific Visualization* (Wiley, 1994), Dr. Pickover's primary interest is finding new ways to continually expand creativity by melding art, science, mathematics, and other seemingly disparate areas of human endeavor.

The *Los Angeles Times* recently proclaimed, "Pickover has published nearly a book a year in which he stretches the limits of computers, art and thought." Pickover received first prize in the Institute of Physics' "Beauty of Physics Photographic Competition." His computer graphics have been featured on the cover of many popular magazines, and his research has recently received considerable attention by the press—including CNN's *Science and Technology Week*, the Discovery Channel, *Science News*, the *Washington Post*, *Wired*, and the *Christian Science Monitor*—and also in international exhibitions and museums. *OMNI* magazine recently described him as "Van Leeuwenhoek's twentieth century equivalent." *Scientific American* several times featured his graphic work, calling it "strange and beautiful, stunningly realistic." *Wired* magazine wrote, "Bucky Fuller thought big, Arthur C. Clarke thinks big, but Cliff Pickover outdoes them both." Among his many patents, Pickover has received U.S. Patent 5,095,302 for a 3-D computer mouse, 5,564,004 for strange computer icons, and 5,682,486 for black-hole transporter interfaces to computers.

Dr. Pickover is currently a Research Staff Member at the IBM T. J. Watson Research Center, where he has received twenty-two invention achievement awards, three research division awards, and four external honor awards. For many years Dr. Pickover was the lead columnist for the Brain-Boggler column in *Discover* magazine, and he is currently the Brain-Strain columnist in *Odyssey*.

Dr. Pickover's hobbies include the practice of Ch'ang-Shih Tai-Chi Ch'uan and Shaolin Kung Fu, raising golden and green severums (large Amazonian fish), and piano playing (mostly jazz). He is also a member of The SETI League, a group of signal processing enthusiasts who systematically search the sky for intelligent, extraterrestrial life. Visit his Web site, which has received over 300,000 visits: http://www.pickover.com. He can be reached at P.O. Box 549, Millwood, New York 10546-0549 USA. ᛗᚱᛗᚴᛗ ᛗᚴ ᚴᛗᚴᚺᛗ

# Index

**445**